decades of
SCIENCE FICTION

decades of
SCIENCE FICTION

APPLEWHITE MINYARD

New York, New York   Columbus, Ohio   Chicago, Illinois   Peoria, Illinois   Woodland Hills, California

For my mother
Alcie Minyard Wood

Executive Editor: Marisa L. L'Heureux
Editor: Lisa A. De Mol
Cover and interior design: Paul Uhl, Design Associates
Cover illustration: François Robert
Design Manager: Ophelia Chambliss
Production Manager: Margo Goia

Acknowledgments begin on page 555, which is to be considered an extension of this copyright page.

 **Glencoe**

The McGraw·Hill Companies

Send all Inquiries to:
Glencoe/McGraw-Hill
8787 Orion Place
Columbus, OH 43240

ISBN : 0-8442-5994-2 (Student Edition)
ISBN : 0-8442-5995-0 (Insructor's Edition)
Printed in the United States of America
8 9 10 QDB 15 14 13 12

Library of Congress Cataloging-in-Publication Data

Minyard, Applewhite, 1946–
     Decades of science fiction / Applewhite Minyard.
          p.   cm.
     Includes index.
     Summary: An anthology of science fiction short stories, grouped by decade from the late 1800s to the present.
     ISBN 0-8442-5994-2
     1. Science fiction, American—Outlines, syllabi, etc. 2. Science fiction, English—Outlines, syllabi, etc. 3. Science fiction, American. 4. Science fiction, English. [1. Science fiction. 2. Short stories.] I. Title
     PS374.S35M56   1997
     813'.0876208[Fic]—dc21   97–348
                                                                                        CIP
                                                                                        AC

CONTENTS

PREFACE

Decades of Science Fiction is a collection of short stories that traces the rise and development of science fiction from its beginnings in the mid-1850s to the present. The authors whose works are included represent some of the best and most well-known writers of the genre. These stories will provide you with a solid introduction to the genre of science fiction.

The Introduction provides an overview of the field of science fiction. Following the chronological theme of the text, it outlines both the development of science fiction itself and explains the various subcategories within science fiction. It also discusses the role of science fiction in our world today.

The stories themselves are arranged in an easy-to-follow chronological sequence. Knowing the historical context of the stories and the events that may have influenced the writers will help you better understand the stories themselves. In addition, scientific aspects often play a role both in the developments within the stories and as speculations about what directions technology may take in light of current knowledge. To help you gain a quick overview of these aspects of science fiction, each chapter of *Decades of Science Fiction* focuses on a particular era. The first chapter covers the entire period through the end of World War I, but each succeeding chapter covers an individual decade. The number of stories per chapter increases as the book progresses, with two stories for each era through the thirties, three stories each for the forties through the sixties, and four each for the seventies through the nineties.

Each chapter begins with a timeline that highlights historical and scientific achievements for the decade, as well as showing some of the most significant science fiction works that appeared. After the timelines, a more detailed look at these three aspects is included. The chapter introductions provide additional information about some of the most noteworthy historical and scientific advances of the decade. Also included is a two-part look at science fiction of the decade. The first part is concerned with major works that appeared in print. Thus, the history of science fiction is written in installments, with enough detail to give an idea of the direction the genre was taking, including notable authors and stories, but not an exhaustive analysis. The second, briefer, segment of the introductions contains a look at science fiction in other media. This includes movies and movie serials, TV shows, comics, and computerized applications.

The short stories in this anthology were selected to represent not only the science fiction of the decade, but also each author's work as a whole. While it is difficult to say that one short story truly represents an author, and realizing that an anthology cannot possibly include everyone's favorite story or author, every attempt was made to cover as wide a range of authors, styles, and themes as possible in an introductory textbook. Each story begins with introductory material about the author, providing biographical information as well as that author's major works and themes.

Following each story are two sets of questions. The discussion questions are meant to prompt your thinking about some of the issues raised by the stories. The writing topics are meant to promote thinking through writing. They may specifically ask for short essay or journal responses, but your instructor may modify those prompts according to his or her desire for emphasis. At least one of the writing topics for each story will ask you to attempt to relate the story to the events of the decade in which it was published. The timelines and chapter introductions will be useful as a starting point for such questions, but you may also want to do additional research to get a more thorough grasp of the historical and scientific context.

A final feature of *Decades of Science Fiction* is the list of reference works about science fiction at the end of the book. You may consult these works to gain a better understanding of science fiction as a whole, or to find out more about a certain aspect, time period, theme, or author. Not all of these reference works will be available at any single library, and some may be out of print. However, if a research paper or annotated essay is required as one of your class assignments, this list will give you a good starting place. Your librarian can give you information about obtaining books through networked databases that may be available, arrangements with a nearby university library, or through interlibrary loan. And, if you want to pursue a particular author or works in a certain time period, your teacher should have a listing of significant books and movies for all the decades.

Science fiction is both fascinating and illuminating. Through this anthology, you can discover and enjoy the world of science fiction, as well as the world in which you live today.

Science fiction is, in a sense, an oxymoron, a phrase consisting of two words that seem to be opposites. *Science* implies that which is true and provable, while *fiction* is that which is fabricated or false. A literal interpretation of science fiction would mean "true false." This may be analyzing words to the point of absurdity, but science fiction does include various definitions. Obviously, to be science fiction, a work must contain both some employment of *science,* or scientific principles and a *fictional* treatment of its use. Science fiction must combine these elements in a meaningful fashion if it is to be relevant to readers. Science fiction is not necessarily about the future, so much as about the possibility of a future or other world alternative. It is not really about predicting the future either, but rather about exploring possibilities by examining present-day events.

In this context, scientific principles must be plausible, and the events described must be valid within the context of currently accepted scientific facts. A working definition for *science fiction,* then, is the exploration of alternate realities taken from present-day events. If desired, *speculative fiction* (a term that many prefer) may be substituted without distorting the meaning.

The use of the name science fiction to describe works that fall into this category didn't become widespread until after Hugo Gernsback introduced it in his pulp magazine *Amazing Stories* in 1929. Fiction appearing before this date may be termed science fiction, of course, since the terminology does not necessarily define the genre. However, some older works that contain elements of what we would now call science fiction might be placed in a separate category—perhaps proto-science fiction. Many critics have pointed to examples of this proto-science fiction going back thousands of years, nearly as far as recorded writing. These examples include passages from the Christian Bible, Plato, Shakespeare, fairy tales, and more recent works such as Jonathan Swift's *Gulliver's Travels* (1726).

Frankenstein, written by an English woman named Mary Shelley, is almost universally regarded as a seminal work. When written in 1818, it was not considered science fiction but rather a Gothic romance that included a morality tale. The Industrial Revolution, beginning around 1775, is also often named as an influence on the early development of science fiction as society became more technologically oriented. It was natural for writers to think about the effects of scientific advances on human society as society changed rapidly.

As technology developed, writers began producing stories using new or proposed mechanical inventions. Proto-science fiction was only one of the many types of writing that American author Edgar Allan Poe produced, including "Hans Pfaal" (1835) and "Mellonta Tauta" (1849). It was really French author Jules Verne, however, who began the scientific-based fiction that has become widely known today as science fiction, with novels such as *Journey to the Center of the Earth* (1864).

The genre was expanded by H. G. Wells in England, with stories such as *The Time Machine* (1895). His stories were frequently called scientific romances, since they featured relationships as much as science. Other early terms for what we now call science fiction included scientific fiction, future fiction, anticipatory tales, and scientifiction. Wells himself said he was more interested in the sociological possibilities than the scientific principles in his fiction. Also in England, Sir Arthur Conan Doyle, who created one of fiction's most memorable characters in Sherlock Holmes, also produced some speculative fiction, including *The Poison Belt* (1913).

The United States emerged as a leader in the science fiction market with pulp writers such as Edgar Rice Burroughs, whose *A Princess of Mars* in 1912 and *Tarzan of the Apes* in 1914 captivated reading audiences throughout the country. When *Amazing Stories* magazine began publication in 1926, America leaped ahead in production of science fiction, and today American science fiction continues to dominate the world market. Perhaps this is because America, as a country, began after an invasion by aliens with a dominating culture and a superior technology, especially in the area of weaponry. Today the United States consists of widely differing cultural and ethnic heritages, so science fiction is naturally popular.

Science fiction has a vast popular appeal, but its academic acceptance has been limited. It has been placed in a subcategory called genre fiction, as opposed to mainstream works considered as having more literary merit. Finding quality science fiction can be difficult due to the large number of titles produced annually, many with little literary value. However, there are diamonds in the broken glass, and their existence and science fiction's longevity contribute to a gradual acceptance of its value, despite the fact that it is considered popular literature. Academia began to accept science fiction in the seventies as universities capitalized on student interest in a popular genre.

Today science fiction is both widely discussed and widely diversified, branching into such subgenres as hard science fiction, space opera, science fantasy, sociological science fiction, dystopian and utopian science fiction, military science fiction, cyberpunk, medical science fiction, psychological science fiction, time travel, alternative histories, future histories, space travel, steampunk, and dimensional travel. The differences among these categorizations are sometimes very slight or are used as advertising gimmicks that have little to do with the actual content of the stories. The following are definitions of some of the important categories of science fiction.

- Hard Science Fiction—Stories often featuring believable scientists or scientific inventions. If the scientific elements are both important to the story and plausible, given today's technology, it is hard science fiction.
- Soft Science Fiction—Stories emphasizing the psychological or sociological sciences. Relationships, more than scientific inventions or principles, are the basis for the action.
- Alternate History—Stories in which history as we know it has been altered in some fundamental way, such as Napoleon winning at Waterloo, or Einstein never unlocking the secrets of atomic power. We see a different society because of such changed events.
- Cyberpunk—Stories set in a computer-dominated environment, usually in the near future, and containing rebellious characters such as street punks.
- Dystopia—Stories in which society is dominated by negative factors.
- Utopia—Stories in which society's ills have, for the most part, been cured and daily life is perfect, or nearly so.
- Future History—Stories set in a distant time and containing a more or less worked out society reflecting the relationships among competing or cooperating species in that universe.
- Steampunk—Stories set in an alternate history when steam power was prominent, such as Victorian England. These stories usually show technology changed in some way by the addition of more modern inventions, and like cyberpunk, most have rebellious characters.
- Fantastic Voyage—Stories where the heroes travel to unknown regions, encountering strange inhabitants.
- Space Opera—Stories with outer space or other planets and galactic war as the center of the action. A soap opera played out in space.

There are also related genres, most notably fantasy and horror, and again the division becomes unclear. A story might contain some fantastic element—such as a flying machine—but the means by which it flies might be magical, scientific, or simply unexplained. Horror can be difficult because works that fit into either of the other two categories could also contain elements that horrify. Thus, *Frankenstein* may be regarded as both science fiction (or proto-science fiction) and horror, as could the *Alien* movies.

A work like J. R. R. Tolkien's *The Lord of the Rings* is also difficult to classify. On one hand, it is clearly rooted in magic and mythology, making it a fantasy. On the other hand, many of the magical elements seem carefully crafted with unknown or lost technology, such as forging the rings in the Crack of Doom. Many of these devices could be considered science fiction, but the overall tone and emphasis of the stories is magic.

The works of Tolkien and others have been called high fantasy or adult fantasy. This gives them an air of respectability above the more commonplace stories in which magic is used to solve any problem the protagonist encounters. Science fiction stories usually features some believable explanation of their devices, whereas fantasy uses magic almost exclusively, and swords and dragons are usually present. The societies depicted in fantasy seem somewhat medieval and have little technology. While these and other categories are not important to enjoyment of science fiction, they do help determine how the genre has been shaped. We must understand where science fiction has been so we may determine where it may go. Since science fiction writings are, in a sense, fictional histories, we must learn from where we have been and head in new directions.

The science fiction of any time reflects that time's own technology and scientific thought. As the level and sophistication of thought have grown, so has science fiction. Thus, some stories become dated, but timeless themes and imaginative situations involving human reactions to difficult issues still keep readers interested in classic works. Indeed, this is why they are regarded as classics.

This book is set up in a historical context. Readers should try to make connections between events that actually happened and those that fiction writers hypothesized. Some of the best science fiction writers have written for many decades, and their ideas changed as they matured as writers and individuals. Science fiction is entering a new age, one that may surpass its supposed Golden Age. Today more than ever, technology is advancing rapidly and the ways that humans adapt or fail to adapt will determine the future.

Several themes run through science fiction stories. Now that the genre has over a century of historical background to draw on and no signs of disappearing in the near future, some of those themes have all but disappeared. Other themes continue to be used, and new ones are emerging as a response to the times that we live in. These themes are broader than the former subgenres; that is, a theme may span several subgenres. Some of the typical science fiction themes are listed here.

- Unexplained Phenomena—Stories featuring UFOs, pyramid power, paranormal abilities, telekinesis, ESP, and other psychic possibilities and how those talents affect humans.
- Self-Knowledge—Stories emphasizing the ability to know and accept our humanity. May include situations challenging gender identities or other preconceived notions.
- The Individual versus Society—Tales where the society has certain guidelines for compatible living, but situations occur that the rules don't cover. A strong individual accomplishes daring feats, and sometimes this requires breaking rules.
- People in Time or Space—Stories involving humans traveling in time or space. Situations include the beings humans encounter, and how the humans react to the unfamiliar surroundings.
- Humans and Technology—Stories describing how humans interact with computers, nanotechnology, bioengineering, virtual reality, artificial intelligences, or other parts of a technologically driven society. These stories often question the concept of what it means to be human.

Science fiction has been a part of literature since at least 1818, and it has been a popular form of entertainment and enlightenment for over a century. There are hundreds of science fiction titles produced each year in the United States alone, and book sales are increasing nationwide. The number of movies, TV shows, comics, and computer games that are aimed at a science fiction audience is growing every year as well. Since this is the information age, people are searching for solutions to show them how to cope with a rapidly changing world. Sometimes we barely know an event has happened before it's over, and the media, especially TV, seems to tell us what is news and what is not.

New electronic equipment is often outdated as soon as it arrives in our homes, and our brains can no longer keep up with the information overload. The soft science fiction stories provide some comfort because they show characters caught in conflicts that mirror many of the things we see happening around us. On the other hand, the post-cyberpunks offer a dismal view of humans becoming tied to their technological inventions, until the division between human and machine almost cannot be found. There are no easy solutions to the complexities of life, and most science fiction stories do not offer an answer but merely a vision. How we choose to use those glimpses into possible futures is up to us, the readers. Science fictional ideas have entered the mainstream of human thought, and our views of the possible future are being shaped by science fiction writers with insightful imaginations. Which path we take can only be determined in the future.

Through World War I

1769	James Watt patents improvements on steam engine
1794	Eli Whitney invents cotton gin
1804	Napoleon becomes Emperor of French Republic
1818	**Mary Shelley publishes *Frankenstein: The Modern Prometheus***
1821	Michael Farraday discovers the fundamentals of electromagnetism
1822	Charles Babbage designs first computer; fails to build working model
1834	Cyrus McCormick patents his reaping machine
1837	L. J. M. Daguerre develops photographic process
1838	**Edgar Allan Poe publishes "The Narrative of Arthur Gordon Pym"**
1844	Samuel Morse lays first telegraph line in the U.S.
1846	Nitroglycerine invented
1851	**Jules Verne publishes *A Voyage in a Balloon***
1860	First practical internal combustion engine produced by Etienne Lenoir
1861–1865	American Civil War
1865	Ku Klux Klan founded
1876	Louis Pasteur invents pasteurization process for wine
1877	Alexander Graham Bell invents telephone
1880	Thomas Edison invents phonograph
1885	First electric lights developed independently by Edison and J. S. Swan
1886	Sir Francis Galton proves individuality of fingerprints
1886	**Robert Louis Stevenson publishes *The Strange Case of Dr. Jekyll and Mr. Hyde***
1888	Nikola Tesla constructs electric motor used by Westinghouse
1892	Rudolf Diesel patents internal combustion engine

1895 — *The Time Machine* by H. G. Wells appears

1896 — First modern-day Olympics held in Athens

1898 — Pierre and Marie Curie discover radium

1900 — Max Planck formulates quantum theory

1902 — **Joseph Conrad produces *The Heart of Darkness***

1903 — Wright Brothers make the first powered flight at Kitty Hawk, North Carolina

1905 — Albert Einstein publishes his Special Theory of Relativity

1906 — First radio programs featuring voice and music in the U.S.

1907 — The first helicopter, designed by Frenchman Paul Cornu, is flown briefly

1908 — **The Iron Heel by Jack London appears**
Henry Ford develops his Model T

1912 — The *Titanic* sinks on its first voyage

1913 — **Arthur Conan Doyle produces *The Lost World***
Federal income tax established

1914 — Archduke Francis Ferdinand, heir to the Austrian throne, is assassinated in Sarajevo, setting off World War I

1915 — Einstein postulates his General Theory of Relativity
First transcontinental telephone call

1917 — Bolshevik revolution in Russia; Tsar abdicates
Sigmund Freud publishes *Introduction to Psychoanalysis*

HISTORICAL CONTEXT

In order to understand science fiction as part of the times during which it was produced, we need to know about actual historical events. The Industrial Revolution is a logical starting point since it advanced civilization with newly invented mechanical devices. It advanced literature by improved printing and distribution techniques.

The Industrial Revolution changed the eighteenth century world tremendously. Mechanized manufacturing made huge strides, changing both workers and the relationship of workers to their workplaces. Previously, societies were based primarily on farming. Cities and towns grew around areas with bountiful crops and favorable trade routes. However, when science and technology concentrated production in urban centers, the role of workers changed to fit the needs of the machinery. Farm production was still important, but just as manufacturing progressed, so did farming. Agricultural tools changed from simple plows to mechanical implements, including Eli Whitney's cotton gin in 1794 and Cyrus McCormick's reaper in 1834.

Other important factors in shaping the Industrial Age were the American Revolution in 1776 and the French Revolution in 1789. These both helped by establishing freedoms for workers, ending rule by monarchs, and increasing power for the middle classes. Common citizens became involved in politics, rather than just slaves to a system into which they had no input. Opportunities for advances in human knowledge were immensely increased, and trade routes opened and expansion undertaken in every imaginable direction.

When locomotives appeared in 1804, the speed and dependability of travel shrunk the time it took for communication, goods,

and people to move across continents. Schedules became standard-
ized so that people could travel and ship items from coast to coast
and know they would arrive reasonably on time. Steam engines
accounted for similar advances in ocean travel. When the first full
steam crossing of the Atlantic Ocean took place in 1838, the time
for an ocean voyage from England to America shrunk from weeks
to days.

These societal changes also changed information and literature. Compulsory education widened the reading audience, and
with most people living in the cities, the middle class became a
potent political force. Formerly, reading and serious literature
were reserved for the upper class. But with the advent of lending
libraries, cheaper paper brought about by the invention of the wood
pulp process, and more automated printing techniques, more
reading material became easily available to the newly literate.

In the United States, books were produced as cheaply as possible, with most popular foreign titles being reprinted without permission. Domestically produced "dime novels" were popular with
less educated readers. As the bookmaking and papermaking processes became even more efficient in the 1880s, "pulp" magazines
began to appear. These magazines used crude paper that quickly
deteriorated and featured flashy color covers to attract unsophisti-
cated readers. The poorly written escapist fantasies were readily
accepted by the expanding population. There were also "slicks,"
so named because they were printed on better quality paper, and
which appealed to the wealthier readers. In nineteenth century
America, scientific romances were almost entirely written as pulps.
Because they were quickly and cheaply produced, little memorable
scientific fiction was published.

In Britain, magazines such as *Blackwood's, Pearson's,* and *The
Strand* commanded a large share of the market. These publications
aimed for respectability and didn't cater to the new "voyages extraordinaires" by Jules Verne or the "scientific romances" of H. G.
Wells. Those works by Wells and Verne were published almost exclusively as hardbacks and competed with other popular literature
of the day. The intellectual climate at that time was quite different
in Britain than the United States. With the expansion of literacy
and the settling of the western parts of America, however, the

demand for stimulating reading soon increased. Reprints of
European titles were popular, but U.S. authors soon became serious literary forces. Nathaniel Hawthorne and Edgar Allan Poe,
most notably, wrote scientific-based fiction pieces.

DEVELOPMENTS IN
SCIENCE FICTION

Though many escapist fantasies had appeared before 1818, Mary
Shelley's *Frankenstein* is often regarded as a beginning in the development of believable, science-based fiction. *Frankenstein* featured
an obsessed scientist intent on completing his experiments regardless of the cost. The novel also combined a creation made by scientific methods and the hideous, criminal side of the single-
minded quest for truth. Shelley doesn't reveal the exact method of
giving the creature life, but electricity is used as a metaphorical
and physical "spark of life." Shelley also included the notion that
sinful actions come back to haunt the sinner. In this case the
wrong is creating life unnaturally, and it ends in the death of both
the creature and its creator. This combination of factors and the
popular and critical acceptance of the novel make *Frankenstein* one
of the seminal works of science fiction.

When Shelley created *Frankenstein,* popular writing already
contained fantastic creatures, impossible voyages, and other highly
imaginary situations. Works such as *Gulliver's Travels* (1726) were
popular, but there was no separate genre to represent science-
based tales. Shelley's only other significant science fiction contribution was *The Last Man,* published in 1826. Although set in the
twenty-fifth century, sailing ships, swordplay, and a medieval way
of life dominate the action. Unlike *Frankenstein,* the book is not
highly regarded as science fiction.

In America, Edgar Allan Poe began producing a wide variety
of original fiction. Included among these were the first detective
stories, Poe's own brand of macabre psychological horror, and scientific articles exploring the origin and makeup of the universe.
Some of his many proto-science fiction pieces include "Ms. Found
in a Bottle" (1833), *The Narrative of Arthur Gordon Pym* (1838), "Hans
Pfaal" (1835), and "Mellonta Tauta" (1849). Poe not only explored

nearly every kind of writing possible, he also almost single-hand-edly defined the short story. He was the first to insist that a short story should have a single focus and effect, and be short enough to be read at a single sitting.

However, it was really Jules Verne's "voyages extraordinaires" that gave science fiction its push toward popularity and respect-ability. Beginning with *Five Weeks in a Balloon* in 1863, Verne created a string of highly successful titles, including *Journey to the Center of the Earth* (1864), *From the Earth to the Moon* (1865), and *20,000 Leagues Under the Sea* (1870). Verne was cautious in exploring the science side of his fiction, choosing to use only proposed or possible cur-rent inventions. He wanted to explore the beneficial aspects that scientific discoveries could have on humankind. Most of his stories depict utopias, or at least optimism for the future.

In England, Robert Louis Stevenson also produced a scientifi-cally based novel. *The Strange Case of Dr. Jekyll and Mr. Hyde* (1886) tells the story of a scientist who creates a potion that splits the good and bad sides of his personality, a twist on the *Frankenstein* theme. Mark Twain, with *A Connecticut Yankee in King Arthur's Court* (1889), wrote one of the first time travel stories, after Charles Dickens' 1842 *A Christmas Carol*. Twain's novel features a technologically minded hero helping progress in the distant past. It all turns out to be a dream and thus is more fantasy than science fiction. The idea of giving past societies modern inventions, though, has been used many times since in science fiction stories.

The popularity that the French Verne achieved with his scientific stories was overshadowed by the English H. G. Wells. Beginning in 1895 with *The Time Machine,* Wells continued with other outstanding titles, including *The Island of Dr. Moreau* (1896), *The Invisible Man* (1897), *War of the Worlds* (1898), and *First Men on the Moon* (1901). Though Wells had more scientific training than Verne, he was more interested in the philosophical concerns, the consequences of ideas represented by new inventions, or taking present events and predicting what might occur if those events formed the basis of a whole society.

For instance, in *The Time Machine,* when the hero travels to the year 800,000, he discovers two classes of people: the Eloi and the Morlocks. The Eloi live above ground and enjoy all the

comforts, while the Morlocks live underground and are forced to
work endlessly to support the Eloi. Wells created many situations,
including insect civilizations, war tanks, diamond making, trans-
dimensional travel, and atomic power, but he used them to make
his point about the basic nature of human beings.

Wells was heavily influenced by the evolutionary theories of
Charles Darwin, first published in 1859, and by the idea of socialism. Wells explored the consequences of humans continuing on
the path they had started with the technological inventions of the
nineteenth century. He thought that humans *could* evolve into a
better species, but they needed to be aware of what mistakes they
had already made and what was likely to occur if they did not learn
from their previous errors. Nearly all his later works are dystopias,
showing human nature in a negative light, as opposed to the optimistic utopias he created in many of his early pieces.

Verne was very careful not to venture far beyond the scientific possibilities of the near future. In *20,000 Leagues Under the Sea,*
Verne featured an advanced submarine, a concept already being
explored. Verne was concerned with the romantic notion that
technology can help humans live better. Wells, on the other hand,
even when he created marvelous inventions, constantly warned
readers of the dangers of science unchecked by moral conscience.
Both authors had tremendous impact on the development of science fiction as a genre, though Wells continues to be more widely
read than Verne, whose stories of the ease science could bring to
everyday life have become dated.

Arthur Conan Doyle, though best known for his creation of
the super detective Sherlock Holmes, also produced some science
fiction, most notably in the Professor Challenger stories *The Lost
World* (1912) and *The Poison Belt* (1913). In the latter, he predicted
the path later taken by the Germans in World War I to attack
England. In America, Edgar Rice Burroughs created an instant
sensation with his first story, *A Princess of Mars,* in 1912. He followed this with his most successful character, *Tarzan of the Apes,*
the same year. His third major series, set inside a hollow Earth,
began with *At the Earth's Core* in 1913. While Burroughs has been
criticized for being a one-plot author, he combined elements of
escapism, heroism, vividly imagined other worlds, and social

commentary in popular adventure stories. He was the most influential of the pulp writers, and nearly all his stories were serialized before they appeared as novels.

Thus, as the century proceeded, science fiction gained in popularity and prominence. By the beginning of World War I, three main categories of science fiction existed: the Extraordinary Voyage, as typified by *Five Weeks in a Balloon* and *The Time Machine;* the Tale of the Future, including Shelley's *The Last Man* and Edward Bellamy's *Looking Backward;* and the Tale of Science or Marvelous Invention, with entries like *Frankenstein, Dr. Jekyll and Mr. Hyde, The Island of Dr. Moreau,* and *20,000 Leagues Under the Sea.* The events and stories that proliferated after the Industrial Revolution laid the foundations for all the speculative fiction that was to follow.

Master Zacharius

1874

JULES VERNE (1828–1905)

The French author Jules Verne began his career writing plays and romantic poetry. His first published story, *A Voyage in a Balloon*, (1851) was a literary flight of fancy. He followed it with *Five Weeks in a Balloon* in 1863, thus beginning a long series of what were termed "voyages extraordinaires." *Journey to the Center of the Earth*, published in 1864, and *From the Earth to the Moon* in 1865, set the pattern for much of Verne's work. He combined an optimism about the future due to scientific progress with emphasis on the basic goodness of human beings.

Although most well known for his novels, Verne also wrote a number of short stories. Many of these, including "Master Zacharius," were collected in *Dr. Ox's Experiment and Other Stories* (1874). Other notable novels include *20,000 Leagues Under the Sea* (1870) and *The Mysterious Island* (1875). Verne's later works featured a grimmer vision of the future, though still proclaiming the rightness of nineteenth-century progress. In *Clipper of the Clouds* (1886), the hero, Robur, invents a flying machine that he puts to good use, but in the sequel, *Master of the World* (1904), Robur becomes an uncontrollable madman. The need to be cautious in accepting scientific marvels is the clear message.

In "Master Zacharius," Jules Verne presents a master clockmaker who gives perhaps too much of himself to his creations and finds that, while science may have many of the answers to life's mysteries, it doesn't have all of them.

CHAPTER 1

A Winter Night

1   The city of Geneva lies at the west end of the lake of the same name. The Rhone, which passes through the town at the outlet of the lake, divides it into two sections, and is itself divided in the centre of the city by an island placed in mid-stream. A topographical feature like this is often found in the great depôts of commerce and industry. No doubt the first inhabitants were influenced by the easy means of transport which the swift currents of the rivers offered them—those "roads which walk along of their own accord," as Pascal puts it. In the case of the Rhone, it would be the road that ran along.

2   Both new and regular buildings were constructed on this island, which was enclosed like a Dutch galley in the middle of the river, the curious mass of houses, piled one on the other, presented a delight-fully confused *coup-d'œil*. The small area of the island had compelled some of the buildings to be perched, as it were, on the piles, which were entangled in the rough currents of the river. The huge beams, blackened by time, and worn by the water, seemed like the claws of an enormous crab, and presented a fantastic appearance. The little yellow streams, which were like cobwebs stretched amid this ancient foundation, quivered in the darkness, as if they had been the leaves of some old oak forest, while the river engulfed in this forest of piles, foamed and roared most mournfully.

3   One of the houses of the island was striking for its curiously aged appearance. It was the dwelling of the old clockmaker, Master Zacharius, whose household consisted of his daughter Gerande, Aubert Thun, his apprentice, and his old servant Scholastique.

4   There was no man in Geneva to compare in interest with this Zacharius. His age was past finding out. Not the oldest inhabitant of the town could tell for how long his thin, pointed head had shaken above his shoulders, nor the day when, for the first time, he had walked through the streets, with his long white locks floating in the wind. The man did not live; he vibrated like the pendulum of his clocks. His spare and cadaverous figure was always clothed in dark colours. Like the pic-tures of Leonardo di Vinci, he was sketched in black.

5   Gerande had the pleasantest room in the whole house, whence, through a narrow window, she had the inspiriting view of the snowy peaks of Jura; but the bedroom and workshop of the old man were a kind of cavern close on to the water, the floor of which rested on the piles.

6   From time immemorial Master Zacharius had never come out ex-cept at meal times, and when he went to regulate the different clocks of

the town. He passed the rest of his time at his bench, which was covered with numerous clockwork instruments, most of which he had invented himself. For he was a clever man; his works were valued in all France and Germany. The best workers in Geneva readily recognized his superiority, and showed that he was an honour to the town, by saying, "To him belongs the glory of having invented the escapement." In fact, the birth of true clock-work dates from the invention which the talents of Zacharius had discovered not many years before.

7   After he had worked hard for a long time, Zacharius would slowly put his tools away, cover up the delicate pieces that he had been adjusting with glasses, and stop the active wheel of his lathe; then he would raise a trap-door constructed in the floor of his workshop, and, stooping down, used to inhale for hours together the thick vapours of the Rhone, as it dashed along under his eyes.

8   One winter's night the old servant Scholastique served the supper, which, according to old custom, she and the young mechanic shared with their master. Master Zacharius did not eat, though the food carefully prepared for him was offered him in a handsome blue and white dish. He scarcely answered the sweet words of Gerande, who evidently noticed her father's silence, and even the clatter of Scholastique herself no more struck his ear than the roar of the river, to which he paid no attention.

9   After the silent meal, the old clockmaker left the table without embracing his daughter, or saying his usual "Good-night" to all. He left by the narrow door leading to his den, and the staircase groaned under his heavy footsteps as he went down.

10   Gerande, Aubert, and Scholastique sat for some minutes without speaking. On this evening the weather was dull; the clouds dragged heavily on the Alps, and threatened rain; the severe climate of Switzerland made one feel sad, while the south wind swept round the house, and whistled ominously.

11   "My dear young lady," said Scholastique, at last, "do you know that our master has been out of sorts for several days? Holy Virgin! I know he has had no appetite, because his words stick in his inside, and it would take a very clever devil to drag even one out of him."

12   "My father has some secret cause of trouble, that I cannot even guess," replied Gerande, as a sad anxiety spread over her face.

13   "Mademoiselle, don't let such sadness fill your heart. You know the strange habits of Master Zacharius. Who can read his secret thoughts in his face? No doubt some fatigue has overcome him, but to-morrow he will have forgotten it, and be very sorry to have given his daughter pain."

14 It was Aubert who spoke thus, looking into Gerande's lovely eyes. Aubert was the first apprentice whom Master Zacharius had ever admitted to the intimacy of his labours, for he appreciated his intelligence, discretion, and goodness of heart; and this young man had attached himself to Gerande with the earnest devotion natural to a noble nature.

15 Gerande was eighteen years of age. Her oval face recalled that of the artless Madonnas whom veneration still displays at the street corners of the antique towns of Brittany. Her eyes betrayed an infinite simplicity. One would love her as the sweetest realization of a poet's dream. Her apparel was of modest colours, and the white linen which was folded about her shoulders had the tint and perfume peculiar to the linen of the church. She led a mystical existence in Geneva, which had not as yet been delivered over to the dryness of Calvinism.

16 While, night and morning, she read her Latin prayers in her iron-clasped missal, Gerande has also discovered a hidden sentiment in Aubert Thun's heart, and comprehended what a profound devotion the young workman had for her. Indeed, the whole world in his eyes was condensed into this old clockmaker's house, and he passed all his time near the young girl, when he left her father's workshop, after his work was over.

17 Old Scholastique saw all this, but said nothing. Her loquacity exhausted itself in preference on the evils of the times, and the little worries of the household. Nobody tried to stop its course. It was with her as with the musical snuff-boxes which they made at Geneva; once wound up, you must break them before you will prevent their playing all their airs through.

18 Finding Gerande absorbed in a melancholy silence, Scholastique left her old wooden chair, fixed a taper on the end of a candlestick, lit it, and placed it near a small waxen Virgin, sheltered in her niche of stone. It was the family custom to kneel before this protecting Madonna of the domestic hearth, and to beg her kindly watchfulness during the coming night; but on this evening Gerande remained silent in her seat.

19 "Well, well, dear demoiselle," said the astonished Scholastique, "supper is over, and it is time to go to bed. Why do you tire your eyes by sitting up late? Ah, Holy Virgin! It's much better to sleep, and to get a little comfort from happy dreams! In these detestable times in which we live, who can promise herself a fortunate day?"

20 "Ought we not to send for a doctor for my father?" asked Gerande.

21 "A doctor!" cried the old domestic. "Has Master Zacharius ever listened to their fancies and pompous sayings? He might accept medicines for the watches, but not for the body!"

22   "What shall we do?" murmured Gerande. "Has he gone to work, or to rest?"

23   "Gerande," answered Aubert softly, "some mental trouble annoys your father, that is all."

24   "Do you know what it is, Aubert?"

25   "Perhaps, Gerande."

26   "Tell us, then," cried Scholastique eagerly, economically extinguishing her taper.

27   "For several days, Gerande," said the young apprentice, "something absolutely incomprehensible has been going on. All the watches which your father has made and sold for some years have suddenly stopped. Very many of them have been brought back to him. He has carefully taken them to pieces; the springs were in good condition, and the wheels well set. He has put them together yet more carefully; but, despite his skill, they will not go."

28   "The devil's in it!" cried Scholastique.

29   "Why say you so?" asked Gerande. "It seems very natural to me. Nothing lasts for ever in this world. The infinite cannot be fashioned by the hands of men."

30   "It is none the less true," returned Aubert, "that there is in this something very mysterious and extraordinary. I have myself been helping Master Zacharius to search for the cause of this derangement of his watches; but I have not been able to find it, and more than once I have let my tools fall from my hands in despair."

31   "But why undertake so vain a task?" resumed Scholastique. "Is it natural that a little copper instrument should go of itself, and mark the hours? We ought to have kept to the sun-dial!"

32   "You will not talk thus, Scholastique," said Aubert, "when you learn that the sun-dial was invented by Cain."

33   "Good heavens! what are you telling me?"

34   "Do you think," asked Gerande simply, "that we might pray to God to give life to my father's watches?"

35   "Without doubt," replied Aubert.

36   "Good! They will be useless prayers," muttered the old servant, "but Heaven will pardon them for their good intent."

37   The taper was relighted. Scholastique, Gerande, and Aubert knelt down together upon the tiles of the room. The young girl prayed for her mother's soul, for a blessing for the night, for travellers and prisoners, for the good and the wicked, and more earnestly than all for the unknown misfortunes of her father.

38   Then the three devout souls rose with some confidence in their hearts, because they had laid their sorrow on the bosom of God.

39   Aubert repaired to his own room; Gerande sat pensively by the window, whilst the last lights were disappearing from the city streets; and Scholastique, having poured a little water on the flickering embers, and shut the two enormous bolts on the door, threw herself upon her bed, where she was soon dreaming that she was dying of fright.

40   Meanwhile the terrors of this winter's night had increased. Sometimes, with the whirlpools of the river, the wind engulfed itself among the piles, and the whole house shivered and shook; but the young girl, absorbed in her sadness, thought only of her father. After hearing what Aubert told her, the malady of Master Zacharius took fantastic proportions in her mind; and it seemed to her as if his existence, so dear to her, having become purely mechanical, no longer moved on its worn-out pivots without effort.

41   Suddenly the pent-house shutter, shaken by the squall, struck against the window of the room. Gerande shuddered and started up without understanding the cause of the noise which thus disturbed her reverie. When she became a little calmer she opened the sash. The clouds had burst, and a torrent-like rain pattered on the surrounding roofs. The young girl leaned out of the window to draw to the shutter shaken by the wind, but she feared to do so. It seemed to her that the rain and the river, confounding their tumultuous waters, were submerging the frail house, the planks of which creaked in every direction. She would have flown from her chamber, but she saw below the flickering of a light which appeared to come from Master Zacharius's retreat, and in one of those momentary calms during which the elements keep a sudden silence, her ear caught plaintive sounds. She tried to shut her window, but could not. The wind violently repelled her, like a thief who was breaking into a dwelling.

42   Gerande thought she would go mad with terror. What was her father doing? She opened the door, and it escaped from her hands, and slammed loudly with the force of the tempest. Gerande then found herself in the dark supper-room, succeeded in gaining, on tiptoe, the staircase which led to her father's shop, and pale and fainting, glided down.

43   The old watchmaker was upright in the middle of the room, which resounded with the roaring of the river. His bristling hair gave him a sinister aspect. He was talking and gesticulating, without seeing or hearing anything. Gerande stood still on the threshold.

44   "It is death!" said Master Zacharius, in a hollow voice; "it is death! Why should I live longer, now that I have dispersed my existence over the earth? For I, Master Zacharius, am really the creator of all the watches that I have fashioned! It is a part of my very soul that I have

shut up in each of these cases of iron, silver, or gold! Every time that one of these accursed watches stops, I feel my heart cease beating, for I have regulated them with its pulsations!"

45   As he spoke in this strange way, the old man cast his eyes on his bench. There lay all the pieces of a watch that he had carefully taken apart. He took up a sort of hollow cylinder, called a barrel, in which the spring is enclosed, and removed the steel spiral, but instead of relaxing itself, according to the laws of its elasticity, it remained coiled on itself like a sleeping viper. It seemed knotted, like impotent old men whose blood has long been congealed. Master Zacharius vainly essayed to uncoil it with his thin fingers, the outlines of which were exaggerated on the wall; but he tried in vain, and soon, with a terrible cry of anguish and rage, he threw it through the trap-door into the boiling Rhone.

46   Gerande, her feet riveted to the floor, stood breathless and motionless. She wished to approach her father, but could not. Giddy hallucinations took possession of her. Suddenly she heard, in the shade, a voice murmur in her ears,—

47   "Gerande, dear Gerande! grief still keeps you awake. Go in again, I beg of you; the night is cold."

48   "Aubert!" whispered the young girl, "You?"

49   These soft words sent the blood back into the young girl's heart. She leaned on Aubert's arm, and said to him, —

50   "My father is very ill, Aubert! You alone can cure him, for this disorder of the mind would not yield to his daughter's consolings. His mind is attacked by a very natural delusion, and in working with him, repairing the watches, you will bring him back to reason. Aubert," she continued, "it is not true, is it, that his life is mixed up with that of his watches?"

51   Aubert did not reply.

52   "But is my father's trade condemned by God?" asked Gerande, trembling.

53   "I know not," returned the apprentice, warming the cold hands of the girl with his own. "But go back to your room, my poor Gerande, and with sleep recover hope!"

54   Gerande slowly returned to her chamber, and remained there till daylight, without sleep closing her eyelids. Meanwhile, Master Zacharius, always mute and motionless, gazed at the river as it rolled turbulently at his feet.

CHAPTER 2
The Pride of Science

55   The severity of the Geneva merchant in business matters has become proverbial. He is rigidly honourable, and excessively just. What must, then, have been the shame of Master Zacharius, when he saw these watches, which he had so carefully constructed, returning to him from every direction?

56   It was certain that these watches had suddenly stopped, and without any apparent reason. The wheels were in a good condition and firmly fixed, but the springs had lost all elasticity. Vainly did the watchmaker try to replace them; the wheels remained motionless. These unaccountable derangements were greatly to the old man's discredit. His noble inventions had many times brought upon him suspicions of sorcery, which now seemed confirmed. These rumours reached Gerande, and she often trembled for her father, when she saw malicious glances directed towards him.

57   Yet on the morning after this night of anguish, Master Zacharius seemed to resume work with some confidence. The morning sun inspired him with some courage. Aubert hastened to join him in the shop, and received an affable "Good-day."

58   "I am better," said the old man. "I don't know what strange pains in the head attacked me yesterday, but the sun has quite chased them away, with the clouds of the night."

59   "In faith, master," returned Aubert, "I don't like the night for either of us!"

60   "And thou art right, Aubert. If you ever become a great man, you will understand that day is as necessary to you as food. A great savant should be always ready to receive the homage of his fellow-men."

61   "Master, it seems to me that the pride of science has possessed you."

62   "Pride, Aubert! Destroy my past, annihilate my present, dissipate my future, and then it will be permitted to me to live in obscurity! Poor boy, who comprehends not the sublime things to which my art is wholly devoted! Art thou not but a tool in my hands?"

63   "Yet, Master Zacharius," resumed Aubert, "I have more than once merited your praise for the manner in which I adjusted the most delicate parts of your watches and clocks."

64   "No doubt, Aubert; thou art a good workman, such as I love; but when thou workest, thou thinkest thou has in thy hands but copper, silver, gold; thou dost not perceive these metals, which my genius animates, palpitating like living flesh! So that thou wilt not die, with the death of thy works!"

65   Master Zacharius remained silent after these words; but Aubert essayed to keep up the conversation.

66   "Indeed, master," said he, "I love to see you work so unceasingly! You will be ready for the festival of our corporation, for I see that the work on this crystal watch is going forward famously."

67   "No doubt, Aubert," cried the old watchmaker, "and it will be no slight honour for me to have been able to cut and shape the crystal to the durability of a diamond! Ah, Louis Berghem did well to perfect the art of diamond–cutting, which has enabled me to polish and pierce the hardest stones!"

68   Master Zacharius was holding several small watch pieces of cut crystal, and of exquisite workmanship. The wheels, pivots, and case of the watch were of the same material, and he had employed remarkable skill in this very difficult task.

69   "Would it not be fine," said he, his face flushing, "to see this watch palpitating beneath its transparent envelope, and to be able to count the beatings of its heart?"

70   "I will wager, sir," replied the young apprentice, "that it will not vary a second in a year."

71   "And you would wager on a certainty! Have I not imparted to it all that is purest of myself? And does my heart vary? My heart, I say?"

72   Aubert did not dare to lift his eyes to his master's face. "Tell me frankly," said the old man sadly. "Have you never taken me for a madman? Do you not think me sometimes subject to dangerous folly? Yes; is it not so? In my daughter's eyes and yours, I have often read my condemnation. Oh!" he cried, as if in pain, "to be misunderstood by those whom one most loves in the world! But I will prove victoriously to thee, Aubert, that I am right! Do not shake thy head, for thou wilt be astounded. The day on which thou understandest how to listen to and comprehend me, thou wilt see that I have discovered the secrets of existence, the secrets of the mysterious union of the soul with the body!"

73   As he spoke thus, Master Zacharius appeared superb in his vanity. His eyes glittered with a supernatural fire, and his pride illumined every feature. And truly, if ever vanity was excusable, it was that of Master Zacharius!

74   The watchmaking art, indeed, down to his time, had remained almost in its infancy. From the day when Plato, four centuries before the Christian era, invented the night watch, a sort of clepsydra which indicated the hours of the night by the sound and playing of a flute, the science had continued nearly stationary. The masters paid more attention to the arts than to mechanics, and it was the period of beautiful watches of iron, copper, wood, silver, which were richly engraved, like

one of Cellini's ewers. They made a masterpiece of chasing, which measured time imperfectly, but was still a masterpiece. When the artist's imagination was not directed to the perfection of modelling, it set to work to create clocks with moving figures and melodious sounds, whose appearance took all attention. Besides, who troubled himself, in those days, with regulating the advance of time? The delays of the law were not as yet invented; the physical and astronomical sciences had not as yet established their calculations on scrupulously exact measurements; there were neither establishments which were shut at a given hour, nor trains which departed at a precise moment. In the evening the curfew bell sounded; and at night the hours were cried amid the universal silence. Certainly people did not live so long, if existence is measured by the amount of business done; but they lived better. The mind was enriched with the noble sentiments born of the contempla-tion of chefs-d'œuvré. They built a church in two centuries, a painter painted but few pictures in the course of his life, a poet only composed one great work; but these were so many masterpieces for after-ages to appreciate.

75   When the exact sciences began at last to make some progress, watch and clock making followed in their path, though it was always arrested by an insurmountable difficulty—the regular and continuous measurement of time.

76   It was in the midst of this stagnation that Master Zacharius invented the escapement, which enabled him to obtain a mathematical regularity by submitting the movement of the pendulum to a sustained force. This invention had turned the old man's head. Pride, swelling in his heart, like mercury in the thermometer, had attained the height of transcendent folly. By analogy he had allowed himself to be drawn to materialistic conclusions, and as he constructed his watches, he fancied that he had discovered the secrets of the union of the soul with the body.

77   Thus, on this day, perceiving that Aubert listened to him attentively, he said to him in a tone of simple conviction,—

78   "Dost thou know what life is, my child? Hast thou comprehended the action of those springs which produce existence? Hast thou examined thyself? No. And yet, with the eyes of science, thou mightest have seen the intimate relation which exists between God's work and my own; for it is from his creature that I have copied the combinations of the wheels of my clocks."

79   "Master," replied Aubert eagerly, "can you compare a copper or steel machine with that breath of God which is called the soul, which animates our bodies as the breeze stirs the flowers? What mechanism could be so adjusted as to inspire us with thought?"

80   "That is not the question," responded Master Zacharius gently, but with all the obstinacy of a blind man walking towards an abyss. "In order to understand me, thou must recall the purpose of the escapement which I have invented. When I saw the irregular working of clocks, I understood that the movements shut up in them did not suffice, and that it was necessary to submit them to the regularity of some independent force. I then thought that the balance-wheel might accomplish this, and I succeeded in regulating the movement! Now, was it not a sublime idea that came to me, to return to it its lost force by the action of the clock itself, which it was charged with regulating?"

81   Aubert made a sign of assent.

82   "Now, Aubert," continued the old man, growing animated, "cast thine eyes upon thyself! Dost thou not understand that there are two distinct forces in us, that of the soul and that of the body—that is, a movement and a regulator? The soul is the principle of life; that is, then, the movement. Whether it is produced by a weight, by a spring, or by an immaterial influence, it is none the less in the heart. But without the body this movement would be unequal, irregular, impossible! Thus the body regulates the soul, and, like the balance-wheel, it is submitted to regular oscillations. And this is so true, that one falls ill when one's drink, food, sleep—in a word, the functions of the body—are not properly regulated; just as in my watches the soul renders to the body the force lost by its oscillations. Well, what produces this intimate union between soul and body, if not a marvellous escapement, by which the wheels of the one work into the wheels of the other? This is what I have discovered and applied; and there are no longer any secrets for me in this life, which is, after all, only an ingenious mechanism!"

83   Master Zacharius looked sublime in this hallucination, which carried him to the ultimate mysteries of the Infinite. But his daughter Gerande, standing on the threshold of the door, had heard all. She rushed into her father's arms, and he pressed her convulsively to his breast.

84   "What is the matter with thee, my daughter?" he asked.

85   "If I had only a spring here," said she, putting her hand on her heart, "I would not love you as I do, father."

86   Master Zacharius looked intently at Gerande, and did not reply. Suddenly he uttered a cry, carried his hand eagerly to his heart, and fell fainting on his old leathern chair.

87   "Father, what is the matter?"

88   "Help!" cried Aubert. "Scholastique!"

89   But Scholastique did not come at once. Some one was knocking at the front door; she had gone to open it, and when she returned to the

shop, before she could open her mouth, the old watchmaker, having recovered his senses, spoke:—

90   "I divine, my old Scholastique, that you bring me still another of
those accursed watches which have stopped."

91   "Lord, it is true enough!" replied Scholastique, handing a watch to
Aubert.

92   "My heart could not be mistaken!" said the old man, with a sigh.

93   Meanwhile Aubert carefully wound up the watch, but it would
not go.

CHAPTER 3
A Strange Visit

94   Poor Gerande would have lost her life with that of her father, had
it not been for the thought of Aubert, who still attached her to the
world.

95   The old watchmaker was, little by little, passing away. His faculties
evidently grew more feeble, as he concentrated them on a single
thought. By a sad association of ideas, he referred everything to his
monomania, and a human existence seemed to have departed from
him, to give place to the extra-natural existence of the intermediate
powers. Moreover, certain malicious rivals revived the sinister rumours
which had spread concerning his labours.

96   The news of the strange derangements which his watches betrayed
had a prodigious effect upon the master clockmakers of Geneva. What
signified this sudden paralysis of their wheels, and why these strange relations which they seemed to have with the old man's life? These were
the kind of mysteries which people never contemplate without a secret
terror. In the various classes of the town, from the apprentice to the
great lord who used the watches of the old horologist, there was no one
who could not himself judge of the singularity of the fact. The citizens
wished, but in vain, to get to see Master Zacharius. He fell very ill; and
this enabled his daughter to withdraw him from those incessant visits
which had degenerated into reproaches and recriminations.

97   Medicines and physicians were powerless in the presence of this
organic wasting away, the cause of which could not be discovered. It
sometimes seemed as if the old man's heart had ceased to beat; then the
pulsations were resumed with an alarming irregularity.

98   A custom existed in those days of publicly exhibiting the works of
the masters. The heads of the various corporations sought to distinguish themselves by the novelty or the perfection of their productions;
and it was among these that the condition of Master Zacharius excited

the most lively, because most interested, commiseration. His rivals
pitied him the more willingly because they feared him the less. They
never forgot the old man's success, when he exhibited his magnificent
clocks with moving figures, his repeaters, which provoked general admiration, and commanded such high prices in the cities of France,
Switzerland, and Germany.

99   Meanwhile, thanks to the constant and tender care of Gerande and
Aubert, his strength seemed to return a little; and in the tranquility in
which his convalescence left him, he succeeded in detaching himself
from the thoughts which had absorbed him. As soon as he could walk,
his daughter lured him away from the house, which was still besieged
with dissatisfied customers. Aubert remained in the shop, vainly adjusting and readjusting the rebel watches; and the poor boy, completely
mystified, sometimes covered his face with his hands, fearful that he,
like his master, might go mad.

100   Gerande led her father towards the more pleasant promenades of
the town. With his arm resting on hers, she conducted him sometimes
through the quarter of Saint Antoine, the view from which extends towards the Cologny hill, and over the lake; on fine mornings they caught
sight of the gigantic peaks of Mount Buet against the horizon. Gerande
pointed out these spots to her father, who had well-nigh forgotten even
their names. His memory wandered; and he took a childish interest in
learning anew what had passed from his mind. Master Zacharius leaned
upon his daughter; and the two heads, one white as snow and the other
covered with rich golden tresses, met in the same ray of sunlight.

101   So it came about that the old watchmaker at last perceived that he
was not alone in the world. As he looked upon his young and lovely
daughter, and on himself old and broken, he reflected that after his
death she would be left alone without support. Many of the young
mechanics of Geneva had already sought to win Gerande's love; but
none of them had succeeded in gaining access to the impenetrable retreat of the watchmaker's household. It was natural, then, that during
this lucid interval, the old man's choice should fall on Aubert Thun.
Once struck with this thought, he remarked to himself that this young
couple had been brought up with the same ideas and the same beliefs;
and the oscillations of their hearts seemed to him, as he said one day to
Scholastique, "isochronous."

102   The old servant, literally delighted with the word, though she did
not understand it, swore by her holy patron saint that the whole town
should hear it within a quarter of an hour. Master Zacharius found it
difficult to calm her; but made her promise to keep on this subject a
silence which she never was known to observe.

103   So, though Gerande and Aubert were ignorant of it, all Geneva was soon talking of their speedy union. But it happened also that, while the worthy folk were gossiping, a strange chuckle was often heard, and a voice saying, "Gerande will not wed Aubert."

104   If the talkers turned round, they found themselves facing a little old man who was quite a stranger to them.

105   How old was this singular being? No one could have told. People conjectured that he must have existed for several centuries, and that was all. His big flat head rested upon shoulders the width of which was equal to the height of his body; this was not above three feet. This personage would have made a good figure to support a pendulum, for the dial would have naturally been placed on his face, and the balance-wheel would have oscillated at its ease in his chest. His nose might readily have been taken for the style of a sun-dial, for it was narrow and sharp; his teeth, far apart, resembled the cogs of a wheel, and ground themselves between his lips; his voice had the metallic sound of a bell, and you could hear his heart beat like the tick of a clock. This little man, whose arms moved like the hands on a dial, walked with jerks, without ever turning round. If any one followed him, it was found that he walked a league an hour, and that his course was nearly circular.

106   This strange being had not long been seen wandering, or rather circulating, around the town; but it had already been observed that, every day, at the moment when the sun passed the meridian, he stopped before the Cathedral of Saint Pierre, and resumed his course after the twelve strokes of noon had sounded. Excepting at this precise moment, he seemed to become a part of all the conversations in which the old watchmaker was talked of; and people asked each other, in terror, what relation could exist between him and Master Zacharius. It was remarked, too, that he never lost sight of the old man and his daughter while they were taking their promenades.

107   One day Gerande perceived this monster looking at her with a hideous smile. She clung to her father with a frightened motion.

108   "What is the matter, my Gerande?" asked Master Zacharius.

109   "I do not know," replied the young girl.

110   "But thou art changed, my child. Art thou going to fall ill in thy turn? Ah, well," he added, with a sad smile, "then I must take care of thee, and I will do it tenderly."

111   "O father, it will be nothing. I am cold, and I imagine that it is—"

112   "What, Gerande?"

113   "The presence of that man, who always follows us," she replied in a low tone.

114   Master Zacharius turned towards the little old man.

115   "Faith, he goes well," said he, with a satisfied air, "for it is just four o'clock. Fear nothing, my child; it is not a man, it is a clock!"

116   Gerande looked at her father in terror. How could Master Zacharius read the hour on this strange creature's visage?

117   "By-the-bye," continued the old watchmaker, paying no further attention to the matter, "I have not seen Aubert for several days."

118   "He has not left us, however, father," said Gerande, whose thoughts turned into a gentler channel.

119   "What is he doing then?"

120   "He is working."

121   "Ah!" cried the old man. "He is at work repairing my watches, is he not? But he will never succeed; for it is not repair they need, but a resurrection!"

122   Gerande remained silent.

123   "I must know," added the old man, "if they have brought back any more of those accursed watches upon which the Devil has sent this epidemic!"

124   After these words Master Zacharius fell into complete silence, till he knocked at the door of his house, and for the first time since his convalescence descended to his shop, while Gerande sadly repaired to her chamber.

125   Just as Master Zacharius crossed the threshold of his shop, one of the many clocks suspended on the wall struck five o'clock. Usually the bells of these clocks—admirably regulated as they were—struck simultaneously, and this rejoiced the old man's heart; but on this day the bells struck one after another, so that for a quarter of an hour the ear was deafened by the successive noises. Master Zacharius suffered acutely; he could not remain still, but went from one clock to the other, and beat the time to them, like a conductor who no longer has control over his musicians.

126   When the last had ceased striking, the door of the shop opened, and Master Zacharius shuddered from head to foot to see before him the little old man, who looked fixedly at him and said,—

127   "Master, may I not speak with you a few moments?"

128   "Who are you?" asked the watchmaker abruptly.

129   "A colleague. It is my business to regulate the sun."

130   "Ah, you regulate the sun?" replied Master Zacharius eagerly, without wincing. "I can scarcely compliment you upon it. Your sun goes badly, and in order to make ourselves agree with it, we have to keep putting our clocks forward so much or back so much."

131   "And by the cloven foot," cried this weird personage, "you are right, my master! My sun does not always mark noon at the same moment as

your clocks; but some day it will be known that this is because of the in-
equality of the earth's transfer, and a mean noon will be invented which
will regulate this irregularity!"

132   "Shall I live till then?" asked the old man, with glistening eyes.

133   "Without doubt," replied the little old man, laughing. "Can you
believe that you will ever die?"

134   "Alas! I am very ill now."

135   "Ah, let us talk of that. By Beelzebub! that will lead to just what I
wish to speak to you about."

136   Saying this, the strange being leaped upon the old leather chair,
and carried his legs one under the other, after the fashion of the bones
which the painters of funeral hangings cross beneath death's heads.
Then he resumed, in an ironical tone,—

137   "Let us see, Master Zacharius, what is going on in this good town
of Geneva? They say that your health is failing, that your watches have
need of a doctor!"

138   "Ah, do you believe that there is an intimate relation between
their existence and mine?" cried Master Zacharius.

139   "Why, I imagine that these watches have faults, even vices. If these
wantons do not preserve a regular conduct, it is right that they should
bear the consequences of their irregularity. It seems to me that they
have need of reforming a little!"

140   "What do you call faults?" asked Master Zacharius, reddening at
the sarcastic tone in which these words were uttered. "Have they not a
right to be proud of their origin?"

141   "Not too proud, not too proud," replied the little old man. "They
bear a celebrated name, and an illustrious signature is graven on their
cases, it is true, and theirs is the exclusive privilege of being introduced
among the noblest families; but for some time they have got out of
order, and you can do nothing in the matter, Master Zacharius; and the
stupidest apprentice in Geneva could prove it to you!"

142   "To me, to me,—Master Zacharius!" cried the old man, with a
flush of outraged pride.

143   "To you, Master Zacharius,—you, who cannot restore life to your
watches!"

144   "But it is because I have a fever, and so have they also!" replied the
old man, as a cold sweat broke out upon him.

145   "Very well, they will die with you, since you cannot impart a little
elasticity to their springs."

146   "Die! No, for you yourself have said it! I cannot die,—I, the first
watchmaker in the world; I, who, by means of these pieces and diverse
wheels, have been able to regulate the movement with absolute precision!

Have I not subjected time to exact laws, and can I not dispose of it like a despot? Before a sublime genius had arranged these wandering hours regularly, in what vast uncertainty was human destiny plunged? At what certain moment could the acts of life be connected with each other? But you, man or devil, whatever you may be, have never considered the magnificence of my art, which calls every science to its aid! No, no! I, Master Zacharius, cannot die, for, as I have regulated time, time would end with me! It would return to the infinite, whence my genius has rescued it, and it would lose itself irreparably in the abyss of nothingness! No, I can no more die than the Creator of this universe, that submitted to His laws! I have become His equal, and I have partaken of His power! If God has created eternity, Master Zacharius has created time!"

147   The old watchmaker now resembled the fallen angel, defiant in the presence of the Creator. The little old man gazed at him, and even seemed to breathe into him this impious transport.

148   "Well said, master," he replied. "Beelzebub had less right than you to compare himself with God! Your glory must not perish! So your servant here desires to give you the method of controlling these rebellious watches."

149   "What is it? what is it?" cried Master Zacharius.

150   "You shall know on the day after that on which you have given me your daughter's hand."

151   "My Gerande?"

152   "Herself!"

153   "My daughter's heart is not free," replied Master Zacharius, who seemed neither astonished nor shocked at the strange demand.

154   "Bah! She is not the least beautiful of watches; but she will end by stopping also—"

155   "My daughter,—my Gerande! No!"

156   "Well, return to your watches, Master Zacharius. Adjust and readjust them. Get ready the marriage of your daughter and your apprentice. Temper your springs with your best steel. Bless Aubert and the pretty Gerande. But remember, your watches will never go, and Gerande will not wed Aubert!"

157   Thereupon the little old man disappeared, but not so quickly that Master Zacharius could not hear six o'clock strike in his breast.

CHAPTER 4
The Church of Saint Pierre

158   Meanwhile Master Zacharius became more feeble in mind and body every day. An unusual excitement, indeed, impelled him to continue his work more eagerly than ever, nor could his daughter entice him from it.

159   His pride was still more aroused after the crises to which his strange visitor had hurried him so treacherously, and he resolved to overcome, by the force of genius, the malign influence which weighed upon his work and himself. He first repaired to the various clocks of the town which were confided to his care. He made sure, by a scrupulous examination, that the wheels were in good condition, the pivots firm, the weights exactly balanced. Every part, even to the bells, was examined with the minute attention of a physician studying the breast of a patient. Nothing indicated that these clocks were on the point of being affected by inactivity.

160   Gerande and Aubert often accompanied the old man on these visits. He would no doubt have been pleased to see them eager to go with him, and certainly he would not have been so much absorbed in his approaching end, had he thought that his existence was to be prolonged by that of these cherished ones, and had he understood that something of the life of a father always remains in his children.

161   The old watchmaker, on returning home, resumed his labours with feverish zeal. Though persuaded that he would not succeed, it yet seemed to him impossible that this could be so, and he unceasingly took to pieces the watches which were brought to his shop, and put them together again.

162   Aubert tortured his mind in vain to discover the causes of the evil.

163   "Master," said he, "this can only come from the wear of the pivots and gearing."

164   "Do you want, then, to kill me, little by little?" replied Master Zacharius passionately. "Are these watches child's work? Was it lest I should hurt my fingers that I worked the surface of these copper pieces in the lathe? Have I not forged these pieces of copper myself, so as to obtain a greater strength? Are not these springs tempered to a rare perfection? Could anybody have used finer oils than mine? You must yourself agree that it is impossible, and you avow, in short, that the devil is in it!"

165   From morning till night discontented purchasers besieged the house, and they got access to the old watchmaker himself, who knew not which of them to listen to.

166   "This watch loses, and I cannot succeed in regulating it," said one.

167   "This," said another, "is absolutely obstinate, and stands still, as did Joshua's sun."

168   "If it is true," said most of them, "that your health has an influence on that of your watches, Master Zacharius, get well as soon as possible."

169   The old man gazed at these people with haggard eyes, and only replied by shaking his head, or by a few sad words,—

170   "Wait till the first fine weather, my friends. The season is coming which revives existence in wearied bodies. We want the sun to warm us all!"

171   "A fine thing, if my watches are to be ill through the winter!" said one of the most angry. "Do you know, Master Zacharius, that your name is inscribed in full on their faces? By the Virgin, you do little honour to your signature!"

172   It happened at last that the old man, abashed by these reproaches, took some pieces of gold from his old trunk, and began to buy back the damaged watches. At news of this, the customers came in a crowd, and the poor watchmaker's money fast melted away; but his honesty remained intact. Gerande warmly praised his delicacy, which was leading him straight towards ruin; and Aubert soon offered his own savings to his master. "What will become of my daughter?" said Master Zacharius, clinging now and then in the shipwreck to his paternal love.

173   Aubert dared not answer that he was full of hope for the future, and of deep devotion to Gerande. Master Zacharius would have that day called him his son-in-law, and thus refuted the sad prophecy, which still buzzed in his ears,—

174   "Gerande will not wed Aubert."

175   By this plan the watchmaker at last succeeded in entirely despoiling himself. His antique vases passed into the hands of strangers; he deprived himself of the richly-carved panels which adorned the walls of his house; some primitive pictures of the early Flemish painters soon ceased to please his daughter's eyes, and everything, even the precious tools that his genius had invented, were sold to indemnify the clamorous customers.

176   Scholastique alone refused to listen to reason on the subject; but her efforts failed to prevent the unwelcome visitors from reaching her master, and from soon departing with some valuable object. Then her shattering was heard in all the streets of the neighbourhood, where she had long been known. She eagerly denied the rumours of sorcery and magic on the part of Master Zacharius, which gained currency; but as at bottom she was persuaded of their truth, she said her prayers over and over again to redeem her pious falsehoods.

177   It had been noticed that for some time the old watchmaker had neglected his religious duties. Time was, when he had accompanied Gerande to church, and had seemed to find in prayer the intellectual charm which it imparts to thoughtful minds, since it is the most sublime exercise of the imagination. This voluntary neglect of holy practices, added to the secret habits of his life, had in some sort confirmed the accusations levelled against his labours. So, with the double purpose of drawing her father back to God, and to the world, Gerande resolved to call religion to her aid. She thought that it might give some vitality to his dying soul; but the dogmas of faith and humility had to combat, in the soul of Master Zacharius, an insurmountable pride, and come into collision with that vanity of science which connects everything with itself, without rising to the infinite source whence first principles flow.

178   It was under these circumstances that the young girl undertook her father's conversion; and her influence was so effective that the old watchmaker promised to attend high mass at the cathedral on the following Sunday. Gerande was in an ecstasy, as if heaven had opened to her view. Old Scholastique could not contain her joy, and at last found irrefutable arguments against the gossiping tongues which accused her master of impiety. She spoke of it to her neighbours, her friends, her enemies, to those whom she knew.

179   "In faith, we scarcely believe what you tell us, dame Scholastique," they replied; "Master Zacharius has always acted in concert with the devil!"

180   "You haven't counted, then," replied the old servant, "the fine bells which strike for my master's clocks? How many times they have struck the hours of prayer and the mass!"

181   "No doubt," they would reply. "But has he not invented machines which go all by themselves, and which actually do the work of a real man?"

182   "Could a child of the devil," exclaimed dame Scholastique wrathfully, "have executed the fine iron clock of the château of Andernatt, which the town of Geneva was not rich enough to buy? A pious motto appeared at each hour, and a Christian who obeyed them, would have gone straight to Paradise! Is that the work of the devil?"

183   This masterpiece, made twenty years before, had carried Master Zacharius's fame to its acme; but even then there had been accusations of sorcery against him. But at least the old man's visit to the Cathedral ought to reduce malicious tongues to silence.

184   Master Zacharius, having doubtless forgotten the promise made to his daughter, had returned to his shop. After being convinced of his

powerlessness to give life to his watches, he resolved to try if he could
not make some new ones. He abandoned all those useless works, and
devoted himself to the completion of the crystal watch, which he intended to be his masterpiece, but in vain did he use his most perfect
tools, and employ rubies and diamonds for resisting friction. The watch
fell from his hands the first time that he attempted to wind it up!

185   The old man concealed this circumstance from every one, even
from his daughter; but from that time his health rapidly declined. There
were only the last oscillations of a pendulum, which goes slower when
nothing restores its original force. It seemed as if the laws of gravity,
acting directly upon him, were dragging him irresistibly down to the
grave.

186   The Sunday so ardently anticipated by Gerande at last arrived. The
weather was fine, and the temperature inspiriting. The people of
Geneva were passing quietly through the streets, gaily chatting about
the return of spring. Gerande, tenderly taking the old man's arm, directed her steps towards the cathedral, while Scholastique followed behind with the prayer-books. People looked curiously at them as they
passed. The old watchmaker permitted himself to be led like a child, or
rather like a blind man. The faithful of Saint Pierre were almost frightened when they saw him cross the threshold, and shrank back at his
approach.

187   The chants of high mass were already resounding through the
church. Gerande went to her accustomed bench, and kneeled with
profound and simple reverence. Master Zacharius remained standing
upright beside her.

188   The ceremonies continued with the majestic solemnity of that
faithful age, but the old man had no faith. He did not implore the pity
of Heaven with cries of anguish of the "Kyrie;" he did not, with the
"Gloria in Excelsis," sing the splendours of the heavenly heights; the
reading of the Testament did not draw him from his materialistic
reverie, and he forgot to join in the homage of the "Credo." This proud
old man remained motionless, as insensible and silent as a stone statue;
and even at the solemn moment when the bell announced the miracle
of transubstantiation, he did not bow his head, but gazed directly at the
sacred host which the priest raised above the heads of the faithful.
Gerande looked at her father, and a flood of tears moistened her missal.
At this moment the clock of Saint Pierre struck half-past eleven.
Master Zacharius turned quickly towards this ancient clock which still
spoke. It seemed to him as if its face was gazing steadily at him; the figures of the hours shone as if they had been engraved in lines of fire, and
the hands shot forth electric sparks from their sharp points.

189   The mass ended. It was customary for the "Angelus" to be said at noon, and the priests, before leaving the altar, waited for the clock to strike the hour of twelve. In a few moments this prayer would ascend to the feet of the Virgin.

190   But suddenly a harsh noise was heard. Master Zacharius uttered a piercing cry.

191   The large hand of the clock, having reached twelve, had abruptly stopped, and the clock did not strike the hour.

192   Gerande hastened to her father's aid. He had fallen down motionless, and they carried him outside the church.

193   "It is the death-blow!" murmured Gerande, sobbing.

194   When he had been borne home, Master Zacharius lay upon his bed utterly crushed. Life seemed only to still exist on the surface of his body, like the last whiffs of smoke about a lamp just extinguished.

195   When he came to his senses, Aubert and Gerande were leaning over him. In these last moments the future took in his eyes the shape of the present. He saw his daughter alone, without a protector.

196   "My son," said he to Aubert, "I give my daughter to thee."

197   So saying, he stretched out his hands towards his two children, who were thus united at his death-bed.

198   But soon Master Zacharius lifted himself up in a paroxysm of rage. The words of the little old man recurred to his mind.

199   "I do not wish to die!" he cried; "I cannot die! I, Master Zacharius, ought not to die! My books—my accounts!—"

200   With these words he sprang from his bed towards a book in which the names of his customers and the articles which had been sold to them were inscribed. He seized it and rapidly turned over its leaves, and his emaciated finger fixed itself on one of the pages.

201   "There!" he cried, "there! this old iron clock, sold to Pittonaccio! It is the only one that has not been returned to me! It still exists—it goes—it lives! Ah, I wish for it—I must find it! I will take such care of it that death will no longer seek me!"

202   And he fainted away.

203   Aubert and Gerande knelt by the old man's bed-side and prayed together.

CHAPTER 5
The Hour of Death

204   Several days passed, and Master Zacharius, though almost dead, rose from his bed and returned to active life under a supernatural excitement.

He lived by pride. But Gerande did not deceive herself; her father's body and soul were for ever lost.

205   The old man got together his last remaining resources, without thought of those who were dependent upon him. He betrayed an incredible energy, walking, ferreting about, and mumbling strange, incomprehensible words.

206   One morning Gerande went down to his shop. Master Zacharius was not there. She waited for him all day. Master Zacharius did not return.

207   Gerande wept bitterly, but her father did not reappear.

208   Aubert searched everywhere through the town, and soon came to the sad conviction that the old man had left it.

209   "Let us find my father!" cried Gerande, when the young apprentice told her this sad news.

210   "Where can he be?" Aubert asked himself.

211   An inspiration suddenly came to his mind. He remembered the last words which Master Zacharius had spoken. the old man only lived now in the old iron clock that had not been returned! Master Zacharius must have gone in search of it.

212   Aubert spoke of this to Gerande.

213   "Let us look at my father's book," she replied.

214   The descended to the shop. The book was open on the bench. All the watches or clocks made by the old man, and which had been returned to him because they were out of order, were stricken out excepting one:—

> *"Sold to M. Pittonaccio,*
>   *an iron clock, with bell and moving figures;*
>   *sent to his château at Andernatt."*

215   It was this "moral" clock of which Scholastique had spoken with so much enthusiasm.

216   "My father is there!" cried Gerande.

217   "Let us hasten thither," replied Aubert. "We may still save him!"

218   "Not for this life," murmured Gerande, "but at least for the other."

219   "By the mercy of God, Gerande! The château of Andernatt stands in the gorge of the 'Dents-du-Midi,' twenty hours from Geneva. Let us go!"

220   That very evening Aubert and Gerande, followed by the old servant, set out on foot by the road which skirts Lake Leman. They accomplished five leagues during the night, stopping neither at Bessinge nor at Ermance, where rises the famous château of the Mayors. They with difficulty forded the torrent of the Dranse, and everywhere they

went they inquired for Master Zacharius, and were soon convinced that they were on his track.

221   The next morning, at daybreak, having passed Thonon, they reached Evian, whence the Swiss territory may be seen extended over twelve leagues. But the two betrothed did not even perceive the enchanting prospect. They went straight forward, urged on by a supernatural force. Aubert, leaning on a knotty stick, offered his arm alternately to Gerande and to Scholastique, and he made the greatest efforts to sustain his companions. All three talked of their sorrow, of their hopes, and thus passed along the beautiful road by the water-side, and across the narrow plateau which unites the borders of the lake with the heights of the Chalais. They soon reached Bouveret, where the Rhone enters the Lake of Geneva.

222   On leaving this town they diverged from the lake, and their weariness increased amid these mountain districts. Vionnaz, Chesset, Collombay, half-lost villages, were soon left behind. Meanwhile their knees shook, their feet were lacerated by the sharp points which covered the ground like a brushwood of granite;—but no trace of Master Zacharius!

223   He must be found, however, and the two young people did not seek repose either in the isolated hamlets or at the château of Monthay, which, with its dependencies, formed the appanage of Margaret of Savoy. At last, late in the day, and half dead with fatigue, they reached the hermitage of Notre-Dame-du-Sex, which is situated at the base of the Dents-du-Midi, six hundred feet above the Rhone.

224   The hermit received the three wanderers as night was falling. They could not have gone another step, and here they must needs rest.

225   The hermit could give them no news of Master Zacharius. They could scarcely hope to find him still living amid these sad solitudes. The night was dark, the wind howled amid the mountains, and the avalanches roared down from the summits of the broken crags.

226   Aubert and Gerande, crouching before the hermit's hearth, told him their melancholy tale. Their mantles, covered with snow, were drying in a corner; and without, the hermit's dog barked lugubriously, and mingled his voice with that of the tempest.

227   "Pride," said the hermit to his guests, "has destroyed an angel created for good. It is the stumbling-block against which the destinies of man strike. You cannot reason with pride, the principal of all the vices, since, by its very nature, the proud man refuses to listen to it. It only remains, then, to pray for your father!"

228   All four knelt down, when the barking of the dog redoubled, and some one knocked at the door of the hermitage.

229 "Open, in the devil's name!"

230 The door yielded under the blows, and a dishevelled, haggard, ill-clothed man appeared.

231 "My father!" cried Gerande.

232 It was Master Zacharius.

233 "Where am I?" said he. "In eternity! Time is ended—the hours no longer strike—the hands have stopped!"

234 "Father!" returned Gerande, with so piteous an emotion that the old man seemed to return to the world of the living.

235 "Thou here, Gerande?" he cried; "and thou, Aubert? Ah, my dear betrothed ones, you are going to be married in our old church!"

236 "Father," said Gerande, seizing him by the arm, "come home to Geneva—come with us!"

237 The old man tore away from his daughter's embrace and hurried towards the door, on the threshold of which the snow was falling in large flakes.

238 "Do not abandon your children!" cried Aubert.

239 "Why return," replied the old man sadly, "to those places which my life has already quitted, and where a part of myself is for ever buried?"

240 "Your soul is not dead," said the hermit solemnly.

241 "My soul? O no,—its wheels are good! I perceive it beating regularly—"

242 "Your soul is immaterial,—your soul is immortal!" replied the hermit sternly.

243 "Yes—like my glory! But it is shut up in the château of Andernatt, and I wish to see it again!"

244 The hermit crossed himself; Scholastique became almost inanimate. Aubert held Gerande in his arms.

245 "The château of Andernatt is inhabited by one who is lost," said the hermit, "one who does not salute the cross of my hermitage."

246 "My father, go not thither!"

247 "I want my soul! My soul is mine—"

248 "Hold him! Hold my father!" cried Gerande.

249 But the old man had leaped across the threshold, and plunged into the night, crying, "Mine, mine, my soul!"

250 Gerande, Aubert, and Scholastique hastened after him. They went by difficult paths, across which Master Zacharius sped like a tempest, urged by an irresistible force. The snow raged around them, and mingled its white flakes with the froth of the swollen torrents.

251 As they passed the chapel erected in memory of the massacre of the Theban legion, they hurriedly crossed themselves. Master Zacharius was not to be seen.

252   At last the village of Evionnaz appeared in the midst of this sterile region. The hardest heart would have been moved to see this hamlet, lost among these horrible solitudes. The old man sped on, and plunged into the deepest gorge of the Dents-du-Midi, which pierce the sky with their sharp peaks.

253   Soon a ruin, old and gloomy as the rocks at its base, rose before him.

254   "It is there—there!" he cried, hastening his pace still more frantically.

255   The château of Andernatt was a ruin even then. A thick, crumbling tower rose above it, and seemed to menace with its downfall the old gables which reared themselves below. The vast piles of jagged stones were gloomy to look on. Several dark halls appeared amid the débris, with caved-in ceilings, now become the abode of vipers.

256   A low and narrow postern opening upon a ditch choked with rubbish, gave access to the château. Who had dwelt there none knew. No doubt some margrave, half lord, half brigand, had sojourned in it; to the margrave had succeeded bandits or counterfeit coiners, who had been hanged on the scene of their crime. The legend went that, on winter nights, Satan came to lead his diabolical dances on the slope of the deep gorges in which the shadow of these ruins was engulfed.

257   But Master Zacharius was not dismayed by their sinister aspect. He reached the postern. No one forbade him to pass. A spacious and gloomy court presented itself to his eyes; no one forbade him to cross it. He passed along the kind of inclined plane which conducted to one of the long corridors, whose arches seemed to banish daylight from beneath their heavy springings. His advance was unresisted. Gerande, Aubert, and Scholastique closely followed him.

258   Master Zacharius, as if guided by an irresistible hand, seemed sure of his way, and strode along with rapid step. He reached an old worm-eaten door, which fell before his blows, whilst the bats described oblique circles around his head.

259   An immense hall, better preserved than the rest, was soon reached. High sculptured panels, on which serpents, ghouls, and other strange figures seemed to disport themselves confusedly, covered its walls. Several long and narrow windows, like loopholes, shivered beneath the bursts of the tempest.

260   Master Zacharius, on reaching the middle of this hall, uttered a cry of joy.

261   On an iron support, fastened to the wall, stood the clock in which now resided his entire life. This unequalled masterpiece represented an ancient Roman church, with buttresses of wrought iron, with its heavy bell-tower, where there was a complete chime for the anthem of the day, the "Angelus," the mass, vespers, compline, and the benediction.

Above the church door, which opened at the hour of the services, was placed a "rose," in the centre of which two hands moved, and the archivault of which reproduced the twelve hours of the face sculptured in relief. Between the door and the rose, just as Scholastique had said, a maxim, relative to the employment of every moment of the day, appeared on a copper plate. Master Zacharius had once regulated this succession of devices with a really Christian solicitude; the hours of prayer, of work, of repast, of recreation, and of repose, followed each other according to the religious discipline, and were to infallibly insure salvation to him who scrupulously observed their commands.

262   Master Zacharius, intoxicated with joy, went forward to take possession of the clock, when a frightful roar of laughter resounded behind him.

263   He turned, and by the light of a smoky lamp recognized the little old man of Geneva.

264   "You are here?" cried he.

265   Gerande was afraid. She drew closer to Aubert.

266   "Good-day, Master Zacharius," said the monster.

267   "Who are you?"

268   "Signor Pittonaccio, at your service! You have come to give me your daughter! You have remembered my words, 'Gerande will not wed Aubert.'"

269   The young apprentice rushed upon Pittonaccio, who escaped from him like a shadow.

270   "Stop, Aubert!" cried Master Zacharius.

271   "Good-night," said Pittonaccio, and he disappeared.

272   "My father, let us fly from this hateful place!" cried Gerande. "My father!"

273   Master Zacharius was no longer there. He was pursuing the phantom of Pittonaccio across the rickety corridors. Scholastique, Gerande, and Aubert remained, speechless and fainting, in the large gloomy hall. The young girl had fallen upon a stone seat; the old servant knelt beside her, and prayed; Aubert remained erect, watching his betrothed. Pale lights wandered in the darkness, and the silence was only broken by the movements of the little animals which live in old wood, and the noise of which marks the hours of "death watch."

274   When daylight came, they ventured upon the endless staircase which wound beneath these ruined masses; for two hours they wandered thus without meeting a living soul, and hearing only a far-off echo responding to their cries. Sometimes they found themselves buried a hundred feet below the ground, and sometimes they reached places whence they could overlook the wild mountains.

275   Chance brought them at last back again to the vast hall, which had sheltered them during this night of anguish. It was no longer empty. Master Zacharius and Pittonaccio were talking there together, the one upright and rigid as a corpse, the other crouching over a marble table.

276   Master Zacharius, when he perceived Gerande, went forward and took her by the hand, and led her towards Pittonaccio, saying, "Behold your lord and master, my daughter. Gerande, behold your husband!"

277   Gerande shuddered from head to foot.

278   "Never!" cried Aubert, "for she is my betrothed."

279   "Never!" responded Gerande, like a plaintive echo.

280   Pittonaccio began to laugh.

281   "You wish me to die, then!" exclaimed the old man. "There, in that clock, the last which goes of all which have gone from my hands, my life is shut up; and this man tells me, 'When I have thy daughter, this clock shall belong to thee.' And this man will not rewind it. He can break it, and plunge me into chaos. Ah, my daughter, you no longer love me!"

282   "My father!" murmured Gerande, recovering consciousness.

283   "If you knew what I have suffered, far away from this principle of my existence!" resumed the old man. "Perhaps no one looked after this timepiece. Perhaps its springs were left to wear out, its wheels to get clogged. But now, in my own hands, I can nourish this health so dear, for I must not die,—I, the great watchmaker of Geneva. Look, my daughter, how these hands advance with certain step. See, five o'clock is about to strike. Listen well, and look at the maxim which is about to be revealed."

284   Five o'clock struck with a noise which resounded sadly in Gerande's soul, and these words appeared in red letters:

YOU MUST EAT OF THE FRUITS OF THE TREE OF SCIENCE.

285   Aubert and Gerande looked at each other stupefied. These were no longer the pious sayings of the Catholic watchmaker. The breath of Satan must have passed over it. But Zacharius paid no attention to this, and resumed—

286   "Dost thou hear, my Gerande? I live, I still live! Listen to my breathing,—see the blood circulating in my veins! No, thou wouldst not kill the father, and thou wilt accept this man for thy husband, so that I may become immortal, and at last attain the power of God!"

287   At these blasphemous words old Scholastique crossed herself, and Pittonaccio laughed aloud with joy.

288   "And then, Gerande, thou wilt be happy with him. See this man,—he is Time! Thy existence will be regulated with absolute precision. Gerande, since I gave thee life, give life to thy father!"

289   "Gerande," murmured Aubert, "I am thy betrothed."

290   "He is my father!" replied Gerande, fainting.

291   "She is thine!" said Master Zacharius. "Pittonaccio, thou wilt keep thy promise!"

292   "Here is the key of the clock," replied the horrible man.

293   Master Zacharius seized the long key, which resembled an uncoiled snake, and ran to the clock, which he hastened to wind up with fantastic rapidity. The creaking of the spring jarred upon the nerves. The old watchmaker wound and wound the key, without stopping a moment, and it seemed as if the movement were beyond his control. He wound more and more quickly, with strange contortions, until he fell from sheer weariness.

294   "There, it is wound up for a century!" he cried.

295   Aubert rushed from the hall is if he were mad. After long wandering, he found the outlet of the hateful château, and hastened into the open air. He returned to the hermitage of Notre-Dame-du-Sex, and talked so despairingly to the holy recluse, that the latter consented to return with him to the château of Andernatt.

296   If, during these hours of anguish, Gerande had not wept, it was because her tears were exhausted.

297   Master Zacharius had not left the hall. He ran every moment to listen to the regular beating of the old clock.

298   Meanwhile the clock had struck, and to Scholastique's great terror, these words had appeared on the silver face:—

MAN OUGHT TO BECOME THE EQUAL OF GOD.

299   The old man had not only not been shocked by these impious maxims, but read them deliriously, and flattered himself with thoughts of pride, whilst Pittonaccio kept close by him.

300   The marriage-contract was to be signed at midnight. Gerande, almost unconscious, saw or heard nothing. The silence was only broken by the old man's words, and the chuckling of Pittonaccio.

301   Eleven o'clock struck. Master Zacharius shuddered, and read in a loud voice:—

MAN SHOULD BE THE SLAVE OF SCIENCE AND SACRIFICE TO IT RELATIVES AND FAMILY.

302   "Yes!" he cried, "there is nothing but science in this world!"

303   The hands slipped over the face of the clock with the hiss of a serpent, and the pendulum beat with accelerated strokes.

304   Master Zacharius no longer spoke. He had fallen to the floor, his throat rattled, and from his oppressed bosom came only these half-broken words: "Life—science!"

305   The scene had now two new witnesses, the hermit and Aubert. Master Zacharius lay upon the floor; Gerande was praying beside him, more dead than alive.

306   Of a sudden a dry, hard noise was heard, which preceded the strike.

307   Master Zacharius sprang up.

308   "Midnight!" he cried.

309   The hermit stretched out his hands towards the old clock,—and midnight did not sound.

310   Master Zacharius uttered a terrible cry, which must have been heard in hell, when these words appeared:—

WHO EVER SHALL ATTEMPT TO MAKE HIMSELF THE
EQUAL OF GOD, SHALL BE FOR EVER DAMNED!

311   The old clock burst with a noise like thunder, and the spring, escaping, leaped across the hall with a thousand fantastic contortions; the old man rose, ran after it, trying in vain to seize it, and exclaiming, "My soul,—my soul!"

312   The spring bounded before him, first on one side, then on the other, and he could not reach it.

313   At last Pittonaccio seized it, and uttering a horrible blasphemy, ingulfed himself in the earth.

314   Master Zacharius fell backwards. He was dead.

315   The old watchmaker was buried in the midst of the peaks of Andernatt.

316   Then Aubert and Gerande returned to Geneva, and during the long life which God accorded to them, they made it a duty to redeem by prayer the soul of the castaway of science.

DISCUSSION QUESTIONS

1. Two people are compared to clocks in this story—Master Zacharius and Pittonaccio. What similarities and differences do these two characters have?
2. There is no scientific reason given for the watches stopping. What does the story imply the reason is?

3. It is claimed in the story that Zacharius invented "true clock work" and is devoted solely to science. Yet, he has a daughter who is devoted to him. How does this element influence your reading of the story?

4. There is a contradiction between Zacharius saying he has turned metals into "living flesh" with "beating hearts" and his insistence on mathematical regularity and faith only in science. In small groups, discuss how these differences can exist together.

5. Why can't physicians and medicines heal Zacharius as he is weakened?

WRITING TOPICS

1. Master Zacharius several times proclaims himself the equal of God. What evidence can you find to support his claim? To contradict it? Explain your findings in a paragraph.

2. Zacharius is completely obsessed with the idea of his soul residing in his creations. In a journal entry, describe other situations where humans put so much of themselves into a project that it may appear to acquire a soul.

3. The late nineteenth century was a time of enormous discovery. Write a short essay describing developments in science or other areas that may have contributed to Verne's ideas for this story.

The Crystal Egg

1899

H . G . W E L L S (1 8 6 6 - 1 9 4 6)

Herbert George Wells, after graduating from the Normal School
of Science in England, wrote two textbooks before he began writing fiction. His first successful novel was *The Time Machine* in 1895.
In this classic, he explored the lives of humans in the far distant
future. He followed this with *The Island of Dr. Moreau* in 1896, a
story about genetically altering people. In 1898 he wrote *The War
of the Worlds,* dealing with an alien invasion of Earth. The alien invaders are overcome, not by superior weaponry or intellect, but
by a common bacterium. His "scientific romances," as they were
called, helped popularize a genre that soon became known by
the label it still holds today: science fiction.

His *When the Sleeper Wakes* (1899) has the hero wakening from
suspended animation, while *The First Men in the Moon* (1901) is
a fantastic visit to a dystopian society. Wells also wrote numerous
essays of prediction and nonfiction, including *The Outline of History*
(1920). His later novels, like *The Shape of Things to Come* (1933) express the idea that a better world will come about only after the
present one is destroyed.

In "The Crystal Egg," H. G. Wells shows a glimpse of a
far-removed civilization, one that may either save or doom humanity. However, it becomes impossible to tell which, given
the circumstances.

1   There was, until a year ago, a little and very grimy-looking shop near Seven Dials, over which, in weather-worn yellow lettering, the name of "C. Cave, Naturalist and Dealer in Antiquities," was inscribed. The contents of its window were curiously variegated. They comprised some elephant tusks and an imperfect set of chessmen, beads and weapons, a box of eyes, two skulls of tigers and one human, several moth-eaten stuffed monkeys (one holding a lamp), an old-fashioned cabinet, a flyblown ostrich egg or so, some fishing-tackle, and an extraordinarily dirty, empty glass fishtank. There was also, at the moment the story begins, a mass of crystal, worked into the shape of an egg and brilliantly polished. And at that two people, who stood outside the window, were looking, one of them a tall, thin clergyman, the other a black-bearded young man of dusky complexion and unobtrusive costume. The dusky young man spoke with eager gesticulation, and seemed anxious for his companion to purchase the article.

2   While they were there, Mr. Cave came into his shop, his beard still wagging with the bread and butter of his tea. When he saw these men and the object of their regard, his countenance fell. He glanced guiltily over his shoulder, and softly shut the door. He was a little old man, with pale face and peculiar watery blue eyes; his hair was a dirty grey, and he wore a shabby blue frock-coat, an ancient high silk hat, and carpet slippers very much down at the heel. He remained watching the two men as they talked. The clergyman went deep into his trouser pocket, examined a handful of money, and showed his teeth in an agreeable smile. Mr. Cave seemed still more depressed when they came into the shop.

3   The clergyman, without any ceremony, asked the price of the crystal egg. Mr. Cave glanced nervously towards the door leading into the parlour, and said five pounds. The clergyman protested that the price was high, to his companion as well as to Mr. Cave—it was, indeed, very much more than Mr. Cave had intended to ask, when he had stocked the article—and an attempt at bargaining ensued. Mr. Cave stepped to the shop-door, and held it open. "Five pounds is my price," he said, as though he wished to save himself the trouble of unprofitable discussion. As he did so, the upper portion of a woman's face appeared above the blind in the glass upper panel of the door leading into the parlour, and stared curiously at the two customers. "Five pounds is my price," said Mr. Cave, with a quiver in his voice.

4   The swarthy young man had so far remained a spectator, watching Cave keenly. Now he spoke. "Give him five pounds," he said. The clergyman glanced at him to see if he were in earnest, and, when he looked at Mr. Cave again, he saw that the latter's face was white. "It's a lot of money," said the clergyman, and, diving into his pocket, began count-

ing his resources. He had little more than thirty shillings, and he appealed to his companion, with whom he seemed to be on terms of considerable intimacy. This gave Mr. Cave an opportunity of collecting his thoughts, and he began to explain in an agitated manner that the crystal was not, as a matter or fact, entirely free for sale. His two customers were naturally surprised at this, and inquired why he had not thought of that before he began to bargain. Mr. Cave became confused, but he stuck to his story, that the crystal was not in the market that afternoon, that a probable purchaser of it had already appeared. The two, treating this as an attempt to raise the price still further, made as if they would leave the shop. But at this point the parlour door opened, and the owner of the dark fringe and the little eyes appeared.

5   She was a coarse-featured, corpulent woman, younger and very much larger than Mr. Cave; she walked heavily, and her face was flushed. "That crystal *is* for sale," she said. "And five pounds is a good enough price for it. I can't think what you're about, Cave, not to take the gentleman's offer!"

6   Mr. Cave, greatly perturbed by the irruption, looked angrily at her over the rims of his spectacles, and, without excessive assurance, asserted his right to manage his business in his own way. An altercation began. The two customers watched the scene with interest and some amusement, occasionally assisting Mrs. Cave with suggestions. Mr. Cave, hard driven, persisted in a confused and impossible story of an enquiry for the crystal that morning, and his agitation became painful. But he stuck to his point with extraordinary persistence. It was the young Oriental who ended this curious controversy. He proposed that they should call again in the course of two days—so as to give the alleged enquirer a fair chance. "And then we must insist," said the clergyman. "Five pounds." Mrs. Cave took it on herself to apologise for her husband, explaining that he was sometimes "a little odd," and as the two customers left, the couple prepared for a free discussion of the incident in all its bearings.

7   Mrs. Cave talked to her husband with singular directness. The poor little man, quivering with emotion, muddled himself between his stories, maintaining on the one hand that he had another customer in view, and on the other asserting that the crystal was honestly worth ten guineas. "Why did you ask five pounds?" said his wife. "*Do* let me manage my business my own way!" said Mr. Cave.

8   Mr. Cave had living with him a step-daughter and a step-son, and at supper that night the transaction was re-discussed. None of them had a high opinion of Mr. Cave's business methods, and this action seemed a culminating folly.

9   "It's my opinion he's refused that crystal before," said the step-son,
a loose-limbed lout of eighteen.

10   "But *Five Pounds!*" said the step-daughter, an argumentative young
women of six-and-twenty.

11   Mr. Cave's answers were wretched; he could only mumble weak
assertions that he knew his own business best. They drove him from his
half-eaten supper into the shop, to close it for the night, his ears aflame
and tears of vexation behind his spectacles. "Why had he left the crystal in the window so long? The folly of it!" That was the trouble closest
in his mind. For a time he could see no way of evading sale.

12   After supper his step-daughter and step-son smartened themselves
up and went out and his wife retired upstairs to reflect upon the business aspects of the crystal, over a little sugar and lemon and so forth in
hot water. Mr. Cave went into the shop, and stayed there until late, os-
tensibly to make ornamental rockeries for gold-fish cases but really for
a private purpose that will be better explained later. The next day Mrs.
Cave found that the crystal had been removed from the window, and
was lying behind some second-hand books on angling. She replaced it
in a conspicuous position. But she did not argue further about it, as a
nervous headache disinclined her from debate. Mr. Cave was always
disinclined. The day passed disagreeably. Mr. Cave was, if anything,
more absent-minded than usual, and uncommonly irritable withal. In
the afternoon, when his wife was taking her customary sleep, he removed the crystal from the window again.

13   The next day Mr. Cave had to deliver a consignment of dog-fish at
one of the hospital schools, where they were needed for dissection. In
his absence Mrs. Cave's mind reverted to the topic of the crystal, and
the methods of expenditure suitable to a windfall of five pounds. She
had already devised some very agreeable expedients, among others a
dress of green silk for herself and a trip to Richmond, when a jangling
of the front door summoned her into the shop. The customer was an
examination coach who came to complain of the non-delivery of certain frogs asked for the previous day. Mrs. Cave did not approve of this
particular branch of Mr. Cave's business, and the gentleman, who had
called in a somewhat aggressive mood, retired after a brief exchange of
words—entirely civil so far as he was concerned. Mrs. Cave's eye then
naturally turned to the window; for the sight of the crystal was an assurance of the five pounds and of her dreams. What was her surprise to
find it gone!

14   She went to the place behind the locker on the counter, where she
had discovered it the day before. It was not there; and she immediately
began an eager search about the shop.

15   When Mr. Cave returned from his business with the dog-fish, about a quarter to two in the afternoon, he found the shop in some confusion, and his wife, extremely exasperated and on her knees behind the counter, routing among his taxidermic material. Her face came up hot and angry over the counter, as the jangling bell announced his return, and she forthwith accused him of "hiding it."

16   "Hid *what?*" asked Mr. Cave.

17   "The crystal!"

18   At that Mr. Cave, apparently much surprised, rushed to the window. "Isn't it here?" he said. "Great Heavens! what has become of it?"

19   Just then, Mr. Cave's step-son re-entered the shop from the inner room—he had come home a minute or so before Mr. Cave—and he was blaspheming freely. He was apprenticed to a second-hand furniture dealer down the road, but he had his meals at home, and he was naturally annoyed to find no dinner ready.

20   But, when he heard of the loss of the crystal, he forgot his meal, and his anger was diverted from his mother to his step-father. Their first idea, of course, was that he had hidden it. But Mr. Cave stoutly denied all knowledge of its fate—freely offering his bedabbled affidavit in the matter—and at last was worked up to the point of accusing, first, his wife and then his step-son of having taken it with a view to a private sale. So began an exceedingly acrimonious and emotional discussion, which ended for Mrs. Cave in a peculiar nervous condition midway between hysterics and amuck, and caused the step-son to be half-an-hour late at the furniture establishment in the afternoon. Mr. Cave took refuge from his wife's emotions in the shop.

21   In the evening the matter was resumed, with less passion and in a judicial spirit, under the presidency of the step-daughter. The supper passed unhappily and culminated in a painful scene. Mr. Cave gave way at last to extreme exasperation, and went out banging the front door violently. The rest of the family, having discussed him with the freedom his absence warranted, hunted the house from garret to cellar, hoping to light upon the crystal.

22   The next day the two customers called again. They were received by Mrs. Cave almost in tears. It transpired that no one *could* imagine all that she had stood from Cave at various times in her married pilgrimage . . . . She also gave a garbled account of the disappearance. The clergyman and the Oriental laughed silently at one another, and said it was very extraordinary. As Mrs. Cave seemed disposed to give them the complete history of her life they made to leave the shop. Thereupon Mrs. Cave, still clinging to hope, asked for the clergyman's address, so that, if she could get anything out of Cave, she might

communicate it. The address was duly given, but apparently was afterwards mislaid. Mrs. Cave can remember nothing about it.

23   In the evening of that day, the Caves seem to have exhausted their
emotions, and Mr. Cave, who had been out in the afternoon, supped in a
gloomy isolation that contrasted pleasantly with the impassioned controversy of the previous days. For some time matters were very badly strained
in the Cave household, but neither crystal nor customer reappeared.

24   Now, without mincing the matter, we must admit that Mr. Cave
was a liar. He knew perfectly well where the crystal was. It was in the
rooms of Mr. Jacoby Wace, Assistant Demonstrator at St. Catherine's
Hospital, Westbourne Street. It stood on the sideboard partially covered
by a black velvet cloth, and beside a decanter of American whisky. It is
from Mr. Wace, indeed, that the particulars upon which this narrative is
based were derived. Cave had taken off the thing to the hospital hidden
in the dog-fish sack, and there had pressed the young investigator to
keep it for him. Mr. Wace was a little dubious at first. His relationship
to Cave was peculiar. He had a taste for singular characters, and he had
more than once invited the old man to smoke and drink in his rooms,
and to unfold his rather amusing views of life in general and of his wife
in particular. Mr. Wace had encountered Mrs. Cave, too, on occasions
when Mr. Cave was not at home to attend to him. He knew the constant interference to which Cave was subjected, and having weighed
the story judicially, he decided to give the crystal a refuge. Mr. Cave
promised to explain the reasons for his remarkable affection for the
crystal more fully on a later occasion, but he spoke distinctly of seeing
visions therein. He called on Mr. Wace the same evening.

25   He told a complicated story. The crystal he said had come into his
possession with other oddments at the forced sale of another curiosity
dealer's effects, and not knowing what its value might be, he had tick-
eted it at ten shillings. It had hung upon his hands at that price for
some months, and he was thinking of "reducing the figure," when he
made a singular discovery.

26   At that time his health was very bad—and it must be borne in
mind that, throughout all this experience, his physical condition was
one of ebb—and he was in considerable distress by reason of negligence, the positive ill-treatment even, he received from his wife and
step-children. His wife was vain, extravagant, unfeeling and had a
growing taste for private drinking; his step-daughter was mean and
over-reaching; and his step-son had conceived a violent dislike for him,
and lost no chance of showing it. The requirements of his business
pressed heavily upon him, and Mr. Wace does not think that he was altogether free from occasional intemperance. He had begun life in a

comfortable position, he was a man of fair education, and he suffered, for weeks at a stretch, from melancholia and insomnia. Afraid to disturb his family, he would slip quietly from his wife's side, when his thoughts became intolerable, and wander about the house. And about three o'clock one morning, late in August, chance directed him into the shop.

27   The dirty little place was impenetrably black except in one spot, where he perceived an unusual glow of light. Approaching this, he discovered it to be the crystal egg, which was standing on the corner of the counter towards the window. A thin ray smote through a crack in the shutters, impinged upon the object, and seemed as it were to fill its entire interior.

28   It occurred to Mr. Cave that this was not in accordance with the laws of optics as he had known them in his younger days. He could understand the rays being refracted by the crystal and coming to a focus in its interior, but this diffusion jarred with his physical conceptions. He approached the crystal nearly, peering into it and round it, with a transient revival of the scientific curiosity that in his youth had determined his choice of a calling. He was surprised to find the light not steady, but writhing within the substance of the egg, as though that object was a hollow sphere of some luminous vapour. In moving about to get different points of view, he suddenly found that he had come between it and the ray, and that the crystal none the less remained luminous. Greatly astonished, he lifted it out of the light ray and carried it to the darkest part of the shop. It remained bright for some four or five minutes, when it slowly faded and went out. He placed it in the thin streak of daylight, and its luminousness was almost immediately restored.

29   So far, at least, Mr. Wace was able to verify the remarkable story of Mr. Cave. He has himself repeatedly held this crystal in a ray of light (which had to be of a less diameter than one millimetre). And in a perfect darkness, such as could be produced by velvet wrapping, the crystal did undoubtedly appear very faintly phosphorescent. It would seem, however, that the luminousness was of some exceptional sort, and not equally visible to all eyes; for Mr. Harbinger—whose name will be familiar to the scientific reader in connection with the Pasteur Institute—was quite unable to see any light whatever. And Mr. Wace's own capacity for its appreciation was out of comparison inferior to that of Mr. Cave's. Even with Mr. Cave the power varied very considerably: his vision was most vivid during states of extreme weakness and fatigue.

30   Now, from the outset this light in the crystal exercised a curious fascination upon Mr. Cave. And it says more for his loneliness of soul than a volume of pathetic writing could do, that he told no human

being of his curious observations. He seems to have been living in such
an atmosphere of petty spite that to admit the existence of a pleasure
would have been to risk the loss of it. He found that as the dawn advanced, and the amount of diffused light increased, the crystal became
to all appearance non-luminous. And for some time he was unable to
see anything in it, except at night-time, in dark corners of the shop.

31   But the use of an old velvet cloth, which he used as a background for
a collection of minerals, occurred to him, and by doubling this, and
putting it over his head and hands, he was able to get a sight of the luminous movement within the crystal even in the day-time. He was very
cautious lest he should be thus discovered by his wife, and he practised
this occupation only in the afternoons, while she was asleep upstairs, and
then circumspectly in a hollow under the counter. And one day, turning
the crystal about in his hands, he saw something. It came and went like a
flash, but it gave him the impression that the object had for a moment
opened to him the view of a wide and spacious and strange country; and,
turning it about, he did, just as the light faded, see the same vision again.

32   Now, it would be tedious and unnecessary to state all the phases of
Mr. Cave's discovery from this point. Suffice that the effect was this: the
crystal, being peered into at an angle of about 137 degrees from the direction of the illuminating ray, gave a clear and consistent picture of a
wide and peculiar country-side. It was not dream-like at all: it produced
a definite impression of reality, and the better the light the more real and
solid it seemed. It was a moving picture: that is to say, certain objects
moved in it, but slowly in an orderly manner like real things, and, according as the direction of the lighting and vision changed, the picture
changed also. It must, indeed, have been like looking through an oval
glass at a view, and turning the glass about to get at different aspects.

33   Mr. Cave's statements, Mr. Wace assures me, were extremely circumstantial, and entirely free from any of that emotional quality that
taints hallucinatory impressions. But it must be remembered that all the
efforts of Mr. Wace to see any similar clarity in the faint opalescence of
the crystal were wholly unsuccessful, try as he would. The difference in
intensity of the impressions received by the two men was very great,
and it is quite conceivable that what was a view to Mr. Cave was a mere
blurred nebulosity to Mr. Wace.

34   The view, as Mr. Cave described it, was invariably of an extensive
plain, and he seemed always to be looking at it from a considerable
height, as if from a tower or a mast. To the east and to the west the
plain was bounded at a remote distance by vast reddish cliffs, which reminded him of those he had seen in some picture; but what the pictures was Mr. Wace was unable to ascertain. These cliffs passed north

and south—he could tell the points of the compass by the stars that
were visible of a night—receding in an almost illimitable perspective
and fading into the mists of the distance before they met. He was
nearer the eastern set of cliffs, on the occasion of his first vision the sun
was rising over them, and black against the sunlight and pale against
their shadow appeared a multitude of soaring forms that Mr. Cave regarded as birds. A vast range of buildings spread below him; he seemed
to be looking down upon them; and, as they approached the blurred
and refracted edge of the picture, they became indistinct. There were
also trees curious in shape, and in colouring, a deep mossy green and
an exquisite grey, beside a wide and shining canal. And something
great and brilliantly coloured flew across the picture. But the first time
Mr. Cave saw these pictures he saw only in flashes, his hands shook, his
head moved, the vision came and went, and grew foggy and indistinct.
And at first he had the greatest difficulty in finding the picture again
once the direction of it was lost.

35   His next clear vision, which came about a week after the first, the
interval having yielded nothing but tantalising glimpses and some useful experience, showed him the view down the length of the valley.
The view was different, but he had a curious persuasion, which his
subsequent observations abundantly confirmed, that he was regarding
this strange world from exactly the same spot, although he was looking
in a different direction. The long façade of the great building, whose
roof he had looked down upon before, was now receding in perspective. He recognised the roof. In the front of the façade was a terrace of
massive proportions and extraordinary length, and down the middle of
the terrace, at certain intervals, stood huge but very graceful masts,
bearing small shiny objects which reflected the setting sun. The import of these small objects did not occur to Mr. Cave until some time
after, as he was describing the scene to Mr. Wace. The terrace over-
hung a thicket of the most luxuriant and graceful vegetation, and beyond this was a wide grassy lawn on which certain broad creatures, in
form like beetles but enormously larger, reposed. Beyond this again
was a richly decorated causeway of pinkish stone; and beyond that, and
lined with dense *red* weeds, and passing up the valley exactly parallel
with the distant cliffs, was a broad and mirror-like expanse of water.
The air seemed full of squadrons of great birds, manœuvering in stately
curves; and across the river was a multitude of splendid buildings,
richly coloured and glittering with metallic tracery and facets, among a
forest of moss-like and lichenous trees. And suddenly something
flapped repeatedly across the vision, like the fluttering of a jewelled fan
or the beating of a wing, and a face, or rather the upper part of a face

with very large eyes, came as it were close to his own and as if on the other side of the crystal. Mr. Cave was so startled and so impressed by the absolute reality of these eyes, that he drew his head back from the crystal to look behind it. He had become so absorbed in watching that he was quite surprised to find himself in the cool darkness of his little shop, with its familiar odour of methyl, mustiness, and decay. And, as he blinked about him, the glowing crystal faded, and went out.

36 Such were the first general impressions of Mr. Cave. The story is curiously direct and circumstantial. From the outset, when the valley first flashed momentarily on his senses, his imagination was strangely affected, and, as he began to appreciate the details of the scene he saw, his wonder rose to the point of a passion. He went about his business listless and distraught, thinking only of the time when he should be able to return to his watching. And then a few weeks after his first sight of the valley came the two customers, the stress and excitement of their offer, and the narrow escape of the crystal from sale, as I have already told.

37 Now, while the thing was Mr. Cave's secret, it remained a mere wonder, a thing to creep to covertly and peep at, as a child might peep upon a forbidden garden. But Mr. Wace has, for a young scientific investigator, a particularly lucid and consecutive habit of mind. Directly the crystal and its story came to him, and he had satisfied himself, by seeing the phosphorescence with his own eyes, that there really was a certain evidence for Mr. Cave's statements, he proceeded to develop the matter systematically. Mr. Cave was only too eager to come and feast his eyes on this wonderland he saw, and he came every night from half-past eight until half-past ten, and sometimes, in Mr. Wace's absence, during the day. On Sunday afternoons, also, he came. From the outset Mr. Wace made copious notes, and it was due to his scientific method that the relation between the direction from which the initiating ray entered the crystal and the orientation of the picture were proved. And, by covering the crystal in a box perforated only with a small aperture to admit the exciting ray, and by substituting black holland for his buff blinds, he greatly improved the conditions of the observations; so that in a little while they were able to survey the valley in any direction they desired.

38 So having cleared the way, we may give a brief account of this visionary world within the crystal. The things were in all cases seen by Mr. Cave, and the method of working was invariably for him to watch the crystal and report what he saw, while Mr. Wace (who as a science student had learnt the trick of writing in the dark) wrote a brief note of his report. When the crystal faded, it was put into its box in the proper position and the electric light turned on. Mr. Wace asked questions,

and suggested observations to clear up difficult points. Nothing, indeed, could have been less visionary and more matter-of-fact.

39   The attention of Mr. Cave had been speedily directed to the bird-like creatures he had seen so abundantly present in each of his earlier visions. His first impression was soon corrected, and he considered for a time that they might represent a diurnal species of bat. Then he thought, grotesquely enough, that they might be cherubs. Their heads were round, and curiously human, and it was the eyes of one of them that had so startled him on his second observation. They had broad, silvery wings, not feathered, but glistening almost as brilliantly as new-killed fish and with the same subtle play of colour, and these wings were not built on the plan of a bird-wing or bat, Mr. Wace learned, but supported by curved ribs radiating from the body. (A sort of butterfly wing with curved ribs seems best to express their appearance.) The body was small, but fitted with two bunches of prehensile organs, like long tentacles, immediately under the mouth. Incredible as it appeared to Mr. Wace, the persuasion at last became irresistible, that it was these creatures which owned the great quasi-human buildings and the magnificent garden that made the broad valley so splendid. And Mr. Cave perceived that the buildings, with other peculiarities, had no doors, but that the great circular windows, which opened freely, gave the creatures egress and entrance. They would alight upon their tentacles, fold their wings to a smallness almost rod-like, and hop into the interior. But among them was a multitude of smaller-winged creatures, like great dragon-flies and moths and flying beetles, and across the greensward brilliantly-coloured gigantic ground-beetles crawled lazily to and fro. Moreover, on the causeways and terraces, large-headed creatures similar to the greater winged flies, but wingless, were visible, hopping busily upon their hand-like tangle of tentacles.

40   Allusion has already been made to the glittering objects upon masts that stood upon the terrace of the nearer building. It dawned upon Mr. Cave, after regarding one of these masts very fixedly on one particularly vivid day, that the glittering object there was a crystal exactly like that into which he peered. And a still more careful scrutiny convinced him that each one in a vista of nearly twenty carried a similar object.

41   Occasionally one of the large flying creatures would flutter up to one, and, folding its wings and coiling a number of its tentacles about the mast, would regard the crystal fixedly for a space,—sometimes for as long as fifteen minutes. And a series of observations, made at the suggestion of Mr. Wace, convinced both watchers that, so far as this visionary world was concerned, the crystal into which they peered actually stood at the summit of the end-most mast on the terrace, and that on

one occasion at least one of these inhabitants of this other world had looked into Mr. Cave's face while he was making these observations.

42   So much for the essential facts of this very singular story. Unless we dismiss it all as the ingenious fabrication of Mr. Wace, we have to believe one of two things: either that Mr. Cave's crystal was in two worlds at once, and that, while it was carried about in one, it remained stationary in the other, which seems altogether absurd; or else that it had some peculiar relation of sympathy with another and exactly similar crystal in this other world, so that what was seen in the interior of the one in this world, was, under suitable conditions, visible to an observer in the corresponding crystal in the other world; and *vice versa*. At present, indeed, we do not know of any way in which two crystals could so come *en rapport*, but nowadays we know enough to understand that the thing is not altogether impossible. This view of the crystals as *en rapport* was the supposition that occurred to Mr. Wace, and to me at least it seems extremely plausible . . . .

43   And where was this other world? On this, also, the alert intelligence of Mr. Wace speedily threw light. After sunset, the sky darkened rapidly—there was a very brief twilight interval indeed—and the stars shone out. They were recognisably the same as those we see, arranged in the same constellations. Mr. Cave recognised the Bear, the Pleiades, Aldebaran, and Sirius: so that the other world must be somewhere in the solar system, and, at the utmost, only a few hundreds of millions of miles from our own. Following up this clue, Mr. Wace learned that the midnight sky was a darker blue even than our midwinter sky, and that the sun seemed a little smaller. *And there were two small moons!* "like our moon but smaller, and quite differently marked" one of which moved so rapidly that its motion was clearly visible as one regarded it. These moons were never high in the sky, but vanished as they rose: that is, every time they revolved they were eclipsed because they were so near their primary planet. And all this answers quite completely, although Mr. Cave did not know it, to what must be the condition of things on Mars.

44   Indeed, it seems an exceedingly plausible conclusion that peering into this crystal Mr. Cave did actually see the planet Mars and its inhabitants. And, if that be the case, then the evening star that shone so brilliantly in the sky of that distant vision, was neither more nor less than our own familiar earth.

45   For a time the Martians—if they were Martians—do not seem to have known of Mr. Cave's inspection. Once or twice one would come to peer, and go away very shortly to some other mast, as though the vision was unsatisfactory. During this time Mr. Cave was able to watch the proceedings of these winged people without being disturbed by their

attentions, and, although his report is necessarily vague and fragmentary, it is nevertheless very suggestive. Imagine the impression of humanity a Martian observer would get who, after a difficult process of preparation and with considerable fatigue to the eyes, was able to peer at London from the steps of St. Martin's Church for stretches, at longest, of four minutes at a time. Mr. Cave was unable to ascertain if the winged Martians were the same as the Martians who hopped about the causeways and terraces, and if the latter could put on wings at will. He several times saw certain clumsy bipeds, dimly suggestive of apes, white and partially translucent, feeding among certain of the lichenous trees, and once some of these fled before one of the hopping, round-headed Martians. The latter caught one in its tentacles, and then the picture faded suddenly and left Mr. Cave most tantalisingly in the dark. On another occasion a vast thing, that Mr Cave thought at first was some gigantic insect, appeared advancing along the causeway beside the canal with extraordinary rapidity. As this drew nearer Mr. Cave perceived that it was a mechanism of shining metals and of extraordinary complexity. And then, when he looked again, it had passed out of sight.

46   After a time Mr. Wace aspired to attract the attention of the Martians, and the next time that the strange eyes of one of the appeared close to the crystal Mr. Cave cried out and sprang away, and they immediately turned on the light and began to gesticulate in a manner suggestive of signalling. But when at last Mr. Cave examined the crystal again the Martian had departed.

47   Thus far these observations had progressed in early November, and then Mr. Cave, feeling that the suspicions of his family about the crystal were allayed, began to take it to and fro with him in order that, as occasion arose in the daytime or night, he might comfort himself with what was fast becoming the most real thing in his existence.

48   In December Mr. Wace's work in connection with a forthcoming examination became heavy, the sittings were reluctantly suspended for a week, and for ten or eleven days—he is not quite sure which—he saw nothing of Cave. He then grew anxious to resume these investigations, and, the stress of his seasonal labours being abated, he went down to Seven Dials. At the corner he noticed a shutter before a bird fancier's window, and then another at a cobbler's. Mr. Cave's shop was closed.

49   He rapped and the door was opened by the step-son in black. He at once called Mrs. Cave, who was, Mr. Wace could not but observe, in cheap but ample widow's weeds of the most imposing pattern. Without any very great surprise Mr. Wace learnt that Cave was dead and already buried. She was in tears, and her voice was a little thick. She had just returned from Highgate. Her mind seemed occupied with

her own prospects and the honourable details of the obsequies, but Mr. Wace was at last able to learn the particulars of Cave's death. He had been found dead in his shop in the early morning, the day after his last visit to Mr. Wace, and the crystal had been clasped in his stone-cold hands. His face was smiling, said Mrs. Cave, and the velvet cloth from the minerals lay on the floor at his feet. He must have been dead five or six hours when he was found.

50   This came as a great shock to Wace, and he began to reproach him-self bitterly for having neglected the plain symptoms of the old man's ill-health. But his chief thought was of the crystal. He approached that topic in a gingerly manner, because he knew Mrs. Cave's peculiarities. He was dumbfounded to learn that it was sold.

51   Mrs. Cave's first impulse, directly Cave's body had been taken up-stairs, had been to write to the mad clergyman who had offered five pounds for the crystal, informing him of its recovery; but after a violent hunt in which her daughter joined her, they were convinced of the loss of his address. As they were without the means required to mourn and bury Cave in the elaborate style the dignity of an old Seven Dials in-habitant demands, they had appealed to a friendly fellow-tradesman in Great Portland Street. He had very kindly taken over a portion of the stock at a valuation. The valuation was his own and the crystal egg was included in one of the lots. Mr. Wace, after a few suitable consolatory observations, a little off-handedly proffered perhaps, hurried at once to Great Portland Street. But there he learned that the crystal egg had al-ready been sold to a tall, dark man in grey. And there the material facts in this curious, and to me at least very suggestive, story come abruptly to an end. The Great Portland Street dealer did not know who the tall dark man in grey was, nor had he observed him with sufficient atten-tion to describe him minutely. He did not even know which way this person had gone after leaving the shop. For a time Mr. Wace remained in the shop, trying the dealer's patience with hopeless questions, vent-ing his own exasperation. And at last, realising abruptly that the whole thing had passed out of his hands, had vanished like a vision of the night, he returned to his own rooms, a little astonished to find the notes he had made still tangible and visible upon his untidy table.

52   His annoyance and disappointment were naturally very great. He made a second call (equally ineffectual) upon the Great Portland Street dealer, and he resorted to advertisements in such periodicals as were likely to come into the hands of a *bric-a-brac* collector. He also wrote letters to *The Daily Chronicle* and *Nature*, but both those periodicals, suspecting a hoax, asked him to reconsider his action before they printed, and he was advised that such a strange story, unfortunately so

bare of supporting evidence, might imperil his reputation as an investigator. Moreover, the calls of his proper work were urgent. So that after a month or so, save for an occasional reminder to certain dealers, he had reluctantly to abandon the quest for the crystal egg, and from that day to this it remains undiscovered. Occasionally, however, he tells me, and I can quite believe him, he has bursts of zeal, in which he abandons his more urgent occupation and resumes the search.

53   Whether or not it will remain lost for ever, with the material and origin of it, are things equally speculative at the present time. If the present purchaser is a collector, one would have expected the enquiries of Mr. Wace to have reached him through the dealers. He has been able to discover Mr. Cave's clergyman and "Oriental"—no other than the Rev. James Parker and the young Prince of Bosso-Kuni in Java. I am obliged to them for certain particulars. The object of the Prince was simply curiousity—and extravagance. He was so eager to buy, because Cave was so oddly reluctant to sell. It is just as possible that the buyer in the second instance was simply a casual purchaser and not a collector at all, and the crystal egg, for all I know, may at the present moment be within a mile of me, decorating a drawing-room or serving as a paper-weight—its remarkable functions all unknown. Indeed, it is partly with the idea of such a possibility that I have thrown this narrative into a form that will give it a chance of being read by the ordinary consumer of fiction.

54   My own ideas in the matter are practically identical with those of Mr. Wace. I believe the crystal on the mast in Mars and the crystal egg of Mr. Cave's to be in some physical, but at present quite inexplicable, way *en rapport,* and we both believe further that the terrestrial crystal must have been—possibly at some remote date—sent hither from that planet, in order to give the Martians a near view of our affairs. Possibly the fellows to the crystals in the other masts are also on our globe. No theory of hallucination suffices for the facts.

DISCUSSION QUESTIONS

1. The sign over the shop reads, "C. Cave, Naturalist and Dealer in Antiquities," an odd combination, by today's standards. How are Cave's name and type of business suitable for the story's setting? What type of store might such a "curiosity dealer" operate today?
2. Why doesn't the shopkeeper want to sell the crystal egg, even at a high price, and against the urgings of his family?

3. The narrator describes an exact set of circumstances for viewing the egg. How does this contribute to the believability of the events?
4. In describing the creatures, what analogy does Wells make most extensive use of? Why do you think he chose this particular comparison?
5. Cave tells only Mr. Wace of his discovery because he thought "to admit the existence of a pleasure would have been to risk the loss of it." In groups of three or four, explore what this might mean.

WRITING TOPICS

1. What do you think killed Cave with a smile on his face? Write a paragraph or two explaining your answer.
2. Write a paragraph explaining which modern invention the crystal is most like. In what ways is it unlike that device?
3. Given today's knowledge of the solar system, Wells and other writers produced some rather outrageous theories about the possibilities of life on Mars. In an essay, explore the dreams and fears this story offers. What historical events might have contributed to its vision?

CHAPTER TWO

The Twenties

1920

Women gain the right to vote in the U.S.

First licensed radio broadcast

Thompson submachine gun patented

The Golem **film is about a clay man reanimated to save the Jews**

1921

First coast-to-coast airmail flights in U.S.

Hitler becomes leader of Nazi Party

Irish War of Independence divides Irish Free State and Northern Ireland

Einstein wins Nobel Prize for discovery of photoelectric effect

Polygraph invented

First use of the word "robot" in print by the Czech Karel Capek in the play *R.U.R.*

1922

Mahatma Gandhi is jailed in India

Mussolini takes power in Italy

Hitler publishes *Mein Kampf*

1923

International Criminal Police Organization (INTERPOL) formed

Freud's *The Ego and the Id* published

H. G. Wells publishes *Men Like Gods*

1924

Self-winding watch patented

Insecticides used for first time

First spiral bound notebook produced

Scopes "Monkey Trial" pits evolutionists against creationists in public schools

Process for manufacturing hydrogen invented

1925

Hugo Gernsback publishes *124 C 41+*

Franz Kafka's *The Trial* **is published posthumously**

First liquid fuel rocket launched in the United States

North Pole flown over by Richard Byrd

First IQ test

First talking motion pictures

Edgar Rice Burroughs publishes *The Moon Maid*

Metropolis novelization of the play appears

Amazing Stories, the premier magazine of science fiction, begins publication

Chinese Civil War begins (ends 1949); Chiang Kai-Shek rises to power

Harlem Globetrotters, all-black basketball team, formed

First "iron lung" developed

Society for Space Travel started in Germany

Charles Lindbergh makes first solo flight over Atlantic

Stalin takes over the Soviet Union

Color TV patented

Penicillin discovered by Alexander Fleming

First color motion picture shown by George Eastman

Bakelite is first plastic to be used commercially

"Scotch" tape introduced

Richard Byrd makes first flight over South Pole

Wall Street crashes, ushering in the Great Depression

Existence of antimatter postulated

"Buck Rogers in the 25th Century" appears in comics

First use of the term *science fiction* in print in the U.S.

HISTORICAL CONTEXT

World War I, or the Great War, as it was called, was the war that
was supposed to end war forever. Instead, it became the greatest
worldwide catastrophe of that time. It destroyed a century of uneasy peace, changed the balance of power, and brought sweeping
economic, social, and political changes. The rate of technological
discoveries also increased, particularly in the area of weaponry.

The ending of World War I didn't make the world safe for
democracy; indeed, before the war, France and Britain were not
noticeably more democratic than Germany or Italy. The first
World War did establish the United States as a major power, but it
was not immediately evident what had been won. The ensuing
treaties actually created tensions that led to World War II.

The aftermath of the war set the stage for both female suffrage
and Prohibition in the United States. The latter backfired for several
reasons. One was that many citizens felt their rights were being
trampled on and drank to spite what they felt was an unjust law.
Another was that there was no way to actually enforce the law, and
local officials were easily bribed. This led to a rise in organized
crime. The administration of President Warren Harding was unable
to stop the illegal activities and was itself riddled with scandal.

It was a decade of contradictions. Despite the post-war
changes, there was an economic boom in the United States
beginning in 1922. Speculation in stocks and payments for goods
arranged on the installment plan fueled the rapid growth. Sigmund
Freud's works on sexuality became available to Americans in translation. Immigration quotas tightened and the Ku Klux Klan resur-
faced during the twenties. Radios became common in nearly every
household, and commercial advertising grew at a tremendous rate,

resulting in, among other things, smoking being perceived as sophisticated. Speakeasies and vaudeville houses sprang up everywhere, and the expression "Anyone who lives only to work is a sucker" gained wide acceptance.

The twenties ended with a crash, though—the stock market crash of 1929. The economic high was followed by a deep low. Wages were cut in half, marriage and birth rates dropped dramatically, college enrollment sank, and the unemployment rate rose to over 35 percent. When Franklin Roosevelt was elected president in 1932, he pushed through his New Deal social reforms and repealed Prohibition in 1933. This eased the crunch, but it wasn't until the beginning of World War II that the United States returned to a level between the highs of the Roaring Twenties and the depths of the Great Depression.

DEVELOPMENTS IN SCIENCE FICTION

In Europe, and Britain particularly, the science fiction that emerged after World War I showed the aftershock of that conflict. Where before there had been many gung-ho tales of future war, the reality of modern warfare became apparent, and stories of ruined civilizations became more prominent. Americans had quite a different war experience from Europeans, since no fighting took place on American soil. This accounts, in part, for the generally optimistic outlook of U.S. science fiction as opposed to the more depressing character of British science fiction after the war.

Much science fiction of the twenties showed the dangers of technology spinning out of control. There was an apathy that settled throughout Europe. The old way had been destroyed and hope for the future was dimmed. Franz Kafka depicted surrealistic nightmares where guilt and oppression ruled. His works show dystopias created from our own inner guilt and despair.

In Karel Capek's *R.U.R.*, which derived the term *robot* from the Czechoslovakian word *robotnik*, the creatures are really organic rather than mechanical, making them technically androids. But soon after, mechanical and organic robots were appearing in numerous science fiction stories. In Fritz Lang's *Metropolis*, for instance, a human woman, Maria, is the protector of underground children. She is replaced by a robot with a flesh-like covering that resembles Maria, until the flesh burns off to reveal the hollow metal core.

The term *scientific romance* was still widely in use in the twenties, meaning a science-based story with an element of romance. The romance concept changed, though, from the romance of adventure—a male model—to romantic love, largely due to the rise in female readership. As World War I was beginning, Hugo Gernsback entered the magazine publishing business. At first he produced technical titles such as *Modern Electrics* and *Electrical Experiments*. He quickly moved on to *Science and Invention,* which featured short technological fantasy stories mixed in with articles on popular science. Gradually he developed the idea for the first magazine devoted entirely to science fiction—*Amazing Stories.* Gernsback at first favored the term *scientifiction,* a shortening of scientific fiction, in order to differentiate these stories from the older scientific romances. Beginning in 1926, he reprinted many of the classic works of Poe, Verne, and Wells, as well as original fiction, mostly from American authors.

The influence of Verne and Wells was widespread (partly due to extensive translations), but science fiction was growing worldwide. There were healthy branches in Russia, France, Germany, Italy, Romania, Japan, Britain, and the United States. Karel Capek's *R.U.R.* (Czech, 1920), Evgenii Zamiatin's *We* (Russian, 1922), and Thea von Harbou's *Metropolis* (German, 1926) are notable contributions to science fiction. Because paper production was down due to wartime shortages, magazines began to dominate the market, with many novels serialized before appearing in book form. Edgar Rice Burroughs' tales of Tarzan of the jungle, John Carter of Mars, Carson Napier of Venus, and David Innes at the Earth's core became immensely popular, and many of Burroughs' novels were serialized by Gernsback.

Burroughs' style is often criticized for being nonscientific and hopelessly romantic, but he gained a following that drew scores of imitators. His work thus had a lasting impact and influence. His works, and many others, began to be called *space opera,* which was essentially an adventure story with love interest, horror, and rescue of a helpless female from bug-eyed monsters from outer space. The hero relied on powerful weapons, making these tales similar to Westerns, except the pistols were replaced by ray guns and horses by rocketships.

Gernsback believed that science fiction should teach readers about scientific possibilities, combined with romance. He also thought that science fiction could predict future scientific developments and spur scientific progress, which he thought was a good thing. He rejected stories which predicted domination of humans by machines, which he thought would stifle progress. Largely through Gernsback's efforts, Abraham Merritt became respected as a writer of scientifically accurate fiction, although his stories employed stock characters and situations and were almost pure fantasy. In stories such as *The Moon Pool* (1918), he attracted readers by including occult powers, evil women, and eventual conquest by a boldly wielded sword.

E. E. "Doc" Smith, another popular pulp writer, wrote about super science rather than sword-wielding feudal societies, but he still appealed to less educated tastes by emphasizing action over thought, power over responsibility, and aggression over consideration. Smith's *The Skylark of Space* appeared in the same issue of *Amazing Stories* (1928) as "Armageddon–2419 A.D.," the first Buck Rogers adventure. With the stock market crash of 1929, Gernsback was forced to abandon many of his magazine titles, but he followed through and produced the first issue of *Science Wonder Stories,* thus establishing a new name for the genre—science fiction.

SCIENCE FICTION IN OTHER MEDIA

While science fiction of the twenties provided a large dose of wish fulfillment, it also established a precedent for the more classic science fiction of the forties and fifties. Even though the pulps increased science fiction readership, movies rose in popularity after the war. The cinema largely ignored science fiction in its early days, focusing instead on contemporary dramas. There were exceptions, such as the 1925 adaptation of Arthur Conan Doyle's *The Lost World,* which captured audiences with its dinosaur model animation, and Fritz Lang's futuristic *Metropolis* in 1926. Despite such successes, the pulps would continue to dominate the science fiction market for another decade.

The Disintegration Machine

1926

ARTHUR CONAN DOYLE (1859–1930)

Doyle is known primarily for his popular Sherlock Holmes stories, but he also wrote historical romances, including *The White Company* (1891), other mysteries, and adventure stories. After World War I he wrote books and essays promoting spiritualism. His significant science fiction works include the Professor Challenger books: *The Lost World* (1912), and *The Poison Belt* (1913). In "Danger" (1914) he predicted the effect German submarines could have on British shipping, much to the chagrin of the British government.

Doyle's first science fiction story was "The Los Amigos Fiasco" (1892). It features an experimental electric chair that supercharges the criminal instead of killing him. He continued to write science fiction sporadically with stories like "The Terror of Blue John Gap" (1910), and after his crusade for spiritualism consumed his energies, he even converted Professor Challenger to that belief in *The Land of Mist* (1926).

In "The Disintegration Machine," Arthur Conan Doyle shows Professor Challenger agreeing to a scientific test, but his real task is much larger, one even the world's greatest living scientist may not be equal to.

1   Professor Challenger was in the worst possible humour. As I stood at the door of his study, my hand upon the handle and my foot upon the mat, I heard a monologue which ran like this, the words booming and reverberating through the house:

2   "Yes, I say it is the second wrong call. The *second* in one morning. Do you imagine that a man of science is to be distracted from essential work by the constant interference of some idiot at the end of a wire? I will not have it. Send this instant for the manager. Oh! you *are* the manager. Well, why don't you manage? Yes, you certainly manage to distract me from work the importance of which your mind is incapable of understanding. I want the superintendent. He is away? So I should imagine. I will carry you to the law courts if this occurs again. Crowing cocks have been adjudicated upon. I myself have obtained a judgment. If crowing cocks, why not jangling bells? The case is clear. A written apology. Very good. I will consider it. *Good* morning."

3   It was at this point that I ventured to make my entrance. It was certainly an unfortunate moment. I confronted him as he turned from the telephone—a lion in its wrath. His huge black beard was bristling, his great chest was heaving with indignation, and his arrogant grey eyes swept me up and down as the backwash of his anger fell upon me.

4   "Infernal, idle, overpaid rascals!" he boomed. "I could hear them laughing while I was making my just complaint. There is a conspiracy to annoy me. And now, young Malone, you arrive to complete a disastrous morning. Are you here, may I ask, on your own account, or has your rag commissioned you to obtain an interview? As a friend you are privileged—as a journalist you are outside the pale."

5   I was hunting in my pocket for McArdle's letter when suddenly some new grievance came to his memory. His great hairy hands fumbled about among the papers upon his desk and finally extracted a press cutting.

6   "You have been good enough to allude to me in one of your recent lucubrations," he said, shaking the paper at me. "It was in the course of your somewhat fatuous remarks concerning the recent Saurian remains discovered in the Solenhofen Slates. You began a paragraph with the words: 'Professor G. E. Challenger, who is among our greatest living scientists—'"

7   "Well, sir?" I asked.

8   "Why these invidious qualifications and limitations? Perhaps you can mention who these other predominant scientific men may be to whom you impute equality, or possibly superiority to myself?"

9   "It was badly worded. I should certainly have said: 'Our greatest living scientist,'" I admitted. It was after all my own honest belief. My words turned winter into summer.

10 "My dear young friend, do not imagine that I am exacting, but surrounded as I am by pugnacious and unreasonable colleagues, one is forced to take one's own part. Self-assertion is foreign to my nature, but I have to hold my ground against opposition. Come now! Sit here! What is the reason of your visit?"

11 I had to tread warily, for I knew how easy it was to set the lion roaring once again. I opened McArdle's letter.

12 "May I read you this, sir? It is from McArdle, my editor."

13 "I remember the man—not an unfavourable specimen of his class."

14 "He has, at least, a very high admiration for you. He has turned to you again and again when he needed the highest qualities in some investigation. That is the case now."

15 "What does he desire?" Challenger plumed himself like some unwieldy bird under the influence of flattery. He sat down with his elbows upon the desk, his gorilla hands clasped together, his beard bristling forward, and his big grey eyes, half covered by his drooping lids, fixed benignly upon me. He was huge in all that he did, and his benevolence was even more overpowering than his truculence.

16 "I'll read you his note to me. He says:

Please call upon our esteemed friend, Professor Challenger, and ask for his co-operation in the following circumstances. There is a Latvian gentleman named Theodore Nemor living at White Friars Mansions, Hampstead, who claims to have invented a machine of a most extraordinary character which is capable of disintegrating any object placed within its sphere of influence. Matter dissolves and returns to its molecular or atomic condition. By reversing the process it can be reassembled. The claim seems to be an extravagant one, and yet there is solid evidence that there is some basis for it and that the man has stumbled upon some remarkable discovery.

I need not enlarge upon the revolutionary character of such an invention, nor of its extreme importance as a potential weapon of war. A force which could disintegrate a battleship, or turn a battalion, if it were only for a time, into a collection of atoms, would dominate the world. For social and for political reasons not an instant is to be lost in getting to the bottom of the affair. The man courts publicity as he is anxious to sell his invention, so that there is no difficulty in approaching him. The enclosed card will open his doors. What I desire is that you and Professor Challenger shall call upon him, inspect his invention, and write for the *Gazette* a considered report upon the value of the discovery. I expect to hear from you tonight.—R. McArdle.

17   "There are my instructions, Professor," I added, as I refolded the letter. "I sincerely hope that you will come with me, for how can I, with my limited capacities, act alone in such a matter?"

18   "True, Malone! True!" purred the great man. "Though you are by no means destitute of natural intelligence, I agree with you that you would be somewhat overweighted in such a matter as you lay before me. These unutterable people upon the telephone have already ruined my morning's work, so that a little more can hardly matter. I am engaged in answering that Italian buffoon, Mazotti, whose views upon the larval development of the tropical termites have excited my derision and contempt, but I can leave the complete exposure of the impostor until evening. Meanwhile, I am at your service."

19   And thus it came about that on that October morning I found myself in the deep level tube with the Professor speeding to the North of London in what proved to be one of the most singular experiences of my remarkable life.

20   I had, before leaving Enmore Gardens, ascertained by the much-abused telephone that our man was at home, and had warned him of our coming. He lived in a comfortable flat in Hampstead, and he kept us waiting for quite half an hour in his ante-room whilst he carried on an animated conversation with a group of visitors, whose voices, as they finally bade farewell in the hall, showed that they were Russians. I caught a glimpse of them through the half-opened door, and had a passing impression of prosperous and intelligent men, with astrakhan collars to their coats, glistening top-hats, and every appearance of that bourgeois well-being which the successful Communist so readily assumes. The hall door closed behind them, and the next instant Theodore Nemor entered our apartment. I can see him now as he stood with the sunlight full upon him, rubbing his long, thin hands together and surveying us with his broad smile and his cunning yellow eyes.

21   He was a short, thick man, with some suggestion of deformity in his body, though it was difficult to say where that suggestion lay. One might say that he was a hunch-back without the hump. His large, soft face was like an underdone dumpling, of the same colour and moist consistency, while the pimples and blotches which adorned it stood out the more aggressively against the pallid background. His eyes were those of a cat, and catlike was the thin, long, bristling moustache above his loose, wet, slobbering mouth. It was all low and repulsive until one came to the sandy eyebrows. From these upwards there was a splendid cranial arch such as I have seldom seen. Even Challenger's hat might have fitted that magnificent head. One might read Theodore Nemor as a vile, crawling conspirator below, but above he might take rank with the great thinkers and philosophers of the world.

22   "Well, gentlemen," said he, in a velvety voice with only the least
trace of a foreign accent, "you have come, as I understand from our
short chat over the wires, in order to learn more of the Nemor
Disintegrator. Is it so?"

23   "Exactly."

24   "May I ask whether you represent the British Government?"

25   "Not at all. I am a correspondent of the *Gazette,* and this is
Professor Challenger."

26   "An honoured name—a European name." His yellow fangs
gleamed in obsequious amiability. "I was about to say that the British
Government has lost its chance. What else it has lost it may find out
later. Possibly its Empire as well. I was prepared to sell to the first
Government which gave me its price, and if it has now fallen into hands
of which you may disapprove, you have only yourselves to blame."

27   "Then you have sold your secret?"

28   "At my own price."

29   "You think the purchaser will have a monopoly?"

30   "Undoubtedly he will."

31   "But others know the secret as well as you."

32   "No, sir." He touched his great forehead. "This is the safe in which
the secret is securely locked—a better safe than any of steel, and secured
by something better than a Yale key. Some may know one side of the
matter: others may know another. No one in the world knows the
whole matter save only I."

33   "And these gentlemen to whom you have sold it."

34   "No, sir; I am not so foolish as to hand over the knowledge until
the price is paid. After that is I whom they buy, and they move this
safe"—he again tapped his brow— "with all its contents to whatever
point they desire. My part of the bargain will then be done—faithfully,
ruthlessly done. After that, history will be made." He rubbed his hands
together and the fixed smile upon his face twisted itself into something
like a snarl.

35   "You will excuse me, sir," boomed Challenger, who had sat in silence up to now, but whose expressive face registered most complete
disapproval of Theodore Nemor, "we should wish before we discuss the
matter to convince ourselves that there is something to discuss. We
have not forgotten a recent case where an Italian, who proposed to explode mines from a distance, proved upon investigation to be an arrant
impostor. History may well repeat itself. You will understand, sir, that I
have a reputation to sustain as a man of science—a reputation which
you have been good enough to describe as European, though I have
every reason to believe that it is not less conspicuous in America.

Caution is a scientific attribute, and you must show us your proofs before we can seriously consider your claims."

36 Nemor cast a particularly malignant glance from the yellow eyes at my companion, but the smile of affected geniality broadened upon his face.

37 "You live up to your reputation, Professor. I had always heard that you were the last man in the world who could be deceived. I am prepared to give you an actual demonstration which cannot fail to convince you, but before we proceed to that I must say a few words upon the general principle.

38 "You will realize that the experimental plant which I have erected here in my laboratory is a mere model, though within its limits it acts most admirably. There would be no possible difficulty, for example, in disintegrating you and reassembling you, but it is not for such a purpose as that a great Government is prepared to pay a price which runs into millions. My model is a mere scientific toy. It is only when the same force is invoked upon a large scale that enormous practical effects could be achieved."

39 "May we see this model?"

40 "You will not only see it, Professor Challenger, but you will have the most conclusive demonstration possible upon your own person, if you have the courage to submit to it."

41 "If!" the lion began to roar. "Your 'if,' sir, is in the highest degree offensive."

42 "Well, well. I had no intention to dispute your courage. I will only say that I will give you an opportunity to demonstrate it. But I would first say a few words upon the underlying laws which govern the matter.

43 "When certain crystals, salt, for example, or sugar, are placed in water they dissolve and disappear. You would not know that they have ever been there. Then by evaporation or otherwise you lessen the amount of water, and lo! there are your crystals again, visible once more and the same as before. Can you conceive a process by which you, an organic being, are in the same way dissolved into the cosmos, and then by a subtle reversal of the conditions reassembled once more?"

44 "The analogy is a false one," cried Challenger. "Even if I make so monstrous an admission as that our molecules could be dispersed by some disrupting power, why should they reassemble in exactly the same order as before?"

45 "The objection is an obvious one, and I can only answer that they do so reassemble down to the last atom of the structure. There is an invisible framework and every brick flies into its true place. You may smile, Professor, but your incredulity and your smile may soon be replaced by quite another emotion."

46   Challenger shrugged his shoulders. "I am quite ready to submit it to the test."

47   "There is another case which I would impress upon you, gentlemen, and which may help you to grasp the idea. You have heard both in Oriental magic and in Western occultism of the phenomenon of the *apport* when some object is suddenly brought from a distance and appears in a new place. How can such a thing be done save by the loosening of the molecules, their conveyance upon an etheric wave, and their reassembling, each exactly in its own place, drawn together by some irresistible law? That seems a fair analogy to that which is done by my machine."

48   "You cannot explain one incredible thing by quoting another incredible thing," said Challenger. "I do not believe in your *apports,* Mr. Nemor, and I do not believe in your machine. My time is valuable, and if we are to have any sort of a demonstration I would beg you to proceed with it without further ceremony."

49   "Then you will be pleased to follow me," said the inventor. He led us down the stair of the flat and across a small garden which lay behind. There was a considerable outhouse, which he unlocked and we entered.

50   Inside was a large whitewashed room with innumerable copper wires hanging in festoons from the ceiling, and a huge magnet balanced upon a pedestal. In front of this was what looked like a prism of glass, three feet in length and about a foot in diameter. To the right of it was a chair which rested upon a platform of zinc, and which had a burnished copper cap suspended above it. Both the cap and the chair had heavy wires attached to them, and at the side was a sort of ratchet with numbered slots and a handle covered with indiarubber which lay at present in the slot marked zero.

51   "Nemor's Disintegrator," said this strange man, waving his hand towards the machine.

52   "This is the model which is destined to be famous, as altering the balance of power among the nations. Who holds this rules the world. Now, Professor Challenger, you have, if I may say so, treated me with some lack of courtesy and consideration in this matter. Will you dare to sit upon that chair and to allow me to demonstrate upon your own body the capabilities of the new force?"

53   Challenger had the courage of a lion, and anything in the nature of a defiance roused him in an instant to a frenzy. He rushed at the machine, but I seized his arm and held him back.

54   "You shall not go," I said. "Your life is too valuable. It is monstrous. What possible guarantee of safety have you? The nearest approach to that apparatus which I have ever seen was the electrocution chair at Sing Sing."

55   "My guarantee of safety," said Challenger, "is that you are a witness and this person would certainly be held for manslaughter at the least should anything befall me."

56   "That would be a poor consolation to the world of science, when you would leave work unfinished which none but you can do. Let me, at least, go first, and then, when the experience proves to be harmless, you can follow."

57   Personal danger would never have moved Challenger, but the idea that his scientific work might remain unfinished hit him hard. He hesitated, and before he could make up his mind I had dashed forward and jumped into the chair. I saw the inventor put his hand to the handle. I was aware of a click. Then for a moment there was a sensation of confusion and a mist before my eyes. When they cleared, the inventor with his odious smile was standing before me, and Challenger, with his apple-red cheeks drained of blood and colour, was staring over his shoulder.

58   "Well, get on with it!" said I.

59   "It is all over. You responded admirably," Nemor replied. "Step out, and Professor Challenger will now, no doubt, be ready to take his turn."

60   I have never seen my old friend so utterly upset. His iron nerve had for a moment completely failed him. He grasped my arm with a shaking hand.

61   "My God, Malone, it is true," said he. "You vanished. There is not a doubt of it. There was a mist for an instant and then vacancy."

62   "How long was I away?"

63   "Two or three minutes. I was, I confess, horrified. I could not imagine that you would return. Then he clicked this lever, if it is a lever, into a new slot and there you were upon the chair, looking a little bewildered but otherwise the same as ever. I thanked God at the sight of you!" He mopped his moist brow with his big red handkerchief.

64   "Now, sir," said the inventor. "Or perhaps your nerve has failed you?"

65   Challenger visibly braced himself. Then, pushing my protesting hand to one side, he seated himself upon the chair. The handle clicked into number three. He was gone.

66   I should have been horrified but for the perfect coolness of the operator. "It is an interesting process, is it not?" he remarked. "When one considers the tremendous individuality of the Professor it is strange to think that he is at present a molecular cloud suspended in some portion of this building. He is now, of course, entirely at my mercy. If I choose to leave him in suspension there is nothing on earth to prevent me."

67   "I would very soon find means to prevent you."

68   The smile once again became a snarl. "You cannot imagine that such a thought ever entered my mind. Good heavens! Think of the permanent dissolution of the great Professor Challenger—vanished into cosmic space and left no trace! Terrible! Terrible! At the same time he has not been as courteous as he might. Don't you think some small lesson—?"

69   "No, I do not."

70   "Well, we will call it a curious demonstration. Something that would make an interesting paragraph in your paper. For example, I have discovered that the hair of the body being on an entirely different vibration to the living organic tissues can be included or excluded at will. It would interest me to see the bear without his bristles. Behold him!"

71   There was the click of the lever. An instant later Challenger was seated upon the chair once more. But what a Challenger! What a shorn lion! Furious as I was at the trick that had been played upon him I could hardly keep from roaring with laughter.

72   His huge head was as bald as a baby's and his chin was as smooth as a girl's. Bereft of his glorious mane the lower part of his face was heavily jowled and ham-shaped, while his whole appearance was that of an old fighting gladiator, battered and bulging, with the jaws of a bulldog over a massive chin.

73   It may have been some look upon our faces—I have no doubt that the evil grin of my companion had widened at the sight—but, however that may be, Challenger's hand flew up to his head and he became conscious of his condition. The next instant he had sprung out of his chair, seized the inventor by the throat, and had hurled him to the ground. Knowing Challenger's immense strength I was convinced that the man would be killed.

74   "For God's sake be careful. If you kill him we can never get matters right again!" I cried.

75   That argument prevailed. Even in his maddest moments Challenger was always open to reason. He sprang up from the floor, dragging the trembling inventor with him. "I give you five minutes," he panted in his fury. "If in five minutes I am not as I was, I will choke the life out of your wretched little body."

76   Challenger in a fury was not a safe person to argue with. The bravest man might shrink from him, and there were no signs that Mr. Nemor was a particularly brave man. On the contrary, those blotches and warts upon his face had suddenly become much more conspicuous as the face behind them changed from the colour of putty, which was normal, to that of a fish's belly. His limbs were shaking and he could hardly articulate.

77   "Really, Professor!" he babbled, with his hand to his throat, "this violence is quite unnecessary. Surely a harmless joke may pass among friends. It was my wish to demonstrate the powers of the machine. I had imagined that you wanted a full demonstration. No offence, I assure you, Professor, none in the world!"

78   For answer Challenger climbed back into the chair.

79   "You will keep your eye upon him, Malone. Do not permit any liberties."

80   "I'll see to it, sir."

81   "Now then, set that matter right or take the consequences."

82   The terrified inventor approached his machine. The reuniting power was turned on to the full, and in an instant, there was the old lion with his tangled mane once more. He stroked his beard affectionately with his hands and passed them over his cranium to be sure that the restoration was complete. Then he descended solemnly from his perch.

83   "You have taken a liberty, sir, which might have had very serious consequences to yourself. However, I am content to accept your explanation that you only did it for the purposes of demonstration. Now, may I ask you a few direct questions upon this remarkable power which you claim to have discovered?"

84   "I am ready to answer anything save what the source of the power is. That is my secret."

85   "And do you seriously inform us that no one in the world knows this except yourself?"

86   "No one has the least inkling."

87   "No assistants?"

88   "No, sir. I work alone."

89   "Dear me! That is most interesting. You have satisfied me as to the reality of the power, but I do not yet perceive its practical bearings."

90   "I have explained, sir, that this is a model. But it would be quite easy to erect a plant upon a large scale. You understand that this acts vertically. Certain currents above you, and certain others below you, set up vibrations which either disintegrate or reunite. But the process could be lateral. If it were so conducted it would have the same effect, and cover a space in proportion to the strength of the current."

91   "Give an example."

92   "We will suppose that one pole was in one small vessel and one in another; a battleship between them would simply vanish into molecules. So also with a column of troops."

93   "And you have sold this secret as a monopoly to a single European Power?"

94   "Yes, sir, I have. When the money is paid over they shall have such power as no nation ever had yet. You don't even now see the full possibilities if placed in capable hands—hands which did not fear to wield the weapon which they held. They are immeasurable." A gloating smile passed over the man's evil face. "Conceive a quarter of London in which such machines have been erected. Imagine the effect of such a current upon the scale which could easily be adopted. Why," he burst into laughter, "I could imagine the whole Thames valley being swept clean, and not one man, woman, or child left of all these teeming millions!"

95   The words filled me with horror—and even more the air of exultation with which they were pronounced. They seemed, however, to produce quite a different effect upon my companion. To my surprise he broke into a genial smile and held out his hand to the inventor.

96   "Well, Mr. Nemor, we have to congratulate you," said he. "There is no doubt that you have come upon a remarkable property of nature which you have succeeded in harnessing for the use of man. That this use should be destructive is no doubt very deplorable, but Science knows no distinctions of the sort, but follows knowledge wherever it may lead. Apart from the principle involved you have, I suppose, no objection to my examining the construction of the machine?"

97   "None in the least. The machine is merely the body. It is the soul of it, the animating principle, which you can never hope to capture."

98   "Exactly. But the mere mechanism seems to be a model of ingenuity." For some time he walked round it and fingered its several parts. Then he hoisted his unwieldy bulk into the insulated chair.

99   "Would you like another excursion into the cosmos?" asked the inventor.

100   "Later, perhaps—later! But meanwhile there is, as no doubt you know, some leakage of electricity. I can distinctly feel a weak current passing through me."

101   "Impossible. It is quite insulated."

102   "But I assure you that I feel it." He levered himself down from his perch.

103   The inventor hastened to take his place.

104   "I can feel nothing."

105   "Is there not a tingling down your spine?"

106   "No, sir. I do not observe it."

107   There was a sharp click and the man had disappeared. I looked with amazement at Challenger. "Good heavens! did you touch the machine, Professor?"

108   He smiled at me benignly with an air of mild surprise.

109   "Dear me! I may have inadvertently touched the handle," said he. "One is very liable to have awkward incidents with a rough model of this kind. This lever should certainly be guarded."

110   "It is in number three. That is the slot which causes disintegration."

111   "So I observed when you were operated upon."

112   "But I was so excited when he brought you back that I did not see which was the proper slot for the return. Did you notice it?"

113   "I may have noticed it, young Malone, but I do not burden my mind with small details. There are many slots and we do not know their purpose. We may make the matter worse if we experiment with the unknown. Perhaps it is better to leave matters as they are."

114   "And you would—"

115   "Exactly. It is better so. The interesting personality of Mr. Theodore Nemor has distributed itself throughout the cosmos, his machine is worthless, and a certain foreign Government has been deprived of knowledge by which much harm might have been wrought. Not a bad morning's work, young Malone. Your rag will no doubt have an interesting column upon the inexplicable disappearance of a Latvian inventor shortly after the visit of its own special correspondent. I have enjoyed the experience. These are the lighter moments which come to brighten the dull routine of study. But life has its duties as well as its pleasures, and I now return to the Italian Mazotti and his preposterous views upon the larval development of the tropical termites."

116   Looking back, it seemed to me that a slight oleaginous mist was still hovering round the chair. "But surely—" I urged.

117   "The first duty of the law-abiding citizen is to prevent murder," said Professor Challenger. "I have done so. Enough, Malone, enough! The theme will not bear discussion. It has already disengaged my thoughts too long from matters of more importance."

DISCUSSION QUESTIONS

1. **The figure of Professor Challenger presents a series of contrasts: a large man with a bristling beard and gruff manners. Yet he likes flattery and is a top-notch scientist. Why do you think Doyle chose such a complex set of characteristics?**

2. **Nemor is repulsive physically, yet gifted intellectually. When he explains his plan, how do these traits combine?**

3. What safeguard has Nemor built around his fantastic machine? How does this eventually work against him?

4. Challenger asks Nemor a question about how his device operates, and Nemor can't answer it directly. Why is his reply so unsatisfactory?

5. What argument does Malone give to Challenger to prevent him from being the first human experimental subject?

WRITING TOPICS

1. What is the danger of the Disintegration Machine? How might such a device be used for good? Write a paragraph or two exploring this idea.

2. How does Challenger finally save the world? What are the moral and technological consequences? Discuss your thoughts in a short essay.

3. This story was written in the uneasy period between World War I and World War II. In an essay, explore how Doyle might have been thinking about what happened and warning about what might be coming.

The Metal Man

1928

JACK WILLIAMSON (1908–)

Jack Williamson was heavily influenced by the pulp fiction in
magazines such as *Amazing Stories*. He published his first science
fiction story, "The Metal Man," in 1928, and by 1940 had written
twelve novels and numerous short stories. In the fifties, Williamson
began collaborating with other science fiction authors. Later he
started producing literary criticism, including a 1973 book on
H. G. Wells (*H. G. Wells: Critic of Progress*). In 1976 he became only
the second recipient of the Grand Master Nebula Award, the first
being Robert Heinlein.

Williamson's *The Legion of Space* (1934) became a series of
five novels, all solidly within the Space Opera tradition. He also
wrote *The Legion of Time* (1938) and its sequel, *After World's End*
(1939). His shorter works were collected in 1978 as *The Best of Jack
Williamson*. His best-known series, however, looks at the positives
and negatives of being a humanoid. He began the series in 1947
with the short story "With Folded Hands." The linked novels
and stories were collected in 1980 as *The Humanoids*.

In "The Metal Man," Jack Williamson's scientist becomes
obsessed with finding a cure for a peculiar affliction. The geologist
may have discovered something wonderful or awful, but he is totally unprepared for the results of his investigations.

> >

1   The Metal Man stands in a dark, dusty corner of the Tyburn College Museum. Just who is responsible for the figure being moved there, or why it was done, I do not know. To the casual eye it looks to be merely an ordinary life-size statue. The visitor who gives it a closer view marvels at the minute perfection of the detail of hair and skin; at the silent tragedy in the set, determined expression and poise; and at the remarkable greenish cast of the metal of which it is composed, but, most of all, at the peculiar mark upon the chest. It is a six-sided blot, of a deep crimson hue, with the surface oddly granular and strange wavering lines radiating from it—lines of a lighter shade of red.

2   Of course it is generally known that the Metal Man was once Professor Thomas Kelvin of the Geology Department. There are current many garbled and inaccurate accounts of the weird disaster that befell him. I believe I am the only one to whom he entrusted his story. It is to put these fantastic tales at rest that I have decided to publish the narrative that Kelvin sent me.

3   For some years he had been spending his summer vacations along the Pacific coast of Mexico, prospecting for radium. It was three months since he had returned from his last expedition. Evidently he had been successful beyond his wildest dreams. He did not come to Tyburn, but we heard stories of his selling millions of dollars worth of salts of radium, and giving as much more to institutions employing radium treatment. And it was said that he was sick of a strange disorder that defied the world's best specialists, and that he was pouring out his millions in the establishment of scholarships and endowments as if he expected to die soon.

4   One cold, stormy day, when the sea was running high on the unprotected coast which the cottage overlooks, I saw a sail out to the north. It rapidly drew nearer until I could tell that it was a small sailing schooner with auxiliary power. She was running with the wind, but a half mile offshore she came up into it and the sails were lowered. Soon a boat had put off in the direction of the shore. The sea was not so rough as to make the landing hazardous, but the proceeding was rather unusual, and, as I had nothing better to do, I went out in the yard before my modest house, which stands perhaps two hundred yards above the beach, in order to have a better view.

5   When the boat touched, four men sprang out and rushed it up higher on the sand. As a fifth tall man arose in the stern, the four picked up a great chest and started up in my direction. The fifth person followed leisurely. Silently, and without invitation, the men brought the chest up the beach, and into my yard, and set it down in front of the door.

6   The fifth man, a hard-faced Yankee skipper, walked up to me and said gruffly, "I am Captain McAndrews."

7   "I'm glad to meet you, Captain," I said, wondering. "There must be some mistake. I was not expecting—"

8   "Not at all," he said abruptly. "The man in that chest was transferred to my ship from the liner *Plutonia* three days ago. He has paid me for my services, and I believe his instructions have been carried out. Good day, sir."

9   He turned on his heel and started away.

10   "A man in the chest!" I exclaimed.

11   He walked on unheeding, and the seamen followed. I stood and watched them walk down to the boat and row back to the schooner. I gazed at its sails until they were lost against the dull blue of the clouds. Frankly, I feared to open the chest.

12   At last I nerved myself to do it. It was unlocked. I threw back the lid. With a shock of uncontrollable horror that left me half sick for hours, I saw in it, stark naked, with the strange crimson mark standing lividly out from the pale green of the breast, the Metal Man, just as you may see him in the Museum.

13   Of course, I knew at once that it was Kelvin. For a long time I bent, trembling and staring at him. Then I saw an old canteen, purple-stained, lying by the head of the figure, and under it, a sheaf of manuscript. I got the latter out, walked with shaken steps to the easy chair in the house, and read the story that follows:

14   "Dear Russell,

15   "You are my best—my only—intimate friend. I have arranged to have my body and this story brought to you. I just drank the last of the wonderful purple liquid that has kept me alive since I came back, and I have scant time to finish this necessarily brief account of my adventure. But my affairs are in order and I die in peace. I had myself transferred to the schooner today, in order to reach you as soon as could be and to avoid possible complications. I trust Captain McAndrews. When I left France, I hoped to see you before the end. But Fate ruled otherwise.

16   "You know that the goal of my expedition was the headwaters of El Rio de la Sangre. 'The River of Blood.' It is a small stream whose strangely red waters flow into the Pacific. On my trip last year I had discovered that its waters were powerfully radioactive. Water has the power of absorbing radium emanations and emitting them in turn, and I hoped to find radium-bearing minerals in the bed of the upper river. Twenty-five miles above the mouth the river emerges from the Cordilleras. There are a few miles of rapids and back of them the river plunges down a magnificent waterfall. No exploring party had ever been back of the falls. I had hired an Indian guide and made a muleback

journey to their foot. At once I saw the futility of attempting to climb
the precipitous escarpment. But the water there was even more powerfully radioactive than at the mouth. There was nothing to do but return.

17   "This summer I bought a small monoplane. Though it was comparatively slow in speed and able to spend only six hours aloft, its light weight
and the small area needed for landing, made it the only machine suitable
for use in so rough a country. The steamer left me again on the dock at the
little town of Vaca Morena, with my stack of crates and gasoline tins. After
a visit to the Alcalde I secured the use of an abandoned shed for a hangar. I
set about assembling the plane and in a fortnight I had completed the task.
It was a beautiful little machine, with a wingspread of only twenty-five feet.

18   "Then, one morning, I started the engine and made a trial flight. It
flew smoothly and in the afternoon I refilled the tanks and set off for the
Rio de la Sangre. The stream looked like a red snake crawling out to the
sea—there was something serpentine in its aspect. Flying high, I followed it, above the falls and into a region of towering mountain peaks.
The river disappeared beneath a mountain. For a moment I thought of
landing, and then it occurred to me that it flowed subterraneously for
only a few miles, and would reappear further inland.

19   "I soared over the cliffs and came over the crater.

20   "A great pool of green fire it was, fully ten miles across to the black
ramparts at the further side. The surface of the green was so smooth that
at first I thought it was a lake, and then I knew that it must be a pool of
heavy gas. In the glory of the evening sun the snow-capped summits
about were brilliant argent crowns, dyed with crimson, tinged with purple and gold, tinted with strange and incredibly beautiful hues. Amid this
wild scenery, nature had placed her greatest treasure. I knew that in the
crater I would find the radium I sought.

21   "I circled about the place, rapt in wonder. As the sun sank lower, a
light silver mist gathered on the peaks, half veiling their wonders, and
flowed toward the crater. It seemed drawn with a strange attraction. And
then the centre of the green lake rose in a shining peak. It flowed up into
a great hill of emerald fire. Something was rising in the green—carrying
it up! Then the vapour flowed back, revealing a strange object, still veiled
faintly by the green and silver clouds. It was a gigantic sphere of deep
red, marked with four huge oval spots of dull black. Its surface was
smooth, metallic, and thickly studded with great spikes that seemed of
yellow fire. It was a machine, inconceivably great in size. It spun slowly as
it rose, on a vertical axis, moving with a deliberate, purposeful motion.

22   "It came up to my own level, paused and seemed to spin faster. And
the silver mist was drawn to the yellow points, condensing, curdling, until
the whole globe was a ball of lambent argent. For a moment it hung,

unbelievably glorious in the light of the setting sun, and then it sank—ever faster—until it dropped like a plummet into the sea of green.

23   "And with its fall a sinister darkness descended upon the desolate wilderness of the peaks, and I was seized by a fear that had been deadened by amazement, and realized that I had scant time to reach Vaca Morena before complete darkness fell. Immediately I put the plane about in the direction of the town. According to my recollections, I had, at the time, no very definite idea of what it was I had seen, or whether the weird exhibition had been caused by human or natural agencies. I remember thinking that in such enormous quantities as undoubtedly the crater contained it, radium might possess qualities unnoticed in small amounts, or, again, that there might be present radioactive minerals at present unknown. It occurred to me also that perhaps some other scientists had already discovered the deposits and that what I had witnessed had been the trial of an airship in which radium was utilized as a propellant. I was considerably shaken, but not much alarmed. What happened later would have seemed incredible to me then.

24   "And then I noticed that a pale bluish luminosity was gathering about the cowl of the cockpit, and in a moment I saw that the whole machine, and even my own person, was covered with it. It was somewhat like St. Elmo's Fire, except that it covered all surfaces indiscriminately, instead of being restricted to sharp points. All at once I connected the phenomenon with the thing I had seen. I felt no physical discomfort, and the motor continued to run, but as the blue radiance continued to increase, I observed that my body felt heavier, and that the machine was being drawn downward! My mind was flooded with wonder and terror. I fought to retain sufficient self-possession to fly the ship. My arms were soon so heavy that I could hold them upon the controls only with difficulty, and I felt a slight dizziness, due, no doubt, to the blood's being drawn from my head. When I recovered, I was already almost upon the green. Somehow, my gravitation had been increased and I was being drawn into the pit! It was possible to keep the plane under control only by diving and keeping at a high speed.

25   "I plunged into the green pool. The gas was not suffocating, as I had anticipated. In fact, I noticed no change in the atmosphere, save that my vision was limited to a few yards around. The wings of the plane were still distinctly discernible. Suddenly a smooth, sandy plain was murkily revealed below, and I was able to level the ship off enough for a safe landing. As I came to a stop I saw that the sand was slightly luminous, as the green mist seemed to be, and red. For a time I was confined to the ship by my own weight, but I noticed that the blue was slowly dissipating, and with it, its effect.

26 "As soon as I was able, I clambered over the side of the cockpit, carrying my canteen and automatic, which were themselves immensely heavy. I was unable to stand erect, but I crawled off over the coarse, shining red sand, stopping at frequent intervals to lie flat and rest. I was in deathly fear of the force that had brought me down. I was sure it had been directed by intelligence. The floor was so smooth and level that I supposed it to be the bottom of an ancient lake.

27 "Sometimes I looked fearfully back, and when I was a hundred yards away I saw a score of lights floating through the green towards the airplane. In the luminous murk each bright point was surrounded by a disc of paler blue. I didn't move, but lay and watched them float to the plane and wheel about it with a slow, heavy motion. Closer and lower they came until they reached the ground about it. The mist was so thick as to obscure the details of the scene.

28 "When I went to resume my flight, I found my excess of gravity almost entirely gone, though I went on hands and knees for another hundred yards to escape possible observation. When I got to my feet, the plane was lost to view. I walked on for perhaps a quarter of a mile and suddenly realized that my sense of direction was altogether gone. I was completely lost in a strange world, inhabited by beings whose nature and disposition I could not even guess! And then I realized that it was the height of folly to walk about when any step might precipitate me into a danger of which I could know nothing. I had a peculiarly unpleasant feeling of helpless fear.

29 "The luminous red sand and the shining green of the air lay about in all directions, unbroken by a single solid object. There was no life, no sound, no motion. The air hung heavy and stagnant. The flat sand was like the surface of a dead and desolate sea. I felt the panic of utter isolation from humanity. The mist seemed to come closer; the strange evil in it seemed to grow more alert.

30 "Suddenly a darting light passed meteor-like through the green above and in my alarm I ran a few blundering steps. My foot struck a light object that rang like metal. The sharpness of the concussion filled me with fear, but in an instant the light was gone. I bent down to see what I had kicked.

31 "It was a metal bird—an eagle formed of metal—with the wings outspread, the talons gripping, the fierce beak set open. The colour was white, tinged with green. It weighed no more than the living bird. At first I thought it was a cast model, and then I saw that each feather was complete and flexible. Somehow, a real eagle had been turned to metal! It seemed incredible, yet here was the concrete proof. I wondered if the radium deposits, which I had already used to explain so much, might

account for this too. I knew that science held transmutation of elements to be possible—had even accomplished it in a limited way, and that radium itself was the product of the disintegration of ionium, and ionium that of uranium.

32 "I was struck with fright for my own safety. Might I be changed to metal? I looked to see if there were other metal things about. And I found them in abundance. Half-buried in the glowing sands were metal birds of every kind—birds that had flown over the surrounding cliffs. And, at the climax of my search, I found a pterosant—a flying reptile that had invaded the pit in ages past—changed to ageless metal. Its wingspread was fully fifteen feet—it would be a treasure in any museum.

33 "I made a fearful examination of myself, and to my unutterable horror, I perceived that the tips of my fingernails, and the fine hairs upon my hands, *were already changed to light green metal!* The shock unnerved me completely. You cannot conceive my horror. I screamed aloud in agony of soul, careless of the terrible foes that the sound might attract. I ran off wildly. I was blind, unreasoning. I felt no fatigue as I ran, only stark terror.

34 "Bright, swift-moving lights passed above in the green, but I heeded them not. Suddenly I came upon the great sphere that I had seen above. It rested motionless in a cradle of black metal. The yellow fire was gone from the spikes, but the red surface shone with a metallic lustre. Lights floated about it. They made little bright spots in the green, like lanterns swinging in a fog. I turned and ran again, desperately. I took no note of direction, nor of the passage of time.

35 "Then I came upon a bank of violet vegetation. Waist-deep it was, grass-like, with thick narrow leaves, dotted with clusters of small pink blooms, and little purple berries. And a score of yards beyond I saw a sluggish red stream—El Rio de la Sangre. Here was cover at last. I threw myself down in the violet growth and lay sobbing with fatigue and terror. For a long time I was unable to stir or think. When I looked again at my fingernails, the tips of metal had doubled in width.

36 "I tried to control my agitation, and to think. Possibly the lights, whatever they were, would sleep by day. If I could find the plane, or scale the walls, I might escape the fearful action of the radioactive minerals before it was too late. I realized that I was hungry. I plucked off a few of the purple berries and tasted them. They had a salty, metallic taste, and I thought they would be valueless for food. But in pulling them I had inadvertently squeezed the juice from one upon my fingers, and when I wiped it off I saw, to my amazement and my inexpressible joy, that the rim of metal was gone from the fingernails it had

touched. I had discovered a means of safety! I suppose that the plants were able to exist there only because they had been so developed that they produced compounds counteracting the metal-forming emanations. Probably their evolution began when the action was far weaker than now, and only those able to withstand the more intense radiations had survived. I lost no time in eating a cluster of the berries, and then I poured the water from my canteen and filled it with their juice. I have analysed the fluid; it corresponds in some ways with the standard formulas for the neutralization of radium burns, and doubtless it saved me from the terrible burns caused by the action of ordinary radium.

37 "I lay there until dawn, dozing a little at times, only to start into wakefulness without cause. It seemed that some daylight filtered through the green, for at dawn it grew paler, and even the red sand appeared less luminous. After eating a few more of the berries, I ascertained the direction in which the stagnant red water was moving, and set off down-stream, towards the west. In order to get an idea of where I was going, I counted my paces. I had walked about two and a half miles, along by the violet plants, when I came to an abrupt cliff. It towered up until it was lost in the green gloom. It seemed to be mostly of black pitchblende. The barrier seemed absolutely unscalable. The red river plunged out of sight by the cliff in a racing whirlpool.

38 "I walked off north around the rim. I had no very definite plan, except to try to find a way out over the cliffs. If I failed in that, it would be time to hunt the plane. I had a mortal fear of going near it, or of encountering the strange lights I had seen floating about it. As I went I saw none of them. I suppose they slept when it was day.

39 "I went on until it must have been noon, though my watch had stopped. Occasionally I passed metal trees that had fallen from above, and once, the metallic body of a bear that had slipped off a path above, some time in past ages. And there were metal birds without number. They must have been accumulating through geological ages. All along up to this, the cliff had risen perpendicularly to the limit of my vision, but now I saw a wide ledge, with a sloping wall beyond it, dimly visible above. But the sheer wall rose a full hundred feet to the shelf, and I cursed at my inability to surmount it. For a time I stood there, devising impractical means for climbing it, driven almost to tears by my impotence. I was ravenously hungry, and thirsty as well.

40 "At last I went on.

41 "In an hour I came upon it. A slender cylinder of black metal, that towered a hundred feet into the greenish mist, and carried at the top, a great mushroom-shaped orange flame. It was a strange thing. The fire was as big as a balloon, bright and steady. It looked much like a great

jet of combustible gas, burning as it streamed from the cylinder. I stood petrified in amazement, wondering vaguely at the what and why of the thing.

42   "And then I saw more of them back of it, dimly—scores of them—a whole forest of flames.

43   "I crouched back against the cliff, while I considered. Here I supposed, was the city of the lights. They were sleeping now, but still I had not the courage to enter. According to my calculations I had gone about fifteen miles. Then I must be, I thought, almost diametrically opposite the place where the crimson river flowed under the wall, with half the rim unexplored. If I wished to continue my journey, I must go around the city, if I may call it that.

44   "So I left the wall. Soon it was lost to view. I tried to keep in view of the orange flames, but abruptly they were gone in the mist. I walked more to the left, but I came upon nothing but the wastes of red sand, with the green murk above. On and on I wandered. Then the sand and the air grew slowly brighter and I knew that night had fallen. The lights were soon passing to and fro. I had seen lights the night before, but they travelled high and fast. These, on the other hand, sailed low, and I felt that they were searching.

45   "I knew that they were hunting for me. I lay down in a little hollow in the sand. Vague, mist-veiled points of light came near and passed. And then one stopped directly overhead. It descended and the circle of radiance grew about it. I knew that it was useless to run, and I could not have done so, for my terror. Down and down it came.

46   "And then I saw its form. The thing was of a glittering, blazing crystal. A great-six-sided, upright prism of red, a dozen feet in length, it was, with a six-pointed structure like a snowflake about the centre, deep blue, with pointed blue flanges running from the points of the star to angles of the prism! Soft scarlet fire flowed from the points. And on each face of the prism, above and below the star, was a purple cone that must have been an eye. Strange pulsating lights flickered in the crystal. It was alive with light.

47   "It fell straight towards me!

48   "It was a terribly, utterly alien form of life. It was not human, not animal—not even life as we know it at all. And yet it had intelligence. But it was strange and foreign and devoid of feeling. It is curious to say that even then, as I lay beneath it, the thought came to me, that the thing and its fellows must have crystallized when the waters of the ancient sea dried out of the crater. Crystallizing salts take intricate forms.

49   "I drew my automatic and fired three times, but the bullets ricocheted harmlessly off the polished facets.

50   "It dropped until the gleaming lower point of the prism was not a
yard above me. Then the scarlet fire reached out caressingly—flowed
over my body. My weight grew less. I was lifted, held against the point.
You may see its mark upon my chest. The thing floated into the air, carrying me. Soon others were drifting about. I was overcome with nausea.
The scene grew black and I knew no more.

51   "I awoke floating free in a brilliant orange light. I touched no solid
object. I writhed, kicked about—at nothingness. I could not move or
turn over, because I could get a hold on nothing. My memory of the
last two days seemed a nightmare. My clothing was still upon me. My
canteen still hung, or rather floated, by my shoulder. And my automatic
was in my pocket. I had the sensation that a great space of time had
passed. There was a curious stiffness in my side. I examined it and
found a red scar. I believe those crystal things had cut into me. And I
found, with a horror you cannot understand, the mark upon my chest.
Presently it dawned upon me that I was floating, devoid of gravity and
free as an object in space, in the orange flame at the top of one of the
black cylinders. The crystals knew the secret of gravity. It was vital to
them. And peering about, I discerned, with infinite repulsion, a great
flashing body, a few yards away. But its inner lights were dead, so I knew
that it was day, and that the strange beings were sleeping.

52   "If I was ever to escape, this was the opportunity. I kicked, clawed
desperately at the air, all in vain. I did not move an inch. If they had
chained me, I could not have been more secure. I drew my automatic, resolved on a desperate measure. They would not find me again, alive. And
as I had it in my hand, an idea came into my mind. I pointed the gun to
the side, and fired six rapid shots. And the recoil of each explosion sent
me drifting faster, rocket-wise, toward the edge.

53   "I shot out into the green. Had my gravity been suddenly restored,
I might have been killed by the fall, but I descended slowly, and felt a
curious lightness for several minutes. And to my surprise, when I struck
the ground, the airplane was right before me! They had drawn it up by
the base of the tower. It seemed to be intact. I started the engine with
nervous haste, and sprang into the cockpit. As I started, another black
tower loomed up abruptly before me, but I veered around it, and took
off in safety.

54   "In a few moments I was above the green. I half expected the
gravitational wave to be turned on me again, but higher and higher I
rose unhindered until the accursed black walls were about me no
longer. The sun blazed high in the heavens. Soon I had landed again at
Vaca Morena.

55 "I had had enough of radium hunting. On the beach, where I landed, I sold the plane to a rancher at his own price, and told him to reserve a place for me on the next steamer, due in three days. Then I went to the town's single inn, ate, and went to bed. At noon the next day, when I got up, I found that my shoes and the pockets of my clothes contained a good bit of the red sand from the crater that had been collected as I crawled about in flight from the crystal lights. I saved some of it for curiosity alone; but when I analysed it, I found it a radium compound so rich that the little handful was worth millions of dollars.

56 "But the fortune was of little value, for, despite frequent doses of the fluid from my canteen, and the best medical aid, I have suffered continually, and now that my canteen is empty, I am doomed.

57 "Your friend, Thomas Kelvin"

58 Thus the manuscript ends. If the reader doubts the truth of the letter, he may see the Metal Man in the Tyburn Museum.

DISCUSSION QUESTIONS

1. Almost all of this story is in the form of a first-person narrative, which is included in the strange box. Russell, who receives the box, does not comment on the events, only on the undeniable evidence he sees. What effect does this technique have on how you perceive the story?

2. There are many references to colors throughout the story: green air, red sand, blue luminosity, orange flame, violet vegetation, black metal, and so on. Why do you think Williamson uses this continuous visual imagery?

3. Professor Kelvin "senses" intelligence in the crystalline creatures, but there is no evidence of communication. Given this, why do you think he believes the creatures of light are evil? Discuss his reasoning and other possible interpretations in a small group.

4. Kelvin eventually discovers an antidote for the transformation, but he doesn't return to get enough to keep himself alive. Why not?

5. What causes Kelvin to assume the lights "sleep" by day?

WRITING TOPICS

1. There are other possible explanations for the behavior of the "creatures" that Kelvin discovers, and many scientific advances could have
   been possible if they had not been feared. How might this story have
   turned out if Kelvin had been able to establish peaceable communication with the aliens? Write a few paragraphs illustrating such an
   alternate ending.
2. Kelvin discovers he's been marked and possibly operated on, making
   this similar in some ways to present-day alien abduction stories.
   Write a journal entry showing how this account is different from
   those more common today.
3. Transmutation of elements, particularly lead into gold, was a goal of
   ancient alchemists. The story mentions uranium being transformed
   into radium, an element whose properties were not well understood
   in the twenties. In a short essay, explore how this radioactive material
   could cause such wild speculations as those Williamson has proposed.

The Thirties

1930	Adolf Hitler's National Socialist Party comes to power
	First jet engine built by Frank Whittle
1931	**Olaf Stapledon's *Last and First Men* published**
1932	***Frankenstein* with Boris Karloff as the creature becomes a movie**
	Franklin Delano Roosevelt announces "New Deal" economic reforms
	Amelia Earhart is the first woman to fly solo across the Atlantic Ocean
	Harold C. Urey discovers heavy hydrogen (deuterium)
	James Chadwick discovers the neutron
	C. D. Anderson discovers the positron
	Aldous Huxley produces *Brave New World*
1933	**The premiere issue of *Astounding Stories* magazine appears**
	Prohibition repealed
	Hitler becomes German Chancellor and forms the Hitler Youth; Germany and Japan withdraw from the League of Nations
	Creation of TVA (Tennessee Valley Authority)
1934	**Movie version of H. G. Wells' *The Invisible Man* premieres**
	Jews deprived of rights and placed in concentration camps in Germany
	U.S.S.R. admitted to League of Nations
	Japan renounces U.S. treaties of 1922 and 1930
1935	Social Security Act takes effect
	Dust storms sweep across Plains states, resulting in massive crop failures
	Alcoholics Anonymous organized
	Radar equipment to detect aircraft built
	***The Bride of Frankenstein* sequel is produced**

HISTORICAL CONTEXT

As the Great Depression tightened its grip on the United States, the repercussions spread around the world. The temporary growth in the economy following WWI came to an abrupt end, and the dissatisfaction with peacetime treaties led to unrest in Europe, and Germany in particular. The worldwide depression actually increased Nazi power as dissatisfied Germans accepted the message that military might was a sign of greatness. Adolf Hitler, on a campaign that appealed to German pride and might, took control of the Nazi party. He then quickly manipulated himself into position as Chancellor of Germany in 1933.

The following year he killed many who disagreed with his policies, ordering 81 executions of party officials. Two years later Germany withdrew from the League of Nations and retook the Rhineland area that had been taken from it at the end of World War I. That same year, 1936, Italy and Germany signed a mutual protection pact. By intervening in the Spanish Civil War, they managed to gain Spain as an ally. Meanwhile, Japan had built up its military forces and invaded China, where Mao Tse-tung had taken over as head of the Chinese Communist Party. During this same time period, Japan also formed an alliance with Germany.

Beginning in 1934, Hitler began persecuting the Jews. Thousands were leaving the country, but millions more couldn't avoid the death camps that were to come. In 1939, when Hitler invaded Poland (with whom Britain and France had protection policies), World War II erupted.

During this decade of increasing German nationalism, the United States was still battling the Great Depression. After Franklin

Roosevelt was inaugurated in 1933, he quickly began sweeping social changes meant to stir the economy and put Americans back to work. He ended Prohibition in 1933 and pushed through the New Deal, the first of his economic packages. These included the Public Works Administration and the Civilian Conservation Corps, which provided jobs for three million Americans who worked on highways and other public projects. Among the most impressive were the Grand Coulee Dam, the largest single public works project ever undertaken in this country, and the Tennessee Valley Authority, which brought electricity to millions of previously isolated Americans.

Roosevelt also instituted the Social Security system, established a minimum wage law, and began the welfare safety net for those unable to support themselves. Those changes were not popular with all citizens, but they began to produce results, and the unemployment rate rolled back steadily. However, the country still harbored resentment from World War I, as well as the lingering effects of the Depression, and demanded a policy of strict neutrality toward the emerging war. The World's Fair of 1939 in New York, labeled The World of Tomorrow, with its optimistic outlook at the future, stood in stark contrast to the horrors happening across the ocean. As the war mounted, public opinion shifted, but America wouldn't enter the conflict until the changing of the decade.

DEVELOPMENTS IN SCIENCE FICTION

The thirties saw a tremendous increase in the amount of science fiction published. The pulp magazines, already established in the twenties, flourished. Hugo Gernsback, forced to sell all his magazine interests following the stock market crash, still continued to publish a great number of science fiction authors in his new *Science Wonder Stories*. He pursued the same directions he had established with *Amazing Stories* and *Astounding Stories,* including stories by many of the same authors. Although he did publish Stanley Weinbaum's "A Martian Odyssey" in 1934, which featured the first instance of a nonbug-eyed monster alien, and the first interspecies friendship, Gernsback paid much more attention to the scientific merits of stories than any literary qualities, such as realistic plots or believable characters. At the same time, he stopped reprinting classic works, and the overall quality of the fiction he printed fell. He published many shallow, uninspired works that appealed to the lowest segment of the mass market. The opinion that many formed of science fiction as juvenile escapism is a direct result of the overall low quality of these pulps, which emphasized action, romance, heroism, fantastic adventures, and upbeat endings. For these reasons, Gernsback's science fiction legacy is a mixed one.

After Gernsback lost control of *Astounding Stories,* F. Orlin Tremaine took over as editor in 1931. At first Tremaine followed Gernsback's direction, but he quickly began choosing stories that relied on gimmicks and sensationalism. He sought out what he called "Thought Variant Stories," where he challenged authors to come up with new, thought-provoking ideas. But Tremaine didn't have the vision or dedication of Gernsback, and after four years, John W. Campbell Jr., a highly respected author in his own right, took control.

Campbell was scientifically trained at M.I.T. and immediately began publishing thoughtful, progressive stories with high standards in writing and thinking. The name of the magazine changed to *Astounding Science Fiction,* and Campbell quickly established a reputation for printing quality fiction. He wanted stories that avoided clichés, featured believable characters, and displayed an inner logic. He divided science fiction into three basic types: the gadget story, featuring technical tricks; the concept story, developed from an original idea; and the character story, dominated by the leading personality in the story.

His ideas and the encouragement he offered to other authors had a major impact on a whole group of science fiction writers who produced many memorable works. His own stories were also excellent examples for others to follow, including his most well known, "Who Goes There" (1938), which was later made into the movie *The Thing* (1951). Authors who either debuted or blossomed under Campbell's wing include Clifford Simak, Robert Heinlein, Theodore Sturgeon, A. E. van Vogt, Isaac Asimov, and Fritz Leiber. For 34 years, Campbell was the top science fiction editor, and he is responsible in large part for the Golden Age of science fiction in the forties.

Under Campbell's leadership, a whole spate of science fiction magazines appeared. Soon there were so many that bookstores reserved special sections for them. The Big Three—*Amazing Stories, Science Wonder Stories,* and *Astounding Science Fiction*—dominated, but there was a great deal of magazine science fiction available during the thirties. Part of the reason for the success of the pulps was readers' needs of escaping, even temporarily, the dreary reality of the Depression, and the general apathy following the unsatisfactory end of World War I. This led, in many cases, to unrestrained escapism, which also contributed to science fiction's poor reputation.

However, even though most of the pulp science fiction was escapist wish fulfillment, there was also much quality science fiction. Olaf Stapledon, a British professor of philosophy, produced *Last and First Men* in 1930, an incredibly detailed future history of mankind. In 1937, he wrote *Star Maker,* a similar fictional historical treatment of the entire universe. These works are highly regarded, complex visions that are difficult to classify, partly because they don't follow the established lines of science fiction or even of storytelling in general.

One author whose work illustrates the best of science fiction in the thirties is Aldous Huxley. His *Brave New World* appeared in 1932, showing a future utopia where people are bred in test tubes, prepared for useful functions in society, and conditioned for happiness. When a throwback "savage" appears, it becomes apparent that this utopia, which allows no individual choice, is fatally flawed and is actually a dystopia. Huxley is promoting individuality, even at the price of unhappiness, as the actual utopian state. Science fiction enthusiasts point to this as an example of good science fiction, whereas the academic community claims that it is an exception, going beyond science fiction and becoming mainstream literature.

Another notable science fiction writer of the thirties is C. S. Lewis. He began his trilogy of philosophical science fiction with *Out of the Silent Planet* in 1938. The silent planet is Earth, and Lewis used the novels to sound warnings against amoral science and materialism.

SCIENCE FICTION IN OTHER MEDIA

Science fiction also came to the comics during the thirties. Buck
Rogers and Flash Gordon both had daily strips, and many of these
were produced as collections in book format. Under names such
as Big Little Books, they became the forerunners of modern comic
books. The big news in comics, though, was Superman, who exploded onto the comic scene in *Action Comics* in 1938. Superman
was followed a year later by Batman in *Detective Comics*. Both of
these characters struck a chord with pre-war Americans who
wanted desperately to believe in all-American virtues and the triumph of good over evil. Ironically, it was an alien Superman who
most clearly stood for these traditional values.

Science fiction was also growing in other directions in the
thirties. More movies were being adapted from science fiction or
written specifically for the screen. H. G. Wells' *Island of Lost Souls*
came out in 1932, followed by *The Invisible Man* in 1933. *King Kong*,
an original screenplay, was a major success in 1933 as well, and
John Hilton's utopian Shangri-la was depicted in the 1934 film
Lost Horizon. "Flash Gordon," starring Buster Crabbe, became a
weekly movie serial in 1936. It also appeared as feature length
productions in 1938 and 1940, and *Buck Rogers*, also starring
Crabbe, became a movie in 1939.

Radio broadcasts of serials also flourished during the thirties, with Buck Rogers beginning in 1932 and others following
soon after. The radio science fiction event of the decade, however,
was Orson Welles' adaptation of H. G. Wells' *The War of the Worlds*.
When he broadcast the dramatization on Halloween eve in 1938,
his description of the alien arrival and takeover was so realistic
that panic swept the East Coast, despite repeated reminders that
it was only a radio play. This illustrates the widespread influence
of radio at that time, as well as the general fear of invasion and
takeover by outside military forces. Germany, Italy, and Japan had
been building up their military might during the decade, and
Americans didn't want to be pulled into another war.

The Mad Moon

1935

STANLEY WEINBAUM (1900–1935)

Stanley Weinbaum's first science fiction story, "A Martian Odyssey,"
was published in *Wonder Stories* in 1934. This was the first story that
attempted to show alien life as other than threatening monsters
intent on killing all humans. The lighthearted, almost comic, style
also helped popularize Weinbaum's story. He quickly followed it
with others, including "The Lotus Eaters" (1935), which features intelligent plant life-forms. His untimely death from lung cancer
shortened a promising career.

Other notable Weinbaum stories include "Flight on Titan"
(1935) and "Parasite Planet" (1935). His "The Worlds of If" (1935)
features an eccentric scientist who designs ridiculous machines.
Many of his stories were collected in a 1936 Memorial Edition,
The Dawn of Flame and Other Stories. The posthumous *The New
Adam* (1939) is a novel of a potential superhuman who is forced
to remain reclusive.

In "The Mad Moon," Stanley Weinbaum explores the fringes
of sanity on one of the moons of Jupiter, where the native species
may be more than what the human traders are prepared to deal
with.

I

1   "Idiots!" howled Grant Calthorpe. "Fools—nitwits—imbeciles!"
He sought wildly for some more expressive terms, failed, and vented his
exasperation in a vicious kick at the pile of rubbish on the ground.

2   Too vicious a kick, in fact; he had again forgotten the one-third
normal gravitation of Io, and his whole body followed his kick in a
long, twelve-foot arc.

3   As he struck the ground the four loonies giggled. Their great, idiotic heads, looking like nothing so much as the comic faces painted on
Sunday balloons for children, swayed in unison on their five-foot necks,
as thin as Grant's wrist.

4   "Get out!" he blazed, scrambling erect. "Beat it, skiddoo, scram! No
chocolate. No candy. Not until you learn that I want ferva leaves, and
not any junk you happen to grab. Clear out!"

5   The loonies—*Lunae Jovis Magnicapites,* or literally, Bigheads of
Jupiter's Moon—backed away, giggling plaintively. Beyond doubt, they
considered Grant fully as idiotic as he considered them, and were quite
unable to understand the reasons for his anger. But they certainly realized that no candy was to be forthcoming, and their giggles took on a
note of keen disappointment.

6   So keen, indeed, that the leader, after twisting his ridiculous blue
face in an imbecilic grin at Grant, voiced a last wild giggle and dashed
his head against a glittering stone-bark tree. His companions casually
picked up his body and moved off, with his head dragging behind them
on its neck like a prisoner's ball on a chain.

7   Grant brushed his hand across his forehead and turned wearily toward his stone-bark log shack. A pair of tiny, glittering red eyes caught
his attention, and a slinker—*Mus Sapiens*—skipped his six-inch form
across the threshold, bearing under his tiny, skinny arm what looked
very much like Grant's clinical thermometer.

8   Grant yelled angrily at the creature, seized a stone and flung it
vainly. At the edge of the brush, the slinker turned its ratlike, semihu-
man face toward him, squeaked its thin gibberish, shook a microscopic
fist in manlike wrath, and vanished, its batlike cowl of skin fluttering
like a cape. It looked, indeed, very much like a black rat wearing a cape.

9   It had been a mistake, Grant knew, to throw the stone at it. Now
the tiny fiends would never permit him any peace, and their diminutive
size and pseudo-human intelligence made them infernally troublesome
as enemies. Yet, neither that reflection nor the loony's suicide troubled
him particularly; he had witnessed instances like the latter too often,
and besides, his head felt as if he were in for another siege of white
fever.

10   He entered the shack, closed the door, and stared down at his pet parcat. "Oliver," he growled, "you're a fine one. Why the devil don't you watch out for slinkers? What are you here for?"

11   The parcat rose on its single, powerful hind leg, clawing at his knees with its two forelegs. "The red jack on the black queen," it observed placidly. "Ten loonies make one half-wit."

12   Grant placed both statements easily. The first was, of course, an echo of his preceding evening's solitaire game, and the second of yesterday's session with the loonies. He grunted abstractedly and rubbed his aching head. White fever again, beyond doubt.

13   He swallowed two ferverin tablets, and sank listlessly to the edge of his bunk, wondering whether this attack of *blancha* would culminate in delirium.

14   He cursed himself for a fool for ever taking this job on Jupiter's third habitable moon, Io. The tiny world was a planet of madness, good for nothing except the production of ferva leaves, out of which Earthly chemists made as many potent alkaloids as they once made from opium.

15   Invaluable to medical science, of course, but what difference did that make to him? What difference, even, did the munificent salary make, if he got back to Earth a raving maniac after a year in the equatorial regions of Io? He swore bitterly that when the plane from Junopolis landed next month for his ferva, he'd go back to the polar city with it, even though his contract with Neilan Drug called for a full year, and he'd get no pay if he broke it. What good was money to a lunatic?

II

16   The whole little planet was mad—loonies, parcats, slinkers and Grant Calthorpe—all crazy. At least, anybody who ever ventured outside either of the two polar cities, Junopolis on the north and Herapolis on the south, was crazy. One could live there in safety from white fever, but anywhere below the twentieth parallel it was worse than the Cambodian jungles on Earth.

17   He amused himself by dreaming of Earth. Just two years ago he had been happy there, known as a wealthy, popular sportsman. He had been just that, too; before he was twenty-one he had hunted knife-kite and threadworm on Titan, and triops and uniped on Venus.

18   That had been before the gold crisis of 2110 had wiped out his fortune. And—well, if he had to work, it had seemed logical to use his interplanetary experience as a means of livelihood. He had really been enthusiastic at the chance to associate himself with Neilan Drug.

19   He had never been on Io before. This wild little world was no
sportsman's paradise with its idiotic loonies and wicked, intelligent, tiny
slinkers. There wasn't anything worth hunting on the feverish little
moon, bathed in warmth by the giant Jupiter only a quarter million
miles away.

20   If he *had* happened to visit it, he told himself ruefully, he'd never
have taken the job; he had visualized Io as something like Titan, cold
but clean.

21   Instead it was as hot as the Venus Hotlands because of its glowing
primary, and subject to half a dozen different forms of steamy daylight—sun day, Jovian day, Jovian and sun day, Europa light, and occasionally actual and dismal night. And most of these came in the course
of Io's forty-two-hour revolution, too—a mad succession of changing
lights. He hated the dizzy days, the jungle, and Idiots' Hills stretching
behind his shack.

22   It was Jovian and solar day at the present moment, and that was the
worst of all, because the distant sun added its modicum of heat to that
of Jupiter. And to complete Grant's discomfort now was the prospect of
a white fever attack. He swore as his head gave an additional twinge,
and then swallowed another ferverin tablet. His supply of these was diminishing, he noticed; he'd have to remember to ask for some when the
plane called—no, he was going back with it.

23   Oliver rubbed against his leg. "Idiots, fools, nitwits, imbeciles," remarked the parcat affectionately. "Why did I have to go to that damn
dance?"

24   "Huh?" said Grant. He couldn't remember having said anything
about a dance. It must, he decided, have been said during his last fever
madness.

25   Oliver creaked like the door, then giggled like a loony. "It'll be all
right," he assured Grant. "Father is bound to come soon."

26   "Father!" echoed the man. His father had died fifteen years before.
"Where'd you get that from, Oliver?"

27   "It must be the fever," observed Oliver placidly. "You're a nice
kitty, but I wish you had sense enough to know what you're saying.
And I wish father would come." He finished with a suppressed gurgle
that might have been a sob.

28   Grant stared dizzily at him. He hadn't said any of those things; he
was positive. The parcat must have heard them from somebody else—
Somebody else? Where within five hundred miles was there anybody
else?

29   "Oliver!" he bellowed. "Where'd you hear that? Where'd you hear
it?"

30   The parcat backed away, startled. "Father is idiots, fools, nitwits, imbeciles," he said anxiously. "The red jack on the nice kitty."

31   "Come here!" roared Grant. "Whose father? Where have you— Come here, you imp!"

32   He lunged at the creature. Oliver flexed his single hind leg and flung himself frantically to the cowl of the wood stove. "It must be the fever!" he squalled. "No chocolate!"

33   He leaped like a three-legged flash for the flue opening. There came a sound of claws grating on metal, and then he had scrambled through.

34   Grant followed him. His head ached from the effort, and with the still sane part of his mind he knew that the whole episode was doubt- less white fever delirium, but he plowed on.

35   His progress was a nightmare. Loonies kept bobbing their long necks above the tall bleeding-grass, their idiotic giggles and imbecilic faces adding to the general atmosphere of madness.

36   Wisps of fetid fever-bearing vapors spouted up at every step on the spongy soil. Somewhere to his right a slinker squeaked and gib- bered; he knew that a tiny slinker village was over in that direction, for once he had glimpsed the neat little buildings, constructed of small, perfectly fitted stones like a miniature medieval town, complete to towers and battlements. It was said that there were even slinker wars.

37   His head buzzed and whirled from the combined effects of ferverin and fever. It was an attack of *blancha,* right enough, and he realized that he was an imbecile, a loony, to wander thus away from his shack. He should be lying on his bunk; the fever was not serious, but more than one man had died on Io in the delirium, with its attendant hallucinations.

38   He was delirious now. He knew it as soon as he saw Oliver, for Oliver was placidly regarding an attractive young lady in perfect evening dress of the style of the second decade of the twenty-second century. Very obviously that was a hallucination, since girls had no business in the Ionian tropics, and if by some wild chance one should appear there, she would certainly not choose formal garb.

39   The hallucination had fever, apparently, for her face was pale with the whiteness that gave *blancha* its name. Her gray eyes regarded him without surprise as he wound his way through the bleeding-grass to her.

40   "Good afternoon, evening, or morning," he remarked, giving a puzzled glance at Jupiter, which was rising, and the sun, which was set- ting. "Or perhaps merely good day, Miss Lee Neilan."

41   She gazed seriously at him. "Do you know," she said, "you're the first one of the illusions that I haven't recognized? All my friends have been around, but you're the first stranger. Or are you a stranger? You know my name—but you ought to, of course, being my own hallucination."

42   "We won't argue about which of us is the hallucination," he suggested. "Let's do it this way. The one of us that disappears first is the illusion. Bet you five dollars you do."

43   "How could I collect?" she said. "I can't very well collect from my own dream."

44   "That is a problem." He frowned. "My problem, of course, not yours. I know I'm real."

45   "How do you know my name?" she demanded.

46   "Ah!" he said. "From intensive reading of the society sections of the newspapers brought by my supply plane. As a matter of fact, I have one of your pictures cut out and pasted next to my bunk. That probably accounts for my seeing you now. I'd like to really meet you some time."

47   "What a gallant remark for an apparition!" she exclaimed. "And who are you supposed to be?"

48   "Why, I'm Grant Calthorpe. In fact, I work for your father, trading with the loonies for ferva."

49   "Grant Calthorpe," she echoed. She narrowed her fever-dulled eyes as if to bring him into better focus. "Why, you are!"

50   Her voice wavered for a moment, and she brushed her hand across her pale brow. "Why should you pop up out of my memories? It's strange. Three or four years ago, when I was a romantic schoolgirl and you the famous sportsman, I was madly in love with you. I had a whole book filled with your pictures—Grant Calthorpe dressed in parka for hunting threadworm on Titan—Grant Calthorpe beside the giant uniped he killed near the Mountains of Eternity. You're—you're really the pleasantest hallucination I've had so far. Delirium would be—fun"— she pressed her hand to her brow again—"if one's head—didn't ache so!"

51   "Gee!" thought Grant, "I wish that were true, that about the book. This is what psychology calls a wish-fulfillment dream." A drop of warm rain plopped on his neck. "Got to get to bed," he said aloud. "Rain's bad for *blancha*. Hope to see you next time I'm feverish."

52   "Thank you," said Lee Neilan with dignity. "It's quite mutual."

53   He nodded, sending a twinge through his head. "Here, Oliver," he said to the drowsing parcat. "Come on."

54   "That isn't Oliver," said Lee. "It's Polly. It's kept me company for two days, and I've named it Polly."

55   "Wrong gender," muttered Grant. "Anyway, it's my parcat, Oliver. Aren't you, Oliver?"

56   "Hope to see you," said Oliver sleepily.

57   "It's Polly. Aren't you, Polly?"

58   "Bet you five dollars," said the parcat. He rose, stretched and loped off into the underbrush. "It must be the fever," he observed as he vanished.

59   "It must be," agreed Grant. He turned away. "Good-by, Miss—or I might as well call you Lee, since you're not real. Good-by, Lee."

60   "Good-by, Grant. But don't go that way. There's a slinker village over in the grass."

61   "No. It's over there."

62   "It's *there*," she insisted. "I've been watching them build it. But they can't hurt you anyway, can they? Not even a slinker could hurt an apparition. Good-by, Grant." She closed her eyes wearily.

III

63   It was raining harder now. Grant pushed his way through the bleeding-grass, whose red sap collected in bloody drops on his boots. He had to get back to his shack quickly, before the white fever and its attendant delirium set him wandering utterly astray. He needed ferverin.

64   Suddenly he stopped short. Directly before him the grass had been cleared away, and in the little clearing were the shoulder-high towers and battlements of a slinker village—a new one, for half-finished houses stood among the others, and hooded six-inch forms toiled over the stones.

65   There was an outcry of squeaks and gibberish. He backed away but a dozen tiny darts whizzed about him. One stuck like a toothpick in his boot, but none, luckily, scratched his skin, for they were undoubtedly poisoned. He moved more quickly, but all around in the thick, fleshy grasses were rustlings, squeakings and incomprehensible imprecations.

66   He circled away. Loonies kept popping their balloon heads over the vegetation, and now and again one giggled in pain as a slinker bit or stabbed it. Grant cut toward a group of the creatures, hoping to distract the tiny fiends in the grass, and a tall, purple-faced loony curved its long neck above him, giggling and gesturing with its skinny fingers at a bundle under its arm.

67   He ignored the thing, and veered toward his shack. He seemed to have eluded the slinkers, so he trudged doggedly on, for he needed a ferverin tablet badly. Yet, suddenly he came to a frowning halt, turned, and began to retrace his steps.

68   "It can't be so," he muttered. "But she told me the truth about the slinker village. I didn't know it was there. Yet how could a hallucination tell me something I didn't know?"

69   Lee Neilan was sitting on the stone-bark log exactly as he had left her, with Oliver again at her side. Her eyes were closed, and two slinkers were cutting at the long skirt of her gown with tiny, glittering knives.

70   Grant knew that they were always attracted by Terrestrial textiles; apparently they were unable to duplicate the fascinating sheen of satin, though the fiends were infernally clever with their tiny hands. As he approached, they tore a strip from thigh to ankle, but the girl made no move. Grant shouted, and the vicious little creatures mouthed unutterable curses at him as they skittered away with their silken plunder.

71   Lee Neilan opened her eyes. "You again," she murmured vaguely. "A moment ago it was father. Now it's you." Her pallor had increased; the white fever was running its course in her body.

72   "Your father! Then that's where Oliver heard—Listen, Lee. I found the slinker village. I didn't know it was there, but I found it just as you said. Do you see what that means? We're both real!"

73   "Real?" she said dully. "There's a purple loony grinning over your shoulder. Make him go away. He makes me feel—sick."

74   He glanced around; true enough, the purple-faced loony was behind him. "Look here," he said, seizing her arm. The feel of her smooth skin was added proof. "You're coming to the shack for ferverin." He pulled her to her feet. "Don't you understand? I'm *real!*"

75   "No, you're not," she said dazedly.

76   "Listen, Lee. I don't know how in the devil you got here or why, but I know Io hasn't driven me that crazy yet. You're real and I'm real." He shook her violently. "I'm *real!*" he shouted.

77   Faint comprehension showed in her dazed eyes. "Real?" she whispered. "Real! Oh, Lord! Then take—me out of this mad place!" She swayed, made a stubborn effort to control herself, then pitched forward against him.

78   Of course on Io her weight was negligible, less than a third Earth normal. He swung her into his arms and set off toward the shack, keeping well away from both slinker settlements. Around him bobbed excited loonies, and now and again the purple-faced one, or another exactly like him, giggled and pointed and gestured.

79   The rain had increased, and warm rivulets flowed down his neck, and to add to the madness, he blundered near a copse of stinging palms, and their barbed lashes stung painfully through his shirt. Those stings were virulent too, if one failed to disinfect them; indeed, it was largely the stinging palms that kept traders from gathering their own ferva instead of depending on the loonies.

80   Behind the low rain clouds, the sun had set, and it was ruddy Jupiter daylight, which lent a false flush to the cheeks of the unconscious Lee Neilan, making her still features very lovely.

81   Perhaps he kept his eyes too steadily on her face, for suddenly Grant was among slinkers again; they were squeaking and sputtering,

and the purple loony leaped in pain as teeth and darts pricked his legs. But, of course, loonies were immune to the poison.

82 The tiny devils were around his feet now. He swore in a low voice and kicked vigorously, sending a ratlike form spinning fifty feet in the air. He had both automatic and flame pistol at his hip, but he could not use them for several reasons.

83 First, using an automatic against the tiny hordes was much like firing into a swarm of mosquitoes; if the bullet killed one or two or a dozen, it made no appreciable impression on the remaining thousands. And as for the flame pistol, that was like using a Big Bertha to swat a fly. Its vast belch of fire would certainly incinerate all the slinkers in its immediate path, along with grass, trees and loonies, but that again would make but little impress on the surviving hordes, and it meant laboriously recharging the pistol with another black diamond and another barrel.

84 He had gas bulbs in the shack, but they were not available at the moment, and besides, he had no spare mask, and no chemist has yet succeeded in devising a gas that would kill slinkers without being also deadly to humans. And, finally, he couldn't use any weapon whatsoever right now, because he dared not drop Lee Neilan to free his hands.

85 Ahead was the clearing around the shack. The space was full of slinkers, but the shack itself was supposed to be slinkerproof, at least for reasonable lengths of time, since stone-bark logs were very resistant to their tiny tools.

86 But Grant perceived that a group of the diminutive devils were around the door, and suddenly he realized their intent. The had looped a cord of some sort over the knob, and were engaged now in twisting it!

87 Grant yelled and broke into a run. While he was yet half a hundred feet distant, the door swung inward and the rabble of slinkers flowed into the shack.

88 He dashed through the entrance. Within was turmoil. Little hooded shapes were cutting at the blankets on his bunk, his extra clothing, the sacks he hoped to fill with ferva leaves, and were pulling at the cooking utensils, or at any and all loose objects.

89 He bellowed and kicked at the swarm. A wild chorus of squeaks and gibberish arose as the creatures skipped and dodged about him. The fiends were intelligent enough to realize that he could do nothing with his arms occupied by Lee Neilan. They skittered out of the way of his kicks, and while he threatened a group at the stove, another rabble tore at his blankets.

90 In desperation he charged at the bunk. He swept the girl's body across it to clear it, dropped her on it, and seized a grass broom he had

made to facilitate his housekeeping. With wide strokes of its handle he attacked the slinkers, and the squeals were checkered by cries and whimpers of pain.

91   A few broke for the door, dragging whatever loot they had. He spun around in time to see half a dozen swarming around Lee Neilan, tearing at her clothing, at the wrist watch on her arm, at the satin evening pumps on her small feet. He roared a curse at them and battered them away, hoping that none had pricked her skin with virulent dagger or poisonous tooth.

92   He began to win the skirmish. More of the creatures drew their black capes close about them and scurried over the threshold with their plunder. At last, with a burst of squeaks, the remainder, laden and empty-handed alike, broke and ran for safety, leaving a dozen furry, impish bodies slain or wounded.

93   Grant swept these after the others with his erstwhile weapon, closed the door in the face of a loony that bobbed in the opening, latched it against any repetition of the slinkers' tricks and stared in dismay about the plundered dwelling.

94   Cans had been rolled or dragged away. Every loose object had been pawed by the slinkers' foul little hands, and Grant's clothes hung in ruins on their hooks against the wall. But the tiny robbers had not succeeded in opening the cabinet nor the table drawer, and there was food left.

95   Six months of Ionian life had left him philosophical; he swore heartily, shrugged resignedly and pulled his bottle of ferverin from the cabinet.

96   His own spell of fever had vanished as suddenly and completely as *blancha* always does when treated, but the girl, lacking ferverin, was paper-white and still. Grant glanced at the bottle; eight tablets remained.

97   "Well, I can always chew ferva leaves," he muttered. That was less effective than the alkaloid itself, but it would serve, and Lee Neilan needed the tablets. He dissolved two of them in a glass of water, and lifted her head.

98   She was not too inert to swallow, and he poured the solution between her pale lips, then arranged her as comfortably as he could. Her dress was a tattered silken ruin, and he covered her with a blanket that was no less a ruin. Then he disinfected his palm stings, pulled two chairs together, and sprawled across them to sleep.

99   He started up at the sound of claws on the roof, but it was only Oliver, gingerly testing the flue to see if it were hot. In a moment the parcat scrambled through, stretched himself, and remarked, "I'm real and you're real."

100   "Imagine that!" grunted Grant sleepily.

I V

101   When he awoke it was Jupiter and Europa light, which meant he had slept about seven hours, since the brilliant little third moon was just rising. He rose and gazed at Lee Neilan, who was sleeping soundly with a tinge of color in her face that was not entirely due to the ruddy daylight. The *blancha* was passing.

102   He dissolved two more tablets in water, then shook the girl's shoulder. Instantly her gray eyes opened, quite clear now, and she looked up at him without surprise.

103   "Hello, Grant," she murmured. "So it's you again. Fever isn't so bad, after all."

104   "Maybe I ought to let you stay feverish," he grinned. "You say such nice things. Wake up and drink this, Lee."

105   She became suddenly aware of the shack's interior. "Why —Where is this? It looks—real!"

106   "It is. Drink this ferverin."

107   She obeyed, then lay back and stared at him perplexedly. "Real?" she said. "And you're real?"

108   "I think I am."

109   A rush of tears clouded her eyes. "Then—I'm out of that place? That horrible place?"

110   "You certainly are." He saw signs of her relief becoming hysteria, and hastened to distract her. "Would you mind telling me how you happened to be there—and dressed for a party, too?"

111   She controlled herself. "I was dressed for a party. A party in Herapolis. But I was in Junopolis, you see."

112   "I don't see. In the first place, what are you doing on Io, anyway? Every time I ever heard of you, it was in connection with New York or Paris society."

113   She smiled. "Then it wasn't all delirium, was it? You did say that you had one of my pictures—Oh, that one!" She frowned at the print on the wall. "Next time a news photographer wants to snap my picture, I'll remember not to grin—like a loony. But as to how I happen to be on Io, I came with father, who's looking over the possibilities of raising ferva on plantations instead of having to depend on traders and loonies. We've been here three months, and I've been terribly bored. I thought Io would be exciting, but it wasn't—until recently."

114   "But what about that dance? How'd you manage to get here, a thousand miles from Junopolis?"

115   "Well," she said slowly, "it was terribly tiresome in Junopolis. No shows, no sport, nothing but an occasional dance. I got restless. When there were dances in Herapolis, I formed the habit of flying over there.

It's only four or five hours in a fast plane, you know. And last week—or whenever it was—I'd planned on flying down, and Harvey—that's father's secretary—was to take me. But at the last minute father needed him, and forbade my flying alone."

116   Grant felt a strong dislike for Harvey. "Well?" he asked.

117   "So I flew alone," she finished demurely.

118   "And cracked up, eh?"

119   "I can fly as well as anybody," she retorted. "It was just that I followed a different route, and suddenly there were mountains ahead."

120   He nodded. "The Idiots' Hills," he said. "My supply plane detours five hundred miles to avoid them. They're not high, but they stick right out above the atmosphere of this crazy planet. The air here is dense but shallow."

121   "I know that. I knew I couldn't fly above them, but I thought I could hurdle them. Work up full speed, you know, and then throw the plane upward. I had a closed plane, and gravitation is so weak here. And besides, I've seen it done several times, especially with rocket-driven craft. The jets help to support the plane even after the wings are useless for lack of air."

122   "What a damn fool stunt!" exclaimed Grant. "Sure it can be done, but you have to be an expert to pull out of it when you hit the air on the other side. You hit fast, and there isn't much falling room."

123   "So I found out," said Lee ruefully. "I almost pulled out, but not quite, and I hit in the middle of some stinging palms. I guess the crash dazed them, because I managed to get out before they started lashing around. But I couldn't reach my plane again, and it was—I only remember two days of it—but it was horrible!"

124   "It must have been," he said gently.

125   "I knew that if I didn't eat or drink, I had a chance of avoiding white fever. The not eating wasn't so bad, but the not drinking—well, I finally gave up and drank out of a brook. I didn't care what happened if I could have a few moments that weren't thirst-tortured. And after that it's all confused and vague."

126   "You should have chewed ferva leaves."

127   "I didn't know that. I wouldn't have even known what they looked like, and beside, I kept expecting father to appear. He must be having a search made by now."

128   "He probably is," rejoined Grant ironically. "Has it occurred to you that there are thirteen million square miles of surface on little Io? And that for all he knows, you might have crashed on any square mile of it? When you're flying from north pole to south pole, there *isn't* any shortest route. You can cross any point on the planet."

129   Her gray eyes started wide. "But I——"

130   "Furthermore," said Grant, "this is probably the *last* place a searching party would look. They wouldn't think any one but a loony would
try to hurdle Idiots' Hills, in which thesis I quite agree. So it looks very
much, Lee Neilan, as if you're marooned here until my supply plane
gets here next month!"

131   "But father will be crazy! He'll think I'm dead!"

132   "He thinks that now, no doubt."

133   "But we can't——" She broke off, staring around the tiny shack's
single room. After a moment she sighed resignedly, smiled and said
softly, "Well, it might have been worse, Grant. I'll try to earn my keep."

134   "Good. How do you feel, Lee?"

135   "Quite normal. I'll start right to work." She flung off the tattered
blanket, sat up, and dropped her feet to the floor. "I'll fix dinn— Good
night! My dress!" She snatched the blanket about her again.

136   He grinned. "We had a little run-in with the slinkers after you had
passed out. They did for my spare wardrobe too."

137   "It's ruined!" she wailed.

138   "Would needle and thread help? They left that, at least, because it
was in the table drawer."

139   "Why, I couldn't make a good swimming suit out of this!" she retorted. "Let me try one of yours."

140   By dint of cutting, patching and mending, she at last managed to
piece one of Grant's suits to respectable proportions. She looked very
lovely in shirt and trousers, but he was troubled to note that a sudden
pallor had overtaken her.

141   It was the *riblancha,* the second spell of fever that usually followed a
severe or prolonged attack. His face was serious as he cupped two of his
last four ferverin tablets in his hand.

142   "Take these," he ordered. "And we've got to get some ferva leaves
somewhere. The plane took my supply away last week, and I've had
bad luck with my loonies ever since. They haven't brought me anything but weeds and rubbish."

143   Lee puckered her lips at the bitterness of the drug, then closed her
eyes against its momentary dizziness and nausea. "Where can you find
ferva?" she asked.

144   He shook his head perplexedly, glancing out at the setting mass of
Jupiter, with its bands glowing creamy and brown, and the Red Spot
boiling near the western edge. Close above it was the brilliant little
disk of Europa. He frowned suddenly, glanced at his watch and then at
the almanac on the inside of the cabinet door.

145   "It'll be Europa light in fifteen minutes," he muttered, "and true
night in twenty-five—the first true night in half a month. I wonder——"

146   He gazed thoughtfully at Lee's face. He knew where ferva grew. One dared not penetrate the jungle itself, where stinging palms and arrow vines and the deadly worms called toothers made such a venture sheer suicide for any creatures but loonies and slinkers. But he knew where ferva grew—

147   In Io's rare true night even the clearing might be dangerous. Not merely from slinkers, either; he knew well enough that in the darkness creatures crept out of the jungle who otherwise remained in the eternal shadows of its depths—toothers, bullet-head frogs and doubtless many unknown slimy, venomous, mysterious beings never seen by man. One heard stories in Herapolis and—

148   But he had to get ferva, and he knew where it grew. Not even a loony would try to gather it there, but in the little gardens or farms around the tiny slinker towns, there was ferva growing.

149   He switched on a light in the gathering dusk. "I'm going outside a moment," he told Lee Neilan. "If the *blancha* starts coming back, take the other two tablets. Wouldn't hurt you to take 'em anyway. The slinkers got away with my thermometer, but if you get dizzy again, you take 'em."

150   "Grant! Where—"

151   "I'll be back," he called, closing the door behind him.

152   A loony, purple in the bluish Europa light, bobbed up with a long giggle. He waved the creature aside and set off on a cautious approach to the neighborhood of the slinker village—the old one, for the other could hardly have had time to cultivate its surrounding ground. He crept warily through the bleeding-grass, but he knew his stealth was pure optimism. He was in exactly the position of a hundred-foot giant trying to approach a human city in secrecy—a difficult matter even in the utter darkness of night.

153   He reached the edge of the slinker clearing. Behind him, Europa, moving as fast as the second hand on his watch, plummeted toward the horizon. He paused in momentary surprise at the sight of the exquisite little town, a hundred feet away across the tiny square fields, with lights flickering in its hand-wide windows. He had not known that slinker culture included the use of lights, but there they were, tiny candles or perhaps diminutive oil lamps.

154   He blinked in the darkness. The second of the ten-foot fields looked like—it was—ferva. He stooped low, crept out, and reached his hand for the fleshy, white leaves. And at that moment came a shrill giggle and the crackle of grass behind him. The loony! The idiotic purple loony!

155   Squeaking shrieks sounded. He snatched a double handful of ferva, rose, and dashed toward the lighted window of his shack. He had no wish to face poisoned barbs or disease-bearing teeth, and the slinkers

were certainly aroused. Their gibbering sounded in chorus; the ground looked black with them.

156   He reached the shack, burst in, slammed and latched the door. "Got it!" He grinned. "Let 'em rave outside now."

157   They were raving. Their gibberish sounded like the creaking of worn machinery. Even Oliver opened his drowsy eyes to listen. "It must be the fever," observed the parcat placidly.

158   Lee was certainly no paler; the *riblancha* was passing safely. "Ugh!" she said, listening to the tumult without. "I've always hated rats, but slinkers are worse. All the shrewdness and viciousness of rats plus the intelligence of devils."

159   "Well," said Grant thoughtfully, "I don't see what they can do. They've had it in for me anyway."

160   "It sounds as if they're going off," said the girl, listening. "The noise is fading."

161   Grant peered out of the window. "They're still around. They've just passed from swearing to planning, and I wish I knew what. Some day, if this crazy little planet ever becomes worth human occupation, there's going to be a show-down between humans and slinkers."

162   "Well? They're not civilized enough to be really a serious obstacle, and they're so small, besides."

163   "But they learn," he said. "They learn so quickly, and they breed like flies. Suppose they pick up the use of gas, or suppose they develop little rifles for their poisonous darts. That's possible, because they work in metals right now, and they know fire. That would put them practically on a par with man as far as offense goes, for what good are our giant cannons and rocket planes against six-inch slinkers? And to be just on even terms would be fatal; one slinker for one man would be a hell of a trade."

164   Lee yawned. "Well, it's not our problem. I'm hungry, Grant."

165   "Good. That's a sign the *blancha*'s through with you. We'll eat and then sleep a while, for there's five hours of darkness."

166   "But the slinkers?"

167   "I don't see what they can do. They couldn't cut through stone-bark walls in five hours, and anyway, Oliver would warn us if one managed to slip in somewhere."

V

168   It was light when Grant awoke, and he stretched his cramped limbs painfully across his two chairs. Something had awakened him, but he didn't know just what. Oliver was pacing nervously beside him, and now looked anxiously up at him.

169   "I've had bad luck with my loonies," announced the parcat plaintively. "You're a nice kitty."

170   "So are you," said Grant. Something had wakened him, but what?

171   Then he knew, for it came again—the merest trembling of the
stone-bark floor. He frowned in puzzlement. Earthquakes? Not on Io,
for the tiny sphere had lost its internal heat untold ages ago. Then
what?

172   Comprehension dawned suddenly. He sprang to his feet with so
wild a yell that Oliver scrambled sideways with an infernal babble. The
startled parcat leaped to the stove and vanished up the flue. His squall
drifted faintly back, "It must be the fever!"

173   Lee had started to a sitting position on the bunk, her gray eyes
blinking sleepily.

174   "Outside!" he roared, pulling her to her feet. "Get out! Quickly!"

175   "Wh—what—why—"

176   "Get out!" He thrust her through the door, then spun to seize his
belt and weapons, the bag of ferva leaves, a package of chocolate. The
floor trembled again, and he burst out of the door with a frantic leap to
the side of the dazed girl.

177   "They've undermined it!" he choked. "The devils undermined
the—"

178   He had no time to say more. A corner of the shack suddenly subsided; the stone-bark logs grated, and the whole structure collapsed like
a child's house of blocks. The crash died into silence, and there was no
motion save a lazy wisp of vapor, a few black, ratlike forms scurrying
toward the grass, and a purple loony bobbing beyond the ruins.

179   "The dirty devils!" he swore bitterly. "The damn little black rats!
The—"

180   A dart whistled so close that it grazed his ear and then twitched a
lock of Lee's tousled brown hair. A chorus of squeaking sounded in the
bleeding-grass.

181   "Come on!" he cried. "They're out to exterminate us this time.
No—this way. Toward the hills. There's less jungle this way."

182   They could outrun the tiny slinkers easily enough. In a few moments they had lost the sound of squeaking voices, and they stopped to
gaze ruefully back on the fallen dwelling.

183   "Now," he said miserably, "we're both where you were to start
with."

184   "Oh, no." Lee looked up at him. "We're together now, Grant. I'm
not afraid."

185   "We'll manage," he said with a show of assurance. "We'll put up a
temporary shack somehow. We'll—"

186   A dart struck his boot with a sharp *blup.* The slinkers had caught up to them.

187   Again they ran toward Idiots' Hills. When at last they stopped, they could look down a long slope and far over the Ionian jungles. There was the ruined shack, and there, neatly checkered, the fields and towers of the nearer slinker town. But they had scarcely caught their breath when gibbering and squeaking came out of the brush.

188   They were being driven into Idiots' Hills, a region as unknown to man as the icy wastes of Pluto. It was as if the tiny fiends behind them had determined that this time their enemy, the giant trampler and despoiler of their fields, should be pursued to extinction.

189   Weapons were useless. Grant could not even glimpse their pursuers, slipping like hooded rats through the vegetation. A bullet, even if chance sped it through a slinker's body, was futile, and his flame pistol, though its lightning stroke should incinerate tons of brush and bleeding-grass, could no more than cut a narrow path through their horde of tormentors. The only weapons that might have availed, the gas bulbs, were lost in the ruins of the shack.

190   Grant and Lee were forced upward. They had risen a thousand feet above the plain, and the air was thinning. There was no jungle here, but only great stretches of bleeding-grass, across which a few loonies were visible, bobbing their heads on their long necks.

191   "Toward—the peaks!" gasped Grant, now painfully short of breath. "Perhaps we can stand rarer air than they."

192   Lee was beyond answer. She panted doggedly along beside him as they plodded now over patches of bare rock. Before them were two low peaks, like the pillars of a gate. Glancing back, Grant caught a glimpse of tiny black forms on a clear area, and in sheer anger he fired a shot. A single slinker leaped convulsively, its cape flapping, but the rest flowed on. There must have been thousands of them.

193   The peaks were closer, no more than a few hundred yards away. They were sheer, smooth, unscalable.

194   "Between them," muttered Grant.

195   The passage that separated them was bare and narrow. The twin peaks had been one in ages past; some forgotten volcanic convulsion had split them, leaving this slender canyon between.

196   He slipped an arm about Lee, whose breath, from effort and altitude, was a series of rasping gasps. A bright dart tinkled on the rocks as they reached the opening, but looking back, Grant could see only a purple loony plodding upward, and a few more to his right. They raced down a straight fifty-foot passage that debouched suddenly into a sizable valley—and there, thunderstruck for a moment, they paused.

197   A city lay there. For a brief instant Grant thought they had burst upon a vast slinker metropolis, but the merest glance showed otherwise. This was no city of medieval blocks, but a poem in marble, classical in beauty, and of human or near-human proportions. White columns, glorious arches, pure curving domes, an architectural loveliness that might have been born on the Acropolis. It took a second look to discern that the city was dead, deserted, in ruins.

198   Even in her exhaustion, Lee felt its beauty. "How—how exquisite!" she panted. "One could almost forgive them—for being—slinkers!"

199   "They won't forgive us for being human," he muttered. "We'll have to make a stand somewhere. We'd better pick a building."

200   But before they could move more than a few feet from the canyon mouth, a wild disturbance halted them. Grant whirled, and for a moment found himself actually paralyzed by amazement. The narrow canyon was filled with a gibbering horde of slinkers, like a nauseous, heaving black carpet. But they came no farther than the valley end, for grinning, giggling and bobbing, blocking the opening with tramping three-toed feet, were our loonies!

201   It was a battle. The slinkers were biting and stabbing at the miserable defenders, whose shrill keenings of pain were less giggles than shrieks. But with a determination and purpose utterly foreign to loonies, their clawed feet trampled methodically up and down, up and down.

202   Grant exploded, "I'll be damned!" Then an idea struck him. "Lee! They're packed in the canyon, the whole devil's brood of 'em!"

203   He rushed toward the opening. He thrust his flame pistol between the skinny legs of a loony, aimed it straight along the canyon and fired.

VI

204   Inferno burst. The tiny diamond, giving up all its energy in one terrific blast, shot a jagged stream of fire that filled the canyon from wall to wall and vomited out beyond to cut a fan of fire through the bleeding-grass of the slope.

205   Idiots' Hills reverberated to the roar, and when the rain of débris settled, there was nothing in the canyon save a few bits of flesh and the head of an unfortunate loony, still bouncing and rolling.

206   Three of the loonies survived. A purple-faced one was pulling his arm, grinning and giggling in imbecile glee. He waved the thing aside and returned to the girl.

207   "Thank goodness!" he said. "We're out of that, anyway."

208   "I wasn't afraid, Grant. Not with you."

209   He smiled. "Perhaps we can find a place here," he suggested. "The fever ought to be less troublesome at this altitude. But—say, this must have been the capital city of the whole slinker race in ancient times. I can scarcely imagine those fiends creating an architecture as beautiful as this—or as large. Why, these buildings are as colossal in proportion to slinker size as the skyscrapers of New York to us!"

210   "But so beautiful," said Lee softly, sweeping her eyes over the glory of the ruins. "One might almost forgive—Grant! Look at those!"

211   He followed the gesture. On the inner side of the canyon's portals were gigantic carvings. But the thing that set him staring in amazement was the subject of the portrayal. There, towering up the cliff sides, were the figures, not of slinkers, but of—loonies! Exquisitely carved, smiling rather than grinning, and smiling somehow sadly, regretfully, pityingly—yet beyond doubt loonies!

212   "Good night!" he whispered. "Do you see, Lee? This must once have been a loony city. The steps, the doors, the buildings, all are on their scale of size. Somehow, some time, they must achieved civilization, and the loonies we know are the degenerate residue of a great race."

213   "And," put in Lee, "the reason those four blocked the way when the slinkers tried to come through is that they still remember. Or probably they don't actually remember, but they have a tradition of past glories, or more likely still, just a superstitious feeling that this place is in some way sacred. They let us pass because, after all, we look more like loonies than like slinkers. But the amazing thing is that they still possess even that dim memory, because this city must have been in ruins for centuries. Or perhaps even for thousands of years."

214   "But to think that loonies could ever have had the intelligence to create a culture of their own," said Grant, waving away the purple one bobbing and giggling at his side. Suddenly he paused, turning a gaze of new respect on the creature. "This one's been following me for days. All right, old chap, what is it?"

215   The purple one extended a sorely bedraggled bundle of bleeding-grass and twigs, giggling idiotically. His ridiculous mouth twisted; his eyes popped in an agony of effort at mental concentration.

216   "Canny!" he giggled triumphantly.

217   "The imbecile!" flared Grant. "Nitwit! Idiot!" He broke off, then laughed. "Never mind. I guess you deserve it." He tossed his package of chocolate to the three delighted loonies. "Here's your candy."

218   A scream from Lee startled him. She was waving her arms wildly, and over the crest of Idiots' Hills a rocket plane roared, circled and nosed its way into the valley.

219   The door opened. Oliver stalked gravely out, remarking casually, "I'm real and you're real." A man followed the parcat—two men.

220   "Father!" screamed Lee.

221   It was some time later that Gustavus Neilan turned to Grant. "I can't thank you," he said. "If there's ever any way I can show my appreciation for—"

222   "There is. You can cancel my contract."

223   "Oh, you work for me?"

224   "I'm Grant Calthorpe, one of your traders, and I'm about sick of this crazy planet."

225   "Of course, if you wish," said Neilan. "If it's a question of pay—"

226   "You can pay me for the six months I've worked."

227   "If you'd care to stay," said the older man, "there won't be trading much longer. We've been able to grow ferva near the polar cities, and I prefer plantations to the uncertainties of relying on loonies. If you'd work out your year, we might be able to put you in charge of a plantation by the end of that time."

228   Grant met Lee Neilan's gray eyes, and hesitated. "Thanks," he said slowly, "but I'm sick of it." He smiled at the girl, then turned back to her father. "Would you mind telling me how you happened to find us? This is the most unlikely place on the planet."

229   "That's just the reason," said Neilan. "When Lee didn't get back, I thought things over pretty carefully. At last I decided, knowing her as I did, to search the least likely places first. We tried the shores of the Fever Sea, and then the White Desert, and finally Idiots' Hills. We spotted the ruins of a shack, and on the debris was this chap"—he indicated Oliver—"remarking that 'Ten loonies make one half-wit.' Well, the half-wit part sounded very much like a reference to my daughter, and we cruised about until the roar of your flame pistol attracted our attention."

230   Lee pouted, then turned her serious gray eyes on Grant. "Do you remember," she said softly, "what I told you there in the jungle?"

231   "I wouldn't even have mentioned that," he replied. "I knew you were delirious."

232   "But—perhaps I wasn't. Would companionship make it any easier to work out your year? I mean if—for instance—you were to fly back with us to Junopolis and return with a wife?"

233   "Lee," he said huskily, "you know what a difference that would make, though I can't understand why you'd ever dream of it."

234   "It must," suggested Oliver, "be the fever."

DISCUSSION QUESTIONS

1. How do the loonies and slinkers differ from each other? Why does Grant find the loonies unsatisfactory workers and helpers?
2. What is the main reason humans are on Io, and what uses do they make of what they find there?
3. Discuss with a classmate the function of the scene where Grant discovers Lee Neilan, yet each considers the other an illusion.
4. What effect does the parcat's imitation of language have on you as a reader? Why does Grant keep him around?
5. Why are human weapons generally ineffective against the slinkers?

WRITING TOPICS

1. The loonies join in the final battle against the slinkers. Why? What does this indicate about them? Write a journal entry explaining your reasoning.
2. When Grant discovers the ruined city, his respect for loonies changes. What does he think may have happened? Do you have any other possible ideas? Write a short essay presenting one or two alternate explanations.
3. In this story the aggressors are shown as rat-like and bent on revenge against the human who started the conflict. In a few paragraphs, show possible comparisons to the military buildup leading to World War II.

Misfit

1939

ROBERT HEINLEIN (1907-1988)

Robert Heinlein served as a naval officer for five years before retiring in 1934. He began writing science fiction in 1939 with "Lifeline" in *Astounding Science Fiction*. He produced quality fiction, and a great deal of it, from 1940 to 1960. Many of his early stories fitted loosely into a somewhat complete future history, the outlines of which John W. Campbell published in *Astounding Science Fiction* in 1941. He wrote mostly short fiction up until 1950. He then switched to novels, including *The Puppet Masters* (1951) and *Starship Troopers* (1959). His most well-known work is *Stranger in a Strange Land* (1961), the story of a human raised on Mars who returns to Earth and becomes a Messiah-like figure. In Heinlein's later period, his works focused on his controversial political views, but his early work helped establish science fiction as adult fiction.

After 1950, Heinlein largely abandoned his future history. *Farnham's Freehold* (1964) is a novel about despotism overcoming the United States, while *The Moon Is a Harsh Mistress* (1966) contains parallels to the American Revolution. *I Will Fear No Evil* (1970) features a rich man transferring his consciousness to his secretary. In the eighties his increasing bitterness is shown in novels like *The Number of the Beast* (1980) and *The Cat Who Walks Through Walls* (1985).

In "Misfit," a group of space recruits gets a second chance to make something of themselves, a chance to contribute something useful to society. They must, however, tap the resources within themselves and overcome the odds against them.

*"... for the purpose of conserving and improving
our interplanetary resources, and providing useful,
healthful occupations for the youth of this planet."*

**Excerpt from the Enabling Act, H. R. 7118,
setting up the Cosmic Construction Corps.**

1   "Attention to muster!" The parade ground voice of a First Sergeant
of Space Marines cut through the fog and drizzle of a nasty New Jersey
morning. "As your names are called, answer 'Here,' step forward with
your baggage, and embark. Atkins!"

2   "Here!"

3   "Austin!"

4   "Hyar!"

5   "Ayres!"

6   "Here!"

7   One by one they fell out of ranks, shouldered the hundred and
thirty pounds of personal possessions allowed them, and trudged up the
gangway. They were young—none more than twenty-two—in some
cases luggage outweighed the owner.

8   "Kaplan!"

9   "Here!"

10   "Keith!"

11   "Heah!"

12   "Libby!"

13   "Here!" A thin gangling blond had detached himself from the
line, hastily wiped his nose, and grabbed his belongings. He slung a fat
canvas bag over his shoulder, steadied it, and lifted a suitcase with his
free hand. He started for the companionway in an unsteady dog trot.
As he stepped on the gangway his suitcase swung against his knees. He
staggered against a short wiry form dressed in the powder-blue of the
Space Navy. Strong fingers grasped his arm and checked his fall.

14   "Steady, son. Easy does it." Another hand readjusted the canvas bag.

15   "Oh, excuse me, uh"—the embarrassed youngster automatically
counted the four bands of silver braid below the shooting star—
"Captain. I didn't—"

16   "Bear a hand and get aboard, son."

17   "Yes, sir."

18   The passage into the bowels of the transport was gloomy. When
the lad's eyes adjusted he saw a gunner's mate wearing the brassard of a
Master-at-Arms, who hooked a thumb towards an open air-tight door.

19   "In there. Find your locker and wait by it." Libby hurried to obey.
Inside he found a jumble of baggage and men in a wide low-ceilinged

compartment. A line of glow-tubes ran around the junction of bulkhead and ceiling and trisected the overhead; the soft roar of blowers made a background to the voices of his shipmates. He picked his way through heaped luggage and located his locker, seven-ten, on the far wall outboard. He broke the seal on the combination lock, glanced at the combination, and opened it. The locker was very small, the middle of a tier of three. He considered what he should keep in it. A loudspeaker drowned out the surrounding voices and demanded his attention:

20   "Attention! Man all space details; first section. Raise ship in twelve minutes. Close air-tight doors. Stop blowers at minus two minutes. Special orders for passengers; place all gear on deck, and lie down on red signal light. Remain down until release is sounded. Masters-at-Arms check compliance."

21   The gunner's mate popped in, glanced around and immediately commenced supervising rearrangement of the baggage. Heavy items were lashed down. Locker doors were closed. By the time each boy had found a place on the deck and the Master-at-Arms had okayed the pad under his head, the glow-tubes turned red and the loudspeaker brayed out.

22   "All hands—Up Ship! Stand by for acceleration." The Master-at-Arms hastily reclined against two cruise bags, and watched the room. The blowers sighed to a stop. There followed two minutes of dead silence. Libby felt his heart commence to pound. The two minutes stretched interminably. Then the deck quivered and a roar like escaping high-pressure steam beat at his ear drums. He was suddenly very heavy and a weight lay across his chest and heart. An indefinite time later the glow-tubes flashed white, and the announcer bellowed:

23   "Secure all getting underway details; regular watch, first section." The blowers droned into life. The Master-at-Arms stood up, rubbed his buttocks and pounded his arms, then said:

24   "Okay, boys." He stepped over and undogged the airtight door to the passageway. Libby got up and blundered into a bulkhead, nearly falling. His legs and arms had gone to sleep, besides which he felt alarmingly light, as if he had sloughed off at least half of his inconsiderable mass.

25   For the next two hours he was too busy to think, or to be homesick. Suitcases, boxes, and bags had to be passed down into the lower hold and lashed against angular acceleration. He located and learned how to use a waterless water closet. He found his assigned bunk and learned that it was his only eight hours in twenty-four; two other boys had the use of it too. The three sections ate in three shifts, nine shifts in all—twenty-four youths and a master-at-arms at one long table which jam-filled a narrow compartment off the galley.

26   After lunch Libby restowed his locker. He was standing before it, gazing at a photograph which he intended to mount on the inside of the locker door, when a command filled the compartment:

27   "Attention!"

28   Standing inside the door was the Captain flanked by the Master-at-Arms. The Captain commenced to speak. "At rest, men. Sit down. McCoy, tell control to shift this compartment to smoke filter." The gunner's mate hurried to the communicator on the bulkhead and spoke into it in a low tone. Almost at once the hum of the blowers climbed a half-octave and stayed there. "Now light up if you like. I'm going to talk to you.

29   "You boys are headed out on the biggest thing so far in your lives. From now on you're men, with one of the hardest jobs ahead of you that men have ever tackled. What we have to do is part of a bigger scheme. You, and hundreds of thousands of others like you, are going out as pioneers to fix up the solar system so that human beings can make better use of it.

30   "Equally important, you are being given a chance to build yourselves into useful and happy citizens of the Federation. For one reason or another you weren't happily adjusted back on Earth. Some of you saw the jobs you were trained for abolished by new inventions. Some of you got into trouble from not knowing what to do with the modern leisure. In any case you were misfits. Maybe you were called bad boys and had a lot of black marks chalked up against you.

31   "But everyone of you starts even today. The only record you have in this ship is your name at the top of a blank sheet of paper. It's up to you what goes on that page.

32   "Now about our job—We didn't get one of the easy repair-and-recondition jobs on the Moon, with week-ends at Luna City, and all the comforts of home. Nor did we draw a high-gravity planet where a man can eat a full meal and expect to keep it down. Instead we've got to go out to Asteroid HS-5388 and turn it into Space Station E-M3. She has no atmosphere at all, and only about two per cent Earth-surface gravity. We've got to play human fly on her for at least six months, no girls to date, no television, no recreation that you don't devise yourselves, and hard work every day. You'll get space sick, and so homesick you can taste it, and agoraphobia. If you aren't careful you'll get ray-burnt. Your stomach will act up, and you'll wish to God you'd never enrolled.

33   "But if you behave yourself, and listen to the advice of the old spacemen, you'll come out of it strong and healthy, with a little credit stored up in the bank, and a lot of knowledge and experience that you wouldn't get in forty years on Earth. You'll be men, and you'll know it.

34   "One last word. It will be pretty uncomfortable to those that aren't
used to it. Just give the other fellow a little consideration, and you'll get
along all right. If you have any complaint and can't get satisfaction any
other way, come see me. Otherwise, that's all. Any questions?"

35   One of the boys put up his hand, "Captain?" he enquired timidly.

36   "Speak up, lad, and give your name."

37   "Rogers, sir. Will we be able to get letters from home?"

38   "Yes, but not very often. Maybe every month or so. The chaplain
will carry mail, and any inspection and supply ships."

39   The ship's loudspeaker blatted out, "All hands! Free flight in ten
minutes. Stand by to lose weight." The Master-at-Arms supervised the
rigging of grab-lines. All loose gear was made fast, and little cellulose
bags were issued to each man. Hardly was this done when Libby felt
himself get light on his feet—a sensation exactly like that experienced
when an express elevator makes a quick stop on an upward trip, except
that the sensation continued and became more intense. At first it was a
pleasant novelty, then it rapidly became distressing. The blood pounded
in his ears, and his feet were clammy and cold. His saliva secreted at an
abnormal rate. He tried to swallow, choked, and coughed. Then his
stomach shuddered and contracted with a violent, painful, convulsive
reflex and he was suddenly, disastrously nauseated. After the first excru-
ciating spasm, he heard McCoy's voice shouting.

40   "Hey! Use your sick-kits like I told you. Don't let that stuff get in
the blowers." Dimly Libby realized that the admonishment included
him. He fumbled for his cellulose bag just as a second temblor shook
him, but he managed to fit the bag over his mouth before the eruption
occurred. When it subsided, he became aware that he was floating near
the overhead and facing the door. The chief Master-at-Arms slithered
in the door and spoke to McCoy.

41   "How are you making out?"

42   "Well enough. Some of the boys missed their kits."

43   "Okay. Mop it up. You can use the starboard lock." He swam out.

44   McCoy touched Libby's arm. "Here, Pinkie, start catching them
butterflies." He handed him a handful of cotton waste, then took another handful himself and neatly dabbed up a globule of the slimy filth
that floated about the compartment. "Be sure your sick-kit is on tight.
When you get sick, just stop and wait until it's over." Libby imitated
him as best as he could. In a few minutes the room was free of the
worst of the sickening debris. McCoy looked it over, and spoke:

45   "Now peel off them dirty duds, and change your kits. Three or
four of you bring everything along to the starboard lock."

46   At the starboard spacelock, the kits were put in first, the inner door closed, and the outer opened. When the inner door was opened again the kits were gone—blown out into space by the escaping air. Pinkie addressed McCoy,

47   "Do we have to throw away our dirty clothes too?"

48   "Huh uh, we'll just give them a dose of vacuum. Take 'em into the lock and stop 'em to those hooks on the bulkheads. Tie 'em tight."

49   This time the lock was opened the garments were bone dry—all the moisture boiled out by the vacuum of space. All that remained of the unpleasant rejecta was a sterile powdery residue. McCoy viewed them with approval. "They'll do. Take them back to the compartment. Then brush them—hard—in front of the exhaust blowers."

50   The next few days were an eternity of misery. Homesickness was forgotten in the all-engrossing wretchedness of spacesickness. The Captain granted fifteen minutes of mild acceleration for each of the nine meal periods, but the respite accentuated the agony. Libby would go to a meal, weak and ravenously hungry. The meal would stay down until free flight was resumed, then the sickness would hit him all over again.

51   On the fourth day he was seated against a bulkhead, enjoying the luxury of a few remaining minutes of weight while the last shift ate, when McCoy walked in and sat down beside him. The gunner's mate fitted a smoke filter over his face and lit a cigarette. He inhaled deeply and started to chat.

52   "How's it going, bud?"

53   "All right, I guess. This spacesickness— Say, McCoy, how do you ever get used to it?"

54   "You get over it in time. Your body acquires new reflexes, so they tell me. Once you learn to swallow without choking, you'll be all right. You even get so you like it. It's restful and relaxing. Four hours sleep is as good as ten."

55   Libby shook his head dolefully. "I don't think I'll ever get used to it."

56   "Yes, you will. You'd better anyway. This here asteroid won't have any surface gravity to speak of; the chief Quartermaster says it won't run over two per cent Earth normal. That ain't enough to cure spacesickness. And there won't be any way to accelerate for meals either."

57   Libby shivered and held his head between his hands.

58   Locating one asteroid among a couple of thousand is not as easy as finding Trafalgar Square in London—especially against the star-crowded backdrop of the galaxy. You take off from Terra with its orbital speed of about nineteen miles per second. You attempt to settle into a composite conoid curve that will not only intersect the orbit of the tiny

fast-moving body, but also accomplish an exact rendezvous. Asteroid HS-5388, 'Eighty-eight,' lay about two and two-tenths astronomical units out from the sun, a little more than two hundred million miles; when the transport took off it lay beyond the sun better than three hundred million miles. Captain Doyle instructed the navigator to plot the basic ellipsoid to tack in free flight around the sun through an elapsed distance of some three hundred forty million miles. The principle involved is the same as used by a hunter to wing a duck in flight by 'leading' the bird in flight. But suppose that you face directly into the sun as you shoot; suppose the bird can not be seen from where you stand, and you have nothing to aim by but some old reports as to how it was flying when last seen?

59   On the ninth day of the passage Captain Doyle betook himself to the chart room and commenced punching keys on the ponderous integral calculator. Then he sent his orderly to present his compliments to the navigator and to ask him to come to the chartroom. A few minutes later a tall heavyset form swam through the door, steadied himself with a grabline and greeted the captain.

60   "Good morning, Skipper."

61   "Hello, Blackie." The Old Man looked up from where he was strapped into the integrator's saddle. "I've been checking your corrections for the meal time accelerations."

62   "It's a nuisance to have a bunch of ground-lubbers on board, sir!"

63   "Yes, it is, but we have to give those boys a chance to eat, or they couldn't work when we got there. Now I want to decelerate starting about ten o'clock, ship's time. What's our eight o'clock speed and co-ordinates?"

64   The Navigator slipped a notebook out of his tunic. "Three hundred fifty-eight miles per second; course is right ascension fifteen hours, eight minutes, twenty-seven seconds, declination minus seven degrees, three minutes; solar distance one hundred and ninety-two million four hundred eighty thousand miles. Our radial position is twelve degrees above course, and almost dead on course in R.A. Do you want Sol's co-ordinates?"

65   "No, not now." The captain bent over the calculator, frowned and chewed the tip of his tongue as he worked the controls. "I want you to kill the acceleration about one million miles inside Eighty-eight's orbit. I hate to waste the fuel, but the belt is full of junk and this damned rock is so small that we will probably have to run a search curve. Use twenty hours on deceleration and commence changing course to port after eight hours. Use normal asymptotic approach. You should have her in a circular trajectory abreast of Eighty-eight, and paralleling her orbit by six o'clock tomorrow morning. I shall want to be called at three."

66   "Aye, aye, sir."

67   "Let me see your figures when you get 'em. I'll send up the order book later."

68   The transport accelerated on schedule. Shortly after three the Captain entered the control room and blinked his eyes at the darkness. The sun was still concealed by the hull of the transport and the midnight blackness was broken only by the dim blue glow of the instrument dials, and the crack of light from under the chart hood. The Navigator turned at the familiar tread.

69   "Good morning, Captain."

70   "Morning, Blackie. In sight yet?"

71   "Not yet. We've picked out half a dozen rocks, but none of them checked."

72   "Any of them close?"

73   "Not uncomfortably. We've overtaken a little sand from time to time."

74   "That can't hurt us—not on a stern chase like this. If pilots would only realize that the asteroids flow in fixed directions at computable speeds nobody would come to grief out here." He stopped to light a cigarette. "People talk about space being dangerous. Sure, it used to be; but I don't know of a case in the past twenty years that couldn't be charged up to some fool's recklessness."

75   "You're right, Skipper. By the way, there's coffee under the chart hood."

76   "Thanks; I had a cup down below." He walked over by the lookouts at stereoscopes and radar tanks and peered up at the star-flecked blackness. Three cigarettes later the lookout nearest him called out.

77   "Light ho!"

78   "Where away?"

79   His mate read the exterior dials of the stereoscope. "Plus point two, abaft one point three, slight drift astern." He shifted to radar and added, "Range seven nine oh four three."

80   "Does that check?"

81   "Could be, Captain. What is her disk?" came the Navigator's muffled voice from under the hood. The first lookout hurriedly twisted the knobs of his instrument, but the Captain nudged him aside.

82   "I'll do this, son." He fitted his face to the double eye guards and surveyed a little silvery sphere, a tiny moon. Carefully he brought two illuminated cross-hairs up until they were exactly tangent to the upper and lower limbs of the disk. "Mark!"

83   The reading was noted and passed to the Navigator, who shortly ducked out from under the hood.

84   "That's our baby, Captain."

85   "Good."

86   "Shall I make a visual triangulation?"

87   "Let the watch officer do that. You go down and get some sleep. I'll
ease her over until we get close enough to use the optical range finder."

88   "Thanks, I will."

89   Within a few minutes the word had spread around the ship that
Eighty-eight had been sighted. Libby crowded into the starboard troop
deck with a throng of excited mess mates and attempted to make out
their future home from the view port. McCoy poured cold water on
their excitement.

90   "By the time that rock shows up big enough to tell anything about
it with your naked eye we'll all be at our grounding stations. She's only
about a hundred miles thick, yuh know."

91   And so it was. Many hours later the ship's announcer shouted:

92   "All hands! Man your grounding stations. Close all air-tight doors.
Stand by to cut blowers on signal."

93   McCoy forced them to lie down throughout the ensuing two
hours. Short shocks of rocket blasts alternated with nauseating weightlessness. Then the blowers stopped and check valves clicked into their
seats. The ship dropped free for a few moments—a final quick blast—
five seconds of falling, and a short, light, grinding bump. A single bugle
note came over the announcer, and the blowers took up their hum.

94   McCoy floated lightly to his feet and poised, swaying, on his toes.
"All out, troops—this is the end of the line."

95   A short chunky lad, a little younger than most of them, awkwardly
emulated him, and bounded toward the door, shouting as he went,
"Come on, fellows! Let's go outside and explore!"

96   The Master-at-Arms squelched him. "Not so fast, kid. Aside from
the fact that there is no air out there, go right ahead. You'll freeze to
death, burn to death, and explode like a ripe tomato. Squad leader, detail
six men to break out spacesuits. The rest of you stay here and stand by."

97   The working party returned shortly loaded down with a couple of
dozen bulky packages. Libby let go the four he carried and watched
them float gently to the deck. McCoy unzipped the envelope from one
suit, and lectured them about it.

98   "This is a standard service type, general issue, Mark IV, Modification
2." He grasped the suit by the shoulders and shook it out so that it hung
like a suit of long winter underwear with the helmet lolling helplessly
between the shoulders of the garment. "It's self-sustaining for eight
hours, having an oxygen supply for that period. It also has a nitrogen
trim tank and a carbon-dioxide-water-vapor cartridge filter."

99   He droned on, repeating practically verbatim the description and instructions given in training regulations. McCoy knew these suits like his tongue knew the roof of his mouth; the knowledge had meant his life on more than one occasion.

100   "The suit is woven from glass fibre laminated with non-volatile asbesto-cellutite. The resulting fabric is flexible, very durable; and will turn all rays normal to solar space outside the orbit of Mercury. It is worn over your regular clothing, but notice the wire-braced accordion pleats at the major joints. They are so designed as to keep the internal volume of the suit nearly constant when the arms or legs are bent. Otherwise the gas pressure inside would tend to keep the suit blown up in an erect position, and movement while wearing the suit would be very fatiguing.

101   "The helmet is moulded from a transparent silicone, leaded and polarized against too great ray penetration. It may be equipped with external visors of any needed type. Orders are to wear not less than a number-two amber on this body. In addition, a lead plate covers the cranium and extends down the back of the suit, completely covering the spinal column.

102   "The suit is equipped with two-way telephony. If your radio quits, as these have a habit of doing, you can talk by putting your helmets in contact. Any questions?"

103   "How do you eat and drink during the eight hours?"

104   "You don't stay in 'em any eight hours. You can carry sugar balls in a gadget in the helmet, but you boys will always eat at the base. As for water, there's a nipple in the helmet near your mouth which you can reach by turning your head to the left. It's hooked to a built-in canteen. But don't drink any more water when you're wearing a suit than you have to. These suits ain't got any plumbing."

105   Suits were passed out to each lad, and McCoy illustrated how to don one. A suit was spread supine on the deck, the front zipper that stretched from neck to crotch was spread wide and one sat down inside this opening, whereupon the lower part was drawn on like long stockings. Then a wiggle into each sleeve and the heavy flexible gauntlets were smoothed and patted into place. Finally an awkward backward stretch of the neck with shoulders hunched enabled the helmet to be placed over the head.

106   Libby followed the motions of McCoy and stood up in his suit. He examined the zipper which controlled the suit's only opening. It was backed by two soft gaskets which would be pressed together by the zipper and sealed by internal air pressure. Inside the helmet a composition mouthpiece for exhalation led to the filter.

107   McCoy bustled around, inspecting them, tightening a belt here and there, instructing them in the use of the external controls. Satisfied, he reported to the conning room that his section had received basic instruction and was ready to disembark. Permission was received to take them out for thirty minutes acclimatization.

108   Six at a time, he escorted them though the air lock, and out on the surface of the planetoid. Libby blinked his eyes at the unaccustomed luster of sunshine on rock. Although the sun lay more than two hundred million miles away and bathed the little planet with radiation only one fifth as strong as that lavished on mother Earth, nevertheless the lack of atmosphere resulted in a glare that made him squint. He was glad to have the protection of his amber visor. Overhead the sun, shrunk to penny size, shone down from a dead black sky in which unwinking stars crowded each other and the very sun itself.

109   The voice of a mess mate sounded in Libby's earphones, "Jeepers! That horizon looks close. I'll bet it ain't more'n a mile away."

110   Libby looked out over the flat bare plain and subconsciously considered the matter. "It's less," he commented, "than a third of a mile away."

111   "What the hell do you know about it, Pinkie? And who asked you, anyhow?"

112   Libby answered defensively, "As a matter of fact, it's one thousand six hundred and seventy feet, figuring that my eyes are five feet three inches above ground level."

113   "Nuts. Pinkie, you are always trying to show off how much you think you know."

114   "Why, I am not," Libby protested. "If this body is a hundred miles thick and as round as it looks: why, naturally the horizon *has* to be just that far away."

115   "Says *who?*"

116   McCoy interrupted.

117   "Pipe down! Libby is a lot nearer right than you were."

118   "He is exactly right," put in a strange voice. "I had to look it up for the navigator before I left control."

119   "Is that so?"—McCoy's voice again— "If the Chief Quartermaster says you're right, Libby, you're right. How did you know?"

120   Libby flushed miserably. "I—I don't know. That's the only way it could be."

121   The gunner's mate and the quartermaster stared at him but dropped the subject.

122   By the end of the 'day' (ship's time, for Eighty-eight had a period of eight hours and thirteen minutes), work was well under way. The transport had grounded close by a low range of hills. The Captain

selected a little bowl-shaped depression in the hills, some thousand feet long and half as broad, in which to establish a permanent camp. This was to be roofed over, sealed, and an atmosphere provided.

123   In the hill between the ship and the valley, quarters were to be excavated; dormitories, mess hall, officers' quarters, sick bay, recreation room, offices, store rooms, and so forth. A tunnel must be bored through the hill, connecting the sites of these rooms, and connecting with a ten foot airtight metal tube sealed to the ship's portside air-lock. Both the tube and tunnel were to be equipped with a continuous conveyor belt for passengers and freight.

124   Libby found himself assigned to the roofing detail. He helped a metalsmith struggle over the hill with a portable atomic heater, difficult to handle because of a mass of eight hundred pounds, but weighing here only sixteen pounds. The rest of the roofing detail were breaking out and preparing to move by hand the enormous translucent tent which was to be the 'sky' of the little valley.

125   The metalsmith located a landmark on the inner slope of the valley, set up his heater, and commenced cutting a deep horizontal groove or step in the rock. He kept it always at the same level by following a chalk mark drawn along the rock wall. Libby enquired how the job had been surveyed so quickly.

126   "Easy," he was answered, "two of the quartermasters went ahead with a transit, leveled it just fifty feet above the valley floor, and clamped a searchlight to it. Then one of 'em ran like hell around the rim, making chalk marks at the height at which the beam struck."

127   "Is this roof going to be just fifty feet high?"

128   "No, it will average maybe a hundred. It bellies up in the middle from the air pressure."

129   "Earth normal?"

130   "Half Earth normal."

131   Libby concentrated for an instant, then looked puzzled. "But look—This valley is a thousand feet long and better than five hundred wide. At half of fifteen pounds per square inch, and allowing for the arch of the roof, that's a load of one and an eighth billion pounds. What fabric can take that kind of a load?"

132   "Cobwebs."

133   "Cobwebs?"

134   "Yeah, cobwebs. Strongest stuff in the world, stronger than the best steel. Synthetic spider silk. This gauge we're using for the roof has a tensile strength of four thousand pounds a running inch."

135   Libby hesitated a second, then replied, "I see. With a rim about eighteen hundred thousand inches around, the maximum pull at the

point of anchoring would be about six hundred and twenty-five pounds per inch. Plenty safe margin."

136   The metalsmith leaned on his tool and nodded, "Something like that. You're pretty quick at arithmetic, aren't you, bud?"

137   Libby looked startled. "I just like to get things straight."

138   They worked rapidly around the slope, cutting a clean smooth groove to which the 'cobweb' could be anchored and sealed. The white-hot lava spewed out of the discharge vent and ran slowly down the hillside. A brown vapor boiled off the surface of the molten rock, arose a few feet and sublimed almost at once into the vacuum to white powder which settled to the ground. The metalsmith pointed to the powder.

139   "That stuff 'ud cause silicosis if we let it stay there, and breathed it later."

140   "What do you do about it?"

141   "Just clean it out with the blowers of the air conditioning plant."

142   Libby took this opening to ask another question. "Mister—?"

143   "Johnson's my name. No mister necessary."

144   "Well, Johnson, where do we get the air for this whole valley, not to mention the tunnels? I figure we must need twenty-five million cubic feet or more. Do we manufacture it?"

145   "Naw, that's too much trouble. We brought it with us."

146   "On the transport?"

147   "Uh huh, at fifty atmospheres."

148   Libby considered this. "I see—that way it would go into a space eighty feet on a side."

149   "Matter of fact it's in three specially constructed holds—giant air bottles. This transport carried air to Ganymede. I was in her then—a recruit, but in the air gang even then."

150   In three weeks the permanent camp was ready for occupancy and the transport cleared of its cargo. The storerooms bulged with tools and supplies. Captain Doyle had moved his administrative offices underground, signed over his command to his first officer, and given him permission to proceed on 'duty assigned'—in this case; return to Terra with a skeleton crew.

151   Libby watched them take off from a vantage point on the hillside. An overpowering homesickness took possession of him. Would he ever go home? He honestly believed at the time that he would swap the rest of his life for thirty minutes each with his mother and with Betty.

152   He started down the hill toward the tunnel lock. At least the transport carried letters to them, and with any luck the chaplain would be by soon with letters from Earth. But tomorrow and the days after that would be no fun. He had enjoyed being in the air gang, but tomorrow

he went back to his squad. He did not relish that—the boys in his squad were all right, he guessed, but he just could not seem to fit in.

153   This company of the C.C.C. started on its bigger job; to pock-mark Eighty-eight with rocket tubes so that Captain Doyle could push this hundred-mile marble out of her orbit and herd her in to a new orbit between Earth and Mars, to be used as a space station—a refuge for ships in distress, a haven for life boats, a fueling stop, a naval outpost.

154   Libby was assigned to a heater in pit H-16. It was his business to carve out carefully calculated emplacements in which the blasting crew then set off the minute charges which accomplished the major part of the excavating. Two squads were assigned to H-16, under the general supervision of an elderly marine gunner. The gunner sat on the edge of the pit, handling the plans, and occasionally making calculations on a circular slide rule which hung from a lanyard around his neck.

155   Libby had just completed a tricky piece of cutting for a three-stage blast, and was waiting for the blasters, when his phones picked up the gunner's instructions concerning the size of the charge. He pressed his transmitter button.

156   "Mr. Larsen! You've made a mistake!"

157   "Who said that?"

158   "This is Libby. You've made a mistake in the charge. If you set off that charge, you'll blow this pit right out of the ground, and us with it."

159   Marine Gunner Larsen spun the dials on his slide rule before re-plying. "You're all het up over nothing, son. That charge is correct."

160   "No, I'm not, sir," Libby persisted, "you've multiplied where you should have divided."

161   "Have you had any experience at this sort of work?"

162   "No, sir."

163   Larsen addressed his next remark to the blasters. "Set the charge."

164   They started to comply. Libby gulped, and wiped his lips with his tongue. He knew what he had to do, but he was afraid. Two clumsy stiff-legged jumps placed him beside the blasters. He pushed between them and tore the electrodes from the detonator. A shadow passed over him as he worked, and Larsen floated down beside him. A hand grasped his arm.

165   "You shouldn't have done that, son. That's direct disobedience of orders. I'll have to report you." He commenced reconnecting the firing circuit.

166   Libby's ears burned with embarrassment, but he answered back with the courage of timidity at bay. "I had to do it, sir. You're still wrong."

167   Larsen paused and ran his eyes over the dogged face. "Well—it's a waste of time, but I don't like to make you stand by a charge you're afraid of. Let's go over the calculation together."

168   Captain Doyle sat at his ease in his quarters, his feet on his desk. He stared at a nearly empty glass tumbler.

169   "That's good beer, Blackie. Do you suppose we could brew some more when it's gone?"

170   "I don't know, Cap'n. Did we bring any yeast?"

171   "Find out, will you?" He turned to a massive man who occupied the third chair. "Well, Larsen, I'm glad it wasn't any worse than it was."

172   "What beats me, Captain, is how I could have made such a mistake. I worked it through twice. If it had been a nitro explosive, I'd have known off hand that I was wrong. If this kid hadn't had a hunch, I'd have set it off."

173   Captain Doyle clapped the old warrant officer on the shoulder. "Forget it, Larsen. You wouldn't have hurt anybody; that's why I require the pits to be evacuated even for small charges. These isotope explosives are tricky at best. Look what happened in pit A-9. Ten days' work shot with one charge, and the gunnery officer himself approved that one. But I want to see this boy. What did you say his name was?"

174   "Libby, A. J."

175   Doyle touched a button on his desk. A knock sounded at the door. A bellowed "Come in!" produced a stripling wearing the brassard of Corpsman Mate-of-the-Deck.

176   "Have Corpsman Libby report to me."

177   "Aye aye, sir."

178   Some few minutes later Libby was ushered into the Captain's cabin. He looked nervously around, and noted Larsen's presence, a fact that did not contribute to his peace of mind. He reported in a barely audible voice, "Corpsman Libby, sir."

179   The Captain looked him over. "Well, Libby, I hear that you and Mr. Larsen had a difference of opinion this morning. Tell me about it."

180   "I—I didn't mean any harm, sir."

181   "Of course not. You're not in any trouble; you did us all a good turn this morning. Tell me, how did you know that the calculation was wrong? Had any mining experience?"

182   "No, sir. I just saw that he had worked it out wrong."

183   "But how?"

184   Libby shuffled uneasily. "Well, sir, it just seemed wrong—It didn't fit."

185   "Just a second, Captain. May I ask this young man a couple of questions?" It was Commander "Blackie" Rhodes who spoke.

186   "Certainly. Go ahead."

187   "Are you the lad they call 'Pinkie'?"

188   Libby blushed. "Yes, sir."

189   "I've heard some rumors about this boy." Rhodes pushed his big frame out of his chair, went over to a bookshelf, and removed a thick volume. He thumbed through it, then with open book before him, started to question Libby.

190   "What's the square root of ninety-five?"

191   "Nine and seven hundred forty-seven thousandths."

192   "What's the cube root?"

193   "Four and five hundred sixty-three thousandths."

194   "What's its logarithm?"

195   "Its what, sir?"

196   "Good Lord, can a boy get through school today without knowing?"

197   The boy's discomfort became more intense. "I didn't get much schooling, sir. My folks didn't accept the Covenant until Pappy died, and we had to."

198   "I see. A logarithm is a name for a power to which you raise a given number, called the base, to get the number whose logarithm it is. Is that clear?"

199   Libby thought hard. "I don't quite get it, sir."

200   "I'll try again. If you raise ten to the second power—square it—it gives one hundred. Therefore the logarithm of a hundred to the base ten is two. In the same fashion the logarithm of a thousand to the base ten is three. Now what is the logarithm of ninety-five?"

201   Libby puzzled for a moment. "I can't make it come out even. It's a fraction."

202   "That's okay."

203   "Then it's one and nine hundred seventy-eight thousandths—just about."

204   Rhodes turned to the Captain. "I guess that about proves it, sir."

205   Doyle nodded thoughtfully. "Yes, the lad seems to have intuitive knowledge of arithmetical relationships. But let's see what else he has."

206   "I am afraid we'll have to send him back to Earth to find out properly."

207   Libby caught the gist of this last remark. "Please, sir, you aren't going to send me home? Maw 'ud be awful vexed with me."

208   "No, no, nothing of the sort. When your time is up, I want you to be checked over in the psychometrical laboratories. In the meantime I wouldn't part with you for a quarter's pay. I'd give up smoking first. But let's see what else you can do."

209   In the ensuing hour the Captain and the Navigator heard Libby: one, deduce the Pythagorean proposition; two, derive Newton's laws of motion and Kepler's laws of ballistics from a statement of the conditions in which they obtained; three, judge length, area, and volume by eye with no measurable error. He had jumped into the idea of relativity and

non-rectilinear space-time continua, and was beginning to pour forth ideas faster than he could talk, when Doyle held up a hand.

210   "That's enough, son. You'll be getting a fever. You run along to bed now, and come see me in the morning. I'm taking you off field work."

211   "Yes, sir."

212   "By the way, what is your full name?"

213   "Andrew Jackson Libby, sir."

214   "No, your folks wouldn't have signed the Covenant. Good night."

215   "Good night, sir."

216   After he had gone, the two older men discussed their discovery.

217   "How do you size it up, Captain?"

218   "Well, he's a genius, of course—one of those wild talents that will show up once in a blue moon. I'll turn him loose among my books and see how he shapes up. Shouldn't wonder if he were a page-at-a-glance reader, too."

219   "It beats me what we turn up among these boys—and not a one of 'em any account back on Earth."

220   Doyle nodded. "That was the trouble with these kids. They didn't feel needed."

221   Eighty-eight swung some millions of miles further around the sun. The pock-marks on her face grew deeper, and were lined with durite, that strange close-packed laboratory product which (usually) would confine even atomic disintegration. Then Eighty-eight received a series of gentle pats, always on the side headed along her course. In a few weeks' time the rocket blasts had their effect and Eighty-eight was plunging in an orbit toward the sun.

222   When she reached her station one and three-tenths the distance from the sun of Earth's orbit, she would have to be coaxed by another series of pats into a circular orbit. Thereafter she was to be known as E-M3, Earth-Mars Space Station Spot Three.

223   Hundreds of millions of miles away two other C.C.C. companies were inducing two other planetoids to quit their age-old grooves and slide between Earth and Mars to land in the same orbit as Eighty-eight. One was due to ride this orbit one hundred and twenty degrees ahead of Eighty-eight, the other one hundred and twenty degrees behind. When E-M1, E-M2, and E-M3 were all on station no hard-pushed traveler of the spaceways on the Earth-Mars passage would ever again find himself far from land—or rescue.

224   During the months that Eighty-eight fell free toward the sun, Captain Doyle reduced the working hours of his crew and turned them to the comparatively light labor of building a hotel and converting the little roofed-in valley into a garden spot. The rock was broken down

into soil, fertilizers applied, and cultures of anaerobic bacteria planted. Then plants, conditioned by thirty-odd generations of low gravity at Luna City, were set out and tenderly cared for. Except for the low gravity, Eighty-eight began to feel like home.

225 But when Eighty-eight approached a tangent to the hypothetical future orbit of E-M3, the company went back to maneuvering routine, watch on and watch off, with the Captain living on black coffee and catching catnaps in the plotting room.

226 Libby was assigned to the ballistic calculator, three tons of thinking metal that dominated the plotting room. He loved the big machine. The Chief Fire Controlman let him help adjust it and care for it. Libby subconsciously thought of it as a person—his own kind of person.

227 On the last day of the approach, the shocks were more frequent. Libby sat in the right-hand saddle of the calculator and droned out the predictions for the next salvo, while gloating over the accuracy with which the machine tracked. Captain Doyle fussed around nervously, occasionally stopping to peer over the Navigator's shoulder. Of course the figures were right, but what if it didn't work? No one had ever moved so large a mass before. Suppose it plunged on and on—and on. Nonsense! It couldn't. Still he would be glad when they were past the critical speed.

228 A marine orderly touched his elbow. "Helio from the Flagship, sir."

229 "Read it."

230 "Flag to Eighty-eight; private message, Captain Doyle; am lying off to watch you bring her in.—Kearney."

231 Doyle smiled. Nice of the old geezer. Once they were on station, he would invite the Admiral to ground for dinner and show him the park.

232 Another salvo cut loose, heavier than any before. The room trembled violently. In a moment the reports of the surface observers commenced to trickle in. "Tube nine, clear!" "Tube ten, clear!"

233 But Libby's drone ceased.

234 Captain Doyle turned on him. "What's the matter, Libby? Asleep? Call the polar stations. I have to have a parallax."

235 "Captain—" The boy's voice was low and shaking.

236 "Speak up, man!"

237 "Captain—the machine isn't tracking."

238 "Spiers!" The grizzled head of the Chief Fire Controlman appeared from behind the calculator.

239 "I'm already on it, sir. Let you know in a moment."

240 He ducked back again. After a couple of long minutes he reappeared. "Gyros tumbled. It's a twelve hour calibration job, at least."

241   The Captain said nothing, but turned away, and walked to the far end of the room. The Navigator followed him with his eyes. He returned, glanced at the chronometer, and spoke to the Navigator.

242   "Well, Blackie, if I don't have that firing data in seven minutes, we're sunk. Any suggestions?"

243   Rhodes shook his head without speaking.

244   Libby timidly raised his voice. "Captain—"

245   Doyle jerked around. "Yes?"

246   "The firing data is tube thirteen, seven point six three; tube twelve, six point nine oh; tube fourteen, six point eight nine."

247   Doyle studied his face. "You sure about that, son?"

248   "It *has* to be that, Captain."

249   Doyle stood perfectly still. This time he did not look at Rhodes but stared straight ahead. Then he took a long pull on his cigarette, glanced at the ash, and said in a steady voice,

250   "Apply the data. Fire on the bell."

251   Four hours later, Libby was still droning out firing data, his face grey, his eyes closed. Once he had fainted but when they revived him he was still muttering figures. From time to time the Captain and the Navigator relieved each other, but there was no relief for him.

252   The salvos grew closer together, but the shocks were lighter.

253   Following one faint salvo, Libby looked up, stared at the ceiling, and spoke.

254   "That's all, Captain."

255   "Call polar stations!"

256   The reports came back promptly, "Parallax constant, sidereal-solar rate constant."

257   The Captain relaxed into a chair. "Well, Blackie, we did it—thanks to Libby!" Then he notice a worried, thoughtful look spread over Libby's face. "What's the matter, man? Have we slipped up?"

258   "Captain, you know you said the other day that you wished you had Earth-normal gravity in the park?"

259   "Yes. What of it?"

260   "If that book on gravitation you lent me is straight dope, I think I know a way to accomplish it."

261   The Captain inspected him as if seeing him for the first time. "Libby, you have ceased to amaze me. Could you stop doing that sort of thing long enough to dine with the Admiral?"

262   "Gee, Captain, that would be swell!"

263   The audio circuit from Communications cut in.

264   "Helio from Flagship: 'Well done, Eighty-eight.'"

265   Doyle smiled around at them all. "That's pleasant confirmation."

266 The audio brayed again.

267 "Helio from Flagship: 'Cancel last signal, stand by for correction.'"

268 A look of surprise and worry sprang into Doyle's face—then the audio continued:

269 "Helio from Flagship: 'Well done, E–M3.'"

DISCUSSION QUESTIONS

1. The scene where the new recruits into the space navy prepare for take off seems futuristic yet at the same time oddly old-fashioned. What does this suggest to you?

2. The youths are constantly referred to as boys. How is this venture supposed to turn them into men?

3. The only females in this story are the ship, the asteroid, and Earth. In small groups, discuss why you think this is so and how it might be different today.

4. The technical jargon describing the space suits and other equipment contrasts with Libby's "knowing" precise mathematical information. What is the purpose of this contrast in the story?

5. Why doesn't Libby fit in with the other recruits?

WRITING TOPICS

1. Space sickness is one problem associated with weightlessness. What other problems might weightlessness cause? Present as many as you can think of in one or two paragraphs.

2. What is the significance of Libby's full name, Andrew Jackson Libby? Why does the commander feel that Libby's family would have resisted signing the Covenant? Explain your answer in a journal entry.

3. In writing about space exploration in the late thirties, Heinlein got some aspects right and others wrong. Make a list of as many of each as you can. What similarities are in the items in each list that suggest why some ideas were more on track than others?

CHAPTER FOUR

The Forties

1940

Paris falls to Germany

F.D.R. elected to unprecedented third presidential term

Electron microscope first used

U.S. savings bonds go on sale

1941

Japan bombs Pearl Harbor; Germany invades Russia

Manhattan Project begins to research atomic weapons possibility

Plutonium discovered

First major science fiction anthology, *Of Other Worlds*, appears

Huge paper shortages curtail SF magazine production. John W. Campbell Jr. suspends publication of *Unknown* in order to preserve publication of *Astounding Science Fiction*

1942

U.S. inters 100,000 Japanese–Americans

Murder of Jews in Nazi gas chambers begins

Enrico Fermi splits the atom

Magnetic recording tape invented

First working computer built at Iowa State University

First U.S. jet tested

1943

Vita Sackville–West's novel *Grand Canyon* predicts a Nazi victory

***The Shadow* series of novels continues, with anti-fascism themes**

Mussolini dismissed, Italy surrenders, then declares war on Germany

U.S. freezes wages and prices and begins rationing goods

Zoot suits become popular

1944

***Batman* movie is shown in theaters**

Operation Overlord (D–Day) involves over 176,000 soldiers

V2 rockets, first remote-controlled missiles, are used in Germany

First uranium pile built

Clifford Simak produces *City* in serial form

HISTORICAL CONTEXT

The Great War (World War I) did not, as claimed, end war forever. Instead, the terms forced on Germany at the end of World War I caused much resentment and led to World War II. Hitler appealed to German pride and equated military strength with greatness, and his ideas steadily gained popular support. Japan was also building up its military power in an attempt to become an Asian Empire. These two nations created an alliance that made World War II a more global and much more destructive war. The death toll doubled from World War I's 20 million to over 45 million in World War II.

When France and Britain aided Poland against German aggression, the war was underway. The Axis Powers, as the German alliance was called, swept to several decisive victories, quickly taking France in 1940 and launching an immense onslaught against Britain. Soon afterwards, Germany invaded Russia. The U.S.S.R. was a huge country, and Hitler, like Napoleon before him, did not plan well for the vicious Russian winter. This double front spread the German forces too thin and they could not dominate in either England or the U.S.S.R. Soon after, Japan bombed American forces in Pearl Harbor, Hawaii. This drew the United States, with its enormous resources and a fresh supply of fighting forces, into the war, boosting the Allied Powers side.

During the war, Hitler began a systematic genocide program designed to rid the world of the "Jewish problem." As the tide of war increasingly turned against Germany, Hitler stepped up his program and began exterminating European Jews by the thousands in the most cost-effective means he could find—gas chambers. His "final solution" resulted in the killing of over six million Jews, more than half the total European Jewish population at that time.

As the war progressed, the Allies overcame Axis forces in Africa and Russia. In June of 1944 the Allies assembled a massive combined force of over 4,000 ships and 176,000 troops off the coast of Normandy, France. The major invasion on D-Day enabled the Allies to quickly retake France, and by the following April, Berlin fell and Germany surrendered. Japan refused to follow suit, however, leading to a devastating act of war. In August of 1945, the United States dropped the first atomic bombs ever used in war over Hiroshima and Nagasaki. Almost 200,000 people were killed instantly, and within five years another 500,000 had died of radiation poisoning. Japan surrendered two days after the second bomb was dropped.

In the aftermath of the war, Russia began absorbing smaller countries such as Poland, Czechoslovakia, and Romania into the Soviet bloc, gaining control of massive portions of eastern Europe. Disputes arose over the division of Germany, and Russia established an East German blockade. The United States responded with an airlift, and after 200,000 flights, Russia finally lifted the block. The result was that Germany was divided into four zones controlled by the U.S.S.R., Britain, France, and the United States. Berlin was split into a Russian-controlled communist section and a U.S.-controlled democratic portion.

The Jews were also attempting to overcome the effects of the Holocaust. The United States and Britain helped set up Israel as an independent state, with Jordan, including Palestine, as a national home for Jews. The Arabs in the region bitterly opposed the creation of the Jewish state, and warring hostilities lasted until 1949, when a grudging peace accord was signed. That same year, Mao Tse-tung led the Chinese Communist Party to power, establishing a single party dictatorship. This forced Chiang Kai-shek and his followers to flee to Formosa (renamed Taiwan) and set up a nationalist government.

In the United States, government loans and the G.I. Bill of Rights made it possible for returning veterans to go to college and buy houses and automobiles. The face of America began to change, from just rural and urban areas to include suburbs (sub urban communities), which sprang up across the country. The threat of war was not gone from the post-war boom, though, and the fear of Soviet communism loomed. It was a Cold War of suspicion and spying that many feared could boil over at any moment, especially as the U.S.S.R. developed its own nuclear weapons.

Americans pointed accusing fingers at the socialistic New
Deal policies of Franklin Roosevelt, even those who had benefited
from them. The feeling that communists were lurking everywhere
occurred in every segment of society, including immigrants eager
to show how "American" they were. When congressional members
suggested loosening movie censorship rules, they were branded communists. When college presidents defended intellectual freedom, they
were accused of promoting communism. Senator Joseph McCarthy
fanned the flames by accusing members of the State Department,
including the Secretary of State, of being communists. He claimed
communists within the department were controlling foreign policy.
These unfounded "witch hunts" continued to influence American
thought for years, but in 1950 a more immediate threat emerged
when communistic North Korea invaded democratic South Korea.

DEVELOPMENTS IN SCIENCE FICTION

The forties are often referred to as the Golden Age of science
fiction, and it is easy to see why. The pulps, under editor John W.
Campbell Jr.'s influence, changed from juvenile fantasies to more
thoughtful stories. More believable technological devices appeared
and women began to play key roles beyond just needing to be rescued. Edgar Rice Burroughs, however, continued to be popular,
producing 12 novelettes and one novel between 1941 and 1943.

By 1940, *Astounding Science Fiction* was the leader in the field.
Through his editing and editorials, Campbell changed the direction
of science fiction. He sometimes referred to science fiction as the
"history that has not yet happened." He defined science fiction by
saying it should include a situation that differs in some technological respects from the present world, and that difference should create problems. Those problems should be basically human ones, and
the situations should not contradict known scientific principles.

Campbell was proud of the large number of scientists and
engineers who subscribed to *Astounding Science Fiction*. His theory
that science fiction could predict future scientific achievements
proved true when a story in the March 1944 issue was about an
atomic bomb. This story set off an FBI investigation into national
security because the Manhattan Project (development of atomic

weapons) was underway and supposedly top secret. Campbell had figured out the location by analyzing subscription data and noticing the high number of scientists in Oak Ridge, Tennessee, that were on his magazine mailing list.

Wartime paper shortages forced the pulps to shrink to 5.5 × 8 inches, the size that the major science fiction magazines still maintain. Many magazines came and went during the decade. In 1940 Frederick Pohl began editing *Astonishing Stories* and *Super Science Stories* together, the publications appearing in alternate months. Campbell, who refused nonscientific-based stories, soon founded *Unknown*, later changing the name to *Unknown Worlds*, as an outlet for fantasy stories. Many of the stories published there were believable fantasy, which influenced science fiction writers. The two branches of the genre then often overlapped. Science fiction anthologies also began to compete with the magazines, and some of the better fiction was picked up by major publishers and appeared in hardcover form. Other writers began to be published in magazines printed on slick paper which were thus more expensive and prestigious. Some of the more prominent "slicks" that published science fiction during the forties included *Collier's, Harper's, Esquire, McCall's,* and occasionally *The New Yorker.*

There were so many talented writers who began in the forties and continued for years to produce quality fiction in a variety of areas that it is no wonder it is referred to as the Golden Age. Even a partial list reads like a Who's Who of science fiction: Isaac Asimov, James Blish, Ray Bradbury, Arthur C. Clarke, Robert Heinlein, Henry Kuttner, C. S. Lewis, C. L. Moore, George Orwell, Frederick Pohl, Clifford Simak, E. E. "Doc" Smith, Olaf Stapledon, and A. E. van Vogt are but some of the authors who contributed to science fiction in the forties.

George Orwell produced two outstanding works during this period—*Animal Farm* in 1945 and *1984* in 1949. *Animal Farm* uses animals for all the characters, but they are thinly veiled representations of human vices. The pigs take over the animal hierarchy and establish a bureaucratic dictatorship similar to Stalinism. By the end of the novel it is apparent that "All animals are created equal, but some are more equal than others."

In his other major work of the decade, *1984*, Orwell shows the horrors of mind control. He creates a society where sex and individuality are outlawed and truth is no longer real but instead shaped by the needs of the government. Those who disobey are relentlessly reprogrammed. Big Brother has eyes and ears everywhere, and no one can escape. This novel gave us words like "doublethink," "newspeak," and "unperson."

Isaac Asimov was prominent among the science fiction authors of the decade. His *I, Robot* series introduced the three laws of robotics. These laws were guaranteed to keep robots in the service of humanity, rather than allowing for the possibility of robots dominating humans. They are:

1. A robot may not injure a human being, or, through inaction, allow a human being to come to harm.
2. A robot must obey the orders given to it by human beings except where such orders would conflict with the First Law.
3. A robot must protect its own existence as long as such protection does not conflict with the First or Second Law.

His *Foundation* series of novels, starting with *Foundation* in 1942, presented a future history. This history included colonization of other planets, humans meeting alien races, the rise of a galactic empire, the decline of that empire, a mass destruction with worlds reverting to primitive conditions, and the rise of new civilizations, which inevitably leads to a repeat of the cycle. Asimov's background in science added to his credibility as a writer, and his humanism tempered the science with a caring attitude.

During this decade the number of science fiction fans increased dramatically, and these fans became a force, with many specialty houses springing up to sell genre fiction by direct mail. Arkham House, founded by August Derleth primarily to publish the fiction of H. P. Lovecraft and fantastic horror stories, also featured stories by Robert Bloch, A. E. van Vogt, and other science fiction authors. Crown Publishers, Viking Press, and Random House all produced science fiction anthologies during the forties. Most of the hardbacks they produced were either anthologies or reprints of previously published magazine material. Few paperbacks appeared until the fifties, when that medium would begin to dominate the market.

The V2 rocket, which Germany had developed in the latter part of the war, also influenced science fiction. The largest rocket ever built, the V2 flew faster, higher, and farther than any before, and it looked great. It was easy to imagine the explosive payload being replaced by a pilot and cargo. The Nazis had actually designed and flown a larger rocket with a human pilot (Hannah Reitsch), which was meant to carry V2s to their delivery point, presumably the United States. After the war, the British Interplanetary Society proposed using a modified V2 to launch a suborbital flight 190 miles high using a human pilot. The capsule would then separate and return to Earth by parachute, much like the space flights of the early sixties. Most illustrations of space ships on science fiction magazine covers in the forties resembled the German V2. Coupling the rockets with the atomic bombs, science fiction writers had clear examples on which to base world-ending catastrophes. Science fiction of the forties matured quickly and gained respectability as it became evident that it was no longer just juvenile escapism.

SCIENCE FICTION IN OTHER MEDIA

Unfortunately, science fiction films did not keep pace with the growing legitimacy and thoughtfulness of books and magazines. Pure escapism, paper-thin plots, horrible special effects, and bad acting combined to produce the poor image that many people still have of early science fiction films. Many movies warned against tampering with nature because it appeared to be tampering with what God (or nature) created, an echo of one of the major themes of *Frankenstein. Dr. Cyclops* (1940) used oversized props to show shrinking humans, and *One Million B.C.* (1940) is set in a distant time with humans battling prehistoric creatures. Batman appeared in a feature length film set in World War II, and Superman and Flash Gordon were serialized for movies. There were also endless sequels, such as *The Invisible Man Returns* (1943) and *The Invisible Woman* (1944), which weakened the theme set in the initial movies, in this case *The Invisible Man* (1933).

Horror films, close cousins to science fiction, were not much better. Titles included *Frankenstein Meets the Wolf Man* (1943), the horror comedy *Abbot and Costello Meet Frankenstein* (1948), and a King Kong spinoff, *Mighty Joe Young* (1949). Overall, the heights of science fiction in print were countered by the dismal quality of the movies. TV hadn't made enough impact during the forties to offer significant science fiction programming.

Robbie

1940

ISAAC ASIMOV (1920–1992)

Isaac Asimov both received his undergraduate degree in chemistry and published his first science fiction story, "Marooned off Vesta," in 1939. He received his Ph.D. in 1948 and worked as an associate professor of biomechanics until he retired in 1958 to write full-time. Asimov was one of the most prolific writers of all time, producing hundreds of titles, including short stories, novels, essays, works in other genres, and science books in his 50-year career. His two major series were the *Robot* and *Foundation* series of novels. The *Robot* series introduced the Three Laws of Robotics, which are still the basis for many science fiction robot stories today. The *Foundation* series features a protagonist who has discovered a way to shorten the period between the fall of one empire and the rise of its replacement. Asimov published over 400 science fiction stories in his lifetime.

Asimov's early stories have been collected in *The Early Asimov, or Eleven Years of Trying* (1972). "Robbie" (1940) was the first story in the *Robot* series. The stories were collected in 1950 as *I, Robot*. The *Foundation* series began with *Foundation* (1942–44), and the novels were collected as *Foundation Trilogy* in 1963. In the eighties, Asimov combined the two series. This was complicated because in the *Foundation* there are no robots, but an empire rising and falling in cycles, whereas the *Robot* series is, of course, full of robots. *The Robots of Dawn* (1983) was Asimov's first combination novel, and he continued the dual series until his death.

In "Robbie," Isaac Asimov uses the Laws of Robotics to show how sometimes robots can be very "human," maybe more so than some humans.

1 "Ninety-eight—ninety-nine—*one hundred*." Gloria withdrew her chubby little forearm from before her eyes and stood for a moment, wrinkling her nose and blinking in the sunlight. Then, trying to watch in all directions at once, she withdrew a few cautious steps from the tree against which she had been leaning.

2 She craned her neck to investigate the possibilities of a clump of bushes to the right and then withdrew farther to obtain a better angle for viewing its dark recesses. The quiet was profound except for the incessant buzzing of insects and the occasional chirrup of some hardy bird, braving the midday sun.

3 Gloria pouted, "I bet he went inside the house, and I've told him a million times that that's not fair."

4 With tiny lips pressed together tightly and a severe frown crinkling her forehead, she moved determinedly toward the two-story building up past the driveway.

5 Too late she heard the rustling sound behind her, followed by the distinctive and rhythmic clump-clump of Robbie's metal feet. She whirled about to see her triumphing companion emerge from hiding and make for the home-tree at full speed.

6 Gloria shrieked in dismay. "Wait, Robbie! That wasn't fair, Robbie! You promised you wouldn't run until I found you." Her little feet could make no headway at all against Robbie's giant strides. Then, within ten feet of the goal, Robbie's pace slowed suddenly to the merest of crawls, and Gloria, with one final burst of wild speed, dashed pantingly past him to touch the welcome bark of home-tree first.

7 Gleefully, she turned on the faithful Robbie, and with the basest of ingratitude, rewarded him for his sacrifice, by taunting him cruelly for a lack of running ability.

8 "Robbie can't run," she shouted at the top of her eight-year-old voice. "I can beat him any day. I can beat him any day." She chanted the words in a shrill rhythm.

9 Robbie didn't answer, of course—not in words. He pantomimed running, instead, inching away until Gloria found herself running after him as he dodged her narrowly, forcing her to veer in helpless circles, little arms outstretched and fanning at the air.

10 "Robbie," she squealed, "stand still!" —And the laughter was forced out of her in breathless jerks.

11 —Until he turned suddenly and caught her up, whirling her round, so that for her the world fell away for a moment with a blue emptiness beneath, and green trees stretching hungrily downward toward the void. Then she was down in the grass again, leaning against Robbie's leg and still holding a hard, metal finger.

12   After a while, her breath returned. She pushed uselessly at her disheveled hair in vague imitation of one of her mother's gestures and twisted to see if her dress were torn.

13   She slapped her hand against Robbie's torso, "Bad boy! I'll spank you!"

14   And Robbie cowered, holding his hands over his face so that she had to add, "No, I won't, Robbie. I won't spank you. But anyway, it's my turn to hide now because you've got longer legs and you promised not to run till I found you."

15   Robbie nodded his head—a small parallelepiped with rounded edges and corners attached to a similar but much larger parallelepiped that served as torso by means of a short, flexible stalk—and obediently faced the tree. A thin, metal film descended over his glowing eyes and from within his body came a steady, resonant ticking.

16   "Don't peek now—and don't skip any numbers," warned Gloria, and scurried for cover.

17   With unvarying regularity, seconds were ticked off, and at the hundredth, up went the eyelids, and the glowing red of Robbie's eyes swept the prospect. They rested for a moment on a bit of colorful gingham that protruded from behind a boulder. He advanced a few steps and convinced himself that it was Gloria who squatted behind it.

18   Slowly, remaining always between Gloria and home-tree, he advanced on the hiding place, and when Gloria was plainly in sight and could no longer even theorize to herself that she was not seen, he extended one arm toward her, slapping the other against his leg so that it rang again. Gloria emerged sulkily.

19   "You peeked!" she exclaimed, with gross unfairness. "Besides I'm tired of playing hide-and-seek. I want a ride."

20   But Robbie was hurt at the unjust accusation, so he seated himself carefully and shook his head ponderously from side to side.

21   Gloria changed her tone to one of gentle coaxing immediately, "Come on, Robbie. I didn't mean it about the peeking. Give me a ride."

22   Robbie was not to be won over so easily, though. He gazed stubbornly at the sky, and shook his head even more emphatically.

23   "Please. Robbie, please give me a ride." She encircled his neck with rosy arms and hugged tightly. Then, changing moods in a moment, she moved away. "If you don't, I'm going to cry," and her face twisted appallingly in preparation.

24   Hard-hearted Robbie paid scant attention to this dreadful possibility, and shook his head a third time. Gloria found it necessary to play her trump card.

25 "If you don't," she exclaimed warmly, "I won't tell you any more stories, that's all. Not one—"

26 Robbie gave in immediately and unconditionally before this ultimatum, nodding his head vigorously until the metal of his neck hummed. Carefully, he raised the little girl and placed her on his broad, flat shoulders.

27 Gloria's threatened tears vanished immediately and she crowed with delight. Robbie's metal skin, kept at a constant temperature of seventy by the high resistance coils within felt nice and comfortable, while the beautifully loud sound her heels made as they bumped rhythmically against his chest was enchanting.

28 "You're an air-coaster, Robbie, you're a big, silver air-coaster. Hold out your arms straight.—You *got* to, Robbie, if you're going to be an air-coaster."

29 The logic was irrefutable. Robbie's arms were wings catching the air currents and he was a silver 'coaster.

30 Gloria twisted the robot's head and leaned to the right. He banked sharply. Gloria equipped the 'coaster with a motor that went "Br-r-r" and then with weapons that went "Powie" and "Sh-sh-shshsh." Pirates were giving chase and the ship's blasters were going into play. The pirates dropped in a steady rain.

31 "Got another one.—Two more," she cried.

32 Then "Faster, men," Gloria said pompously, "we're running out of ammunition." She aimed over her shoulder with undaunted courage and Robbie was a blunt-nosed spaceship zooming through the void at maximum acceleration.

33 Clear across the field he sped, to the patch of tall grass on the other side, where he stopped with a suddenness that evoked a shriek from his flushed rider, and then tumbled her onto the soft, green carpet.

34 Gloria gasped and panted, and gave voice to intermittent whispered exclamations of "That was *nice!*"

35 Robbie waited until she had caught her breath and then pulled gently at a lock of hair.

36 "You want something?" said Gloria, eyes wide in an apparently artless complexity that fooled her huge "nursemaid" not at all. He pulled the curl harder.

37 "Oh, I know. You want a story."

38 Robbie nodded rapidly.

39 "Which one?"

40 Robbie made a semi-circle in the air with one finger.

41 The little girl protested, "*Again?* I've told you Cinderella a million times. Aren't you tired of it?—It's for babies."

42   Another semi-circle.

43   "Oh, well," Gloria composed herself, ran over the details of the tale in her mind (together with her own elaborations, of which she had several) and began:

44   "Are you ready? Well—once upon a time there was a beautiful little girl whose name was Ella. And she had a terribly cruel step-mother and two very ugly and *very* cruel step-sisters and—"

45   Gloria was reaching the very climax of the tale—midnight was striking and everything was changing back to the shabby originals lickety-split, while Robbie listened tensely with burning eyes—when the interruption came.

46   "Gloria!"

47   It was the high-pitched sound of a woman who has been calling not once, but several times; and had the nervous tone of one in whom anxiety was beginning to overcome impatience.

48   "Mamma's calling me," said Gloria, not quite happily. "You'd better carry me back to the house, Robbie."

49   Robbie obeyed with alacrity for somehow there was that in him which judged it best to obey Mrs. Weston, without as much as a scrap of hesitation. Gloria's father was rarely home in the daytime except on Sunday—today, for instance—and when he was, he proved a genial and understanding person. Gloria's mother, however, was a source of uneasiness to Robbie and there was always the impulse to sneak away from her sight.

50   Mrs. Weston caught sight of them the minute they rose above the masking tufts of long grass and retired inside the house to wait.

51   "I've shouted myself hoarse, Gloria," she said, severely. "Where were you?"

52   "I was with Robbie," quavered Gloria. "I was telling him Cinderella, and I forgot it was dinner-time."

53   "Well, it's a pity Robbie forgot, too." Then, as if that reminded her of the robot's presence, she whirled upon him. "You may go, Robbie. She doesn't need you now." Then, brutally, "And don't come back till I call you."

54   Robbie turned to go, but hesitated as Gloria cried out in his defense, "Wait, Mamma, you got to let him stay. I didn't finish Cinderella for him. I said I would tell him Cinderella and I'm not finished."

55   "Gloria!"

56   "Honest and truly, Mamma, he'll stay so quiet, you won't even know he's here. He can sit on the chair in the corner, and he won't say a word,—I mean he won't *do* anything. Will you, Robbie?"

57   Robbie, appealed to, nodded his massive head up and down once.

58   "Gloria, if you don't stop this at once, you shan't see Robbie for a
whole week."

59   The girl's eyes fell, "All right! But Cinderella is his favorite story
and I didn't finish it.—And he likes it so much."

60   The robot left with a disconsolate step and Gloria choked back a sob.

61   George Weston was comfortable. It was a habit of his to be comfortable on Sunday afternoons. A good, hearty dinner below the
hatches; a nice, soft, dilapidated couch on which to sprawl; a copy of the
Times; slippered feet and shirtless chest;—how could anyone help but be
comfortable?

62   He wasn't pleased, therefore, when his wife walked in. After ten
years of married life, he still was so unutterably foolish as to love her,
and there was no question that he was always glad to see her—still
Sunday afternoons just after dinner were sacred to him and his idea of
solid comfort was to be left in utter solitude for two or three hours.
Consequently, he fixed his eye firmly upon the latest reports of the
Lefebre-Yoshida expedition to Mars (this one was to take off from
Lunar Base and might actually succeed) and pretended she wasn't there.

63   Mrs. Weston waited patiently for two minutes, then impatiently
for two more, and finally broke the silence.

64   "George!"

65   "Hmpph?"

66   "George I say! Will you put down that paper and look at me?"

67   The paper rustled to the floor and Weston turned a weary face toward his wife, "What is it, dear?"

68   "You know what it is, George. It's Gloria and that terrible
machine."

69   "What terrible machine?"

70   "Now don't pretend you don't know what I'm talking about. It's
that robot Gloria calls Robbie. He doesn't leave her for a moment."

71   "Well, why should he? He's not supposed to. And he certainly isn't a
terrible machine. He's the best darn robot money can buy and I'm
damned sure he set me back half a year's income. He's worth it, though—
darn sight cleverer than half my office staff."

72   He made a move to pick up the paper again, but his wife was
quicker and snatched it away.

73   "You listen to me, George. I won't have my daughter entrusted to a
machine—and I don't care how clever it is. It has no soul, and no one
knows what it may be thinking. A child just isn't made to be guarded
by a thing of metal."

74   Weston frowned, "When did you decide this? He's been with
Gloria two years now and I haven't seen you worry till now."

75   "It was different at first. It was a novelty; it took a load off me, and—and it was a fashionable thing to do. But now I don't know. The neighbors—"

76   "Well, what have the neighbors to do with it? Now, look. A robot is infinitely more to be trusted than a human nursemaid. Robbie was constructed for only one purpose really—to be the companion of a little child. His entire 'mentality' has been created for the purpose. He just can't help being faithful and loving and kind. He's a machine—*made so*. That's more than you can say for humans."

77   "But something might go wrong. Some—some—" Mrs. Weston was a bit hazy about the insides of a robot, "some little jigger will come loose and the awful thing will go berserk and—and—" She couldn't bring herself to complete the quite obvious thought.

78   "Nonsense," Weston denied, with an involuntary nervous shiver. "That's completely ridiculous. We had a long discussion at the time we bought Robbie about the First Law of Robotics. You *know* that it is impossible for a robot to harm a human being; that long before enough can go wrong to alter that First Law, a robot would be completely inoperable. It's a mathematical impossibility. Besides I have an engineer from U. S Robots here twice a year to give the poor gadget a complete overhaul. Why, there's no more chance of anything at all going wrong with Robbie than there is of you or I suddenly going looney—considerably less, in fact. Besides, how are you going to take him away from Gloria?"

79   He made another futile stab at the paper and his wife tossed it angrily into the next room.

80   "That's just it, George! She won't play with anyone else. There are dozens of little boys and girls that she should make friends with, but she won't. She won't go *near* them unless I make her. That's no way for a little girl to grow up. You want her to be normal, don't you? You want her to be able to take her part in society."

81   "You're jumping at shadows, Grace. Pretend Robbie's a dog. I've seen hundreds of children who would rather have their dog than their father."

82   "A dog is different, George. We *must* get rid of that horrible thing. You can sell it back to the company. I've asked, and you can."

83   "You've *asked?* Now look here, Grace, let's not go off the deep end. We're keeping the robot until Gloria is older and I don't want the subject brought up again." And with that he walked out of the room in a huff.

84   Mrs. Weston met her husband at the door two evenings later. "You'll have to listen to this, George. There's bad feeling in the village."

85   "About what?" asked Weston. He stepped into the washroom and drowned out any possible answer by the splash of water.

86   Mrs. Weston waited. She said, "About Robbie."

87   Weston stepped out, towel in hand, face red and angry, "What are you talking about?"

88   "Oh, it's been building up and building up. I've tried to close my eyes to it, but I'm not going to any more. Most of the villagers consider Robbie dangerous. Children aren't allowed to go near our place in the evenings."

89   "We trust *our* child with the thing."

90   "Well, people aren't reasonable about these things."

91   "Then to hell with them."

92   "Saying that doesn't solve the problem. I've got to do my shopping down there. I've got to meet them every day. And it's even worse in the city these days when it comes to robots. New York has just passed an ordinance keeping all robots off the streets between sunset and sunrise."

93   "All right, but they can't stop us from keeping a robot in our home.—Grace, this is one of your campaigns. I recognize it. But it's no use. The answer is still, no! We're keeping Robbie!"

94   And yet he loved his wife—and what was worse, his wife knew it. George Weston, after all, was only a man—poor thing—and his wife made full use of every device which a clumsier and more scrupulous sex has learned, with reason and futility, to fear.

95   Ten times in the ensuing week, he cried, "Robbie stays, —and that's *final!*" and each time it was weaker and accompanied by a louder and more agonized groan.

96   Came the day at last, when Weston approached his daughter guiltily and suggested a "beautiful" visivox show in the village.

97   Gloria clapped her hands happily, "Can Robbie go?"

98   "No, dear," he said, and winced at the sound of his voice, "they won't allow robots at the visivox—but you can tell him all about it when you get home." He stumbled all over the last few words and looked away.

99   Gloria came back from town bubbling over with enthusiasm, for the visivox had been a gorgeous spectacle indeed.

100   She waited for her father to maneuver the jet-car into the sunken garage. "Wait till I tell Robbie, Daddy. He would have liked it like anything.—Especially when Francis Fran was backing away so-o-o quietly, and backed right into one of the Leopard-Men and had to run." She laughed again, "Daddy, are there really Leopard-Men on the Moon?"

101   "Probably not," said Weston absently. "It's just funny make-believe." He couldn't take much longer with the car. He'd have to face it.

102   Gloria ran across the lawn. "Robbie.—Robbie!"

103   Then she stopped suddenly at the sight of a beautiful collie which regarded her out of serious brown eyes as it wagged its tail on the porch.

104   "Oh, what a nice dog!" Gloria climbed the steps, approached cautiously and patted it. "Is it for me, Daddy?"

105   Her mother had joined them. "Yes, it is, Gloria. Isn't it nice—soft and furry. It's very gentle. It *likes* little girls."

106   "Can he play games?"

107   "Surely. He can do any number of tricks. Would you like to see some?"

108   "Right away. I want Robbie to see him, too.—*Robbie!*" She stopped, uncertainly, and frowned, "I'll bet he's just staying in his room because he's mad at me for not taking him to the visivox. You'll have to explain to him, Daddy. He might not believe me, but he knows if you say it, it's so."

109   Weston's lips grew tighter. He looked toward his wife but could not catch her eye.

110   Gloria turned precipitously and ran down the basement steps, shouting as she went, "Robbie—Come and see what Daddy and Mamma brought me. They brought me a dog, Robbie."

111   In a minute she had returned, a frightened little girl. "Mamma, Robbie isn't in his room. Where is he?" There was no answer and George Weston coughed and was suddenly extremely interested in an aimlessly drifting cloud. Gloria's voice quavered on the verge of tears, "Where's Robbie, Mamma?"

112   Mrs. Weston sat down and drew her daughter gently to her, "Don't feel bad, Gloria. Robbie has gone away, I think."

113   "Gone *away?* Where? Where's he gone away, Mamma?"

114   "No one knows, darling. He just walked away. We've looked and we've looked and we've looked for him, but we can't find him."

115   "You mean he'll never come back again?" Her eyes were round with horror.

116   "We may find him soon. We'll keep looking for him. And meanwhile you can play with your nice new doggie. Look at him! His name is Lightning and he can—"

117   But Gloria's eyelids had overflown, "I don't want the nasty dog—I want Robbie. I want you to find me Robbie." Her feelings became too deep for words, and she spluttered into a shrill wail.

118   Mrs. Weston glanced at her husband for help, but he merely shuffled his feet morosely and did not withdraw his ardent stare from the heavens, so she bent to the task of consolation, "Why do you cry,

Gloria? Robbie was only a machine, just a nasty old machine. He wasn't alive at all."

119   "He was *not* no machine!" screamed Gloria, fiercely and ungrammatically. "He was a *person* just like you and me and he was my *friend*. I want him back. Oh, Mamma, I want him back."

120   Her mother groaned in defeat and left Gloria to her sorrow.

121   "Let her have her cry out," she told her husband. "Childish griefs are never lasting. In a few days, she'll forget that awful robot ever existed."

122   But time proved Mrs. Weston a bit too optimistic. To be sure, Gloria ceased crying, but she ceased smiling, too, and the passing days found her ever more silent and shadowy. Gradually, her attitude of passive unhappiness wore Mrs. Weston down and all that kept her from yielding was the impossibility of admitting defeat to her husband.

123   Then, one evening, she flounced into the living room, sat down, folded her arms and looked boiling mad.

124   Her husband stretched his neck in order to see her over his newspaper, "What now, Grace?"

125   "It's that child, George. I've had to send back the dog today. Gloria positively couldn't stand the sight of him, she said. She's driving me into a nervous breakdown."

126   Weston laid down the paper and a hopeful gleam entered his eye, "Maybe—Maybe we ought to get Robbie back. It might be done, you know. I can get in touch with—"

127   "No!" she replied, grimly. "I won't hear of it. We're not giving up that easily. My child shall *not* be brought up by a robot if it takes years to break her of it."

128   Weston picked up his paper again with a disappointed air. "A year of this will have me prematurely gray."

129   "You're a big help, George," was the frigid answer. "What Gloria needs is a change of environment. Of course she can't forget Robbie here. How can she when every tree and rock reminds her of him? It is really the *silliest* situation I have ever heard of. Imagine a child pining away for the loss of a robot."

130   "Well, stick to the point. What's the change in environment you're planning?"

131   "We're going to take her to New York."

132   "The city! In August! Say, do you know what New York is like in August? It's unbearable."

133   "Millions do bear it."

134   "They don't have a place like this to go to. If they didn't have to stay in New York, they wouldn't."

135   "Well, *we* have to. I say we're leaving now—or as soon as we can make the arrangements. In the city, Gloria will find sufficient interests and sufficient friends to perk her up and make her forget that machine."

136   "Oh, Lord," groaned the lesser half, "those frying pavements!"

137   "We have to," was the unshaken response. "Gloria has lost five pounds in the last month and my little girl's health is more important to me than your comfort."

138   "It's a pity you didn't think of your little girl's health before you deprived her of her pet robot," he muttered—but to himself.

139   Gloria displayed immediate signs of improvement when told of the impending trip to the city. She spoke little of it, but when she did, it was always with lively anticipation. Again, she began to smile and to eat with something of her former appetite.

140   Mrs. Weston hugged herself for joy and lost no opportunity to triumph over her still skeptical husband.

141   "You see, George, she helps with the packing like a little angel, and chatters away as if she hadn't a care in the world. It's just as I told you—all we need to do is substitute other interests."

142   "Hmpph," was the skeptical response, "I hope so."

143   Preliminaries were gone through quickly. Arrangements were made for the preparation of their city home and a couple were engaged as housekeepers for the country home. When the day of the trip finally did come, Gloria was all but her old self again, and no mention of Robbie passed her lips at all.

144   In high good-humor the family took a taxi-gyro to the airport (Weston would have preferred using his own private 'gyro, but it was only a two-seater with no room for baggage) and entered the waiting liner.

145   "Come, Gloria," called Mrs. Weston. "I've saved you a seat near the window so you can watch the scenery."

146   Gloria trotted down the aisle cheerily, flattened her nose into a white oval against the thick clear glass, and watched with an intentness that increased as the sudden coughing of the motor drifted backward into the interior. She was too young to be frightened when the ground dropped away as if let through a trap-door and she herself suddenly became twice her usual weight, but not too young to be mightily interested. It wasn't until the ground had changed into a tiny patch-work quilt that she withdrew her nose, and faced her mother again.

147   "Will we soon be in the city, Mamma?" she asked, rubbing her chilled nose, and watching with interest as the patch of moisture which her breath had formed on the pane shrank slowly and vanished.

148   "In about half an hour, dear." Then, with just the faintest trace of anxiety, "Aren't you glad we're going? Don't you think you'll be very

happy in the city with all the buildings and people and things to see? We'll go to the visivox every day and see shows and go to the circus and the beach and—"

149   "Yes, Mamma," was Gloria's unenthusiastic rejoinder. The liner passed over a bank of clouds at the moment, and Gloria was instantly absorbed in the unusual spectacle of clouds underneath one. Then they were over clear sky again, and she turned to her mother with a sudden mysterious air of secret knowledge.

150   "*I* know why we're going to city, Mamma."

151   "Do you?" Mrs. Weston was puzzled. "Why, dear?"

152   "You didn't tell me because you wanted it to be a surprise, but *I* know." For a moment, she was lost in admiration at her own acute penetration, and then she laughed gaily. "We're going to New York so we can find Robbie, aren't we?—With detectives."

153   The statement caught George Weston in the middle of a drink of water, with disastrous results. There was a sort of strangled gasp, a geyser of water, and then a bout of choking coughs. When all this was over, he stood there, a red-faced, water-drenched and very, very annoyed person.

154   Mrs. Weston maintained her composure, but when Gloria repeated her question in a more anxious tone of voice, she found her temper rather bent.

155   "Maybe," she retorted, tartly. "Now sit and be still, for Heaven's sake."

156   New York City, 1998 A.D., was a paradise for the sightseer more than ever in its history. Gloria's parents realized this and made the most of it.

157   On direct orders from his wife, George Weston arranged to have his business take care of itself for a month or so, in order to be free to spend the time in what he termed "dissipating Gloria to the verge of ruin." Like everything else Weston did, this was gone about in an efficient, thorough, and business-like way. Before the month had passed, nothing that could be done had not been done.

158   She was taken to the top of the half-mile-tall Roosevelt Building, to gaze down in awe upon the jagged panorama of rooftops that blended far off in the fields of Long Island and the flatlands of New Jersey. They visited the zoos where Gloria stared in delicious fright at the "real live lion" (rather disappointed that the keepers fed him raw steaks, instead of human beings, as she had expected), and asked insistently and peremptorily to see "the whale."

159   The various museums came in for their share of attention, together with the parks and the beaches and the aquarium.

160   She was taken halfway up the Hudson in an excursion steamer fitted out in the archaism of the mad Twenties. She travelled into the

stratosphere on an exhibition trip, where the sky turned deep purple and the stars came out and the misty earth below looked like a huge concave bowl. Down under the waters of the Long Island Sound she was taken in a glass-walled sub-sea vessel, where in a green and wavering world, quaint and curious sea-things ogled her and wiggled suddenly away.

161   On a more prosaic level, Mrs. Weston took her to the department stores where she could revel in another type of fairyland.

162   In fact, when the month had nearly sped, the Westons were convinced that everything conceivable had been done to take Gloria's mind once and for all off the departed Robbie—but they were not quite sure they had succeeded.

163   The fact remained that wherever Gloria went, she displayed the most absorbed and concentrated interest in such robots as happened to be present. No matter how exciting the spectacle before her, nor how novel to her girlish eyes, she turned away instantly if the corner of her eye caught a glimpse of metallic movement.

164   Mrs. Weston went out of her way to keep Gloria away from all robots.

165   And the matter was finally climaxed in the episode at the Museum of Science and Industry. The Museum had announced a special "children's program" in which exhibits of scientific witchery scaled down to the child mind were to be shown. The Westons, of course, placed it upon their list of "absolutely."

166   It was while the Westons were standing totally absorbed in the exploits of a powerful electro-magnet that Mrs. Weston suddenly became aware of the fact that Gloria was no longer with her. Initial panic gave way to calm decision and, enlisting the aid of three attendants, a careful search was begun.

167   Gloria, of course, was not one to wander aimlessly, however. For her age, she was an unusually determined and purposeful girl, quite full of the maternal genes in that respect. She had seen a huge sign on the third floor, which had said, "This Way to the Talking Robot." Having spelled it out to herself and having noticed that her parents did not seem to wish to move in the proper direction, she did the obvious thing. Waiting for an opportune moment of parental distraction, she calmly disengaged herself and followed the sign.

168   The Talking Robot was a *tour de force,* a thoroughly impractical device, possessing publicity value only. Once an hour, an escorted group stood before it and asked questions of the robot engineer in charge in careful whispers. Those the engineer decided were suitable for the robot's circuits were transmitted to the Talking Robot.

169   It was rather dull. It may be nice to know that the square of four-teen is one hundred ninety-six, that the temperature at the moment is 72 degrees Fahrenheit, and the air-pressure 30.02 inches of mercury, that the atomic weight of sodium is 23, but one doesn't really need a robot for that. One especially does not need an unwieldy, totally immo-bile mass of wires and coils spreading over twenty-five square yards.

170   Few people bothered to return for a second helping, but one girl in her middle teens sat quietly on a bench waiting for a third. She was the only one in the room when Gloria entered.

171   Gloria did not look at her. To her at the moment, another human being was but an inconsiderable item. She saved her attention for this large thing with the wheels. For a moment, she hesitated in dismay. It didn't look like any robot she had ever seen.

172   Cautiously and doubtfully she raised her treble voice, "Please, Mr. Robot, sir, are you the Talking Robot, sir?" She wasn't sure, but it seemed to her that a robot that actually talked was worth a great deal of politeness.

173   (The girl in her mid-teens allowed a look of intense concentration to cross her thin, plain face. She whipped out a small notebook and began writing in rapid pot-hooks.)

174   There was an oily whir of gears and a mechanically-timbred voice boomed out in words that lacked accent and intonation, "I—am—the—robot—that—talks."

175   Gloria stared at it ruefully. It *did* talk, but the sound came from in-side somewhere. There was no *face* to talk to. She said, "Can you help me, Mr. Robot, sir?"

176   The Talking Robot was designed to answer questions, and only such questions as it could answer had ever been put to it. It was quite confident of its ability, therefore, "I—can—help—you."

177   "Thank you, Mr. Robot, sir. Have you seen Robbie?"

178   "Who—is—Robbie?"

179   "He's a robot, Mr. Robot, sir." She stretched to tip-toes. "He's about so high, Mr. Robot, sir, only higher, and he's very nice. He's got a head, you know. I mean you haven't, but he has, Mr. Robot, sir."

180   The Talking Robot had been left behind, "A—robot?"

181   "Yes, Mr. Robot, sir. A robot just like you, except he can't talk, of course, and—looks like a real person."

182   "A—robot—like—me?"

183   "Yes, Mr. Robot, sir."

184   To which the Talking Robot's only response was an erratic splutter and an occasional incoherent sound. The radical generalization offered it, i.e., its existence, not as a particular object, but as a member of a general

group, was too much for it. Loyally, it tried to encompass the concept and half a dozen coils burnt out. Little warning signals were buzzing.

185   (The girl in her mid-teens left at that point. She had enough for her Physics-1 paper on "Practical Aspects of Robotics." This paper was Susan Calvin's first of many on the subject.)

186   Gloria stood waiting, with carefully concealed impatience, for the machine's answer when she heard the cry behind her of "There she is," and recognized that cry as her mother's.

187   "What are you doing here, you bad girl?" cried Mrs. Weston, anxiety dissolving at once into anger. "Do you know you frightened your mamma and daddy almost to death? Why did you run away?"

188   The robot engineer had also dashed in, tearing his hair, and demanding who of the gathering crowd had tampered with the machine. "Can't anybody read signs?" he yelled. "You're not allowed in here without an attendant."

189   Gloria raised her grieved voice over the din, "I only came to see the Talking Robot, Mamma. I thought he might know where Robbie was because they're both robots." And then, as the thought of Robbie was suddenly brought forcefully home to her, she burst into a sudden storm of tears, "And I *got* to find Robbie, Mamma. I *got* to."

190   Mrs. Weston strangled a cry, and said, "Oh, good Heavens. Come home, George. This is more than I can stand."

191   That evening, George Weston left for several hours, and the next morning, he approached his wife with something that looked suspiciously like smug complacence.

192   "I've got an idea, Grace."

193   "About what?" was the gloomy, uninterested query.

194   "About Gloria."

195   "You're not going to suggest buying back that robot?"

196   "No, of course not."

197   "Then go ahead. I might as well listen to you. Nothing *I've* done seems to have done any good."

198   "All right. Here's what I've been thinking. The whole trouble with Gloria is that she thinks of Robbie as a *person* and not as a *machine*. Naturally, she can't forget him. Now if we managed to convince her that Robbie was nothing more than a mess of steel and copper in the form of sheets and wires with electricity its juice of life, how long would her longings last? It's the psychological attack, if you see my point."

199   "How do you plan to do it?"

200   "Simple. Where do you suppose I went last night? I persuaded Robertson of U.S. Robots and Mechanical Men Corporation to

arrange for a complete tour of his premises tomorrow. The three of us will go, and by the time we're through, Gloria will have it drilled into her that a robot is *not* alive."

201   Mrs. Weston's eyes widened gradually and something glinted in her eyes that was quite like sudden admiration, "Why, George, that's a *good* idea."

202   And George Weston's vest buttons strained. "Only kind I have," he said.

203   Mr. Struthers was a conscientious General Manager and naturally inclined to be a bit talkative. The combination, therefore, resulted in a tour that was fully explained, perhaps even overabundantly explained, at every step. However, Mrs. Weston was not bored. Indeed, she stopped him several times and begged him to repeat his statements in simpler language so that Gloria might understand. Under the influence of this appreciation of his narrative powers, Mr. Struthers expanded genially and became ever more communicative, if possible.

204   George Weston, himself, showed a gathering impatience.

205   "Pardon me, Struthers," he said, breaking into the middle of a lecture on the photo-electric cell, "haven't you a section of the factory where only robot labor is employed?"

206   "Eh? Oh, yes! Yes, indeed!" He smiled at Mrs. Weston. "A vicious circle in a way, robots creating more robots. Of course, we are not making a general practice out of it. For one thing, the unions would never let us. But we can turn out a very few robots using robot labor exclusively, merely as a sort of scientific experiment. You see," he tapped his pince-nez into one palm argumentatively, "what the labor unions don't realize—and I say this as a man who has always been very sympathetic with the labor movement in general—is that the advent of the robot, while involving some dislocation to begin with, will, inevitably—"

207   "Yes, Struthers," said Weston, "but about that section of the factory you speak of—may we see it? It would be very interesting, I'm sure."

208   "Yes! Yes, of course!" Mr. Struthers replaced his pince-nez in one convulsive movement and gave vent to a soft cough of discomfiture. "Follow me, please."

209   He was comparatively quiet while leading the three through a long corridor and down a flight of stairs. Then, when they had entered a large well-lit room that buzzed with metallic activity, the sluices opened and the flood of explanation poured forth again.

210   "There you are!" he said with pride in his voice. "Robots only! Five men act as overseers and they don't even stay in this room. In five years, that is, since we began this project, not a single accident has

occurred. Of course, the robots here assembled are comparatively simple, but . . ."

211   The General Manager's voice had long died to a rather soothing murmur in Gloria's ears. The whole trip seemed rather dull and pointless to her, though there *were* many robots in sight. None were even remotely like Robbie, though, and she surveyed them with open contempt.

212   In this room, there weren't any people at all, she noticed. Then her eyes fell upon six or seven robots busily engaged at a round table halfway across the room. They widened in incredulous surprise. It was a big room. She couldn't see for sure, but one of the robots looked like—looked like—it *was!*

213   "*Robbie!*" Her shriek pierced the air, and one of the robots about the table faltered and dropped the tool he was holding. Gloria went almost mad with joy. Squeezing through the railing before either parent could stop her, she dropped lightly to the floor a few feet below, and ran toward her Robbie, arms waving and hair flying.

214   And the three horrified adults, as they stood frozen in their tracks, saw what the excited little girl did not see,—a huge, lumbering tractor bearing blindly down upon its appointed track.

215   It took split-seconds for Weston to come to his senses, and those split-seconds meant everything, for Gloria could not be overtaken. Although Weston vaulted the railing in a wild attempt, it was obviously hopeless. Mr. Struthers signalled wildly to the overseers to stop the tractor, but the overseers were only human and it took time to act.

216   It was only Robbie that acted immediately and with precision.

217   With metal legs eating up the space between himself and his little mistress he charged down from the opposite direction. Everything then happened at once. With one sweep of an arm, Robbie snatched up Gloria, slackening his speed not one iota, and, consequently, knocking every breath of air out of her. Weston, not quite comprehending all that was happening, felt, rather than saw, Robbie brush past him, and came to a sudden bewildered halt. The tractor intersected Gloria's path half a second after Robbie had, rolled on ten feet further and came to a grinding, long-drawn-out stop.

218   Gloria regained her breath, submitted to a series of passionate hugs on the part of both her parents and turned eagerly toward Robbie. As far as she was concerned, nothing had happened except that she had found her friend.

219   But Mrs. Weston's expression had changed from one of relief to one of dark suspicion. She turned to her husband, and despite her disheveled and undignified appearance, managed to look quite formidable, "*You* engineered this, *didn't* you?"

220   George Weston swabbed at a hot forehead with his handkerchief. His hand was unsteady, and his lips could curve only into a tremulous and exceedingly weak smile.

221   Mrs. Weston pursued the thought, "Robbie wasn't designed for engineering or construction work. He couldn't be of any use to them. You had him placed there deliberately so that Gloria would find him. You know you did."

222   "Well, I did," said Weston. "But, Grace, how was I to know the reunion would be so violent? And Robbie has saved her life; you'll have to admit that. You *can't* send him away again."

223   Grace Weston considered. She turned toward Gloria and Robbie and watched them abstractedly for a moment. Gloria had a grip about the robot's neck that would have asphyxiated any creature but one of metal, and was prattling nonsense in half-hysterical frenzy. Robbie's chrome-steel arms (capable of bending a bar of steel two inches in diameter into a pretzel) wound about the little girl gently and lovingly, and his eyes glowed a deep, deep red.

224   "Well," said Mrs. Weston, at last, "I guess he can stay with us until he rusts."

———————

DISCUSSION QUESTIONS

1. Robbie wants desperately to be told stories. Why do you think Cinderella is his favorite?
2. Why, even though he is programmed with sophisticated actions and movements, can't Robbie talk?
3. When Grace Weston tells Gloria her robot is gone, why does she lie about the reason? What does she do to try to make Gloria happy?
4. Robbie is presented as emotional, childlike, loving, caring, and kind. Yet Mrs. Weston claims he has no *soul* because he isn't a *person*. In small groups, discuss the possibility of robots acquiring souls.
5. The trip to the city doesn't "cure" Gloria of her loneliness, even though it's packed with activities. Why not?

WRITING TOPICS

1. George Weston tries to defend Robbie, but his wife wears him down. How does Mr. Weston finally win in the end? In a short essay, discuss what this reveals about both Mr. and Mrs. Weston.

2. Write a paragraph explaining the significance of Mrs. Weston's final remark.

3. Asimov's 1998, envisioned in 1940, is a far cry from today's reality. Which of his ideas have not happened? Are there any that have? In your journal, make a list of both categories and speculate about why his vision was so unlike today's world.

Desertion

1944

CLIFFORD D. SIMAK (1904–1988)

Clifford D. Simak was primarily a journalist who began writing science fiction as a sideline in the early thirties. Under the guidance of John W. Campbell, he began to produce limited and nostalgic work that was emotionally charged beneath the surface. His most well-known work began as a series of short stories, the first of which, "City" (1944), also became the title of the novel that linked together several of the sequential stories. *City* (1952) is a novel about a time when humans have deserted the cities and eventually Earth itself. Robots and animals, the only things left, begin evolving into sentient life forms. In the sixties Simak produced several excellent novels, including *Time Is the Simplest Thing* (1961) and *All Flesh Is Grass* (1965). Simak preferred rural life and when that became unpopular, so did his stories. Unfortunately, the quality of his writing also declined in his later works.

A Choice of Gods (1972) features some of his favorite themes: a depopulated world, a wise old man, and robots liberated from servitude. *A Heritage of Stars* (1977) is another look at a post-technological society, and in *The Visitors* (1980), aliens visit Earth bearing gifts. Typically, the gifts eventually cause new problems.

In "Desertion," Clifford Simak looks at communication with other life-forms, but in this case, the viewpoint is everything.

1   Four men, two by two, had gone into the howling maelstrom that was Jupiter and had not returned. They had walked into the keening gale—or rather, they had loped, bellies low against the ground, wet sides gleaming in the rain.

2   For they did not go in the shape of men.

3   Now the fifth man stood before the desk of Kent Fowler, head of Dome No. 3, Jovian Survey Commission.

4   Under Fowler's desk, old Towser scratched a flea, then settled down to sleep again.

5   Harold Allen, Fowler saw with a sudden pang, was young—too young. He had the easy confidence of youth, the straight back and eyes, the face of one who never had known fear. And that was strange. For men in the domes of Jupiter did know fear—fear and humility. It was hard for Man to reconcile his puny self with the mighty forces of the monstrous planet.

6   "You understand," said Fowler, "that you need not do this. You understand that you need not go."

7   It was formula, of course. The other four had been told the same thing, but they had gone. This fifth one, Fowler knew, would go too. But suddenly he felt a dull hope stir within him that Allen wouldn't go.

8   "When do I start?" asked Allen.

9   There was a time when Fowler might have taken quiet pride in that answer, but not now. He frowned briefly.

10   "Within the hour," he said.

11   Allen stood waiting, quietly.

12   "Four other men have gone out and have not returned," said Fowler. "You know that, of course. We want you to return. We don't want you going off on any heroic rescue expedition. The main thing, the only thing, is that you come back, that you prove Man can live in a Jovian form. Go to the first survey stake, no farther, then come back. Don't take any chances. Don't investigate anything. Just come back."

13   Allen nodded. "I understand all that."

14   "Miss Stanley will operate the converter," Fowler went on. "You need have no fear on that particular point. The other men were converted without mishap. They left the converter in apparently perfect condition. You will be in thoroughly competent hands. Miss Stanley is the best qualified conversion operator in the Solar System. She had had experience on most of the other planets. That is why she's here."

15   Allen grinned at the woman and Fowler saw something flicker across Miss Stanley's face—something that might have been pity, or rage—or just plain fear. But it was gone again and she was smiling back at the youth who stood before the desk. Smiling in that prim, school-

teacherish way she had of smiling, almost as if she hated herself for doing it.

16   "I shall be looking forward," said Allen, "to my conversion."

17   And the way he said it, he made it all a joke, a vast, ironic joke.

18   But it was no joke.

19   It was serious business, deadly serious. Upon these tests, Fowler knew, depended the fate of men on Jupiter. If the tests succeeded, the resources of the giant planet would be thrown open. Man would take over Jupiter as he already had taken over the smaller planets. And if they failed—

20   If they failed, Man would continue to be chained and hampered by the terrific pressure, the greater force of gravity, the weird chemistry of the planet. He would continue to be shut within the domes, unable to set actual foot upon the planet, unable to see it with direct, unaided vision, forced to rely upon the awkward tractors and the televisor, forced to work with clumsy tools and mechanisms or through the medium of robots that themselves were clumsy.

21   For Man, unprotected and in his natural form, would be blotted out by Jupiter's terrific pressure of fifteen thousand pounds per square inch, pressure that made Terrestrial sea bottoms seem a vacuum by comparison.

22   Even the strongest metal Earthmen could devise couldn't exist under pressure such as that, under the pressure and the alkaline rains that forever swept the planet. It grew brittle and flaky, crumbling like clay, or it ran away in little streams and puddles of ammonia salts. Only by stepping up the toughness and strength of that metal, by increasing its electronic tension, could it be made to withstand the weight of thousands of miles of swirling, choking gases that made up the atmosphere. And even when that was done, everything had to be coated with tough quartz to keep away the rain—the bitter rain that was liquid ammonia.

23   Fowler sat listening to the engines in the sub-floor of the dome. Engines that ran on endlessly, the dome never quiet of them. They had to run and keep on running. For if they stopped, the power flowing into the metal walls of the dome would stop, the electronic tension would ease up and that would be the end of everything.

24   Towser roused himself under Fowler's desk and scratched another flea, his leg thumping hard against the floor.

25   "Is there anything else?" asked Allen.

26   Fowler shook his head. "Perhaps there's something you want to do," he said. "Perhaps you—"

27   He had meant to say write a letter and he was glad he caught himself quick enough so he didn't say it.

28   Allen looked at his watch. "I'll be there on time," he said. He swung around and headed for the door.

29   Fowler knew Miss Stanley was watching him and he didn't want to turn and meet her eyes. He fumbled with a sheaf of papers on the desk before him.

30   "How long are you going to keep this up?" asked Miss Stanley and she bit off each word with a vicious snap.

31   He swung around in his chair and faced her then. Her lips were drawn into a straight, thin line, and her hair seemed skinned back from her forehead tighter than ever, giving her face that queer, almost startling death-mask quality.

32   He tried to make his voice cool and level. "As long as there's any need of it," he said. "As long as there's any hope."

33   "You're going to keep on sentencing them to death," she said. "You're going to keep marching them out face to face with Jupiter. You're going to sit in here safe and comfortable and send them out to die."

34   "There is no room for sentimentality, Miss Stanley," Fowler said, trying to keep the note of anger from his voice. "You know as well as I do why we're doing this. You realize that Man in his own form simply cannot cope with Jupiter. The only answer is to turn men into the sort of things that can cope with it. We've done it on the other planets.

35   "If a few men die, but we finally succeed, the price is small. Through the ages men have thrown away their lives on foolish things, for foolish reasons. Why should we hesitate, then, at a little death in a thing as great as this?"

36   Miss Stanley sat stiff and straight, hands folded in her lap, the lights shining on her graying hair and Fowler, watching her, tried to imagine what she might feel, what she might be thinking. He wasn't exactly afraid of her, but he didn't feel quite comfortable when she was around. Those sharp blue eyes saw too much, her hands looked far too competent. She should be somebody's Aunt sitting in a rocking chair with her knitting needles. But she wasn't. She was the top-notch conversion unit operator in the Solar System and she didn't like the way he was doing things.

37   "There is something wrong, Mr. Fowler," she declared.

38   "Precisely," agreed Fowler. "That's why I'm sending young Allen out alone. He may find out what it is."

39   "And if he doesn't?"

40   "I'll send someone else."

41   She rose slowly from her chair, started toward the door, then stopped before his desk.

42   "Some day," she said, "you will be a great man. You never let a chance go by. This is your chance. You knew it was when this dome

was picked for the tests. If you put it through, you'll go up a notch or two. No matter how many men may die, you'll go up a notch or two."

43   "Miss Stanley," he said and his voice was curt, "young Allen is going out soon. Please be sure that your machine——"

44   "My machine," she told him, icily, "is not to blame. It operates along the coordinates the biologists set up."

45   He sat hunched at his desk, listening to her footsteps go down the corridor.

46   What she said was true, of course. The biologists had set up the co-ordinates. But the biologists could be wrong. Just a hairbreadth of difference, one iota of digression and the converter would be sending out something that wasn't the thing they meant to send. A mutant that might crack up, go haywire, come unstuck under some condition or stress of circumstance wholly unsuspected.

47   For Man didn't know much about what was going on outside. Only what his instruments told him was going on. And the samplings of those happenings furnished by those instruments and mechanisms had been no more than samplings, for Jupiter was unbelievably large and the domes were very few.

48   Even the work of the biologists in getting the data on the Lopers, apparently the highest form of Jovian life, had involved more than three years of intensive study and after that two years of checking to make sure. Work that could have been done on Earth in a week or two. But work that, in this case, couldn't be done on Earth at all, for one couldn't take a Jovian life form to Earth. The pressure here on Jupiter couldn't be duplicated outside of Jupiter and at Earth pressure and temperature the Lopers would simply have disappeared in a puff of gas.

49   Yet it was work that had to be done if Man ever hoped to go about Jupiter in the life form of the Lopers. For before the converter could change a man to another life form, every detailed physical characteristic of that life form must be known—surely and positively, with no chance of mistake.

50   Allen did not come back.

51   The tractors, combing the nearby terrain, found no trace of him, unless the skulking thing reported by one of the drivers had been the missing Earthman in Loper form.

52   The biologists sneered their most accomplished academic sneers when Fowler suggested the co-ordinates might be wrong. Carefully they pointed out, the co-ordinates worked. When a man was put into the converter and the switch was thrown, the man became a Loper. He left the machine and moved away, out of sight, into the soupy atmosphere.

53   Some quirk, Fowler had suggested; some tiny deviation from the thing a Loper should be, some minor defect. If there were, the biologists said, it would take years to find it.

54   And Fowler knew that they were right.

55   So there were five men now instead of four and Harold Allen had walked out into Jupiter for nothing at all. It was as if he'd never gone so far as knowledge was concerned.

56   Fowler reached across his desk and picked up the personal file, a thin sheaf of papers neatly clipped together. It was a thing he dreaded but a thing he had to do. Somehow the reason for these strange disappearances must be found. And there was no other way than to send out more men.

57   He sat for a moment listening to the howling of the wind above the dome, the everlasting thundering gale that swept across the planet in boiling, twisting wrath.

58   Was there some threat out there, he asked himself? Some danger they did not know about? Something that lay in wait and gobbled up the Lopers, making no distinction between Lopers that were *bona fide* and Lopers that were men? To the gobblers, of course, it would make no difference.

59   Or had there been a basic fault in selecting the Lopers as the type of life best fitted for existence on the surface of the planet? The evident intelligence of the Lopers, he knew, had been one factor in that determination. For if the thing Man became did not have capacity for intelligence, Man could not for long retain his own intelligence in such a guise.

60   Had the biologists let that one factor weigh too heavily, using it to offset some other factor that might be unsatisfactory, even disastrous? It didn't seem likely. Stiffnecked as they might be, the biologists knew their business.

61   Or was the whole thing impossible, doomed from the very start? Conversion to other life forms had worked on other planets, but that did not necessarily mean it would work on Jupiter. Perhaps Man's intelligence could not function correctly through the sensory apparatus provided Jovian life. Perhaps the Lopers were so alien there was no common ground for human knowledge and the Jovian conception of existence to meet and work together.

62   Or the fault might lie with Man, be inherent in the race. Some mental aberration which, coupled with what they found outside, wouldn't let them come back. Although it might not be an aberration, not in the human sense. Perhaps just one ordinary human mental trait, accepted as commonplace on Earth, would be so violently at odds with Jovian existence that it would blast all human intelligence and sanity.

63   Claws rattled and clicked down the corridor. Listening to them, Fowler smiled wanly. It was Towser coming back from the kitchen, where he had gone to see his friend, the cook.

64   Towser came into the room, carrying a bone. He wagged his tail at Fowler and flopped down beside the desk, bone between his paws. For a long moment his rheumy old eyes regarded his master and Fowler reached down a hand to ruffle a ragged ear.

65   "You still like me, Towser?" Fowler asked and Towser thumped his tail.

66   "You're the only one," said Fowler. "All through the dome they're cussing me. Calling me a murderer, more than likely."

67   He straightened and swung back to the desk. His hand reached out and picked up the file.

68   Bennett? Bennett had a girl waiting for him back on Earth.

69   Andrews? Andrews was planning on going back to Mars Tech just as soon as he earned enough to see him through a year.

70   Olson? Olson was nearing pension age. All the time telling the boys how he was going to settle down and grow roses.

71   Carefully, Fowler laid the file back on the desk.

72   Sentencing men to death. Miss Stanley had said that, her pale lips scarcely moving in her parchment face. Marching men out to die while he, Fowler, sat here safe and comfortable.

73   They were saying it all through the dome, no doubt, especially since Allen had failed to return. They wouldn't say it to his face, of course. Even the man or men he called before this desk and told they were the next to go, wouldn't say it to him.

74   They would only say: "When do we start?" For that was the formula.

75   But he would see it in their eyes.

76   He picked up the file again. Bennett, Andrews, Olson. There were others, but there was no use in going on.

77   Kent Fowler knew that he couldn't do it, couldn't face them, couldn't send more men out to die.

78   He leaned forward and flipped up the toggle on the inter-communicator.

79   "Yes, Mr. Fowler."

80   "Miss Stanley, please."

81   He waited for Miss Stanley, listening to Towser chewing half-heartedly on the bone. Towser's teeth were getting bad.

82   "Miss Stanley," said Miss Stanley's voice.

83   "Just wanted to tell you, Miss Stanley, to get ready for two more."

84   "Aren't you afraid," asked Miss Stanley, "that you'll run out of them? Sending out one at a time, they'd last longer, give you twice the satisfaction."

85   "One of them," said Fowler, "will be a dog."

86   "A dog?"

87   "Yes, Towser."

88   He heard the quick, cold rage that iced her voice. "Your own dog! He's been with you all these years—"

89   "That's the point," said Fowler. "Towser would be unhappy if I left him behind."

90   It was not the Jupiter he had known through the televisor. He had expected it to be different, but not like this. He had expected a hell of ammonia rain and stinking fumes and the deafening, thundering tumult of the storm. He had expected swirling clouds and fog and the snarling flicker of monstrous thunderbolts.

91   He had not expected the lashing downpour would be reduced to drifting purple mist that moved like fleeing shadows over a red and purple sward. He had not even guessed the snaking bolts of lightning would be flares of pure ecstasy across a painted sky.

92   Waiting for Towser, Fowler flexed the muscles of his body, amazed at the smooth, sleek strength he found. Not a bad body, he decided, and grimaced at remembering how he had pitied the Lopers when he glimpsed them through the television screen.

93   For it had been hard to imagine a living organism based upon ammonia and hydrogen rather than upon water and oxygen, hard to believe that such a form of life could know the same quick thrill of life that humankind could know. Hard to conceive of life out in the soupy maelstrom that was Jupiter, not knowing, of course, that through Jovian eyes it was no soupy maelstrom at all.

94   The wind brushed against him with what seemed gentle fingers and he remembered with a start that by Earth standards the wind was a roaring gale, a two-hundred-mile an hour howler laden with deadly gases.

95   Pleasant scents seeped into his body. And yet scarcely scents, for it was not the sense of smell as he remembered it. It was as if his whole being was soaking up the sensation of lavender—and yet not lavender. It was something, he knew, for which he had no word, undoubtedly the first of many enigmas in terminology. For the words he knew, the thought symbols that served him as an Earthman would not serve him as a Jovian.

96   The lock in the side of the dome opened and Towser came tumbling out—at least he thought it must be Towser.

97   He started to call to the dog, his mind shaping the words he meant to say. But he couldn't say them. There was no way to say them. He had nothing to say them with.

98 For a moment his mind swirled in muddy terror, a blind fear that eddied in little puffs of panic through his brain.

99 How did Jovians talk? How—

100 Suddenly he was aware of Towser, intently aware of the bumbling, eager friendliness of the shaggy animal that had followed him from Earth to many planets. As if the thing that was Towser had reached out and for a moment sat within his brain.

101 And out of the bubbling welcome that he sensed, came words.

102 "Hiya, pal."

103 Not words really, better than words. Thought symbols in his brain, communicated thought symbols that had shades of meaning words could never have.

104 "Hiya, Towser," he said.

105 "I feel good," said Towser. "Like I was a pup. Lately I've been feeling pretty punk. Legs stiffening up on me and teeth wearing down to almost nothing. Hard to mumble a bone with teeth like that. Besides, the fleas give me hell. Used to be I never paid much attention to them. A couple of fleas more or less never meant much in my early days."

106 "But . . . but—" Fowler's thoughts tumbled awkwardly. "You're talking to me!"

107 "Sure thing," said Towser. "I always talked to you, but you couldn't hear me. I tried to say things to you, but I couldn't make the grade."

108 "I understood you sometimes," Fowler said.

109 "Not very well," said Towser. "You knew when I wanted food and when I wanted a drink and when I wanted out, but that's about all you ever managed."

110 "I'm sorry," Fowler said.

111 "Forget it," Towser told him. "I'll race you to the cliff."

112 For the first time, Fowler saw the cliff, apparently many miles away, but with a strange crystalline beauty that sparkled in the shadow of the many-colored clouds.

113 Fowler hesitated. "It's a long way—"

114 "Ah, come on," said Towser and even as he said it he started for the cliff.

115 Fowler followed, testing his legs, testing the strength in that new body of his, a bit doubtful at first, amazed a moment later, then running with a sheer joyousness that was one with the red and purple sward, with the drifting smoke of the rain across the land.

116 As he ran the consciousness of music came to him, a music that beat into his body, that surged throughout his being, that lifted him on wings of silver speed. Music like bells might make from some steeple on a sunny, springtime hill.

117   As the cliff drew nearer the music deepened and filled the universe with a spray of magic sound. And he knew the music came from the tumbling waterfall that feathered down the face of the shining cliff.

118   Only, he knew, it was no waterfall, but an ammonia-fall and the cliff was white because it was oxygen, solidified.

119   He skidded to a stop beside Towser where the waterfall broke into a glittering rainbow of many hundred colors. Literally many hundred, for here, he saw, was no shading of one primary to another as human beings saw, but a clear-cut selectivity that broke the prism down to its last ultimate classification.

120   "The music," said Towser.

121   "Yes, what about it?"

122   "The music," said Towser, "is vibrations. Vibrations of water falling."

123   "But, Towser, you don't know about vibrations."

124   "Yes, I do," contended Towser. "It just popped into my head."

125   Fowler gulped mentally. "Just popped!"

126   And suddenly, within his own head, he held a formula—the formula for a process that would make metal to withstand the pressure of Jupiter.

127   He stared, astounded, at the waterfall and swiftly his mind took the many colors and placed them in their exact sequence in the spectrum. Just like that. Just out of blue sky. Out of nothing, for he knew nothing either of metals or of colors.

128   "Towser," he cried. "Towser, something's happening to us!"

129   "Yeah, I know," said Towser.

130   "It's our brains," said Fowler. "We're using them, all of them, down to the last hidden corner. Using them to figure out things we should have known all the time. Maybe the brains of Earth things naturally are slow and foggy. Maybe we are the morons of the universe. Maybe we are fixed so we have to do things the hard way."

131   And, in the new sharp clarity of thought that seemed to grip him, he knew that it would not only be the matter of colors in a waterfall or metals that would resist the pressure of Jupiter, he sensed other things, things not yet quite clear. A vague whispering that hinted of greater things, of mysteries beyond the pale of human thought, beyond even the pale of human imagination. Mysteries, fact, logic built on reasoning. Things that any brain should know if it used all its reasoning power.

132   "We're still mostly Earth," he said. "We're just beginning to learn a few of the things we are to know—a few of the things that were kept from us as human beings, perhaps because we were human beings. Because our human bodies were poor bodies. Poorly equipped for

thinking, poorly equipped in certain senses that one has to have to know. Perhaps even lacking in certain senses that are necessary to true knowledge."

133 He stared back at the dome, a tiny black thing dwarfed by the distance.

134 Back there were men who couldn't see the beauty that was Jupiter. Men who thought that swirling clouds and lashing rain obscured the face of the planet. Unseeing human eyes. Poor eyes. Eyes that could not see the beauty in the clouds, that could not see through the storms. Bodies that could not feel the thrill of trilling music stemming from the rush of broken water.

135 Men who walked alone, in terrible loneliness, talking with their tongue like Boy Scouts wigwagging out their messages, unable to reach out and touch one another's mind as he could reach out and touch Towser's mind. Shut off forever from that personal, intimate contact with other living things.

136 He, Fowler, had expected terror inspired by alien things out here on the surface, had expected to cower before the threat of unknown things, had steeled himself against disgust of a situation that was not of Earth.

137 But instead he had found something greater than Man had ever known. A swifter, surer body. A sense of exhilaration, a deeper sense of life. A sharper mind. A world of beauty that even the dreamers of the Earth had not yet imagined.

138 "Let's get going," Towser urged.

139 "Where do you want to go?"

140 "Anywhere," said Towser. "Just start going and see where we end up. I have feeling. . .well, a feeling—"

141 "Yes, I know," said Fowler.

142 For he had the feeling, too. The feeling of high destiny. A certain sense of greatness. A knowledge that somewhere off beyond the horizons lay adventure and things greater than adventure.

143 Those other five had felt it, too. Had felt the urge to go and see, the compelling sense that here lay a life of fullness and of knowledge.

144 That, he knew, was why they had not returned.

145 "I won't go back," said Towser.

146 "We can't let them down," said Fowler.

147 Fowler took a step or two, back toward the dome, then stopped.

148 Back to the dome. Back to that aching, poison-laden body he had left. It hadn't seemed aching before, but now he knew it was.

149 Back to the fuzzy brain. Back to muddled thinking. Back to flapping mouths that formed signals others understood. Back to eyes that now would be worse than no sight at all. Back to squalor, back to crawling, back to ignorance.

150   "Perhaps some day," he said, muttering to himself.

151   "We got a lot to do and a lot to see," said Towser. "We got a lot to learn. We'll find things—"

152   Yes, they could find things. Civilizations, perhaps. Civilizations that would make the civilization of Man seem puny by comparison. Beauty and more important—an understanding of that beauty. And a comradeship no one had ever known before—that no man, no dog had ever known before.

153   And life. The quickness of life after what seemed a drugged existence.

154   "I can't go back," said Towser.

155   "Nor I," said Fowler.

156   "They would turn me back into a dog," said Towser.

157   "And me," said Fowler, "back into a man."

_____

DISCUSSION QUESTIONS

1. In order to withstand the tremendous pressures on Jupiter, what steps must the Earth explorers take? Why are they unsuccessful?
2. As the fifth volunteer for conversion presents himself, both Fowler and Stanley display many emotions. Why?
3. Why do you think the Jovians are termed "Lopers"?
4. Why does Fowler think the human-Jovian changeover always fails?
5. References are made to Man having a right (and perhaps a responsibility) to conquer the solar system. In small groups, examine this as if "Man" did not include women. How does this reading contribute to the irony of the story?

WRITING TOPICS

1. Fowler experiences Jupiter quite differently once he is converted. What other experiences can you compare to his change of reality? Write a short essay detailing one or more such experiences.
2. In a journal entry, explain why Fowler doesn't go back to the Earth station.
3. As they become more aware of their Jovian forms, both Fowler and Towser begin purposely distancing themselves from humanity. In a few paragraphs, discuss what events in the mid-forties could have prompted Simak to write such a story.

That Only a Mother

1948

JUDITH MERRIL (b. 1923)

**Judith Merril was married to Frederick Pohl from 1949 until
1953, during which time her first novel, *Shadow on the Hearth*
(1950), was published. It was later made into a television movie
entitled *Atomic Attack*. Her story "Dead Center" (1954) was an-
thologized in *The Best American Short Stories: 1955*. During the
fifties, she began editing science fiction anthologies, and in 1956
she became editor of *SF: The Year's Greatest Science-Fiction and
Fantasy* series, a position she held for twelve years.**

**In 1952 Merril collaborated with C. M. Kornbluth on two
stories, "Outpost Mars," about the colonization of Mars, and
"Gunner Cade," showing a society where war is a spectator
sport. In 1960 she produced the psychological mystery *The
Tomorrow People*. Merril published little of her own fiction after
1960, though her stories have been collected in *A Judith Merril
Omnibus: Daughters of the Earth and Other Stories* (1968) and
The Best of Judith Merril (1976).**

**In "That Only a Mother," Judith Merril's first published
story, she explores a mother's love for her newborn baby.**

1   Margaret reached over to the other side of the bed where Hank should have been. Her hand patted the empty pillow, and then she came altogether awake, wondering that the old habit should remain after so many months. She tried to curl up, cat-style, to hoard her own warmth, found she couldn't do it anymore, and climbed out of bed with a pleased awareness of her increasingly clumsy bulkiness.

2   Morning motions were automatic. On the way through the kitchenette, she pressed the button that would start breakfast cooking—the doctor had said to eat as much breakfast as she could—and tore the paper out of the facsimile machine. She folded the long sheet carefully to the "National News" section, and propped it on the bathroom shelf to scan while she brushed her teeth.

3   No accidents. No direct hits. At least none that had been officially released for publication. *Now, Maggie, don't get started on that. No accidents. No hits. Take the nice newspaper's word for it.*

4   The three clear chimes from the kitchen announced that breakfast was ready. She set a bright napkin and cheerful colored dishes on the table in a futile attempt to appeal to a faulty morning appetite. Then, when there was nothing more to prepare, she went for the mail, allowing herself the full pleasure of prolonged anticipation, because today there would *surely* be a letter.

5   There was. There were. Two bills and a worried note from her mother: "Darling. Why didn't you write and tell me sooner? I'm thrilled, of course, but, well, one hates to mention these things, but are you *certain* the doctor was right? Hank's been around all that uranium or thorium or whatever it is all these years, and I know you say he's a designer, not a technician, and he doesn't get near anything that might be dangerous, but you know he used to, back at Oak Ridge. Don't you think . . . well, of course, I'm just being a foolish old woman, and I don't want you to get upset. You know much more about it than I do, and I'm sure your doctor was right. He *should* know . . ."

6   Margaret made a face over the excellent coffee, and caught herself refolding the paper to the medical news.

7   *Stop it, Maggie, stop it! The radiologist said Hank's job couldn't have exposed him. And the bombed area we drove past . . . No, no. Stop it, now! Read the social notes or the recipes, Maggie girl.*

8   A well-known geneticist, in the medical news, said that it was possible to tell with absolute certainty, at five months, whether the child would be normal, or at least whether the mutation was likely to produce anything freakish. The worst cases, at any rate, could be prevented. Minor mutations, of course, displacements in facial features, or

changes in brain structure could not be detected. And there had been some cases recently, of normal embryos with atrophied limbs that did not develop beyond the seventh or eighth month. But, the doctor concluded cheerfully, the *worst* cases could now be predicted and prevented.

9   *"Predicted and prevented." We predicted it, didn't we? Hank and the others, they predicted it. But we didn't prevent it. We could have stopped it in '46 and '47. Now . . .*

10   Margaret decided against the breakfast. Coffee had been enough for her in the morning for ten years; it would have to do for today. She buttoned herself into interminable folds of material that, the salesgirl had assured her, was the *only* comfortable thing to wear during the last few months. With a surge of pure pleasure, the letter and newspaper forgotten, she realized she was on the next to the last button. It wouldn't be long now.

11   The city in the early morning had always been a special kind of excitement for her. Last night it had rained, and the sidewalks were still damp-gray instead of dusty. The air smelled the fresher, to a city-bred woman, for the occasional pungency of acrid factory smoke. She walked the six blocks to work, watching the lights go out in the all-night hamburger joints, where the plate-glass walls were already catching the sun, and the lights go on in the dim interiors of cigar stores and dry-cleaning establishments.

12   The office was in a new Government building. In the rolovator, on the way up, she felt, as always, like a frankfurter roll in the ascending half of an old-style rotary toasting machine. She abandoned the air-foam cushioning gratefully at the fourteenth floor, and settled down behind her desk, at the rear of a long row of identical desks.

13   Each morning the pile of papers that greeted her was a little higher. These were, as everyone knew, the decisive months. The war might be won or lost on these calculations as well as any others. The manpower office had switched her here when her old expediter's job got to be too strenuous. The computer was easy to operate, and the work was absorbing, if not as exciting as the old job. But you didn't just stop working these days. Everyone who could do anything at all was needed.

14   *And*—she remembered the interview with the psychologist—*I'm probably the unstable type. Wonder what sort of neurosis I'd get sitting home reading that sensational paper . . .*

15   She plunged into the work without pursuing the thought.

February 18.

Hank darling,

16 Just a note—from the hospital, no less. I had a dizzy spell at work, and the doctor took it to heart. Blessed if I know what I'll do with myself lying in bed for weeks, just waiting—but Dr. Boyer seems to think it may not be so long.

17 There are too many newspapers around here. More infanticides all the time, and they can't seem to get a jury to convict any of them. It's the fathers who do it. Lucky thing you're not around, in case—

18 Oh, darling, that wasn't a very *funny* joke, was it? Write as often as you can, will you? I have too much time to think. But there really isn't anything wrong, and nothing to worry about.

19 Write often, and remember I love you.

Maggie.

SPECIAL SERVICE TELEGRAM

FEBRUARY 21, 1953

22:04 LK37G

FROM: TECH. LIEUT. H. MARVELL

X47-016 GCNY

TO: MRS. H. MARVELL

WOMEN'S HOSPITAL

NEW YORK CITY

20 HAD DOCTOR'S GRAM STOP WILL ARRIVE FOUR OH TEN STOP SHORT LEAVE STOP YOU DID IT MAGGIE STOP LOVE HANK

February 25.

Hank dear,

21 So you didn't see the baby either? You'd think a place this size would at least have visiplates on the incubators, so the fathers could get a look, even if the poor benighted mommas can't. They tell me I won't see her for another week, or maybe more—but of course, mother always warned me if I didn't slow my pace, I'd probably even have my babies too fast. Why must she *always* be right?

22 Did you meet that battle-ax of a nurse they put on here? I imagine they save her for people who've already had theirs, and don't let her get too near the prospectives—but a woman like that simply shouldn't be allowed in a maternity ward. She's obsessed with mutations, can't seem to talk about anything else. Oh, well, *ours* is all right, even if it was in an unholy hurry.

23   I'm tired. They warned me not to sit up so soon, but I *had*
to write you. All my love, darling,

                                                            Maggie.

                                                    February 29.
Darling,

24   I finally got to see her! It's all true, what they say about new
babies and the face that only a mother could love—but it's all
there, darling, eyes, ears, and noses—no, only one!—all in the
right places. We're so *lucky*, Hank.

25   I'm afraid I've been a rambunctious patient. I kept telling that
hatchet-faced female with the mutation mania that I wanted to
see the baby. Finally the doctor came in to "explain" everything to
me, and talked a lot of nonsense, most of which I'm sure no one
could have understood, any more than I did. The only thing I got
out of it was that she didn't actually *have* to stay in the incubator;
they just thought it was "wiser."

26   I think I got a little hysterical at that point. Guess I was more
worried than I was willing to admit, but I threw a small fit about
it. The whole business wound up with one of those hushed medical conferences outside the door, and finally the Woman in
White said: "Well, we might as well. Maybe it'll work out better
that way."

27   I'd heard about the way doctors and nurses in these places develop a God complex, and believe me it is as true figuratively as it
is literally that a mother hasn't got a leg to stand on around here.

28   I *am* awfully weak, still. I'll write again soon. Love,

                                                            Maggie.

                                                        March 8
Dearest Hank,

29   Well, the nurse was wrong if she told you that. She's an idiot
anyhow. It's a girl. It's easier to tell with babies than with cats, and
I know. How about Henrietta?

30   I'm home again, and busier than a betatron. They got *everything* mixed up at the hospital, and I had to teach myself how to
bathe her and do just about everything else. She's getting prettier,
too. When can you get a leave, a *real* leave?

                                                            Love,
                                                            Maggie.

                                                    May 26.

Hank dear,

31   You should see her now—and you shall. I'm sending along a
reel of color movie. My mother sent her those nighties with
drawstrings all over. I put one on, and right now she looks like a
snow-white potato sack with that beautiful, beautiful flower-face
blooming on top. Is that *me* talking? Am I a doting mother? But
wait till you *see* her!

                                                    July 10.

32   . . . Believe it or not, as you like, but your daughter can talk,
and I don't mean baby talk. Alice discovered it—she's a dental assistant in the WACs, you know—and when she heard the baby
giving out what I thought was a string of gibberish, she said the
kid knew words and sentences, but couldn't say them clearly because she has no teeth yet. I'm taking her to a speech specialist.

                                                    September 13.

33   . . . We have a prodigy for real! Now that all her front teeth are
in, her speech is perfectly clear and—a new talent now—she can
sing! I mean really carry a tune! At seven months! Darling, my
world would be perfect if you could only get home.

                                                    November 19.

34   . . . at least. The little goon was so busy being clever, it took
her all this time to crawl. The doctor says development in these
cases is always erratic . . .

                         SPECIAL SERVICE TELEGRAM
                                                    DECEMBER 1, 1953
                                                    08:47 LK59F

FROM: TECH. LIEUT. H. MARVELL
        X47-016 GCNY
TO: MRS. H. MARVELL
        APT. K-17
        504 E. 19 ST.
        N.Y. N.Y.

35   WEEK'S LEAVE STARTS TOMORROW STOP WILL ARRIVE AIRPORT
        TEN OH FIVE STOP DON'T MEET ME STOP LOVE LOVE LOVE HANK

36   Margaret let the water run out of the bathinette until only a few
inches were left, and then loosed her hold on the wriggling baby.

37   "I think it was better when you were retarded, young woman," she informed her daughter happily. "You *can't* crawl in a bathinette, you know."

38   "Then why can't I go in the bathtub?" Margaret was used to her child's volubility by now, but every now and then it caught her unawares. She swooped the resistant mass of pink flesh into a towel and began to rub.

39   "Because you're too little, and your head is very soft, and bathtubs are very hard."

40   "Oh. Then when can I go in the bathtub?"

41   "When the outside of your head is as hard as the inside, brainchild." She reached toward a pile of fresh clothing. "I cannot understand," she added, pinning a square of cloth through the nightgown, "why a child of your intelligence can't learn to keep a diaper on the way other babies do. They've been used for centuries, you know, with perfectly satisfactory results."

42   The child disdained to reply; she had heard it too often. She waited patiently until she had been tucked, clean and sweet-smelling, into a white-painted crib. Then she favored her mother with a smile that inevitably made Margaret think of the first golden edge of the sun bursting into a rosy predawn. She remembered Hank's reaction to the color pictures of his beautiful daughter, and with the thought, realized how late it was.

43   "Go to sleep, puss. When you wake up, you know, your *daddy* will be here."

44   "Why?" asked the four-year-old mind, waging a losing battle to keep the ten-month-old body awake.

45   Margaret went into the kitchenette and set the timer for the roast. She examined the table and got her clothes from the closet, new dress, new shoes, new slip, new everything, bought weeks before and saved for the day Hank's telegram came. She stopped to pull a paper from the facsimile and, with clothes and news, went into the bathroom and lowered herself gingerly into the steaming luxury of a scented tub.

46   She glanced through the paper with indifferent interest. Today at least there was no need to read the national news. There was an article by a geneticist. The same geneticist. Mutations, he said, were increasing disproportionately. It was too soon for recessives; even the first mutants, born near Hiroshima and Nagasaki in 1946 and 1947, were not old enough yet to breed. *But my baby's all right.* Apparently, there was some degree of free radiation from atomic explosions causing the trouble. *My baby's fine. Precocious, but normal.* If more attention had been paid to the first Japanese mutations, he said ...

47   *There was that little notice in the paper in the spring of '47. That was when Hank quit at Oak Ridge.* "Only 2 or 3 percent of those guilty of infanticide are being caught and punished in Japan today . . ." *But* MY BABY'S *all right.*

48   She was dressed, combed, and ready to the last light brush-on of lip paste, when the door chime sounded. She dashed for the door and heard for the first time in eighteen months the almost-forgotten sound of a key turning in the lock before the chime had quite died away.

49   "Hank!"

50   "Maggie!"

51   And then there was nothing to say. So many days, so many months, of small news piling up, so many things to tell him, and now she just stood there, staring at a khaki uniform and a stranger's pale face. She traced the features with the finger of memory. The same high-bridged nose, wide-set eyes, fine feathery brows; the same long jaw, the hair a little farther back now on the high forehead, the same tilted curve to his mouth. Pale . . . Of course, he'd been underground all this time. And strange, stranger because of lost familiarity than any newcomer's face could be.

52   She had time to think of all that before his hand reached out to touch her, and spanned the gap of eighteen months. Now, again, there was nothing to say, because there was no need. They were together, and for the moment that was enough.

53   "Where's the baby?"

54   "Sleeping. She'll be up any minute."

55   No urgency. Their voices were as casual as though it were a daily exchange, as though war and separation did not exist. Margaret picked up the coat he'd thrown on the chair near the door and hung it carefully in the hall closet. She went to check the roast, leaving him to wander through the rooms by himself, remembering and coming back. She found him, finally, standing over the baby's crib.

56   She couldn't see his face, but she had no need to.

57   "I think we can wake her just this once." Margaret pulled the covers down and lifted the white bundle from the bed. Sleepy lids pulled back heavily from smoky brown eyes.

58   "Hello." Hank's voice was tentative.

59   "Hello." The baby's assurance was more pronounced.

60   He had heard about it, of course, but that wasn't the same as hearing it. He turned eagerly to Margaret. "She really can—?"

61   "Of course she can, darling. But what's more important, she can even do nice normal things like other babies do, even stupid ones. Watch her crawl!" Margaret set the baby on the big bed.

62   For a moment young Henrietta lay and eyed her parents dubiously.

63   "Crawl?" she asked.

64   "That's the idea. Your daddy is new around here, you know. He wants to see you show off."

65   "Then put me on my tummy."

66   "Oh, of course." Margaret obligingly rolled the baby over.

67   "What's the matter?" Hank's voice was still casual, but an undercurrent in it began to charge the air of the room. "I thought they turned over first."

68   "This baby"—Margaret would not notice the tension—"*This* baby does things when she wants to."

69   This baby's father watched with softening eyes while the head advanced and the body hunched up propelling itself across the bed.

70   "Why, the little rascal." He burst into relieved laughter. "She looks like one of those potato-sack racers they used to have on picnics. Got her arms pulled out of the sleeves already." He reached over and grabbed the knot at the bottom of the long nightie.

71   "I'll do it, darling." Margaret tried to get there first.

72   "Don't be silly, Maggie. This may be *your* first baby, but *I* had five kid brothers." He laughed her away, and reached with his other hand for the string that closed one sleeve. He opened the sleeve bow and groped for an arm.

73   "The way you wriggle," he addressed his child sternly, as his hand touched a moving knob of flesh at the shoulder, "anyone might think you are a worm, using your tummy to crawl on, instead of your hands and feet."

74   Margaret stood and watched, smiling. "Wait till you hear her sing, darling—"

75   His right hand traveled down from the shoulder to where he thought an arm would be, traveled down, and straight down, over firm small muscles that writhed in an attempt to move against the pressure of his hand. He let his fingers drift up again to the shoulder. With infinite care he opened the knot at the bottom of the nightgown. His wife was standing by the bed, saying. "She can do 'Jingle Bells,' and—"

76   His left hand felt along the soft knitted fabric of the gown, up toward the diaper that folded, flat and smooth, across the bottom end of his child. No wrinkles. No kicking. *No* . . .

77   "Maggie." He tried to pull his hands from the neat fold in the diaper, from the wriggling body. "Maggie." His throat was dry; words came hard, low and grating. He spoke very slowly, thinking the sound of each word to make himself say it. His head was spinning, but he had to *know* before he let it go. "Maggie, why . . . didn't you . . . tell me?"

78   "Tell you what darling?" Margaret's poise was the immemorial patience of woman confronted with man's childish impetuosity. Her sudden laugh sounded fantastically easy and natural in that room; it was all
clear to her now. "Is she wet? I didn't know."

79   *She didn't know.* His hands, beyond control, ran up and down the
soft-skinned baby body, the sinuous, limbless body. *Oh God, dear God—*
his head shook and his muscles contracted in a bitter spasm of hysteria.
His fingers tightened on his child—*Oh God, she didn't know . . .*

DISCUSSION QUESTIONS

1. Throughout the story there are hints of what has caused the
   alarming mutations. What probably happened?
2. There are early warning signs about her baby, but Maggie discounts
   or ignores them. Why?
3. Maggie sees her child as a prodigy, talking and singing at seven
   months, yet unable to crawl for two more. Why doesn't this dis-
   crepancy bother her?
4. Why do juries refuse to convict fathers of the increasing crime of
   infanticide?
5. The story takes place in 1953, and Maggie says they could have
   stopped "it" in 1946 and 1947. What is "it"?

WRITING TOPICS

1. Why doesn't Maggie even *know* the truth about her baby? Do you
   know of any other situations where someone has refused to admit the
   truth, even to him or herself? Write a short essay with specific examples to illustrate your answer.
2. The story is told from Maggie's point of view. In your journal, show
   how her letters to her husband Hank provide clues that Maggie isn't
   being entirely honest.
3. The story takes place in New York City, yet Hiroshima, Nagasaki,
   and Oak Ridge, Tennessee, are referred to more than once. In a paragraph or two, explain how these cities are significant to the story.

CHAPTER FIVE

The Fifties

1950

Douglas MacArthur named Commander of U.N. forces when Korean War breaks out

U.S.S.R. and Communist China sign 30-year pact

Riots occur in Johannesburg against apartheid

U.S. sends arms and advisors to Vietnam

Severe restrictions put on communists in U.S. via McCarlan Act

Einstein's General Field Theory expands his Theory of Relativity

Antihistamines gain widespread use for colds and allergies

Doubleday begins publishing major science fiction authors including Isaac Asimov and Ray Bradbury

Fifteen science fiction magazines begin production, including *Galaxy* and *Science Fantasy*

1951

Color TV introduced

Electric atomic power produced

Jules Verne's *Mysterious Island* is serialized

1952

Britain produces its first atomic bomb

U.S. explodes first hydrogen bomb

Oral contraceptives introduced

1953

Korean War ends

Lung cancer attributed to cigarette smoking

Frederick Pohl's *Star Science Fiction Stories* anthology published by Ballantine, which begins producing quality paperback originals

First Hugo Award, named after Hugo Gernsback, given

1954

Senator Joseph McCarthy begins communist "witch hunts" on TV

Segregation by color in U.S. public schools ruled unconstitutional

U.S. submarine *Nautilis* converted to nuclear power

Dr. Jonas Salk produces polio vaccine and begins injecting schoolchildren

***Them!*, a movie about giant ants, stars James Arness**

Disney studios produces *20,000 Leagues Under the Sea*, a film version of the Jules Verne novel

African Americans in Montgomery, Alabama, boycott segregated city bus line

First atomic power plant built at Schenectady, New York

Rock and roll begins

Martin Luther King Jr. emerges as civil rights leader

F.W. Muller develops ion microscope

Oral polio vaccine developed by Dr. Albert Sabin

Forbidden Planet features the first cinematic use of Isaac Asimov's Three Laws of Robotics

Bobby Fischer is national junior chess champion at 13

Sputnik I launched by Russians

Sputnik II carries a dog into space

Beatnik movement spreads from California across U.S.

Wernher von Braun, German scientist who designed the V2 rockets, helps U.S. develop the *Explorer* satellite

U.S. *Explorer* weighs 31 lbs; U.S.S.R. *Sputnik III* weighs 3,000 lbs.

Stereophonic recordings begin

U.S. establishes NASA

Van Allen radiation belts discovered around Earth

The Fly, with Vincent Price, is a popular science fiction film

Fidel Castro, after overthrowing dictator Fulgencio Batista, becomes Premier of Cuba

Hawaii becomes 50th state

Russian *Lunik III* takes the first moon photos from space; *Lunik II* reaches the moon

U.S.S.R. launches two monkeys in one rocket

Fiction publishes first French science fiction anthology

1955

1956

1957

1958

1959

HISTORICAL CONTEXT

At the end of World War II, Korea was divided at the 38th parallel into Soviet-controlled North Korea and U.S.-managed South Korea. In 1950, the North launched a surprise attack. The United States and the United Nations supplied troops, and General Douglas MacArthur was appointed commander. By the end of 1950, U.N. forces had driven the communist forces back, but then China entered the war on behalf of North Korea. This caused MacArthur to call for all-out war, including the use of nuclear weapons. However, President Truman wasn't willing to use the atomic bomb again, and he eventually fired MacArthur for quarreling with his commander-in-chief and possibly triggering a worldwide nuclear catastrophe. An uneasy cease-fire finally ended the war in 1953, at a cost of over three million lives.

Meanwhile, nations around the globe began to assert their independence from colonial rule. Kenyan nationalists rebelled against British rule, leading to Kenyan independence. Algeria faced a similar situation as the Muslim population, which was prohibited from voting because of French colonial rule, began its struggle for independence. Because of the cost in money and lives, the French later gave up control and allowed Algeria to become independent.

In Vietnam, Ho Chi Minh and his communist government seized power from French forces in 1954, and Vietnam was then divided similarly to Korea. North Vietnam was communistic, and the United States formed the Southeast Asian Treaty Organization (SEATO) to defend against communism in South Vietnam. Meanwhile, the bordering countries of Laos and Cambodia gained independence from outside rule.

Communist-ruled Hungary also attempted social reforms in 1956, but when Hungarians demanded withdrawal of Soviet troops, Soviet premier Nikita Khrushchev quickly stopped the rebellion with tanks and troops. This established the harsh manner of dealing with rebellions that would dominate Soviet politics for years and continues to some extent today.

In the United States, the Supreme Court ruled in 1954 in *Brown v. Board of Education* that school segregation based on race was unconstitutional, throwing out the previous "separate but equal" doctrine. As a result, in 1957 the governor of Arkansas called the National Guard to prevent African Americans from enrolling in public schools, forcing President Eisenhower to send in federal troops. By 1960 five southern states still had no integrated schools. Meanwhile, in 1955 an African-American woman, Rosa Parks, refused to give up her bus seat to a white man in Montgomery, Alabama, touching off protests in that city. Martin Luther King Jr. organized bus boycotts by the city's African-American residents. The resulting economic losses eventually forced the city to rescind its laws giving preference to white citizens.

The Soviets made international headlines in 1957 when they launched *Sputnik,* the world's first space satellite. It weighed 184 pounds, was 23 inches in diameter, and transmitted clear radio signals to Earth. A month later they sent a live dog into orbit. The following year the United States put its first satellite, *Explorer,* into space and the space race was on.

Trouble was brewing between Soviet and Chinese communists. When Khrushchev gave an anti-Stalin speech in 1956, Mao broke relations with the U.S.S.R. and started economic reforms based on his ideas of true communism. He formed 24,000 agricultural communes of about 30,000 people each, hoping to establish a "Great Leap Forward" by putting the people to work in manageable units, organized for the benefit of all. But by 1960 his experiment was in ruins and millions died of starvation due to poor administrative control and a series of agricultural disasters.

The United States, however, was busy trying to stop communism closer to home. In 1952, General Fulgencio Batista suspended Cuba's democratic constitution and set himself up as a dictator. At that time the United States backed Fidel Castro in his guerrilla campaign to take back the country and restore civil liberties and free elections. However, when Castro successfully got rid of Batista in 1959, those reforms didn't appear. It soon became obvious that Castro was setting himself up as a communistic head of state.

After World War II, anticommunist fever swept rapidly throughout the United States, fueled in part by the renewed attacks of Senator Joseph McCarthy. He accused many prominent people, including World War II hero George C. Marshall, of being involved in a communist conspiracy. Senator Robert Taft and congressman Richard Nixon joined in the attacks. Soon the State Department was forbidding distribution of books, artwork, and music by suspected communists. Libraries got rid of suspected texts, often burning books by John Steinbeck, Dashiell Hammett, and even tales of Robin Hood. In 1954, McCarthy attacked the army in a series of televised hearings. When the secretary of the navy leveled counter charges, McCarthy labeled the secretary a communist. The army hearings quickly exposed the senator's complete lack of evidence, and Americans saw on national TV broadcasts that he was using the accusations to promote himself. McCarthy's career ended in ruin.

Also in the fifties, President Eisenhower began planning and constructing the freeway systems for civilian travel and emergency troop transport, as he had seen the *autobahns* used in Germany. Americans were moving to the suburbs in increasing numbers, and the freeways contributed to the ease of automobile transportation. Parents who had children in the postwar baby boom were trying to provide opportunities for their children that they themselves had not had. As the population became increasingly mobile, integration moved slowly across the country. Soon American pop music began to change as black rhythm and blues and white country music influenced each other. The result was a new musical mixture—rock and roll.

DEVELOPMENTS IN SCIENCE FICTION

The Golden Age of the forties was followed by the Nuclear Age of the fifties. As the threat of nuclear war loomed, many families constructed backyard fallout shelters stocked with canned food,

water, guns, radios, and Geiger counters to detect radiation.
Schools regularly practiced atomic air raid drills, and science
fiction writers portrayed postapocalyptic futures. Most of these
presumed that a period of rebuilding would follow a worldwide
catastrophe, and that eventually a drastically changed civilization
would emerge after the fall of established societies.

Science fiction was riding a wave of popularity for several
reasons. One was that more people were worried about the state
of global affairs following World War II. The world was in a state
of cultural and social upheaval as a new generation struggled to
understand the political balance of power and the factors which
might at any moment plunge the world into catastrophe. Another
was that as the birth rate increased following the war, parents were
lavishing attention and consumable goods on their children, and
the postwar economic boom provided young people with more
disposable income. A rising, politically aware youth culture was
beginning to perceive that the older generation had created an
unstable world. This situation would lead to divisive protest riots
across the United States in the sixties as these youths came of age.
Teenagers in the fifties were reading speculative fiction about what
might happen to the world situation they had no hand in creating
and pondering what, if any, their options were.

Another factor that contributed to the expanding science
fiction market was a significant change in the magazine distribution network. The collapse of American News Company, a major
distributor, the growing popularity of TV, and the establishment
of original paperback fiction were additional factors in the disappearance of the pulps. Magazines that relied heavily on advertising
were hardly affected, but the cheaply produced pulps depended
almost entirely on volume sales for profit. They soon disappeared
as book-length novels and anthologies began going straight to
paperback. There were still hardback science fiction books, but
those were mostly published after a successful magazine serial-
ization created demand for reprints. In 1940 only a few million
paperback books were published in the United States; by 1955
this had risen to over 220 million. Likewise, in 1944, a total of 44
paperback publishers produced 4,500 titles; in 1962, some 198
publishers produced 17,900 titles. Of the huge number of science
fiction magazines in existence at the beginning of the fifties, only

six survived until 1960: *Amazing Stories, Astounding Science Fiction, The Magazine of Fantasy and Science Fiction, Galaxy, Fantastic,* and *If.*

The Magazine of Fantasy and Science Fiction actually started in the fall of 1949, with Anthony Boucher and J. Francis McComas as editors. It emphasized quality new fiction as well as reprints by prestigious authors. Beginning in 1958, every issue featured a science article by Isaac Asimov. It won the Hugo award for best science novel in 1958 and 1959. It is one of the few major science fiction magazines that continues to be published today.

The writers who were prominent in the fifties expanded on and deepened the themes introduced during the thirties and forties. The writers of this decade were generally more mature and writing for a more knowledgeable audience, including many college-educated ex-GIs. Writers and readers were enthusiastic about the growing amount of quality science fiction, and patterns soon emerged. The most prominent was nuclear disaster. H. L. Gold, editor of *Galaxy,* said that in 1952, about 90 percent of the stories submitted to that magazine were about postatomic or biological war, and this recurring idea can be seen in several major works of the decade.

Clifford Simak, in his highly regarded *City* (1952), depicts a time after human beings have disappeared. Robots and intelligent dogs gather and tell legends about humans, though none know for certain if these are fact or fiction. The overall pessimistic tone of the novel reflects Simak's disillusionment with the horrors of war and its aftermath.

Ray Bradbury's *The Martian Chronicles* (1952), a loosely connected series of short stories, tells the history of the colonization of Mars. The Martians ignore the humans, but eventually the humans bring disease and ruin to the Martian culture. This compares with the displacement of Native Americans by European settlers in America's past. In *Fahrenheit 451* (1953), books are banned and firemen exist to burn books, rather than to stop burnings. One day a fireman actually reads one of the books he is supposed to burn and discovers knowledge he doesn't want to destroy. He is hunted and finally discovers a group of rebel intellectuals who are trying to preserve great literature. These people memorize it, hoping for a time when people will again value great ideas. This was written at the time that the McCarthy "witch hunts" were in full swing, causing libraries to actually burn books. *Fahrenheit 451* is clearly an anti-McCarthyism novel that would have been difficult to publish in any other genre without being banned itself.

Isaac Asimov also produced an anti-McCarthy novel, *The Martian Way* (1952); a protest against the Korean War, *C-Chute* (1951); an H-bomb warning, *Silly Asses* (1957); and an allegory about the relationship between blacks and whites, *Caves of Steel* (1954), in which robots take people's jobs and "pass" for human. William Golding's *The Lord of the Flies* (1954) is a deeply disturbing story about children who are stranded after a nuclear holocaust. They set up their own government and proceed to reenact the same horrors as their adult role models did on each other. John Wyndam's *The Day of the Triffids* (1951) features sentient, ambulatory plants (triffids) who hunt humans. After a meteor shower leaves most people blind and helpless, the remaining survivors huddle together on the Isle of Wight, leaving England to the triffids. Walter Miller's *A Canticle for Leibowitz* (1959) shows three stages in the development of civilization: small communities struggle to preserve the past; someone finds a way to restart civilization; and the apocalypse repeats.

Philip Jose Farmer challenged one of the taboos in science fiction in the fifties. Science fiction had avoided dealing with sexual situations, partly because much of it had been relegated to the youth category. Women, when they did appear in the male-dominated genre, generally existed either to be rescued by men, or lectured to by them, though this had eased somewhat in the forties under Campbell's leadership. The heritage of science fiction as "scientific romance" was the romance of adventure, not love, and when women were part of early science fiction, there was little attention to realistic relationships or sex.

Women hadn't yet taken a prominent role in society, and science fiction writers seemed intent on keeping it that way, regardless of their forward thinking in other areas. Thus, when Farmer's novella *The Lovers* was published in *Startling Stories* in 1952, it created an avalanche of criticism. Farmer made the story of a human falling in love with an alien in human form quite explicit, unlike authors such as Edgar Rice Burroughs, who avoided the sexual side of any relationship. The protests regarding Farmer's preoccupation with

the physical side of relationships did not deter him, and he
produced a string of other similarly oriented novels, including
Flesh (1960).

SCIENCE FICTION IN OTHER MEDIA

Illustrators did not show this same reluctance toward the human
form, though, and magazine and book covers regularly featured
scantily clad women and implied sexual situations. Comics went
through a difficult time in the fifties, partly due to a book by psychiatrist Frederic Wertham. His seven-year study of the effects of
comics on children was a devastating condemnation. In Britain,
horror comics were banned, and in the United States, comic publishers joined together to form the Comics Code Authority, tout-
ing "wholesome" comics. This forced E.C. (Educational Comics),
a producer of quality science fiction, horror, Western, and romance titles, to cancel production. The desire to protect children
against the adult content of the material, the widespread fear of
communist influence on the comics industry, and the threat of nuclear war all added to the push to rid the newsstands of objection-
able material. E.C. was able to stay in business only by reorganiz-
ing and producing a satire periodical, *Mad Magazine*, employing
many of the same E.C. artists and writers.

Movies and TV also produced more science fiction in the
fifties. *The Day the Earth Stood Still* (1951) portrayed a realistic flying
saucer and peace-loving aliens who are attacked by the fear-har-
boring humans. James Arness starred as the vegetable-based creature in the movie adaptation of John W. Campbell Jr.'s "Who Goes
There," titled *The Thing* for its 1951 release. *The War of the Worlds*,
adapted from H. G. Wells' book, also appeared that year, as did an
intelligent Disney production of *20,000 Leagues Under the Sea*, based
on Jules Verne's novel. *When Worlds Collide* (1953) shows the reaction to an imminent worldwide catastrophe and the decision making that determines who gets to start over on another planet.

Invasion of the Body Snatchers (1955), a low-budget horror
movie, presents a metaphorical depiction of alien communist
invaders. In 1956, George Orwell's *1984* presented a chilling, gov-

ernment-controlled police state, and in 1959, *On the Beach* showed a pessimistic but moving account of the last people on Earth after an atomic disaster. On the whole, though, science fiction was plagued by a number of monster movies and mindless thrills, increasing the public perception that this was not serious literature. When *Godzilla* premiered in 1955, it spawned a whole host of sequels and imitations, featuring badly dubbed Japanese dialogue and a complete lack of believability. However, many of these struck a chord with audiences, perhaps because of the inherent antinuclear message they contained.

A few half hour TV programs aired during the fifties. *Captain Video* (1949-53 and 1955–56), *Tales of Tomorrow* (1951–56), and *Science Fiction Theater* (1955 57) all had low budgets, almost nonexistent special effects, and mostly juvenile plots. Occasionally, though, *Science Fiction Theater* treated its subject matter seriously, and the debut of *The Twilight Zone* in 1959 was promising.

The Exiles

1950

RAY BRADBURY (b. 1920)

Ray Bradbury began writing for the pulp magazines, with his first
published story, "Pendulum," appearing in the 1941 issue of *Super
Science Stories*. A collection of his stories, loosely linked, appeared
under the title *The Martian Chronicles* in 1950. With the success of this
venture, his reputation rose and he found a market in the "slicks,"
including *Esquire, The Saturday Evening Post,* and *McCall's*. He soon
followed this with *Fahrenheit 451* (1951), a story about books being
banned and burned publicly. It was a haunting reminder of the
search for and destruction of communist-influenced books
in this country at that time.

Important collections of his stories include *The Illustrated Man*
(1951) which was made into a movie in 1968, *The Golden Apples of
the Sun* (1953), and the double volume *The Stories of Ray Bradbury*
(1980). Other significant collections of Bradbury stories include
The Machineries of Joy (1964), *I Sing the Body Electric* (1969), and
The Toynbee Convector (1988). His works have also been adapted to
both series of *The Twilight Zone* (1959–64, 1985–87) as well as the
Ray Bradbury Theatre (1985-86). His works have appeared in over
800 anthologies and he is highly regarded as a literary figure.
Although a prolific writer, Bradbury's total science fiction output
is small because he also writes crime fiction, mainstream fiction,
poetry, and screenplays. The latter include *Moby Dick* (1956) and
Picasso Summer (1972). Graphic novels featuring his stories include
The Autumn People (1965) and *Tomorrow Midnight* (1966).

In "The Exiles," Ray Bradbury takes a playful look at what
might happen if certain traditions and literary texts were examined under the harsh microscope of science. In the process, he
speculates about the relationship of authors to their audiences.

1   Their eyes were fire and the breath flamed out the witches' mouths as they bent to probe the caldron with greasy stick and bony finger.

> *"When shall we three meet again*
> *In thunder, lightning, or in rain?"*

2   They danced drunkenly on the shore of an empty sea, fouling the air with their three tongues, and burning it with their cats' eyes malevolently aglitter:

> *"Round about the cauldron go;*
> *In the poison'd entrails throw. . . .*
> *Double, double, toil and trouble;*
> *Fire burn, and cauldron bubble!"*

3   They paused and cast a glance about. "Where's the crystal? Where the needles?"

4   "Here!"

5   "Good!"

6   "Is the yellow wax thickened?"

7   "Yes!"

8   "Pour it in the iron mold!"

9   "Is the wax figure done?" They shaped it like molasses adrip on their green hands.

10   "Shove the needle through the heart!"

11   "The crystal, the crystal; fetch it from the tarot bag. Dust it off; have a look!"

12   They bent to the crystal, their faces white.

> *"See, see, see . . ."*

13   A rocket ship moved through space from the planet Earth to the planet Mars. On the rocket ship men were dying.

14   The captain raised his head, tiredly. "We'll have to use the morphine."

15   "But, Captain—"

16   "You see yourself this man's condition." The captain lifted the wool blanket and the man restrained beneath the wet sheet moved and groaned. The air was full of sulphurous thunder.

17   "I saw it—I saw it." The man opened his eyes and stared at the port where there were only black spaces, reeling stars, Earth far removed, and the planet Mars rising large and red. "I saw it—a bat, a huge thing, a bat

with a man's face, spread over the front port. Fluttering and fluttering, fluttering and fluttering."

18 "Pulse?" asked the captain.

19 The orderly measured it. "One hundred and thirty."

20 "He can't go on with that. Use the morphine. Come along, Smith."

21 They moved away. Suddenly the floor plates were laced with bone and white skulls that screamed. The captain did not dare look down, and over the screaming he said, "Is this where Perse is?" turning in at a hatch.

22 A white-smocked surgeon stepped away from a body. "I just don't understand it."

23 "How did Perse die?"

24 "We don't know, Captain. It wasn't his heart, his brain, or shock. He just—died."

25 The captain felt the doctor's wrist, which changed to a hissing snake and bit him. The captain did not flinch. "Take care of yourself. You've a pulse too."

26 The doctor nodded. "Perse complained of pains—needles, he said—in his wrists and legs. Said he felt like wax, melting. He fell. I helped him up. He cried like a child. Said he had a silver needle in his heart. He died. Here he is. We can repeat the autopsy for you. Everything's physically normal."

27 "That's impossible! He died of *something!*"

28 The captain walked to a port. He smelled of menthol and iodine and green soap on his polished and manicured hands. His white teeth were dentifriced, and his ears scoured to a pinkness, as were his cheeks. His uniform was the color of new salt, and his boots were black mirrors shining below him. His crisp crewcut hair smelled of sharp alcohol. Even his breath was sharp and new and clean. There was no spot to him. He was a fresh instrument, honed and ready, still hot from the surgeon's oven.

29 The men with him were from the same mold. One expected huge brass keys spiraling slowly from their backs. They were expensive, talented, well-oiled toys, obedient and quick.

30 The captain watched the planet Mars grow very large in space.

31 "We'll be landing in an hour on that damned place. Smith, did you see any bats, or have other nightmares?"

32 "Yes, sir. The month before our rocket took off from New York, sir. White rats biting my neck, drinking my blood. I didn't tell. I was afraid you wouldn't let me come on this trip."

33 "Never mind," sighed the captain. "I had dreams too. In all of my fifty years I never had a dream until that week before we took off from Earth.

And then every night I dreamed I was a white wolf. Caught on a snowy hill. Shot with a silver bullet. Buried with a stake in my heart." He moved his head toward Mars. "Do you think, Smith, *they* know we're coming?"

34   "We don't know if there *are* Martian people, sir."

35   "Don't we? They began frightening us off eight weeks ago, before we started. They've killed Perse and Reynolds now. Yesterday they made Grenville go blind. How? I don't know. Bats, needles, dreams, men dying for no reason. I'd call it witchcraft in another day. But this is the year 2120, Smith. We're rational men. This all can't be happening. But it is! Whoever they are, with their needles and their bats, they'll try to finish us all." He swung about. "Smith, fetch those books from my file. I want them when we land."

36   Two hundred books were piled on the rocket deck.

37   "Thank you, Smith. Have you glanced at them? Think I'm insane? Perhaps. It's a crazy hunch. At that last moment I ordered these books from the Historical Museum. Because of my dreams. Twenty nights I was stabbed, butchered, a screaming bat pinned to a surgical mat, a thing rotting underground in a black box; bad, wicked dreams. Our whole crew dreamed of witch-things and were-things, vampires and phantoms, things they *couldn't* know anything about. Why? Because books on such ghastly subjects were destroyed a century ago. By law. Forbidden for any-one to own the grisly volumes. These books you see here are the *last* copies, kept for historical purposes in the locked museum vaults."

38   Smith bent to read the dusty titles:

39   "*Tales of Mystery and Imagination*, by Edgar Allan Poe. *Dracula*, by Bram Stoker. *Frankenstein*, by Mary Shelley. *The Turn of the Screw*, by Henry James. *The Legend of Sleepy Hollow*, by Washington Irving. *Rappaccini's Daughter*, by Nathaniel Hawthorne. *An Occurrence at Owl Creek Bridge*, by Ambrose Bierce. *Alice in Wonderland*, by Lewis Carroll. *The Willows*, by Algernon Blackwood. *The Wizard of Oz*, by L. Frank Baum. *The Weird Shadow Over Innsmouth*, by H. P. Lovecraft. And more! Books by Walter de la Mare, Wakefield, Harvey, Wells, Asquith, Huxley—all forbidden authors. All burned in the same year that Halloween was outlawed and Christmas was banned! But, sir, what good are these to us on the rocket?"

40   "I don't know," sighed the captain, "yet."

41   The three hags lifted the crystal where the captain's image flick-ered, his tiny voice tinkling out of the glass:

42   "I don't know," sighed the captain, "yet."

43   The three witches glared redly into one another's faces.

44   "We haven't much time," said one.

45   "Better warn *Them* in the City."

46   "They'll want to know about the books. It doesn't look good. That fool of a captain."

47   "In an hour they'll land their rocket."

48   The three hags shuddered and blinked up at the Emerald City by the edge of the dry Martian sea. In its highest window a small man held a blood-red drape aside. He watched the wastelands where the three witches fed their caldron and shaped the waxes. Farther along, ten thousand other blue fires and laurel incenses, black tobacco smokes and fir weeds, cinnamons and bone dusts rose soft as moths through the Martian night. The man counted the angry, magical fires. Then, as the three witches stared, he turned. The crimson drape, released, fell, causing the distant portal to wink, like a yellow eye.

49   Mr. Edgar Allan Poe stood in the tower window, a faint vapor of spirits upon his breath. "Hecate's friends are busy tonight," he said, seeing the witches, far below.

50   A voice behind him said, "I saw Will Shakespeare at the shore, earlier, whipping them on. All along the sea Shakespeare's army alone, tonight, numbers thousands: the three witches, Oberon, Hamlet's father, Puck—all, all of them—thousands! Good lord, a regular sea of people."

51   "Good William." Poe turned. He let the crimson drape fall shut. He stood for a moment to observe the raw stone room, the black-timbered table, the candle flame, the other man, Mr. Ambrose Bierce, sitting very idly there, lighting matches and watching them burn down, whistling under his breath, now and then laughing to himself.

52   "We'll have to tell Mr. Dickens now," said Mr. Poe. "We've put it off too long. It's a matter of hours. Will you go down to his home with me, Bierce?"

53   Bierce glanced up merrily. "I've just been thinking—what'll happen to us?"

54   "If we can't kill the rocket men off, frighten them away, then we'll have to leave, of course. We'll go on to Jupiter, and when they come to Jupiter, we'll go on to Saturn, and when they come to Saturn, we'll go to Uranus, or Neptune, and then on out to Pluto—"

55   "Where then?"

56   Mr. Poe's face was weary; there were fire coals remaining, fading, in his eyes, and a sad wildness in the way he talked, and a uselessness of his hand and the way his hair fell lankly over his amazing white brow. He was like a satan of some lost dark cause, a general arrived from a derelict invasion. His silky, soft, black mustache was worn away by his musing lips. He was so small his brow seemed to float, vast and phosphorescent, by itself, in the dark room.

57   "We have the advantages of superior forms of travel," he said. "We can always hope for one of their atomic wars, dissolution, the dark ages come again. The return of superstition. We could go back then to Earth, all of us, in one night." Mr. Poe's black eyes brooded under his round and luminant brow. He gazed at the ceiling. "So they're coming to ruin *this* world too? They won't leave *anything* undefiled, will they?"

58   "Does a wolf pack stop until it's killed its prey and eaten the guts? It should be quite a war. I shall sit on the side lines and be the scorekeeper. So many Earthmen boiled in oil, so many Mss. Found in Bottles burnt, so many Earthmen stabbed with needles, so many Red Deaths put to flight by a battery of hypodermic syringes—ha!"

59   Poe swayed angrily, faintly drunk with wine. "What did we do? Be *with* us, Bierce, in the name of God! Did we have a fair trial before a company of literary critics? No! Our books were plucked up by neat, sterile, surgeon's pliers, and flung into vats, to boil, to be killed of all their mortuary germs. Damn them all!"

60   "I find our situation amusing," said Bierce.

61   They were interrupted by a hysterical shout from the tower stair.

62   "Mr. Poe! Mr. Bierce!"

63   "Yes, yes, we're coming!" Poe and Bierce descended to find a man gasping against the stone passage wall.

64   "Have you heard the news?" he cried immediately, clawing at them like a man about to fall over a cliff. "In an hour they'll land! They're bringing books with them—*old* books, the witches said! What're you doing in the tower at a time like this? Why aren't you acting?"

65   Poe said: "We're doing everything we can, Blackwood. You're new to all this. Come along, we're going to Mr. Charles Dickens' place—"

66   "—to contemplate our doom, our black doom," said Mr. Bierce, with a wink.

67   They moved down the echoing throats of the castle, level after dim green level, down into mustiness and decay and spiders and dreamlike webbing. "Don't worry," said Poe, his brow like a huge white lamp before them, descending, sinking. "All along the dead sea tonight I've called others. Your friends and mine, Blackwood—Bierce. They're all there. The animals and the old women and the tall men with the sharp white teeth. The traps are waiting; the pits, yes, and the pendulums. The Red Death." Here he laughed quietly. "Yes, even the Red Death. I never thought—no, I never thought the time would come when a thing like the Red Death would actually *be*. But *they* asked for it, and they shall have it!"

68   "But are we strong enough?" wondered Blackwood.

69   "How strong is strong? They won't be prepared for us, at least. They haven't the imagination. Those clean young rocket men with their anti-septic bloomers and fish-bowl helmets, with their new religion. About their necks, on gold chains, scalpels. Upon their heads, a diadem of microscopes. In their holy fingers, steaming incense urns which in reality are only germicidal ovens for steaming out superstition. The names of Poe, Bierce, Hawthorne, Blackwood—blasphemy to their clean lips."

70   Outside the castle they advanced through a watery space, a tarn that was not a tarn, which misted before them like the stuff of nightmares. The air filled with wing sounds and whirring, a motion of winds and blacknesses. Voices changed, figures swayed at campfires. Mr. Poe watched the needles knitting, knitting, knitting, in the firelight; knitting pain and misery, knitting wickedness into wax marionettes, clay puppets. The caldron smells of wild garlic and cayenne and saffron hissed up to fill the night with evil pungency.

71   "Get on with it!" said Poe. "I'll be back!"

72   All down the empty seashore black figures spindled and waned, grew up and blew into black smoke on the sky. Bells rang in mountain towers and licorice ravens spilled out with the bronze sounds and spun away to ashes.

73   Over a lonely moor and into a small valley Poe and Bierce hurried, and found themselves quite suddenly on a cobbled street, in cold, bleak, biting weather, with people stomping up and down stony courtyards to warm their feet; foggy withal, and candles flaring in the windows of offices and shops where hung the Yuletide turkeys. At a distance some boys, all bundled up, snorting their pale breaths on the wintry air, were trilling, "God Rest Ye Merry, Gentlemen," while the immense tones of a great clock continuously sounded midnight. Children dashed by from the baker's with dinners all asteam in their grubby fists, on trays and under silver bowls.

74   At a sign which red SCROOGE, MARLEY AND DICKENS, Poe gave the Marley-faced knocker a rap, and from within, as the door popped open a few inches, a sudden gust of music almost swept them into a dance. And there, beyond the shoulder of the man who was sticking a trim goatee and mustaches at them, was Mr. Fezziwig clapping his hands, and Mrs. Fezziwig, one vast substantial smile, dancing and colliding with other merrymakers, while the fiddle chirped and laughter ran about a table like chandelier crystals given a sudden push of wind. The large table was heaped with brawn and turkey and holly and geese; with mince pies, suckling pigs, wreaths of sausages, oranges and apples; and

there was Bob Cratchit and Little Dorrit and Tiny Tim and Mr. Fagin himself, and a man who looked as if he might be an undigested bit of beef, a blot of mustard, a crumb of cheese, a fragment of an underdone potato—who else but Mr. Marley, chains and all, while the wine poured and the brown turkeys did their excellent best to steam!

75   "What do you want?" demanded Mr. Charles Dickens.

76   "We've come to plead with you again, Charles; we need your help," said Poe.

77   "Help? Do you think I would help you fight against those good men coming in the rocket? I don't belong here, anyway. My books were burned by mistake. I'm no supernaturalist, no writer of horrors and terrors like you, Poe; you, Bierce, or the others. I'll have nothing to do with you terrible people!"

78   "You are a persuasive talker," reasoned Poe. "You could go to meet the rocket men, lull them, lull their suspicions and then—then we would take care of them."

79   Mr. Dickens eyed the folds of the black cape which hid Poe's hands. From it, smiling, Poe drew forth a black cat. "For *one* of our visitors."

80   "And for the others?"

81   Poe smiled again, well pleased. "The Premature Burial?"

82   "You are a grim man, Mr. Poe."

83   "I am a frightened and an angry man. I am a god, Mr. Dickens, even as you are a god, even as we all are gods, and our inventions—our people, if you wish—have not only been threatened, but banished and burned, torn up and censored, ruined and done away with. The worlds we created are falling into ruin. Even gods must fight!"

84   "So?" Mr. Dickens tilted his head, impatient to return to the party, the music, the food. "Perhaps you can explain why we are here? How did we come here?"

85   "War begets war. Destruction begets destruction. On Earth, a century ago, in the year 2020 they outlawed our books. Oh, what a horrible thing—to destroy our literary creations that way! It summoned us out of—what? Death? The Beyond? I don't like abstract things. I don't know. I only know that our worlds and our creations called us and we tried to save them, and the only saving thing we could do was wait out the century here on Mars, hoping Earth might overweight itself with these scientists and their doubtings; but now they're coming to clean us out of here, us and our dark things, and all the alchemists, witches, vampires, and were-things that, one by one, retreated across space as science made inroads through every country on Earth and finally left no alternative at all but exodus. You must help us. You have a good speaking manner. We need you."

86   "I repeat, I am not of you. I don't approve of you and the others,"
cried Dickens angrily. "I was no player with witches and vampires and
midnight things."

87   "What of *A Christmas Carol?*"

88   "Ridiculous! *One* story. Oh, I wrote a few others about ghosts, perhaps, but what of that? My basic works had none of that nonsense!"

89   "Mistaken or not, they grouped you with us. They destroyed your
books—your worlds too. You must hate them, Mr. Dickens!"

90   "I admit they are stupid and rude, but that is all. Good day!"

91   "Let Mr. Marley come, at least!"

92   "*No!*"

93   The door slammed. As Poe turned away, down the street, skim-
ming over the frosty ground, the coachman playing a lively air on a
bugle, came a great coach, out of which, cherry-red, laughing and
singing, piled the Pickwickians, banging on the door, shouting Merry
Christmas good and loud, when the door was opened by the fat boy.

94   Mr. Poe hurried along the midnight shore of the dry sea. By fires
and smoke he hesitated, to shout orders, to check the bubbling cal-
drons, the poisons and the chalked pentagrams. "Good!" he said, and
ran on. "Fine!" he shouted, and ran again. People joined him and ran
with him. Here were Mr. Coppard and Mr. Machen running with him
now. And there were hating serpents and angry demons and fiery
bronze dragons and spitting vipers and trembling witches like the barbs
and nettles and thorns and all the vile flotsam and jetsam of the retreating sea of imagination, left on the melancholy shore, whining and
frothing and spitting.

95   Mr. Machen stopped. He sat like a child on the cold sand. He
began to sob. They tried to soothe him, but he would not listen. "I just
thought," he said. "What happens to us on the day when the *last* copies
of our books are destroyed?"

96   The air whirled.

97   "Don't speak of it!"

98   "We must," wailed Mr. Machen. "Now, now, as the rocket comes
down, you, Mr. Poe; you, Coppard; you, Bierce—all of you grow faint.
Like wood smoke. Blowing away. Your faces melt—"

99   "Death! *Real* death for all of us."

100   "We exist only through Earth's sufferance. If a final edict tonight
destroyed our last few works we'd be like lights put out."

101   Coppard brooded gently. "I wonder who I am. In what Earth mind
tonight do I exist? In some African hut? Some hermit, reading my
tales? Is he the lonely candle in the wind of time and science? The

flickering orb sustaining me here in rebellious exile? Is it him? Or some boy in a discarded attic, finding me, only just in time! Oh, last night I felt ill, ill, ill to the marrows of me, for there is a body of the soul as well as a body of the body, and this soul body ached in all of its blowing parts, and last night I felt myself a candle, guttering. When suddenly I sprang up, given new light! As some child, sneezing with dust, in some yellow garret on Earth once more found a worn, time-specked copy of me! And so I'm given a short respite!"

102   A door banged wide in a little hut by the shore. A thin short man, with flesh hanging from him in folds, stepped out and, paying no attention to the others, sat down and stared into his clenched fists.

103   "There's the one I'm sorry for," whispered Blackwood. "Look at him, dying away. He was once more real than we, who were men. They took him, a skeleton thought, and clothed him in centuries of pink flesh and snow beard and red velvet suit and black boot; made him reindeers, tinsel, holly. And after centuries of manufacturing him they drowned him in a vat of Lysol, you might say."

104   The men were silent.

105   "What must it be on Earth?" wondered Poe. "Without Christmas? No hot chestnuts, no tree, no ornaments or drums or candles—nothing; nothing but the snow and wind and the lonely, factual people. . . ."

106   They all looked at the thin little old man with the scraggly beard and faded red velvet suit.

107   "Have you heard his story?"

108   "I can imagine it. The glitter-eyed psychiatrist, the clever sociologist, the resentful, froth-mouthed educationalist, the antiseptic parents—"

109   "A regrettable situation," said Bierce, smiling, "for the Yuletide merchants who, toward the last there, as I recall, were beginning to put up holly and sing Noel the day before Halloween. With any luck at all this year they might have started on Labor Day!"

110   Bierce did not continue. He fell forward with a sigh. As he lay upon the ground he had time to say only, "How interesting." And then, as they all watched, horrified, his body burned into blue dust and charred bone, the ashes of which fled through the air in black tatters.

111   "Bierce, Bierce!"

112   "Gone!"

113   "His last book gone. Someone on Earth just now burned it."

114   "God rest him. Nothing of him left now. For what are we but books, and when those are gone, nothing's to be seen."

115   A rushing sound filled the sky.

116   They cried out, terrified, and looked up. In the sky, dazzling it with sizzling fire clouds, was the rocket! Around the men on the seashore

lanterns bobbed; there was a squealing and a bubbling and an odor of cooked spells. Candle-eyed pumpkins lifted into the cold clear air. Thin fingers clenched into fists and a witch screamed from her withered mouth:

> *"Ship, ship, break, fall!*
> *Ship, ship, burn all!*
> *Crack, flake, shake, melt!*
> *Mummy dust, cat pelt!"*

117   "Time to go," murmured Blackwood. "On to Jupiter, on to Saturn or Pluto."

118   "Run away?" shouted Poe in the wind. "Never!"

119   "I'm a tired old man!"

120   Poe gazed into the old man's face and believed him. He climbed atop a huge boulder and faced the ten thousand gray shadows and green lights and yellow eyes on the hissing wind.

121   "The powders!" he shouted.

122   A thick hot smell of bitter almond, civet, cumin, wormseed and orris!

123   The rocket came down—steadily down, with the shriek of a damned spirit! Poe raged at it! He flung his fists up and the orchestra of heat and smell and hatred answered in symphony! Like stripped tree fragments, bats flew upward! Burning hearts, flung like missiles, burst in bloody fireworks on the singed air. Down, down, relentlessly down, like a pendulum the rocket came. And Poe howled, furiously, and shrank back with every sweep and sweep of the rocket cutting and ravening the air! All the dead sea seemed a pit in which, trapped, they waited the sinking of the dread machinery, the glistening ax; they were people under the avalanche!

124   "The snakes!" screamed Poe.

125   And luminous serpentines of undulant green hurtled toward the rocket. But it came down, a sweep, a fire, a motion, and it lay panting out exhaustions of red plumage on the sand, a mile away.

126   "At it!" shrieked Poe. "The plan's changed! Only one chance! Run! At it! At it! Drown them with our bodies! Kill them!"

127   And as if he had commanded a violent sea to change its course, to suck itself free from primeval beds, the whirls and savage gouts of fire spread and ran like wind and rain and stark lightning over the sea sands, down empty river deltas, shadowing and screaming, whistling and whining, sputtering and coalescing toward the rocket which, extinguished, lay like a clean metal torch in the farthest hollow. As if a great charred caldron of sparkling lava had been overturned, the boiling people and snapping animals churned down the dry fathoms.

128   "Kill them!" screamed Poe, running.

129   The rocket men leaped out of their ship, guns ready. They stalked about, sniffing the air like hounds. They saw nothing. They relaxed.

130   The captain stepped forth last. He gave sharp commands. Wood was gathered, kindled, and a fire leapt up in an instant. The captain beckoned his men into a half circle about him.

131   "A new world," he said, forcing himself to speak deliberately, though he glanced nervously, now and again, over his shoulder at the empty sea. "The old world left behind. A new start. What more symbolic than that we here dedicate ourselves all the more firmly to science and progress." He nodded crisply to his lieutenant. "The books."

132   Firelight lined the faded gilt titles: *The Willows, The Outsider, Behold, the Dreamer, Dr. Jekyll and Mr. Hyde, The Land of Oz, Pellucidar, The Land That Time Forgot, A Midsummer Night's Dream,* and the monstrous names of Machen and Edgar Allan Poe and Cabell and Dunsany and Blackwood and Lewis Carroll; the names, the old names, the evil names.

133   "A new world. With a gesture, we burn the last of the old."

134   The captain ripped pages from the books. Leaf by seared leaf, he fed them into the fire.

135   A scream!

136   Leaping back, the men stared beyond the firelight at the edges of the encroaching and uninhabited sea.

137   Another scream! A high and wailing thing, like the death of a dragon and the thrashing of a bronzed whale left gasping when the waters of a leviathan's sea drain down the shingles and evaporate.

138   It was the sound of air rushing in to fill a vacuum, where, a moment before, there had been *something!*

139   The captain neatly disposed of the last book by putting it into the fire.

140   The air stopped quivering.

141   Silence!

142   The rocket men leaned and listened.

143   "Captain, did you hear it?"

144   "No."

145   "Like a wave, sir. On the sea bottom! I thought I saw something. Over there. A black wave. Big. Running at us."

146   "You were mistaken."

147   "There, sir!"

148   "What?"

149   "See it? There! The city! Way over! That green city near the lake! It's splitting in half. It's falling!"

150   The men squinted and shuffled forward.

151   Smith stood trembling among them. He put his hand to his head as if to find a thought there. "I remember. Yes, now I do. A long time

back. When I was a child. A book I read. A story. Oz, I think it was. Yes, Oz. *The Emerald City of Oz* . . ."

152   "Oz? Never heard of it."

153   "Yes, Oz, that's what it was. I saw it just now, like in the story. I saw it fall."

154   "Smith!"

155   "Yes, sir?"

156   "Report for psychoanalysis tomorrow."

157   "Yes, sir!" A brisk salute.

158   "Be careful."

159   The men tiptoed, guns alert, beyond the ship's aseptic light to gaze at the long sea and the low hills.

160   "Why," whispered Smith, disappointed, "there's no one here at all, is there? No one here at all."

161   The wind blew sand over his shoes, whining.

DISCUSSION QUESTIONS

1. It is easy to understand why Halloween might be banned, but why Christmas as well? And why is Santa Claus in the worst shape of all the spirit characters?

2. Why are the medics depicted as so sterile and antiseptic?

3. In small groups, determine why Charles Dickens' books and *Alice in Wonderland* are forbidden texts. Under this system, what other books might be banned? Why?

4. Why does Edgar Allan Poe's spirit say facts are no comfort, only producing lonely people? With a classmate, discuss what this means.

5. What finally "kills" the dead authors for good?

WRITING TOPICS

1. In a few paragraphs, show how science can be compared to a belief system similar to a religion.

2. Do people *need* a belief in the supernatural? Why? Write a journal entry explaining your response.

3. What was happening in the early fifties similar to what Bradbury describes? Write a short essay, describing how his shift of the focus to Mars and the future gives the story more than one level.

Scanners Live in Vain

1950

CORDWAINER SMITH (1913–1966)

Cordwainer Smith was the pseudonym of Paul Myron Anthony
Linebarger, a U.S. diplomat and military adviser in Korea and
Malaysia. He spent much of his youth in Japan and China and was
interested in psychoanalysis and brainwashing techniques. His
unique perspective and background contributed to the complexity
of his stories. Just after World War II, Smith published three sus-
pense novels, but after "Scanners Live in Vain" appeared in 1950,
he published only science fiction. All his stories from that date fit
into a complex universe called the Instrumentality. There is not
much revealed, but a fully developed Future History is implied.
The interconnected stories deal with the complications arising
from the changes in the scanners. They have become distanced
from other humans, and the type of space travel the scanners have
been adapted to is ending. The stories have been collected into
*The Rediscovery of Man: The Complete Short Stories of Cordwainer
Smith* (1994).

    In "Scanners Live in Vain," Cordwainer Smith offers a fasci-
nating view of a possible future where humanity has been divided
into distinct classes, and what might happen when those divisions
are challenged.

1   Martel was angry. He did not even adjust his blood away from anger. He stamped across the room by judgment, not by sight. When he saw the table hit the floor, and could tell by the expression on Luci's face that the table must have made a loud crash, he looked down to see if his leg was broken. It was not. Scanner to the core, he had to scan himself. The action was reflex and automatic. The inventory included his legs, abdomen, chestbox of instruments, hands, arms, face and back with the mirror. Only then did Martel go back to being angry. He talked with his voice, even though he knew that his wife hated its blare and preferred to have him write.

2   "I tell you, I must cranch. I have to cranch. It's my worry, isn't it?"

3   When Luci answered, he saw only a part of her words as he read her lips: "Darling . . . you're my husband . . . right to love you . . . dangerous . . . do it . . . dangerous . . . wait . . ."

4   He faced her, but put sound in his voice, letting the blare hurt her again: "I tell, I'm going to cranch."

5   Catching her expression, he became rueful and a little tender: "Can't you understand what it means to me? To get out of this horrible prison in my own head? To be a man again—hearing your voice, smelling smoke? To *feel* again—to feel my feet on the ground, to feel the air move against my face? Don't you know what it means?"

6   Her wide-eyed worrisome concern thrust him back into pure annoyance. He read only a few words as her lips moved: ". . . love you . . . your own good . . . don't you think I want you to be human? . . . your own good . . . too much . . . he said . . . they said . . ."

7   When he roared at her, he realized that his voice must be particularly bad. He knew that the sound hurt her no less than did the words: "Do you think I wanted you to marry a scanner? Didn't I tell you we're almost as low as the habermans? We're dead, I tell you. We've got to be dead to do our work. How can anybody go to the up-and-out? Can you dream what raw space is? I warned you. But you married me. All right, you married a man. Please, darling, let me be a man. Let me hear your voice, let me feel the warmth of being alive, of being human. Let me!"

8   He saw by her look of stricken assent that he had won the argument. He did not use his voice again. Instead, he pulled his tablet up from where it hung against his chest. He wrote on it, using the pointed fingernail of his right forefinger—the talking nail of a scanner—in quick cleancut script: *Pls, drlng, whrs crnchng wire?*

9   She pulled the long gold-sheathed wire out of the pocket of her apron. She let its field sphere fall to the carpeted floor. Swiftly, dutifully, with the deft obedience of a scanner's wife, she wound the cranching wire around his head, spirally around his neck and chest. She avoided

the instruments set in his chest. She even avoided the radiating scars around the instruments, the stigmata of men who had gone up and into the out. Mechanically he lifted a foot as she slipped the wire between his feet. She drew the wire taut. She snapped the small plug into the high-burden control next to his heart-reader. She helped him to sit down, arranging his hands for him, pushing his head back into the cup at the top of the chair. She turned then, full-face toward him, so that he could read her lips easily. Her expression was composed.

10 She knelt, scooped up the sphere at the other end of the wire, stood erect calmly, her back to him. He scanned her, and saw nothing in her posture but grief which would have escaped the eye of anyone but a scanner. She spoke: he could see her chest-muscles moving. She realized that she was not facing him, and turned so that he could see her lips.

11 "Ready at last?"

12 He smiled a *yes*.

13 She turned her back to him again. (Luci could never bear to watch him go under the wire.) She tossed the wire-sphere into the air. It caught in the force-field, and hung there. Suddenly it glowed. That was all. All—except for the sudden red stinking roar of coming back to his senses. Coming back, across the wild threshold of pain.

14 When he awakened, under the wire, he did not feel as though he had just cranched. Even though it was the second cranching within the week, he felt fit. He lay in the chair. His ears drank in the sound of air touching things in the room. He heard Luci breathing in the next room, where she was hanging up the wire to cool. He smelt the thousand and one smells that are in anybody's room: the crisp freshness of the germ-burner, the sour-sweet tang of the humidifier, the odor of the dinner they had just eaten, the smells of clothes, furniture, of people themselves. All these were pure delight. He sang a phrase or two of his favorite song:

> *"Here's to the haberman, up-and-out!*
> *Up—oh! and out—oh!—up-and-out!...."*

15 He heard Luci chuckle in the next room. He gloated over the sounds of her dress as she swished to the doorway.

16 She gave him her crooked little smile. "You sound all right. Are you all right, really?"

17 Even with this luxury of senses, he scanned. He took the flash-quick inventory which constituted his professional skill. His eyes swept in the news of the instruments. Nothing showed off scale, beyond the

nerve compression hanging in the edge of *Danger*. But he could not worry about the nervebox. That always came through cranching. You couldn't get under the wire without having it show on the nervebox. Some day the box would go to *Overload* and drop back down to *Dead*. That was the way a haberman ended. But you couldn't have everything. People who went to the up-and-out had to pay the price for space.

18   Anyhow, he should worry! He was a scanner. A good one, and he knew it. If he couldn't scan himself, who could? This cranching wasn't too dangerous. Dangerous, but not too dangerous.

19   Luci put out her hand and ruffled his hair as if she had been reading his thoughts, instead of just following them: "But you know you shouldn't have! You shouldn't!"

20   "But I did!" He grinned at her.

21   Her gaiety still forced, she said: "Come on, darling, let's have a good time. I have almost everything there is in the icebox—all your favorite tastes. And I have two new records just full of smells. I tried them out myself, and even I liked them. And you know me—"

22   "Which?"

23   "Which what, you old darling?"

24   He slipped his hand over her shoulders as he limped out of the room. He could never go back to feeling the floor beneath his feet, feeling the air against his face, without being bewildered and clumsy. As if cranching was real, and being a haberman was a bad dream. But he *was* a haberman, and a scanner. "You know what I meant, Luci . . . the smells, which you have. Which one did you like, on the record?"

25   "Well-l-l," said she, judiciously, "there were some lamb chops that were the strangest things—"

26   He interrupted: "What are lambtchots?"

27   "Wait till you smell them. Then guess. I'll tell you this much. It's a smell hundreds and hundreds of years old. They found out about it in the old books."

28   "Is a lambtchot a beast?"

29   "I won't tell you. You've got to wait," she laughed, as she helped him sit down and spread his tasting dishes before him. He wanted to go back over the dinner first, sampling all the pretty things he had eaten, and savoring them this time with his now-living lips and tongue.

30   When Luci had found the music wire and had thrown its sphere up into the force-field, he reminded her of the new smells. She took out the long glass records and set the first one into a transmitter.

31   "Now sniff!"

32   A queer, frightening, exciting smell came over the room. It seemed like nothing in this world, nor like anything from the up-and-out. Yet

it was familiar. His mouth watered. His pulse beat a little faster; he scanned his heartbox. (Faster, sure enough.) But that smell, what was it? In mock perplexity, he grabbed her hands, looked into her eyes, and growled:

33 "Tell me, darling! Tell me, or I'll eat you up!"

34 "That's just right!"

35 "What?"

36 "You're right. It should make you want to eat me. It's meat."

37 "Meat. Who?"

38 "Not a person," said she, knowledgeably, "a Beast. A Beast which people used to eat. A lamb was a small sheep—you've seen sheep out in the Wild, haven't you?—and a chop is part of its middle—here!" She pointed at her chest.

39 Martel did not hear her. All his boxes had swung over toward *Alarm,* some to *Danger.* He fought against the roar of his own mind, forcing his body into excess excitement. How easy it was to be a scanner when you really stood outside your own body, haberman-fashion, and looked back into it with your eyes alone. Then you could manage the body, rule it coldly even in the enduring agony of space. But to realize that you *were* a body, that this thing was ruling you, that the mind could kick the flesh and send it roaring off into panic! That was bad.

40 He tried to remember the days before he had gone into the haberman device, before he had been cut apart for the up-and-out. Had he always been subject to the rush of his emotions from his mind to his body, from his body back to his mind, confounding him so that he couldn't scan? But he hadn't been a scanner then.

41 He knew what had hit him. Amid the roar of his own pulse, he knew. In the nightmare of the up-and-out, that smell had forced its way through to him, while their ship burned off Venus and the habermans fought the collapsing metal with their bare hands. He had scanned then: all were in *Danger.* Chestboxes went up to *Overload* and dropped to *Dead* all around him as he had moved from man to man, shoving the drifting corpses out of his way as he fought to scan each man in turn, to clamp vises on unnoticed broken legs, to snap the sleeping valve on men whose instruments showed they were hopelessly near *Overload.* With men trying to work and cursing him for a scanner while he, professional zeal aroused, fought to do his job and keep them alive in the great pain of space, he had smelled that smell. It had fought its way along his rebuilt nerves, past the haberman cuts, past all the safeguards of physical and mental discipline. In the wildest hour of tragedy, he had smelled aloud. He remembered it was like a bad cranching, connected with the fury and nightmare all around him. He had even stopped his

work to scan himself, fearful that the first effect might come, breaking past all haberman cuts and ruining him with the pain of space. But he had come through. His own instruments stayed and stayed at *Danger,* without nearing *Overload.* He had done his job, and won a commendation for it. He had even forgotten the burning ship.

42   All except the smell.

43   And here the smell was all over again—the smell of meat-with-fire ...

44   Luci looked at him with wifely concern. She obviously thought he had cranched too much, and was about to haberman back. She tried to be cheerful: "You'd better rest, honey."

45   He whispered to her: "Cut—off—that—smell."

46   She did not question his word. She cut the transmitter. She even crossed the room and stepped up the room controls until a small breeze flitted across the floor and drove the smells up to the ceiling.

47   He rose, tired and stiff. (His instruments were normal, except that heart was fast and nerves still hanging on the edge of *Danger.*) He spoke sadly:

48   "Forgive me, Luci. I suppose I shouldn't have cranched. Not so soon again. But darling, I have to get out from being a haberman. How can I ever be near you? How can I be a man—not hearing my own voice, not even feeling my own life as it goes through my veins? I love you, darling. Can't I ever be near you?"

49   Her pride was disciplined and automatic: "But you're a scanner!"

50   "I know I'm a scanner. But so what?"

51   She went over the words, like a tale told a thousand times to reassure herself: "You are the bravest of the brave, the most skillful of the skilled. All mankind owes most honor to the scanner, who unites the Earths of mankind. Scanners are the protectors of the habermans. They are the judges in the up-and-out. They make men live in the place where men need desperately to die. They are the most honored of mankind, and even the chiefs of the Instrumentality are delighted to pay them homage!"

52   With obstinate sorrow he demurred: "Luci, we've heard that all before. But does it pay us back—"

53   " 'Scanners work for more than pay. They are the strong guards of mankind.' Don't you remember that?"

54   "But our lives, Luci. What can you get out of being the wife of a scanner? Why did you marry me? I'm human only when I cranch. The rest of the time—you know what I am. A machine. A man turned into a machine. A man who has been killed and kept alive for duty. Don't you realize what I miss?"

55   "Of course, darling, of course—"

56 He went on: "Don't you think I remember my childhood? Don't you think I remember what it is to be a man and not a haberman? To walk and feel my feet on the ground? To feel a decent clean pain instead of watching my body every minute to see if I'm alive? How will I know if I'm dead? Did you ever think of that, Luci? How will I know if I'm dead?"

57 She ignored the unreasonableness of his outburst. Pacifiyingly, she said: "Sit down, darling. Let me make you some kind of a drink. You're overwrought."

58 Automatically, he scanned: "No I'm not! Listen to me. How do you think it feels to be in the up-and-out with the crew tied-for-space all around you? How do you think it feels to watch them sleep? How do you think I like scanning, scanning, scanning month after month, when I can feel the pain of space beating against every part of my body, trying to get past my haberman blocks? How do you think I like to wake the men when I have to, and have them hate me for it? Have you ever seen habermans fight—strong men fighting, and neither knowing pain, fighting until one touches *Overload?* Do you think about that, Luci?" Triumphantly he added: "Can you blame me if I cranch, and come back to being a man, just two days a month?"

59 "I'm not blaming you, darling. Let's enjoy your cranch. Sit down now, and have a drink."

60 He was sitting down, resting his face in his hands, while she fixed the drink, using natural fruits out of bottles in addition to the secure alkaloids. He watched her restlessly and pitied her for marrying a scanner; and then, though it was unjust, resented having to pity her.

61 Just as she turned to hand him the drink, they both jumped a little as the phone rang. It should not have rung. They had turned it off. It rang again, obviously on the emergency circuit. Stepping ahead of Luci, Martel strode over to the phone and looked into it. Vomact was looking at him.

62 The custom of scanners entitled him to be brusque, even with a senior scanner, on certain given occasions. This was one.

63 Before Vomact could speak, Martel spoke two words into the plate, not caring whether the old man could read lips or not:

64 "Cranching. Busy."

65 He cut the switch and went back to Luci.

66 The phone rang again.

67 Luci said, gently, "I can find out what it is, darling. Here, take your drink and sit down."

68 "Leave it alone," said her husband. "No one has a right to call when I'm cranching. He knows that. He ought to know that."

69   The phone rang again. In a fury, Martel rose and went to the plate. He cut it back on. Vomact was on the screen. Before Martel could speak, Vomact held up his talking nail in line with his heartbox. Martel reverted to discipline:

70   "Scanner Martel present and waiting, sir."

71   The lips moved solemnly: "Top emergency."

72   "Sir, I am under the wire."

73   "Top emergency."

74   "Sir, don't you understand?" Martel mouthed his words, so he could be sure that Vomact followed. "I . . . am . . . under . . . the . . . wire. Unfit . . . for . . . Space!"

75   Vomact repeated: "Top emergency. Report to Central Tie-in."

76   "But, sir, no emergency like this—"

77   "Right, Martel. No emergency like this, ever before. Report to Tie-in." With a faint glint of kindliness, Vomact added: "No need to de-cranch. Report as you are."

78   This time it was Martel whose phone was cut out. The screen went gray.

79   He turned to Luci. The temper had gone out of his voice. She came to him. She kissed him, and rumpled his hair. All she could say was,

80   "I'm sorry."

81   She kissed him again, knowing his disappointment. "Take good care of yourself, darling. I'll wait."

82   He scanned, and slipped into his transparent aircoat. At the window he paused, and waved. She called, "Good luck!" As the air flowed past him he said to himself,

83   "This is the first time I've felt flight in—eleven years. Lord, but it's easy to fly if you can feel yourself live!"

84   Central Tie-in lowed white and austere far ahead. Martel peered. He saw no glare of incoming ships from the up-and-out, no shuddering flare of space-fire out of control. Everything was quiet, as it should be on an off-duty night.

85   And yet Vomact had called. He had called an emergency higher than space. There was no such thing. But Vomact had called it.

86   When Martel got there, he found about half the scanners present, two dozen or so of them. He lifted the talking finger. Most of the scanners were standing face to face, talking in pairs as they read lips. A few of the old, impatient ones were scribbling on their tablets and then thrusting the tablets into other people's faces. All the faces wore the dull dead relaxed look of a haberman. When Martel entered the room, he knew that most of the others laughed in the deep isolated privacy of

their minds, each thinking things it would be useless to express in formal words. It had been a long time since a scanner showed up at a meeting cranched.

87   Vomact was not there: probably, thought Martel, he was still on the phone calling others. The light of the phone flashed on and off; the bell rang. Martel felt odd when he realized that of all those present, he was the only one to hear that loud bell. It made him realize why ordinary people did not like to be around groups of habermans or scanners. Martel looked around for company.

88   His friend Chang was there, busy explaining to some old and testy scanner that he did not know why Vomact had called. Martel looked farther and saw Parizianski. He walked over, threading his way past the others with a dexterity that showed he could feel his feet from the inside, and did not have to watch them. Several of the others stared at him with their dead faces, and tried to smile. But they lacked full muscular control and their faces twisted into horrid masks. (Scanners usually knew better than to show expression on faces which they could no longer govern. Martel added to himself, *I swear I'll never smile again unless I'm cranched.*)

89   Parizianski gave him the sign of the talking finger. Looking face to face, he spoke:

90   "You come here cranched?"

91   Parizianski could not hear his own voice, so the words roared like the words on a broken and screeching phone; Martel was startled, but knew that the inquiry was well meant. No none could be better-natured than the burly Pole.

92   "Vomact called. Top emergency."

93   "You told him you were cranched?"

94   "Yes."

95   "He still made you come?"

96   "Yes."

97   "Then all this—it is not for Space? You could not go up-and-out? You are like ordinary men?"

98   "That's right."

99   "Then why did he call us?" Some pre-haberman habit made Parizianski wave his arms in inquiry. The hand struck the back of the old man behind them. The slap could be heard throughout the room, but only Martel heard it. Instinctively, he scanned Parizianski and the old scanner, and they scanned him back. Only then did the old man ask why Martel had scanned him. When Martel explained that he was under the wire, the old man moved swiftly away to pass on the news that there was a cranched scanner present at the tie-in.

100   Even this minor sensation could not keep the attention of most of the scanners from the worry about the top emergency. One young man, who had scanned his first transit just the year before, dramatically interposed himself between Parizianski and Martel. He dramatically flashed his tablet at them:

101   *Is Vmct mad?*

102   The older men shook their heads. Martel, remembering that it had not been too long that the young man had been haberman, mitigated the dead solemnity of the denial with a friendly smile. He spoke in a normal voice, saying:

103   "Vomact is the senior of scanners. I am sure that he could not go mad. Would he not see it on his boxes first?"

104   Martel had to repeat the question, speaking slowly and mouthing his words before the young scanner could understand the comment. The young man tried to make his face smile, and twisted it into a comic mask. But he took up his tablet and scribbled:

105   *Yr rght.*

106   Chang broke away from his friend and came over, his half-Chinese face gleaming in the warm evening. (It's strange, thought Martel, that more Chinese don't become scanners. Or not so strange perhaps, if you think that they never fill their quota of habermans. Chinese love good living too much. The ones who do scan are all good ones.) Chang saw that Martel was cranched, and spoke with voice:

107   "You break precedents. Luci must be angry to lose you?"

108   "She took it well. Chang, that's strange."

109   "What?"

110   "I'm cranched, and I can hear. Your voice sounds all right. How did you learn to talk like—like an ordinary person?"

111   "I practiced with soundtracks. Funny you noticed it. I think I am the only scanner in or between the Earths who can pass for an ordinary man. Mirrors and soundtracks. I found out how to act."

112   "But you don't . . ?"

113   "No. I don't feel, or taste, or hear, or smell things, any more than you do. Talking doesn't do me much good. But I notice that it cheers up the people around me."

114   "It would make a difference in the life of Luci."

115   Chang nodded sagely. "My father insisted on it. He said, 'You may be proud of being a scanner. I am sorry you are not a man. Conceal your defects.' So I tried. I wanted to tell the old boy about the up-and-out, and what we did there, but it did not matter. He said, 'Airplanes were good enough for Confucius, and they are for me too.' The old humbug! He tries so hard to be a Chinese when he can't even read Old

Chinese. But he's got wonderful good sense, and for somebody going on two hundred he certainly gets around."

116   Martel smiled at the thought: "In his airplane?"

117   Chang smiled back. This discipline of his facial muscles was amazing; a bystander would not think that Chang was a haberman, controlling his eyes, cheeks, and lips by cold intellectual control. The expression had the spontaneity of life. Martel felt a flash of envy of Chang when he looked at the dead cold faces of Parizianski and the others. He knew that he himself looked fine: but why shouldn't he? He was cranched. Turning to Parizianski he said,

118   "Did you see what Chang said about his father? The old boy uses an airplane."

119   Parizianski made motions with his mouth, but the sounds meant nothing. He took up his tablet and showed it to Martel and Chang.

120   *Bzz bzz. Ha ha. Gd ol' boy.*

121   At that moment, Martel heard steps out in the corridor. He could not help looking toward the door. Other eyes followed the direction of his glance.

122   Vomact came in.

123   The group shuffled to attention in four parallel lines. They scanned one another. Numerous hands reached across to adjust the electrochemical controls on chestboxes which had begun to load up. One scanner held out a broken finger which his counter-scanner had discovered, and submitted it for treatment and splinting.

124   Vomact had taken out his staff of office. The cube at the top flashed red light through the room, the lines re-formed, and all scanners gave the sign meaning, *Present and ready!*

125   Vomact countered with the stance signifying, *I am the senior and take command.*

126   Talking fingers rose in the counter-gesture, *We concur and commit ourselves.*

127   Vomact raised his right arm, dropped the wrist as though it were broken, in a queer searching gesture, meaning: *Any men around? Any habermans not tied? All clear for the scanners?*

128   Alone of all those present, the cranched Martel heard the queer rustle of feet as they all turned completely around without leaving position, looking sharply at one another and flashing their beltlights into the dark corners of the great room. When again they faced Vomact, he made a further sign:

129   *All clear. Follow my words.*

130   Martel noticed that he alone relaxed. The others could not know the meaning of relaxation with the minds blocked off up there in their

skulls, connected only with the eyes, and the rest of the body connected with the mind only by controlling non-sensory nerves and the instrument boxes on their chests. Martel realized that, cranched as he was, he had expected to hear Vomact's voice: the senior had been talking for some time. No sound escaped his lips. (Vomact never bothered with sound.)

131   "... and when the first men to go up-and-out went to the moon, what did they find?"

132   "Nothing," responded the silent chorus of lips.

133   "Therefore they went farther, to Mars and to Venus. The ships went out year by year, but they did not come back until the Year One of Space. Then did a ship come back with the first effect. Scanners, I ask you, what is the first effect?"

134   "No one knows. No one knows."

135   "No one will ever know. Too many are the variables. By what do we know the first effect?"

136   "By the great pain of space," came the chorus.

137   "And by what further sign?"

138   "By the need, oh the need for death."

139   Vomact again: "And who stopped the need for death?"

140   "Henry Haberman conquered the first effect, in the Year Eighty-three of Space."

141   "And, Scanners, I ask you, what did he do?"

142   "He made the habermans."

143   "How, O Scanners, are habermans made?"

144   "They are made with the cuts. The brain is cut from the heart, the lungs. The brain is cut from the ears, the nose. The brain is cut from the mouth, the belly. The brain is cut from desire, and pain. The brain is cut from the world. Save for the eyes. Save for the control of the living flesh."

145   "And how, O Scanners, is flesh controlled?"

146   "By the boxes set in the flesh, the controls set in the chest, the signs made to rule the living body, the signs by which the body lives."

147   "How does a haberman live and live?"

148   "The haberman lives by control of the boxes."

149   "Whence come the habermans?"

150   Martel felt in the coming response a great roar of broken voices echoing through the room as the scanners, habermans themselves, put sound behind their mouthings:

151   "Habermans are the scum of mankind. Habermans are the weak, the cruel, the credulous, and the unfit. Habermans are the sentenced-to-more-than-death. Habermans live in the mind alone. They are killed for

space but they live for space. They master the ships that connect the Earths. They live in the great pain while ordinary men sleep in the cold, cold sleep of the transit."

152   "Brothers and Scanners, I ask you now: are we habermans or are we not?"

153   "We are habermans in the flesh. We are cut apart, brain and flesh. We are ready to go to the up-and-out. All of us have gone through the haberman device."

154   "We are habermans then?" Vomact's eyes flashed and glittered as he asked the ritual question.

155   Again the chorused answer was accompanied by a roar of voices heard only by Martel: "Habermans we are, and more, and more. We are the chosen who are habermans by our own free will. We are the agents of the Instrumentality of Mankind."

156   "What must the others say to us?"

157   "They must say to us, 'You are the bravest of the brave, the most skillful of the skilled. All mankind owes most honor to the scanner, who unites the Earths of mankind. Scanners are the protectors of the habermans. They are the judges in the up-and-out. They make men live in the place where men need desperately to die. They are the most honored of mankind, and even the chiefs of the Instrumentality are delighted to pay them homage!'"

158   Vomact stood more erect: "What is the secret duty of the scanner?"

159   "To keep secret our law, and to destroy the acquirers thereof."

160   "How to destroy?"

161   "Twice to the *Overload,* back and *Dead.*"

162   "If habermans die, what the duty then?"

163   The scanners all compressed their lips for answer. (Silence was the code.) Martel, who—long familiar with the code—was a little bored with the proceedings, noticed that Chang was breathing too heavily; he reached over and adjusted Chang's lung-control and received the thanks of Chang's eyes. Vomact observed the interruption and glared at them both. Martel relaxed, trying to imitate the dead cold stillness of the others. It was hard to do, when you were cranched.

164   "If others die, what the duty then?" asked Vomact.

165   "Scanners together inform the Instrumentality. Scanners together accept the punishment. Scanners together settle the case."

166   "And if the punishment be severe?"

167   "Then no ships go."

168   "And if scanners be not honored?"

169   "Then no ships go."

170   "And if a scanner goes unpaid?"

171   "Then no ships go!"

172   "And if the Others and the Instrumentality are not in all ways at all
times mindful of their proper obligation to the scanners?"

173   "Then no ships go."

174   "And what, O Scanners, if no ships go?"

175   "The Earths fall apart. The Wild comes back in. The Old Machines
and the Beasts return."

176   "What is the first known duty of a scanner?"

177   "Not to sleep in the up-and-out."

178   "What is the second duty of a scanner?"

179   "To keep forgotten the name of fear."

180   "What is the third duty of a scanner?"

181   "To use the wire of Eustace Cranch only with care, only with mod-
eration." Several pair of eyes looked quickly at Martel before the
mouthed chorus went on. "To cranch only at home, only among friends,
only for the purpose or remembering, of relaxing, or of begetting."

182   "What is the word of the scanner?"

183   "Faithful though surrounded by death."

184   "What is the motto of the scanner?"

185   "Awake though surrounded by silence."

186   "What is the work of the scanner?"

187   "Labor even in the heights of the up-and-out, loyalty even in the
depths of the Earths."

188   "Who do you know a scanner?"

189   "We know ourselves. We are dead though we live. And we talk
with the tablet and the nail."

190   "What is this code?"

191   "This code is the friendly ancient wisdom of scanners, briefly put
that we may be mindful and cheered by our loyalty to one another."

192   At this point the formula should have run: "We complete the code.
Is there work or word for the scanners?" But Vomact said, and he
repeated:

193   "Top emergency. Top emergency."

194   They gave him the sign, *Present and ready!*

195   He said with every eye straining to follow his lips:

196   "Some of you know the work of Adam Stone?"

197   Martel saw lips move, saying: "The Red Asteroid. The Other who
lives at the edge of Space."

198   "Adam Stone has gone to the Instrumentality, claiming success
for his work. He says that he has found how to screen out the pain of
space. He says that the up-and-out can be made safe for ordinary
men to work in, to stay awake in. He says that there need be no more
scanners."

199   Beltlights flashed on all over the room as scanners sought the right to speak. Vomact nodded to one of the older men. "Scanner Smith will speak."

200   Smith stepped slowly up into the light, watching his own feet. He turned so that they could see his face. He spoke: "I say that this is a lie. I say that Stone is a liar. I say that the Instrumentality must not be deceived."

201   He paused. Then, in answer to some question from the audience which most of the others did not see, he said:

202   "I invoke the secret duty of the scanners."

203   Smith raised his right hand for emergency attention:

204   "I say that Stone must die."

205   Martel, still cranched, shuddered as he heard the boos, groans, shouts, squeaks, grunts and moans which came from the scanners who forgot noise in their excitement and strove to make their dead bodies talk to one another's deaf ears. Beltlights flashed wildly all over the room. There was a rush for the rostrum and scanners milled around at the top, vying for attention until Parizianski—by sheer bulk—shoved the others aside and down, and turned to mouth at the group.

206   "Brother Scanners, I want your eyes."

207   The people on the floor kept moving, with their numb bodies jostling one another. Finally Vomact stepped up in front of Parizianski, faced the others, and said:

208   "Scanners, be scanners! Give him your eyes."

209   Parizianski was not good at public speaking. His lips moved too fast. He waved his hands, which took the eyes of the others away from his lips. Nevertheless, Martel was able to follow most of the message:

210   ". . . can't do this. Stone may have succeeded. If he has succeeded, it means the end of the scanners. It means the end of the habermans, too. None of us will have to fight in the up-and-out. We won't have anybody else going under the wire for a few hours or days of being human. Everybody will be Other. Nobody will have to cranch, never again. Men can be men. The habermans can be killed decently and properly, the way men were killed in the old days, without anybody keeping them alive. They won't have to work in the up-and-out! There will be no more great pain—think of it! No . . . more . . . great . . . pain! How do we know that Stone is a liar—" Lights began flashing directly into his eyes. (The rudest insult of scanner to scanner was this.)

211   Vomact again exercised authority. He stepped in front of Parizianski and said something which the others could not see. Parizianski stepped down from the rostrum. Vomact again spoke:

212   "I think that some of the scanners disagree with our brother Parizianski. I say that the use of the rostrum be suspended till we have

had a chance for private discussion. In fifteen minutes I will call the meeting back to order."

213   Martel looked around for Vomact when the senior had rejoined the group on the floor. Finding the senior, Martel wrote swift script on his tablet, waiting for a chance to thrust the tablet before the senior's eyes. He had written:

214   *Am crnchd. Rspctfly requst prmissn lv now, stnd by fr orders.*

215   Being cranched did strange things to Martel. Most meetings that he attended seemed formal, hearteningly ceremonial, lighting up the dark inward eternities of habermanhood. When he was not cranched, he noticed his body no more than a marble bust notices its marble pedestal. He had stood with them before. He had stood with them effortless hours, while the long-winded ritual broke through the terrible loneliness behind his eyes, and made him feel that the scanners, though a confraternity of the damned, were none the less forever honored by the professional requirements of their mutilation.

216   This time, it was different. Coming cranched, and in full possession of smell-sound-taste-feeling, he reacted more or less as a normal man would. He saw his friends and colleagues as a lot of cruelly driven ghosts, posturing out the meaningless ritual of their indefeasible damnation. What difference did anything make, once you were a haberman? Why all this talk about habermans and scanners? Habermans were criminals or heretics, and scanners were gentlemen-volunteers, but they were all in the same fix—except that scanners were deemed worthy of the short-time return of the cranching wire, while habermans were simply disconnected while the ships lay in port and were left suspended until they should be awakened, in some hour of emergency or trouble, to work out another spell of their damnation. It was a rare haberman that you saw on the street—someone of special merit or bravery, allowed to look at mankind from the terrible prison of his own mechanified body. And yet, what scanner ever pitied a haberman? What scanner ever honored a haberman except perfunctorily in the line of duty? What had the scanners as a guild and a class ever done for the habermans, except to murder them with a twist of the wrist whenever a haberman, too long beside a scanner, picked up the tricks of the scanning trade and learned how to live at his own will, not the will the scanners imposed? What could the Others, the ordinary men, know of what went on inside the ships? The Others slept in their cylinders, mercifully unconscious until they woke up on whatever other Earth they had consigned themselves to. What could the Others know of the men who had to stay alive within the ship?

217   What could any Other know of the up-and-out? What Other could look at the biting acid beauty of the stars in open space? What could they tell of the great pain, which started quietly in the marrow, like an ache, and proceeded by the fatigue and nausea of each separate nerve cell, brain cell, touchpoint in the body, until life itself became a terrible aching hunger for silence and for death?

218   He was a scanner. All right, he *was* a scanner. He had been a scanner from the moment when, wholly normal, he had stood in the sunlight before a subchief of the Instrumentality, and had sworn:

219   "I pledge my honor and my life to mankind. I sacrificed myself willingly for the welfare of mankind. In accepting the perilous austere honor, I yield all my rights without exception to the honorable chiefs of the Instrumentality and to the honored Confraternity of Scanners."

220   He had pledged.

221   He had gone into the haberman device.

222   He remembered his hell. He had not had such a bad one, even though it had seemed to last a hundred-million years, all of them without sleep. He had learned to feel with his eyes. He had learned to see despite the heavy eyeplates set back of his eyeballs to insulate his eyes from the rest of him. He had learned to watch his skin. He still remembered the time he had noticed dampness on his shirt, and had pulled out his scanning mirror only to discover that he had worn a hole in his side by leaning against a vibrating machine. (A thing like that could not happen to him now; he was too adept at reading his own instruments.) He remembered the way that he had gone up-and-out, and the way that the great pain beat into him, despite the fact that his touch, smell, feeling, and hearing were gone for all ordinary purposes. He remembered killing habermans, and keeping others alive, and standing for months beside the honorable scanner-pilot while neither of them slept. He remembered going ashore on Earth Four, and remembered that he had not enjoyed it, and had realized on that day that there was no reward.

223   Martel stood among the other scanners. He hated their awkwardness when they moved, their immobility when they stood still. He hated the queer assortment of smells which their bodies yielded unnoticed. He hated the grunts and groans and squawks which they emitted from their deafness. He hated them, and himself.

224   How could Luci stand him? He had kept his chestbox reading *Danger* for weeks while he courted her, carrying the cranch wire about with him most illegally, and going direct from one cranch to the other without worrying about the fact his indicators all crept up to the edge of *Overload*. He had wooed her without thinking of what would happen if she did say, "Yes." She had.

225   "And they lived happily ever after." In old books they did, but how could they, in life? He had had eighteen days under the wire in the whole of the past year! Yet she had loved him. She still loved him. He knew it. She fretted about him through the long months that he was in the up-and-out. She tried to make home mean something to him even when he was haberman, make food pretty when it could not be tasted, make herself lovable when she could not be kissed—or might as well not, since a haberman body meant no more than furniture. Luci was patient.

226   And now, Adam Stone! (He let his tablet fade: how could he leave, now?)

227   God bless Adam Stone!

228   Martel could not help feeling a little sorry for himself. No longer would the high keen call of duty carry him through two hundred or so years of the Others' time, two million private eternities of his own. He could slouch and relax. He could forget high space, and let the up-and-out be tended by Others. He could cranch as much as he dared. He could be almost normal—almost—for one year or five years or no years. But at least he could stay with Luci. He could go with her into the Wild, where there were Beasts and Old Machines still roving the dark places. Perhaps he would die in the excitement of the hunt, throwing spears at an ancient manshonyagger as it leapt from its lair, or tossing hot spheres at the tribesmen of the Unforgiven who still roamed the Wild. There was still life to live, still a good normal death to die, not the moving of a needle out in the silence and agony of space!

229   He had been walking about restlessly. His ears were attuned to the sounds of normal speech, so that he did not feel like watching the mouthings of his brethren. Now they seemed to have come to a decision. Vomact was moving to the rostrum. Martel looked about for Chang, and went to stand beside him. Chang whispered.

230   "You're as restless as water in mid-air! What's the matter? Decranching?"

231   They both scanned Martel, but the instruments held steady and showed no sign of the cranch giving out.

232   The great light flared in its call to attention. Again they formed ranks. Vomact thrust his lean old face into the glare, and spoke:

233   "Scanners and Brothers, I call for a vote." He held himself in the stance which meant: *I am the senior and take command.*

234   A beltlight flashed in protest.

235   It was old Henderson. He moved to the rostrum, spoke to Vomact, and—with Vomact's nod of approval—turned full-face to repeat his question:

236   "Who speaks for the scanners out in space?"

237   No beltlight or hand answered.

238   Henderson and Vomact, face to face, conferred for a few moments. Then Henderson faced them again:

239   "I yield to the senior in command. But I do not yield to a meeting of the Confraternity. There are sixty-eight scanners, and only forty-seven present, of whom one is cranched and U.D. I have therefore proposed that the senior in command assume authority only over an emergency committee of the Confraternity, not over a meeting. Is that agreed and understood by the honorable scanners?"

240   Hands rose in assent.

241   Chang murmured in Martel's ear, "Lot of difference that makes! Who can tell the difference between a meeting and a committee?" Martel agreed with the words, but was even more impressed with the way that Chang, while haberman, could control his own voice.

242   Vomact resumed chairmanship: "We now vote on the question of Adam Stone.

243   "First, we can assume that he has not succeeded, and that his claims are lies. We know that from our practical experience as scanners. The pain of space is only part of scanning" (*But the essential part, the basis of it all,* thought Martel) "and we can rest assured that Stone cannot solve the problem of space discipline."

244   "That tripe again," whispered Chang, unheard save by Martel.

245   "The space discipline of our confraternity has kept high space clean of war and dispute. Sixty-eight disciplined men control all high space. We are removed by our oath and our haberman status from all Earthly passions.

246   "Therefore, if Adam Stone has conquered the pain of space, so that Others can wreck our confraternity and bring to space the trouble and ruin which afflicts Earths, I say that Adam Stone is wrong. If Adam Stone succeeds, scanners live in vain!

247   "Secondly, if Adam Stone has not conquered the pain of space, he will cause great trouble in all the Earths. The Instrumentality and the subchiefs may not give us as many habermans as we need to operate the ships of mankind. There will be wild stories, and fewer recruits, and, worst of all, the discipline of the Confraternity may relax if this kind of nonsensical heresy is spread around.

248   "Therefore, if Adam Stone has succeeded, he threatens the ruin of the Confraternity and should die.

249   "I move the death of Adam Stone."

250   And Vomact made the sign, *The honorable scanners are pleased to vote.*

251   Martel grabbed wildly for his beltlight. Chang, guessing ahead, had his light out and ready; its bright beam, voting *No,* shone straight up at

the ceiling. Martel got his light out and threw its beam upward in dissent. Then he looked around. Out of the forty-seven present, he could see only five or six glittering.

252   Two more lights went on. Vomact stood as erect as a frozen corpse. Vomact's eyes flashed as he stared back and forth over the group, looking for lights. Several more went on. Finally Vomact took the closing stance:

253   *May it please the scanners to count the vote.*

254   Three of the older men went up on the rostrum with Vomact. They looked over the room. (Martel thought: *These damned ghosts are voting on the life of a real man, a live man! They have no right to do it. I'll tell the Instrumentality!* But he knew that he would not. He thought of Luci and what she might gain by the triumph of Adam Stone: the heart-breaking folly of the vote was then almost too much for Martel to bear.)

255   All three of the tellers held up their hands in unanimous agreement on the sign of the number: *Fifteen against.*

256   Vomact dismissed them with a bow of courtesy. He turned and again took the stance: *I am the senior and take command.*

257   Marveling at his own daring, Martel flashed his beltlight on. He knew that any one of the bystanders might reach over and twist his heartbox to *Overload* for such an act. He felt Chang's hand reaching to catch him by the aircoat. But he eluded Chang's grasp and ran, faster than a scanner should, to the platform. As he ran, he wondered what appeal to make. It was no use talking common sense. Not now. It had to be law.

258   He jumped up on the rostrum beside Vomact, and took the stance: *Scanners, an Illegality!*

259   He violated good custom while speaking, still in the stance: "A committee has no right to vote death by a majority vote. It takes two-thirds of a full meeting."

260   He felt Vomact's body lunge behind him, felt himself falling from the rostrum, hitting the floor, hurting his knees and his touch-aware hands. He was helped to his feet. He was scanned. Some scanner he scarcely knew took his instruments and toned him down.

261   Immediately Martel felt more calm, more detached, and hated himself for feeling so.

262   He looked up at the rostrum. Vomact maintained the stance signifying: *Order!*

263   The scanners adjusted their ranks. The two scanners next to Martel took his arms. He shouted at them, but they looked away, and cut themselves off from communication altogether.

264   Vomact spoke again when he saw the room was quiet: "A scanner came here cranched. Honorable Scanners, I apologize for this. It is not the fault of our great and worthy scanner and friend, Martel. He came

here under orders. I told him not to de-cranch. I hoped to spare him an unnecessary haberman. We all know how happily Martel is married, and we wish his brave experiment well. I like Martel. I respect his judgment. I wanted him here. I knew you wanted him here. But he is cranched. He is in no mood to share in the lofty business of the scanners. I therefore propose a solution which will meet all the requirements of fairness. I propose that we rule Scanner Martel out of order for his violation of the rules. This violation would be inexcusable if Martel were not cranched.

265 "But at the same time, in all fairness to Martel, I further propose that we deal with the points raised so improperly by our worthy but disqualified brother."

266 Vomact gave the sign, *The honorable scanners are pleased to vote.* Martel tried to reach his own beltlight; the dead strong hands held him tightly and he struggled in vain. One lone light shone high: Chang's, no doubt.

267 Vomact thrust his face into the light again: "Having the approval of our worthy scanners and present company for the general proposal, I now move that this committee declare itself to have the full authority of a meeting, and that this committee further make me responsible for all misdeeds which this committee may enact, to be held answerable before the next full meeting, but not before any other authority beyond the closed and secret ranks of scanners."

268 Flamboyantly this time, his triumph evident, Vomact assumed the *vote* stance.

269 Only a few lights shone: far less, patently, than a minority of one-fourth.

270 Vomact spoke again. The light shone on his high calm forehead, on his dead relaxed cheekbones. His lean cheeks and chin were halfshadowed, save where the lower light picked up and spotlighted his mouth, cruel even in repose. (Vomact was said to be a descendant of some ancient lady who had traversed, in an illegitimate and inexplicable fashion, some hundreds of years of time in a single night. Her name, the Lady Vomact, had passed into legend; but her blood and her archaic lust for mastery lived on in the mute masterful body of her descendant. Martel could believe the old tales as he stared at the rostrum, wondering what untraceable mutation had left the Vomact kin as predators among mankind.) Calling loudly with the movement of his lips, but still without sound, Vomact appealed:

271 "The honorable committee is now pleased to reaffirm the sentence of death issued against the heretic and enemy, Adam Stone." Again the *vote* stance.

272   Again Chang's light shone lonely in its isolated protest.

273   Vomact then made his final move:

274   "I call for the designation of the senior scanner present as the manager of the sentence. I call for authorization to him to appoint execu-
tioners, one or many, who shall make evident the will and majesty of
scanners. I ask that I be accountable for the deed, and not for the
means. The deed is a noble deed, for the protection of mankind and for
the honor of the scanners; but of the means it must be said that they are
to be the best at hand, and no more. Who knows the true way to kill an
Other, here on a crowded and watchful Earth? This is no mere matter
of discharging a cylindered sleeper, no mere question of upgrading the
needle of a haberman. When people die down here, it is not like the
up-and-out. They die reluctantly. Killing within the Earth is not our
usual business, O Brothers and Scanners, as you know well. You must
choose me to choose my agent as I see fit. Otherwise the common
knowledge will become the common betrayal whereas if I alone know
the responsibility, I alone could betray us, and you will not have far to
look in case the Instrumentality comes searching." (*What about the killer
you choose?* thought Martel. *He too will know unless—unless you silence
him forever.*)

275   Vomact went into the stance: *The honorable scanners are pleased to vote.*

276   One light of protest shone: Chang's, again.

277   Martel imagined that he could see a cruel joyful smile on Vomact's
dead face—the smile of a man who knew himself righteous and who
found his righteousness upheld and affirmed by militant authority.

278   Martel tried one last time to come free.

279   The dead hands held. They were locked like vises until their owners' eyes unlocked them: how else could they hold the piloting month
by month?

280   Martel then shouted: "Honorable Scanners, this is judicial murder."

281   No ear heard him. He was cranched, and alone.

282   Nonetheless, he shouted again: "You endanger the Confraternity."

283   Nothing happened.

284   The echo of his voice sounded from one end of the room to the
other. No head turned. No eyes met his.

285   Martel realized that as they paired for talk, the eyes of the scanners
avoided him. He saw that no one desired to watch his speech. He knew
that behind the cold faces of his friends there lay compassion or amusement. He knew that they knew him to be cranched—absurd, normal,
manlike, temporarily no scanner. But he knew that in this matter the
wisdom of scanners was nothing. He knew that only a cranched scanner could feel with his very blood the outrage and anger which delib-

erate murder would provoke among the Others. He knew that the Confraternity endangered itself, and knew that the most ancient prerogative of law was the monopoly of death. Even the ancient nations, in the times of the Wars, before the Beasts, before men went into the up-and-out—even the ancients had known this. How did they say it? *Only the state shall kill.* The states were gone but the Instrumentality remained, and the Instrumentality could not pardon things which occurred with the Earths but beyond its authority. Death in space was the business, the right of the scanners: how could the Instrumentality enforce its laws in a place where all men who wakened, wakened only to die in the great pain? Wisely did the Instrumentality leave space to the scanners, wisely had the Confraternity not meddled inside the Earths. And now the Confraternity itself was going to step forth as an outlaw band, as a gang of rogues as stupid and reckless as the tribes of the Unforgiven!

286   Martel knew this because he was cranched. Had he been haberman, he would have thought only with his mind, not with his heart and guts and blood. How could the other scanners know?

287   Vomact returned for the last time to the rostrum: *The committee has met and its will shall be done.* Verbally he added: "Senior among you, I ask your loyalty and your silence."

288   At that point, the two scanners let his arms go. Martel rubbed his numb hands, shaking his fingers to get the circulation back into the cold fingertips. With real freedom, he began to think of what he might still do. He scanned himself: the cranching held. He might have a day. Well, he could go on even if haberman, but it would be inconvenient, have to talk with finger and tablet. He looked about for Chang. He saw his friend standing patient and immobile in a quiet corner. Martel moved slowly, so as not to attract any more attention to himself than could be helped. He faced Chang, moved until his face was in the light, and then articulated:

289   "What are we going to do? You're not going to let them kill Adam Stone, are you? Don't you realize what Stone's work will mean to us, if it succeeds? No more scanners. No more habermans. No more pain in the up-and-out. I tell you, if the others were all cranched, as I am, they would see it in a human way, not with the narrow crazy logic which they used in the meeting. We've got to stop them. How can we do it? What are we going to do? What does Parizianski think? Who has been chosen?"

290   "Which question do you want me to answer?"

291   Martel laughed. (It felt good to laugh, even then; it felt like being a man.) "Will you help me?"

292   Chang's eyes flashed across Martel's face as Chang answered: "No. No. No."

293   "You won't help?"

294   "No."

295   "Why not, Chang? Why not?

296   "I am a scanner. The vote has been taken. You would do the same if you were not in this unusual condition."

297   "I'm not in an unusual condition. I'm cranched. That merely means that I see things the way that the Others would. I see the stupidity. The recklessness. The selfishness. It is murder."

298   "What is murder? Have you not killed? You are not one of the Others. You are a scanner. You will be sorry for what you are about to do, if you do not watch out."

299   "But why did you vote against Vomact then? Didn't you too see what Adam Stone means to all of us? Scanners will live in vain. Thank God for that! Can't you see it?"

300   "No."

301   "But you talk to me, Chang. You are my friend?"

302   "I talk to you. I am your friend. Why not?"

303   "But what are you going to do?"

304   "Nothing, Martel. Nothing."

305   "Will you help me?"

306   "No."

307   "Not even to save Stone?"

308   "No."

309   "Then I will go to Parizianski for help."

310   "It will do you no good."

311   "Why not? He's more human than you, right now."

312   "He will not help you, because he has the job. Vomact designated him to kill Adam Stone."

313   Martel stopped speaking in mid-movement. He suddenly took the stance: *I thank you, Brother, and I depart.*

314   At the window he turned and faced the room. He saw that Vomact's eyes were upon him. He gave the stance, *I thank you, Brother, and I depart,* and added the flourish of respect which is shown when seniors are present. Vomact caught the sign, and Martel could see the cruel lips move. He thought he saw the words ". . . take good care of yourself . . ." but did not wait to inquire. He stepped backward and dropped out the window.

315   Once below the window and out of sight, he adjusted his aircoat to a maximum speed. He swam lazily in the air, scanning himself thoroughly, and adjusting his adrenal intake down. He then made the movement of release, and felt the cold air rush past his face like running water.

316   Adam Stone had to be at Chief Downport.

317   Adam Stone had to be there.

318   Wouldn't Adam Stone be surprised in the night? Surprised to meet the strangest of beings, the first renegade among scanners. (Martel suddenly appreciated that it was of himself he was thinking. Martel the Traitor to Scanners! That sounded strange and bad. But what of Martel, the Loyal to Mankind? Was that not compensation? And if he won, he won Luci. If he lost, he lost nothing—an unconsidered and expendable haberman. It happened to be himself. But in contrast to the immense reward, to mankind, to the Confraternity, to Luci, what did it matter?)

319   Martel thought to himself: "Adam Stone will have two visitors tonight. Two scanners, who are the friends of one another." He hoped that Parizianski was still his friend.

320   "And the world," he added, "depends on which of us gets there first."

321   Multifaceted in their brightness, the lights of Chief Downport began to shine through the mist ahead. Martel could see the outer towers of the city and glimpsed the phosphorescent periphery which kept back the Wild, whether Beasts, Machines, or the Unforgiven.

322   Once more Martel invoked the lords of his chance: "Help me to pass for an Other!"

323   Within the Downport, Martel had less trouble than he thought. He draped his aircoat over his shoulder so that it concealed the instruments. He took up his scanning mirror, and made up his face from the inside, by adding tone and animation to his blood and nerves until the muscles of his face glowed and the skin gave out a healthy sweat. That way he looked like an ordinary man who had just completed a long night flight.

324   After straightening out his clothing, and hiding his tablet within his jacket, he faced the problem of what to do about the talking finger. If he kept the nail, it would show him to be a scanner. He would be respected, but he would be identified. He might be stopped by the guards whom the Instrumentality had undoubtedly set around the person of Adam Stone. If he broke the nail—But he couldn't! No scanner in the history of the Confraternity had ever willingly broken his nail. That would be resignation, and there was no such thing. The only way out, was in the up-and-out! Martel put his finger to his mouth and bit off the nail. He looked at the now-queer finger, and sighed to himself.

325   He stepped toward the city gate, slipping his hand into his jacket and running up his muscular strength to four times normal. He started to scan, and then realized that his instruments were masked. *Might as well take all the chances at once,* he thought.

326   The watcher stopped him with a searching wire. The sphere thumped suddenly against Martel's chest.

327   "Are you a man?" said the unseen voice. (Martel knew that as a scanner in haberman condition, his own field-charge would have illuminated the sphere.)

328   "I am a man." Martel knew that the timbre of his voice had been good; he hoped that it would not be taken for that of a manshonyagger or a Beast or an Unforgiven one, who with mimicry sought to enter the cities and ports of mankind.

329   "Name, number, rank, purpose, function, time departed."

330   "Martel." He had to remember his old number, not Scanner 34. "Sunward 4234, 782nd Year of Space. Rank, rising subchief." That was no lie, but his substantive rank. "Purpose, personal and lawful within the limits of this city. No function of the Instrumentality. Departed Chief Outport 2019 hours." Everything now depended on whether he was believed, or would be checked against Chief Outport.

331   The voice was flat and routine: "Time desired within the city."

332   Martel used the standard phrase: "Your honorable sufferance is requested."

333   He stood in the cool night air, waiting. Far above him, through a gap in the mist, he could see the poisonous glittering in the sky of scanners. *The stars are my enemies*, he thought: *I have mastered the stars but they hate me. Ho, that sounds ancient! Like a book. Too much cranching.*

334   The voice returned: "Sunward 4234 dash 782 rising subchief Martel, enter the lawful gates of the city. Welcome. Do you desire food, raiment, money, or companionship?" The voice had no hospitality in it, just business. This was certainly different from entering a city in a scanner's role! Then the petty officers came out, and threw their beltlights on their fretful faces, and mouthed their words with preposterous deference, shouting against the stone deafness of scanner's ears. So that was the way that a subchief was treated: matter of fact, but not bad. Not bad.

335   Martel replied: "I have that which I need, but beg of the city a favor. My friend Adam Stone is here. I desire to see him, on urgent and personal lawful affairs."

336   The voice replied: "Did you have an appointment with Adam Stone?"

337   "No."

338   "The city will find him. What is his number?"

339   "I have forgotten it."

340   "You have forgotten it? Is not Adam Stone a magnate of the Instrumentality? Are you truly his friend?"

341   "Truly." Martel let a little annoyance creep into his voice. "Watcher, doubt me and call your subchief."

342   "No doubt implied. Why do you not know the number? This must go into the record," added the voice.

343   "We were friends in childhood. He has crossed the—" Martel started to say "the up-and-out" and remembered that the phrase was current only among scanners. "He has leapt from Earth to Earth, and has just now returned. I knew him well and I seek him out. I have word of his kith. May the Instrumentality protect us!"

344   "Heard and believed. Adam Stone will be searched."

345   At a risk, though a slight one, of having the sphere sound an alarm for *nonhuman*, Martel cut in on his scanner speaker within his jacket. He saw the trembling needle of light await his words and he started to write on it with his blunt finger. *That won't work*, he thought, and had a moment's panic until he found his comb, which had a sharp enough tooth to write. He wrote: "Emergency none. Martel Scanner calling Parizianski Scanner."

346   The needle quivered and the reply glowed and faded out: "Parizianski Scanner on duty and D.C. Calls taken by Scanner Relay."

347   Martel cut off his speaker.

348   Parizianski was somewhere around. Could he have crossed the direct way, right over the city wall, setting off the alert, and invoking official business when the petty officers overtook him in mid-air? Scarcely. That meant that a number of other scanners must have come in with Parizianski, all of them pretending to be in search of a few of the tenuous pleasures which could be enjoyed by a habermans, such as the sight of the newspictures or the viewing of beautiful women in the Pleasure Gallery. Parizianski was around, but he could not have moved privately, because Scanner Central registered him on duty and recorded his movements city by city.

349   The voice returned. Puzzlement was expressed in it. "Adam Stone is found and awakened. He has asked pardon of the Honorable, and says he knows no Martel. Will you see Adam Stone in the morning? The city will bid you welcome."

350   Martel ran out of resources. It was hard enough mimicking a man without having to tell lies in the guise of one. Martel could only repeat: "Tell him I am Martel. The husband of Luci."

351   "It will be done."

352   Again the silence, and the hostile stars, and the sense that Parizianski was somewhere near and getting nearer; Martel felt his heart beating faster. He stole a glimpse at his chestbox and set his heart down a point. He felt calmer, even though he had not been able to scan with care.

353   The voice this time was cheerful, as though an annoyance had been settled: "Adam Stone consents to see you. Enter Chief Downport, and welcome."

354   The little sphere dropped noiselessly to the ground and the wire whispered away into the darkness. A bright arc of narrow light rose from the ground in front of Martel and swept through the city to one of the higher towers—apparently a hostel, which Martel had never entered. Martel plucked his aircoat to his chest for ballast, stepped heel-and-toe on the beam, and felt himself whistle through the air to an entrance window which sprang up before him as suddenly as a devouring mouth.

355   A tower guard stood in the doorway. "You are awaited, sir. Do you bear weapons, sir?"

356   "None," said Martel, grateful that he was relying on his own strength.

357   The guard led him past the check-screen. Martel noticed the quick flight of a warning across the screen as his instruments registered and identified him as a scanner. But the guard had not noticed it.

358   The guard stopped at a door. "Adam Stone is armed. He is lawfully armed by the authority of the Instrumentality and by the liberty of this city. All those who enter are given warning."

359   Martel nodded in understanding at the man and went in.

360   Adam Stone was a short man, stout and benign. His gray hair rose stiffly from a low forehead. His whole face was red and merry-looking. He looked like a jolly guide from the Pleasure Gallery, not like a man who had been at the edge of the up-and-out, fighting the great pain without haberman protection.

361   He stared at Martel. His look was puzzled, perhaps a little annoyed, but not hostile.

362   Martel came to the point. "You do not know me. I lied. My name is Martel, and I mean you no harm. But I lied. I beg the honorable gift of your hospitality. Remain armed. Direct your weapon against me—"

363   Stone smiled: "I am doing so," and Martel noticed the small wire-point in Stone's capable, plump hand.

364   "Good. Keep on guard against me. It will give you confidence in what I shall say. But do, I beg you, give us a screen of privacy. I want no casual lookers. This is a matter of life and death."

365   "First: whose life and death?" Stone's face remained calm, his voice even.

366   "Yours, and mine, and the worlds'."

367   "You are cryptic but I agree." Stone called through the doorway: "Privacy please." There was a sudden hum, and all the little noises of the night quickly vanished from the air of the room.

368   Said Adam Stone: "Sir, who are you? What brings you here?"

369   "I am Scanner 34."

370   "You a scanner? I don't believe it."

371   For answer, Martel pulled his jacket open, showing his chestbox. Stone looked up at him, amazed. Martel explained:

372   "I am cranched. Have you never seen it before?"

373   "*Not with men.* On animals. Amazing! But—what do you want?"

374   "The truth. Do you fear me?"

375   "Not with this," said Stone, grasping the wirepoint. "But I shall tell you the truth."

376   "Is it true that you have conquered the great pain?"

377   Stone hesitated, seeking words for an answer.

378   "Quick, can you tell me how you have done it, so that I may believe you?"

379   "I have loaded the ships with life."

380   "Life?"

381   "Life. I don't know what the great pain is, but I did find that in the experiments, when I sent out masses of animals or plants, the life in the center of the mass lived longest. I built ships—small ones, of course—and sent them out with rabbits, with monkeys—"

382   "Those are Beasts?"

383   "Yes. With small Beasts. And the Beasts came back unhurt. They came back because the walls of the ships were filled with life. I tried many kinds, and finally found a sort of life which lives in the waters. Oysters. Oysterbeds. The outermost oysters died in the great pain. The inner ones lived. The passengers were unhurt."

384   "But they were Beasts?"

385   "Not only Beasts. Myself."

386   "You!"

387   "I came through space alone. Through what you call the up-and-out, alone. Awake and sleeping. I am unhurt. If you do not believe me, ask your brother scanners. Come and see my ship in the morning. I will be glad to see you then, along with your brother scanners. I am going to demonstrate before the chiefs of the Instrumentality."

388   Martel repeated his question: "You came here alone?"

389   Adam Stone grew testy: "Yes, alone. Go back and check your scanner's register if you do not believe me. You never put me in a bottle to cross Space."

390   Martel's face was radiant. "I believe you now. It is true. No more scanners. No more habermans. No more cranching."

391   Stone looked significantly toward the door.

392   Martel did not take the hint. "I must tell you that—"

393   "Sir, tell me in the morning. Go enjoy your cranch. Isn't it supposed to be pleasure? Medically I know it well. But not in practice."

394   "It is pleasure. It's normality—for a while. But listen. The scanners have sworn to destroy you, and your work."

395   "What!"

396   "They have met and have voted and sworn. You will make scanners unnecessary, they say. You will bring the ancient wars back to the world, if scanning is lost and the scanners live in vain."

397   Adam Stone was nervous but kept his wits about him: "You're a scanner. Are you going to kill me—or try?"

398   "No, you fool. I have betrayed the Confraternity. Call guards the moment I escape. Keep guards around you. I will try to intercept the killer."

399   Martel saw a blur in the window. Before Stone could turn, the wirepoint was whipped out of his hand. The blur solidified and took form as Parizianski.

400   Martel recognized what Parizianski was doing: *High speed.*

401   Without thinking of his cranch, he thrust his hand to his chest, set himself up to *High speed* too. Waves of fire, like the great pain, but hotter, flooded over him. He fought to keep his face readable as he stepped in front of Parizianski and gave the sign.

402   *Top emergency.*

403   Parizianski spoke, while the normally moving body of Stone stepped away from them as slowly as a drifting cloud: "Get out of my way. I am on a mission."

404   "I know it. I stop you here and now. Stop. Stop. Stop. Stone is right."

405   Parizianski's lips were barely readable in the haze of pain which flooded Martel. (He thought: *God, God, God of the ancients! Let me hold on! Let me live under* Overload *just long enough!*) Parizianski was saying: "Get out of my way. By order of the Confraternity, get out of my way!" And Parizianski gave the sign, *Help I demand in the name of my duty!*

406   Martel choked for breath in the syruplike air. He tried one last time:

407   "Parizianski, friend, friend, my friend. Stop. Stop." (No scanner had ever murdered scanner before.)

408   Parizianski made the sign: *You are unfit for duty, and I will take over.*

409   Martel thought, *For the first time in the world!* as he reached over and twisted Parizianski's brainbox up to *Overload.* Parizianski's eyes glittered in terror and understanding. His body began to drift down toward the floor.

410   Martel had just strength to reach his own chestbox. As he faded into haberman or death, he knew not which, he felt his fingers turning on the control of speed, turning down. He tried to speak, to say, "Get a scanner. I need help, get a scanner . . ."

411   But the darkness rose about him, and the numb silence clasped him.

412 Martel awakened to see the face of Luci near his own.

413 He opened his eyes wider, and found that he was hearing—hearing the sound of her happy weeping, the sound of her chest as she caught the air back into her throat.

414 He spoke weakly: "Still cranched? Alive?"

415 Another face swam into the blur beside Luci's. It was Adam Stone. His deep voice rang across immensities of space before coming to Martel's hearing. Martel tried to read Stone's lips, but could not make them out. He went back to listening to the voice:

416 "... not cranched. Do you understand me? Not cranched!"

417 Martel tried to say: "But I can hear! I can feel!" The others got his sense if not his words.

418 Adam Stone spoke again:

419 "You have gone back through the haberman. I put you back first. I didn't know how it would work in practice, but I had the theory all worked out. You don't think the Instrumentality would waste the scanners, do you? You go back to normality. We are letting the habermans die as fast as the ships come in. They don't need to live any more. But we are restoring the scanners. You are the first. Do you understand? You are the first. Take it easy, now."

420 Adam Stone smiled. Dimly behind Stone, Martel thought that he saw the face of one of the chiefs of the Instrumentality. That face, too, smiled at him, and then both faces disappeared upward and away.

421 Martel tried to lift his head, to scan himself. He could not. Luci stared at him, calming herself, but with an expression of loving perplexity. She said,

422 "My darling husband! You're back again, to stay!"

423 Still, Martel tried to see his box. Finally he swept his hand across his chest with a clumsy motion. There was nothing there. The instruments were gone. He was back to normality but still alive.

424 In the deep weak peacefulness of his mind, another troubling thought took shape. He tried to write with his finger, the way that Luci wanted him to, but he had neither pointed fingernail nor scanner's tablet. He had to use his voice. He summoned up his strength and whispered:

425 "Scanners?"

426 "Yes, darling? What is it?"

427 "Scanners?"

428 "Scanners. Oh, yes, darling, they're all right. They had to arrest some of them for going into High speed and running away. But the Instrumentality caught them all—all those on the ground—and they're happy now. Do you know, darling," she laughed, "some of them didn't want to be restored to normality. But Stone and the chiefs persuaded them."

429   "Vomact?"

430   "He's fine, too. He's staying cranched until he can be restored. Do
you know, he has arranged for scanners to take new jobs. You're all to be
deputy chiefs for Space. Isn't that nice? But he got himself made chief for
Space. You're all going to be pilots, so that your fraternity and guild can
go on. And Chang's getting changed right now. You'll see him soon."

431   Her face turned sad. She looked at him earnestly and said: "I might as
well tell you now. You'll worry otherwise. There has been one accident.
Only one. When you and your friend called on Adam Stone, your friend
was so happy that he forgot to scan, and he let himself die of *Overload*."

432   "Called on Stone?"

433   "Yes. Don't you remember? Your friend."

434   He still looked surprised, so she said:

435   "Parizianski."

DISCUSSION QUESTIONS

1. What is the difference between habermans and scanners?

2. If there is no reward for being a scanner because there is no enjoyment, why do they do it? Would you choose to be a scanner? Why?
   Discuss your responses with one or two classmates.

3. When the scanners vote on the fate of a real man without the right
   to do so, why does Martel claim he won't report them?

4. Why did Henry Haberman create the first habermans?

5. How are the scanners a fraternity of the damned?

WRITING TOPICS

1. Why does Martel decide at the meeting that scanners live in vain?
   Explain what he means in your journal.

2. The scene where the scanners recite their ritualistic code has two
   purposes. What is its purpose in the context of the story? What is
   its purpose for readers? Write a short essay exploring the importance
   of rituals for humans.

3. What other types of societies might the scanners (minus the technological trappings) be compared to, especially those prominent in the
   fifties? List and briefly describe as many as you can think of, then
   compare them to the society of the scanners.

Death between the Stars

1956

MARION ZIMMER BRADLEY (b. 1930)

Marion Zimmer Bradley began her writing career in 1953 with
"Women Only" and produced her first novel, *The Door Through
Space*, in 1957. In 1958 she began her most ambitious project,
the *Darkover* series, a chain of dozens of novels with an internal
chronology of events. As the series progressed, the emphasis on
feminist concerns became a stronger element in her stories. One
of the nonseries works Bradley is noted for is *Mists of Avalon*
(1983), a revisionist look at Arthurian legends.

Her short stories have been collected in *The Dark Intruder
and Other Stories* (1964) and *The Best of Marion Zimmer Bradley* (1985).
In the *Darkover* series the inhabitants are descended from previous
human colonists who resist the empire's enticements to join.
Darkover combines antitechnology with telepathy. The novels have
an internal chronology that differs from the publishing dates. *The
Planet Savers* (1958) was first in publication, but *Darkover Landfall*
(1972) is first in chronology. Bradley's husband, Leigh Brackett,
wrote *The Darkover Concordance: A Reader's Guide* (1979) to help sort
out the complexities of the series. Bradley continues to write the
Darkover series, with the latest contribution being *Towers of
Darkover* (1993).

In "Death between the Stars," Marion Zimmer Bradley
shows how two unlikely cabinmates struggle with their accom-
modations and end up in an even more unlikely circumstance.

1   They asked me about it, of course, before I boarded the starship. All through the Western sector of the Galaxy, few rules are stricter than the one dividing human from nonhuman, and the little captain of the *Vesta*—he was Terran, too, and proud in the black leather of the Empire's merchant-man forces—hemmed and hawed about it, as much as was consistent with a spaceman's dignity.

2   "You see, Miss Vargas," he explained, not once but as often as I would listen to him, "this is not, strictly speaking, a passenger ship at all. Our charter is only to carry cargo. But, under the terms of our franchise, we are required to transport an occasional passenger, from the more isolated planets where there is no regular passenger service. Our rules simply don't permit us to discriminate, and the Theradin reserved a place on this ship for our last voyage."

3   He paused, and reemphasized, "We have only the one passenger cabin, you see. We're a cargo ship, and we are not allowed to make any discrimination between our passengers."

4   He looked angry about it. Unfortunately, I'd run up against that attitude before. Some Terrans won't travel on the same ship with nonhumans even when they're isolated in separate ends of the ship.

5   I understood his predicament, better than he thought. The Theradin seldom travel in space. No one could have foreseen that Haalvordhen, the Theradin from Samarra, who had lived on the forsaken planet of Deneb IV for eighteen of its cycles, would have chosen this particular flight to go back to its own world.

6   At the same time, I had no choice. I had to get back to an Empire planet—*any* planet—where I could take a starship for Terra. With war about to explode in the Procyon sector, I had to get home before communications were knocked out altogether. Otherwise—well, a Galactic war can last up to eight hundred years. By the time regular transport service was reestablished, I wouldn't be worrying about getting home.

7   The *Vesta* could take me well out of the dangerous sector, and all the way to Samarra—Sirius Seven—which was, figuratively speaking, just across the street from the Solar System and Terra. Still, it was a questionable solution. The rules about segregation are strict, the antidiscriminatory laws are stricter, and the Theradin had made a prior reservation.

8   The captain of the *Vesta* couldn't have refused him transportation, even if fifty human Terran women had been left stranded on Deneb IV. And sharing a cabin with the Theradin was ethically, morally, and socially out of the question. Haalvordhen was a nonhuman telepath; and no human in his right senses will get any closer than necessary even to a human telepath. As for a nonhuman one—

9   And yet, what other way was there?

10   The captain said tentatively, "We *might* be able to squeeze you into the crewmen's quarters—" He paused uneasily and glanced up at me.

11   I bit my lip, frowning. That was worse yet. "I understand," I said slowly, "that this Theradin—Haalvordhen—has offered to allow me to share *its* quarters."

12   "That's right. But, Miss Vargas—"

13   I made up my mind in a rush. "I'll do it," I said. "It's the best way, all around."

14   At the sight of his scandalized face, I almost regretted my decision. It was going to cause an interplanetary scandal, I thought wryly. A human woman—and a Terran citizen—spending forty days in space and sharing a cabin with a nonhuman!

15   The Theradin, although male in form, had no single attribute which one could remotely refer to as sex. But of course that wasn't the problem. The nonhuman were specifically prohibited from mingling with the human races. Terran custom and taboo were binding, and I faced, resolutely, the knowledge that by the time I got to Terra, the planet might be made too hot to hold me.

16   Still, I told myself defiantly, it was a big Galaxy. And conditions weren't normal just now and that made a big difference. I signed a substantial check for my transportation and made arrangements for the shipping and stowing of what few possessions I could safely transship across space.

17   But I still felt uneasy when I went aboard the next day—so uneasy that I tried to bolster up my flagging spirits with all sorts of minor comforts. Fortunately, the Theradin were oxygen breathers, so I knew there would be no trouble about atmosphere mixtures or the air pressure to be maintained in the cabin. And the Theradin were Type Two nonhumans, which meant that the acceleration of a hyperspeed ship would knock my shipmate into complete prostration without special drugs. In fact, he would probably stay drugged in his skyhook during most of the trip.

18   The single cabin was far up toward the nose of the starship. It was a queer little spherical cubbyhole, a nest. The walls were foam-padded all around the sphere, for passengers never develop a spaceman's skill at maneuvering their bodies in free fall, and cabins had to be designed so that an occupant, moving unguardedly, would not dash out his or her brains against an unpadded surface. Spaced at random on the inside of the sphere were three skyhooks—nested cradles on swinging pivots— into which the passenger was snagged during blastoff in shock-absorbing foam and a complicated Garensen pressure apparatus and was thus enabled to sleep secure without floating away.

19   A few screw-down doors were marked LUGGAGE. I immediately unscrewed one door and stowed my personal belongings in the bin. Then I screwed the top down securely and carefully fastened the padding over it. Finally, I climbed around the small cubbyhole, seeking to familiarize myself with it before my unusual roommate arrived.

20   It was about fourteen feet in diameter. A sphincter lock opened from the narrow corridor to cargo bays and crewmen's quarters, while a second led into the cabin's functional equivalent of a bathroom. Planetbound men and women are always surprised and a little shocked when they see the sanitary arrangements on a spaceship. But once they've tried to perform normal bodily functions in free fall, they understand the peculiar equipment very well.

21   I've made six trips across the Galaxy in as many cycles. I'm practically an old hand, and can even wash my face in free fall without drowning. The trick is to use a sponge and suction. But, by and large, I understand perfectly why spacemen, between planets, usually look a bit unkempt.

22   I stretched out on the padding of the main cabin, and waited with growing uneasiness for the nonhuman to show. Fortunately, it wasn't long before the diaphragm on the outer sphincter lock expanded and a curious, peaked face peered through.

23   "Vargas Miss Hel-len?" said the Theradin in a sibilant whisper.

24   "That's my name," I replied instantly. I pulled upward, and added, quite unnecessarily, "You are Haalvordhen, of course."

25   "Such is my identification," confirmed the alien, and the long, lean, oddly muscled body squirmed through after the peaked head. "It is kind, Vargas Miss, to share accommodation under this necessity."

26   "It's kind of you," I said vigorously. "We've all got to get home before this war breaks out!"

27   "That war may be prevented, I have all hope," the nonhuman said. He spoke comprehensibly in Galactic Standard, but expressionlessly, for the vocal cords of the Theradins are located in an auxiliary pair of inner lips, and their voices seem reedy and lacking in resonance to human ears.

28   "Yet know you, Vargas Miss, they would have hurled me from this ship to make room for an Empire citizen, had you not been heart-kind to share."

29   "Good heavens!" I exclaimed, shocked. "I didn't know that!"

30   I stared at him, disbelieving. The captain couldn't have legally done such a thing—or even seriously have entertained the thought. Had he been trying to intimidate the Theradin into giving up his reserved place?

31   "I—I was meaning to thank *you*," I said, to cover my confusion.

32   "Let us thank we-other, then, and be in accord," the reedy voice mouthed.

33   I looked the nonhuman over, unable to hide completely my curiosity. In form the Theradin was vaguely humanoid—but only
vaguely—for the squat arms terminated in mittened "hands" and the
long, sharp face was elfin and perpetually grimacing.

34   The Theradin have no facial muscles to speak of, and no change of
expression or of vocal inflection is possible for them. Of course, being
telepathic, such subtleties of visible or auditory expression would be
superfluous on the face of it.

35   I felt—as yet—none of the revulsion which the mere presence of
the Theradin was *supposed* to inspire. It was not much different from
being in the presence of a large humanoid animal. There was nothing
inherently fearful about the alien. Yet he was a telepath—and of a nonhuman breed my species had feared for a thousand years.

36   Could he read my mind?

37   "Yes," said the Theradin from across the cabin. "You must forgive
me. I try to put up barrier, but it is hard. You broadcast your thought
so strong it is impossible to shut it out." The alien paused. "Try not to
be embar-rass. It bother me, too."

38   Before I could think of anything to say to that, a crew member in
black leather thrust his head, unannounced, through the sphincter and
said with an air of authority. "In skyhooks, please." He moved confidently into the cabin. "Miss Vargas, can I help you strap down?" he asked.

39   "Thanks, but I can manage," I told him.

40   Hastily I clambered into the skyhook, buckling the inner straps
and fastening the suction tubes of the complicated Garensen apparatus
across my chest and stomach. The nonhuman was awkwardly drawing
his hands from their protective mittens and struggling with the
Garensens.

41   Unhappily, the Theradin have a double thumb, and handling the
small-size Terran equipment is an almost impossibly delicate task. It is
made more difficult by the fact that the flesh of their "hands" is mostly
thin mucous membrane which tears easily on contact with leather and
raw metal.

42   "Give Haalvordhen a hand," I urged the crewman. "I've done this
dozens of times!"

43   I might as well have saved my breath. The crewman came and assured himself that *my* straps and tubes and cushions were meticulously
tightened. He took what seemed to me a long time, and used his hands
somewhat excessively. I lay under the heavy Garensen equipment, too
inwardly furious to even give him the satisfaction of protest.

44   It was far too long before he finally straightened and moved toward Haalvordhen's skyhook. He gave the alien's outer straps only a

perfunctory tug or two and then turned his head to grin at me with a totally uncalled-for familiarity.

45   "Blastoff in ninety seconds," he said, and wriggled himself rapidly out through the lock.

46   Haalvordhen exploded in a flood of Samarran which I could not follow. The vehemence of his voice, however, was better than a dictionary. For some strange reason I found myself sharing his fury. The unfairness of the whole procedure was shameful. The Theradin had paid passage money and deserved in any case the prescribed minimum of decent attention.

47   I said forthrightly, "Never mind the fool, Haalvordhen. Are you strapped down all right?"

48   "I don't know," he replied despairingly. "The equipment is unfamiliar—"

49   "Look—" I hesitated, but in common decency I had to make the gesture. "If I examine carefully my own Garensens, can you read my mind and see how they should be adjusted?"

50   He mouthed, "I'll try," and immediately I fixed my gaze steadily on the apparatus.

51   After a moment, I felt a curious sensation. It was something like the faint, sickening feeling of being touched and pushed about, against my will, by a distasteful stranger.

52   I tried to control the surge of almost physical revulsion. No wonder that humans kept as far as possible from the telepathic races. . . .

53   And then I saw—did I see, I wondered, or was it a direct telepathic interference with my perceptions?—a second image superimpose itself on the Garensens into which I was strapped. And the realization was so disturbing that I forgot the discomfort of the mental rapport completely.

54   "You aren't nearly fastened in," I warned. "You haven't begun to fasten the suction tubes—oh, damn the man. He must have seen in common humanity—" I broke off abruptly and fumbled in grim desperation with my own straps. "I think there's just time—"

55   But there wasn't. With appalling suddenness a violent clamor—the final warning—hit my ears. I clenched my teeth and urged frantically: "Hang on! Here we go!"

56   And then the blast hit us! Under the sudden sickening pressure I felt my lungs collapse and struggled to remain upright, choking for breath. I heard a queer, gagging grunt from the alien, and it was far more disturbing than a human scream would have been. Then the second shock wave struck with such violence that I screamed aloud in completely human terror. Screamed—and blacked out.

57   I wasn't unconscious very long. I'd never collapsed during takeoff before, and my first fuzzy emotion when I felt the touch of familiar

things around me again was one of embarrassment. What had happened? Then, almost simultaneously, I became reassuringly aware that we were in free fall and that the crewman who had warned us to alert ourselves was stretched out on the empty air near my skyhook. He looked worried.

58   "Are you all right, Miss Vargas?" he asked, solicitously. "The blastoff wasn't any rougher than usual—"

59   "I'm all right," I assured him woozily. My shoulders jerked and the Garensens shrieked as I pressed upward, undoing the apparatus with tremulous fingers. "What about the Theradin?" I asked urgently. "His Garensens weren't fastened. You barely glanced at them."

60   The crewman spoke slowly and steadily, with a deliberation I could not mistake. "Just a minute, Miss Vargas," he said. "Have you forgotten? I spent *every moment* of the time I was in here fastening the Theradin's belts and pressure equipment."

61   He gave me a hand to assist me up, but I shook it off so fiercely that I flung myself against the padding on the opposite side of the cabin. I caught apprehensively at a handhold and looked down at the Theradin.

62   Haalvordhen lay flattened beneath the complex apparatus. His peaked pixie face was shrunken and ghastly, and his mouth looked badly bruised. I bent closer, then jerked upright with a violence that sent me cascading back across the cabin, almost into the arms of the crewman.

63   "You must have fixed those belts *just now,*" I said accusingly. "They *were not* fastened before blastoff! It's malicious criminal negligence, and if Haalvordhen dies—"

64   The crewman gave me a slow, contemptuous smile. "It's my word against yours, sister," he reminded me.

65   "In common decency, in common humanity—" I found that my voice was hoarse and shaking, and could not go on.

66   The crewman said humorlessly, "I should think you'd be glad if the geek died in blastoff. You're awfully concerned about the geek—and you know how *that* sounds?"

67   I caught the frame of the skyhook and anchored myself against it. I was almost too faint to speak. "What were you trying to do?" I brought out at last. "*Murder* the Theradin?"

68   The crewman's baleful gaze did not shift from my face. "Suppose you close your mouth," he said, without malice but with an even inflection that was far more frightening. "If you don't, we may have to close it for you. I don't think much of humans who fraternize with geeks."

69   I opened and shut my mouth several times before I could force myself to reply. All I finally said was, "You know, of course, that I intend to speak to the captain."

70 "Suit yourself." He turned and strode contemptuously toward the door. "We'd have been doing you a favor if the geek had died in blastoff. But, as I say, suit yourself. I think your geek's alive, anyhow. They're hard to kill."

71 I clutched the skyhook, unable to move, while he dragged his body through the sphincter lock and it contracted behind him.

72 Well, I thought bleakly, I had known what I would be letting myself in for when I'd made the arrangement. And since I was already committed, I might as well see if Haalvordhen was alive or dead. Resolutely I bent over his skyhook, angling sharply to brace myself in free fall.

73 He wasn't dead. While I looked, I saw the bruised and bleeding "hands" flutter spasmodically. Then, abruptly, the alien made a queer, rasping noise. I felt helpless, and for some reason I was stirred to compassion.

74 I bent and laid a hesitant hand on the Garensen apparatus, which was now neatly and expertly fastened. I was bitter about the fact that for the first time in my life I had lost consciousness! Had I not done so, the crewman could not have so adroitly covered his negligence. But it was important to remember that the circumstance would not have helped Haalvordhen much either.

75 "Your feelings do you nothing but credit!" The reedy, flat voice was almost a whisper. "If I may trespass once more on your kindness—can you unfasten these instruments again?"

76 I bent to comply, asking helplessly as I did so, "Are you sure you're all right?"

77 "Very far from all right," the alien mouthed, slowly and without expression.

78 I had the feeling that he resented being compelled to speak aloud, but I didn't think I could stand that telepath touch again. The alien's flat, slitted eyes watched me while I carefully unfastened the suction tubes and cushioning devices.

79 At this distance I could see that the eyes had lost their color and that the raw "hands" were flaccid and limp. There were also heavily discolored patches about the alien's throat and head. He pronounced, with a terribly thick effort:

80 "I should have—been drugged. Now it's too late. *Argha maci*—" The words trailed off into blurred Samarran, but the discolored patch in his neck still throbbed sharply, and the hands twitched in an agony which, being dumb, seemed the more fearful.

81 I clung to the skyhook, dismayed at the intensity of my own emotion. I thought that Haalvordhen had spoken again when the sharp jolt of command sounded, clear and imperative, in my brain.

82   *"Procalamine!"* For an instant the shock was all I could feel—the shock, and the overwhelming revulsion at the telepathic touch. There was no hesitation or apology in it now, for the Theradin was fighting for his life. Again the sharp, furious command came: *"Give me procalamine!"*

83   And with a start of dismay I realized that most nonhumans needed the drug, which was kept on all spaceships to enable them to live in free fall.

84   Few nonhuman races have the stubbornly persistent heart of the Terrans, which beats by muscular contraction alone. The circulation of the Theradin, and similar races, is dependent on gravity to keep the vital fluid pulsing. Procalamine gives their main blood organ just enough artificial muscular spasm to keep the blood moving and working.

85   Hastily I propelled myself into the "bathroom"—wiggled hastily through the diaphragm and unscrewed the top of the bin marked First Aid. Neatly pigeonholed beneath transparent plastic were sterile bandages, antiseptics clearly marked Human and—separately, for the three main types of nonhuman races, in one deep bin—the small plastic globules of vital stimulants.

86   I sorted out two purple fluorescent ones—little globes marked *procalamine*—and looked at the warning, in raised characters on the globule. It read: For Administration by Qualified Space Personnel Only. A touch of panic made my diaphragm catch. Should I call the *Vesta*'s captain or one of the crew?

87   Then a cold certainty grew in me. If I did, Haalvordhen wouldn't get the stimulant he needed. I sorted out a fluorescent needle for nonhuman integument, pricked the globule, and sucked the dose into the needle. Then, with its tip still enclosed in the plastic globe, I wriggled myself back to where the alien lay loosely confined by one of the inner straps.

88   Panic touched me again, with the almost humorous knowledge that I didn't know where to inject the stimulant and that a hypodermic injection in space presents problems which only space-trained men are able to cope with. But I reached out notwithstanding and gingerly picked up one of the unmittened "hands." I didn't stop to think how I knew that this was the proper site for the injection. I was too overcome with strong physical loathing.

89   Instinct from man's remote past on Earth told me to drop the nonhuman flesh and cower, gibbering and howling as my simian antecedents would have done. The raw membrane was feverishly hot and unpleasantly slimy to touch. I fought rising queasiness as I tried to think how to stead him for the injection.

90   In free fall there is no steadiness, no direction. The hypodermic needle, of course, worked by suction, but piercing the skin would be the big problem. Also, I was myself succumbing to the dizziness of

no-gravity flight and realized coldly that if I couldn't make the injection in the next few minutes, I wouldn't be able to accomplish it at all.

91　　For a minute I didn't care, a primitive part of myself reminding me that if the alien died, I'd be rid of a detestable cabinmate and have a decent trip between planets.

92　　Then, stubbornly, I threw off the temptation. I steadied the needle in my hand, trying to conquer the disorientation which convinced me that I was looking both up and down at the Theradin.

93　　My own center of gravity seemed to be located in the pit of my stomach, and I fought the familiar space voyaging instinct to curl up in the fetal position and float. I moved slightly closer to the Theradin. I knew that if I could get close enough, our two masses would establish a common center of gravity and I would have at least a temporary orientation while I made the injection.

94　　The maneuver was unpleasant, for the alien seemed unconscious, flaccid and still, and mere physical closeness to the creature was repellent. The feel of the thick, wettish "hand" pulsing feebly in my own was almost sickeningly intimate. But at last I managed to maneuver myself close enough to establish a common center of gravity between us— an axis on which I seemed to hover briefly suspended.

95　　I pulled Haalvordhen's "hand" into this weight center in the bare inches of space between us, braced the needle, and resolutely stabbed with it.

96　　The movement disturbed the brief artificial gravity, and Haalvordhen floated and bounced a little weightlessly in his skyhook. The "hand" went sailing back, the needle recoiling harmlessly. I swore out loud, now quite foolishly angry, and my own jerky movement of annoyance flung me partially across the cabin.

97　　Inching slowly back, I tried to grit my teeth but only succeeded with a snap that jarred my skull. In tense anger, I seized Haalvordhen's "hand," which had almost stopped its feverish pulsing, and with a painfully slow effort—any quick or sudden movement would have thrown me, in recoil, across the cabin again—I wedged Haalvordhen's "hand" under the strap and anchored it there.

98　　It twitched faintly—the Theradin was apparently still sensible to pain—and my stomach rose at that sick pulsing. But I hooked my feet under the skyhook's frame and flung my free arm down and across the alien, holding tight to the straps that confined him.

99　　Still holding him thus wedged down securely, I jabbed again with the needle. It touched, pricked—and then, in despair, I realized it could not penetrate the Theradin integument without weight and pressure behind it.

100   I was too absorbed now in what had to be done to care just how I did it. So I wrenched forward with a convulsive movement that threw me, full-length, across the alien's body. Although I still had no weight, the momentum of the movement drove the hypodermic needle deeply into the flesh of the "hand."

101   I pressed the catch, then picked myself up slowly and looked around to see the crewman who had jeered at me with his head thrust through the lock again, regarding me with the distaste he had displayed toward the Theradin from the first. To him I was lower than the Theradin, having degraded myself by close contact with a nonhuman.

102   Under that frigid, contemptuous stare, I was unable to speak. I could only silently withdraw the needle and hold it up. The rigid look of condemnation altered just a little, but not much. He remained silent, looking at me with something halfway between horror and accusation.

103   It seemed years, centuries, eternities that he clung there, just looking at me, his face an elongated ellipse above the tight collar of his black leathers. Then, without even speaking, he slowly withdrew his head and the lock contracted behind him, leaving me alone with my sickening feeling of contamination and an almost hysterical guilt.

104   I hung the needle up on the air, curled myself into a ball, and, entirely unstrung, started sobbing like a fool.

105   It must have been a long time before I managed to pull myself together, because before I even looked to see whether Haalvordhen was still alive, I head the slight buzzing noise which meant that it was a meal period and that food had been sent through the chute to our cabin. I pushed the padding listlessly aside and withdrew the heat-sealed containers—one set colorless, the other set nonhuman fluorescent.

106   Tardily conscious of what a fool I'd been making of myself, I hauled my rations over to the skyhook and tucked them into a special slot, so that they wouldn't float away. Then, with a glance at the figure stretched out motionless beneath the safety strap of the other skyhook, I shrugged, pushed myself across the cabin again, and brought the fluorescent containers to Haalvordhen.

107   He made a weary, courteous noise which I took for acknowledgment. By now heartily sick of the whole business, I set them before him with a bare minimum of politeness and withdrew to my own skyhook, occupying myself with the always-ticklish problem of eating in free fall.

108   At last I drew myself up to return the containers to the chute, knowing we wouldn't leave the cabin during the entire trip. Space, on a starship, is held to a rigid minimum. There is simply no room for untrained outsiders moving around in the cramped ship, perhaps getting

dangerously close to critically delicate equipment, and the crew is far too busy to stop and keep an eye on rubbernecking tourists.

109   In an emergency, passengers can summon a crewman by pressing a call-button. Otherwise, as far as the crew was concerned, we were in another world.

110   I paused in midair to Haalvordhen's skyhook. His containers were untouched, and I felt moved to say, "Shouldn't you try to eat something?"

111   The flat voice had become even weaker and more rasping now, and the nonhuman's careful enunciation was slurred. Words of his native Samarran intermingled with queer turns of phrase which I expected were literally rendered from mental concepts.

112   "Heart-kind of you, *thakkava* Varga Miss, but late. Haalvordhen-I deep in grateful wishing—" A long spate of Samarran, thickly blurred, followed, then as if to himself, "Theradin-we, die nowhere only on Samarra, and only a little time ago Haalvordhen-I knowing must die, and must returning to home planet. *Saata.* Knowing to return and die there where Theradin-we around dying—" The jumble of words blurred again, and the limp "hands" clutched spasmodically, in and out.

113   Then, in a queer, careful tone, the nonhuman said, "But I am not living to return where I can stop-die. Not so long Haalvordhen-I be lasting, although Vargas-you Miss be helping most like *real* instead of alien. Sorry your people be most you unhelping—" he stopped again, and with a queer little grunting noise, continued, "Now Haalvordhen-I be giving Vargas-you stop-gift of heritage, be needful it is."

114   The flaccid form of the nonhuman suddenly stiffened, went rigid. The drooping lids over the Theradin's eyes seemed to unhood themselves, and in a spasm of fright I tried to fling myself backward. But I did not succeed. I remained motionless, held in a dumb fascination.

115   I felt a sudden, icy cold, and the sharp physical nausea crawled over me again at the harsh and sickening touch of the alien on my mind, not in words this time, but in a rapport even closer—a hateful touch so intimate that I felt my body go limp in helpless fits and spasms of convulsive shuddering under the deep, hypnotic contact.

116   Then a wave of darkness almost palpable surged up in my brain. I tried to scream, "*Stop it, stop it!*" and a panicky terror flitted in my last conscious thought through my head. *This is why, this is the reason humans and telepaths don't mix—*

117   And then a great dark door opened under my senses and I plunged again into unconsciousness.

118   It was not more than a few seconds, I suppose, before the blackness swayed and lifted and I found myself floating, curled helplessly in

midair, and seeing, with a curious detachment, the Theradin's skyhook below me. Something in the horrid limpness of that form stirred me wide awake.

119   With a tight band constricting my breathing, I arrowed downward. I had never seen a dead Theradin before, but I needed no one to tell me that I saw one now. The constricting band still squeezed my throat in dry gasps, and in a frenzy of hysteria I threw myself wildly across the cabin, beating and battering on the emergency button, shrieking and sobbing and screaming. . . .

120   They kept me drugged all the rest of the trip. Twice I remember waking and shrieking out things I did not understand myself, before the stab of needles in my arm sent me down into comforting dreams again. Near the end of the flight, while my brain was still fuzzy, they made me sign a paper, something to do with witnessing that the crew held no responsibility for the Theradin's death.

121   It didn't matter. There was something clear and cold and shrewd in my mind, behind the surface fuzziness, which told me I must do exactly what they wanted, or I would find myself in serious trouble with the Terran authorities. At the time I didn't even care about that and supposed it was the drugs. Now, of course, I know the truth.

122   When the ship made planetfall at Samarra, I had to leave the *Vesta* and transship for Terra. The *Vesta*'s little captain shook me by the hand and carefully avoided my eyes, without mentioning the dead Theradin. I had the feeling—strange, how clear it was to my perceptions—that he regarded me in the same way he would regard a loaded time bomb that might explode at any moment.

123   I knew he was anxious to hurry me aboard a ship for Terra. He offered me special reservations on a linocruiser at a nominal price, with the obvious lie that he owned a part interest in it. Detachedly I listened to his floundering lies, ignored the hand he offered again, and told a lie or two of my own. He was angry. I knew he didn't want me to linger on Samarra.

124   Even so, he was glad to be rid of me.

125   Descending at last from the eternal formalities of the Terran landing zone, I struck out quickly across the port city and hailed a Theradin ground car. The Theradin driving it looked at me curiously, and in a buzzing voice informed me that I could find a human conveyance at the opposite corner. Surprised at myself, I stopped to wonder what I was doing. And then—

126   And then I identified myself in a way the Theradin could not mistake. He was nearly as surprised as I was. I clambered into the car, and he drove me to the queer, block-shaped building which my eyes had

never seen before but which I now knew as intimately as the blue sky of Terra.

127   Twice, as I crossed the twisting ramp, I was challenged. Twice, with the same shock of internal surprise, I answered the challenge correctly.

128   At last I came before a Theradin whose challenge crossed mine like a sure, sharp lance, and the result was startling. The Theradin Haalvamphrenan leaned backward twice in acknowledgment and said— not in words—"Haalvordhen!"

129   I answered in the same fashion. "Yes. Due to certain blunders, I could not return to our home planet and was forced to use the body of this alien. Having made the transfer unwillingly, under necessity, I now see certain advantages. Once within this body, it does not seem at all re- pulsive, and the host is highly intelligent and sympathetic.

130   "I regret the feeling that I am distasteful to you, dear friend. But, consider. I can now contribute my services as messenger and courier, without discrimination by these mind-blind Terrans. The law which pre- vents Theradin from dying on any other planet should now be changed."

131   "Yes, yes," the other acquiesced, quickly grasping my meaning. "But now to personal matters, my dear Haalvordhen. Of course your possessions are held intact for you."

132   I became aware that I possessed five fine residences upon the planet, a private lake, a grove of Theirry-trees, and four hattel-boats. Inheritance among the Theradin, of course, is dependent upon conti- nuity of the mental personality, regardless of the source of the young. When any Theradin died, transferring his mind into a new and younger host, the new host at once possessed all of those things which had be- longed to the former personality. Two Theradin, unsatisfied with their individual wealth, sometimes pooled their personalities into a single hostbody, thus accumulating modest fortunes.

133   Continuity of memory, of course, was perfect. As Helen Vargas, I had certain rights and privileges as a Terran citizen, certain possessions, certain family rights, certain Empire privileges. And as Haalvordhen, I was made free of Samarra as well.

134   In a sense of strict justice, I "told" Haalvamphrenan how the original host had died. I gave him the captain's name. I didn't envy him, when the *Vesta* docked again at Samarra.

135   "On second thought," Haalvamphrenan said reflectively, "I shall merely commit suicide in his presence."

136   Evidently, Helen-Haalvordhen-I had a very long and interesting life ahead of me.

137   So did all the other Theradin.

DISCUSSION QUESTIONS

1. Why would people avoid a human telepath? Why even more so an alien one?
2. Helen Vargas submits in silent protest to the overly physical strapping in by the crew member, but when her mind is touched by Haalvordhen she feels even more revulsion. Why? In small groups, examine the basis for her disgust.
3. Even though she initially regrets her decision to share a cabin with an alien, what circumstances contribute to Vargas's overcoming her discomfiture?
4. Upon leaving the *Vesta*, why does the captain regard Vargas as "a loaded time bomb"? Discuss the meaning of this with a classmate.
5. Why does the second Theradin say he will commit suicide in the presence of the *Vesta*'s captain the next time he arrives on Samarra?

WRITING TOPICS

1. There are conflicting regulations concerning segregation and discrimination in human–alien interactions. In your journal, explain why any intermingling might be so strongly prohibited.
2. How is Vargas changed once she reaches Samarra? Why does she decide to remain there instead of returning to Earth? In a few paragraphs, examine the ramifications of her decisions.
3. In an essay, discuss how this story reflects, in many ways, the civil rights situation in the United States in the mid-fifties.

CHAPTER SIX

The Sixties

1960	American Heart Association attributes higher death rates to smoking
	H. G. Wells' *The Time Machine* is made into a movie
	Astounding Science Fiction magazine changes its name to Analog Science Fact and Fiction
1961	Berlin Wall erected
	U.S.-trained Cuban rebels unsuccessfully attempt to overthrow Castro
	U.S.S.R. puts first man—Yuri Gagarin—in space
	Alan Shepard is the first man to make a U.S. space flight
	Robert Heinlein publishes *Stranger in a Strange Land*
	Irwin Allen's Voyage to the Bottom of the Sea movie
1962	Cuban missile crisis ends with U.S.S.R. withdrawing missiles from Cuba
	Rachel Carson publishes *Silent Spring*, warning of chemical pesticide use
	Telstar relays first live transatlantic pictures
	The Manchurian Candidate is made into a film
1963	**In Philip K. Dick's *The Man in the High Castle*, Hitler wins World War II**
	President Kennedy assassinated
	South Vietnamese government overthrown; U.S. sends aid
	Soviets put first woman—Valentina Tereshkova—in space
1964	***Dr. Who* begins 26–year TV career**
	Nelson Mandela imprisoned in South Africa
	Mods and Rockers clash in Britain

1965
- Malcolm X assassinated
- U.S. sends combat troops to Vietnam
- Protesters march in Washington against Vietnam War
- Soviet cosmonauts take first space walk
- **Frank Herbert's *Dune* is published**

1966
- Color TV becomes popular
- Chinese cultural revolution begins
- Soviet and U.S. remote-controlled spacecraft land on moon
- **The Nebula awards begin**

1967
- **The original *Star Trek* series begins on TV**
- Martin Luther King Jr. leads anti-Vietnam War demonstration
- U.S. scientists produce artificial DNA
- China explodes its first hydrogen bomb
- Race riots and anti-Vietnam War protests spread across country
- First human heart transplant by Dr. Christiaan Barnard
- *The Prisoner* begins airing on British TV

1968
- Martin Luther King Jr. assassinated
- Robert Kennedy assassinated
- *2001: A Space Odyssey* movie
- Woodstock festival in New York promotes love and music
- Charles Manson's brutal murders shock the nation
- Protestants and Catholics clash in Northern Ireland

1969
- *Apollo 11* lands two men on the moon
- U.S. removes cyclamates (food additive) from market and restricts use of DDT
- First use of an artificial human heart

HISTORICAL CONTEXT

The sixties were dominated by unrest and worldwide mounting
political tensions. In 1960, blacks in South Africa marched in protest
of laws restricting their freedom of movement. Police fired on
crowds, killing 67 and wounding hundreds more. The U.N. called
for economic sanctions, and the protests focused on the injustice
of apartheid. The next year trouble arose in Germany as increasing
numbers of East Berliners, under Soviet jurisdiction, were prevented
from working in U.S.-controlled West Berlin. The Soviets responded
by building the Berlin Wall, a concrete structure topped with barbed
wire and patrolled by troops. Though it was declared illegal by the
United States, the wall remained in place until 1989.

Conflicts between the Super Powers—the United States and
U.S.S.R.—also occurred in Cuba. Fidel Castro had established close
ties with the U.S.S.R. as well as Cuban communists. Cuban freedom fighters, trained by the CIA, attacked the Bay of Pigs in 1961
in an attempt to overthrow Castro. They were repelled, and soon
afterward Castro announced that the Communist Party was the
only legal party in Cuba. The next year the United States detected
nuclear missile bases on Cuba. The U.S.S.R. claimed these were for
defense only, but President John Kennedy demanded their removal.
Kennedy then blockaded Cuba by both air and sea to prevent more
Soviet missiles from arriving. For six tension-filled days the world
stood on the brink of nuclear war as the two forces squared off.
Finally, Nikita Khrushchev backed down and dismantled the bases
in return for a U.S. agreement not to invade Cuba. The following
year, 1963, Kennedy was assassinated by Lee Harvey Oswald.

In Vietnam, civil war had been brewing since the French withdrew in 1954. The United States saw Vietnam as a bulwark against the spread of communism in Southeast Asia, and believed that if a communist takeover of South Vietnam were to occur, other countries in Southeast Asia would fall like dominoes. From 1961 until 1963 Americans were officially only offering technical aid and advice to the South Vietnamese. When American warships were allegedly attacked by the Vietcong in 1964, however, President Lyndon Johnson was given full executive authority to defend the SEATO nations. The next year, bombing of North Vietnam began, and 150,000 U.S. troops were deployed. By 1966, that number had risen to 400,000.

As fighting in Southeast Asia escalated, anti-war campaigns sprouted in the United States, primarily among young people who doubted the wisdom of the war. When Richard Nixon took office and extended the battle to Laos and Cambodia, the protests increased in number and stridency.

After Mao Tse-tung's "Great Leap Forward" failed, he mounted a Cultural Revolution to lead the Chinese on the path to true communism. Schools and universities were closed as the army tortured and killed dissidents, and students who didn't enlist were sent to work in the fields. The army established committees to run the country, and Mao was named Supreme Commander in 1970.

In France, students inspired by the youth power movement in the United States forced universities to close. They demanded more government spending on education and less funding for nuclear weapons. The resulting conflict brought a virtual halt to the French economy for weeks, until President Charles de Gaulle promised reforms.

Violence returned to Northern Ireland after a decade of relative peace when Catholics marched to protest discrimination in housing and employment. British troops were sent at the request of the provincial government to restore order. Trouble was also brewing in the Mideast as Israel attacked its Arab neighbors, including Syria, Jordan, and Egypt. After a stunning victory in the Six-Day War, Israel occupied Jerusalem and Palestine.

In the United States, more than half of Americans were
under 30 by 1960. Postwar prosperity had empowered youth as
more went to college, had cars, and had more money to spend than
previous generations. When youths began protesting against the
society that had elevated them to this position, older Americans
were mystified. The youth, fueled by the beatnik era and the rock
and roll frenzy of the fifties, disregarded many of the teachings
of their parents and began advocating free love, drugs, and mysti-
cism. They organized their emerging social consciousness into
political activism and supported the civil rights movement, help
for the poor and minorities, and protested visibly and loudly
against the war in Vietnam. "Never trust anyone over 30" was
often repeated, along with, "Hell no, we won't go," referring
to the widespread refusal to obey draft laws.

The space race was dramatically highlighted in 1969 when
the United States, after trailing the Soviets for a decade, landed
the first human beings on the moon. Neil Armstrong's "one giant
leap for mankind" echoed in the consciousness of the world. The
technological progress highlighted by the moon landing was tempered by the realization that countries could not act in isolation;
repercussions would be felt around the world.

DEVELOPMENTS IN SCIENCE FICTION

Many of the established science fiction writers had been writing
since before World War II and were over 30 by the 1960s. A new
generation of writers, many of whom identified with the hippie
movement of the mid-sixties, reacted against the "conservative"
writers of the previous generation. These new writers were inspired by the social experiments sweeping the nation, including
mind-altering drugs, communes, free love, civil rights, and
nonviolence.

The pulps were gone, and with them the emphasis on the
short story as the basic form of science fiction. Instead, book-
length fiction that went straight to paperback dominated the market. Few science fiction magazines remained, and although John
W. Campbell Jr. remained as editor at *Astounding Science Fiction*

(renamed *Analog Science Fact and Fiction* in 1960), other editors began to eclipse him. Newer writers explored areas different from the hard science fiction that Campbell upheld as the ideal. Campbell still clung to his belief that science fiction was "very strictly and literally, analogous to science facts."

While Campbell continued to promote hard science fiction, Michael Moorcock, known for his Elric series of sword and sorcery novels and as editor of *Tarzan's Adventures* magazine, became editor of the *New Worlds* magazine in Britain in 1964. Moorcock encouraged experimentation, freedom from previous formulas, and stories with wide scope. He believed science fiction should be introspective and examine the "soft" sciences, such as psychology and sociology. "Interior space" became a buzzword as hard and soft science fiction battled on the open market.

J. G. Ballard was a leading proponent of the "New Wave" of science fiction writers, and his stories featured stream of consciousness, present tense, out-of-time sequences, and interior monologues. Ballard called his own writing during the sixties "psychological wish fulfillment." He created three linked-world novels, *The Drowned World* (1962), *The Burning World* (1964), and *The Crystal World* (1966). The setting is a near, rather than a distant, future, and these novels tell of individual reactions to doomsday catastrophes. One character, for instance, chooses suicide in the ruined world as a logical wish fulfillment, something unheard of in scientific-dominated hard science fiction.

In *Beta-2* (1965), Samuel Delany (another of the New Wave writers) has characters in a spaceship confronting sociological problems that mirror the racial and ethnic strife that our country was experiencing. The sealed environment becomes a microcosm, not only of the United States but of the rest of the world during the sixties. Roger Zelazny, on the other hand, in *This Immortal* (1966), wrote about aliens who are intent on turning Earth into a giant amusement park while the hero recites poetry and practices martial arts. Zelazny preferred to use reconstructed mythological figures in future settings, making his fiction a curious mixture of fantasy and science fiction.

Many fans objected to the New Wave, though the criticisms were often directed against Moorcock's editorials as much as against the stories themselves. Others simply ignored the attempt to change the direction of science fiction, but Norman Spinrad's "Bug Jack Barron" brought howls of protest in 1969 because of its use of profanity and emphasis on sex. As Moorcock's crusade against literary staleness caused battles with censorship, the resulting financial difficulties made the New Wave stumble. By the end of the decade, both the New Wave phase and its main vehicle, *New Worlds,* were out of business.

Other, more mainstream science fiction writers continued to publish engrossing stories in the sixties. Robert Heinlein's *Stranger in a Strange Land* (1961), the best known of all his works, is the story of a human raised as a Martian. When he returns to Earth, he is regarded as a cult figure whose proclamations incite religious, political, and sexual revolutions. This book was considered by many to be a "hippie Bible."

While Kurt Vonnegut wasn't labeled a science fiction writer, he occasionally used science fiction when it suited his satirical or literary purposes. In *Cat's Cradle* (1963), he presents telling lies as a necessary ingredient to promoting happiness. In *Slaughterhouse 5* (1969) he writes against war by showing mental patients assuming control of the post-apocalyptic Dresden, Germany, where he himself had been hospitalized as a POW during World War II.

Frank Herbert's *Dune* series of seven novels, beginning in 1965, is the story of a genetically engineered Messiah who uses powers to terraform (to add life to) a world. Politics, sociology, ecology, and metaphysics are all woven into an enormously complicated world with so many transformations, each carefully planned out, that readers almost need a guidebook. It set a hallmark example of the meticulous world building that other science fiction writers would strive for.

Philip K. Dick, in his fiction, pondered the conflicts between humans and machines. Reality changes in Dick's stories, and the characters are just as likely to be victims as heroes. He often wrote novels at breakneck speed, each examining in detail some part of his own struggle with the nature of reality. *The Three Stigmata of Palmer Eldritch* (1964) was his first popular science fiction novel.

Women began to get some recognition for their writing as the feminist movement gathered momentum. Women's voices added a dimension missing from previous treatments of science fiction themes by showcasing strong female characters coping with difficult situations. Joanna Russ' *Picnic on Paradise* was well received in 1968, and Ursula K. LeGuin's *The Left Hand of Darkness* (1969) added a new twist to gender roles. The characters in that novel change genders without any control or knowledge of what they will be in the next metamorphosis, causing the Earth characters much consternation and difficulty in trying to deal with their own perceptions about fixed gender roles.

SCIENCE FICTION IN OTHER MEDIA

Several good science fiction movies were produced during the sixties. Alfred Hitchcock's *The Birds* (1963), based on the 1952 Daphne du Maurier story, shows a seacoast town attacked by birds who seem bent on revenge, perhaps for ecological mistreatment. Ray Bradbury's *Fahrenheit 451* was also transferred to the screen, and while it is somewhat stilted, the film's message about the need for intellectual freedom is clear. Adaptations of stories by both Wells and Verne appeared in 1964. Wells' *First Men on the Moon* and Verne's *From the Earth to the Moon* suffer in the translation to the screen, with the screenplay and special effects vying for bottom place.

Fantastic Voyage (1966), though it had a somewhat unbelievable plot of shrinking humans to microscopic size and putting them inside a human body, did have some drama and humor, and much more attention was paid to the special effects. *Planet of the Apes* (1967) was set in a time when apes are the dominant species who keep humans, whom they regard as unintelligent, as slaves. The original movie, based on Pierre Boulle's 1963 novel, spurred a host of sequels.

The movie event of the decade, though, was Stanley Kubrick's *2001: A Space Odyssey* in 1968, which brought science fiction to the screen in a grand style. The detailed sets, special effects, and the haunting music set a new standard in quality. Arthur C. Clarke, whose story "The Sentinel" was the basis for the movie, was the script consultant.

TV also brought science fiction into millions of homes. *The Outer Limits* (1953–66), even though uneven in quality, was often excellent and provocative. *Voyage to the Bottom of the Sea* (1964–68), a spinoff from the 1961 movie of the same name, had drama and undersea monsters galore. *The Twilight Zone* (1959–64) didn't always feature science fiction themes, but the talented Rod Serling's imagination produced some vivid stories. The series was also hampered by low budgets, but it contained some of the most thought-provoking episodes ever aired. *Lost in Space* (1965–68) was a space opera featuring the Space Family Robinsons and the eternally obnoxious Dr. Smith.

The science fiction TV event, though, was *Star Trek* (1966–69), the brainchild of Gene Roddenberry. This series was the first to feature a multiracial and ethnic crew, and to use established science fiction writers like Harlan Ellison, Robert Bloch, Theodore Sturgeon, and Norman Spinrad for scripts. While the series was certainly in the Space Opera tradition of the pulps of the thirties and forties, it has moments of brilliance and eventually established a remarkably loyal following. When the series was cancelled after the second season, the massive number of letters to NBC convinced them to renew it for a third season. Subsequently released in syndication, the series is the most profitable TV show in history and has spawned several movies and spinoff TV series.

The Ship Who Sang

1961

ANNE MᶜCAFFREY (b. 1926)

Anne McCaffrey's shorter works began appearing in the fifties, but her first novel, *Restoree,* didn't appear until 1967. Much of her work is tenuously balanced on the bridge between science fiction and fantasy, including the work for which she is most well known, the *Pern* novels. Though fantasy in tone and treatment, the *Pern* novels do have a science fiction basis. The planet Pern is a distant Earth colony and has dragons genetically engineered to defend the planet. The dragons bond and team up with humans to battle the planet's deadly falling Threads.

The individual novels *Dragonquest* (1968), *Dragonflight* (1971), and *The White Dragon* (1978) also appeared as a series called *The Dragonriders of Pern* in 1978. And in 1988, she produced a prequel, *Dragonsdawn.* In 1989, a guidebook, *The Dragonlover's Guide to Pern,* was published. McCaffrey's works are primarily romantic adventures with sentimental overtones, and while the tone is fantasy, she maintains science fiction as a premise. She is also noted for the trilogy of *The Crystal Singer* (1982), *Killashandra* (1985), and *The Crystal Line* (1992). Some of her books are being converted into graphic novels, with *Dragonflight* (1991) the first to appear.

In "The Ship Who Sang," Anne McCaffrey explores a technological development that is far advanced from our present capabilities. We also see, though, that such science must be tempered with compassion when dealing with human emotions.

1   She was born a thing and as such would be condemned if she failed to pass the encephalograph test required of all newborn babies. There was always the possibility that though the limbs were twisted, the mind was not, that though the ears would hear only dimly, the eyes see vaguely, the mind behind them was receptive and alert.

2   The electroencephalogram was entirely favorable, unexpectedly so, and the news was brought to the waiting, grieving parents. There was the final, harsh decision: to give their child euthanasia or permit it to become an encapsulated "brain," a guiding mechanism in any one of a number of curious professions. As such, their offspring would suffer no pain, live a comfortable existence in a metal shell for several centuries, performing unusual service to Central Worlds.

3   She lived and was given a name, Helva. For her first three vegetable months she waved her crabbed claws, kicked weakly with her clubbed feet and enjoyed the usual routine of the infant. She was not alone, for there were three other such children in the big city's special nursery. Soon they all were removed to Central Laboratory School, where their delicate transformation began.

4   One of the babies died in the initial transferral, but of Helva's "class," seventeen thrived in the metal shells. Instead of kicking feet, Helva's neural responses started her wheels; instead of grabbing with hands, she manipulated mechanical extensions. As she matured, more and more neural synapses would be adjusted to operate other mechanisms that went into the maintenance and running of a spaceship. For Helva was destined to be the "brain" half of a scout ship, partnered with a man or a woman, whichever she chose, as the mobile half. She would be among the elite of her kind. Her initial intelligence tests registered above normal and her adaptation index was unusually high. As long as her development within her shell lived up to expectations, and there were no side-effects from the pituitary tinkering, Helva would live a rewarding, rich, and unusual life, a far cry from what she would have faced as an ordinary, "normal" being.

5   However, no diagram of her brain patterns, no early IQ tests recorded certain essential facts about Helva that Central must eventually learn. They would have to bide their official time and see, trusting that the massive doses of shell–psychology would suffice her, too, as the necessary bulwark against her unusual confinement and the pressures of her profession. A ship run by a human brain could not run rogue or insane with the power and resources Central had to build into their scout ships. Brain ships were, of course, long past the experimental stages. Most babies survived the perfected techniques of pituitary manipulation that kept their bodies small, eliminating the necessity of transfers from smaller to larger shells. And very, very few were lost when the final connection

was made to the control panels of ship or industrial combine. Shell-people resembled mature dwarfs in size whatever their natal deformities were, but the well-oriented brain would not have changed places with the most perfect body in the Universe.

6   So, for happy years, Helva scooted around in her shell with her classmates, playing such games as Stall, Power-Seek, studying her lessons in trajectory, propulsion techniques, computation, logistics, mental hygiene, basic alien psychology, philology, space history, law, traffic codes: all the et ceteras that eventually became compounded into a reasoning, logical, informed citizen. Not so obvious to her, but of more importance to her teachers, Helva ingested the precepts of her conditioning as easily as she absorbed her nutrient fluid. She would one day be grateful to the patient drone of the subconscious-level instruction.

7   Helva's civilization was not without busy, do-good associations, exploring possible inhumanities to terrestrial as well as extraterrestrial citizens. One such group—Society for the Preservation of the Rights of Intelligent Minorities—got all incensed over shelled "children" when Helva was just turning fourteen. When they were forced to, Central Worlds shrugged its shoulders, arranged a tour of the Laboratory Schools, and set the tour off to a big start by showing the members case histories, complete with photographs. Very few committees ever looked past the first few photos. Most of their original objections about "shells" were overridden by the relief that these hideous (to them) bodies *were* mercifully concealed.

8   Helva's class was doing fine arts, a selective subject in her crowded program. She had activated one of her microscopic tools, which she would later use for minute repairs to various parts of her control panel. Her subject was large—a copy of *The Last Supper*—and her canvas, small—the head of a tiny screw. She had turned her sight to the proper degree. As she worked she absentmindedly crooned, producing a curious sound. Shell-people used their own vocal cords and diaphragms, but sound issued through microphones rather than mouths. Helva's hum, then, had a curious vibrancy, a warm, dulcet quality even in its aimless chromatic wanderings.

9   "Why, what a lovely voice you have," said one of the female visitors.

10   Helva "looked" up and caught a fascinating panorama of regular, dirty craters on a flaky pink surface. Her hum became a gurgle of surprise. She instinctively regulated her "sight" until the skin lost its cratered look and the pores assumed normal proportions.

11   "Yes, we have quite a few years of voice training, madam," remarked Helva calmly. "Vocal peculiarities often become excessively irritating during prolonged interstellar distances and must be eliminated. I enjoyed my lessons."

12   Although this was the first time that Helva had seen unshelled people, she took this experience calmly. Any other reaction would have been reported instantly.

13   "I meant that you have a nice singing voice . . . dear," the lady said.

14   "Thank you. Would you like to see my work?" Helva asked politely. She instinctively sheered away from personal discussions, but she filed the comment away for further meditation.

15   "Work?" asked the lady.

16   "I am currently reproducing *The Last Supper* on the head of a screw."

17   "Oh, I say," the lady twittered.

18   Helva turned her vision back to magnification and surveyed her copy critically. "Of course, some of my color values do not match the old Master's and the perspective is faulty, but I believe it to be a fair copy."

19   The lady's eyes, unmagnified, bugged out.

20   "Oh, I forget," and Helva's voice was really contrite. If she could have blushed, she would have. "You people don't have adjustable vision."

21   The monitor of this discourse grinned with pride and amusement as Helva's tone indicated pity for the unfortunate.

22   "Here, this will help," said Helva, substituting a magnifying device in one extension and holding it over the picture.

23   In a kind of shock, the ladies and gentlemen of the committee bent to observe the incredibly copied and brilliantly executed *Last Supper* on the head of a screw.

24   "Well," remarked one gentleman who had been forced to accompany his wife, "the good Lord can eat where angels fear to tread."

25   "Are you referring, sir," asked Helva politely, "to the Dark Age discussions of the number of angels who could stand on the head of a pin?"

26   "I had that in mind."

27   "If you substitute 'atom' for 'angel,' the problem is not insoluble, given the metallic content of the pin in question."

28   "Which you are programmed to compute?"

29   "Of course."

30   "Did they remember to program a sense of humor, as well, young lady?"

31   "We are directed to develop a sense of proportion, sir, which contributes the same effect."

32   The good man chortled appreciatively and decided the trip was worth his time.

33   If the investigation committee spent months digesting the thoughtful food served them at the Laboratory School, they left Helva with a morsel as well.

34   "Singing" as applicable to herself required research. She had, of course, been exposed to and enjoyed a music-appreciation course that had included the better-known classical works, such as *Tristan und Isolde, Candide, Oklahoma!,* and *Le nozze di Figaro,* along with the atomic-age singers, Birgit Nilsson, Bob Dylan, and Geraldine Todd, as well as the curious rhythmic progressions of the Venusians, Capellan visual chromatics, the sonic concerti of the Altairians and Reticulan croons. But "singing" for any shell-person posed considerable technical difficulties. Shell-people were schooled to examine every aspect of a problem or situation before making a prognosis. Balanced properly between optimism and practicality, the nondefeatist attitude of the shell-people led them to extricate themselves, their ships, and personnel, from bizarre situations. Therefore to Helva, the problem that she couldn't open her mouth to sing, among other restrictions, did not bother her. She would work out a method, bypassing her limitations, whereby she could sing.

35   She approached the problem by investigating the methods of sound reproduction through the centuries, human and instrumental. Her own sound-production equipment was essentially more instrumental than vocal. Breath control and the proper enunciation of vowel sounds within the oral cavity appeared to require the most development and practice. Shell-people did not, strictly speaking, breathe. For their purposes, oxygen and other gases were not drawn from the surrounding atmosphere through the medium of lungs but sustained artificially by solution in their shells. After experimentation, Helva discovered that she could manipulate her diaphragmic unit to sustain tone. By relaxing the throat muscles and expanding the oral cavity well into the frontal sinuses, she could direct the vowel sounds into the most felicitous position for proper reproduction through her throat microphone. She compared the results with tape recordings of modern singers and was not unpleased, although her own tapes had a peculiar quality about them, not at all unharmonious, merely unique. Acquiring a repertoire from the Laboratory library was no problem to one trained to perfect recall. She found herself able to sing any role and any song which struck her fancy. It would not have occurred to her that it was curious for a female to sing bass, baritone, tenor, mezzo, soprano, and coloratura as she pleased. It was, to Helva, only a matter of the correct reproduction and diaphragmatic control required by the music attempted.

36   If the authorities remarked on her curious avocation, they did so among themselves. Shell-people were encouraged to develop a hobby so long as they maintained proficiency in their technical work.

37   On the anniversary of her sixteenth year, Helva was unconditionally graduated and installed in her ship, the XH–834. Her permanent titanium shell was recessed behind an even more indestructible barrier in the central shaft of the scout ship. The neural, audio, visual, and sensory connections were made and sealed. Her extendibles were diverted, connected, or augmented, and the final, delicate-beyond-description brain taps were completed while Helva remained anesthetically unaware of the proceedings. When she woke, she *was* the ship. Her brain and intelligence controlled every function from navigation to such loading as a scout ship of her class needed. She could take care of herself and her ambulatory half in any situation already recorded in the annals of Central Worlds and any situation its most fertile minds could imagine.

38   Her first actual flight, for she and her kind had made mock flights on dummy panels since she was eight, showed her to be a complete master of the techniques of her profession. She was ready for her great adventures and the arrival of her mobile partner.

39   There were nine qualified scouts sitting around collecting base pay the day Helva reported for active duty. There were several missions that demanded instant attention, but Helva had been of interest to several department heads in Central for some time and each bureau chief was determined to have her assigned to *his* section. No one had remembered to introduce Helva to the prospective partners. The ship always chose its own partner. Had there been another "brain" ship at the base at the moment, Helva would have been guided to make the first move. As it was, while Central wrangled among itself, Robert Tanner sneaked out of the pilots' barracks, out to the field, and over to Helva's slim metal hull.

40   "Hello, anyone at home?" Tanner said.

41   "Of course," replied Helva, activating her outside scanners. "Are you my partner?" she asked hopefully, as she recognized the Scout Service uniform.

42   "All you have to do is ask," he retorted in a wistful tone.

43   "No one has come. I thought perhaps there were no partners available and I've had no directives from Central."

44   Even to herself Helva sounded a little self-pitying, but the truth was she was lonely, sitting on the darkened field. She had always had the company of other shells and more recently, technicians by the score. The sudden solitude had lost its momentary charm and become oppressive.

45   "No directives from Central is scarcely a cause for regret, but there happen to be eight other guys biting their fingernails to the quick just waiting for an invitation to board you, you beautiful thing."

46   Tanner was inside the central cabin as he said this, running apprecia-
tive fingers over her panel, the scout's gravity-chair, poking his head into
the cabins, the galley, the head, the pressured-storage compartments.

47   "Now, if you want to goose Central and do *us* a favor all in one,
call up the barracks and let's have a ship-warming partner-picking
party. Hmmmm?"

48   Helva chuckled to herself. He was so completely different from
the occasional visitors or the various Laboratory technicians she had
encountered. He was so gay, so assured, and she was delighted by his
suggestion of a partner-picking party. Certainly it was not against anything in her understanding of regulations.

49   "Cencom, this is XH–834. Connect me with Pilot Barracks."

50   "Visual?"

51   "Please."

52   A picture of lounging men in various attitudes of boredom came
on her screen.

53   "This is XH–834. Would the unassigned scouts do me the favor of
coming aboard?"

54   Eight figures were galvanized into action, grabbing pieces of
wearing apparel, disengaging tape mechanisms, disentangling themselves from bedsheets and towels.

55   Helva dissolved the connection while Tanner chuckled gleefully
and settled down to await their arrival.

56   Helva was engulfed in an unshell-like flurry of anticipation. No
actress on her opening night could have been more apprehensive, fearful, or breathless. Unlike the actress, she could throw no hysterics, china
objets d'art, or greasepaint to relieve her tension. She could, of course,
check her stores for edibles and drinks, which she did, serving Tanner
from the virgin selection of her commissary.

57   Scouts were colloquially known as "brawns" as opposed to their ship
"brains." They had to pass as rigorous a training program as the brains
and only the top 1 percent of each contributory world's highest scholars
were admitted to Central Worlds Scout Training Program. Consequently
the eight young men who came pounding up the gantry into Helva's
hospitable lock were unusually fine-looking, intelligent, well-coordi-
nated, and well-adjusted young men, looking forward to a slightly
drunken evening, Helva permitting, and all quite willing to do each
other dirt to get possession of her.

58   Such a human invasion left Helva mentally breathless, a luxury she
thoroughly enjoyed for the brief time she felt she should permit it.

59   She sorted out the young men. Tanner's opportunism amused but
did not specifically attract her; the blond Nordsen seemed too simple;

dark-haired Alatpay had a kind of obstinacy for which she felt no compassion; Mir-Ahnin's bitterness hinted an inner darkness she did not wish to lighten, although he made the biggest outward play for her attention. Hers was a curious courtship—this would be only the first of several marriages for her, for brawns retired after seventy-five years of service, or earlier if they were unlucky. Brains, their bodies safe from any deterioration, were indestructible. In theory, once a shell-person had paid off the massive debt of early care, surgical adaptation, and maintenance charges, he or she was free to seek employment elsewhere. In practice, shell-people remained in the Service until they chose to self-destruct or died in line of duty. Helva had actually spoken to one shell-person 322 years old. She had been so awed by the contact she hadn't presumed to ask the personal questions she had wanted to.

60   Her choice of a brawn did not stand out from the others until Tanner started to sing a scout ditty recounting the misadventures of the bold, dense, painfully inept Billy Brawn. An attempt at harmony resulted in cacophony and Tanner wagged his arms wildly for silence.

61   "What we need is a roaring good lead tenor. Jennan, besides palming aces, what do you sing?"

62   "Sharp," Jennan replied with easy good humor.

63   "If a tenor is absolutely necessary, I'll attempt it," Helva volunteered.

64   "My good *woman*," Tanner protested.

65   "Sound your A," said Jennan, laughing.

66   Into the stunned silence that followed the rich, clear, high A, Jennan remarked quietly, "Such an A Caruso would have given the rest of his notes to sing."

67   It did not take them long to discover her full range.

68   "All Tanner asked for was one roaring good lead tenor," Jennan said jokingly, "and our sweet mistress supplied us an entire repertory company. The boy who gets this ship will go far, far, far."

69   "To the Horsehead Nebula?" asked Nordsen, quoting an old Central saw.

70   "To the Horsehead Nebula and back, we shall make beautiful music," said Helva, chuckling.

71   "Together," Jennan said. "Only you'd better make the music and, with my voice, I'd better listen."

72   "I rather imagined it would be I who listened," suggested Helva.

73   Jennan executed a stately bow with an intricate flourish of his crush-brimmed hat. He directed his bow toward the central control pillar where Helva *was*. Her own personal preference crystallized at that precise moment and for that particular reason: Jennan, alone of the men, had addressed his remarks directly at her physical presence, regardless of

the fact that he knew she could pick up his image wherever he was in the ship and regardless of the fact that her body was behind massive metal walls. Throughout their partnership, Jennan never failed to turn his head in her direction no matter where he was in relation to her. In response to this personalization, Helva at that moment and from then on always spoke to Jennan only through her central mike, even though that was not always the most efficient method.

74   Helva didn't know that she fell in love with Jennan that evening. As she had never been exposed to love or affection, only the drier cousins, respect and admiration, she could scarcely have recognized her reaction to the warmth of his personality and thoughtfulness. As a shell-person, she considered herself remote from emotions largely connected with physical desires.

75   "Well, Helva, it's been swell meeting you," said Tanner suddenly as she and Jennan were arguing about the baroque quality of "Come All Ye Sons of Art." "See you in space sometime, you lucky dog, Jennan. Thanks for the party, Helva."

76   "You don't have to go so soon?" asked Helva, realizing belatedly that she and Jennan had been excluding the others from this discussion.

77   "Best man won," Tanner said wryly. "Guess I'd better go get a tape on love ditties. Might need 'em for the next ship, if there're any more at home like you."

78   Helva and Jennan watched them leave, both a little confused.

79   "Perhaps Tanner's jumping to conclusions?" Jennan asked.

80   Helva regarded him as he slouched against the console, facing her shell directly. His arms were crossed on his chest and the glass he held had been empty for some time. He was handsome—they all were—but his watchful eyes were unwary, his mouth assumed a smile easily, his voice (to which Helva was particularly drawn) was resonant, deep, and without unpleasant overtones or accent.

81   "Sleep on it, at any rate, Helva. Call me in the morning if it's your opt."

82   She called him at breakfast, after she had checked her choice through Central. Jennan moved his things aboard, received their joint commission, had his personality and experience file locked into her reviewer, gave her the coordinates of their first mission. The XH–834 officially became the JH–834.

83   Their first mission was a dull but necessary crash priority (Medical got Helva), rushing a vaccine to a distant system plagued with a virulent spore disease. They had only to get to Spica as fast as possible.

84   After the initial, thrilling forward surge at her maximum speed, Helva realized her muscles were to be given less of a workout than her

brawn on this tedious mission. But they did have plenty of time for exploring each other's personalities. Jennan, of course, knew what Helva was capable of as a ship and partner, just as she knew what she could expect from him. But these were only facts, and Helva looked forward eagerly to learning that human side of her partner which could not be reduced to a series of symbols. Nor could the give-and-take of two personalities be learned from a book. It had to be experienced.

85   "My father was a scout, too, or is that programmed?" began Jennan their third day out.

86   "Naturally."

87   "Unfair, you know. You've got all my family history and I don't know one blamed thing about yours."

88   "I've never known either," Helva said. "Until I read yours, it hadn't occurred to me I must have one, too, someplace in Central's files."

89   Jennan snorted. "Shell psychology!"

90   Helva laughed. "Yes, and I'm even programmed against curiosity about it. You'd better be, too."

91   Jennan ordered a drink, slouched into the gravity couch opposite her, put his feet on the bumpers, turning himself idly from side to side on the gimbals.

92   "Helva—a made up name . . ."

93   "With a Scandinavian sound."

94   "You aren't blond," Jennan said positively.

95   "Well, then, there're dark Swedes."

96   "And blond Turks and this one's harem is limited to one."

97   "Your woman in purdah, yes, but you can comb the pleasure houses—" Helva found herself aghast at the edge to her carefully trained voice.

98   "You know," Jennan interrupted her, deep in some thought of his own, "my father gave me the impression he was a lot more married to his ship, the Silvia, than to my mother. I know I used to think Silvia was my grandmother. She was a low number, so she must have been a great-great-grandmother at least. I used to talk to her for hours."

99   "Her registry?" asked Helva, unwittingly jealous of everyone and anyone who had shared his hours.

100   "422. I think she's TS now. I ran into Tom Burgess once."

101   Jennan's father had died of a planetary disease, the vaccine for which his ship had used up in curing the local citizens.

102   "Tom said she'd got mighty tough and salty. You lose your sweetness and I'll come back and haunt you, girl," Jennan threatened.

103   Helva laughed. He startled her by stamping up to the column panel, touching it with light, tender fingers.

104   "I *wonder* what you look like," he said softly, wistfully.

105   Helva had been briefed about this natural curiosity of scouts. She didn't know anything about herself and neither of them ever would or could.

106   "Pick any form, shape, and shade and I'll be yours obliging," she countered, as training suggested.

107   "Iron Maiden, I fancy blondes with long tresses," and Jennan pantomimed Lady Godiva-like tresses. "Since you're immolated in titanium, I'll call you Brunehilde, my dear," and he made his bow.

108   With a chortle, Helva launched into the appropriate aria just as Spica made contact.

109   "What'n'ell's that yelling about? Who are you? And unless you're Central Worlds Medical, go away. We've got a plague. No visiting privileges."

110   "My ship is singing, we're the JH–834 of Worlds, and we've got your vaccine. What are our landing coordinates?"

111   "Your *ship* is singing?"

112   "The greatest SATB in organized space. Any requests?"

113   The JH–834 delivered the vaccine but no more arias and received immediate orders to proceed to Leviticus IV. By the time they got there, Jennan found a reputation awaiting him and was forced to defend the 834's virgin honor.

114   "I'll stop singing," murmured Helva contritely as she ordered up poultices for his third black eye in a week.

115   "You will not," Jennan said through gritted teeth. "If I have two black eyes from here to the Horsehead to keep the snicker out of the title, we'll be the ship who sings."

116   After the "ship who sings" tangled with a minor but vicious narcotic ring in the Lesser Magellanics, the title became definitely respectful. Central was aware of each episode and punched out a "special interest" key on JH–834's file. A first-rate team was shaking down well.

117   Jennan and Helva considered themselves a first-rate team, too, after their tidy arrest.

118   "Of all the vices in the universe, I *hate* drug addiction," Jennan remarked as they headed back to Central Base. "People can go to hell quick enough without that kind of help."

119   "Is that why you volunteered for Scout Service? To redirect traffic?"

120   "I'll bet my official answer's on your review."

121   "In far too flowery wording. 'Carrying on the traditions of my family, which has been proud of four generations in Service,' if I may quote you your own words."

122   Jennan groaned. "I was *very* young when I wrote that. I certainly hadn't been through Final Training. And once I was in Final Training, my pride wouldn't let me fail . . .

123   "As I mentioned, I used to visit Dad on board the Silvia and I've a very good idea she might have had her eye on me as a replacement for my father because I had had massive doses of scout-oriented propaganda. It took. From the time I was seven, I was going to be a scout or else." He shrugged as if deprecating a youthful determination that had taken a great deal of mature application to bring to fruition.

124   "Ah, so? Scout Sahir Silan on the JS–422 penetrating into the Horsehead Nebula?"

125   Jennan chose to ignore her sarcasm.

126   "With *you*, I may even get that far. But even with Silvia's nudging *I* never daydreamed myself *that* kind of glory in my wildest flights of fancy. I'll leave the whoppers to your agile brain henceforth. I have in mind a smaller contribution to space history."

127   "So modest?"

128   "No. Practical. We also serve, et cetera." He placed a dramatic hand on his heart.

129   "Glory hound!" scoffed Helva.

130   "Look who's talking, my Nebula-bound friend. At least I'm not greedy. There'll only be one hero like my dad at Parsaea, but I *would* like to be remembered for some kudos. Everyone does. Why else do or die?"

131   "Your father died on his way back from Parsaea, if I may point out a few cogent facts. So he could never have known he was a hero for damming the flood with his ship. Which kept the Parsaean colony from being abandoned. Which gave them a chance to discover the antiparalytic qualities of Parsaea. Which *he* never knew."

132   "I know," said Jennan softly.

133   Helva was immediately sorry for the tone of her rebuttal. She knew very well how deep Jennan's attachment to his father had been. On his review a note was made that he had rationalized his father's loss with the unexpected and welcome outcome of the Affair at Parsaea.

134   "Facts are not human, Helva. My father was and so am I. And *basically*, so are you. Check over your dial, 834. Amid all the wires attached to you is a heart, an underdeveloped human heart. Obviously!"

135   "I apologize, Jennan," she said.

136   Jennan hesitated a moment, threw out his hands in acceptance, and then tapped her shell affectionately.

137   "If they ever take us off the milk runs, we'll make a stab at the Nebula, huh?"

138   As so frequently happened in the Scout Service, within the next hour they had orders to change course, not to the Nebula, but to a recently colonized system with two habitable planets, one tropical, one glacial. The sun, named Ravel, had become unstable; the spectrum was that of a rapidly expanding shell, with absorption lines rapidly displacing toward violet. The augmented heat of the primary had already forced evacuation of the nearer world, Daphnis. The pattern of spectral emissions gave indication that the sun would sear Chloe as well. All ships in the immediate spatial vicinity were to report to Disaster Headquarters on Chloe to effect removal of the remaining colonists.

139   The JH–834 obediently presented itself and was sent to outlying areas on Chloe to pick up scattered settlers who did not appear to appreciate the urgency of the situation. Chloe, indeed, was enjoying the first temperatures above freezing since it had been flung out of its parent. Since many of the colonists were religious fanatics who had settled on rigorous Chloe to fit themselves for a life of pious reflection, Chloe's abrupt thaw was attributed to sources other than a rampaging sun.

140   Jennan had to spend so much time countering specious arguments that he and Helva were behind schedule on their way to the fourth and last settlement.

141   Helva jumped over the high range of jagged peaks that surrounded and sheltered the valley from the former raging snows as well as the present heat. The violent sun with its flaring corona was just beginning to brighten the deep valley as Helva dropped down to a landing.

142   "They'd better grab their toothbrushes and hop aboard," Helva said. "HQ says speed it up."

143   "All women," remarked Jennan in surprise as he walked down to meet them. "Unless the men on Chloe wear furred skirts."

144   "Charm 'em but pare the routine to the bare essentials. And turn on your two-way private."

145   Jennan advanced smiling, but his explanation of his mission was met with absolute incredulity and considerable doubt as to his authenticity. He groaned inwardly as the matriarch paraphrased previous explanations of the warming sun.

146   "Revered mother, there's been an overload on that prayer circuit and the sun is blowing itself up in one obliging burst. I'm here to take you to the spaceport at Rosary—"

147   "That Sodom?" The worthy woman glowered and shuddered disdainfully at his suggestion. "We thank you for your warning but we have no wish to leave our cloister for the rude world. We must go about our morning meditation, which has been interrupted—"

148   "It'll be permanently interrupted when that sun starts broiling you. You must come now," Jennan said firmly.

149   "Madame," said Helva, realizing that perhaps a female voice might carry more weight in this instance than Jennan's very masculine charm.

150   "Who spoke?" cried the nun, startled by the bodiless voice.

151   "I, Helva, the ship. Under my protection you and your sisters-in-faith may enter safely and be unprofaned by association with a male. I will guard you and take you safely to a place prepared for you."

152   The matriarch peered cautiously into the ship's open port. "Since only Central Worlds is permitted the use of such ships, I acknowledge that you are not trifling with us, young man. However, we are in no danger here."

153   "The temperature at Rosary is now ninety-nine degrees," said Helva. "As soon as the sun's rays penetrate directly into this valley, it will also be ninety-nine degrees, and it is due to climb to approximately one hundred eighty degrees today. I noticed your buildings are made of wood with moss chinking. Dry moss. It should fire around noontime."

154   The sunlight was beginning to slant into the valley through the peaks, and the fierce rays warmed the restless group behind the matriarch. Several opened the throats of their furry parkas.

155   "Jennan," said Helva privately to him, "our time is very short."

156   "I can't leave them, Helva. Some of those girls are barely out of their teens."

157   "Pretty, too. No wonder the matriarch doesn't want to get in."

158   "Helva."

159   "It will be the Lord's will," said the matriarch stoutly and turned her back squarely on rescue.

160   "To burn to death?" shouted Jennan as she threaded her way through her murmuring disciples.

161   "They want to be martyrs? Their opt, Jennan," said Helva dispassionately. "We must leave and that is no longer a matter of option."

162   "How can I leave, Helva?"

163   "Parsaea?" Helva asked tauntingly as he stepped forward to grab one of the women. "You can't drag them all aboard and we don't have time to fight it out. Get on board, Jennan, or I'll have you on report."

164   "They'll die," muttered Jennan dejectedly as he reluctantly turned to climb on board.

165   "You can risk only so much," Helva said sympathetically. "As it is we'll just have time to make a rendezvous. Lab reports a critical speedup in spectral evolution."

166   Jennan was already in the air lock when one of the younger women, screaming, rushed to squeeze in the closing port. Her action

set off the others. They stampeded through the narrow opening. Even crammed back to breast, there was not enough room inside for all the women. Jennan broke out space suits for the three who would have to remain with him in the air lock. He wasted valuable time explaining to the matriarch that she must put on the suit because the air lock had no independent oxygen or cooling units.

167   "We'll be caught," said Helva in a grim tone to Jennan on their private connection. "We've lost eighteen minutes in this last-minute rush. I am now overloaded for maximum speed and I must attain maximum speed to outrun the heat wave."

168   "Can you lift? We're suited."

169   "Lift? Yes," she said, doing so. "Run? I stagger."

170   Jennan, bracing himself and the women, could feel her sluggishness as she blasted upward. Heartlessly, Helva applied thrust as long as she could, despite the fact that the gravitational force mashed her cabin passengers brutally and crushed two fatally. It was a question of saving as many as possible. The only one for whom she had any concern was Jennan and she was in desperate terror about his safety. Airless and uncooled, protected by only one layer of metal, not three, the air lock was not going to be safe for the four trapped there, despite their space suits. These were only the standard models, not built to withstand the excessive heat to which the ship would be subjected.

171   Helva ran as fast as she could but the incredible wave of heat from the explosive sun caught them halfway to cold safety.

172   She paid no heed to the cries, moans, pleas, and prayers in her cabin. She listened only to Jennan's tortured breathing, to the missing throb in his suit's purifying system and the sucking of the overloaded cooling unit. Helpless, she heard the hysterical screams of his three companions as they writhed in the awful heat. Vainly, Jennan tried to calm them, tried to explain they would soon be safe and cool if they could be still and endure the heat. Undisciplined by their terror and torment, they tried to strike out at him despite the close quarters. One flailing arm became entangled in the leads to his power pack and the damage was quickly done. A connection, weakened by heat and the dead weight of the arm, broke.

173   For all the power at her disposal, Helva was helpless. She watched as Jennan fought for his breath, as he turned his head beseechingly toward *her*, and died.

174   Only the iron conditioning of her training prevented Helva from swinging around and plunging back into the cleansing heart of the exploding sun. Numbly she made rendezvous with the refugee convoy.

She obediently transferred her burned, heat-prostrated passengers to the assigned transport.

175   "I will retain the body of my scout and proceed to the nearest base for burial," she informed Central dully.

176   "You will be provided escort," was the reply.

177   "I've no need of escort."

178   "Escort is provided, XH–834," she was told curtly. The shock of hearing Jennan's initial severed from her call number cut off her half-formed protest. Stunned, she waited by the transport until her screens showed the arrival of two other slim brain ships. The cortege proceeded homeward at unfunereal speeds.

179   "834? The ship who sings?"

180   "I have no more songs."

181   "Your scout was Jennan."

182   "I do not wish to communicate."

183   "I'm 422."

184   "Silvia?"

185   "Silvia died a long time ago. I'm 422. Currently MS," the ship rejoined curtly. "AH–640 is our other friend, but Henry's not listening in. Just as well—he wouldn't understand it if you wanted to turn rogue. But I'd stop *him* if he tried to deter you."

186   "Rogue?" The term snapped Helva out of her apathy.

187   "Sure. You're young. You've got power for years. Skip. Others have done it. 732 went rogue twenty years ago after she lost her scout on a mission to that white dwarf. Hasn't been seen since."

188   "I never head about rogues."

189   "As it's exactly the thing we're conditioned against, you sure wouldn't hear about it in school, my dear," 422 said.

190   "Break conditioning?" cried Helva, anguished, thinking longingly of the white, white furious hot heart of the sun she had just left.

191   "For you, I don't think it would be hard at the moment," 422 said quietly, her voice devoid of her earlier cynicism. "The stars are out there, winking."

192   "Alone?" cried Helva from her heart.

193   "Alone!" 422 confirmed bleakly.

194   Alone with all of space and time. Even the Horsehead Nebula would not be far enough away to daunt her. Alone with a hundred years to live with her memories and nothing . . . nothing more.

195   "Was Parsaea worth it?" she asked 422 softly.

196   "Parsaea?" 422 repeated, surprised. "With his father? Yes. We were there, at Parsaea when we were needed. Just as you . . . and his son . . .

were at Chloe. When you were needed. The crime is not knowing where need is and not being there."

197   "But *I* need *him*. Who will supply my need?" said Helva bitterly. . . .

198   "834," said 422 after a day's silent speeding. "Central wishes your report. A replacement awaits your opt at Regulus Base. Change course accordingly."

199   "A replacement?" That was certainly not what she needed . . . a reminder inadequately filling the void Jennan left. Why, her hull was barely cool of Chloe's heat. Atavistically, Helva wanted time to mourn Jennan.

200   "Oh, none of them are impossible if *you're* a good ship," 422 remarked philosophically. "And it is just what you need. The sooner the better."

201   "You told them I wouldn't go rogue, didn't you?" Helva said.

202   "The moment passed you even as it passed me after Parsaea, and before that, after Glen Arthur, and Betelgeuse."

203   "We're conditioned to go on, aren't we? We *can't* go rogue. You were testing."

204   "Had to. Orders. Not even Psych knows why a rogue occurs. Central's very worried, and so, daughter, are your sister ships. I asked to be your escort. I . . . don't want to lose you both."

205   In her emotional nadir, Helva could feel a flood of gratitude for Silvia's rough sympathy.

206   "We've all known this grief, Helva. It's no consolation, but if we couldn't feel with our scouts, we'd only be machines wired for sound."

207   Helva looked at Jennan's still form stretched before her in its shroud and heard the echo of his rich voice in the quiet calm.

208   "Silvia! I *couldn't* help him," she cried from her soul.

209   "Yes, dear, I know," 422 murmured gently and then was quiet.

210   The three ships sped on, wordless, to the great Central Worlds base at Regulus. Helva broke silence to acknowledge landing instructions and the officially tendered regrets.

211   The three ships set down simultaneously at the wooded edge where Regulus's gigantic blue trees stood sentinel over the sleeping dead in the small Service cemetery. The entire Base complement approached with measured step and formed an aisle from Helva to the burial ground. The honor detail, out of step, walked slowly into her cabin. Reverently they placed the body of her dead love on the wheeled bier, covered it honorably with the deep-blue, star-splashed flag of the Service. She watched as it was driven slowly down the living aisle, which closed in behind the bier in last escort.

212   Then, as the simple words of interment were spoken, as the atmosphere planes dipped in tribute over the open grave, Helva found voice for her lonely farewell.

213   Softly, barely audible at first, the strains of the ancient song of evening and requiem swelled to the final poignant measure until black space itself echoed back the sound of the song the ship sang.

———————

DISCUSSION QUESTIONS

1. In discussing art and religion in her first contact with unshelled people, Helva thinks of problems in mathematical terms. What does this say about her development at this stage?

2. After she is complimented on her unconscious singing, Helva thinks about singing from a logical rather than emotional perspective. What is her *purpose* in eventually learning to sing?

3. What is meant by the phrase, "She (Helva) *was* the ship"?

4. Brain ships choose their partners. Why is this referred to as a marriage, with built-in divorce or widowhood?

5. Jennan says he'd like to be remembered well after he's gone. He says, "Why else do or die?" What does he mean?

WRITING TOPICS

1. Love is commonly associated with physical attraction. How does the story show that emotional bonding can lead to love even when people are very different physically? Discuss your response in an essay.

2. In your journal, discuss what Helva's *real* needs are, especially after Jennan is gone.

3. Research the tremendous scientific advances made in the sixties, especially in the area of space travel. Then share with your class the ways this story might be a reaction to or warning against unrestrained development.

"Repent, Harlequin!" Said the Ticktockman

1966

HARLAN ELLISON (b. 1934)

After briefly attending Ohio State University, Harlan Ellison moved to New York. In early 1956 he produced his first science fiction story, "Glowworm," which appeared in *Infinity Science Fiction;* by 1958 he had written more than 150 stories. He quickly produced novels, including *Web of the City* (1958), *The Sound of a Scythe* (1960), and *Spider Kiss* (1961), and collections of stories, including *The Deadly Streets* (1958) and *Gentleman Junkie and Other Stories of the Hung-up Generation* (1961), focusing on the harshness of urban life. After serving in the Army (1957–59), he moved to Chicago and then, in 1962, to Los Angeles, where he established himself as a film and TV writer, producing scripts for *The Outer Limits* and *Star Trek,* as well as many non-science-fiction series. He also served as creative consultant for the revived *The Twilight Zone* (1985–87).

In the late sixties, as one of the founders of the New Wave, Ellison edited the *Dangerous Visions* anthologies. He produced two volumes (1967, 1972), containing hundreds of original stories on the cutting edge of speculation. He has won numerous awards for his stories, including "I Have No Mouth and I Must Scream" (1967), and "A Boy and His Dog" (1969), which was later made into a successful movie. He has also written film criticism, essays, and other nonfiction. Much of his best work has been collected in *The Essential Ellison: A 35 Year Retrospective* (1987).

In "'Repent, Harlequin!' said the Ticktockman," Harlan Ellison shows what happens when an obsession with conformity is carried to extremes, and what a society of compulsive clock-watchers might be like.

1   There are always those who ask, what is it all about? For those who
    need to ask, for those who need points sharply made, who need to
    know "where it's at," this:

> The mass of men serve the state thus, not as men mainly,
> but as machines, with their bodies. They are the standing
> army, and the militia, jailors, constables, posse comitatus,
> etc. In most cases there is no free exercise whatever of the
> judgment or of the moral sense; but they put themselves on a
> level with wood and earth and stones; and wooden men can
> perhaps be manufactured that will serve the purpose as well.
> Such command no more respect than men of straw or a lump
> of dirt. They have the same sort of worth only as horses and
> dogs. Yet such as these even are commonly esteemed good
> citizens. Others—as most legislators, politicians, lawyers,
> ministers, and officeholders—serve the state chiefly with their
> heads; and, as they rarely make any moral distinctions, they
> are as likely to serve the Devil, without intending it, as God.
> A very few, as heroes, patriots, martyrs, reformers in the great
> sense, and men, serve the state with their consciences also,
> and so necessarily resist it for the most part; and they are
> commonly treated as enemies by it.
>
> Henry David Thoreau
> *Civil Disobedience*

2   That is the heart of it. Now begin in the middle, and later learn the
    beginning; the end will take care of itself.

3   But because it was the very world it was, the very world they had allowed
    it to *become,* for months his activities did not come to the alarmed atten-
    tion of The Ones Who Kept The Machine Functioning Smoothly, the
    ones who poured the very best butter over the cams and mainsprings of
    the culture. Not until it had become obvious that somehow, someway, he
    had become a notoriety, a celebrity, perhaps even a hero for (what
    Officialdom inescapably tagged) "an emotionally disturbed segment of
    the populace," did they turn it over to the Ticktockman and his legal ma-
    chinery. But by then, because it was the very world it was, and they had
    no way to predict he would happen—possibly a strain of disease long-
    defunct, now, suddenly, reborn in a system where immunity had been
    forgotten, had lapsed—he had been allowed to become too real. Now he
    had form and substance.

4   He had become a *personality,* something they had filtered out of the
    system many decades before. But there it was, and there *he* was, a very

definitely imposing personality. In certain circles—middle-class circles—it was thought disgusting. Vulgar ostentation. Anarchistic. Shameful. In others, there was only sniggering: those strata where thought is subjugated to form and ritual, niceties, proprieties. But down below, ah, down below, where the people always needed their saints and sinners, their bread and circuses, their heroes and villains, he was considered a Bolivar; a Napoleon; a Robin Hood; a Dick Bong (Ace of Aces); a Jesus; a Jomo Kenyatta.

5 And at the top—where, like socially-attuned Shipwreck Kellys, every tremor and vibration threatening to dislodge the wealthy, powerful and titled from their flagpoles—he was considered a menace; a heretic; a rebel; a disgrace; a peril. He was known down the line, to the very heart-meat core, but the important reactions were high above and far below. At the very top, at the very bottom.

6 So his file was turned over, along with his time-card and his cardioplate, to the office of the Ticktockman.

7 The Ticktockman: very much over six feet tall, often silent, a soft purring man when things went timewise. The Ticktockman.

8 Even in the cubicles of the hierarchy, where fear was generated, seldom suffered, he was called the Ticktockman. But no one called him that to his mask.

9 You don't call a man a hated name, not when that man, behind his mask, is capable of revoking the minutes, the hours, the days and nights, the years of your life. He was called the Master Timekeeper to his mask. It was safer that way.

10 "This is *what* he is," said the Ticktockman with genuine softness, "but not *who* he is. This time-card I'm holding in my left hand has a name on it, but it is the name of *what* he is, not *who* he is. The cardioplate here in my right hand is also named, but not *whom* named, merely *what* named. Before I can exercise proper revocation, I have to know *who* this *what* is."

11 To his staff, all the ferrets, all the loggers, all the finks, all the commex, even the mineez, he said, "Who is this Harlequin?"

12 He was not purring smoothly. Timewise, it was jangle.

13 However, it *was* the longest single speech they had ever heard him utter at one time, the staff, the ferrets, the loggers, the finks, the commex, but not the mineez, who usually weren't around to know, in any case. But even they scurried to find out.

14 Who is the Harlequin?

15 High above the third level of the city, he crouched on the humming aluminum-frame platform of the air-boat (foof! air-boat, indeed! swizzleskid is what it was, with a tow-rack jerry-rigged) and stared down at the neat Mondrian arrangement of the buildings.

16   Somewhere nearby, he could hear the metronomic left-right-left of the 2:47 PM shift, entering the Timkin roller-bearing plant in their sneakers. A minute later, precisely, he heard the softer right-left-right of the 5:00 AM formation, going home.

17   An elfin grin spread across his tanned features, and his dimples appeared for a moment. Then, scratching at his thatch of auburn hair, he shrugged within his motley, as though girding himself for what came next, and threw the joystick forward, and bent into the wind as the air-boat dropped. He skimmed over a slidewalk, purposely dropping a few feet to crease the tassels of the ladies of fashion, and—inserting thumbs in large ears—he stuck out his tongue, rolled his eyes and went wugga-wugga-wugga. It was a minor diversion. One pedestrian skittered and tumbled, sending parcels everywhichway, another wet herself, a third keeled slantwise and the walk was stopped automatically by the servitors till she could be resuscitated. It was a minor diversion.

18   Then he swirled away on a vagrant breeze, and was gone. Hi-ho.

19   As he rounded the cornice of the Time-Motion Study Building, he saw the shift, just boarding the slidewalk. With practiced motion and an absolute conservation of movement, they sidestepped up onto the slow-strip and (in a chorus line reminiscent of a Busby Berkeley film of the antidiluvian 1930s) advanced across the strips ostrich-walking till they were lined up on the expresstrip.

20   Once more, in anticipation, the elfin grin spread, and there was a tooth missing back there on the left side. He dipped, skimmed, and swooped over them; and then, scrunching about on the air-boat, he released the holding pins that fastened shut the ends of the home-made pouring troughs that kept his cargo from dumping prematurely. And as he pulled the trough-pins, the air-boat slid over the factory workers and one hundred and fifty thousand dollars' worth of jelly beans cascaded down on the expresstrip.

21   Jelly beans! Millions and billions of purples and yellows and greens and licorice and grape and raspberry and mint and round and smooth and crunchy outside and soft-mealy inside and sugary and bouncing jouncing tumbling clittering clattering skittering fell on the heads and shoulders and hardhats and carapaces of the Timkin workers, tinkling on the slidewalk and bouncing away and rolling about underfoot and filling the sky on their way down with all the colors of joy and childhood and holidays, coming down in a steady rain, a solid wash, a torrent of color and sweetness out of the sky from above, and entering a universe of sanity and metronomic order with quite-mad coocoo newness. Jelly beans!

22   The shift workers howled and laughed and were pelted, and broke ranks, and the jelly beans managed to work their way into the mecha-

nism of the slidewalks after which there was a hideous scraping as the sound of a million fingernails rasped down a quarter of a million blackboards, followed by a coughing and a sputtering, and then the slidewalks all stopped and everyone was dumped thisawayandthataway in a jackstraw tumble, still laughing and popping little jelly bean eggs of childish color into their mouths. It was a holiday, and a jollity, an absolute insanity, a giggle. But . . .

23 The shift was delayed seven minutes.

24 They did not get home for seven minutes.

25 The master schedule was thrown off by seven minutes.

26 Quotas were delayed by inoperative slidewalks for seven minutes.

27 He had tapped the first domino in the line, and one after another, like chik chik chik, the others had fallen.

28 The System had been seven minutes' worth of disrupted. It was a tiny matter, one hardly worthy of note, but in a society where the single driving force was order and unity and equality and promptness and clocklike precision and attention to the clock, reverence of the gods of the passage of time, it was a disaster of major importance.

29 So he was ordered to appear before the Ticktockman. It was broadcast across every channel of the communications web. He was ordered to be *there* at 7:00 dammit on time. And they waited, and they waited, but he didn't show up till almost ten-thirty, at which time he merely sang a little song about moonlight in a place no one had ever heard of, called Vermont, and vanished again. But they had all been waiting since seven, and it wrecked *hell* with their schedules. So the question remained: Who is the Harlequin?

30 But the *unasked* question (more important of the two) was: how did we get *into* this position, where a laughing, irresponsible japer of jabberwocky and jive could disrupt our entire economic and cultural life with a hundred and fifty thousand dollars' worth of jelly beans . . .

31 *Jelly* for God's sake *beans!* This is madness! Where did he get the money to buy a hundred and fifty thousand dollars' worth of jelly beans? (They knew it would have cost that much, because they had a team of Situation Analysts pulled off another assignment, and rushed to the slidewalk scene to sweep up and count the candies, and produce findings, which disrupted *their* schedules and threw their entire branch at least a day behind.) Jelly beans! Jelly . . . *beans?* Now wait a second— a second accounted for—no one has manufactured jelly beans for over a hundred years. Where did he get jelly beans?

32 That's another good question. More than likely it will never be answered to your complete satisfaction. But then, how many questions ever are?

33 The middle you know. Here is the beginning. How it starts:

34   A desk pad. Day for day, and turn each day. 9:00—open the mail. 9:45—appointment with planning commission board. 10:30—discuss installation progress charts with J. L. 11:15—pray for rain. 12:00—lunch. *And so it goes.*

35   "I'm sorry, Miss Grant, but the time for interviews was set at 2:30, and it's almost five now. I'm sorry you're late, but those are the rules. You'll have to wait till next year to submit application for this college again." *And so it goes.*

36   The 10:10 local stops at Cresthaven, Galesville, Tonawanda Junction, Selby and Farnhurst, but not at Indiana City, Lucasville and Colton, except on Sunday. The 10:35 express stops at Galesville, Selby and Indiana City, except on Sundays & Holidays, at which time it stops at . . . *and so it goes.*

37   "I couldn't wait, Fred. I had to be at Pierre Cartain's by 3:00, and you said you'd meet me under the clock in the terminal at 2:45, and you weren't there, so I had to go on. You're always late, Fred. If you'd been there, we could have sewed it up together, but as it was, well, I took the order alone . . ." *And so it goes.*

38   Dear Mr. and Mrs. Atterley: In reference to your son Gerald's constant tardiness, I am afraid we will have to suspend him from school unless some more reliable method can be instituted guaranteeing he will arrive at his classes on time. Granted he is an exemplary student, and his marks are high, his constant flouting of the schedules of this school make it impractical to maintain him in a system where the other children seem capable of getting where they are supposed to be on time *and so it goes.*

39   YOU CANNOT VOTE UNLESS YOU APPEAR AT 8:45 AM.

40   "I don't care if the script is *good,* I need it Thursday!"

41   CHECK-OUT TIME IS 2:00 PM.

42   "You got here late. The job's taken. Sorry."

43   YOUR SALARY HAS BEEN DOCKED FOR TWENTY MINUTES TIME LOST.

44   "God, what time is it, I've gotta run!"

45   And so it goes. And so it goes. And so it goes. And so it goes goes goes goes goes tick tock tick tock tick tock and one day we no longer let time serve us, we serve time and we are slaves of the schedule, worshippers of the sun's passing, bound into a life predicated on restrictions because the system will not function if we don't keep the schedule tight.

46   Until it becomes more than a minor inconvenience to be late. It becomes a sin. Then a crime. Then a crime punishable by this:

47   EFFECTIVE 15 JULY 2389, 12:00:00 midnight, the office of the Master Timekeeper will require all citizens to submit their time-cards and car-

dioplates for processing. In accordance with Statute 555–7–SGH–999 governing the revocation of time per capita, all cardioplates will be keyed to the individual holder and—

48   What they had done, was devise a method of curtailing the amount of life a person could have. If he was ten minutes late, he lost ten minutes of his life. An hour was proportionately worth more revocation. If someone was consistently tardy, he might find himself, on a Sunday night, receiving a communiqué from the Master Timekeeper that his time had run out, and he would be "turned off" at high noon on Monday, please straighten your affairs, sir, madame or bisex.

49   And so, by this simple scientific expedient (utilizing a scientific process held dearly secret by the Ticktockman's office) the System was maintained. It was the only expedient thing to do. It was, after all, patriotic. The schedules had to be met. After all, there *was* a war on!

50   But, wasn't there always?

51   "Now that is really disgusting," the Harlequin said, when Pretty Alice showed him the wanted poster. "Disgusting and *highly* improbable. After all, this isn't the Day of the Desperado. A *wanted* poster!"

52   "You know," Pretty Alice noted, "you speak with a great deal of inflection."

53   "I'm sorry," said the Harlequin, humbly.

54   "No need to be sorry. You're always saying 'I'm sorry.' You have such massive guilt, Everett, it's really very sad."

55   "I'm sorry," he said again, then pursed his lips so the dimples appeared momentarily. He hadn't wanted to say that at all. "I have to go out again. I have to *do* something."

56   Pretty Alice slammed her coffee-bulb down on the counter. "Oh for God's *sake,* Everett, can't you stay home just *one* night! Must you always be out in that ghastly clown suit, running around annoying people?"

57   "I'm—" He stopped, and clapped the jester's hat onto his auburn thatch with a tiny tingling of bells. He rose, rinsed out his coffee-bulb at the spray, and put it into the drier for a moment. "I have to go."

58   She didn't answer. The faxbox was purring, and she pulled a sheet out, read it, threw it toward him on the counter. "It's about you. Of course. You're ridiculous."

59   He read it quickly. It said the Ticktockman was trying to locate him. He didn't care, he was going out to be late again. At the door, dredging for an exit line, he hurled back petulantly, "Well, *you* speak with inflection, *too!*"

60   Pretty Alice rolled her pretty eyes heavenward. "You're ridiculous." The Harlequin stalked out, slamming the door, which sighed shut softly, and locked itself.

61   There was a gentle knock, and Pretty Alice got up with an exhalation of exasperated breath, and opened the door. He stood there. "I'll be back about ten-thirty, okay?"

62   She pulled a rueful face. "Why do you tell me that? Why? You *know* you'll be late! You *know* it! You're *always* late, so why do you tell me these dumb things?" She closed the door.

63   On the other side, the Harlequin nodded to himself. *She's right. She's always right. I'll be late. I'm always late. Why do I tell her these dumb things?*

64   He shrugged again, and went off to be late once more.

65 He had fired off the firecracker rockets that said: I will attend the 115th annual International Medical Association Invocation at 8:00 PM precisely. I do hope you will all be able to join me.

66   The words had burned in the sky, and of course the authorities were there, lying in wait for him. They assumed, naturally, that he would be late. He arrived twenty minutes early, while they were setting up the spiderwebs to trap and hold him. Blowing a large bullhorn, he frightened and unnerved them so, their own moisturized encirclement webs sucked closed, and they were hauled up, kicking and shrieking, high above the amphitheater's floor. The Harlequin laughed and laughed, and apologized profusely. The physicians, gathered in solemn conclave, roared with laughter, and accepted the Harlequin's apologies with exaggerated bowing and posturing, and a merry time was had by all, who thought the Harlequin was a regular foofaraw in fancy pants; all, that is, but the authorities, who had been sent out by the office of the Ticktockman; they hung there like so much dockside cargo, hauled up above the floor of the amphitheater in a most unseemly fashion.

67   (In another part of the same city where the Harlequin carried on his "activities," totally unrelated in every way to what concerns us here, save that it illustrates the Ticktockman's power and import, a man named Marshall Delahanty received his turn-off notice from the Ticktockman's office. His wife received the notification from the gray-suited minee who delivered it, with the traditional "look of sorrow" plastered hideously across his face. She knew what it was, even without unsealing it. It was a billet-doux of immediate recognition to everyone these days. She gasped, and held it as though it was a glass slide tinged with botulism, and prayed it was not for her. Let it be for Marsh, she thought, brutally, realistically, or one of the kids, but not for me, please dear God, not for me. And then she opened it, and it *was* for Marsh, and she was at one and the same time horrified and relieved. The next trooper in the line

had caught the bullet. "Marshall," she screamed, "Marshall! Termination, Marshall! OhmiGod, Marshall, whattl we do, whattl we do, Marshall, omigodmarshall . . ." and in their home that night was the sound of tearing paper and fear, and the stink of madness went up the flue and there was nothing, absolutely nothing they could do about it.

68   (But Marshall Delahanty tried to run. And early the next day, when turn-off time came, he was deep in the Canadian forest two hundred miles away, and the office of the Ticktockman blanked his cardioplate, and Marshall Delahanty keeled over, running, and his heart stopped, and the blood dried up on its way to his brain, and he was dead that's all. One light went out on the sector map in the office of the Master Timekeeper, while notification was entered for fax reproduction, and Georgette Delahanty's name was entered on the dole roles till she could remarry. Which is the end of the footnote, and all the point that need be made, except don't laugh, because that is what would happen to the Harlequin if ever the Ticktockman found out his real name. It isn't funny.)

69   The shopping level of the city was thronged with the Thursday-colors of the buyers. Women in canary yellow chitons and men in pseudo-Tyrolean outfits that were jade and leather and fit very tightly, save for the balloon pants.

70   When the Harlequin appeared on the still-being-constructed shell of the new Efficiency Shopping Center, his bullhorn to his elfishly-laughing lips, everyone pointed and stared, and he berated them:

71   "Why let them order you about? Why let them tell you to hurry and scurry like ants or maggots? Take your time! Saunter a while! Enjoy the sunshine, enjoy the breeze, let life carry you at your own pace! Don't be slaves of time, it's a helluva way to die, slowly, by degrees . . . down with the Ticktockman!"

72   Who's the nut? most of the shoppers wanted to know. Who's the nut oh wow I'm gonna be late I gotta run . . .

73   And the construction gang on the Shopping Center received an urgent order from the office of the Master Timekeeper that the dangerous criminal known as the Harlequin was atop their spire, and their aid was urgently needed in apprehending him. The work crew said no, they would lose time on their construction schedule, but the Ticktockman managed to pull the proper threads of governmental webbing, and they were told to cease work and catch that nitwit up there on the spire with the bullhorn. So a dozen and more burly workers began climbing into their construction platforms, releasing the a-grav plates, and rising toward the Harlequin.

74 After the debacle (in which, through the Harlequin's attention to personal safety, no one was seriously injured), the workers tried to reassemble, and assault him again, but it was too late. He had vanished. It had attracted quite a crowd, however, and the shopping cycle was thrown off by hours, simply hours. The purchasing needs of the system were therefore falling behind, and so measures were taken to accelerate the cycle for the rest of the day, but it got bogged down and speeded up and they sold too many float-valves and not nearly enough wegglers, which meant that the popli ratio was off, which made it necessary to rush cases and cases of spoiling Smash-O to stores that usually needed a case only every three or four hours. The shipments were bollixed, the transshipments were misrouted, and in the end, even the swizzleskid industries felt it.

75 "Don't come back till you have him!" the Ticktockman said, very quietly, very sincerely, extremely dangerously.

76 They used dogs. They used probes. They used cardioplate crossoffs. They used teepers. They used bribery. They used stiktytes. They used intimidation. They used torment. They used torture. They used finks. They used cops. They used search&seizure. They used fallaron. They used betterment incentive. They used fingerprints. They used the Bertillon system. They used cunning. They used guile. They used treachery. They used Raoul Mitgong, but he didn't help much. They used applied physics. They used techniques of criminology.

77 And what the hell: they caught him.

78 After all, his name was Everett C. Marm, and he wasn't much to begin with, except a man who had no sense of time.

79 "Repent, Harlequin!" said the Ticktockman.

80 "Get stuffed!" the Harlequin replied, sneering.

81 "You've been late a total of sixty-three years, five months, three weeks, two days, twelve hours, forty-one minutes, fifty-nine seconds, point oh three six one one one microseconds. You've used up everything you can, and more. I'm going to turn you off."

82 "Scare someone else. I'd rather be dead than live in a dumb world with a bogeyman like you."

83 "It's my job."

84 "You're full of it. You're a tyrant. You have no right to order people around and kill them if they show up late."

85 "You can't adjust. You can't fit in."

86 "Unstrap me, and I'll fit my fist into your mouth."

87 "You're a nonconformist."

88   "That didn't used to be a felony."

89   "It is now. Live in the world around you."

90   "I hate it. It's a terrible world."

91   "Not everyone thinks so. Most people enjoy order."

92   "I don't, and most of the people I know don't."

93   "That's not true. How do you think we caught you?"

94   "I'm not interested."

95   "A girl named Pretty Alice told us who you were."

96   "That's a lie."

97   "It's true. You unnerve her. She wants to belong, she wants to conform, I'm going to turn you off."

98   "Then do it already, and stop arguing with me."

99   "I'm not going to turn you off."

100   "You're an idiot!"

101   "Repent, Harlequin!" said the Ticktockman.

102   "Get stuffed."

103   So they sent him to Coventry. And in Coventry they worked him over. It was just like what they did to Winston Smith in NINETEEN EIGHTY-FOUR, which was a book none of them knew about, but the techniques are really quite ancient, and so they did it to Everett C. Marm, and one day, quite a long time later, the Harlequin appeared on the communications web, appearing elfin and dimpled and bright-eyed, and not at all brainwashed, and he said he had been wrong, that it was a good, a very good thing indeed, to belong, to be right on time hip-ho and away we go, and everyone stared up at him on the public screens that covered an entire city block, and they said to themselves, well, you see, he was just a nut after all, and if that's the way the system is run, then let's do it that way, because it doesn't pay to fight city hall, or in this case, the Ticktockman. So Everett C. Marm was destroyed, which was a loss, because of what Thoreau said earlier, but you can't make an omelet without breaking a few eggs, and in every revolution a few die who shouldn't, but they have to, because that's the way it happens, and if you make only a little change, then it seems to be worthwhile. Or, to make the point lucidly:

104   "Uh, excuse me, sir, I, uh, don't know how to uh, to uh, tell you this, but you were three minutes late. The schedule is a little, uh, bit off."

105   He grinned sheepishly.

106   "That's ridiculous!" murmured the Ticktockman behind his mask. "Check your watch." And then he went into his office, going *mrmee, mrmee, mrmee, mrmee.*

DISCUSSION QUESTIONS

1. How does the epigraph by Thoreau at the beginning of the story eventually make sense as a controlling idea behind the story?
2. The narrator frequently intrudes into the events of the story. Explain how this affects you as a reader and why.
3. How does the situation in the story help create the Harlequin?
4. What happens to those who are late? Why is it such a serious crime?
5. What does the title of the story mean?

WRITING TOPICS

1. Read about the book *1984* by George Orwell. Write a short essay about how what happens to Winston Smith has a bearing on this story.
2. In an essay, write about what circumstances you think could lead to nonconformity becoming a felony. Do you think our country is moving in that direction?
3. In 1966, youth protests were gaining worldwide momentum. In small groups, find out more about this cultural phenomenon. Write a report on what possible correlations those events have with the story.

The Electric Ant

1969

PHILIP K. DICK (1928–1982)

Philip K. Dick's first short story was "Beyond the Wub" (1952).
In his lifetime he produced an enormous number of short works,
as well as novels that were often expanded versions of the shorter
stories. There are twin themes which run throughout much of
Dick's fiction: paranoia about manipulations of reality by some
powerful outside source, and the shifting levels of those realities.
There is usually one more or less objective reality in his universes,
and another artificially imposed by drugs or psychic means.

One of his first novels to win acclaim was *The Man in the High
Castle* (1962), an alternate history in which Hitler wins World War II.
In this tale, one of the characters discovers a reality in which the
Allies win. The reality is not the reality we know, however, but yet
another variation. In *The Three Stigmata of Palmer Eldritch* (1965),
Dick shows competing drug companies marketing products that
produce believable escapes from the dreariness colonists face on
Mars. It becomes increasingly unclear, though, whether they are
truly altering the perceptions of those taking their medications
or removing a mask that prevents them from seeing the true "reality." The novel Dick is best known for is *Do Androids Dream
of Electric Sheep* (1968), which was made into the 1982 movie
Bladerunner, a film credited with bringing cyberpunk to the screen.

In "The Electric Ant," Philip K. Dick toys with one of his
favorite themes, the fabric of reality. In this case reality is tied in a
very tangible sense to the information the main character receives.

1   At four-fifteen in the afternoon, T.S.T., Garson Poole woke up in his hospital bed, knew that he lay in a hospital bed in a three-bed ward and realized in addition two things: that he no longer had a right hand and that he felt no pain.

2   They had given me a strong analgesic, he said to himself as he stared at the far wall with its window showing downtown New York. Webs in which vehicles and peds darted and wheeled glimmered in the late afternoon sun, and the brilliance of the aging light pleased him. It's not yet out, he thought. And neither am I.

3   A fone lay on the table beside his bed; he hesitated, then picked it up and dialed for an outside line. A moment later he was faced by Louis Danceman, in charge of Tri-Plan's activities while he, Garson Poole, was elsewhere.

4   "Thank God you're alive," Danceman said, seeing him; his big, fleshy face with its moon's surface of pock marks flattened with relief. "I've been calling all—"

5   "I just don't have a right hand," Poole said.

6   "But you'll be okay, I mean, they can graft another one on."

7   "How long have I been here?" Poole said. He wondered where the nurses and doctors had gone to; why weren't they clucking and fussing about him making a call?

8   "Four days," Danceman said. "Everything here at the plant is going splunkishly. In fact we've splunked orders from three separate police systems, all here on Terra. Two in Ohio, one in Wyoming. Good solid orders, with one third in advance and the usual three-year lease-option."

9   "Come get me out of here," Poole said.

10   "I can't get you out until the new hand—"

11   "I'll have it done later." He wanted desperately to get back to familiar surroundings; memory of the mercantile squib looming grotesquely on the pilot screen careened at the back of his mind; if he shut his eyes he felt himself back in his damaged craft as it plunged from one vehicle to another, piling up enormous damage as it went. The kinetic sensations . . . he winced, recalling them. I guess I'm lucky, he said to himself.

12   "Is Sarah Benton there with you?" Danceman asked.

13   "No." Of course; his personal secretary—if only for job considerations—would be hovering close by, mothering him in her jejune, infantile way. All heavy-set women like to mother people, he thought. And they're dangerous; if they fall on you they can kill you. "Maybe that's what happened to me," he said aloud. "Maybe Sarah fell on my squib."

14   "No, no; a tie rod in the steering fin of your squib split apart during the heavy rush-hour traffic and you—"

15   "I remember." He turned in his bed as the door of the ward opened; a white-clad doctor and two blue-clad nurses appeared, making their way toward his bed. "I'll talk to you later," Poole said and hung up the fone. He took a deep, expectant breath.

16   "You shouldn't be foning quite so soon," the doctor said as he studied his chart. "Mr. Garson Poole, owner of Tri-Plan Electronics. Maker of random ident darts that track their prey for a circle-radius of a thousand miles, responding to unique enceph wave patterns. You're a successful man, Mr. Poole. But, Mr. Poole, you're not a man. You're an electric ant."

17   "Christ," Poole said, stunned.

18   "So we can't really treat you here, now that we've found out. We knew, of course, as soon as we examined your injured right hand; we saw the electronic components and then we made torso x-rays and of course they bore out our hypothesis."

19   "What," Poole said, "is an 'electric ant'?" But he knew; he could decipher the term.

20   A nurse said, "An organic robot."

21   "I see," Poole said. Frigid perspiration rose to the surface of his skin, across all his body.

22   "You didn't know," the doctor said.

23   "No." Poole shook his head.

24   The doctor said, "We get an electric ant every week or so. Either brought in here from a squib accident—like yourself—or one seeking voluntary admission . . . one who, like yourself, has never been told, who has functioned alongside humans, believing himself—itself—human. As to your hand—" He paused.

25   "Forget my hand," Poole said savagely.

26   "Be calm." The doctor leaned over him, peered acutely down into Poole's face. "We'll have a hospital boat convey you over to a service facility where repairs, or replacement, on your hand can be made at a reasonable expense, either to yourself, if you're self-owned, or to your owners, if such there are. In any case you'll be back at your desk at Tri-Plan functioning just as before."

27   "Except," Poole said, "now I know." He wondered if Danceman or Sarah or any of the others at the office knew. Had they—or one of them—purchased him? Designed him? A figurehead, he said to himself; that's all I've been. I must never really have run the company; it was a delusion implanted in me when I was made . . . along with the delusion that I am human and alive.

28   "Before you leave for the repair facility," the doctor said, "could you kindly settle your bill at the front desk?"

29   Poole said acidly, "How can there be a bill if you don't treat ants here?"

30   "For our services," the nurse said. "Up until the point we knew."

31   "Bill me," Poole said, with furious, impotent anger. "Bill my firm." With massive effort he managed to sit up; his head swimming, he stepped haltingly from the bed and onto the floor. "I'll be glad to leave here," he said as he rose to a standing position. "And thank you for your humane attention."

32   "Thank you, too, Mr. Poole," the doctor said. "Or rather I should say just Poole."

33   At the repair facility he had his missing hand replaced.

34   It proved fascinating, the hand; he examined it for a long time before he let the technicians install it. On the surface it appeared organic—in fact on the surface, it was. Natural skin covered natural flesh, and true blood filled the veins and capillaries. But, beneath that, wires and circuits, miniaturized components, gleamed . . . looking deep into the wrist he saw surge gates, motors, multi-stage valves, all very small. Intricate. And—the hand cost forty frogs. A week's salary, insofar as he drew it from the company payroll.

35   "Is this guaranteed?" he asked the technicians as they fused the "bone" section of the hand to the balance of his body.

36   "Ninety days, parts and labor," one of the technicians said. "Unless subjected to unusual or intentional abuse."

37   "That sounds vaguely suggestive," Poole said.

38   The technician, a man—all of them were men—said, regarding him keenly, "You've been posing?"

39   "Unintentionally," Poole said.

40   "And now it's intentional?"

41   Poole said, "Exactly."

42   "Do you know why you never guessed? There must have been signs . . . clickings and whirrings from inside you, now and then. You never guessed because you were programmed not to notice. You'll now have the same difficulty finding out why you were built and for whom you've been operating."

43   "A slave," Poole said. "A mechanical slave."

44   "You've had fun."

45   "I've lived a good life," Poole said. "I've worked hard."

46   He paid the facility its forty frogs, flexed his new fingers, tested them out by picking up various objects such as coins, then departed. Ten minutes later he was aboard a public carrier, on his way home. It had been quite a day.

47   At home, in his one-room apartment, he poured himself a shot of Jack Daniel's Purple Label—sixty years old—and sat sipping it, meanwhile gazing through his sole window at the building on the opposite side of the street. Shall I go to the office? he asked himself. If so, why? If not, why? Choose one. Christ, he thought, it undermines you, knowing this. I'm a freak, he realized. An inanimate object mimicking an animate one. But—he felt alive. Yet . . . he felt differently, now. About himself. Hence about everyone, especially Danceman and Sarah, everyone at Tri-Plan.

48   I think I'll kill myself, he said to himself. But I'm probably programmed not to do that; it would be a costly waste which my owner would have to absorb. And he wouldn't want to.

49   Programmed. In me somewhere, he thought, there is a matrix fitted in place, a grid screen that cuts me off from certain thoughts, certain actions. And forces me into others. I am not free. I never was, but now I know it; that makes it different.

50   Turning his window to opaque, he snapped on the overhead light, carefully set about removing his clothing, piece by piece. He had watched carefully as the technicians at the repair facility had attached his new hand: he had a rather clear idea, now, of how his body had been assembled. Two major panels, one in each thigh; the technicians had removed the panels to check the circuit complexes beneath. If I'm programmed, he decided, the matrix probably can be found there.

51   The maze of circuitry baffled him. I need help, he said to himself. Let's see . . . what's the fone code for the class BBB computer we hire at the office?

52   He picked up the fone, dialed the computer at its permanent location in Boise, Idaho.

53   "Use of this computer is prorated at a five frogs per minute basis," a mechanical voice from the fone said. "Please hold your mastercredit-chargeplate before the screen."

54   He did so.

55   "At the sound of the buzzer you will be connected with the computer," the voice continued. "Please query it as rapidly as possible, taking into account the fact that its answer will be given in terms of a microsecond, while your query will—" He turned the sound down, then. But quickly turned it up as the blank audio input of the computer appeared on the screen. At this moment the computer had become a giant ear, listening to him—as well as fifty thousand other queriers throughout Terra.

56   "Scan me visually," he instructed the computer. "And tell me where I will find the programming mechanism which controls my

thoughts and behavior." He waited. On the fone's screen a great active eye, multi-lensed, peered at him; he displayed himself for it, there in his one-room apartment.

57   The computer said, "Remove your chest panel. Apply pressure at your breastbone and then ease outward."

58   He did so. A section of his chest came off; dizzily, he set it down on the floor.

59   "I can distinguish control modules," the computer said, "but I can't tell which—" It paused as its eye roved about on the fone screen. "I distinguish a roll of punched tape mounted above your heart mechanism. Do you see it?" Poole craned his neck, peered. He saw it, too. "I will have to sign off," the computer said. "After I have examined the data available to me I will contact you and give you an answer. Good day," The screen died out.

60   I'll yank the tape out of me, Poole said to himself. Tiny . . . no larger than two spools of thread, with a scanner mounted between the delivery drum and the take-up drum. He could not see any sign of motion; the spools seemed inert. They must cut in as override, he reflected, when specific situations occur. Override to my encephalic processes. And they've been doing it all my life.

61   He reached down, touched the delivery drum. All I have to do is tear this out, he thought, and—

62   The fone screen relit. "Mastercreditchargeplate number 3–BNX–883–HQR446–T," the computer's voice came. "This is BBB–307DR recontacting you in response to your query of sixteen seconds lapse, November 4, 1992. The punched tape roll above your heart mechanism is not a programming turret but is in fact a reality-supply construct. All sense stimuli received by your central neurological system emanate from that unit and tampering with it would be risky if not terminal." It added, "You appear to have no programming circuit. Query answered. Good day." It flicked off.

63   Poole, standing naked before the fone screen, touched the tape drum once again, with calculated, enormous caution. I see, he thought wildly. Or do I see? This unit—

64   If I cut the tape, he realized, my world will disappear. Reality will continue for others, but not for me. Because my reality, my universe, is coming to me from this minuscule unit. Fed into the scanner and then into my central nervous system as it snailishly unwinds.

65   It has been unwinding for years, he decided.

66   Getting his clothes, he redressed, seated himself in his big armchair—a luxury imported into his apartment from Tri-Plan's main offices—and lit a tobacco cigarette. His hands shook as he laid down his

initialed lighter; leaning back, he blew smoke before himself, creating a nimbus of gray.

67   I have to go slowly, he said to himself. What am I trying to do? Bypass my programming? But the computer found no programming circuit. Do I want to interfere with the reality tape? And if so, *why?*

68   Because, he thought, if I control that, I control reality. At least so far as I'm concerned. My subjective reality . . . but that's all there is. Objective reality is a synthetic construct, dealing with a hypothetical universalization of a multitude of subjective realities.

69   My universe is lying within my fingers, he realized. If I can just figure out how the damn thing works. All I set out to do originally was to search for and locate my programming circuit so I could gain true homeostatic functioning: control of myself. But with this—

70   With this he did not merely gain control of himself, he gained control over everything.

71   And this sets me apart from every human who ever lived and died, he thought somberly.

72   Going over to the fone he dialed his office. When he had Danceman on the screen he said briskly, "I want you to send a complete set of microtools and enlarging screen over to my apartment. I have some microcircuitry to work on." Then he broke the connection, not wanting to discuss it.

73   A half hour later a knock sounded on his door. When he opened up he found himself facing one of the shop foremen, loaded down with microtools of every sort. "You didn't say exactly what you wanted," the foreman said, entering the apartment. "So Mr. Danceman had me bring everything."

74   "And the enlarging-lens system?"

75   "In the truck, up on the roof."

76   Maybe what I want to do, Poole thought, is die. He lit a cigarette, stood smoking and waiting as the shop foreman lugged the heavy enlarging screen, with its power-supply and control panel, into the apartment. This is suicide, what I'm doing here. He shuddered.

77   "Anything wrong, Mr. Poole?" the shop foreman said as he rose to his feet, relieved of the burden of the enlarging-lens system. "You must still be rickety on your pins from your accident."

78   "Yes," Poole said quietly. He stood tautly waiting until the foreman left.

79   Under the enlarging-lens system the plastic tape assumed a new shape: a wide track along which hundreds of thousands of punch-holes worked their way. I thought so, Poole thought. Not recorded as charges on a ferrous oxide layer but actually punched-free slots.

80   Under the lens the strip of tape visibly oozed forward. Very slowly, but it did, at uniform velocity, move in the direction of the scanner.

81   The way I figure it, he thought, is that the punched holes are *on* gates. It functions like a player piano; solid is no, punch-hole is yes. How can I test this?

82   Obviously by filling in a number of holes.

83   He measured the amount of tape left on the delivery spool, calculated—at great effort—the velocity of the tape's movement, and then came up with a figure. If he altered the tape visible at the in-going edge of the scanner, five to seven hours would pass before that particular time period arrived. He would in effect be painting out stimuli due a few hours from now.

84   With a microbrush he swabbed a large—relatively large—section of tape with opaque varnish . . . obtained from the supply kit accompanying the microtools. I have smeared out stimuli for about half an hour, he pondered. Have covered at least a thousand punches.

85   It would be interesting to see what change, if any, overcame his environment, six hours from now.

86   Five and a half hours later he sat at Krackter's, a superb bar in Manhattan, having a drink with Danceman.

87   "You look bad," Danceman said.

88   "I am bad," Poole said. He finished his drink, a Scotch sour, and ordered another.

89   "From the accident?"

90   "In a sense, yes."

91   Danceman said, "Is it—something you found out about yourself?"

92   Raising his head, Poole eyed him in the murky light of the bar. "Then you know."

93   "I know," Danceman said, "that I should call you 'Poole' instead of 'Mr. Poole.' But I prefer the latter, and will continue to do so."

94   "How long have you known?" Poole said.

95   "Since you took over the firm. I was told that the actual owners of Tri-Plan, who are located in the Prox System, wanted Tri-Plan run by an electric ant whom they could control. They wanted a brilliant and forceful—"

96   "The real owners?" This was the first he had heard about that. "We have two thousand stockholders. Scattered everywhere."

97   "Marvis Bey and her husband Ernan, on Prox 4, control fifty-one percent of the voting stock. This has been true from the start."

98   "Why didn't I know?"

99   "I was told not to tell you. You were to think that you yourself made all company policy. With my help. But actually I was feeding you what the Beys fed to me."

100   "I'm a figurehead," Poole said.

101   "In a sense, yes." Danceman nodded. "But you'll always be 'Mr. Poole' to me."

102   A section of the far wall vanished. And with it, several people at tables nearby. And—

103   Through the big glass side of the bar, the skyline of New York City flickered out of existence.

104   Seeing his face, Danceman said, "What is it?"

105   Poole said hoarsely, "Look around. Do you see any changes?"

106   After looking around the room, Danceman said, "No. What like?"

107   "You still see the skyline?"

108   "Sure. Smoggy as it is. The lights wink—"

109   "Now I know," Poole said. He had been right; every punch-hole covered up meant the disappearance of some object in his reality world. Standing, he said, "I'll see you later, Danceman. I have to get back to my apartment; there's some work I'm doing. Goodnight." He strode from the bar and out onto the street, searching for a cab.

110   No cabs.

111   Those, too, he thought. I wonder what else I painted over. Prostitutes? Flowers? Prisons?

112   There, in the bar's parking lot, Danceman's squib. I'll take that, he decided. There are still cabs in Danceman's world; he can get one later. Anyhow it's a company car, and I hold a copy of the key.

113   Presently he was in the air, turning toward his apartment.

114   New York City had not returned. To the left and right vehicles and buildings, streets, ped-runners, signs . . . and in the center nothing. How can I fly into that? he asked himself. I'd disappear.

115   Or would I? He flew toward the nothingness.

116   Smoking one cigarette after another he flew in a circle for fifteen minutes . . . and then, soundlessly, New York reappeared. He could finish his trip. He stubbed out his cigarette (a waste of something so valuable) and shot off in the direction of his apartment.

117   If I insert a narrow opaque strip, he pondered as he unlocked his apartment door, I can—

118   His thoughts ceased. Someone sat in his living room chair, watching a captain kirk on the TV "Sarah," he said, nettled.

119   She rose, well-padded but graceful. "You weren't at the hospital, so I came here. I still have that key you gave me back in March after we

had that awful argument. Oh … you look so depressed." She came up to him, peeped into his face anxiously. "Does your injury hurt that badly?"

120   "It's not that." He removed his coat, tie, shirt, and then his chest panel; kneeling down he began inserting his hands into the microtool gloves. Pausing, he looked up at her and said, "I found out I'm an electric ant. Which from one standpoint opens up certain possibilities, which I am exploring now." He flexed his fingers and, at the far end of the left waldo, a micro screwdriver moved, magnified into visibility by the enlarging-lens system. "You can watch," he informed her. "If you so desire."

121   She had begun to cry.

122   "What's the matter?" he demanded savagely, without looking up from his work.

123   "I—it's just so sad. You've been such a good employer to all of us at Tri-Plan. We respect you so. And now it's all changed."

124   The plastic tape had an unpunched margin at top and bottom; he cut a horizontal strip, very narrow, then, after a moment of great concentration, cut the tape itself four hours away from the scanning head. He then rotated the cut strip into a right-angle piece in relation to the scanner, fused it in place with a micro heat element, then reattached the tape reel to its left and right sides. He had, in effect, inserted a dead twenty minutes into the unfolding flow of his reality. It would take effect—according to his calculations—a few minutes after midnight.

125   "Are you fixing yourself?" Sarah asked timidly.

126   Poole said, "I'm freeing myself." Beyond this he had several alterations in mind. But first he had to test his theory; blank, unpunched tape meant no stimuli, in which case the *lack* of tape …

127   "That look on your face," Sarah said. She began gathering up her purse, coat, rolled-up aud-vid magazine. "I'll go; I can see how you feel about finding me here."

128   "Stay," he said. "I'll watch the captain kirk with you." He got into his shirt. "Remember years ago when there were—what was it?—twenty or twenty-two TV channels? Before the government shut down the independents?"

129   She nodded.

130   "What would it have looked like," he said, "if this TV set projected all channels onto the cathode ray screen *at the same time?* Could we have distinguished anything, in the mixture?"

131   "I don't think so."

132   "Maybe we could learn to. Learn to be selective; do our own job of perceiving what we wanted to and what we didn't. Think of the possibilities, if our brains could handle twenty images at once; think of the

amount of knowledge which could be stored during a given period. I wonder if the brain, the human brain—" He broke off. "The human brain couldn't do it," he said, presently, reflecting to himself. "But in theory a quasi-organic brain might."

133   "Is that what you have?" Sarah asked.

134   "Yes," Poole said.

135   They watched the captain kirk to its end, and then they went to bed. But Poole sat up against his pillows, smoking and brooding. Beside him, Sarah stirred restlessly, wondering why he did not turn off the light.

136   Eleven-fifty. It would happen anytime, now.

137   "Sarah," he said. "I want your help. In a very few minutes something strange will happen to me. It won't last long, but I want you to watch me carefully. See if I " He gestured. "Show any changes. If I seem to go to sleep, or if I talk nonsense, or—" He wanted to say, if I disappear. But he did not. "I won't do you any harm, but I think it might be a good idea if you armed yourself. Do you have your anti-mugging gun with you?"

138   "In my purse." She had become fully awake now; sitting up in bed, she gazed at him with wild fright, her ample shoulders tanned and freckled in the light of the room.

139   He got her gun for her.

140   The room stiffened into paralyzed immobility. Then the colors began to drain away. Objects diminished until, smoke-like, they flitted away into shadows. Darkness filmed everything as the objects in the room became weaker and weaker.

141   The last stimuli are dying out, Poole realized. He squinted, trying to see. He made out Sarah Benton, sitting in the bed: a two-dimensional figure that doll-like had been propped up, there to fade and dwindle. Random gusts of dematerialized substance eddied about in unstable clouds; the elements collected, fell apart, then collected once again. And then the last heat, energy and light dissipated; the room closed over and fell into itself, as if sealed off from reality. And at that point absolute blackness replaced everything, space without depth, not nocturnal but rather stiff and unyielding. And in addition he heard nothing.

142   Reaching, he tried to touch something. But he had nothing to reach with. Awareness of his own body had departed along with everything else in the universe. He had no hands, and even if he had, there would be nothing for them to feel.

143   I am still right about the way the damn tape works, he said to himself, using a nonexistent mouth to communicate an invisible message.

144   Will this pass in ten minutes? he asked himself. Am I right about that, too? He waited . . . but knew intuitively that his time sense had departed with everything else. I can only wait, he realized. And hope it won't be long.

145   To pace himself, he thought, I'll make up an encyclopedia; I'll try to list everything that begins with an "a." Let's see. He pondered. Apple, automobile, acksetron, atmosphere, Atlantic, tomato aspic, advertising—he thought on and on, categories slithering through his fright-haunted mind.

146   All at once light flickered on.

147   He lay on the couch in the living room, and mild sunlight spilled in through the single window. Two men bent over him, their hands full of tools. Maintenance men, he realized. They've been working on me.

148   "He's conscious," one of the technicians said. He rose, stood back; Sarah Benton, dithering with anxiety, replaced him.

149   "Thank God!" she said, breathing wetly in Poole's ear. "I was so afraid; I called Mr. Danceman finally about—"

150   "What happened?" Poole broke in harshly. "Start from the beginning and for God's sake speak slowly. So I can assimilate it all."

151   Sarah composed herself, paused to rub her nose, and then plunged on nervously, "You passed out. You just lay there, as if you were dead. I waited until two-thirty and you did nothing. I called Mr. Danceman, waking him up unfortunately, and he called the electric-ant maintenance—I mean, the organic-roby maintenance people, and these two men came about four forty-five, and they've been working on you ever since. It's now six fifteen in the morning. And I'm very cold and I want to go to bed; I can't make it in to the office today; I really can't." She turned away, sniffling. The sound annoyed him.

152   One of the uniformed maintenance men said, "You've been playing around with your reality tape."

153   "Yes," Poole said. Why deny it? Obviously they had found the inserted solid strip. "I shouldn't have been out that long," he said. "I inserted a ten minute strip only."

154   "It shut off the tape transport," the technician explained. "The tape stopped moving forward; your insertion jammed it, and it automatically shut down to avoid tearing the tape. Why would you want to fiddle around with that? Don't you know what you could do?"

155   "I'm not sure," Poole said.

156   "But you have a good idea."

157   Poole said acridly, "That's why I'm doing it."

158   "Your bill," the maintenance man said, "is going to be ninety-five frogs. Payable in installments, if you so desire."

159   "Okay," he said; he sat up groggily, rubbed his eyes and grimaced. His head ached and his stomach felt totally empty.

160   "Shave the tape next time," the primary technician told him. "That way it won't jam. Didn't it occur to you that it had a safety factor built into it? So it would stop rather than—"

161   "What happens," Poole interrupted, his voice low and intently careful, "if no tape passed under the scanner? No tape—nothing at all. The photocell shining upward without impedance?"

162   The technicians glanced at each other. One said, "All the neuro circuits jump their gaps and short out."

163   "Meaning what?" Poole said.

164   "Meaning it's the end of the mechanism."

165   Poole said, "I've examined the circuit. It doesn't carry enough voltage to do that. Metal won't fuse under such slight loads of current, even if the terminals are touching. We're talking about a millionth of a watt along a cesium channel perhaps a sixteenth of an inch in length. Let's assume there are a billion possible combinations at one instant arising from the punch-outs on the tape. The total output isn't cumulative; the amount of current depends on what the battery details for that module, and it's not much. With all gates open and going."

166   "Would we lie?" one of the technicians asked wearily.

167   "Why not?" Poole said. "Here I have an opportunity to experience everything. Simultaneously. To know the universe and its entirety, to be momentarily in contact with all reality. Something that no human can do. A symphonic score entering my brain outside of time, all notes, all instruments sounding at once. And all symphonies. Do you see?"

168   "It'll burn you out," both technicians said, together.

169   "I don't think so," Poole said.

170   Sarah said, "Would you like a cup of coffee, Mr. Poole?"

171   "Yes," he said; he lowered his legs, pressed his cold feet against the floor, shuddered. He then stood up. His body ached. They had me lying all night on the couch, he realized. All things considered, they could have done better than that.

172   At the kitchen table in the far corner of the room, Garson Poole sat sipping coffee across from Sarah. The technicians had long since gone.

173   "You're not going to try any more experiments on yourself, are you?" Sarah asked wistfully.

174   Poole grated, "I would like to control time. To reverse it." I will cut a segment of tape out, he thought, and fuse it in upside down. The causal sequences will then flow the other way. Thereupon I will walk

backward down the steps from the roof field, back up to my door, push a
locked door open, walk backward to the sink, where I will get out a
stack of dirty dishes. I will seat myself at this table before the stack, fill
each dish with food produced from my stomach . . . I will then transfer
the food to the refrigerator. The next day I will take the food out of the
refrigerator, pack it in bags, carry the bags to a supermarket, distribute
the food here and there in the store. And at last, at the front counter,
they will pay me money for this, from their cash register. The food will
be packed with other food in big plastic boxes, shipped out of the city
into the hydroponic plants on the Atlantic, there to be joined back
to trees and bushes or the bodies of dead animals or pushed deep into
the ground. But what would all that prove? A video tape running backward . . . I would know no more than I know now, which is not enough.

175   What I want, he realized, is ultimate and absolute reality, for one
microsecond. After that it doesn't matter, because all will be known;
nothing will be left to understand or see.

176   I might try one other change, he said to himself. Before I try cutting the tape. I will prick new punch-holes in the tape and see what
presently emerges. It will be interesting because I will not know what
the holes I make mean.

177   Using the tip of a microtool, he punched several holes, at random,
on the tape. As close to the scanner as he could manage . . . he did not
want to wait.

178   "I wonder if you'll see it," he said to Sarah. Apparently not, insofar
as he could extrapolate. "Something may show up," he said to her. "I
just want to warn you; I don't want you to be afraid."

179   "Oh dear," Sarah said tinnily.

180   He examined his wristwatch. One minute passed, then a second, a
third. And then—

181   In the center of the room appeared a flock of green and black
ducks. They quacked excitedly, rose from the floor, fluttered against the
ceiling in a dithering mass of feathers and wings and frantic in their vast
urge, their instinct, to get away.

182   "Ducks," Poole said, marveling. "I punched a hole for a flight of
wild ducks."

183   Now something else appeared. A park bench with an elderly, tattered man seated on it, reading a torn, bent newspaper. He looked up,
dimly made out Poole, smiled briefly at him with badly made dentures,
and then returned to his folded-back newspaper. He read on.

184   "Do you see him?" Poole asked Sarah. "And the ducks." At that
moment the ducks and the park bum disappeared. Nothing remained
of them. The interval of their punch-holes had quickly passed.

185   "They weren't real," Sarah said. "Were they? So how——"

186   "You're not real," he told Sarah. "You're a stimulus-factor on my reality tape. A punch-hole that can be glazed over. Do you also have an existence in another reality tape, or one in an objective reality?" He did not know; he couldn't tell. Perhaps Sarah did not know, either. Perhaps she existed in a thousand reality tapes; perhaps on every reality tape ever manufactured. "If I cut the tape," he said, "you will be everywhere and nowhere. Like everything else in the universe. At least as far as I am aware of it."

187   Sarah faltered, "I am real."

188   "I want to know you completely," Poole said. "To do that I must cut the tape. If I don't do it now, I'll do it some other time; it's inevitable that eventually I'll do it." So why wait? he asked himself. And there is always the possibility that Danceman has reported back to my maker, that they will be making moves to head me off. Because, perhaps, I'm endangering their property—myself.

189   "You make me wish I had gone to the office after all," Sarah said, her mouth turned down with dimpled gloom.

190   "Go," Poole said.

191   "I don't want to leave you alone."

192   "I'll be fine," Poole said.

193   "No, you're not going to be fine. You're going to unplug yourself or something, kill yourself because you've found out you're just an electric ant and not a human being."

194   He said, presently, "Maybe so." Maybe it boiled down to that.

195   "And I can't stop you," she said.

196   "No." He nodded in agreement.

197   "But I'm going to stay," Sarah said. "Even if I can't stop you. Because if I do leave and you do kill yourself, I'll always ask myself for the rest of my life what would have happened if I had stayed. You see?"

198   Again he nodded.

199   "Go ahead," Sarah said.

200   He rose to his feet. "It's not pain I'm going to feel," he told her. "Although it may look like that to you. Keep in mind the fact that organic robots have minimal pain-circuits in them. I will be experiencing the most intense——"

201   "Don't tell me any more," she broke in. "Just do it if you're going to, or don't do it if you're not."

202   Clumsily—because he was frightened—he wriggled his hands into the microglove assembly, reached to pick up a tiny tool: a sharp cutting blade. "I am going to cut a tape mounted inside my chest panel," he said, as he gazed through the enlarging-lens system. "That's all." His

hand shook as it lifted the cutting blade. In a second it can be done, he realized. All over. And—I will have time to fuse the cut ends of the tape back together, he realized. A half hour at least. If I change my mind.

203   He cut the tape.

204   Staring at him, cowering, Sarah whispered, "Nothing happened."

205   "I have thirty or forty minutes." He reseated himself at the table, having drawn his hands from the gloves. His voice, he noticed, shook; undoubtedly Sarah was aware of it, and he felt anger at himself, knowing that he had alarmed her. "I'm sorry," he said, irrationally; he wanted to apologize to her. "Maybe you ought to leave," he said in panic; again he stood up. So did she, reflexively, as if imitating him; bloated and nervous she stood there palpitating. "Go away," he said thickly. "Back to the office where you ought to be. Where we both ought to be." I'm going to fuse the tape-ends together, he told himself; the tension is too great for me to stand.

206   Reaching his hands toward the gloves he groped to pull them over his straining fingers. Peering into the enlarging screen, he saw the beam from the photoelectric gleam upward, pointed directly into the scanner; at the same time he saw the end of the tape disappearing under the scanner . . . he saw this, understood it; I'm too late, he realized. It has passed through. God, he thought, help me. It has begun winding at a rate greater than I calculated. So it's *now* that—

207   He saw apples, and cobblestones and zebras. He felt warmth, the silky texture of cloth; he felt the ocean lapping at him and a great wind, from the north, plucking at him as if to lead him somewhere. Sarah was all around him, so was Danceman. New York glowed in the night, and the squibs about him scuttled and bounced through night skies and daytime and flooding and drought. Butter relaxed into liquid on his tongue, and at the same time hideous odors and tastes assailed him: the bitter presence of poisons and lemons and blades of summer grass. He drowned; he fell; he lay in the arms of a woman in a vast white bed which at the same time dinned shrilly in his ear: the warning noise of a defective elevator in one of the ancient, ruined downtown hotels. I am living, I have lived, I will never live, he said to himself, and with his thoughts came every word, every sound; insects squeaked and raced, and he half sank into a complex body of homeostatic machinery located somewhere in Tri-Plan's labs.

208   He wanted to say something to Sarah. Opening his mouth he tried to bring forth words—a specific string of them out of the enormous mass of them brilliantly lighting his mind, scorching him with their utter meaning.

209   His mouth burned. He wondered why.

210   Frozen against the wall, Sarah Benton opened her eyes and saw the curl of smoke ascending from Poole's half-opened mouth. Then the roby sank down, knelt on elbows and knees, then slowly spread out in a broken, crumpled heap. She knew without examining it that it had "died."

211   Poole did it to itself, she realized. And it couldn't feel pain; it said so itself. Or at least not very much pain; maybe a little. Anyhow, now it is over.

212   I had better call Mr. Danceman and tell him what's happened, she decided. Still shaky, she made her way across the room to the fone; picking it up, she dialed from memory.

213   It thought I was a stimulus-factor on its reality tape, she said to herself. So it thought I would die when it "died." How strange, she thought. Why did it imagine that? It had never been plugged into the real world; it had "lived" in an electronic world of its own. How bizarre.

214   "Mr. Danceman," she said when the circuit to his office had been put through. "Poole is gone. It destroyed itself right in front of my eyes. You'd better come over."

215   "So we're finally free of it."

216   "Yes, won't it be nice?"

217   Danceman said, "I'll send a couple of men over from the shop." He saw past her, made out the sight of Poole lying by the kitchen table. "You go home and rest," he instructed Sarah. "You must be worn out by all this."

218   "Yes," she said. "Thank you, Mr. Danceman." She hung up and stood, aimlessly.

219   And then she noticed something.

220   My hands, she thought. She held them up. Why is it I can see through them?

221   The walls of the room, too, had become ill-defined.

222   Trembling, she walked back to the inert roby, stood by it, not knowing what to do. Through her legs the carpet showed, and then the carpet became dim, and she saw, through it, farther layers of disintegrating matter beyond.

223   Maybe if I can fuse the tape-ends back together, she thought. But she did not know how. And already Poole had become vague.

224   The wind of early morning blew about her. She did not feel it; she had begun, now, to cease to feel.

225   The winds blew on.

DISCUSSION QUESTIONS

1. Why aren't the "organic robots" told they're not human?
2. Why do you think the owner of a successful business in New York City lives in a one-room, one-window apartment?
3. When Poole discovers he has a "reality-supply" system and not programmed circuitry, how does he interpret this information?
4. What makes New York City disappear? What brings it back?
5. By removing his tape, Poole faces two distinct possibilities: receive *all* stimuli at once or none at all. In small groups, discuss how these are similar in concept.

WRITING TOPICS

1. Once he realizes the truth, Poole thinks of himself as a slave held by his programming. In your journal, discuss how all humans face a similar dilemma.
2. In an essay, discuss the difference between objective reality and subjective reality. How can that distinction be blurred?
3. In the late sixties, many young people were experimenting with "mind expanding" drugs. In a paragraph or two, discuss how Poole's search for the ultimate reality is a reflection of this or a prediction of the virtual reality experiments of the eighties and nineties.

CHAPTER SEVEN

The Seventies

1970

Four students at Kent State University in Ohio are killed by National Guardsmen during Vietnam War protests

Women outnumber men for the first time in the U.S.

First complete synthesis of a gene

First nuclear-powered heart pacemakers installed

Soviets land a spacecraft on Venus

Mariner 9 orbits Mars

1971

George Lucas makes the movie *THX 1138*

Cigarette ads banned from U.S. TV

Britain switches to metric system

U.S.S.R. *Soyuz* docks with space station *Salyut*

1972

Stanley Kubrick adapts Anthony Burgess' *A Clockwork Orange* to film

Burglars hired by Nixon campaign officials caught breaking into National Democratic headquarters at Watergate

Britain imposes direct rule on Northern Ireland in attempt to control ongoing violence between Protestants and Catholics

Ms. magazine for liberated women begins publication

Equal Rights Amendment guaranteeing women equal consideration passed by Congress but fails to gain ratification by states

1973

Watergate defendants plead guilty; Vice President Spiro Agnew resigns

East and West Germany establish diplomatic relations

U.S. involvement in Vietnam war ends

Oil prices rise dramatically due to Mideast oil embargo

Supreme Court decision *Roe v. Wade* makes abortions legal in the United States

Bahamas become independent after 300 years of British rule

Pioneer 10 transmits TV pictures from 81,000 miles above Jupiter

John W. Campbell Memorial Award established

1974

***Billion Year Spree*, Brian Aldiss' critical history of science fiction published**

Energy crisis spawns worldwide inflation

Nixon resigns when his role in the Watergate scandal is revealed

Skylab 3 astronauts set record of 84 days in space

Mariner 10 transmits pictures of Venus and Mercury

1975

American scientists discover a new subatomic particle, the psi

Japanese *Science Fiction Magazine* begins publishing Japanese originals in addition to American reprints

Soyuz and *Apollo* meet in space, marking the first international space cooperation

First video cassette recorder produced for home use in the U.S.

1976

Harlan Ellison's *A Boy and His Dog* becomes a movie

North and South Vietnam reunite as Socialist Republic of Vietnam

Rioting against apartheid spreads across South Africa

U.S. and U.S.S.R. agree to limit underground testing of nuclear weapons with mutual inspections

1977

National Academy of Science reports that CFC gases from spray cans damage the Earth's ozone layer

Neil Barron's major critical work on science fiction, *Anatomy of Wonder*, published

U.S. forms Department of Energy in response to oil crisis

Refugees flee Vietnam by boat

U.S. space shuttle *Enterprise* makes first test flight

British scientists determine the complete genetic structure of a living organism

Neutron bomb, which kills people but leaves buildings intact, tested

U.S. scientists detect first quark

Star Wars—the first in the movie trilogy by George Lucas—appears

Close Encounters of the Third Kind, a Steven Spielberg movie, depicts nonthreatening aliens

1978

Bob Guccione founds *Omni Magazine* with a budget for quality fiction, including science fiction

U.S. and People's Republic of China establish full diplomatic relations

Three Mile Island nuclear reactor spews radioactive gases

First test tube baby born

1979

Shah of Iran forced into exile; replaced by Ayatollah Khomeini; 53 U.S. Embassy members held hostage

Soviet cosmonauts return to Earth after spending a record 175 days in space

Voyager I and *Voyager II* fly by Jupiter, revealing new information about its atmosphere

Skylab, an abandoned U.S. attempt to establish a space station, tumbles onto Australia and adjacent ocean

Ridley Scott directs *Alien*, using set designs by illustrator G. R. Giger

HISTORICAL CONTEXT

The space race continued throughout the seventies, with the
United States launching more *Apollo* spacecraft. There were additional trips to the moon and one historic docking with the Soviets'
Soyuz 19 in space. The *Skylab* research station, *Voyager 1* and *Voyager 2*
heading out of the solar system, and *Pioneer 1* and *Pioneer 2* heading
to Venus were other important space explorations during the
decade. The need for smaller equipment for space travel led to the
development of the microprocessor computer chip in 1971. This
chip stored tremendous amounts of information on a few square
millimeters of silicon with a retrieval time of less than 100 microseconds. Soon this revolutionary breakthrough would affect
every aspect of daily life, including medicine, the military, the
communications industry, entertainment, and transportation.

However, even though some attempt at cooperation was made
between the United States and the Soviet Union, including the limit
of nuclear weapons testing, conflicts continued to flare up threatening
world peace. In 1972 Palestinian terrorists attacked the Israeli compound at the Olympics in Munich, Germany, killing one athlete
and taking nine others hostage. Their demand for the release of
Palestinian prisoners ended in a shoot-out with German police. All
the hostages, five Palestinians, and one German police officer were
killed. Live TV carried the terrorist activity around the globe, advertising their cause and sparking indignation and demands for an
end to Arab terrorism.

In South America, Salvador Allende became the first freely
elected Marxist in the world when he was elected head of state of

Chile in 1970. After assuming office, he quickly dismantled much of the capitalistic economy. This upset both the Chilean middle class and the U.S. corporations that had interests there. The CIA encouraged opposition to Allende, and he was killed in a coup three years after he took office. He was replaced by a military junta headed by General Pinochet, who later assumed dictatorial powers.

An Arab-Israeli war broke out in the Middle East in 1973 as Egypt and Syria attacked Sinai and the Golan Heights of Israel in an attempt to retake the territory taken from them in 1967. They emphasized the religious nature of the war by attacking on Yom Kippur, the most sacred Jewish holy day. After the Yom Kippur war, Israel, backed by the United States, mounted a retaliatory campaign and achieved a limited military victory. The Arab countries, acting together, cut oil production and limited exports to the United States in retaliation. As the embargo progressed, Yasser Arafat, head of the Palestine Liberation Organization, negotiated for a partial Palestine free state. The U.N. recognized the PLO as the legitimate representative of Palestine, but Israel refused to acknowledge their right to democratic rule.

In the United States, burglars funded by Richard Nixon's presidential re-election campaign were caught breaking into Democratic National Headquarters in the Watergate hotel and placing electronic surveillance devices in the offices of George McGovern, the Democratic presidential candidate. Many of Nixon's top aides were indicted and eventually served prison time for the break-in and cover-up. Nixon himself was charged with conspiracy when secret White House tapes were discovered. This led to the threat of impeachment proceedings, forcing Nixon to become the first U.S. president ever to resign from the office. His vice president, Spiro Agnew, had previously resigned due to a tax scandal, and Nixon's appointed vice president, Gerald Ford, quickly pardoned Nixon from any criminal proceedings. This action angered many across the country.

Though Nixon achieved a cease-fire in Vietnam and withdrew U.S. troops in 1973, civil war was brewing in Cambodia. The Khmer Rouge communist party, with dictator Pol Pot as its leader, took power in 1975 and conducted a campaign of ethnic genocide against anyone not Khmer. In an attempt to rid the country of religion, half the country's 60,000 Buddhist monks were murdered, and one fourth of the total population was killed.

President Jimmy Carter, in an attempt to establish peace in the Middle East, invited Egyptian president Anwar Sadat and Israeli prime minister Menachem Begin to Camp David in 1978. The result was the first peace accord ever established between Israel and an Arab state. The agreement included provisions for withdrawal of Israeli troops from the Sinai, demilitarization of the Israeli-Egyptian border, and an attempt at establishing Palestinian autonomy. Arafat, however, denounced the Camp David accord and refused to be bound by it.

In 1975, the Shah of Iran formed a new political party and banned all opposition parties. Iranian Muslims disliked the Shah's secularism and his dependence on the United States. A Muslim religious fundamentalist, Ayatollah Khomeini, cultivated this unrest and gained the support of the Iranian army to oust the Shah and set up an Islamic republic, ushering in an era of anti-U.S. sentiment.

Meanwhile, the Nicaraguan government in Central America, which had close ties to the United States, was overthrown in 1979 by the Marxist Sandinista movement. When Anastasio Somoza Debayle took power in 1974, his violations of human rights were so severe that he lost the support of the middle class, the trade unions, and the church. The United States then helped set Daniel Ortega in place to realign the Sandinista party. Ortega began a program of land reform and nationalization of interests.

By the 1970s, the baby boom generation that had protested in the sixties against those over 30 was itself beginning to turn 30. The generation that had sought to change the world began to show signs of disillusionment, and turned its attention inward to health clubs, therapy sessions, jogging, and consciousness raising. The six-ties visionaries had lost their faith in the future and were instead focusing on more personal changes. The new generation maturing during this decade chose to ignore the social activism of the sixties. Instead their attention shifted toward acquiring wealth and pres-tige, and they were dubbed the "me" generation by the press. Voter turnout dropped as faith in the political system waned.

In the sixties, a Youth International Party had been formed. These "yippies" vowed never to grow up or forget their youthful ideas, and they were repeatedly in the news through much of the decade. Late in the decade, however, a new emphasis on materialism began. This trend would develop more fully in the eighties.

The country, however, was losing its isolationist tendencies, and foreign policy became a top priority. The United States was clearly the world power by the seventies. Thus, when President Carter agreed to let the exiled Shah of Iran into the country for medical treatment in 1979, Khomeini's followers stormed the U.S. embassy in Tehran and took 53 hostages. They held these hostages for 444 days and didn't release them until the day Carter left office.

DEVELOPMENTS IN SCIENCE FICTION

As the New Wave wavered and crumbled from its top position, science fiction teetered on the brink of possibilities. Science fiction writers and audiences did not attempt another "movement" but rather diversified in a number of directions. When John W. Campbell Jr. died in 1971, Ben Bova took over as editor of *Analog*. He continued to publish New Wave–type stories that emphasized psychological explorations rather than technological inventions. Frederick Pohl's "The Gold at Starbow's End" (1972), for instance, disgusted many staunch hard science fiction fans with its use of drugs, sex, and Eastern religions. The biggest complaint, however, was the emphasis on the ideal man portrayed, not as an action hero, but as loving, compassionate, and nonviolent.

Analog remained primarily the domain of hard science fiction, including stories such as Larry Niven's "Cloak of Anarchy" (1972). This tale features a future history set in California at a time when violence and anarchy are held in check by high-tech enforcing devices called copseyes.

The use of computers as science fiction fixtures expanded rapidly during the seventies with the advent of the microprocessor and microcomputer. Vacuum tubes and punch cards disappeared as size was no longer an important element of computers. Stories about artificial intelligence, like Isaac Asimov's "The Bicentennial

Man" (1976) began to appear. Computer terminology became more common in science fiction stories, as in John Brunner's *The Shockwave Rider* (1975). In that novel, Brunner employs the then-novel concepts of computer viruses and wormholes.

In addition to hard and soft science fiction, fantasy fiction rose in popularity in the seventies. Science fiction and fantasy had always had close ties, with many writers producing works in both genres. Even Campbell had produced *Unknown Stories* as an outlet for fantasy stories, and many of the same authors frequently contributed to both it and *Astounding Science Fiction*. Science fiction promotes the idea of scientific plausibility, while fantasy freely makes use of magic. However, time travel and faster-than-light travel, both staples of science fiction, are scientifically impossible and thus fantasy elements. Arthur C. Clarke said of this dilemma, "Any sufficiently advanced technology is indistinguishable from magic."

The republication of J. R. R. Tolkien's *The Lord of the Rings* trilogy in paperback in 1965 touched off the fantasy boom. Sales of the books climbed steadily until by the end of the seventies more than eight million copies had been sold. Tolkien created a land of elves, dwarves, hobbits, wizards, and walking trees in a time of limited technology amidst a warrior culture. The story featured fully developed societies with ancient traditions, complete languages, and carefully detailed histories. It is distinctly a step removed from typical sword and sorcery fantasy.

Fritz Leiber's *Farhrd and the Gray Mouser* series was also popular. His *Ill Met in Lankhmar* won the Hugo award as the best science fiction novella of 1971, though most critics consider it primarily fantasy. The surge in popularity of fantasy also resulted in reprints of Robert E. Howard's sword-wielding *Conan the Barbarian* books. H. P. Lovecraft's stories of *Cthullo* where horrific creatures try to invade Earth through a dimensional warp were also reprinted.

As fantasy fiction became more popular, opportunities grew for more women authors to publish both fantasy and science fiction. Anne McCaffrey's *Dragonriders of Pern* series of novels were enormously popular. Pern is a planet colonized by Earthlings who then develop their own culture. The level of technology is low and the society is organized along feudal guidelines.

Marion Zimmer Bradley's *Darkover* stories, though begun much earlier, had a renewed popularity with the fantasy boom. There is telepathy on Darkover, but Bradley shows the workings of a fantastic alien culture much as Edgar Rice Burroughs did in his Mars and Venus novels of the thirties.

However, in proportion to males, the number of female readers (and writers) of science fiction was still small. For one thing, there were few believable female characters, even those created by women authors. The emphasis on technological hardware and the lack of relationship-oriented stories also distanced many women from the genre. Fantasy, though it contains a fair amount of violence and bloodshed, usually emphasizes the moral dilemmas that provoke the fighting, while hard science fiction devotes more attention to the gadgetry used in battling foes.

The civil rights movement begun in the sixties now grew to include campaigns for women's rights. Science fiction of the seventies began to encompass feminist visions, both in fantasy and more traditional science fiction categories. Ursula K. LeGuin's *The Left Hand of Darkness* in 1969 was a forerunner, and her *The Dispossessed* (1974) relates the story of a physician on a barren planet who relocates to another planet so he can continue his research. In the course of the novel, he examines the consumerism and disrespect for women that are prevalent on the second, more prosperous planet. Joanna Russ, Marge Piercy, and James Tiptree Jr. (Alice Sheldon) were also important feminist voices of the seventies.

Russ' "When it Changed" (1972) shows a world where there are no men. The women have learned the secret of reproduction without them, making men obsolete. When men do reappear from Earth, the inhabitants of Whileaway are sure their own traditions are endangered by the "aliens." *The Female Man* (1975) shows four female characters who really represent four different sides of the same person. Though difficult to follow because of shifting viewpoints, its insights into the female psyche had not been explored in science fiction until the seventies.

Piercy's *Woman on the Edge of Time* (1976) depicts a woman in a mental institution. She is in touch with a different world, where gender roles are significantly different from the world where she is institutionalized. This novel looks at both sex stereotyping and our concept of mental health and normalcy, especially as it applies to women.

Tiptree's feminist vision is evident in "The Women Men Don't See" (1973), a story about the alienation of women in a world dominated by men. "Houston, Houston, Do You Read?" (1976) is a story about three male astronauts transported to a world where men have died out and only women remain. They fantasize about the sexual possibilities, but the astronauts' lustful visions turn to naught as they die one by one.

Science fiction in the seventies had matured enough that science fiction courses began to appear in college catalogs, though many academics still had to prove their subject was worthy of serious literary merit. *Extrapolation* was the only academic journal devoted to science fiction before 1970, the year the Science Fiction Research Association was established, followed by the Science Fiction Foundation in Britain in 1971, which began publishing *The Review of Science Fiction Stories* in 1972. It remains a serious academic journal with critical and literary analysis of science fiction works. *Science Fiction Studies* was founded at Indiana State University in 1973 and is the most academic of the journals. These associations and journals enhanced the credibility and reputation of science fiction. Soon new publications and collections were springing up in great numbers, including *Introduction to Psychology Through Science Fiction* (1974). The text included stories grouped to show seven areas of psychological development, with explanatory notes. It was used as a supplementary psychology text in many college classrooms.

SCIENCE FICTION IN OTHER MEDIA

Science fiction was also expanding into other areas. In 1974 *Dungeons and Dragons* became the first fantasy role playing boardgame, and that same year the fantasy computer game *Adventure* was created. At first this was only text-based, but succeeding generations would include graphics and sound as well. It wasn't long before the computer game field was booming and many science fiction titles were included. Science fiction appeared on TV, in comics, and in increasingly sophisticated movies during the seventies.

Science fiction TV shows of the seventies were uneven. *Rod Serling's Night Gallery* (1970–72) included horror, occult, and some science fiction stories, though Serling's imagination and creative control were less evident than in *The Twilight Zone*. *The Six Million Dollar Man* (1973–78) featured a human pilot infused with increased powers by the use of cybernetic replacement parts. Interesting plot twists and good action sequences saved *Wonder Woman* (1974–79) from triteness, and *Mork and Mindy* (1978–82), with the comic ability of Robin Williams, showed that there was a place for comedy in science fiction. *Battlestar Galactica* (1978), inspired by the success of *Star Wars*, had ponderously huge sets and detailed special effects. Repetitive story lines and high production costs, however, combined to limit its run to a single season.

Comics, which had grown in popularity during the late sixties, continued to expand in scope, complexity, and price. Marvel and D.C. had a virtual war of superheroes during the seventies. Nearly all superheroes began to have personality quirks, something hardly ever explored before, as heroes were expected to be perfect role models without human feelings or failings. This changed drastically during the comic book boom. Soon multi-story comics were the rule rather than the exception, as comic artists and writers strained at the boundaries of the single issue story. Soon collections of linked stories began appearing so fans could have access to an entire story line under one cover. These paved the way for longer, more sustained works called graphic novels, which further extended the comics format by introducing complexities not previously possible.

Movies, though, were the most improved area for science fiction during the seventies. So many good movies appeared it is difficult to mention them all in a text emphasizing print media. Stanley Kubrick adapted Anthony Burgess' *A Clockwork Orange* (1971) for the screen. In it, a criminal is given therapy that forces him to do good, taking away his freedom to choose his own destiny. Harlan Ellison's *A Boy and His Dog* was made into a movie in 1975, showing a new use for dogs, and women, in a post-apocalyptic world. *The Man Who Fell to Earth* was the story of an alien from a dry planet coming to Earth in search of water for his dying planet. As in the Walter Tevis novel, though, the alien is discovered and absorbed into human culture.

Logan's Run (1976), a story where no one can live past thirty because of overpopulation pressures, showed the distrust of the older generation expressed by the youth of the sixties. Star Wars (1977), the first of a trilogy of space operas by George Lucas, set a new standard in science fiction film making. It had revolutionary special effects, universe spanning scope, attention to detail, and a resounding fairytale-like story line. Its tremendous popularity boosted the science fiction film industry by showing it as not only popular entertainment, but something that could be presented intelligently as well. The same year Steven Spielberg presented benign, though mysterious, aliens in Close Encounters of the Third Kind.

In 1979, Alien, in what became another trilogy, featured a tough woman hero who eventually overcomes an extraordinarily tenacious creature. Her biggest enemy, though, turns out to be the corporation that wants to exploit the potential of the dangerous creature, regardless of the cost in human lives. That same year Mad Max, the beginning of yet another trilogy, depicted a postnuclear world where punks and power rule, and the only way to stay alive is to be ruthless. The crew of the Enterprise also appeared on the big screen in 1979 in Star Trek: The Motion Picture. The attention to detail and character translated well to the cinema, leading to many sequels.

The Sliced-Crosswise Only-on-Tuesday World

1971

PHILIP JOSÉ FARMER (b. 1918)

Philip José Farmer began his science fiction career by exploring a topic that had not been approached directly before—sex. His *The Lovers* was shocking to 1952 readers not used to open talk about such taboo topics. Even though he produced a number of good stories and a few other novels in the fifties, his career languished until the sixties. In 1965 he began a series of novels with *The Maker of Universes*. These novels set the stage for his even more popular *Riverworld* series in the seventies. Riverworld is a planet where a godlike race has resurrected humans along the banks of an incredibly long river. Figures from throughout history meet and try to discover the nature of the universe they find themselves in.

Farmer also wrote a number of pseudo-history novels which presented seemingly rational explanations for the existence of characters such as Tarzan, Doc Savage, Sherlock Holmes, and James Bond. In *Tarzan Alive* (1972) he creates an elaborate genealogy and explains why Tarzan has kept the truth of his existence secret. Farmer explains these characters by theorizing that a meteorite landed at some time in the past and irradiated a number of pregnant women, who then gave birth to a race of mutant supermen.

In "The Sliced-Crosswise Only-on-Tuesday World," Philip José Farmer shows what can happen when love at first sight disrupts the normality of an otherwise orderly world.

1   Getting into Wednesday was almost impossible. Tom Pym had
thought about living on other days of the week. Almost everybody with
any imagination did. There were even TV shows speculating on this.
Tom Pym had even acted in two of these. But he had no genuine desire
to move out of his own world. Then his house burned down.

2   This was on the last day of the eight days of spring. He awoke to
look out the door at the ashes and the firemen. A man in a white asbestos
suit motioned for him to stay inside. After fifteen minutes, another man
in a suit gestured that it was safe. He pressed the button by the door, and
it swung open. He sank down in the ashes to his ankles: they were a trifle
warm under the inch-thick coat of water-soaked crust.

3   There was no need to ask what had happened, but he did, anyway.

4   The fireman said, "A short-circuit, I suppose. Actually, we don't
know. It started shortly after midnight, between the time that Monday
quit and we took over."

5   Tom Pym thought that it must be strange to be a fireman or a po-
liceman. Their hours were so different, even though they were still limited by the walls of midnight.

6   By then the others were stepping out of their stoners or "coffins" as
they were often called. That left sixty still occupied.

7   They were due for work at 08:00. The problem of getting new
clothes and a place to live should have to be put off until off-hours, because the TV studio where they worked was behind in the big special it
was due to put on in 144 days.

8   They ate breakfast at an emergency center. Tom Pym asked a grip
if he knew of any place he could stay. Though the government would
find one for him, it might not look very hard for a convenient place.

9   The grip told him about a house only six blocks from his former
house. A makeup man had died, and as far as he knew the vacancy had
not been filled. Tom got onto the phone at once, since he wasn't needed
at that moment, but the office wouldn't be open until ten, as the recording informed him. The recording was a very pretty girl with red hair,
tourmaline eyes, and a very sexy voice. Tom would have been more impressed if he had not known her. She had played in some small parts in
two of his shows, and the maddening voice was not hers. Neither was
the color of her eyes.

10   At noon he called again, got through after a ten-minute wait, and
asked Mrs. Bellefield if she would put through a request for him. Mrs.
Bellefield reprimanded him for not having phoned sooner; she was not
sure that anything could be done today. He tried to tell her his circumstances and then gave up. Bureaucrats! That evening he went to a public
emergency place, slept for the required four hours while the inductive

field speeded up his dreaming, woke up and got into the upright cylinder of eternium. He stood for ten seconds, gazing out through the
transparent door at other cylinders with their still figures, and then
he pressed the button. Approximately fifteen seconds later he became
unconscious.

11   He had to spend three more nights in the public stoner. Three
days of fall were gone; only five left. Not that that mattered in
California so much. When he had lived in Chicago, winter was like a
white blanket being shaken by a madwoman. Spring was a green explosion. Summer was a bright roar and a hot breath. Fall was the topple
of a drunken jester in garish motley.

12   The fourth day, he received notice that he could move into the
very house he had picked. This surprised and pleased him. He knew of
a dozen who had spent a whole year—forty-eight days or so—in a
public station while waiting. He moved in the fifth day with three days
of spring to enjoy. But he would have to use up his two days off to
shop for clothes, bring in groceries and other goods and get acquainted
with his housemates. Sometimes, he wished he had not been born with
the compulsion to act. TV'ers worked five days at a stretch, sometimes
six, while a plumber, for instance, only put in three days out of seven.

13   The house was as large as the other, and the six extra blocks to
walk would be good for him. It held eight people per day, counting
himself. He moved in that evening, introduced himself and got Mabel
Curta, who worked as a secretary for a producer, to fill him in on the
household routine. After he made sure that his stoner had been moved
into the stoner room, he could relax somewhat.

14   Mabel Curta had accompanied him into the stoner room, since
she had appointed herself his guide. She was a short, overly curved
woman of about thirty-five (Tuesday time). She had been divorced
three times, and marriage was no more for her unless, of course, Mr.
Right came along. Tom was between marriages himself, but he did not
tell her so.

15   "We'll take a look at your bedroom," Mabel said. "It's small but it's
soundproofed, thank God."

16   He started after her, then stopped. She looked back through the
doorway and said, "What is it?"

17   "This girl . . ."

18   There were sixty-three of the tall gray eternium cylinders. He was
looking through the door of the nearest at the girl within.

19   "Wow! Really beautiful!"

20   If Mabel felt any jealousy, she suppressed it.

21   "Yes, isn't she?"

22   The girl had long, black, slightly curly hair, a face that could have launched him a thousand times a thousand times, a figure that had enough but not too much and long legs. Her eyes were open; in the dim light they looked a purplish-blue. She wore a thin silvery dress.

23   The plate by the top of the door gave her vital data. Jennie Marlowe. Born 2031 A.D., San Marino, California. She would be twenty-four years old. Actress. Unmarried. Wednesday's child.

24   "What's the matter?" Mabel said.

25   "Nothing."

26   How could he tell her that he felt sick in his stomach from a desire that could never be satisfied? Sick from beauty?

> *For will in us is over-ruled by fate.*
> *Who ever loved, that loved not at first sight?*

27   "What?" Mabel said, and then, after laughing, "You must be kidding?"

28   She wasn't angry. She realized that Jennie Marlowe was no more competition than if she were dead. She was right. Better for him to busy himself with the living of this world. Mabel wasn't too bad, cuddly, really, and after a few drinks, rather stimulating.

29   The went downstairs after 18:00 to the TV room. Most of the others were there, too. Some had their ear plugs in; some were looking at the screen but talking. The newscast was on, of course. Everybody was filling up on what had happened last Tuesday and today. The Speaker of the House was retiring after his term was up. His days of usefulness were over and his recent ill health showed no signs of disappearing. There was a shot of the family graveyard in Mississippi with the pedestal reserved for him. When science someday learned how to rejuvenate, he would come out of stonerment.

30   "That'll be the day!" Mabel said. She squirmed on his lap.

31   "Oh, I think they'll crack it," he said. "They're already on the track; they've succeeded in stopping the aging of rabbits."

32   "I don't mean that," she said. "Sure, they'll find out how to rejuvenate people. But then what? You think they're going to bring them all back? With all the people they got now and then they'll double, maybe triple, maybe quadruple, the population? You think they won't just leave them standing there?" She giggled, and said, "What would the pigeons do without them?"

33   He squeezed her waist. At the same time, he had a vision of himself squeezing *that* girl's waist. Hers would be soft enough but with no hint of fat.

34   Forget about her. Think of now. Watch the news.

35   A Mrs. Wilder had stabbed her husband and then herself with a kitchen knife. Both had been stonered immediately after the police arrived, and they had been taken to the hospital. An investigation of a work slowdown in the county government offices was taking place. The complaints were that Monday's people were not setting up the computers for Tuesday's. The case was being referred to the proper authorities of both days. The Ganymede base reported that the Great Red Spot of Jupiter was emitting weak but definite pulses that did not seem to be random.

36   The last five minutes of the program was a precis devoted to outstanding events of the other days. Mrs. Cuthmar, the housemother, turned the channel to a situation comedy with no protests from anybody.

37   Tom left the room, after telling Mabel that he was going to bed early—alone, and to sleep. He had a hard day tomorrow.

38   He tiptoed down the hall and the stairs and into the stoner room. The lights were soft, there were many shadows, and it was quiet. The sixty-three cylinders were like ancient granite columns of an underground chamber of a buried city. Fifty-five faces were white blurs behind the clear metal. Some had their eyes open; most had closed them while waiting for the field radiated from the machine in the base. He looked through Jennie Marlowe's door. He felt sick again. Out of his reach; never for him. Wednesday was only a day away. No, it was only a little less than four and a half hours away.

39   He touched the door. It was slick and only a little cold. She stared at him. Her right forearm was bent to hold the strap of a large purse. When the door opened, she would step out, ready to go. Some people took their showers and fixed their faces as soon as they got up from their sleep and then went directly into the stoner. When the field was automatically radiated at 05:00, they stepped out a minute later, ready for the day.

40   He would like to step out of his "coffin," too, at the same time.

41   But he was barred by Wednesday.

42   He turned away. He was acting like a sixteen-year-old kid. He had been sixteen about one hundred and six years ago, not that that made any difference. Physiologically, he was thirty.

43   As he started up to the second floor, he almost turned around and went back for another look. But he took himself by his neck-collar and pulled himself up to his room. There he decided he would get to sleep at once. Perhaps he would dream about her. If dreams were wish-fulfillments, they would bring her to him. It still had not been "proved" that dreams always expressed wishes, but it had been proved that man

deprived of dreaming did go mad. And so the somniums radiated a field that put man into a state in which he got all the sleep, and all the dreams, that he needed within a four-hour period. Then he was awakened and a little later went into the stoner where the field suspended all atomic and subatomic activity. He would remain in that state forever unless the activating field came on.

44   He slept, and Jennie Marlowe did not come to him. Or, if she did, he did not remember. He awoke, washed his face, went down eagerly to the stoner, where he found the entire household standing around, getting in one last smoke, talking, laughing. Then they would step into their cylinders, and a silence like that at the heart of a mountain would fall.

45   He had often wondered what would happen if he did not go into the stoner. How would he feel? Would he be panicked? All his life, he had known only Tuesdays. Would Wednesday rush at him, roaring, like a tidal wave? Pick him up and hurl him against the reefs of a strange time?

46   What if he made some excuse and went back upstairs and did not go back down until the field had come on? By then, he could not enter. The door to his cylinder would not open again until the proper time. He could still run down to the public emergency stoners only three blocks away. But if he stayed in his room, waiting for Wednesday?

47   Such things happened. If the breaker of the law did not have a reasonable excuse, he was put on trial. It was a felony second only to murder to "break time," and the unexcused were stonered. All felons, sane or insane, were stonered. Or *mañanaed*, as some said. The *mañanaed* criminal waited in immobility and unconsciousness, preserved unharmed until science had techniques to cure the insane, the neurotic, the criminal, the sick. *Mañana.*

48   "What was it like in Wednesday?" Tom had asked a man who had been unavoidably left behind because of an accident.

49   "How would I know? I was knocked out except about fifteen minutes. I was in the same city, and I had never seen the faces of the ambulance men, of course, but then I've never seen them here. They stonered me and left me in the hospital for Tuesday to take care of."

50   He must have it bad, he thought. Bad. Even to think of such a thing was crazy. Getting into Wednesday was almost impossible. Almost. But it could be done. It would take time and patience, but it could be done.

51   He stood in front of his stoner for a moment. The others said, "See you! So long! Next Tuesday!" Mabel called, "Good night, lover!"

52   "Good night," he muttered.

53   "What?" she shouted.

54   "Good night!"

55   He glanced at the beautiful face behind the door. Then he smiled. He had been afraid that she might hear him say good night to a woman who called him lover.

56   He had ten minutes left. The intercom alarms were whooping. Get going, everybody! Time to take the six-day trip! Run! Remember the penalties!

57   He remembered, but he wanted to leave a message. The recorder was on a table. He activated it, and said, "Dear *Miss* Jennie Marlowe. My name is Tom Pym, and my stoner is next to yours. I am an actor, too; in fact, I work at the same studio as you. I know this is presumptuous of me, but I have never seen anybody so beautiful. Do you have a talent to match your beauty? I would like to see some run-offs of your shows. Would you please leave some in room five? I'm sure the occupant won't mind. Yours, Tom Pym."

58   He ran it back. It was certainly bald enough, and that might be just what was needed. Too flowery or too pressing would have made her leery. He had commented on her beauty twice but not overstressed it. And the appeal to her pride in her acting would be difficult to resist. Nobody knew better than he about that.

59   He whistled a little on his way to the cylinder. Inside, he pressed the button and looked at his watch. Five minutes to midnight. The light on the huge screen above the computer in the police station would not be flashing for him. Ten minutes from now, Wednesday's police would step out of their stoners in the precinct station, and they would take over their duties.

60   There was a ten-minute hiatus between the two days in the police station. All hell could break loose in these few minutes and it sometimes did. But a price had to be paid to maintain the walls of time.

61   He opened his eyes. His knees sagged a little and his head bent. The activation was a million microseconds fast—from eternium to flesh and blood almost instantaneously and the heart never knew that it had been stopped for such a long time. Even so, there was a little delay in the muscles' response to a standing position.

62   He pressed the button, opened the door, and it was as if his button had launched the day. Mabel had made herself up last night so that she looked dawn-fresh. He complimented her and she smiled happily. But he told her he would meet her for breakfast. Halfway up the staircase, he stopped, and waited until the hall was empty. Then he sneaked back down and into the stoner room. He turned on the recorder.

63   A voice, husky but also melodious, said, "Dear Mister Pym. I've had a few messages from other days. It was fun to talk back and forth across the abyss between the worlds, if you don't mind my exaggerating a little. But there is really no sense in it, once the novelty has worn off.

If you become interested in the other person, you're frustrating yourself. That person can only be a voice in a recorder and a cold waxy face
in a metal coffin. I wax poetic. Pardon me. If the person doesn't interest
you, why continue to communicate? There is no sense in either case.
And I *may* be beautiful. Anyway, I thank you for the compliment, but I
am also sensible.

64   "I should have just not bothered to reply. But I want to be nice;
I didn't want to hurt your feelings. So please don't leave any more
messages."

65   He waited while silence was played. Maybe she was pausing for effect. Now would come a chuckle or a low honey-throated laugh, and
she would say, "However, I don't like to disappoint my public. The run-
offs are in your room."

66   The silence stretched out. He turned off the machine and went to
the dining room for breakfast.

67   Siesta time at work was from 14:40 to 14:45. He lay down on the
bunk and pressed the button. Within a minute he was asleep. He did
dream of Jennie this time; she was a white shimmering figure solidify-
ing out of the darkness and floating toward him. She was even more
beautiful than she had been in her stoner.

68   The shooting ran overtime that afternoon so that he got home just
in time for supper. Even the studio would not dare keep a man past his
supper hour, especially since the studio was authorized to serve food
only at noon.

69   He had time to look at Jennie for a minute before Mrs. Cuthmar's
voice screeched over the intercom. As he walked down the hall, he
thought, "I'm getting barnacled on her. It's ridiculous. I'm a grown
man. Maybe . . . maybe I should see a psycher."

70   Sure, make your petition, and wait until a psycher has time for you.
Say about three hundred days from now, if you are lucky. And if the
psycher doesn't work out for you, then petition for another, and wait
six hundred days.

71   Petition. He slowed down. Petition. What about a request, not to
see a psycher, but to move? Why not? What did he have to lose? It
would probably be turned down, but he could at least try.

72   Even obtaining a form for the request was not easy. He spent two
nonwork days standing in line at the Center City Bureau before he got
the proper forms. The first time, he was handed the wrong form and
had to start all over again. There was no line set aside for those who
wanted to change their days. There were not enough who wished to do
this to justify such a line. So he had to queue up before the Miscella-
neous office counter of the Mobility Section of the Vital Exchange

Department of the Interchange and Cross Transfer Bureau. None of these titles had anything to do with emigration to another day.

73   When he got his form the second time, he refused to move from the office window until he had checked the number of the form and asked the clerk to doublecheck. He ignored the cries and the mutterings behind him. Then he went to one side of the vast room and stood in line before the punch machines. After two hours, he got to sit down at a small rolltop desk-shaped machine, above which was a large screen. He inserted the form into the slot, looked at the projection of the form, and punched buttons to mark the proper spaces opposite the proper questions. After that, all he had to do was to drop the form into a slot and hope it did not get lost. Or hope he would not have to go through the same procedure because he had improperly punched the form.

74   That evening, he put his head against the hard metal and murmured to the rigid face behind the door. "I must really love you to go through all this. And you don't even know it. And, worse, if you did, you might not care one bit."

75   To prove to himself that he had kept his gray stuff, he went out with Mabel that evening to a party given by Sol Voremwolf, a producer. Voremwolf had just passed a civil service examination giving him an A–13 rating. This meant that, in time, with some luck and the proper pull, he would become an executive vice-president of the studio.

76   The party was a qualified success. Tom and Mabel returned about half an hour before stoner time. Tom had managed to refrain from too many blowminds and liquor, so he was not tempted by Mabel. Even so, he knew that when he became unstoned, he would be half-loaded and he'd have to take some dreadful counteractives. He would look and feel like hell at work, since he had missed his sleep.

77   He put Mabel off with an excuse, and went down to the stoner room ahead of the others. Not that that would do him any good if he wanted to get stoned early. The stoners only activated within narrow time limits.

78   He leaned against the cylinder and patted the door. "I tried not to think about you all evening. I wanted to be fair to Mabel, it's not fair to go out with her and think about you all the time."

All's fair in love . . .

79   He left another message for her, then wiped it out. What was the use? Besides, he knew that his speech was a little thick. He wanted to appear at his best for her.

80   Why should he? What did she care for him?

81   The answer was, he did care, and there was no reason or logic connected with it. He loved this forbidden, untouchable, far-away-in-time, yet-so-near woman.

82   Mabel had come in silently. She said, "You're sick!"

83   Tom jumped away. Now why had she done that? He had nothing to be ashamed of. Then why was he so angry with her? His embarrassment was understandable but his anger was not.

84   Mabel laughed at him, and he was glad. Now he could snarl at her. He did so, and she turned away and walked out. But she was back in a few minutes with the others. It would soon be midnight.

85   By then he was standing inside the cylinder. A few seconds later, he left it, pushed Jennie's backward on its wheels, and pushed his around so that it faced hers. He went back in, pressed the button and stood there. The double doors only slightly distorted his view. But she seemed even more removed in distance, in time, and in unattainability.

86   Three days later, well into winter, he received a letter. The box inside the entrance hall buzzed just as he entered the front door. He went back and waited until the letter was printed and had dropped from the slot. It was the reply to his request to move to Wednesday.

87   Denied. Reason: he had no reasonable reason to move.

88   That was true. But he could not give his real motive. It would have been even less impressive than the one he had given. He had punched the box opposite No. 12. REASON: TO GET INTO AN ENVIRONMENT WHERE MY TALENTS WILL BE MORE LIKELY TO BE ENCOURAGED.

89   He cursed and he raged. It was his human, his civil right to move into any day he pleased. That is, it should be his right. What if a move did cause much effort? What if it required a transfer of his I.D. and all the records connected with him from the moment of his birth? What if . . .?

90   He could rage all he wanted to, but it would not change a thing. He was stuck in the world of Tuesday.

91   Not yet, he muttered. Not yet. Fortunately, there is no limit to the number of requests I can make in my own day. I'll send out another. They think they can wear me out, huh? Well, I'll wear them out. Man against the machine. Man against the system. Man against the bureaucracy and the hard cold rules.

92   Winter's twenty days had sped by. Spring's eight days rocketed by. It was summer again. On the second day of the twelve days of summer, he received a reply to his second request.

93   It was neither a denial nor an acceptance. It stated that if he thought he would be better off psychologically in Wednesday because his astrologer said so, then he would have to get a psycher's critique of the astrologer's analysis. Tom Pym jumped into the air and clicked his sandaled

heels together. Thank God that he lived in an age that did not classify astrologers as charlatans! The people—the masses—had protested that astrology was a necessity and that it should be legalized and honored. So laws were passed, and because of that, Tom Pym had a chance.

94   He went down to the stoner room and kissed the door of the cylinder and told Jennie Marlowe the good news. She did not respond, though he thought he saw her eyes brighten just a little. That was, of course, only his imagination, but he liked his imagination.

95   Getting a psycher for a consultation and getting through the three sessions took another year, another forty-eight days. Doctor Sigmund Traurig was a friend of Doctor Stelhela, the astrologer, and so that made things easier for Tom.

96   "I've studied Doctor Stelhela's chart carefully and analyzed carefully your obsession for this woman," he said. "I agree with Doctor Stelhela that you will always be unhappy in Tuesday, but I don't quite agree with him that you will be happier in Wednesday. However, you have this thing going for this Miss Marlowe, so I think you should go to Wednesday. But only if you sign papers agreeing to see a psycher there for extended therapy."

97   Only later did Tom Pym realize that Doctor Traurig might have wanted to get rid of him because he had too many patients. But that was an uncharitable thought.

98   He had to wait while the proper papers were transmitted to Wednesday's authorities. His battle was only half-won. The other officials could turn him down. And if he did get to his goal, then what? She could reject him without giving him a second chance.

99   It was unthinkable, but she could.

100   He caressed the door and then pressed his lips against it.

101   "Pygmalion could at least touch Galatea," he said. "Surely, the gods—the big dumb bureaucrats—will take pity on me, who can't even touch you. Surely."

102   The psycher had said that he was incapable of a true and lasting bond with a woman, as so many men were in this world of easy-come-easy-go liaisons. He had fallen in love with Jennie Marlowe for several reasons. She may have resembled somebody he had loved when he was very young. His mother, perhaps? No? Well, never mind. He would find out in Wednesday—perhaps. The deep, the important, truth was that he loved Miss Marlowe because she could never reject him, kick him out or become tiresome, complain, weep, yell, insult and so forth. He loved her because she was unattainable and silent.

103   "I love her as Achilles must have loved Helen when he saw her on top of the walls of Troy," Tom said.

104   "I wasn't aware that Achilles was ever in love with Helen of Troy,"
Doctor Traurig said drily.

105   "Homer never said so, but I *know* that he must have been! Who
could see her and *not* love her?"

106   "How the hell would I know? I never saw her! If I had suspected
these delusions would intensify . . ."

107   "I am a poet!" Tom said.

108   "Overimaginative, you mean! Hmmmm. She must be a douser! I
don't have anything particular to do this evening. I'll tell you what . . .
my curiosity is aroused. . . . I'll come down to your place tonight and
take a look at this fabulous beauty, your Helen of Troy."

109   Doctor Traurig appeared immediately after supper, and Tom Pym
ushered him down the hall and into the stoner room at the rear of the
big house as if he were a guide conducting a famous critic to a just-dis-
covered Rembrandt.

110   The doctor stood for a long time in front of the cylinder. He
hmmmmed several times and checked her vital-data plate several times.
Then he turned and said, "I see what you mean, Mr. Pym. Very well.
I'll give the go-ahead."

111   "Ain't she something?" Tom said on the porch. "She's out of this
world, literally and figuratively, of course."

112   "Very beautiful. But I believe that you are facing a great disappointment, perhaps heartbreak, perhaps, who knows, even madness,
much as I hate to use that unscientific term."

113   "I'll take the chance," Tom said. "I know I sound nuts, but where
would we be if it weren't for nuts. Look at the man who invented the
wheel, at Columbus, at James Watt, at the Wright brothers, at Pasteur,
you name them."

114   "You can scarcely compare these pioneers of science with their
passion for truth with you and your desire to marry a woman. But, as I
have observed, she is strikingly beautiful. Still, that makes me exceedingly cautious. Why isn't she married? What's wrong with her?"

115   "For all I know, she may have been married a dozen times!" Tom
said. "The point is, she isn't now! Maybe she's disappointed and she's
sworn to wait until the right man comes along. Maybe . . ."

116   "There's no maybe about it, you're neurotic," Traurig said. "But I
actually believe that it would be more dangerous for you *not* to go to
Wednesday than it would be *to* go."

117   "Then you'll say yes!" Tom said, grabbing the doctor's hand and
shaking it.

118   "Perhaps. I have some doubts."

119   The doctor had a faraway look. Tom laughed and released the hand and slapped the doctor on the shoulder. "Admit it! You were really struck by her! You'd have to be dead not to!"

120   "She's all right," the doctor said. "But you must think this over. If you do go there and she turns you down, you might go off the deep end, much as I hate to use such a poetical term."

121   "No, I won't. I wouldn't be a bit the worse off. Better off, in fact. I'll at least get to see her in the flesh."

122   Spring and summer zipped by. Then, a morning he would never forget, the letter of acceptance. With it, instructions on how to get to Wednesday. These were simple enough. He was to make sure that the technicians came to his stoner sometime during the day and readjusted the timer within the base. He could not figure out why he could not just stay out of the stoner and let Wednesday catch up to him, but by now he was past trying to fathom the bureaucratic mind.

123   He did not intend to tell anyone at the house, mainly because of Mabel. But Mabel found out from someone at the studio. She wept when she saw him at supper time, and she ran upstairs to her room. He felt badly, but he did not follow to console her.

124   That evening, his heart beating hard, he opened the door to his stoner. The others had found out by then; he had been unable to keep the business to himself. Actually, he was glad that he had told them. They seemed happy for him, and they brought in drinks and had many rounds of toasts. Finally, Mabel came downstairs, wiping her eyes, and she said she wished him luck, too. She had known that he was not really in love with her. But she did wish someone would fall in love with her just by looking inside her stoner.

125   When she found out that he had gone to see Doctor Traurig, she said, "He's a very influential man. Sol Voremwolf had him for his analyst. He says he's even got influence on other days. He edits the *Psyche Crosscurrents,* you know, one of the few periodicals read by other people."

126   *Other,* of course, meant those who lived in Wednesdays through Mondays.

127   Tom said he was glad he had gotten Traurig. Perhaps he had used his influence to get the Wednesday authorities to push through his request so swiftly. The walls between the worlds were seldom broken, but it was suspected that the very influential did it when they pleased.

128   Now, quivering, he stood before Jennie's cylinder again. The last time, he thought, that I'll see her stonered. Next time, she'll be warm, colorful, touchable flesh.

129   *"Ave atque vale!"* he said aloud. The others cheered. Mabel said,
"How corny!" They thought he was addressing them, and perhaps he
had included them.

130   He stepped inside the cylinder, closed the door and pressed the
button. He would keep his eyes open, so that ...

131   And today was Wednesday. Though the view was exactly the same,
it was like being on Mars.

132   He pushed open the door and stepped out. The seven people had
faces he knew and names he had read on their plates. But he did not
know them.

133   He started to say hello, and then he stopped.

134   Jennie Marlowe's cylinder was gone.

135   He seized the nearest man by the arm.

136   "Where's Jennie Marlowe?"

137   "Let go. You're hurting me. She's gone. To Tuesday."

138   *"Tuesday! Tuesday?"*

139   "Sure. She'd been trying to get out of here for a long time. She had
something about this day being unlucky for her. She was unhappy, that's
for sure. Just two days ago, she said her application had finally been accepted. Apparently, some Tuesday psycher had used his influence. He
came down and saw her in her stoner and that was it, brother."

140   The walls and the people and the stoners seemed to be distorted.
Time was bending itself this way and that. He wasn't in Wednesday; he
wasn't in Tuesday. He wasn't in *any* day. He was stuck inside himself at
some crazy date that should never have existed.

141   "She can't do that!"

142   "Oh, no! She just did that!"

143   "But ... you can't transfer more than once!"

144   "That's her problem."

145   It was his, too.

146   "I should never have brought him down to look at her!" Tom said.
"The swine! The unethical swine!"

147   Tom Pym stood there for a long time, and then he went into the
kitchen. It was the same environment, if you discounted the people.
Later, he went to the studio and got a part in a situation play which
was, really, just like all those in Tuesday. He watched the newscaster that
night. The President of the U.S.A. had a different name and face, but
the words of his speech could have been those of Tuesday's President.
He was introduced to a secretary of a producer; her name wasn't
Mabel, but it might as well have been.

148   The difference here was that Jennie was gone, and oh, what a world
of difference it made to him.

DISCUSSION QUESTIONS

1. What problems does this one-day-a-week world present for fire
   and police services? Why do they accept these difficulties without
   complaint?
2. What is the significance of the eternium cylinders being referred
   to as "stoners" or "coffins"?
3. What causes Tom Pym to fall in love with Jennie Marlowe? What
   is the reason according to his psycher?
4. Pym says Marlowe is "out of this world, literally and figuratively."
   Discuss what he means with a classmate.
5. Why, after getting his transfer granted, is Pym even more miserable
   than he was before?

WRITING TOPICS

1. Although most people want to live for a long time, there are some
   possible drawbacks to longevity. In an essay, discuss the disadvantages of a long life. Compare your findings with others in your class.
2. In a journal entry, examine the use of personal ads for meeting
   potential dates/mates. Can astrology be a possible indicator of
   compatibility among those seeking relationships?
3. The decade of the seventies was an era of advancing technology and
   withdrawal from personal responsibility. In an essay, explore how the
   concerns and attitudes of that decade are reflected in this story.

Cloak of Anarchy

1972

LARRY NIVEN (b . 1 9 3 8)

Beginning with his first short story in 1967, Larry Niven created a universe centered around his *Tales of Known Space*. He gained recognition for his 1970 novel *Ringworld,* which won both the Hugo and Nebula awards for that year. Niven's mathematical background adds to the realism that he brings to his hard science fiction. He presents technology as being ultimately beneficial to progress. Humans, only slightly evolved, quickly learn about genetic engineering, teleportation, and faster-than-light travel and use these advances to achieve an intergalactic maturity.

Niven alludes to a complex background for his *Tales of Known Space.* The background includes Protectors, some of whom despise humans, while others strive to protect them. Other aliens include Puppeteers who are fleeing from their exploded world and who eventually construct a huge satellite as a replacement.

Only in collaboration with others has Niven ventured outside his created universe. He teamed up with Jerry Pournelle on *The Mote in God's Eye* (1974) and *Lucifer's Hammer* (1977), and with Steven Barnes for *The Barsoom Project* (1989) and *The Voodoo Game* (1991).

In "Cloak of Anarchy," Larry Niven shows how freedom is important to humans, but also how freedom, if carried too far, can become a threat.

1   Square in the middle of what used to be the San Diego Freeway, I leaned back against a huge, twisted oak. The old bark was rough and powdery against my bare back. There was dark green shade shot with tight parallel beams of white gold. Long grass tickled my legs.

2   Forty yards away across a wide strip of lawn was a clump of elms, and a small grandmotherly woman sitting on a green towel. She looked like she'd grown there. A stalk of grass protruded between her teeth. I felt we were kindred spirits, and once when I caught her eye I wiggled a forefinger at her, and she waved back.

3   In a minute now I'd have to be getting up. Jill was meeting me at the Wilshire exits in half an hour. But I'd started walking at the Sunset Boulevard ramps, and I was tired. A minute more . . .

4   It was a good place to watch the world rotate.

5   A good day for it, too. No clouds at all. On this hot blue summer afternoon, King's Free Park was as crowded as it ever gets.

6   Someone at police headquarters had expected that. Twice the usual number of copseyes floated overhead, waiting. Gold dots against blue, basketball-sized, twelve feet up. Each a television eye and a sonic stunner, each a hookup to police headquarters, they were there to enforce the law of the Park.

7   *No violence.*

8   No hand to be raised against another—and no other laws whatever. Life was often entertaining in a Free Park.

9   North towards Sunset, a man carried a white rectangular sign, blank on both sides. He was parading back and forth in front of a square-jawed youth on a plastic box, who was trying to lecture him on the subject of fusion power and the heat pollution problem. Even this far away I could hear the conviction and the dedication in his voice.

10   South, a handful of yelling marksmen were throwing rocks at a copseye, directed by a gesticulating man with wild black hair. The golden basketball was dodging the rocks, but barely. Some cop was baiting them. I wondered where they had got the rocks. Rocks were scarce in King's Free Park.

11   The black-haired man looked familiar. I watched him and his horde chasing the copseye . . . then forgot them when a girl walked out of a clump of elms.

12   She was lovely. Long, perfect legs, deep red hair worn longer than shoulder length, the face of an arrogant angel, and a body so perfect that it seemed unreal, like an adolescent's daydream. Her walk showed training; possibly she was a model, or dancer. Her only garment was a cloak of glowing blue velvet.

13   It was fifteen yards long, that cloak. It trailed back from two big gold discs that were stuck somehow to the skin of her shoulders. It trailed back

and back, floating at a height of five feet all the way, twisting and turning to trace her path through the trees. She seemed like the illustration in a book of fairy tales, bearing in mind that the original fairy tales were not intended for children.

14   Neither was she. You could hear neck vertebrae popping all over the Park. Even the rock-throwers had stopped to watch.

15   She could sense the attention, or hear it in a whisper of sighs. It was what she was here for. She strolled along with a condescending angel's smile on her angel's face, not overdoing the walk, but letting it flow. She turned, regardless of whether there were obstacles to avoid, so that fifteen yards of flowing cloak could follow the curve.

16   I smiled, watching her go. She was lovely from the back, with dimples.

17   The man who stepped up to her a little farther on was the same one who had led the rock-throwers. Wild black hair and beard, hollow cheeks and deep-set eyes, a diffident smile and a diffident walk . . . Ron Cole. Of course.

18   I didn't hear what he said to the girl in the cloak, but I saw the result. He flinched, then turned abruptly and walked away with his eyes on his feet.

19   I got up and moved to intercept him. "Don't take it personal," I said.

20   He looked up, startled. His voice, when it came, was bitter. "How should I take it?"

21   "She'd have turned any man off the same way. She's to look at, not to touch."

22   "You know her?"

23   "Never saw her before in my life."

24   "Then—"

25   "Her cloak. Now you *must* have noticed her cloak."

26   The tail end of her cloak was just passing us, its folds rippling an improbable deep, rich blue. Ronald Cole smiled as if it hurt his face. "Yah."

27   "All right. Now suppose you made a pass, and suppose the lady liked your looks and took you up on it. What would she do next? Bearing in mind that she can't stop walking even for a second."

28   He thought it over first, then asked, "Why not?"

29   "If she stops walking, she loses the whole effect. Her cloak just hangs there like some kind of tail. It's supposed to wave. If she lies down, it's even worse. A cloak floating at five feet, then swooping into a clump of bushes and bobbing frantically—" Ron laughed helplessly in falsetto. I said, "See? Her audience would get the giggles. That's not what she's after."

30   He sobered. "But if she really wanted to, she wouldn't *care* about . . . oh. Right. She must have spent a fortune to get that effect."

31   "Sure. She wouldn't ruin it for Jacques Casanova himself." I thought
unfriendly thoughts towards the girl in the cloak. There are polite ways to
turn down a pass. Ronald Cole was easy to hurt.

32   I asked, "Where did you get the rocks?"

33   "Rocks? Oh, we found a place where the centre divider shows
through. We knocked off some chunks of concrete." Ron looked down
the length of the Park just as a kid bounced a missile off a golden ball.
"They got one! Come on!"

34   The fastest commercial shipping that ever sailed was the clipper ship;
yet the world stopped building them after just twenty-five years. Steam
had come. Steam was faster, safer, more dependable and cheaper.

35   The freeways served America for almost fifty years. Then modern
transportation systems cleaned the air and made traffic jams archaic and
left the nation with an embarrassing problem. What to do with ten
thousand miles of unsightly abandoned freeways?

36   King's Free Park had been part of the San Diego Freeway, the section
between Sunset and the Santa Monica interchange. Decades ago the concrete had been covered with topsoil. The borders had been landscaped
from the start. Now the Park was as thoroughly covered with green as the
much older Griffith Free Park.

37   Within King's Free Park was an orderly approximation of anarchy.
People were searched at the entrances. There were no weapons inside.
The copseyes, floating overhead and out of reach, were the next best thing
to no law at all.

38   There was only one law to enforce. All acts of attempted violence
carried the same penalty for attacker and victim. Let anyone raise his
hands against his neighbour, and one of the golden basketballs would stun
them both. They would wake separately, with copseyes watching. It was
usually enough.

39   Naturally people threw rocks at copseyes. It was a Free Park, wasn't it?

40   "They got one! Come on!" Ron tugged at my arm. The felled copseye
was hidden, surrounded by those who had destroyed it. "I hope they don't
kick it apart. I told them I need it intact, but that might not stop them."

41   "It's a Free Park. And they bagged it."

42   "With my missiles!"

43   "Who are they?"

44   "I don't know. They were playing baseball when I found them. I told
them I needed a copseye. They said they'd get me one."

45   I remembered Ron quite well now. Ronald Cole was an artist and an
inventor. It would have been two sources of income for another man, but

Ron was different. He invented new art forms. With solder and wire and diffraction gratings and several makes of plastics kit, and an incredible collection of serendipitous junk, Ron Cole made things the like of which had never been seen on Earth.

46   The market for new art forms has always been low, but now and then he did make a sale. It was enough to keep him in raw materials, especially since many of his raw materials came from basements and attics. Rarely there came a *big* sale, and then, briefly, he would be rich.

47   There was this about him: he knew who I was, but he hadn't remembered my name. Ron Cole had better things to think about than what name belonged with whom. A name was only a tag and a conversational gambit. "Russel! How are you?" A signal. Ron had developed a substitute.

48   Into a momentary gap in the conversation he would say, "Look at this," and hold out—miracles.

49   Once it had been a clear plastic sphere, golf-ball size, balanced on a polished silver concavity. When the ball rolled around on the curved mirror, the reflections were *fantastic*.

50   Once it had been a twisting sea serpent engraved on a Michelob beer bottle, the lovely vase-shaped bottle of the early 1960s that was too big for standard refrigerators.

51   And once it had been two strips of dull silvery metal, unexpectedly heavy. "What's this?"

52   I'd held them in the palm of my hand. They were heavier than lead. Platinum? But nobody carries that much platinum around. Joking, I'd asked, "U–235?"

53   "Are they warm?" he'd asked apprehensively. I'd fought off an urge to throw them as far as I could and dive behind a couch.

54   But they *had* been platinum. I never did learn why Ron was carrying them about. Something that didn't pan out.

55   Within a semicircle of spectators, the felled copseye lay on the grass. It was intact; possibly because two cheerful, conspicuously large men were standing over it, waving everyone back.

56   "Good," said Ron. He knelt above the golden sphere, turned it with his long artist's fingers. To me he had said, "Help me get it open."

57   "What for? What are you after?"

58   "I'll tell you in a minute. Help me get—Never mind." The hemispherical cover came off. For the first time ever, I looked into a copseye.

59   It was impressively simple. I picked out the stunner by its parabolic reflector, the cameras, and a toroidal coil that had to be part of the floater device. No power source. I guessed that the shell itself was a power beam antenna. With the cover cracked there would be no way for a damn fool to electrocute himself.

60   Ron knelt and studied the strange guts of the copseye. From his pocket he took something made of glass and metal. He suddenly remembered my existence and held it out to me, saying, "Look at this."

61   I took it, expecting a surprise, and I got it. It was an old hunting watch, a big wind-up watch on a chain, with a protective case. They were in common use a couple of hundred years ago. I looked at the face, said "Fifteen minutes slow. You didn't repair the whole works, did you?"

62   "Oh, no." He clicked the back open for me.

63   The works looked modern. I guessed, "Battery and tuning fork?"

64   "That's what the guard thought. Of course that's what I made it from. But the hands don't move; I set them just before they searched me."

65   "Aah. What does it do?"

66   "If I work it right, I think it'll knock down every copseye in King's Free Park."

67   For a minute or so I was laughing too hard to speak. Ron watched me with his head on one side, clearly wondering if I thought he was joking.

68   I managed to say, "That ought to cause all *kinds* of excitement."

69   Ron nodded vigorously. "Of course it all depends on whether they use the kind of circuits I think they use. Look for yourself; the copseyes aren't supposed to be foolproof. They're supposed to be cheap. If one gets knocked down, the taxes don't go up much. The other way is to make them expensive and foolproof, and frustrate a lot of people. People aren't supposed to be frustrated in a Free Park."

70   "So?"

71   "Well, there's a cheap way to make the circuitry for the power system. If they did it that way, I can blow the whole thing. We'll see." Ron pulled thin copper wire from the cuffs of his shirt.

72   "How long will this take?"

73   "Oh, half an hour—maybe more."

74   That decided me. "I've got to be going. I'm meeting Jill Hayes at the Wilshire exits. You've met her, a big blond girl, my height—"

75   But he wasn't listening. "OK, see you," he muttered. He began placing the copper wire inside the copseye, with tweezers. I left.

76   Crowds tend to draw crowds. A few minutes after leaving Ron, I joined a semicircle of the curious to see what they were watching.

77   A balding, lantern-jawed individual was putting something together—an archaic machine, with blades and a small gasoline motor. The T-shaped wooden handle was brand new and unpainted. The metal parts were dull with the look of ancient rust recently removed.

78   The crowd speculated in half-whispers. What was it? Not part of a car; not an outboard motor, though it had blades; too small for a motor scooter, too big for a motor skateboard—

79   "Lawn mower," said the white-haired lady next to me. She was one of those small, birdlike people who shrivel and grow weightless as they age, and live forever. Her words meant nothing to me. I was about to ask, when—

80   The lantern-jawed man finished his work, and twisted something, and the motor started with a roar. Black smoke puffed out. In triumph he gripped the handles. Outside, it was a prison offence to build a working internal-combustion machine. Here—

81   With the fire of dedication burning in his eyes, he wheeled his infernal machine across the grass. He left a path as flat as a rug. It was a Free Park, wasn't it?

82   The smell hit everyone at once: black dirt in the air, a stink of half-burned hydrocarbons attacking nose and eyes. I gasped and coughed. I'd never smelled anything like it.

83   The crowd roared and converged.

84   He squawked when they picked up his machine. Someone found a switch and stopped it. Two men confiscated the tool kit and went to work with screwdriver and hammer. The owner objected. He picked up a heavy pair of pliers and tried to commit murder.

85   A copseye zapped him and the man with the hammer, and they both hit the lawn without bouncing. The rest of them pulled the lawn mower apart and bent and broke the pieces.

86   "I'm half sorry they did that," said the old woman. "Sometimes I miss the sound of lawn mowers. My dad used to mow the lawn on Sunday mornings."

87   I said, "It's a Free Park."

88   "Then why can't he build anything he pleases?"

89   "He can. He did. Anything he's free to build, we're free to kick apart." And my mind finished, *Like Ron's rigged copseye.*

90   Ron was good with tools. It would not surprise me a bit if he knew enough about copseyes to knock out the whole system.

91   Maybe someone ought to stop him.

92   But knocking down copseyes wasn't illegal. It happened all the time. It was part of the freedom of the Park. If Ron could knock them all down at once, well—

93   Maybe someone ought to stop him. I passed a flock of high-school girls, all chittering like birds, all about sixteen. It might have been their first trip inside a Free Park. I looked back because they were so cute, and caught them staring in awe and wonder at the dragon on my back.

94   A few years and they'd be too blasé to notice. It had taken Jill almost half an hour to apply it this morning: a glorious red-and-gold dragon breathing flames across my shoulder, flames that seemed to glow by their own light. Lower down were a princess and a knight in golden armour,

the princess tied to a stake, the knight fleeing for his life. I smiled back at the girls, and two of them waved.

95 Short blond hair and golden skin, the tallest girl in sight, wearing not even a nudist's shoulder pouch: Jill Hayes stood squarely in front of the Wilshire entrance, visibly wondering where I was. It was five minutes after three.

96 There was this about living with a physical culture nut. Jill insisted on getting me into shape. The daily exercises were part of that, and so was this business of walking half the length of King's Free Park.

97 I'd balked at doing it briskly, though. Who walks briskly in a Free Park? There's too much to see. She'd given me an hour; I'd held out for three. It was a compromise, like the paper slacks I was wearing despite Jill's nudist beliefs.

98 Sooner or later she'd find someone with muscles, or I'd relapse into laziness, and we'd split. Meanwhile . . . we got along. It seemed only sensible to let her finish my training.

99 She spotted me, yelled, "Russel! Here!" in a voice that must have reached both ends of the Park.

100 In answer I lifted my arm, semaphore-style, slowly over my head and back down.

101 And every copseye in King's Free Park fell out of the sky, dead.

102 Jill looked about her at all the startled faces and all the golden bubbles resting in bushes and on the grass. She approached me somewhat uncertainly. She asked, "Did you do that?"

103 I said, "Yah. If I wave my arms again, they'll all go back up."

104 "I think you'd better do it," she said primly. Jill had a fine poker face. I waved my arm grandly over my head and down, but, of course, the copseyes stayed where they had fallen.

105 Jill said, "I wonder what happened to them?"

106 "It was Ron Cole. You remember him. He's the one who engraved some old Michelob beer bottles for Steuben—"

107 "Oh, yes. But how?"

108 We went off to ask him.

109 A brawny college man howled and charged past us at a dead run. We saw him kick a copseye like a soccer ball. The golden cover split, but the man howled again and hopped up and down hugging his foot.

110 We passed dented golden shells and broken resonators and bent parabolic reflectors. One woman looked flushed and proud; she was wearing several of the copper toroids as bracelets. A kid was collecting the cameras. Maybe he thought he could sell them outside.

111 I never saw an intact copseye after the first minute.

112   They weren't all busy kicking copseyes apart. Jill stared at the conservatively dressed group carrying POPULATION BY COPULATION signs, and wanted to know if they were serious. Their grim-faced leader handed us pamphlets that spoke of the evil and the blasphemy of Man's attempts to alter himself through gene tampering and extra-uterine growth experiments. If it was a put-on, it was a good one.

113   We passed seven little men, each three to four feet high, travelling with a single, tall pretty brunette. They wore medieval garb. We both stared; but I was the one who noticed the makeup and the use of UnTan. African pigmies, probably part of a UN-sponsored tourist group; and the girl must be their guide.

114   Ron Cole was not where I had left him.

115   "He must have decided that discretion is the better part of cowardice. May be right, too," I surmised. "Nobody's ever knocked down *all* the copseyes before."

116   "It's not illegal, is it?"

117   "Not illegal, but excessive. They can bar him from the Park, at the very least."

118   Jill stretched in the sun. She was all golden, and *big*. She said, "I'm thirsty. Is there a fountain around?"

119   "Sure, unless someone's plugged it by now. It's a—"

120   "Free Park. Do you mean to tell me they don't even protect the *fountains?*"

121   "You make one exception, it's like a wedge. When someone ruins a fountain, they wait and fix it that night. That way ... If I see someone trying to wreck a fountain, I'll generally throw a punch at him. A lot of us do. After a guy's lost enough of his holiday to the copseye stunners, he'll get the idea sooner or later."

122   The fountain was a solid cube of concrete with four spigots and a hand-sized metal button. It was hard to jam, hard to hurt. Ron Cole stood near it, looking lost.

123   He seemed glad to see me, but still lost. I introduced him—"You remember Jill Hayes." He said, "Certainly. Hello, Jill." And, having put her name to its intended purpose, promptly forgot it.

124   Jill said, "We thought you'd made a break for it."

125   "I did."

126   "Oh?"

127   "You know how complicated the exits are. They have to be, to keep anyone from getting in through an exit with—like a shotgun." Ron ran both hands through his hair, without making it any more or less neat. "Well, all the exits have stopped working. They must be on the same circuits as the copseyes. I wasn't expecting that."

128   "Then we're locked in," I said. That was irritating. But underneath the irritation was a funny feeling in the pit of my stomach. "How long do you think—"

129   "No telling. They'll have to get new copseyes in somehow. And repair the beamed power system, and figure out how I bollixed it, and fix it so it doesn't happen again. I suppose someone must have kicked my rigged copseye to pieces by now, but the police don't know that."

130   "Oh, they'll just send in some cops," said Jill.

131   "Look around you."

132   There were pieces of copseyes in all directions. Not one remained whole. A cop would have to be out of his mind to enter a Free Park.

133   Not to mention the damage to the spirit of the Park.

134   "I wish I'd brought a bag lunch," said Ron.

135   I saw the cloak off to my right: a ribbon of glowing blue velvet hovering at five feet, like a carpeted path in the air. I didn't yell, or point, or anything. For Ron it might be pushing the wrong buttons.

136   Ron didn't see it. "Actually I'm kind of glad this happened," he said animatedly. "I've always thought that anarchy ought to be a viable form of society."

137   Jill made polite sounds of encouragement.

138   "After all, anarchy is only the last word in free enterprise. What can a government do for people that people can't do for themselves? Protection from other countries? If all the other countries are anarchies, too, you don't need armies. Police, maybe; but what's wrong with privately owned police?"

139   "Fire departments used to work that way," Jill remembered. "They were hired by the insurance companies. They only protected houses that belonged to their own clients."

140   "Right! So you buy theft and murder insurance, and the insurance companies hire a police force. The client carries a credit card—"

141   "Suppose the robber steals the card, too?"

142   "He can't use it. He doesn't have the right retina prints."

143   "But if the client doesn't have the credit card, he can't sic the cops on the thief."

144   "Oh." A noticeable pause, "Well—"

145   Half-listening, for I had heard it all before, I looked for the end points of the cloak. I found empty space at one end and a lovely red-haired girl at the other. She was talking to two men as outré as herself.

146   One can get the impression that a Free Park is one gigantic costume party. It isn't. Not one person in ten wears anything but street clothes; but the costumes are what get noticed.

147   These guys were part bird.

148   Their eyebrows and eyelashes were tiny feathers, green on one, golden on the other. Larger feathers covered their heads, blue and green

and gold, and ran in a crest down their spines. They were bare to the waist, showing physiques Jill would find acceptable.

149   Ron was lecturing. "What does a government do for *anyone* except the people who run the government? Once there were private post offices, and they were cheaper than what we've got now. Anything the government takes over gets more expensive, *immediately*. There's no reason why private enterprise can't do anything a government—"

150   Jill gasped. She said, "Ooh! How lovely."

151   Ron turned to look.

152   As if on cue, the girl in the cloak slapped one of the feathered men hard across the mouth. She tried to hit the other one, but he caught her wrist. Then all three froze.

153   I said, "See? Nobody wins. She doesn't even like standing still. She—" and I realized why they weren't moving.

154   In a Free Park it's easy for a girl to turn down an offer. If the guy won't take No for an answer, he gets slapped. The stun beam gets him and the girl. When she wakes up, she walks away.

155   Simple.

156   The girl recovered first. She gasped and jerked her wrist loose and turned to run. One of the feathered men didn't bother to chase her; he simply took a double handful of the cloak.

157   This was getting serious.

158   The cloak jerked her sharply backward. She didn't hesitate. She reached for the big gold discs at her shoulders, ripped them loose and ran on. The feathered men chased her, laughing.

159   The redhead wasn't laughing. She was running all out. Two drops of blood ran down her shoulders. I thought of trying to stop the feathered men, decided in favour of it—but they were already past.

160   The cloak hung like a carpeted path in the air, empty at both ends.

161   Jill hugged herself uneasily. "Ron, just how does one go about hiring your private police force?"

162   "Well, you can't expect it to form spontaneously—"

163   "Let's try the entrances. Maybe we can get out."

164   It was slow to build. Everyone knew what a copseye did. Nobody thought it through. Two feathered men chasing a lovely nude? A pretty sight; and why interfere? If she didn't want to be chased, she need only . . . what? And nothing else had changed. The costumes, the people with causes, the people looking for causes, the peoplewatchers, the pranksters—

165   Blank Sign had joined the POPULATION BY COPULATION faction. His grass-stained pink street tunic jarred strangely with their conservative suits, but he showed no sign of mockery; his face was as preternaturally solemn as theirs. None the less they did not seem glad of his company.

166   It was crowded near the Wilshire entrance. I saw enough bewildered and frustrated faces to guess that it was closed. The little vestibule area was so packed that we didn't even try to find out what was wrong with the doors.

167   "I don't think we ought to stay here," Jill said uneasily.

168   I noticed the way she was hugging herself. "Are you cold?"

169   "No." She shivered. "But I wish I were dressed."

170   "How about a strip of that velvet cloak?"

171   "Good!"

172   We were too late. The cloak was gone.

173   It was a warm September day, near sunset. Clad only in paper slacks, I was not cold in the least. I said, "Take my slacks."

174   "No, hon, I'm the nudist." But Jill hugged herself with both arms.

175   "Here," said Ron, and handed her his sweater. She flashed him a grateful look, then, clearly embarrassed, she wrapped the sweater around her waist and knotted the sleeves.

176   Ron didn't get it at all. I asked him, "Do you know the difference between nude and naked?"

177   He shook his head.

178   "Nude is artistic. Naked is defenceless."

179   Nudity was popular in a Free Park. That night, nakedness was not. There must have been pieces of that cloak all over King's Free Park. I saw at least four that night: one worn as a kilt, two being used as crude sarongs, and one as a bandage.

180   On a normal day, the entrances to King's Free Park close at six. Those who want to stay, stay as long as they like. Usually there are not many, because there are no lights to be broken in a Free Park; but light does seep in from the city beyond. The copseyes float about, guided by infrared, but most of them are not manned.

181   Tonight would be different.

182   It was after sunset, but still light. A small and ancient lady came stumping toward us with a look of murder on her lined face. At first I thought it was meant for us; but that wasn't it. She was so mad she couldn't see straight.

183   She saw my feet and looked up. "Oh, it's you. The one who helped break the lawn mower," she said—which was unjust. "A Free Park, is it? A Free Park! Two men just took away my dinner!"

184   I spread my hands. "I'm sorry. I really am. If you still had it, we could try to talk you into sharing it."

185   She lost some of her mad; which brought her embarrassingly close to tears. "Then we're all hungry together. I brought it in a plastic bag. Next time I'll use something that isn't transparent, by d-damn!" She noticed Jill

and her improvised sweater-skirt, and added, "I'm sorry, dear, I gave my towel to a girl who needed it even more."

186   "Thank you anyway."

187   "Please, may I stay with you people until the copseyes start working again? I don't feel safe, somehow. I'm Glenda Hawthorne."

188   We introduced ourselves. Glenda Hawthorne shook our hands. By now it was quite dark. We couldn't see the city beyond the high green hedges, but the change was startling when the lights of Westwood and Santa Monica flashed on.

189   The police were taking their own good time getting us some copseyes.

190   We reached the grassy field sometimes used by the Society for Creative Anachronism for their tournaments. They fight on foot with weighted and padded weapons designed to behave like swords, broadaxes, morningstars, et cetera. The weapons are bugged so that they won't fall into the wrong hands. The field is big and flat and bare of trees, sloping upward at the edges.

191   On one of the slopes, something moved.

192   I stopped. It didn't move again, but it showed clearly in light reflected down from the white clouds. I made out something man-shaped and faintly pink, and a pale rectangle nearby.

193   I spoke low. "Stay here."

194   Jill said, "Don't be silly. There's nothing for anyone to hide under. Come on."

195   The blank sign was bent and marked with shoe prints. The man who had been carrying it looked up at us with pain in his eyes. Drying blood ran from his nose. With effort he whispered, "I think they dislocated my shoulder."

196   "Let me look." Jill bent over him. She probed him a bit, then set herself and pulled hard and steadily on his arm. Blank Sign yelled in pain and despair.

197   "That'll do it." Jill sounded satisfied. "How does it feel?"

198   "It doesn't hurt as much." He smiled, almost.

199   "What happened?"

200   "They started pushing me and kicking me to make me go away. I was *doing* it, I was walking away. I *was*. Then someone snatched away my sign—" He stopped for a moment, then went off at a tangent. "I wasn't hurting anyone with my sign. I'm a Psych Major. I'm writing a thesis on what people read into a blank sign. Like the blank sheets in the Rorschach tests."

201   "What kind of reactions do you get?"

202   "Usually hostile. But nothing like *that*." Blank Sign sounded bewildered. "Wouldn't you think a Free Park is the one place you'd find freedom of speech?"

203   Jill wiped at his face with a tissue from Glenda Hawthorne's purse. She said, "Especially when you're not saying anything. Hey, Ron, tell us more about your government by anarchy."

204   Ron cleared his throat. "I hope you're not judging it by *this*. King's Free Park hasn't been an anarchy for more than a couple of hours. It needs time to develop."

205   Glenda Hawthorne and Blank Sign must have wondered what the hell he was talking about. I wished him joy in explaining it to them, and wondered if he would explain who had knocked down the copseyes.

206   This field would be a good place to spend the night. It was open, with no cover and no shadows, no way for anyone to sneak up on us.

207   And I was learning to think like a true paranoid.

208   We lay on wet grass, sometimes dozing, sometimes talking. Two other groups no bigger than ours occupied the jousting field. They kept their distance, we kept ours. Now and then we heard voices, and knew that they were not asleep; not all at once, anyway.

209   Blank Sign dozed restlessly. His ribs were giving him trouble, though Jill had said none of them were broken. Every so often he whimpered and tried to move and woke himself up. Then he had to hold himself still until he fell asleep again.

210   "Money," said Jill. "It takes a government to print money."

211   "But you could get IOUs printed. Standard denominations, printed for a fee and notarized. Backed by your good name."

212   Jill laughed softly. "Thought of everything, haven't you? You couldn't travel very far that way."

213   "Credit cards, then."

214   I had stopped believing in Ron's anarchy. I said, "Ron, remember the girl in the long blue cloak?"

215   A little gap of silence. "Yah?"

216   "Pretty, wasn't she? Fun to watch."

217   "Granted."

218   "If there weren't any laws to stop you from raping her, she'd be muffled to the ears in a long dress and carrying a tear gas pen. What fun would that be? I *like* the nude look. Look how fast it disappeared after the copseyes fell."

219   "Mm-m," said Ron.

220   The night was turning cold. Faraway voices; occasional distant shouts, came like thin grey threads in a black tapestry of silence. Mrs. Hawthorne spoke into that silence.

221   "What was that boy really saying with his blank sign?"

222   "He wasn't saying anything," said Jill.

223   "Now, just a minute, dear. I think he was, even if he didn't know it."

Mrs. Hawthorne talked slowly, using the words to shape her thoughts. "Once there was an organization to protest the forced contraception bill. I was one of them. We carried signs for hours at a time. We printed leaflets. We stopped people passing so that we could talk to them. We gave up our time, we went to considerable trouble and expense, because we wanted to get our ideas across.

224   "Now, if a man had joined us with a blank sign, he would have *been saying* something.

225   "His sign says that he has no opinion. If he joins us, he says that we have no opinion either. He's saying our opinions aren't worth anything."

226   I said, "Tell him when he wakes up. He can put it in his notebook."

227   "But his notebook is *wrong*. He wouldn't push his blank sign in among people he agreed with, would he?"

228   "Maybe not."

229   "I ... suppose I don't like people with no opinions." Mrs. Hawthorne stood up. She had been sitting tailor-fashion for some hours. "Do you know if there's a pop machine nearby?"

230   There wasn't, of course. No private company would risk getting their machines smashed once or twice a day. But she had reminded the rest of us that we were thirsty. Eventually we all got up and trooped away in the direction of the fountain.

231   All but Blank Sign.

232   I'd *liked* that blank sign gag. How odd, how ominous, that so basic a right as freedom of speech could depend on so slight a thing as a floating copseye.

233   I was thirsty.

234   The park was bright by city light, crossed by sharp-edged shadows. In such light it seems that one can see much more than he really can. I could see into every shadow; but, though there were stirrings all around us, I could see nobody until he moved. We four, sitting under an oak with our backs to the tremendous trunk, must be invisible from any distance.

235   We talked little. The Park was quiet except for occasional laughter from the fountain.

236   I couldn't forget my thirst. I could feel others being thirsty around me. The fountain was right out there in the open, a solid block of concrete with five men around it.

237   They were dressed alike, in paper shorts with big pockets. They looked alike: like first-string athletes. Maybe they belonged to the same order, or frat, or ROTC class.

238   They had taken over the fountain.

239   When someone came to get a drink, the tall ash-blond one would step forward with his arm held stiffly out, palm forward. He had a wide

mouth and a grin that might otherwise have been infectious, and a deep, echoing voice. He would intone, "Go back. None may pass here but the immortal Cthulhu—" or something equally silly.

240   Trouble was, they weren't kidding. Or: they were kidding, but they wouldn't let anyone have a drink.

241   When we arrived, a girl dressed in a towel had been trying to talk some sense into them. It hadn't worked. It might even have boosted their egos: a lovely half-naked girl begging them for water. Eventually she'd given up and gone away.

242   In that light her hair might have been red. I hoped it was the girl in the cloak.

243   And a beefy man in a yellow business jumper had made the mistake of demanding his Rights. It was not a night for Rights. The blond kid had goaded him into screaming insults, a stream of unimaginative profanity, which ended when he tried to hit the blond kid. Then three of them had swarmed over him. The man had left crawling, moaning of police and lawsuits.

244   Why hadn't somebody done something?

245   I had watched it all from sitting position. I could list my own reasons. One: it was hard to face the fact that a copseye would not zap them both, any second now. Two: I didn't like the screaming fat man much. He talked dirty. Three: I'd been waiting for someone else to step in.

246   Mrs. Hawthorne said, "Ronald, what time is it?"

247   Ron may have been the only man in King's Free Park who knew the time. People generally left their valuables in lockers at the entrances. But years ago, when Ron was flush with money from the sale of the engraved beer bottles, he'd bought an implant-watch. He told time by one red mark and two red lines glowing beneath the skin of his wrist.

248   We had put the women between us, but I saw the motion as he glanced at his wrist. "Quarter of twelve."

249   "Don't you think they'll get bored and go away? It's been twenty minutes since anyone tried to get a drink," Mrs. Hawthorne said.

250   Jill shifted against me in the dark. They can't be any more bored than we are. I think they'll get bored and stay anyway. Besides—" She stopped.

251   I said, "Besides that, we're thirsty *now*.

252   "Right."

253   "Ron, have you seen any sign of those rock throwers you collected? Especially the one who knocked down the copseye."

254   "No."

255   I wasn't surprised. In this darkness? "Do you remember his ..." and I didn't even finish.

256   "...Yes!" Ron said suddenly.

257   "You're kidding."

258   "No. His name was Bugeyes. You don't forget a name like that."

259   "I take it he had bulging eyes?"

260   "I didn't notice."

261   Well, it was worth a try. I stood and cupped my hands for a mega-
phone and shouted, "Bugeyes!"

262   One of the Water Monopoly shouted, "Let's keep the noise down out
there!"

263   *"Bugeyes!"*

264   A chorus of remarks from the Water Monopoly. "Strange habits these
peasants—" "Most of them are just thirsty. *This* character—"

265   From off to the side: "What do you want?"

266   "We want to talk to you! Stay where you are!" To Ron I said, "Come
on." To Jill and Mrs. Hawthorne, "Stay here. Don't get involved."

267   We moved out into the open space between us and Bugeyes' voice.

268   Two of the five kids came immediately to intercept us. They must
have been bored, all right, and looking for action.

269   We ran for it. We reached the shadows of the trees before those two
reached us. They stopped, laughing like maniacs, and moved back to the
fountain.

270   Ron and I, we lay on our bellies in the shadows of low bushes. Across
too much shadowless grass, four men in paper shorts stood at parade rest at
the four corners of the fountain. The fifth man watched for a victim.

271   A boy walked out between us into the moonlight. His eyes were shining, big, expressive eyes, maybe a bit too prominent. His hands were big,
too—with knobby knuckles. One hand was full of acorns.

272   He pitched them rapidly, one at a time, overhand. First one, then another of the Water Monopoly twitched and looked in our direction.
Bugeyes kept throwing.

273   Quite suddenly, two of them started toward us at a run. Bugeyes kept
throwing until they were almost on him; then he threw his acorns in a
handful and dived into the shadows.

274   The two of them ran between us. We let the first go by: the wide-
mouthed blond spokesman, his expression low and murderous now. The
other was short and broad-shouldered, an intimidating silhouette, seemingly all muscle. A tackle. I stood up in front of him, expecting him to
stop in surprise; and he did, and I hit him in the mouth as hard as I could.

275   He stepped back in shock. Ron wrapped an arm around his throat.

276   He bucked. Instantly. Ron hung on. I did something I'd seen often
enough on television: linked my fingers and brought both hands down on
the back of his neck.

277   The blond spokesman should be back by now; and I turned, and he was. He was on me before I could get my hands up. We rolled on the ground, me with my arms pinned to my sides, him unable to use his hands without letting go. It was lousy planning for both of us. He was squeezing the breath out of me. Ron hovered over us, waiting for a chance to hit him.

278   Suddenly there were others, a lot of others. Three of them pulled the blond kid off me, and a beefy, bloody man in a yellow business jumper stepped forward and crowned him with a rock.

279   The blond kid went limp.

280   The man squared off and threw a straight left hook with the rock in his hand. The blond kid's head snapped back, fell forward.

281   I yelled, "Hey!" Jumped forward, got hold of the arm that held the rock.

282   Someone hit me solidly in the side of the neck.

283   I dropped. It felt like all my strings had been cut. Someone was helping me to my feet—Ron—voices babbling in whispers, one shouting, "Get him—"

284   I couldn't see the blond kid. The other one, the tackle, was up and staggering away. Shadows came from between the trees to play pileup on him. The woods were alive, and it was just a *little* patch of woods. Full of angry, thirsty people.

285   Bugeyes reappeared, grinning widely. "Now what? Go somewhere else and try it again?"

286   "Oh, no. It's getting very vicious out tonight. Ron, we've got to stop them. They'll kill him!"

287   "It's a Free Park. Can you stand now?"

288   "Ron, they'll *kill* him!"

289   The rest of the Water Trust was charging to the rescue. One of them had a tree branch with the leaves stripped off. Behind them, shadows converged on the fountain.

290   We fled.

291   I had to stop after a dozen paces. My head was trying to explode. Ron looked back anxiously, but I waved him on. Behind me the man with the branch broke through the trees and ran towards me to do murder.

292   Behind him, all the noise suddenly stopped.

293   I braced myself for the blow.

294   And fainted.

295   He was lying across my legs, with the branch still in his hand. Jill and Ron were pulling at my shoulders. A pair of golden moons floated overhead.

296   I wriggled loose. I felt my head. It seemed intact.

297   Ron said, "The copseyes zapped him before he got to you."

298   "What about the others? Did they kill them?"

299   "I don't know." Ron ran his hands through his hair. "I was wrong.
Anarchy isn't stable. It comes apart too easily."

300   "Well, don't do any more experiments, OK?"

301   People were beginning to stand up. They streamed towards the exits,
gathering momentum, beneath the yellow gaze of the copseyes.

DISCUSSION QUESTIONS

1. What is free in the Free Parks? What is the single exception?
2. Why does Ron Cole want to disable the copseyes?
3. Why does one man carry a blank sign? What reactions does he
   usually get? Why?
4. What is the distinction made between nudity and nakedness?
   Why does it become significant?
5. Why does Cole think anarchy is the highest form of free
   enterprise? What causes him to change his mind?

WRITING TOPICS

1. In your journal, speculate about a world without rules or government. What are the possible advantages and disadvantages
   of such a system?
2. In a paragraph or two, explore the concept of freedom of speech,
   especially as it relates to the right to not say *anything*. What do
   you *really* say when you say (or do) nothing?
3. In the seventies, social activism was declining and personal freedoms were being sought. In an essay, examine the ways that Niven
   is exploring both the need for individual expression and regulation
   of that expression.

The Hunting

1976

DORIS BEETEM (b. 1951)

In 1969 the popular TV show *Star Trek* aired its last episode, a
cancellation that was stalled for a year by the outcry of the show's
fans. After a final unsuccessful season, though, its fate was sealed.
The following year a new novel, *Spock Must Die,* was published,
and print versions of the broadcast episodes continued from
1967 to 1975. These were joined by adaptations of the animated
series from 1974 to 1975. In 1976, this was continued with *Star Trek:
The New Voyages,* a collection of stories written by fans and published in small "fanzines." Soon afterward, novels featuring the
series' characters began proliferating and continue to appear
regularly today.

    Doris Beetem was a college student in 1972 at the University
of Colorado when she wrote "The Hunting." It was originally
published in *Eridani Triad* along with another of her stories, "And
Maybe Tell You About Phaedra." She continued to write for amateur publications while pursuing a career as a librarian. In 1989
she produced, with Jamie Ritchey, the novella *Half-Life,* a story
that, like much of her fiction, features strong female characters
and brings characters or situations from two universes together.
In this case, she used *Blake's Seven,* a British TV series that was originally broadcast from 1978 to 1981 as the backdrop, but also included a concept from the *Star Trek* episode "The Enemy Within."

    In 1995 she published, in collaboration with Margaret
McNickle, "Image of a Rebel" in *Texas Revelations,* this time featuring a crossover between *Blake's Seven* and *Star Wars.* Today she
works as a Texas Medical Center Librarian in Houston, Texas, and
continues to write stories and articles for amateur "fanzines."

She has produced dozens of such stories, but does not pursue professional publication.

In "The Hunting," Doris Beetem explores the roles of "civilized" rites in adapting humans (or Vulcans) for entry into the complex world of adulthood.

————————

1 Rhinegelt. It was a frontier planet—a few hundred kilometers of settlement surrounded by barely surveyed terra incognita. Shore leave would be limited either to hiking, hunting, and camping in the primitive areas, or to drinking and carousing in port towns reminiscent of the American West of three hundred years ago.

2 "You're getting old, McCoy," the *Enterprise*'s chief medical officer told himself. Roughing it, either in the forests or the port towns, didn't appeal to him. Perhaps he wouldn't bother leaving the ship this stop.

3 The Sickbay door swished open. "What shore party shall I assign you to, Bones?" Captain James Kirk asked. To the captain, nothing was more relaxing than a stable orbit around a safe planet, and a lessening of responsibility for the 430 crewmen he commanded: so the captain could always approach shore leave with considerable energy.

4 "I don't need leave," McCoy said. "Give it to somebody who can use it."

5 "A little rest'll do you good, Doctor," Kirk replied. "That's what you always tell the crew, anyway. Even Spock's taking leave."

6 "He is?" McCoy was startled by this unusual occurrence.

7 The captain was obviously greatly pleased. "Spock's been under too much stress lately—even for a Vulcan. He's been stretched both physically and mentally, although he'd never admit it. We've both seen it."

8 "And you know how stubborn Spock is about taking shore leave. He says it's illogical."

9 "By his own request, I put him down for shore party three. And Lieutenant Uhura tells me that he's already contacted Rhinegelt Port Control and arranged to take out a Primitive Area hunting permit."

10 Dr. McCoy reviewed four years of poking, prodding, and psychologically dissecting the *Enterprise*'s Vulcan science officer. "Something's wrong there, Jim. Spock wouldn't kill a fly. A hunting permit, you said?"

11 "Why not ask him about it?" answered Kirk, apparently untroubled. "Sure you don't want shore leave?"

12 "Ye-es," McCoy answered slowly. "Guess I will, at that. Put me down for party three."

13   Kirk foresaw another McCoy/Spock bout, but complied with the request.

14   "Fool Vulcan! He can't be gone already!" McCoy, waiting impatiently outside Spock's door, signaled for admittance again.

15   "Yes, Doctor?" Imperturbably the Vulcan surveyed McCoy's collection of camping equipment, which was piled lumpily in the hall. McCoy was determined to be well prepared, and had packed everything from medikit to insect repellent to a small tent.

16   "Spock, I'm going with you," McCoy asserted, too proud to soften his statement to a request. "I'm all packed and ready to go."

17   Spock, staring quizzically at the heap of equipment compiled by the tenderfoot woodsman, replied, "I can see no logical reason—"

18   "Blast it, I've got a hunch," McCoy interrupted. "A Human, irrational hunch that you'll need my help. Now am I going with you or not?"

19   Spock, after considering the matter carefully, answered, "You have the right. And I should have a companion. A Vulcan preferably, but you will do." While McCoy was deciding whether or not to be insulted, Mr. Spock, after picking up a small green sack of his own, slung a good part of McCoy's camping equipment over his shoulder. "Come, Doctor," he ordered, starting down the hall.

20   "But what about your supplies?" McCoy spluttered. "Don't you need to get ready?"

21   Spock shook his head and continued on his way. McCoy picked up the remainder of his equipment and followed Spock to the Transporter chamber. Once again he checked to make sure that his medikit was still securely packed.

22   Three days later McCoy was still puzzled, although he was learning more about Spock's character than ever. He'd discovered that, given half a chance, the Vulcan would keep his mouth shut forever. However, no new information had been offered about the hunting expedition.

23   "Dr. McCoy, you have turned up your sonic screen to the point that it is audible to me." Both the doctor and Spock had edged quite close to their campfire—McCoy for protection against the native animals, and Spock because he found nights on the Rhinegelt savannah chilly.

24   McCoy grudgingly turned down the protective device. "By the time it's low enough for you, the wild animals it's supposed to ward off won't notice it," he complained.

25   "I am somewhat dubious about the value of a supersonic transmitter as protection. Were I a wild beast, I suspect that I would more likely be irritated into attacking than retreating," Spock said politely, but with

a trace of resentment against the machine. Since the beginning of the hunt, he'd used no tools at all, and was eating various tubers he'd collected, without even bothering to roast them in the fire.

26   "Hasn't eaten anything but native plants since we came here," McCoy thought. "Some hunter!"

27   Above them, the giant planet Fafnir glowed green in the sky. It provided as much light as Earth's full moon, but in coloring, the landscape distorted vision. McCoy peered gloomily out into the savannah. "What game animals are found on Rhinegelt, Spock?" he asked suddenly.

28   "Scissorbuck, white mammoth, and owltiger. We are hunting an owltiger," Spock replied, answering the question that had been bothering McCoy more and more with time.

29   Scissorbuck were the brown antelope types with prongy white horns, McCoy knew, and the mammoth would be farther north. But . . . "How big are owltigers, Spock?"

30   "Approximately the same size as the Terran Bengal tiger."

31   "Then why," McCoy exploded, "are you hunting one with no weapon? What are you going to do—give it the kiss of death?"

32   "I can stun it with a nerve pinch long enough to accomplish my purpose."

33   "What purpose, Spock?" McCoy asked. "You've got to let me know, or I'm likely to be a hindrance when the time comes." He was determined, this time, not to let the Vulcan lapse back into silence again.

34   Spock settled back, nodding reluctantly at McCoy's request. "I am engaging in a ritual hunt—one of the more important rituals of my people. Since I am a male of full physical strength and dexterity, I seek out the most dangerous beast of all. It is the *mok farr*—the time of remembrance."

35   "Another Vulcan ritual—and me with only a medikit," thought McCoy, appalled.

36   "The hunt does not end in a killing. Instead, I shall meld minds with the animal, as you have seen me do before. The purpose of the tradition is to see and understand, in the ferocity of the beast, the savagery of the Vulcan nature, which we have hidden and controlled so carefully."

37   "And then what?" McCoy asked skeptically, thinking privately that Spock, unlike young men on Vulcan, had doubtless already encountered more savage ferocity than he would ever require.

38   "Then I shall officially be an adult."

39   "You mean you're not?" McCoy asked, amazed.

40   Spock shook his head, shamefaced. "My human heritage impeded my telepathic ability, and I was quite young when I left Vulcan. I could not have successfully completed the ritual. Since then, I have had mind

contact with many aliens—Humans, the Horta, a Medusan. Now I am prepared. I do not wish to further postpone the rite."

41   "Wouldn't it be safer to put it off until you could get to Vulcan?" McCoy ventured tentatively.

42   "Doctor. The *mok farr* is the Vulcan rite of passage into adulthood. If our positions were reversed, would you put it off?"

43   "I guess you've got a point."

44   Spock curled up like a cat on a pile of leaves—he was carrying primitivism a bit too far, McCoy thought resentfully—and prepared for sleep. "The correct phrase would be 'Good night, Doctor,'" Spock said sleepily. McCoy crawled into his sleeping bag, and for a long time listened to the voice of the warm wind.

45   As usual, Spock was up at dawn, irritatingly alert, and as usual, McCoy slept half an hour longer, savoring each precious moment of sleep with an intensity he had not previously possessed. Once McCoy was finally wakened, Spock had them ready for the trail in practically no time at all.

46   In three days the Vulcan had taught McCoy something of the rudiments of stalking—enough to tiptoe quietly down the trail. Spock, who by this time had appropriated the carrying of nearly all of McCoy's pack, was more silent still.

47   "How long until we find your owltiger?" McCoy panted.

48   "We have been following a scissorbuck herd for two days now," Spock replied. "Eventually, one will make an appearance."

49   "Mmmph. Maybe."

50   "Dr. McCoy, do you know nothing of hunting?" Spock was watching the lithe brown forms of the scissorbucks move slowly in the distance.

51   "I've fished a little."

52   "I have never been able to comprehend the Terran attitude that fishing is a sport. Considering the mass ratio between man and fish, it can hardly be called an equal contest. At any rate, you may trust me. I know what I am doing."

53   At that moment Spock's keen eyes caught the leaders of the herd sniffing the air nervously. "Wait here," he commanded, slipping off the bulky pack and moving quietly toward the herd. After a few minutes, McCoy crept after him, clutching the medikit firmly in hand.

54   From a slight rise he watched Spock approach the now skittish herd. The Vulcan's Star Fleet uniform was relatively easy to spot— McCoy recollected the incredulous eyebrow-raising he'd encountered when he had suggested wearing different clothes for the occasion. Apparently Spock considered his uniform an auxiliary skin.

55   McCoy strained his eyes looking for an owltiger, then finally flipped open his medikit to check its life-form-sensor. He hadn't wanted to take one of the *Enterprise's* tricorders on a private excursion, but the medikit would perform the same function.

56   Yes. Spock was cautiously approaching the location of a large animal only a few hundred yards from the herd. Then McCoy saw the owltiger.

57   It was huge, a mottled dun color, with a small white ruff. The owlish ears were what gave the beast the name owltiger, McCoy knew, that and the two wicked fangs placed close together, which gave the impression of a beak.

58   Had it seen Spock? The scissorbucks were beginning to scatter. Then McCoy saw Spock fling himself toward the giant carnivore at a dead run. The great cat roared, and responded by leaping toward him.

59   As the two closed, McCoy cursed the government regulation that made phasers in Primitive Areas forbidden. He watched helplessly as the beast attacked. Spock was almost under its paws, and then suddenly standing over the brute, which was twitching convulsively. "He's safe!" McCoy shouted thankfully, then added, "Knock on wood."

60   The owltiger's short red thoughts flooded into Spock's mind. Spock struggled with the problem of handling its bestial emotions without suppressing them, and attempted to calm the beast by mentally asserting, "We are one mind. Our thoughts are moving together." *Hurt, pain, attack, slash.* "No! We are unity—no need for that!" *Run, leap, bite, hurt.* "The twitching in the legs will stop. . . ." *Flesh rending food, the hunting* . . . Fascinating—all thoughts the same. Monomania . . . monom . . . mon . . . *Teeth, claws, kill,* kill, *kill* kill*kill*kill . . .

61   The owltiger shook itself and bounded off. McCoy watched it go with a feeling of great relief. "Well, that's that," he told himself, satisfied. He was startled, then, to hear an unearthly roar.

62   Or was it a scream? It's Spock! McCoy realized. "I'm coming," he yelled, and recklessly scrambled down the slope toward his comrade.

63   Spock was crouching on all fours, flexing and unflexing his hands, looking at the strange blunt claws. He felt clumsy and off-balance. The whole landscape was full of confusingly different colors, sounds, and odors. Out of the corner of his eye he saw the scissorbuck herd, alerted and on the run, and he growled in irritation.

64   Some creature was crashing down the hill at him. Suspiciously, he prepared to spring. But foggily, from the back of his mind, he remembered that the creature had something to do with sickness and whirring things that hurt, and his own blood. Rattled, he got up on two feet and fled.

65   "Wait, Spock, wait!" McCoy puffed. He'd known that catching Spock was impossible from the moment that Spock had started to run,

but had continued until the last glimpse of the blue shirt was gone in the distance.

66   "Damn!" McCoy remembered bitterly Spock's tendency to get so tied up in the mind of the being he was contacting that he had to be pried loose. "I'll have to bring him back to himself, or he'll be yowling at the moon for the rest of his shore leave." McCoy grumbled. Nagging at him was the recollection of Simon van Gelder. Spock had snapped back to normal immediately after being pulled away from him. Never before had Spock maintained mental identity with a being so far away from him. Worriedly, McCoy reached for his communicator to summon help.

67   It wasn't there. He'd let Spock carry it, along with most of his gear. The doctor scrambled over the dusty grasses to where Spock had dropped his pack, opened it, and rifled through. No—Spock had carried both their communicators securely on his belt. And they were both lost with him.

68   Glumly McCoy considered the situation. The nearest Wilderness Station was about twenty miles back along the river. By the time he could get there and call the *Enterprise,* Spock could wander off so far that the search operation might take months. And heaven only knew what would be happening to Spock, mentally and physically, in the meantime.

69   Grinding his teeth quietly, McCoy decided to follow the herd. Maybe Spock would return. He had to!

70   Midday. The sun's warmth comforted Spock, even as it disturbed him by revealing colors he'd forgotten how to name. Night was best, when the violent stars lit a gray landscape and he could prowl, scenting sharp living odors on the wind. It was too cold to hunt then, though.

71   He tried to doze, well hidden in the tall grass, lying with his head on his hands. Both legs were drawn up awkwardly to his body, showing great rents at the knees of his trousers where the dura-fiber had been worn away by too much clumsy scrambling on all fours. His knees were scratched and gashed, and his hands.

72   Spock's eyes gleamed ferally as his ears flattened at a small, suspicious sound. He had been hunted. Something was following his trail. Some . . . what? He couldn't remember what, but he didn't want it to find him.

73   He sighed. No way to hunt and run away at once, and now he was so tired. He kept wary guard regardless, but trusted his ears more than his eyes, which constantly drooped and closed. Suddenly his eyes snapped open. There was a rustle in the grass, and a small, foolish rodent ran in front of him. It was small . . . but he was *hungry!* Spock carefully lifted one paw.

74   McCoy watched the sun flee over the mountained horizon. His back straightened painfully as he unfastened the heavy pack. The light would soon be gone; he'd try again tomorrow.

75   "Why didn't I go back and call out the search parties?" he asked himself for the thousandth time. "Nine days—we'll be absent without leave in two more. Anything could be happening to him out there."

76   He rubbed a grubby sleeve against grainy eyes, and strove to see one flicker of blue somewhere on the savannah in the fading light. Hopeless. Spock's Vulcan stamina could probably keep him ahead of McCoy indefinitely. Scrabbling through his pack, McCoy searched for a nutri-bar. He sat on a rock in the rapidly fading twilight and bit at the food concentrate. It would be another bad, cold night. His sleeping bag was at least fifty miles back, and he didn't dare light a fire for fear Spock would see it and run. Using the sonic screen was definitely out, too— Spock's sensitive ears might pick it up.

77   "Wait a minute . . ." McCoy smiled ephemerally. Then he searched out the screen projector in his kit. It had been too small and light to be worth leaving behind. Scrutinizing its control dial carefully, he saw that it allowed a considerably stronger broadcast than the labeled "protection" range.

78   "Wouldn't this just be audible to those Vulcan ears, though!" McCoy chuckled grimly. "And that feline fiend inside him will be madder than a wet hen when it hears this. Maybe even mad enough," he speculated, "to come and try to stop it!"

79   His plan was risky, McCoy knew. The supersonics might frighten Spock into running off. "But what choice do I have? I could be following him till doomsday." Decided, McCoy flicked the sonic device on and up to maximum.

80   The vibration made McCoy's teeth grate rustily in his mouth. He couldn't hear the sound, but it was palpable, and pushed on every nerve relentlessly. From far off toward the mountains he heard a bloodcurdling screech, and another, and another echoing it, from much closer locations.

81   McCoy considered morbidly the chance that his trick might prove fatal. Some maddened owltiger leaping on him with bloodlust . . . Or even Spock. McCoy formed the grotesque picture of himself as King Pentheus in reverse—ripped apart by a man who thought he was a lion.

82   Then McCoy remembered Spock, standing stiffly, and saying in a thin, precise voice, "Nothing can excuse the crime of which I am guilty. I intend to offer no defense. I must . . . surrender myself to the authorities."

83   "And he would," McCoy thought savagely. He grabbed his ever-present medikit, pushed the med-record button, and spoke "To whom it may concern—Jim, I guess. About the events occurring to Mr. Spock

and me on Rhinegelt." He paused and then added peripherally, almost idly, "Damnit, Spock, don't try to deny that I brought this on myself!"

84 Outlined on a ridge, a scissordoe trembled and twitched her ears nervously. Then she ran toward the mountains, as if scenting the acridness of a grass fire, and nearly bowled Spock over in her uncautious flight.

85 The rasping shriek caused even more pain to Spock's sensitive ears than the doe's. He stood his ground, wondering. No! It was not like a fire, or a flood . . . something natural, to hide from. It was—Spock searched through his muddled thoughts—*him!* The following one, Spock remembered other times of pain, when he had been strapped down so he couldn't run, and the face of the following one. A face that smiled too much.

86 "I will stop him!" And Spock, gathering up all his will, waded painfully through the tall grasses in the direction of the hurting.

87 McCoy thumbed his medikit and peered toward the hills, deathly afraid. Hypnospray . . . sedative . . . knockout drugs. He considered them all, then muttered, "Nothing organic's wrong with him . . . nothing but the sanity of that alien Vulcan mind. What am I going to do for him? And my God, what will I do if I guess wrong?"

88 Over the absolute silence of the hypersound, McCoy heard a sound—a branch snapping. And then hoarse heavy breathing, as if every intake of breath was half a sob. Before McCoy could take a reading on his kit, Spock appeared, gliding swiftly toward him, looking ragged, muddy . . . and homicidal.

89 McCoy had been expecting savagery, belligerence—all the emotions written nakedly on Spock's face—but not, somehow, the Vulcan's incredible, pantherlike speed. Before the doctor had time to more than yell, "Spock!", Spock had sprung. The lunge carried them both to the ground where Spock dug his fingers cruelly into McCoy's neck with slowly increasing force.

90 "S-s-pock . . . s-s-stop . . ." McCoy hissed breathlessly. Then, as the Vulcan's lethal grip did not slacken, McCoy kneed him in the stomach. Spock panted, and released him. McCoy scrabbled off, feeling a little more confident, until he looked into the Vulcan's face to see a vicious smile. And recollected, with a dreadful certainty, how the cat toys with its prey.

91 The screen projector was sitting on a rock. Twisting desperately, McCoy reached it before Spock became aware of his intent, and grabbed it as his only protection. The projector vibrated fiercely in McCoy's hand as he jabbed it toward Spock. The diabolically feral look faded, and Spock covered his ears with shaking hands, pacing backward fearfully.

92   The doctor had tasted his moment of triumph for only an instant, when he realized that Spock was about to bolt again. Swallowing hard, he flicked the screen projector off, gambling on Spock's mental controls for his life.

93   It was still Spock—nothing could change that. The Vulcan seemed confused, as if memories were being awakened, or perhaps because he was being pushed into an entirely different pattern than the days of chase on the savannah; Spock would have to choose now, to think. McCoy waited.

94   He found himself looking into eyes that were neither bestial nor logical, neither a Star Fleet officer's nor an owltiger's. Spock simply stood immobile, projecting a mute doubt and horror. It seemed to McCoy in that moment that all the gambles had been lost.

95   Then Spock stepped forward and pleaded in an awkward voice, *"Alab hwallir k'len?"* McCoy could practically have hugged him for every incomprehensible, tongue-twisting Vulcan syllable. Spock was acting Human again!

96   The doctor had pried the communicator off Spock's belt, and they were coalescing out of golden sparkles onto the comfortingly safe Transporter platforms, before he remembered to amend that description.

97   It was nice to have the authority to certify yourself medically fit for duty, McCoy thought. The captain, after grasping the situation's seriousness, if not its nature, had wanted to argue that with him. The doctor recollected how Kirk's grin at his friend's bewhiskered appearance had faded when Spock had toppled unceremoniously to the floor. He was worried about them both.

98   McCoy thankfully tugged on a clean shirt and hurried out of his office into Sickbay. Whether he'd be able to certify Spock medically fit was another matter. His med-scan had revealed Spock to be in acceptable, if not perfect, physical condition, and Dr. M'benga had agreed that he was suffering from no more than shock. But whether Spock would snap out of it quickly was another matter.

99   As Dr. McCoy entered the ward, M'benga approached him and whispered, "Mr. Spock has an unusually resilient mind, for either a Vulcan or a Human. He should recover quickly now." He paused, then asked, "It's not a medical question, Doctor, but this wasn't anything you did to him?" Scowling, McCoy returned to his patient.

100   McCoy sighed with relief as he saw Spock eye with loathing the sponge bath M'benga was taking away. The Vulcan was already back in thermal underwear and was finishing dressing rapidly. "Look at it this way," McCoy said soothingly. "It's better than a belly full of fur balls."

101   Spock looked up at him sharply, and McCoy was immediately aware that Spock was in no mood for the usual feuding back and forth; he just wanted to talk. "I believe I understand now the purpose of the ritual, Doctor."

102   "To understand how to control emotion?" McCoy ventured.

103   "No, to demonstrate that the alternative is attractive. I have wondered from time to time why there are such extensive game preserves on Vulcan. It seemed to me that the 'track and stalk' that is favored there had no logical value, since the prey was not killed. Now I know that there must be many who wish to re-create the experience of the *mok farr.*"

104   McCoy, as usual, was not quite sure that he knew what the Vulcan was getting at. "Wait a minute! You can't tell me that you liked running around in the bush regressed back to an animal."

105   "As you should know, not all of that was intended to be in the ritual." The Vulcan's face was unusually somber. "It is what you have always advocated—a life ruled by the nerve endings. More pleasurable, in some ways, than my own. But I shall not choose it."

106   "Why?" McCoy asked.

107   "Doctor. Choose the life of a wild animal?"

108   "No," McCoy explained, "not that. But you might live a little more according to your nerve endings, Spock."

109   "The end result would be essentially the same."

110   The Sickbay door whistled, and the captain of the *Enterprise* walked in, anxious about the condition of his friends. Catching the polite battle stance of his science officer and chief medical officer, Kirk extrapolated, "You must be all right, Spock. Bones never argues with seriously ill patients."

111   "Have him tell you someday, Jim, about the time he tried to walk out and go back to duty in the middle of an operation," McCoy cracked.

112   "All right, what's been going on, and why didn't either of you take my advice to rest during shore leave?" Captain Kirk demanded.

113   Dr. McCoy opened his mouth and prepared to give a long, aggrieved account of Vulcan rituals, uncomfortable nights of reversion to Boy Scouting, and a companion who alternated ignoring him and pouncing on him. The frozen look on Spock's face stopped him, and he closed his mouth carefully. "He wants to tell Jim slowly. In his own time. Or maybe not at all." Out loud he answered, "There was a Vulcan custom Spock wanted to go through. What was its name again, Spock?"

114   "The *mok farr,*" Mr. Spock replied thankfully.

115   "Oh," Kirk said, mystified. "Well, I hope it worked out all right."

116   "There was . . . some difficulty." Spock said seriously. "But Dr. McCoy solved the problem."

117   "How?"

118   McCoy grinned. "I took a thorn out of his paw!"

DISCUSSION QUESTIONS

1. Why does Spock apply for a primitive area hunting permit, even though he is a vegetarian?

2. Why does Spock say the protective sonic screen might actually become a liability? How does McCoy eventually use that liability to his advantage?

3. What is the ultimate gamble McCoy takes to protect himself from the bestial Spock?

4. Why are game animals not killed in Vulcan hunting?

5. Spock describes using his emotions for guiding his life choices as the same as reverting to a wild animal. Yet his decision is, in essence, an emotional one. Why does the author present this repudiation of the basis for an important value judgment? In small groups, discuss this apparent contradiction.

WRITING TOPICS

1. The Vulcan mind-meld is a step beyond telepathy, causing a joining of two consciousnesses. In a short essay, discuss the inherent impossibilities of this process, as well as its possible advantages and disadvantages.

2. Rites of passage into adulthood are common in most cultures. In a journal entry, develop the idea of the value of one or two of these rites and how they help or harm the transition from adolescence into adulthood.

3. Write a newspaper article discussing the *Star Trek* phenomenon of the seventies and why it has continued up to the present day. Also look at how fan networks and fan-supported publications have contributed to that popularity.

The Thaw

1979

TANITH LEE (b. 1947)

Tanith Lee began her writing career with *The Dragon Hoard* (1971), a children's fantasy novel. Her *Don't Bite the Sun* (1976) and *Drinking Sapphire Wine* (1977) are set in a future world, and the citizens, though free to change shapes at will, are virtual prisoners of their protective environment.

Many of her plots focus on the difficulties of young women who must control self-destructive urges while living in a hostile or repressive environment. For instance, in *Shadowfire* (1979) the protagonist wakens with amnesia and discovers she has caused immense damage to the world by use of her powers. And in *The Silver Metal Lover* (1981), a teenage girl must determine how to tell her mother that her soul mate is a robot.

Lee's short fiction has been collected in several volumes, including *Dreams of Dark and Light: The Great Short Fiction* (1986) and *Women as Dreams: The Male Perception of Women through Space and Time* (1989). Lee makes use of many science fiction conventions, but treats all of them as elements in her storytelling, rather than as symbols in an unusual universe.

In "The Thaw," Tanith Lee looks at a technological advancement that produces difficulties when the impulse to improve is not tempered with caution.

1   Ladies first, they said.

2   That was O.K. Then they put a histotrace on the lady in question, and called me.

3   "No, thanks," I said.

4   "Listen," they said, "you're a generative blood-line descendant of Carla Brice. Aren't you interested, for God's sake? This is a unique moment, a unique experience. She's going to need support, understanding. A contact. Come on. Don't be frigid about it."

5   "I guess Carla is more frigid than I'm ever likely to be."

6   They laughed, to keep up the informalities. Then they mentioned the Institute grant I'd receive, just for hanging around and being supportive. To a quasi-unemployed artist, that was temptation and a half. They also reminded me that on this initial bout there wouldn't be much publicity, so later, if I wanted to capitalize as an eyewitness, and providing good old Carla was willing—I had a sudden vision of getting very rich, very quick, and with the minimum of effort, and I succumbed ungracefully.

7   Which accurately demonstrates my three strongest qualities: laziness, optimism, and blind stupidity. Which in turn sums up the whole story, more or less. And that's probably why I was told to write it down for the archives of the human race. I can't think of a better way to depress and wreck the hopes of frenzied, shackled, bleating humanity.

8   But to return to Carla. She was, I believe, my great-great-great-great-great grandmother. Give or take a great. Absolute accuracy isn't one of my talents, either. The relevant part is, however, that at thirty-three, Carla had developed the rare heart complaint valu—val—well, she'd developed it. She had a few months, or less, and so she opted, along with seventy other people that year, to undergo Cryogenic Suspension till a cure could be found. Cry Sus had been getting progressively more popular, ever since the 1980s. Remember? It's the freezing method of holding a body in refrigerated stasis, indefinitely preserving thereby flesh, bones, organs and the rest, perfect and pristine, in a frosty crystal box. (Just stick a tray of water in the freezer and see for yourself.) It may not strike you as cozy anymore, but that's hardly surprising. In 1993, seventy-one persons, of whom four-or-five-or-six-great granny Carla was one, saw it as the only feasible alternative to death. In the following two hundred years, four thousand others copied their example. They froze their malignancies, their unreliable hearts, and their corroding tissues, and as the light faded from their snowed-over eyes, they must have dreamed of waking up in the fabulous future.

9   Funny thing about the future. Each next second is the future. And now it's the present. And now it's the past.

10   Those all-together four thousand and ninety-one who deposited their physiognomies in the cold-storage compartments of the world were looking forward to the future. And here it was. And we were it.

11   And smack in the middle of this future, which I naively called Now, was I, Tacey Brice, a rotten little unskilled artist, painting gimcrack flying saucers for the spacines. There was a big flying saucer sighting boom that year of 2193. Either you recollect that, or you don't. Nearly as big as the historic boom between the 1930s and '90s. Psychologists had told us it was our human inadequacy, searching all over for a father-mother figure to replace God. Besides, we were getting desperate. We'd penetrated our solar system to a limited extent, but without meeting anybody on the way.

12   That's another weird thing. When you read the speculativia of the 1900s, you can see just how much they expected of us. It was going to be all or nothing. Either the world would become a miracle of rare device with plastisteel igloos balanced on the stratosphere and metal giblets, or we'd have gone out in a blast of radiation. Neither of which had happened. We'd had problems, of course. Over two hundred years, problems occur. There had been the Fission Tragedy, and the World Flood of '14. There'd been the huge pollution clear-ups complete with the rationing that entailed, and one pretty nasty pandemic. They had set us back, that's obvious. But not halted us. So we reached 2193 mostly unscathed, with a whizz-bang technology not quite as whizz, or bang, as prophesied. A place where doors opened when they saw who you were, and with a colony on Mars, but where they hadn't solved the unemployment problem or the geriatric problem. Up in the ether there were about six hundred buzz-whuzzes headed out into nowhere, bleeping information about earth. But we hadn't landed on Alpha Centauri yet. And if the waste-disposal jammed, brother, it jammed. What I'm trying to say (superfluously, because you're ahead of me), is that their future, those four thousand and ninety-one, their future which was our present, wasn't as spectacular as they'd trusted or feared. Excepting the Salenic Vena-derivative drugs, which had rendered most of the diseases of the 1900s and the 2000s obsolete.

13   And suddenly, one day, someone had a notion.

14   "Hey, guys," this someone suggested, "you recall all those sealed frosty boxes the medic centers have? You know, with the on-ice carcinomas and valu-diddums in 'em? Well, don't you think it'd be grand to defrost the lot of them and pump 'em full of health?"

15   "Crazy," said everybody else, and wet themselves with enthusiasm.

16   After that, they got the thing organized on a global scale. And first off, not wanting to chance any public mishaps, they intended to unfreeze

a single frost box, in relative privacy. Perhaps they put all the names in a
hat. Whatever, they picked Carla Brice, or Brr-Ice, if you liked that
Newsies' tablotape pun.

17   And since Carla Brr-Ice might feel a touch extra chilly, coming
back to life two hundred years after she's cryonised out of it, they
dredged up a blood-line descendant to hold her cold old thirty-three-
year hand. And that was Tacey Brr-Ice. Me.

18   The room below was pink but the cold pink of strawberry ice
cream. There were forty doctors of every gender prowling about in it
and round the crystal slab. It put me in mind of a pack of wolves with a
carcass they couldn't quite decide when to eat. But then, I was having a
nervous attack, up on the spectator gallery where they'd sat me. The
countdown had begun two days ago, and I'd been ushered in at noon
today. For an hour now, the crystal had been clear. I could see a sort of
blob in it, which gradually resolved into a naked woman. Straight off,
even with her lying there stiff as a board and utterly defenseless, I could
tell she was the sort of lady who scared me dizzy. She was large and
well-shaped, with a mane of dark red hair. She was the type that goes
outdoor swimming at all seasons, skis, shoots rapids in a canoe, becomes
the co-ordinator of a moon colony. The type that bites. Valu-diddums
had got her, but nothing else cold have done. Not child, beast, nor man.
Certainly not another woman. Oh, my. And this was my multiple-great
granny that I was about to offer the hand of reassurance.

19   Another hour, and some dial and click mechanisms down in the
strawberry ice room started to dicker. The wolves flew in for the kill. A
dead lioness, that was Carla. Then the box rattled and there was a yell. I
couldn't see for scrabbling medics.

20   "What happened?"

21   The young medic detailed to sit on the spec gallery with me
sighed.

22   "I'd say she's opened her eyes."

23   The young medic was black as space and beautiful as the stars
therein. But he didn't give a damn about me. You could see he was in
love with Carla the lioness. I was simply a pain he had to put up with
for two or three hours, while he stared at the goddess beneath.

24   But now the medics had drawn off. I thought of the Sleeping
Beauty story, and Snow White. Her eyes were open indeed. Coppery
brown to tone with the mane. She didn't appear dazed. She appeared
contemptuous. Precisely as I'd anticipated. Then the crystal box lid
began to rise.

25   "Jesus," I said.

26   "Strange you should say that," said the black medic. His own wonderful eyes fixed on Carla, he'd waxed profound and enigmatic. "The
manner in which we all still use these outdated religious expletives:
God, Christ, Hell, long after we've ceased to credit their religious basis
as such. The successful completion of this experiment in life-suspense
and restoration has a bearing on the same matter," he murmured, his
inch-long lashes brushing the plastase pane. "You've read of the controversy regarding this process? It was seen at one era as an infringement of religious faith."

27   "Oh, yes?"

28   I kept on staring at him. Infinitely preferable to Carla, with her
open eyes, and the solitary bending medic with the supadermic.

29   "The idea of the soul," said the medic on the gallery. "The immortal part which survives death. But what befalls a soul trapped for years,
centuries, in a living yet statically frozen body? In a physical limbo, a
living death. You see the problem this would pose for the religious?"

30   "I—uh—"

31   "But, of course, today . . ." he spread his hands. "There is no such
barrier to lucid thought. The life force, we now know, resides purely in
the brain, and thereafter in the motor nerves, the spinal cord, and attendant reflexive centers. There is no *soul.*"

32   Then he shut up and nearly swooned away, and I realized Carla
had met his eye.

33   I looked, and she was sitting, part reclined against some medic's
arm. The medic was telling her where she was and what year it was and
how, by this evening, the valu-diddums would be no more than a bad
dream, and then she could go out into the amazing new world with her
loving descendant, who she could observe up there on the gallery.

34   She did spare a glance for me. It lasted about .09 of a mini-instant. I
tried to unglue my mouth and flash her a warming welcoming grin, but
before I could manage it, she was back to studying the black medic.

35   At that moment somebody came and whipped me away for cele-
bratory alcohol, and two hours later, when I'd celebrated rather too
much, they took me up a plushy corridor to meet Carla, skin to skin.

36   Actually, she was dressed on this occasion. She'd had a shower and
a couple of post-defrosting tests and some shots and the anti-valu-did-
dums stuff. Her hair was smouldering like a fire in a forest. She wore
the shiny smock medical centers insisted that you wore, but on her it
was like a design original. She'd even had a tan frozen in with her, or
maybe it was my dazzled eyes that made her seem all bronzed and
glowing. Nobody could look that good, that *healthy,* after two hundred
years on ice. And if they did, they shouldn't. Her room was crammed

with flowers and bottles of scent and exotic light paintings, courtesy of the Institute. And then they trundled me in.

37   Not astoundingly, she gazed at me with bored amusement. Like she'd come to the dregs at the bottom of the wine.

38   "This is Tacey," somebody said, making free with my forename.

39   Carla spoke, in a voice of maroon velvet.

40   "Hallo, er, Tacey." Patently, my cognomen was a big mistake. Never mind, she'd overlook it for now. "I gather we are related."

41   I was drunk, but it wasn't helping.

42   "I'm your gr—yes, we are, but—" I intelligently blurted. The "but" was going to be a prologue to some nauseating, placatory, crawler's drivel about her gorgeousness and youth. It wasn't necessary, not even to let her know how scared I was. She could tell that easily, plus how I'd shrunk to a shadow in her high-voltage glare. Before I could complete my hiccupping sycophancy, anyway, the medic in charge said: "Tacey is your link, Mz Brice, with civilization as it currently is."

43   Carla couldn't resist it. She raised one manicured eyebrow, frozen exquisite for two centuries. If Tacey was the link, civilization could take a walk.

44   "My apartment," I went on blurting, "it's medium, but—"

45   What was I going to say now? About how all my grant from the Institute I would willingly spend on gowns and perfumes and skis and automatic rifles, or whatever Carla wanted. How I'd move out and she could have the apartment to herself. (She wouldn't like the spacine murals on the walls.)

46   "It's just a bri—a bridge," I managed. "Till you get acclimatosed—atised."

47   She watched me as I made a fool of myself, or rather, displayed my true foolishness. Finally I comprehended the message in her copper eyes: Don't bother. That was all: Don't bother. You're a failure, Carla's copper irises informed me, as if I didn't know. Don't make excuses. You can alter nothing. I expect nothing from you. I will stay while I must in your ineffectual vicinity, and you may fly round me and scorch your wings if you like. When I am ready, I shall leave immediately, soaring over your sky like a meteor. You can offer no aid, no interest, no grain I cannot garner for myself.

48   "How kind of Tacey," Carla's voice said. "Come, darling, and let me kiss you."

49   Somehow, I'd imagined her still as very cold from the frosty box, but she was blood heat. Ashamed, I let her brush my cheek with her meteoric lips. Perhaps I'd burn.

50   "I'd say this calls for a toast," said the medic in charge. "But just rose-juice for Mz Brice, I'm afraid, at present."

51   Carla smiled at him, and I hallucinated a rose-bush, thorns too, eviscerated by her teeth. Lions drink blood, not roses.

52   I got home paralyzed and floundered about trying to change things. In the middle of attempting to re-spray-paint over a wall, I sank on a pillow and slept. Next day I was angry, the way you can only be angry over something against which you are powerless. So damn it. Let her arrive and see space-shuttles, motherships, and whirly bug-eyed monsters all across the plastase. And don't pull the ready-cook out of the alcove to clean the feed-pipes behind it that I hadn't seen for three years. Or dig the plant out of the cooled-water dispenser. Or buy any new garments, blinds, rugs, sheets. And don't conceal the Wage-Increment cheques when they skitter down the chute. Or prop up the better spacines I'd illustrated, on the table where she won't miss them.

53   I visited her one more time during the month she stayed at the Institute. I didn't have the courage not to take her anything, although I knew that whatever I offered would be wrong. Actually, I had an impulse to blow my first grant cheque and my W-I together and buy her a little antique stiletto of Toledo steel. It was blatantly meant to commit murder with, and as I handed it to her I'd bow and say, "For you, Carla. I just know you can find a use for it." But naturally I didn't have the bravura. I bought her a flagon of expensive scent she didn't need and was rewarded by seeing her put it on a shelf with three other identically packaged flagons, each twice the size of mine. She was wearing a re-clinerobe of amber silk, and I almost reached for sunglasses. We didn't say much. I tottered from her room, sunburned and peeling. And that night I painted another flying saucer on the wall.

54   The day she left the Institute, they sent a mobile for me. I was supposed to collect and ride to the apartment with Carla, to make her feel homey. I felt sick.

55   Before I met her, though, the medic in charge wafted me into his office.

56   "We're lucky," he said. "Mz Brice is a most independent lady. Her readjustment has been, in fact, remarkable. None of the traumas or rebuttals we've been anxious about. I doubt if most of the other subjects to be revived from Cryogenesis will demonstrate the equivalent rate of success."

57   "They're really reviving them then?" I inquired lamely. I was glad to be in here, putting off my fourth congress with inadequacy.

58   "A month from today. Dependent on the ultimately positive results of our post-resuscitation analysis of Mz Brice. But, as I intimated, I hardly predict any hitch there."

59   "And how long," I swallowed, "how long do you think Carla will want to stay with me?"

60   "Well, she seems to have formed quite an attachment for you, Tacey. It's a great compliment, you know, from a woman like that. A proud, volatile spirit. But she needs an anchor for a while. We all need our anchors. Probably, her proximity will benefit you, in return. Don't you agree?"

61   I didn't answer, and he concluded I was overwhelmed. He started to describe to me that glorious scheduled event, the global link-up, when every single cryogone was to be revived, as simultaneously with each other as they could arrange it. The process would be going out on five channels of the Spatials, visible to us all. Technology triumphant yet again, bringing us a minute or two of transcendental catharsis. I thought about the beautiful black medic and his words on religion. And this is how we replaced it, presumably (when we weren't saucer-sighting), shedding tears sentimentally over four thousand and ninety idiots fumbling out of the deep-freeze.

62   "One last, small warning," the medic in charge added. "You may notice—or you may not, I can't be positive—the occasional lapse in the behavioural patterns of Mz Brice."

63   There was a fantasy for me. Carla, *lapsed.*

64   "In what way?" I asked, miserably enjoying the unlikelihood.

65   "Mere items. A mood, an aberration—a brief disorientation even. These are to be expected in a woman reclaimed by life after two hundred years, and in a world she is no longer familiar with. As I explained, I looked for much worse and far greater quantity. The odd personality slip is inevitable. You mustn't be alarmed. At such moments the most steadying influence on Mz Brice will be a non-Institutional normalcy of surroundings. And the presence of yourself."

66   I nearly laughed.

67   I would have, if the door hadn't opened, and if Carla, in mock red-lynx fur, hadn't stalked into the room.

68   I didn't even try to create chatter. Alone in the mobile, with the auto driving us along the cool concrete highways, there wasn't any requirement to pretend for the benefit of others. Carla reckoned I was a schmoil, and I duly schmoiled. Mind you, now and again, she put out a silk paw and gave me a playful tap. Like when she asked me where I got my hair *done.* But I just told her about the ready-set parlours and she quit. Then again, she asked a couple of less abstract questions. Did libraries still exist, that was one. The second one was if I slept well.

69   I went along with everything in a dank stupor. I think I was half kidding myself it was going to be over soon. Then the mobile drove into the auto-lift of my apartment block, the gates gaped and we got out. As my door recognized me and split wide, it abruptly hit me that

Carla and I were going to be hand in glove for some while. A month at least, while the Institute computed its final tests. Maybe more, if Carla had my lazy streak somewhere in her bronze and permasteel frame.

70   She strode into my apartment and stood flaming among the flying saucers and the wine-ringed furniture. The fake-fur looked as if she'd shot it herself. She was a head taller than I was ever going to be. And then she startled me, about the only way she could right then.

71   "I'm tired, Tacey," said Carla.

72   No wise-cracks, no vitriol, no stare from Olympus.

73   She glided to the bedroom. O.K. I'd allocated the bed as hers, the couch as mine. She paused, gold digit on the panel that I'd pre-set to respond to her finger.

74   "Will you forgive me?" she wondered aloud.

75   Her voice was soporific. I yawned.

76   "Sure, Carla."

77   She stayed behind the closed panels for hours. The day reddened over the city, colours as usual heightened by the weather control that operates a quarter of a mile up. I slumped here and there, unable to eat or rest or read or doodle. I was finding out what it was going to be like, having an apartment and knowing it wasn't mine anymore. Even through a door, Carla dominated.

78   Around 19, I knocked. No reply.

79   Intimidated, I slunk off. I wouldn't play the septophones, even with the ear-pieces only, even with the volume way down. Might wake Granny. You see, if you could wake her from two hundred years in the freezer, you could certainly wake her after eight hours on a dormadais.

80   At twenty-four midnight, she still hadn't come out.

81   Coward, I knocked again, and feebly called: "Night, Carla. See you tomorrow."

82   On the couch I had nightmares, or nightcarlas to be explicit. Some were very realistic, like the one where the trust bonds Carla's estate had left for her hadn't accumulated after all and she was destitute, and going to remain with me for ever and ever. Or there were the comic-strip ones where the fake red-lynx got under the cover and bit me. Or the surreal ones where Carla came floating towards me, clad only in her smouldering hair, and everything caught fire from it, and I kept saying, "Please, Carla, don't set the rug alight. Please, Carla, don't set the couch alight." In the end there was merely a dream where Carla bent over me, hissing something like an anaconda—if they do hiss. She wanted me to stay asleep, apparently, and for some reason I was fighting her, though I was almost comatose. The strange thing in this dream was that Carla's eyes had altered from copper to a brilliant topaz yellow, like the lynx's.

83 It must have been about four in the morning that I woke up. I think it was the washer unit that woke me. Or it could have been the septophones. Or the waste-disposal. Or the drier. Or any of the several gadgets a modern apartment was equipped with. Because they were all on. It sounded like a madhouse. Looked like one. All the lights were on, too. In the middle of chaos: Carla. She was quite naked, the way I'd seen her at the first, but she had the sort of nakedness that seems like clothes, clean-cut, firm and flawless. The sort that makes me want to hide inside a stone. She was reminiscent of a sorceress in the midst of her sorcery, the erupting mechanisms sprawling round her in the fierce light. I had a silly thought: *Carla's going nova.* Then she turned and saw me. My mouth felt as if it had been security-sealed, but I got out, "You O.K., Carla?"

84 "I am, darling. Go back to sleep now."

85 That's the last thing I remember till 10 A.M. the next day.

86 I wondered initially if Carla and the gadgets had been an additional dream. But when I checked the energy-meter I discovered they hadn't. I was plodding to the ready-cook when Carla emerged from the bedroom in her amber reclinerobe.

87 She didn't say a word. She just relaxed at the counter and let me be her slave. I got ready to prepare her the large breakfast she outlined. Then I ran her bath. When the water-meter shut off half through, Carla suggested I put in the extra tags to ensure the tub was filled right up.

88 As she bathed, I sat at the counter and had another nervous attack.

89 Of course, Carla was predictably curious. Back in 1993, many of our gadgets hadn't been invented, or at least not developed to their present standard. Why not get up in the night and turn everything on? Why did it have to seem sinister? Maybe my sleeping through it practically non-stop was the thing that troubled me. All right. So Carla was a hypnotist. Come to consider, should I run a histotrace myself, in an attempt to learn what Carla was—had been?

90 But let's face it, what really upset me was the low on the energy-meter, the water-meter taking a third of my week's water tags in one morning. And Carla luxuriously wallowing, leaving me to foot the bill.

91 Could I say anything? No. I knew she'd immobilize me before I'd begun.

92 When she came from the bathroom, I asked her did she want to go out. She said no, but I could visit the library, if I would, and pick up this book and tape list she'd called through to them. I checked the call-meter. That was down, too.

93 "I intend to act the hermit for a while, Tacey," Carla murmured behind me as I guiltily flinched away from the meter. "I don't want to get involved in a furor of publicity. I gather the news of my successful revival

will have been leaked today. The tablotapes will be sporting it. But I understand, by the news publishing codes of the '80s, that unless I approach the Newsies voluntarily, they are not permitted to approach me."

94   "Yes, that's right." I gazed pleadingly into the air. "I guess you wouldn't ever reconsider that, Carla? It could mean a lot of money. That is, not for you to contact the Newsies. But if you'd all—allow me to on your beh—half."

95   She chuckled like a lioness with her throat full of gazelle. The hair rose on my neck as she slunk closer. When her big, warm, elegant hand curved over my skull, I shuddered.

96   "No, Tacey. I don't think I'd care for that. I don't need the cash. My estate investments, I hear, are flourishing."

97   "I was thinking of m—I was thinking of me, Carla, I cou—could use the tags."

98   The hand slid from my head and batted me lightly. Somehow, I was glad I hadn't given her the Toledo knife after all.

99   "No, I don't think so. I think it will do you much more good to continue as you are. Now, run along to the library, darling."

100   I went mainly because I was glad to get away from her. To utter the spineless whining I had had drained entirely my thin reserves of courage. I was shaking when I reached the auto-lift. I had a wild plan of leaving town, and leaving my apartment with Carla in it, and going to ground. It was more than just inadequacy now. Hunter and hunted. And as I crept through the long grass, her fiery breath was on my heels.

101   I collected the twenty books and the fifty tapes and paid for the loan. I took them back to the apartment and laid them before my astonishing amber granny. I was too scared even to hide. Much too scared to disobey.

102   I sat on the sun-patio, though it was the weather control day for rain. Through the plastase panels I heard the tapes educating Carla on every aspect of contemporary life; social, political, economic, geographical, and carnal.

103   When she summoned me, I fixed lunch. Later, drinks and supper.

104   Then I was too nervous to go to sleep. I passed out in the bathroom, sitting in the shower cubicle. Had nightcarlas Carla eating salad. Didn't wake up till 10 A.M. Checked. All meters down again.

105   When I trod on smashed plastase I thought it was sugar. Then I saw the cooled-water dispenser was in ninety-five bits. Where the plant had been, there was only soil and condensation and trailing roots.

106   I looked, and everywhere beheld torn-off leaves and tiny clots of earth. There was a leaf by Carla's bedroom. I knocked and my heart knocked to keep my hand company.

107   But Carla wasn't interested in breakfast, wasn't hungry.

108   I knew why not. She'd eaten my plant.

109   You can take a bet I meant to call up the Institute right away. Somehow, I didn't. For one thing, I didn't want to call from the apartment and risk Carla catching me at it. For another, I didn't want to go out and leave her, in case she did something worse. Then again, I was terrified to linger in her vicinity. A *lapse,* the medic in charge had postulated. It was certainly that. Had she done anything like it at the Institute? Somehow I had the idea she hadn't. She'd saved it for me. Out of playful malice.

110   I dithered for an hour, till I panicked, pressed the call button and spoke the digits. I never heard the door open. She seemed to know exactly when to—*strike;* yes, that *is* the word I want. I sensed her there. She didn't even touch me. I let go the call button.

111   "Who were calling?" Carla asked.

112   "Just a guy I used to pair with," I said, but it came out husky and gulped and quivering.

113   "Well, go ahead. Don't mind me."

114   Her maroon voice, bored and amused and indifferent to anything I might do, held me like a steel claw. And I discovered I had to turn around and face her. I had to stare into her eyes.

115   The scorn in them was killing. I wanted to shrivel and roll under the rug, but I couldn't look away.

116   "But if you're not going to call anyone, run my bath, darling," Carla said.

117   I ran her bath.

118   It was that easy. Of course.

119   She was magnetic. Irresistible.

120   I couldn't—

121   I could *not*—

122   Partly, it had all become incredible. I couldn't picture myself accusing Carla of house-plant-eating to the medics at the Institute. Who'd believe it? It was nuts. I mean, too nuts even for them. And presently, I left off quite believing it myself.

123   Nevertheless, somewhere in my brain I kept on replaying those sentences of the medic in charge: *the occasional lapse in the behavioural patterns . . . a mood, an aberration . . .* And against that, point counterpoint, there kept on playing that phrase the beautiful black medic had reeled off enigmatically as a cultural jest: *But what befalls a soul trapped for years, centuries, in a living yet statically frozen body?*

124   Meanwhile, by sheer will, by the force of her persona, she'd stopped me calling. And that same thing stopped me talking about her to any-

body on the street, sent me tongue-tied to fetch groceries, sent me grovelling to conjure meals. It was almost as if it also shoved me asleep when she wanted and brought me awake ditto.

125   Doesn't time fly when you're having fun?

126   Twenty days, each more or less resembling each, hurried by. Carla didn't do anything else particularly weird, at least not that I saw or detected. But then, I never woke up nights anymore. And I had an insane theory that the meters had been fiddled, because they weren't low, but they felt as if they should be. I hadn't got any more plants. I missed some packaged paper lingerie, but it turned up under Carla's bed, where I'd kicked it when the bed was mine. Twenty days, twenty-five. The month of Carla's post-resuscitation tests was nearly through. One morning, I was stumbling about like a zombie, cleaning the apartment because the dustease had jammed and Carla had spent five minutes in silent comment on the dust. I was moving in that combined sludge of terror, mindlessness and masochistic cringing she'd taught me, when the door signal went.

127   When I opened the door, there stood the black medic with a slim case of file-tapes. I felt transparent, and that was how he treated me. He gazed straight through me to the empty room where he had hoped my granny would be.

128   "I'm afraid your call doesn't seem to be working," he said. (Why had I the notion Carla had done something to the call?) "I'd be grateful to see Mz Brice, if she can spare me a few minutes. Just something we'd like to check for the files."

129   That instant, splendid on her cue, Carla manifested from the bathroom. The medic had seen her naked in the frosty box, but not a naked that was vaguely and fluently sheathed in a damp towel. It had the predictable effect. As he paused transfixed, Carla bestowed her most gracious smile.

130   "Sit down," she said. "What check is this? Tacey, darling, why not arrange some fresh coffee?"

131   Tacey darling went to the coffee cone. Over its bubbling, I heard him say to her, "It's simply that Doctor Something was a little worried by a possible amnesia. Certainly, none of the memory areas seem physically impaired. But you see, here and there on the tape—"

132   "Give me an example, please," drawled Carla.

133   The black medic lowered his lashes as if to sweep the tablotape.

134   "Some confusion over places, and names. Your second husband, Francis, for instance, who you named as Frederick. And there, the red mark—Doctor Something-Else mentioned the satellite disaster of '91, and it seems you did not recall—"

135   "You're referring to the malfunction of the Ixion 11, which broke
up and crashed in the midwest, taking three hundred lives," said Carla.
She sounded like a purring textbook. She leaned forward, and I could
watch him tremble all the way across from the coffee cone. "Doctor
Something and Doctor Something-Else," said Carla, "will have to make
allowances for my excitement at rebirth. Now, I can't have you driving
out this way for nothing. How about you come to dinner, the night before the great day. Tacey doesn't see nearly enough people her own age.
As for me, let's say you'll make a two-hundred-year-old lady very happy."

136   The air between them was electric enough to form sparks. By the
"Great day" she meant, patently, the five-channel Spatial event when
her four thousand and ninety confrères got liberated from the sub-zero.
But he plainly didn't care so much about defrosting anymore.

137   The coffee cone boiled over. I noticed with a shock I was crying.
Nobody else did.

138   What I wanted to do was program the ready-cook for the meal, get
in some wine, and get the hell out of the apartment and leave the two
of them alone. I'd pass the night at one of the all-night Populars, and
creep in around 10 A.M. the next morning. That's the state I frankly ac-
knowledged she had reduced me to. I'd have been honestly grateful to
have done that. But Carla wouldn't let me.

139   "Out?" she inquired. "But this whole party is for you, darling."

140   There was nobody about. She didn't have to pretend. She and I
knew I was the slave. She and I knew her long-refrigerated soul, returning in fire, had scalded me into a melty on the ground. So it could only
be a cruelty, this. She seemed to be experimenting, even, as she had
with the gadgets. The psychological dissection of an inferior inhabitant
of the future.

141   What I had to do therefore, was to visit the ready-set hair parlour,
and buy a dress with my bi-monthly second W-I cheque. Carla, though
naturally she didn't go with me, somehow instigated and oversaw these
ventures. Choosing the dress, she was oddly at my elbow. *That* one, her
detached and omnipresent aura instructed me. It was expensive, and it
was scarlet and gold. It would have looked wonderful on somebody else.
But not me. That dress just sucked the little life I've got right out of me.

142   Come the big night (before the big day, for which the countdown
must already have, in fact, begun), there I was, done up like a New Year
parcel, and with my own problematical soul wizened within me. The
door signal went, and the slave accordingly opened the door, and the
dark angel entered, politely thanking me as he nearly walked straight
through me.

143   He looked so marvellous, I practically bolted. But still the aura of Carla, and Carla's wishes, which were beginning to seem to be communicating themselves telepathically, held me put.

144   Then Carla appeared. I hadn't seen her before, that evening. The dress was lionskin, and it looked real, despite the anti-game-hunting laws. Her hair was a smooth auburn waterfall that left bare an ear with a gold star dependent from it. I just went into the cooking area and uncorked a bottle and drank most of it straight off.

145   They both had good appetites, though hers was better than his. She'd eaten a vast amount since she'd been with me, presumably ravenous after that long fast. I was the waitress, so I waited on them. When I reached my plate, the food had congealed because the warmer in the table on my side was faulty. Anyway, I wasn't hungry. There were two types of wine. I drank the cheap type. I was on the second bottle now, and sufficiently sad I could have howled, but I'd also grown uninvolved, viewing my sadness from a great height.

146   They danced together to the septophones. I drank some more wine. I was going to be very, very ill tomorrow. But that was tomorrow. Verily. When I looked up, they'd danced themselves into the bedroom and the panels were shut. Carla's cruelty had had its run and I wasn't prepared for any additions, such as ecstatic moans from the interior, to augment my frustration. Accordingly, garbed in my New Year parcel frock, hair in curlicues, and another bottle in my hand, I staggered forth into the night.

147   I might have met a thug, a rapist, a murderer, or even one of the numerous polipatrols that roam the city to prevent the activities of such. But I didn't meet anyone who took note of me. Nobody cared. Nobody was interested. Nobody wanted to be my friend, rob me, abuse me, give me a job or a goal, or make me happy, or make love to me. So if you thought I was a Judas, just you remember that. If one of you slobs had taken any notice of me that night—

148   I didn't have to wait for morning to be ill. There was a handsome washroom on Avenue East. I'll never forget it. I was there quite a while.

149   When the glamourous weather-control dawn irradiated the city, I was past the worst. And by 10 A.M. I was trudging home, queasy, embittered, hard-done-by, but sober. I was even able to register the tabloes everywhere and the holoid neons, telling us all that the great day was here. The day of the four thousand and ninety. Thawday. I wondered dimly if Carla and the Prince of Darkness were still celebrating it in my bed. She should have been cold. Joke. All right. It isn't.

150   The door to my apartment let me in. The place was as I'd abandoned it. The window-blinds were down, the table strewn with plates and glasses. The bedroom door firmly shut.

151   I pressed the switch to raise the blinds, and nothing happened, which didn't surprise me. That in itself should have proved to me how far the influence had gone and how there was no retreat. But I only had this random desultory urge to see what the apartment door would do now. What it did was not react. Not even when I put my hand on the panel, which method was generally reserved for guests. It had admitted me, but wouldn't let me out again. Carla had done something to it. As she had to the call, the meters, and to me. But how—personal power? Ridiculous. I was a spineless dope, that was why she'd been able to negate me. Yet—forty-one medics, with a bevy of tests and questions, some of which, apparently, she hadn't got right, ate from her hand. And maybe her psychic ability had increased. Practice makes perfect.

152   . . . *What befalls a soul trapped for years, centuries, in a living, yet statically frozen body?*

153   It was dark in the room, with the blinds irreversibly staying down and the lights irreversibly off.

154   Then the bedroom door slid wide, and Carla slid out. Naked again, and glowing in the dark. She smiled at me, pityingly.

155   "Tacey, darling, now you've gotten over your sulks, there's something in here I'd like you to clear up for me."

156   Dichotomy once more. I wanted to take root where I was, but she had me walking to the bedroom. She truly was glowing. As if she'd lightly sprayed herself over with something mildly luminous. I guessed what would be in the bedroom, and I'd begun retching, but, already despoiled of filling, that didn't matter. Soon I was in the doorway and she said, "Stop that, Tacey." And I stopped retching and stood and looked at what remained of the beautiful black medic, wrapped up in the bloodstained lionskin.

157   Lions drink blood, not roses.

158   Something loosened inside me then. It was probably the final submission, the final surrender of the fight. Presumably I'd been fighting her subconsciously from the start, or I wouldn't have gained the ragged half-freedoms I had. But now I was limp and sodden, so I could ask humbly: "The plant was salad. But a man—what was he?"

159   "You don't quite get it, darling, do you?" Carla said. She stroked my hair friendlily. I didn't shudder anymore. Cowed dog, I was relaxed under the contemptuous affection of my mistress. "One was green and vegetable. One was black, male, and meat. Different forms. Local dishes. I had no inclination to sample you, you comprehend, since you were approximate to my own appearance. But of course, others who find themselves to be black and male, may wish to sample pale-skinned females. Don't worry, Tacey. You'll be safe. You entertain me. You're mine. Protected species."

160   "Still don't understand, Carla," I whispered meekly.

161   "Well, just clear up for me, and I'll explain."

162   I don't have to apologize to you for what I did then, because, of course, you know all about it, the will-less indifference of the absolute slave. I bundled up the relics of Carla's lover-breakfast, and dumped them in the waste-disposal, which dealt with them pretty efficiently.

163   Then I cleaned the bedroom, and had a shower, and fixed Carla some coffee and biscuits. It was almost noon, the hour when the four thousand and ninety were going to be roused, and to step from their frost boxes in front of seven-eighths of the world's Spatial-viewers. Carla wanted to see it too, so I switched on my set, minus the sound. Next Carla told me I might sit, and I sat on a pillow, and she explained.

164   For some reason, I don't remember her actual words. Perhaps she put it in a technical way and I got the gist but not the sentences. I'll put it in my own words here, despite the fact that a lot of you know now anyway. After all, under supervision, we still have babies sometimes. When they grow up they'll need to know. Know why they haven't got a chance, and why we hadn't. And, to level with you, know why I'm not a Judas, and that I didn't betray us, because I didn't have a chance either.

165   Laziness, optimism, and blind stupidity.

166   I suppose optimism more than anything.

167   Four thousand and ninety-one persons lying down in frozen stasis, aware they didn't have souls and couldn't otherwise survive, dreaming of a future of cures, and of a reawakening in that future. And the earth dreaming of benevolent visitors from other worlds, father-mother figures to guide and help us. Sending them buzz-whuzzes to bleep, over and over, *Here* we are. *Here. Here.*

168   I guess we do have souls. Or we have something that has nothing to do with the brain, or the nerve centers, or the spinal cord. Perhaps that dies too, when we die. Or perhaps it escapes. Whatever happens, that's the one thing you can't retain in Cryogenic Suspension. The body, all its valves and ducts and organs, lies pristine in limbo, and when you wake it up with the correct drugs, impulses, stimuli, it's live again, can be cured of its diseases, becoming a flawless vessel of—nothing. It's like an empty room, a vacant lot. The tenant's skipped.

169   Somewhere out in the starry night of space, one of the bleeping buzz-whuzzes was intercepted. Not by pater-mater figures, but by a predatory, bellicose alien race. It was simple to get to us—hadn't we given comprehensive directions? But on arrival they perceived a world totally unsuited to their fiery, gaseous, incorporeal forms. That was a blow, that was. But they didn't give up hope. Along with their superior technology they developed a process whereby they reckoned they could transfer inside of human bodies, and thereafter live off the fat of the Terrain.

However, said process wouldn't work. Why not? The human consciousness (soul?) was too strong to overcome, it wouldn't let them through.
Even asleep, they couldn't oust us. Dormant, the consciousness (soul?) is
still present, or at least linked. As for dead bodies, no go. A man who had
expired of old age, or with a mobile on top of him was no use. The body
had to be a whole one, or there was no point. Up in their saucers, which
were periodically spotted, they spat and swore. They gazed at the earth
and drooled, pondering mastery of a globe, and entire races of slaves at
their disposal. But there was no way they could achieve their aims—until
they learned of all those Cryogenic Suspensions in their frost boxes, all
those soulless lumps of ice, waiting on the day when science would release and cure them and bring them forth healthy and *void*.

170   If you haven't got a tenant, advertize for a new tenant. We had.
And they'd come.

171   Carla was the first. As her eyes opened under the crystal, something
looked out of them. Not Carla Brice. Not anymore. But something.

172   Curious, cruel, powerful, indomitable, alien, deadly.

173   Alone, she could handle hundreds of us humans, for her influence
ascended virtually minute by minute. Soon there were going to be four
thousand and ninety of her kind, opening their eyes, smiling their
scornful thank-yous through the Spatials at the world they had come to
conquer. The world they did conquer.

174   We gave them beautiful, healthy, moveable houses to live in, and billions to serve them and be toyed with by them, and provide them with
extra bodies to be frozen and made fit to house any leftover colleagues
of theirs. And our green depolluted meadows wherein to rejoice.

175   As for Carla, she'd kept quiet and careful as long as she had to. Long
enough for the tests to go through and for her to communicate back,
telepathically, to her people, all the data they might require on earth,
prior to their arrival.

176   And now she sat and considered me, meteoric fiery Carla-who-
wasn't-Carla, her eyes, in the dark, gleaming topaz yellow through their
copper irises, revealing her basic inflammable nature within the veil of
a dead woman's living flesh.

177   They can make me do whatever they want, and they made me
write this. Nothing utterly bad has been done to me, and maybe it
never will. So I've been lucky there.

178   To them, I'm historically interesting, as Carla had been historically
interesting to us, as a first. I'm the first Slave. Possibly, I can stay alive on
the strength of that and not be killed for a whim.

179   Which, in a way, I suppose, means I'm a sort of success, after all.

DISCUSSION QUESTIONS

1. The narrator is self-deprecating throughout the story. What effect does this have on your perception of her? On the outcome of the story?
2. In the world of 2193, Tacey Brice says some problems, like diseases, are solved; but others, like unemployment and geriatrics, are not. In small groups, discuss why this might be the case.
3. Why is Tacey so intimidated by her revived relative?
4. Why are the saucer sightings relevant, in retrospect, to the revival efforts?
5. The medic brings up the outdated concept of revivifying as a possible religious infringement. What is he most concerned about?

WRITING TOPICS

1. The body and brain, in the story, can be retained in pristine condition. In your journal, write about how the aliens can become the souls of the emptied vessels, and what implications this has for today's world.
2. The Newsies in this story aren't allowed to approach subjects. Instead, they must wait for people to approach them voluntarily. Explore how this is comparable to the way news is gathered today. Write a brief essay on whether Lee's idea is logical or is more of a way to advance the plot.
3. In an essay, research the UFO phenomena, especially in relationship to the increased sightings in the late seventies. Couple this with the search for extraterrestrial life that gained momentum then. How much of the UFO sighting information can be believed? What problems might we encounter if we do actually make contact with alien species?

CHAPTER EIGHT

The Eighties

Eight Americans killed in rescue attempt of 53 U.S. hostages in Iran

Iraq attacks Iran, beginning an eight-year war that ends in a stalemate

World Health Organization announces worldwide eradication of smallpox

The Empire Strikes Back, second in the Star Wars movie trilogy, is released

Hostages released when Ronald Reagan inaugurated as president

Sandra Day O'Connor becomes first woman Supreme Court Justice

Columbia becomes first re-used U.S. space shuttle

IBM introduces the personal computer (PC) with disk operating system (DOS)

AIDS recognized as a disease by the U.S. Center for Disease Control

Chinese scientists successfully clone a fish (golden carp)

The Road Warrior film shows a post-apocalyptic world with gritty realism

American Telephone and Telegraph ordered to end its telephone monopoly

First artificial heart implanted; patient lives 112 days

Blade Runner, the first movie adapted from a Philip K. Dick novel, debuts the same year Dick dies

Jesse Jackson is the first African American to make a serious bid for the White House

President Reagan proposes Strategic Defense Initiative ("Star Wars") antimissile defense system to stave off threat of Soviets, whom he dubs "The Evil Empire"

France tests neutron bomb

Music CDs first appear on market

Return of the Jedi completes the Star Wars trilogy

Indian Prime Minister Indira Gandhi assassinated by her Sikh bodyguards

Apple introduces Macintosh computers, using a mouse

HIV virus identified

William Gibson's Neuromancer novel wins the Hugo, Nebula, and Philip K. Dick awards

The Terminator movie combines time travel and war between humans and machines

Mikhail Gorbachev becomes general secretary of Communist party; introduces *glasnost* and *perestroika*, leading to the end of the Cold War and the breakup of the Soviet Union

Video cameras produced for home use

Lasers first used to clean out clogged arteries

Orson Scott Card begins *Ender's Game* series of novels with *Ender's Game*

President Reagan admits arms were traded for hostages in Iran

U.S. begins banning lead in water pipes

Challenger shuttle explodes on takeoff, killing all seven crew members

The Russian nuclear power plant at Chernobyl suffers a partial meltdown, causing massive radiation damage

International agreement reached to phase out ozone-destroying propellants

Frank Miller's *Batman: The Dark Knight Returns* is published as a graphic novel

***Star Trek: The Next Generation* begins on TV**

Airline flight from London to New York exploded by terrorists over Lockerbie, Scotland, killing all 259 aboard

Mikhail Gorbachev becomes president of U.S.S.R., begins cutting troops and reducing nuclear arsenal

First transatlantic fiber optic cable put into service

Chinese pro-democracy dissidents occupy Tiananmen Square in Peking; government imposes martial law, killing thousands

Berlin Wall comes down

Greenhouse effect blamed for warmest winter ever recorded

***Locus* magazine reports a 50 percent rise in the number of science fiction titles published each year from 1980–1989**

HISTORICAL CONTEXT

Trouble continued to brew in the Mideast, Soviet satellites, and South America during the eighties. In 1979 Saddam Hussein became president of Iraq. The next year he invaded Iran in an attempt to gain further control in the Persian Gulf region. Iraq had greater military strength, but Iran had more people and the support of Syria. Even after Hussein used chemical weapons, neither side could achieve a decisive victory. An uneasy cease-fire was declared in 1988.

In 1982 the Israeli ambassador to Great Britain was shot by PLO assassins, and Israel launched a major attack on Beirut, the capital of Lebanon. Beirut was half Christian, half Muslim, and the headquarters of the PLO. Syria and Jordan joined in the battle against Israel, and the United States supplied arms to Israel while the Soviets supplied them to the Syrians. Arafat was driven from Beirut and 2,000 Palestinians were massacred by Christians.

Poland, which was under communist rule, was in a state of economic crisis in 1980. Lech Walesa formed a Solidarity Union and united workers in a massive strike, eventually gaining limited freedom. When Solidarity called for similar trade unions in other communist countries, however, Walesa was imprisoned. He remained there until 1989 when the Soviets relented. The following year Walesa was elected president of Poland in that country's first free elections since before World War II.

Soon after Hungary and Poland established free elections, Hungary and Czechoslovakia opened their borders to East Germans who were seeking to flee from East Germany. In the face of the mass exodus and escalating protest rallies, East German President Erich Honecker resigned. The authorities opened the Berlin Wall in 1989 and within weeks the entire wall was torn down and free communication and travel between the eastern and western portions was restored. The following year East and West Germany reunited.

In South America, Argentina invaded the Falkland Islands in 1982 in a dispute with Britain over ownership of the islands. The British quickly squelched the takeover and retained possession of the Falklands. The socialist government of the Caribbean island of Grenada was overthrown soon afterward in a military coup backed by the U.S. marines, even though it was a member of the British Commonwealth. The Marxist resistance collapsed and Paul Scoon assumed authority as governor general. He restored the 1974 constitution and the next year Grenada had free elections.

Ferdinand Marcos had controlled the Philippines since 1965. In 1972 he suspended the constitution, imposed martial law, and assumed near dictatorial powers. In 1983 the leader of the opposition party, Benigno Aquino, was assassinated. His widow Corazon assumed his position, and as Marcos' corrupt government drew increasing international criticism, he called for an election in 1986. He won against Aquino, but only by bribery and fraudulent ballot counting. Marcos was forced to resign and left for the United States, which granted him asylum.

In the Soviet Union, a substantial quantity of radioactive material was released into the atmosphere at the Chernobyl nuclear power plant in 1986. At first the Soviets denied the accident had happened. However, satellite photos showed the top of the reactor had blown off and the plant was in flames. At least 30 people died immediately and thousands were treated for radiation sickness. Contaminated meat and dairy products were embargoed and livestock destroyed in an attempt to prevent the radiation from spreading. Over 300 square miles had to be evacuated in the most severe nuclear accident in history.

Electronic communications expanded during the eighties. Fiber optic cables were laid, satellite transmissions carried live TV around the globe, fax machines became common, and computers spread to nearly every facet of life. The technology had been developed in the United States, but the production was predominately centered in Japan. It became nearly impossible to buy a TV set made in America, and Japanese automobiles began to dominate the U.S. market as well. The unexpected strength of competition from a foreign market hurt many American companies.

These companies had to devise different manufacturing and marketing strategies in order to remain viable.

In 1986 Ronald Reagan admitted that the United States had
secretly sold arms to Iran during the hostage crisis, but he denied
the weapons were bribes for hostage release. The funds from the
sale had been diverted to Nicaragua whose Sandinista government
was hostile to the United States. Reagan supported their oppo-
nents—the Contras, who had little support in their own country.
The United States Congress, fearing another Vietnam-type situation, banned all military aid to the Contras. The Reagan administration solicited funds from other countries and negotiations for
arms sales were turned over to private citizens.

But the fact that more than a thousand U.S. missiles were
shipped to Iran for its war against Iraq and the funds were then
diverted to the Contras caused a Senate investigation. Reagan
declared he didn't know the details. The investigation ended in
1987 with Oliver North taking most of the blame. For many
Americans, though, the questions raised were never satisfactorily
answered.

The AIDS crisis began and quickly built up momentum
during the eighties, and homelessness was on the rise as Reagan's
trickle down economic policies didn't trickle much below the
upper class. The wealthiest one percent of the population increased their wealth by an average of 74 percent during his eight
years in office. At the same time, the federal deficit ballooned to
triple what it had been in 1980. As the wealthy increased their
holdings, other Americans were forced to tighten their belts and
face rising unemployment and reduced income. When Reagan's
vice president George Bush was elected president in 1988, he
continued many of the policies Reagan had established.

DEVELOPMENTS IN SCIENCE FICTION

A new movement in science fiction appeared in the eighties in
response to the increasing complexities of the U.S. government
and the turbulent state of global affairs. The philosophy reflected a
growing disregard for politics and increasing apathy among young
people. The multi-layered society that Americans were living in,

and the impersonalization brought about by more technology, contributed to isolated groups with little or no sense of community.

The term *cyberpunk* combined the word *cyber*, from cybernetics—the study of machine and animal systems of communication—and *punk*, from rock music terminology—aggressive youth and alienation. The person most associated with the cyberpunk movement is William Gibson and his *Neuromancer* universe. Bruce Sterling edited the 1986 anthology *Mirrorshades: The Cyberpunk Anthology*, which defined the subgenre and its world of disaffected youth.

Cyberpunk stories repeatedly feature bodily implanted circuitry, genetic alterations, brain-computer interfaces, and artificial intelligence. They are usually set in urban locations in the near future. The cities are invariably run down or infested with street gangs or slums. Japan is often shown as a dominant economic force, and the urban spread is a decaying organism. Gibson's *Neuromancer* (1984) is considered the classic cyberpunk text. It depicts Case, a "cowboy on an adrenaline high." Case is physically connected to a cyberspace deck that projects his disembodied consciousness into a virtual reality inhabited by computer simulations which he both explores and exploits.

Gibson and other cyberpunk writers drew from current events in much the same way that other science fiction writers had been doing, but their vision of the near future was darker and grittier. They depicted America falling from world dominance and succumbing to human problems which could not be fixed by space exploration or technological solutions.

The explosion of the space shuttle *Challenger* in 1986 highlighted the end of the traditional science fiction dream and ushered in the dark pessimism of the cyberpunks. John Brunning, a prominent cyberpunk writer, said, "Science fiction used to be the most optimistic form of literature, apart from inspirational propaganda, [but] too many of us are behaving too stupidly down here on Earth for those worn visions to be any longer credible."

While these cyberpunk visions of a crumbling world were growing in science fiction, President Reagan in 1983 began a Strategic Defense Initiative. Popularly known as Star Wars, the idea was that the free world could be defended from nuclear attack by a group of satellite-based anti-missile weapons. This

effort to use a technological solution to overcome the threat of nuclear war cost U.S. taxpayers over $32 billion before it was finally
abandoned in 1993. The cyberpunk writers didn't offer these kind
of pie-in-the-sky type of solutions to global problems. Instead they
suggested the dismal paths down which humanity was headed.

Like punk music, which stripped away the shallowness of
seventies progressive rock, cyberpunk was a return to science fiction's roots—struggling with ideas suggested by current events
without the gloss of optimism. The advances in computer technology became such a part of the culture in the seventies that the
emergence of a counterculture was inevitable. The rise in popularity of rock music videos was advanced by the fast-paced MTV
presentations which began in 1981. Rock's influence on disen-
chanted urban youth and the increasing anarchy created by inner
city street gangs also influenced many writers to predict decen-
tralization of power, especially as more groups attempted to
establish dominance over their own "turf."

This unease was fueled by the possibility that a single computer hacker might be able to start a nuclear war, as portrayed
in the 1983 science fiction movie *War Games*. With the emphasis
shifting away from technology as a good development and toward
science as an alienating feature of society, it became evident that
a darker vision was gaining prominence in science fiction.

Nanotechnology, the concept of creating machines on a
molecular level, was another theme advanced during the cyberpunk
years. Greg Bear's *Blood Music* (1985) involves a scientist who uses genetic engineering to transform a virus into an intelligent nanocom-
puter which proceeds to take over and transform the scientist's body.

Other science fiction writers of the eighties, though, tried
to distance themselves from the new movement and set novels in
the far future when Earth's civilization had been, or is in the process of being, destroyed. Douglas Adam's *The Hitchhiker's Guide to
the Galaxy* series (1979–93), for instance, has the planet destroyed
in the first novel and creates an interstellar "freeway" for intergalactic travel. The series began as lighthearted and satiric, but as
the number of novels increased, the point became hard to follow
and they turned into fluff.

More science fiction was written by women during the eighties, though most were avoiding cyberpunk and emphasizing feminist

or humanistic concerns instead. Even though more women were moving into positions of power in business and politics, science fiction continued to be dominated by male writers. The emphasis in cyberpunk on hard science fiction and hard characters scrambling for survival in an impersonal world did not appeal to a majority of readers, either, though the movement was extremely influential.

Pat Cadigan is one of the few female writers considered a cyberpunk. Her *Mindplayers* (1987) features female characters just as hard-hitting as male street punks. Other women science fiction writers, like Joan Slonczewski, contributed more human-centered, optimistic works. Her 1986 novel *The Door into Ocean* depicts a pacifist female society in conflict with an aggressive male one. Margaret Atwood's *The Handmaid's Tale* (1988) shows a future where women have no legal rights and actually assist in their own repression. Sherri Tepper in *The Gate to Women's Country* (1988) presents a world where it has been discovered that men carry genetic patterning for a preference for war, a trait that is being selectively bred out. All these works show societies where gender issues and the relationship between men and women is more important than technological progress, which is worthless without some concern for what impact it will have on humans.

Lois McMaster Bujold produced *Falling Free* (1988), a novel about humans genetically altered to work in space and who would be physically handicapped on Earth. It is neither feminist nor cyberpunk, but a more mainstream science fiction piece. Many authors were dissatisfied with being referred to as a "type," causing Orson Scott Card, even though he wrote the cyberpunk story "Dogwalker" in 1989, to criticize the subgenre as more style than content. By the end of the eighties the newest "movement" in science fiction was on its way out, and by the nineties it had virtually disappeared.

SCIENCE FICTION IN OTHER MEDIA

Science fiction made strides in other media in the eighties. Comics became more involved, and in 1985 to 1986 Frank Miller revamped the Batman figure with *The Dark Knight Returns*. This is the story of an aging hero facing streetwise punks and a climactic battle with Superman. Finally, Batman must fake his own death in order to remain effective behind the scenes, leaving the action to younger heroes. With this classic work, the graphic novel came into its own as an art form. In 1986 Alan Moore and David Gibbons began a twelve-part graphic novel called *Watchmen* set in an alternate history where costumed superheroes exist as vigilantes. In many ways, it is an essay on the kind of society that needs such heroes, though it is a multi-layered story, with complex characters and situations.

The quality of TV science fiction improved during the eighties as well. *V* (1983-85) featured aliens who take on human form to disguise their lizard-like appearance. It was essentially a violent soap opera, though expensive to produce. *The Twilight Zone* (1985–87) was a revival of Rod Serling's series, which had to battle with producers over airing controversial themes on network television. *Star Trek: The Next Generation* (1987–94) avoided many of those problems by being produced for syndication. It had a new cast, a new ship, better special effects, and consistently good story lines. It eventually became the highest rated dramatic series on TV.

Alien Nation (1989–90), based on the movie of the same name, was a human and alien buddy series. Its major achievement was its sensitivity to depiction of aliens fleeing from enslavement and fighting against discrimination. *Quantum Leap* (1989–94) showed a time traveler trapped in other people's bodies, but always attempting to return to his own time in the future. He was helped by a holographic guide in his quest to right wrongs so he could move a step closer to achieving his goal.

The greatest advances in science fiction, though, were in the movies. A host of good science fiction appeared during the decade. *The Empire Strikes Back* (1980) was a worthy sequel to *Star Wars*. *The Road Warrior* (1981) showed Max, from *Mad Max,* in a radically altered post-apocalyptic world. *Bladerunner* (1982), based on Philip K. Dick's novel *Do Androids Dream of Electric Sheep,* featured intricately detailed sets, a prominent Asian presence, high-tech vehicles alongside bicycles, futuristic buildings coexisting with slums, and the story of a cop who hunts down artificial humans. It was the debut of cyberpunk in the cinema.

E. T.: The Extraterrestrial (1982) shows a friendly alien befriended by kids, who can relate to his dilemma as an outsider wishing to return home. *Star Trek: The Wrath of Khan* (1982) elaborated on a 1967 TV episode about a genetically altered group of exiled humans. *Videodrome* (1982) featured bodily metamorphosis, media overload leading to mind control, and destructive sex. The final part of the *Star Wars* trilogy, *Return of the Jedi* (1983), completed the storyline and remained consistent with the others in the series. *1984* (1984) was a remake of George Orwell's future vision of a media-controlled world. *The Terminator* (1984) is a time travel story about a robot-controlled society in the near future and the human battle to regain supremacy. In order to do this, they send a human back in time to prevent an assassination.

Aliens (1986) is a rare sequel, in that it is better than its predecessor, rather than just a continuation of the success of the original. *Batman* (1989), though not the dark knight of Miller's graphic novel, is a return to the urban vigilante's roots. Gotham is a dark, foreboding city with huge Gothic sculptures and a hero who obsessively questions why he needs to be Batman.

Valhalla

1986

GREGORY BENFORD (b. 1941)

Gregory Benford holds a Ph.D. in physics and has been a professor of physics as well as a science fiction writer since the mid-sixties. His first science fiction story, "Stand-In," was published in *The Magazine of Fantasy and Science Fiction* in 1965. He also was a regular contributor to the science column in *Amazing Stories* from 1969 to 1976.

With his background in science, Benford turned naturally to hard science fiction. His first novel was *Deeper than the Darkness* (1970), in which humans confront aliens with less than ideal results. He later revised this to fit into his *Ocean* novel series, all of which contain references to water. In the series, there is a continuing struggle between organic life and self-replicating machines, with the machines appearing to have the edge. He develops a similar theme in a trilogy begun with *Great Sky River* in 1987.

His 1980 novel *Timescape* won both the Hugo and John W. Campbell Memorial awards. Although his fiction is notable for its realistic scientific content, Benford's fiction has also been praised for its lyrical content, and critic Gary K. Wolfe even compared Benford's fiction with that of William Faulkner.

Much of the best of his short fiction has been collected in *In Alien Flesh* (1986), and he has also co-edited a number of anthologies, including *Hitler Victorious* (1986), *Nuclear War* (1988), and two alternate history collections, bound together as *What Might Have Been, Volumes I and II* (1990).

In "Valhalla," Gregory Benford explores an alternate history, one in which Hitler's World War II campaigns are much more successful, but with unexpected consequences.

1   Adolf Hitler worked the action of the pistol. He clacked a round into the chamber. He stared at it.

2   Eva Braun numbly picked up the cyanide capsule from the table in front of them. She opened her mouth slightly and stared glassily at the small pill.

3   They sat on a rich red couch that stood out from the bleak gray concrete of the bunker walls. Hitler's face was puffy and waxen.

4   "Bite down hard," he said in a flat, rough way that was barely like the famous harsh, powerful voice of the ancient films.

5   He raised the muzzle of the Lüger to his temple. Eva sighed softly and opened her mouth again. So there were to be no last, loving words.

6   That was when I chose to materialize.

7   Hitler caught the ultraviolet flicker as I came into being before them. *"Ich sagt—"* he said harshly, rasping, and my pickups translated, "I said we were to be left for ten minutes—" and then he saw me.

8   I was gratified at his shock. I looked exactly like him.

9   I wore the same clothes, the general's gray field uniform, with the high-peaked hat. All details were correct, even down to the pale, sickly face and the trembling hand, a reminder of the assassination attempt by his own Army officers.

10   He pressed it against his left side. Echoing him, I did the same. I stepped over a broken wine bottle, my boots crunching on the glass, and said, *"Führer!* I have come to you across a thousand years to this, your supreme moment."

11   It was a perhaps a bit florid, but our analysts had calculated that it would strike the correct note. There had been much high-flown, desperate rhetoric in these final days in Berlin. In his state of depression and nervous collapse Hitler could respond only to the most exaggerated of statements. He had ignored Albert Speer when the man came to make his farewell some days ago. Speer was an exact, cool type. Such a manner would not work for my purposes.

12   "I . . . you look. . . ." He waved the Lüger vaguely, eyes watery.

13   I moved swiftly and took the pistol. The primary thing to avoid was any sound that would cause the staff officers outside to open the heavy door. If they came in and found us, history would be altered and our entire scheme would fail. I would be flung forward into the future. Hitler would still kill himself, most probably, but the perturbation of the time flow would prevent us from ever returning to this moment.

14   "Yes, I can explain that," I murmured. "Madame?"

15   I leaned over Eva and gently lowered the hand that held the cyanide. She would not disturb events if she was treated formally; that much was clear from the personality profile we had reconstructed from historical

data. She glanced at Hitler and began wringing her hands. On her face conflicting emotions warred, but there was no resoluteness, no projection of focused intelligence. I could see the psychotheorists had been wrong about her. She was no canny power behind the throne.

16   Hitler said, "If this is a plan of Goebbels—"

17   *"Führer*, this is no futile attempt—"

18   "I will *not* leave Berlin. I will not allow a, a *dummy* to take my place." He raised a trembling finger and shouted. "I will *not* run and sneak and hide from my subhuman enemies who—"

19   "Of course not. The world will respect what you do here."

20   "This cheap joke! You dressed up!—I will not have it!"

21   Hitler leaped to his feet, full of raving bantam energy. His eyes bulged with a sudden fury, more like the old films. I had to cut him off before the staff outside heard. It would mean a change in the scenario we had worked out, but that could not be helped.

22   "Immortality, *Führer!* That is what I offer. I have come to you from the future!"

23   He paused. "What . . . ?"

24   I rushed ahead. "Think of the times ahead, *Führer.* There will be glorious days again—I know. I have come from there. More than a thousand years from now you will be the most famous of all men from this time."

25   He faltered and the rage in him burned away. Exhaustion returned to the ruined face. "I . . . a thousand . . ."

26   I had lied only slightly about his fame. There was a physicist whose name had greater weight in our time, but it would not be wise to mention it. It was an odd coincidence that they both lived in the same land at the same time.

27   And a larger lie: I was not merely from a future age. Physics was not so simple. But subtleties such as that could scarcely penetrate the swarming mad mind I addressed.

28   Still, my own code of honor demanded that I make only minor excursions from the truth. I would have to be careful.

29   "Your world goals, *Führer*—would you like to know how they fared?"

30   "I . . . goals . . . ?" He seemed in a daze. "Jewry . . ."

31   "Yes! To cleanse Europe of Jewry! And the destiny of Germany, sir?"

32   "Deutschland . . . it is finished . . . their own weakness . . . not my do-ing . . . I gave my all . . . but there were . . . cowards . . . traitors . . . spies . . ."

33   "You fought to make Germany the dominant power in Europe, yes? I am able to tell you, *Führer,* that fifty years after this dark day, it was done!"

34   "Deutschland . . . destroyed . . . Berlin . . . ."

35   "Jewry never returned to the body of Europe, *Führer!* They never returned to your homeland in such numbers again, ever." This was true, but

not for the reasons he would imagine. "And Germany shall rise from its ashes. Its economy shall excel the Bolsheviks, equal the American capitalists within four decades."

36   He brightened. He looked at me and then at Eva. "Is this . . . can you be . . . Eva . . ."

37   "That is how the future of Europe will be. You have done your great task." I smiled and clicked my bootheels together.

38   He would not catch the irony in the gesture, or in the word "great"— he was too embedded in his own fantasies. Yet I had quite strictly told the truth. He had broken down the whole structure of the world he was born into, and left behind a Germany and a Europe deeply divided. These events were great in the sense of their size and implications. He would, of course, interpret the word in a different sense. That was what I expected, but it did not alter the fact that I had told the truth. To achieve a noble end one must keep to the truth.

39   Eva Braun said in a strained, thin voice, "Adolf, it is as you said it would be. Your faith . . ."

40   Hitler brightened, his eyes rolling with sudden fresh excitement. The man still had some crazed inner reserves. "Yes! I knew it! I held to the dream of Deutschland when all those around me failed. Indomitable! And this, this—"

41   "*Führer*, there is little time," I said rapidly, soothingly. "I come from a society you cannot envision, but in my time you are understood better than now." This, too, was true. We could analyze the past with the tools of exact sociometric theory. "We are devoted to justice. We look backward to your time and we see errors, great unfairness. My people have sent me to you, to correct injustice."

42   He frowned, blinked. He wavered, almost reeled. What fresh fantasies did my words summon up for him? His hands jerked, clasping at empty air.

43   As we had suspected, though there would be bursts of the old energy, he was near collapse. Probably he was unable to understand much of what I said. My subtle phrasings surely eluded him.

44   "For you to die here by your own hand, *Führer,* after all that you have done—such an outcome is, to my society, unthinkable." I smiled again.

45   Hitler's gaze shifted. For a moment I thought he was going to faint and all our hopes would be dashed.

46   But no—he was staring at the room behind me. It was the sitting room of his personal suite, crowded with curious wooden furniture. The dregs of parties—pieces of discarded clothing, bottles, half-finished plates of animal-flesh food—were scattered through it. But Hitler was staring at the blue aura behind me. I saw suddenly that it framed me in a halo of fire.

47   Hitler's eyes widened as this registered. He took a step forward. "Valkyrie!" he cried.

48   I calculated swiftly. *Valkyrie.* My translating subsystem told me that this meant, literally, the chooser of the slain. They were maidens who conducted the souls of heroes slain in battle to Valhalla.

49   In some deranged way Hitler thought the future I was describing was a Nordic heaven.

50   I was tempted to let him think so. But then I saw that to do so would be unjust to him. He had to make as informed a choice as was possible. Honor demanded that.

51   "No, *Führer,*" I said quickly. "You are not destined for Valhalla yet. There is no need to die. I—"

52   "I am the greatest warrior the world has ever seen!" He stiffened. Spine straight, he thrust out his chest. The smoldering fury kindled again. "I destroyed the Poles, the simpering French, the—"

53   "Of course, in our time we know this," I said in soothing tones. "Have no doubts. Though I come from more than a millennium in the future, this war remains the largest the world has ever seen." I did not add that the explosions to come in a few months would end forever the possibility of a rational large-scale conflict, and this fact more than any other made the Second World War so important an event.

54   "Adolf," Eva said soothingly, "this man is not a god. He says he is from the—"

55   "I heard! I saw a vision once ... on the Rhine ... the blue ..."

56   He moved unsteadily to touch the ultraviolet shimmer behind me. I stepped aside, but the glow followed me. The portal was still centered on me and Hitler could not reach it. He grasped at it a few times and then vaguely let his arms drop.

57   "She is correct, sir," I said. "My society has sent me back to this moment to rescue you. Your life should not end here. I will take you into the far future, *Führer.* Into a more just world, where—"

58   His head snapped up. Abruptly he was the man he had once been, vibrant, possessed. "Very well! I see a glowing blue Valhalla and you tell me it is the future. These are names! Only names! I saw it there on the Rhine and now I see it for what it truly *is*—" He raised a finger, wagging it dramatically, as in the old days."—And the dreams, my dreams are not finished. I knew it! Goebbels told me never to submit, and I have not! I have held on, and now you come for me. It is as I—"

59   There was a hollow knock at the door.

60   Hitler blinked and then smiled. He turned toward the door. "They... outside ... if they can see this it will put backbone into my generals ... I will ..."

61   This was crucial. I put out a restraining hand. "No, it is not possible."

62   "What? If they see you, see——"

63   "*Führer,* history—the history of this particular world—depends on your staff never seeing you again. In their eyes you will die in here."

64   "I ... do not ..."

65   "It is the natural order of things. I have come to save you for the future. There is nothing more you can do for Germany, this land that did not deserve you."

66   I spoke passionately, for I believed these words. They had their effect. Hitler nodded wearily and said raggedly, "Deutschland . . . did not stand by me ... deserves this ...."

67   Eva Braun said clearly, "This is why you are dressed so."

68   I nodded. She was more clever than the historians had thought. Intellectuals, they always underestimate the natural shrewdness of those in the distant past.

69   But Hitler ignored her remark. Perhaps with his damaged ears he had not even heard it. He smiled, mouth twisted into an arrogant smirk.

70   "I rescued Mussolini, yes? It is only right that some higher power should in turn save me, eh?" He paused, lost in his dulled thoughts. I remembered that Mussolini had been captured by partisans only a few days before, and shot, and then hung upside down in a marketplace with his mistress, for all the crowd to see. That memory was, we thought, the reason why Hitler and Eva Braun were taking this way out. But Hitler chose now to remember only his troops' rescue. This was typical of the irreality that pervaded his bunker in these last days.

71   "I am the architect of National Socialism and without me it will die, die, and ..."

72   He was rambling now. I stepped backward, knocking aside a broken chair, and checked the parameter matrices around the blue corona of the portal. It detached from me and filled with motes of orange and yellow.

73   "I built it ... there was no one else who saw the vision ..." He was right, of course. The other great doomed movement of the era had Marx and Lenin and Stalin, but National Socialism was the work of a single figure.

74   And all that was still roughly true, in my own timeline. The truth—far too technical to convey to this addled tyrant—was that I was not from *his* future. The laws of causality and of mass-energy conservation prevented me from diving directly into my own past. I had to trans-slip sidewise to this similar world, to move both in time and in probability-space. Otherwise causality paradoxes would rend me, atom from atom, in one curt crimson flash.

75   I came from an alternate world, in which Hitler's legions had mastered the Soviets. The crucial difference lay in the 1942 Churchill Treaty,

which resolved the sluggish war on the western front, giving the German General Staff a free hand in the vast steppes of the East.

76   Only the American entrance in 1943, prompted by the hugely stupid Japanese attack at Pearl Harbor, kept the war going. German submarine attacks on American shipping renewed the western war, leading to a final, crushing defeat for Germany in 1947.

77   By then the Final Solution had been carried out in full. The Gypsies, the Jews, millions of assorted Slavs . . .

78   Those years left a black stain on all civilization, one far worse than in this particular probability-world. Yet this Hitler before me was cut from the same cloth. In my world he had been victorious for longer, done darker deeds. And left even deeper hatreds that had simmered a century without diminishing.

79   In our world Hitler had grown fat in the stalemate of the middle 1940s, toasted by the occupied nations, honored as a demigod in vast torchlit rites in the thronged streets of Munich. His pudgy, satisfied face beamed down from posters, content, serenely presiding over the muffled cries of the continuing slaughter that spread through all of Europe. When German engineers began the first television broadcasts, Hitler used them with the intuitive genius he had displayed in his stadium speeches, manipulating his people with a dark, skillful fury.

80   Its job finished in Germany, the SS became more systematic and careful in the extermination of a new general category of hapless souls, the *Reichs*-criminals. Hitler victorious had not mellowed, but he directed the press to portray him that way. The propaganda campaign did much to undermine the Allied resolve, delaying the German defeat by years.

81   And in turn, carving the horror of that decade of catastrophe into the memory of the survivors.

82   This world had gotten off easy . . .

83   A pounding on the door. In another instant the generals might force it open.

84   *"Führer!* Go now!"

85   "I . . ." He turned slowly to the couch. "Eva . . ."

86   She did not rise. She knew.

87   I had to seize the moment, to deflect his thoughts toward his destiny. "There is a greater end awaiting you. Take it now!"

88   I laid a hand on his shoulder and urged him forward. I did not push. I merely helped.

89   Eva Braun did not rise. As I helped the old man forward, I saw her pick up the capsule from the table.

90   I felt the fields clutch at him, pull him away from me. There.

91   Quickly I sat on the couch.

92   The Lüger!—there it was, on the table.

93   He had been holding it in his right hand. I grasped it the way he had and checked the action. It was ready.

94   Eva Braun was holding the cyanide, looking at me.

95   I said to her, "You must understand. There are reasons why he must go alone. It is—" I had difficulty looking into her eyes. "It is for the best. The best for you."

96   She said nothing. I knew I should force her but that would be wrong. And I could not pull the trigger for myself until she had taken the poison. The texts were clear on that point—she had died of poison.

97   I spoke rapidly, fixing her watery eyes with mine to keep her from looking toward the murmuring blue aura.

98   "You see, we are a society devoted to justice. We have perfected it in our time to a degree you cannot imagine. It is the consuming passion of our age. We indulge ourselves, perhaps. This era was a great, warping trial, in my world. We must expunge its traces in our collective psyche."

99   "You make no sense . . ." she said wanly, clasping the pill.

100   "I cannot explain. Our ways are alien to you. We cannot alter the history of this era, and we are blocked from visiting our own past. Yet our people cry out for, for . . ."

101   I could not go on, could not summon up the words to name the emotions I—great-grandson of a man who had stayed in Europe then, despite his Gypsy origins—I felt sweep over me.

102   I gestured mutely at the blue corona. Hitler was partway through it now, moving in slow motion like a swimmer in deep water, as the tangled timelines warped around him, sucking him forward.

103   I looked at her beseechingly, and somehow she caught some flicker of my meaning. Eva Braun murmured, "I believe I understand."

104   She put the capsule in her mouth and bit down. I think she smiled at the last instant.

105   A sound from the door. I raised the muzzle to my temple. They would find the two bodies, as history said.

106   I looked up at Hitler swimming in the fluxlines and he rotated back toward me. He had seen ahead of him, into the room we had prepared for him.

107   He turned toward me and on his face I saw the surprise and the terror, witnessed the yawning scream begin. I would join him in an instant, when the bullet crashed into my brain and the life-essence that this ugly vat-grown body carried, the life-essence that was truly me, would return, drawn in through the closing portal and forward into my unforgetting future, where Hitler would be trapped.

108   No sound escaped from that pocket of folded space-time. Only cool blue, remorseless light poured through.

109   For a last abiding moment I savored the image of Hitler turning, spinning in the crackling blue aura, his mouth stretched wide, trying to flee from the sight of the devices and machines and animals ahead of him. Turning fruitlessly away from the things that would do justice at last, and could bring bubbling up in him an infinite pain, infinitely prolonged.

110   I pulled the trigger, eager to slip through the portal, eager to hear Hitler's scream.

DISCUSSION QUESTIONS

1. The opening conversations between Hitler and his visitor hint at a hidden agenda. How are both history and sociology important to the protagonist?

2. What does the narrator mean when he says that "To achieve a noble end one must keep to the truth"? Discuss your response with a classmate.

3. Hitler sees his savior as a Valkyrie—one who is sent to transport him to Valhalla, or the Nordic Heaven. How does this differ from the reality he eventually faces?

4. Why is it important that the protagonist not force Hitler into the future, but merely help him?

5. Why must Eva Braun stay behind? Why does she "almost smile" at the end?

WRITING TOPICS

1. Hitler is given credit for establishing National Socialism, an accomplishment compared to the creation of communism in the Soviet Union. In two or three paragraphs, discuss how such a movement could act as a strong unifying force for a struggling country, and what disadvantages it could also present.

2. The justice the narrator brings to Hitler comes from a thousand years in the future. In an essay, show how the crimes he is credited with in the story could cause such incredible perseverance in pursuit of justice. Can you think of any situations where such tenacity would be justifiable? Could such a solution turn out to be double-edged?

3. In your journal, explain why you think a story about Hitler and justice would appear in 1986 instead of 1946.

Skin Deep

1987

KRISTINE KATHRYN RUSCH (b. 1960)

Kristine Kathryn Rusch's first science fiction story, "Sing," was published in *Aboriginal Science Fiction* in 1987, and in 1990 she won the John W. Campbell Memorial award for Best New Writer. Her work is strongly emotional and often features characters going through rites of passage. She writes both fantasy and science fiction pieces. Her first novel, *The White Mists of Power* (1991) is fantasy, while her second, *The Gallery of His Dreams* (1991) is a science fiction time travel novel which features the noted Civil War photographer Matthew B. Brady.

Rusch is also a prominent editor and anthologist. She cofounded Pulphouse Publishing with Dean Wesley Smith in 1987 and edited the magazine *Pulphouse: The Hardback Magazine*. She also produced the anthology of that magazine's stories, *The Best of Pulphouse: The Hardback Magazine,* in 1991. In addition, she has been the editor of *The Magazine of Fantasy and Science Fiction* since 1991.

In "Skin Deep," Kristine Kathryn Rusch explores how deep beneath the surface our humanity runs.

1   "More pancakes, Colin?"

2   Cullaene looked down at his empty plate so that he wouldn't have to meet Mrs. Fielding's eyes. The use of his alias bothered him more than usual that morning.

3   "Thank you, no, ma'am. I already ate so much I could burst. If I take another bite, Jared would have to carry me out to the fields."

4   Mrs. Fielding shot a glance at her husband. Jared was using the last of his pancake to sop up the syrup on his plate.

5   "On a morning as cold as this, you should eat more," she said as she scooped up Cullaene's plate and set it in the sterilizer. "You could use a little fat to keep you warm."

6   Cullaene ran his hand over the stubble covering his scalp. Not taking thirds was a mistake, but to take some now would compound it. He would have to watch himself for the rest of the day.

7   Jared slipped the dripping bit of pancake into his mouth. He grinned and shrugged as he inclined his head toward his wife's back. Cullaene understood the gesture. Jared had used it several times during the week Cullaene worked for them. The farmer knew that his wife seemed pushy, but he was convinced that she meant well.

8   "More coffee, then?" Mrs. Fielding asked. She stared at him as if she were waiting for another mistake.

9   "Please." Cullaene handed her his cup. He hated the foreign liquid that colonists drank in gallons. It burned the back of his throat and churned restlessly in his stomach. But he didn't dare say no.

10 Mrs. Fielding poured his coffee, and Cullaene took a tentative sip as Lucy entered the kitchen. The girl kept tugging her loose sweater over her skirt. She slipped into her place at the table and rubbed her eyes with the heel of her hand.

11 "You're running late, little miss," her father said gently.

12 Lucy nodded. She pushed her plate out of her way and rested both elbows on the table. "I don't think I'm going today, Dad."

13 "Going?" Mrs. Fielding exclaimed. "Of course, you'll go. You've had a perfect attendance record for three years, Luce. It's no time to break it now—"

14 "Let her be, Elsie," Jared said. "Can't you see she doesn't feel well?"

15 The girl's skin was white, and her hands were trembling. Cullaene frowned. She made him nervous this morning. If he hadn't known her parentage, he would have thought she was going to have her first Change. But the colonists had hundreds of diseases with symptoms like hers. And she was old enough to begin puberty. Perhaps she was about to begin her first menstrual period.

16   Apparently, Mrs. Fielding was having the same thoughts, for she placed her hand on her daughter's forehead. "Well, you don't have a fever," she said. Then her eyes met Cullaene's. "Why don't you men get busy? You have a lot to do today."

17   Cullaene slid his chair back, happy to leave his full cup of coffee sitting on the table. He pulled on the thick jacket that he had slung over the back of his chair and let himself out the back door.

18   Jared joined him on the porch. "Think we can finish plowing under?"

19   Cullaene nodded. The great, hulking machine sat in the half-turned field like a sleeping monster. In a few minutes, Cullaene would climb into the cab and feel the strange gears shiver under his fingers. Jared had said that the machine was old and delicate, but it had to last at least three more years—colonist's years—or they would have to do the seeding by hand. There was no industry on the planet yet. The only way to replace broken equipment was to send to Earth for it, and that took time.

20   Just as Cullaene turned toward the field, a truck floated onto the landing. He began to walk, as if the arrival of others didn't concern him, but he knew they were coming to see him. The Fieldings seldom had visitors.

21   "Colin!" Jared was calling to him. Cullaene stopped, trying not to panic. He had been incautious this time. Things had happened too fast. He wondered what the colonists would do. Would they imprison him, or would they hurt him? Would they give him a chance to explain the situation and then let him go?

22   Three colonists, two males and a female, were standing outside the truck. Jared was trying to get them to go toward the house.

23   "I'll meet you inside," Cullaene shouted back. For a moment he toyed with running. He stared out over the broad expanse of newly cultivated land, toward the forest and rising hills beyond it. Somewhere in there he might find an enclave of his own people, a group of Abandoned Ones who hadn't assimilated, but the chances of that were small. His people had always survived by adaptation. The groups of Abandoned Ones had grown smaller every year.

24   He rubbed his hands together. His skin was too dry. If only he could pull off this self-imposed restraint for an hour, he would lie down in the field and encase himself in mud. Then his skin would emerge as soft and pure as the fur on Jared's cats. But he needed his restraint now more than ever. He pulled his jacket tighter and let himself into the kitchen once more.

25   He could hear the voices of Lucy and her mother rise in a heated discussion from upstairs. Jared had pressed the recycle switch on the old coffee maker, and it was screeching in protest. The three visitors were seated around the table, the woman in Cullaene's seat, and all of them turned as he entered the room.

26   He nodded and sat by the sterilizer. The heat made his back tingle, and the unusual angle made him feel like a stranger in the kitchen where he had supped for over a week. The visitors stared at him with the same cold look he had seen on the faces of the townspeople.

27   "This is Colin," Jared said. "He works for me."

28   Cullaene nodded again. Jared didn't introduce the visitors, and Cullaene wondered if it was an intentional oversight.

29   "We would like to ask you a few questions about yourself," the woman said. She leaned forward as she spoke, and Cullaene noted that her eyes were a vivid blue.

30   "May I ask why?"

31   Jared's hand shook as he poured the coffee. "Colin, it's customary around here—"

32   "No," the woman interrupted. "It is not customary. We're talking with all the strangers. Surely your hired man has heard of the murder."

33   Cullaene started. He took the coffee cup Jared offered him, relieved that his own hand did not shake. "No, I hadn't heard."

34   "We don't talk about such things in this house, Marlene," Jared said to the woman.

35   Coffee cups rattled in the silence as Jared finished serving everyone. The older man, leaning against the wall behind the table, waited until Jared was through before he spoke.

36   "It's our first killing in *this* colony, and it's a ghastly one. Out near the ridge, we found the skin of a man floating in the river. At first, we thought it was a body because the water filled the skin like it would fill a sack. Most of the hair was in place, hair so black that when it dried its highlights were blue. We couldn't find any clothes—"

37   "—or bones for that matter," the other man added.

38   "That's right," the spokesman continued. "He had been gutted. We scoured the area for the rest of him, and up on the ridge we found blood."

39   " A great deal of it," Marlene said. "As if they had skinned him while he was still alive."

40   Cullaene had to wrap his fingers around the hot cup to keep them warm. He hadn't been careful enough. Things had happened so swiftly that he hadn't had a chance to go deeper into the woods. He felt the fear that had been quivering in the bottom of his stomach settle around his heart.

41 "And so you're questioning all of the strangers here to see if they could have done it." He spoke as if he were more curious than frightened.

42 Marlene nodded. She ran a long hand across her hairline to catch any loose strands.

43 "I didn't kill anyone," Cullaene said. "I'll answer anything you ask."

44 They asked him careful, probing questions about his life before he had entered their colony, and he answered with equal care, being as truthful as he possibly could. He told them that the first colony he had been with landed on ground unsuitable for farming. The colonists tried hunting and even applied for a mining permit, but nothing worked. Eventually, most returned to Earth. He remained, traveling from family to family, working odd jobs while he tried to find a place to settle. As he spoke, he mentioned occasional details about himself, hoping that the sparse personal comments would prevent deeper probing. He told them about the Johansens whose daughter he had nearly married, the Cassels who taught him how to cultivate land, and the Slingers who nursed him back to health after a particularly debilitating illness. Cullaene told them every place he had ever been except the one place they were truly interested in—the woods that bordered the Fieldings' farm.

45 He spoke in a gentle tone that Earthlings respected. And he watched Jared's face because he knew that Jared, of any of them, would be the one to realize that Cullaene was not and never had been a colonist. Jared had lived on the planet for fifteen years. Once he had told Cullaene proudly that Lucy, though an orphan, was the first member of this colony born on the planet.

46 The trust in Jared's eyes never wavered. Cullaene relaxed slightly. If Jared didn't recognize him, no one would.

47 "They say that this is the way the natives commit murder," Marlene said when Cullaene finished. "We've heard tales from other colonies of bodies—both human and Riiame—being found like this."

48 Cullaene realized that she was still questioning him. "I never heard of this kind of murder before."

49 She nodded. As if by an unseen cue, all three of them stood. Jared stood with them. "Do you think Riiame could be in the area?" he asked.

50 "It's very likely," Marlene said. "Since you live so close to the woods, you should probably take extra precautions."

51 "Yes." Jared glanced over at his well-stocked gun cabinet. "I plan to."

52 The men nodded their approval and started out the door. Marlene turned to Cullaene. "Thank you for your cooperation," she said. "We'll let you know if we have any further questions."

53 Cullaene stood to accompany them out, but Jared held him back. "Finish your coffee. We have plenty of time to get to the fields later."

54   After they went out the door, Cullaene took his coffee and moved to
his own seat. Lucy and her mother were still arguing upstairs. He took
the opportunity to indulge himself in a quick scratch of his hands and
arms. The heat had made the dryness worse.

55   He wondered if he had been convincing. The three looked as if they
had already decided what happened. A murder. He shook his head.

56   A door slammed upstairs, and the argument grew progressively
louder. Cullaene glanced out the window over the sterilizer. Jared was
still talking with the three visitors. Cullaene hoped they'd leave soon.
Then maybe he'd talk to Jared, explain as best he could why he could no
longer stay.

57   "Where are you going?" Mrs. Fielding shouted. Panic touched the
edge of her voice.

58   "Away from you!" Lucy sounded on the verge of tears. Cullaene
could hear her stamp her way down the stairs. Suddenly, the footsteps
stopped. "No! You stay away from me! I need time to think!"

59   "You can't have time to think! We've got to find out what's wrong."

60   "Nothing's wrong!"

61   "Lucy—"

62   "You take another step and I swear I'll leave!" Lucy backed her way
into the kitchen, slammed the door, and leaned on it. Then she noticed
Cullaene, and all the fight left her face.

63   "How long have you been here?" she whispered.

64   He poured his now-cold coffee into the recycler that they had set
aside for him. "I won't say anything to your father, if that's what you're
worried about. I don't even know why you were fighting."

65   There was no room left in the sterilizer, so he set the cup next to the
tiny boiler that purified the ground water. Lucy slid a chair back, and it
creaked as she sat in it. Cullaene took another glance out the window.
Jared and his visitors seemed to be arguing.

66   What would he do if they decided he was guilty? He couldn't disappear. They had a description of him that they would send to other
colonies. He could search for the Abandoned Ones, but even if he found
them, they might not take him in. He had lived with the colonists all his
life. He looked human, and sometimes, he even felt human.

67   Something crashed behind him. Cullaene turned in time to see Lucy
stumble over her chair as she backed away from the overturned coffee
maker. Coffee ran down the wall, and the sterilizer hissed. He hurried to
her side, moved the chair, and got her to a safer corner of the kitchen.

68   "Are you all right?" he asked.

69   She nodded. A tear slipped out of the corner of her eye. "I didn't
grab it tight, I guess."

70   "Why don't you sit down. I'll clean it up—" Cullaene stopped as Lucy's tear landed on the back of his hand. The drop was heavy and lined with red. He watched it leave a pink trail as it rolled off his skin onto the floor. Slowly, he looked up into her frightened eyes. More blood-filled tears threatened. He wiped one from her eyelashes and rolled it around between his fingertips.

71   Suddenly, she tried to pull away from him, and he tightened his grip on her arm. He slid back the sleeve of her sweater. The flesh hung in folds around her elbow and wrist. He touched her wrist lightly and noted that the sweat from her pores was also rimmed in blood.

72   "How long?" he whispered. "How long has this been happening to you?"

73   The tears began to flow easily now. It looked as if she were bleeding from her eyes. "Yesterday morning."

74   He shook his head. "It had to start sooner than that. You would have itched badly. Like a rash."

75   "A week ago."

76   He let her go. Poor girl. A week alone without anyone telling her anything. She would hurt by now. The pain and the weakness would be nearly intolerable.

77   "What is it?" Her voice was filled with fear.

78   Cullaene stared at her, then, as the full horror finally reached him. He had been prepared from birth for the Change, but Lucy thought she was human. And suddenly he looked out the window again at Jared. Jared, who had found the orphaned girl without even trying to discover anything about the type of life form he raised. Jared, who must have assumed that because the child looked human, she was human.

79   She was rubbing her wrist. The skin was already so loose that the pressure of his hand hadn't left a mark on it.

80   "It's normal," he said. "It's the Change. The first time—the first time can be painful, but I can help you through it."

81   The instant he said the words, he regretted them. If he helped her, he'd have to stay. He was about to contradict himself when the kitchen door clicked shut.

82   Mrs. Fielding looked at the spilled coffee, then at the humped skin on Lucy's arm. The older woman seemed frightened and vulnerable. She held out her hand to her daughter, but Lucy didn't move. "She's sick," Mrs. Fielding said.

83   "Sick?" Cullaene permitted himself a small ironic smile. These people didn't realize what they had done to Lucy. "How do you know? You've never experienced anything like this before, have you?"

84   Mrs. Fielding was flushed. "Have you?"

85   "Of course, I have. It's perfectly normal development in an adult Riiame."

86   "And you'd be able to help her?"

87   The hope in her voice mitigated some of his anger. He could probably trust Mrs. Fielding to keep his secret. She had no one else to turn to right now. "I was able to help myself."

88   "You're Riiame?" she whispered. Suddenly, the color drained from her face. "Oh, my God."

89   Cullaene could feel a chill run through him. He'd made the wrong choice. Before he was able to stop her, she had pulled the porch door open. "Jared!" she called. "Get in here right away! Colin—Colin says he's a Riiame!"

90   Cullaene froze. She couldn't be saying that. Not now. Not when her daughter was about to go through one of life's most painful experiences unprepared. Lucy needed him right now. Her mother couldn't help her, and neither could the other colonists. If they tried to stop the bleeding, it would kill her.

91   He had made his decision. He grabbed Lucy and swung her horizontally across his back, locking her body in position with his arms. She was kicking and pounding on his side. Mrs. Fielding started to scream. Cullaene let go of Lucy's legs for a moment, grabbed the doorknob, and let himself out into the hallway. Lucy had her feet braced against the floor, forcing him to drag her. He continued to move swiftly toward the front door. When he reached it, he yanked it open and ran into the cold morning air.

92   Lucy had almost worked herself free. He shifted her slightly against his back and managed to capture her knees again. The skin had broken where he touched her. She would leave a trail of blood.

93   The girl was so frightened that she wasn't even screaming. She hit him in the soft flesh of his side, then leaned over and bit him. The pain almost made him drop her. Suddenly, he spun around and tightened his grip on her.

94   "I'm trying to help you," he said. "Now stop it."

95   She stopped struggling and rested limply in his arms. Cullaene found himself hating the Fieldings. Didn't they know there would be questions? Perhaps they could explain the Change as a disease, but what would happen when her friends began to shrivel with age and she remained as young and lovely as she was now? Who would explain that to her?

96   He ran on a weaving path through the trees. If Jared was thinking, he would know where Cullaene was taking Lucy. But all Cullaene needed was time. Lucy was so near the Change now that it wouldn't take too

long to help her through it. But if the others tried to stop it, no matter how good their intentions, they could kill or disfigure the girl.

97 Cullaene was sobbing air into his lungs. His chest burned. He hadn't run like this in a long time, and Lucy's extra weight was making the movements more difficult. As if the girl could read his thoughts, she began struggling again. She bent her knees and jammed them as hard as she could into his kidneys. He almost tripped, but managed to right himself just in time. The trees were beginning to thin up ahead, and he smelled the thick spice of the river. It would take the others a while to reach him. They couldn't get the truck in here. They would have to come by foot. Maybe he'd have enough time to help Lucy and to get away.

98 Cullaene broke into the clearing. Lucy gasped as she saw the ridge. He had to bring her here. She needed the spicy water—and the height. He thought he could hear someone following him now, and he prayed he would have enough time. He had so much to tell her. She had to know about the pigmentation changes, and the possibilities of retaining some skin. But most of all, she had to do what he told her, or she'd be deformed until the next Change, another ten years away.

99 He bent in half and lugged her up the ridge. The slope of the land was slight enough so that he kept his balance, but great enough to slow him down. He could feel Lucy's heart pounding against his back. The child thought he was going to kill her, and he didn't know how he would overcome that.

100 When he reached the top of the ridge, he stood, panting, looking over the caramel-colored water. He didn't dare release Lucy right away. They didn't have much time, and he had to explain what was happening to her.

101 She had stopped struggling. She gripped him as if she were determined to drag him with her when he flung her into the river. In the distance, he could hear faint shouts.

102 "Lucy, I brought you up here for a reason," he said. Her fingers dug deeper into his flesh. "You're going through what my people call the Change. It's normal. It—"

103 "I'm not one of your people," she said. "Put me down!"

104 He stared across the sluggish river into the trees beyond. Even though he had just begun, he felt defeated. The girl had been human for thirteen years. He couldn't alter that in fifteen minutes.

105 "No, you're not." He set her down, but kept a firm grasp of her wrists. Her sweater and skirt were covered with blood. "But you were born here. Have you ever seen this happen to anyone else?"

106   He grabbed a loose fold of skin and lifted it. There was a sucking release as the skin separated from the wall of the body. Lucy tried to pull away from him. He drew her closer. "Unfortunately, you believe you are human and so the first one to undergo this. I'm the only one who can help you. I'm a Riiame. This has happened to me."

107   "You don't look like a Riiame."

108   He held back a sharp retort. There was so much that she didn't know. Riiame were a shape-shifting people. Parents chose the form of their children at birth. His parents had had enough foresight to give him a human shape. Apparently, so had hers. But she had only seen the Abandoned Ones who retained the shape of the hunters that used to populate the planet's forests.

109   A cry echoed through the woods. Lucy looked toward it, but Cullaene shook her to get her attention again. "I am Riiame," he said. "Your father's friends claimed to have found a body here. But that body they found wasn't a body at all. It was my skin. I just went through the Change. I shed my skin just as you're going to. And then I came out to find work in your father's farm."

110   "I don't believe you," she said.

111   "Lucy, you're bleeding through every pore in your body. Your skin is loose. You feel as if you're floating inside yourself. You panicked when you saw your form outlined in blood on the sheets this morning, didn't you? And your mother, she noticed it, too, didn't she?"

112   Lucy nodded.

113   "You have got to trust me because in a few hours the blood will go away, the skin you're wearing now will stick to the new skin beneath it, and you will be ugly and deformed. And in time, the old skin will start to rot. Do you want that to happen to you?"

114   A bloody tear made its way down Lucy's cheek. "No," she whispered.

115   "All right then." Cullaene wouldn't let himself feel relief. He could hear unnatural rustling coming from the woods. "You're going to have to leave your clothes here. Then go to the edge of the ridge, reach your arms over your head to stretch the skin as much as you can, and jump into the river. It's safe, the river is very deep here. As soon as you can feel the cold water on every inch of your body, surface, go to shore, and wrap yourself in mud. That will prevent the itching from starting again."

116   The fear on her face alarmed him. "You mean I have to strip?"

117   He bit back his frustration. They didn't have time to work through human taboos. "Yes. Or the old skin won't come off."

118   Suddenly, he saw something flash in the woods below. It looked like the muzzle of a heat gun. Panic shot through him. Why was he risking his life to help this child? As soon as he emerged at the edge of

the ridge, her father would kill him. Cullaene let go of Lucy's wrists. Let her run if she wanted to. He was not going to let himself get killed. Not yet.

119   But to his surprise, Lucy didn't run. She turned her back and slowly pulled her sweater over her head. Then she slid off the rest of her clothes and walked to the edge of the ridge. Cullaene knew she couldn't feel the cold right now. Her skin was too far away from the nerve endings.

120   She reached the edge of the ridge, her toes gripping the rock as tightly as her fingers had gripped his arm, and then she turned to look back at him. "I can't," she whispered.

121   She was so close. Cullaene saw the blood working under the old skin, trying to separate all of it. "You have to," he replied, keeping himself in shadow. "Jump."

122   Lucy looked down at the river below her, and a shiver ran through her body. She shook her head.

123   "Do—?" Cullaene stopped himself. If he went into the open, they'd kill him. Then he stared at Lucy for a moment, and felt his resolve waver. "Do you want me to help you?"

124   He could see the fear and helplessness mix on her face. She wasn't sure what he was going to do, but she wanted to believe him. Suddenly, she set her jaw with determination. "Yes," she said softly.

125   Cullaene's hands went cold. "All right. I'm going to do this quickly. I'll come up behind you and push you into the river. Point your toes and fall straight. The river is deep and it moves slow. You'll be all right."

126   Lucy nodded and looked straight ahead. The woods around them were unnaturally quiet. He hurried out of his cover and grabbed her waist feeling the blood slide away from the pressure of his hands. He paused for a moment, knowing that Jared and his companions would not shoot while he held the girl.

127   "Point," he said, then pushed.

128   He could feel the air rush through his fingers as Lucy fell. Suddenly, a white heat blast stabbed his side, and he tumbled after her, whirling and flipping in the icy air. He landed on his stomach in the thick, cold water, knocking the wind out of his body. Cullaene knew that he should stay under and swim away from the banks, but he needed to breathe. He clawed his way to the surface, convinced he would die before he reached it. The fight seemed to take forever, and suddenly he was there, bobbing on top of the river, gasping air into his empty lungs.

129   Lucy's skin floated next to him, and he felt a moment of triumph before he saw Jared's heat gun leveled at him from the bank.

130   "Get out," the farmer said tightly. "Get out and tell me what you did with the rest of her before I lose my head altogether."

131   Cullaene could still go under and swim for it, but what would be the use? He wouldn't be able to change his pigmentation for another ten years or so, and if he managed to swim out of range of their heat guns, he would always be running.

132   With two long strokes, Cullaene swam to the bank and climbed out of the water. He shivered. It was cold, much too cold to be standing wet near the river. The spice aggravated his new skin's dryness.

133   Marlene, gun in hand, stood next to Jared, and the two other men were coming out of the woods.

134   "Where's the rest of her?" Jared asked. His arm was shaking. "On the ridge?"

135   Cullaene shook his head. He could have hit the gun from Jared's hand and run, but he couldn't stand to see the sadness, the defeat in the man who had befriended him.

136   "She'll be coming out of the water in a minute."

137   "You lie!" Jared screamed, and Cullaene saw with shock that the man had nearly snapped.

138   "No, she will." Cullaene hesitated for a moment. He didn't want to die to keep his people's secret. The Riiame always adapted. They'd adapt this time, too. "She's Riiame. You know that. This is normal for us."

139   "She's my daughter!"

140   "No, she's not. She can't be. This doesn't happen to humans."

141   A splash from the river bank drew his attention. Lucy pulled herself up alongside the water several feet from them. Her skin was fresh, pink and clean, and her bald head reflected patches of sunlight. She gathered herself into a fetal position and began to rock.

142   Cullaene started to go to her, but Jared grabbed him. Cullaene tried to shake his arm free, but Jared was too strong for him.

143   "She's not done yet," Cullaene said.

144   Marlene had come up beside them. "Let him go, Jared."

145   "He killed my daughter." Jared's grip tightened on Cullaene's arm.

146   "No, he didn't. She's right over there."

147   Jared didn't even look. "That's not my Lucy."

148   Cullaene swallowed hard. His heart was beating in his throat. He should have run when he had the chance. Now Jared was going to kill him.

149   "That is Lucy," Marlene said firmly. "Let him go, Jared. He has to help her."

150   Jared looked over at the girl rocking at the edge of the river bank. His hold loosened, and finally he let his hands drop. Cullaene took two steps backward and rubbed his arms. Relief was making him dizzy.

151   Marlene had put her arm around Jared as if she, too, didn't trust him. She was watching Cullaene to see what he'd do next. If he ran,

she'd get the other two to stop him. Slowly, he turned away from them and went to Lucy's side.

152 "You need mud, Lucy," he said as he dragged her higher onto the bank. She let him roll her into a cocoon. When he was nearly through, he looked at the man behind him.

153 Jared had dropped his weapon and was staring at Lucy's skin as it made its way down the river. Marlene still clutched her gun, but her eyes were on Jared, not Cullaene.

154 "Is she Riiame?" Marlene asked Jared.

155 The farmer shook his head. "I thought she was human!" he said. Then he raised his voice as if he wanted Cullaene to hear. "I thought she was human!"

156 Cullaene took a handful of mud and started painting the skin on Lucy's face. She had closed her eyes and was lying very still. She would need time to recover from the shock.

157 "I thought they were going to kill her," Jared said brokenly. "There were two of them and she was so little and I thought they were going to kill her." His voice dropped. "So I killed them first."

158 Cullaene's fingers froze on Lucy's cheek. Jared had killed Lucy's parents because they didn't look human. Cullaene dipped his hands in more mud and continued working. He hoped they would let him leave when he finished.

159 He placed the last of the mud on the girl's face. Jared came up beside him. "You're Riiame too, aren't you? And you look human."

160 Cullaene washed the mud from his shaking hands. He was very frightened. What would he do now? Leave with Lucy, and try to teach the child that she wasn't human at all? He turned to face Jared. "What are you going to do with Lucy?"

161 "Will she be okay?" the farmer asked.

162 Cullaene stared at Jared for a moment. All the color had drained from the farmer's face, and he looked close to tears. Jared had finally realized what he had done.

163 "She should be," Cullaene said. "But someone has to explain this to her. It'll happen again. And there are other things."

164 He stopped, remembering his aborted love affair with a human woman. Ultimately, their forms had proven incompatible. He wasn't really human, although it was so easy to forget that. He only appeared human.

165 "Other things?"

166 "Difficult things." Cullaene shivered again. He would get ill from these wet clothes. "If you want, I'll take her with me. You won't have to deal with her then."

167   "No." Jared reached out to touch the mud-encased girl, but his hand hovered over her shell, never quite resting on it. "She's my daughter. I raised her. I can't just let her run off and disappear."

168   Cullaene swallowed heavily. He didn't understand these creatures. They killed Abandoned Ones on a whim, professed fear and hatred of the Riiame, and then would offer to keep one in their home.

169   "That was your skin that they found, wasn't it?" Jared asked. "This just happened to you."

170   Cullaene nodded. His muscles were tense. He wasn't sure what Jared was going to do.

171   "Why didn't you tell us?"

172   Cullaene looked at Jared for a moment. Because, he wanted to say, the woman I loved screamed and spat at me when she found out. Because one farmer nearly killed me with an axe. Because your people don't know how to cope with anything different, even when *they* are the aliens on a new planet.

173   "I didn't think you'd understand," he said. Suddenly, he grabbed Jared's hand and set it on the hardening mud covering Lucy's shoulder. Then he stood up. There had to be Abandoned Ones in these woods. He would find them if Jared didn't kill him first. He started to walk.

174   "Colin," Jared began, but Cullaene didn't stop. Marlene reached his side and grabbed him. Cullaene glared at her, but she didn't let go. He was too frightened to hit her, too frightened to try to break free. If she held him, maybe they weren't going to kill him after all.

175   She ripped open the side of Cullaene's shirt and examined the damage left by the heat blast. The skin was puckered and withered, and Cullaene suddenly realized how much it ached.

176   "Can we treat this?" she asked.

177   "Are you asking for permission?" Cullaene could barely keep the sarcasm from his voice.

178   "No." The woman looked down and blushed deeply as some humans did when their shame was fullest. "I was asking if we had the skill."

179   Cullaene relaxed enough to smile. "You have the skill."

180   "Then," she asked. "May we treat you?"

181   Cullaene nodded. He allowed himself to be led back to Jared's side. Jared was staring at his daughter, letting tears fall onto the cocoon of mud.

182   "You can take her out of there soon," Cullaene said. "Her clothes are up on the ridge. I'll get them."

183   And before anyone could stop him, Cullaene went into the woods and started up the ridge. He could escape now. He could simply turn around and run away. But he wasn't sure he wanted to do that.

184   When he reached the top of the ridge, he peered down at Jared, his frightened daughter, and the woman who protected them. They had a lot

of explaining to do to Lucy. But if she was strong enough to survive the Change, she was strong enough to survive anything.

185   Cullaene draped her bloody clothes over his arm and started back down the ridge. When he reached the others, he handed the clothes to Marlene. Then Cullaene crouched beside Jared. Carefully, Cullaene made a hole in the mud and began to peel it off Lucy. Jared watched him for a moment. Then, he slipped his fingers into a crack, and together the alien and the native freed the girl from her handmade shell.

DISCUSSION QUESTIONS

1. Cullaene, as the narrator, early in the story identifies himself as an alien. Why is he hiding among the humans?
2. What reasons could there be for Cullaene being an outsider both among his own species and the human colonists?
3. The Fieldings see Lucy's condition as a disease. How does Cullaene perceive it?
4. After Lucy begins to change, Jared and Marlene react quite differently toward the Riiame. Show how both reactions are validated by the events of the story.
5. Cullaene gets a chance to escape at the end of the story. Why does he choose not to?

WRITING TOPICS

1. In your journal, discuss what it means to be human. Then share some of your thoughts with the entire class.
2. The inhabitants of Riiame are able to choose the shape of their off-spring, who then undergo a visible transformation at puberty, and periodically afterwards. In a paragraph or two, examine this analogy of change to manifestations exhibited by cultures that you are familiar with, and how it may relate to the point of this story.
3. In an essay, explore Rusch's emphasis on compassion and acceptance. Is it a reflection primarily of the growing concern over cultural diversity and political correctness of the late eighties, or is it mainly her personal vision of desirable human traits?

For I Have Touched the Sky

1989

MIKE RESNICK (b. 1942)

Mike Resnick began his writing career with a short book in the
Edgar Rice Burroughs vein called *The Forgotten Sea of Mars* (1965).
He continued this approach with *The Goddess of Ganymede* (1968)
and *Pursuit on Ganymede* (1968). He then produced a post-holocaust
novel, *Redbeard* (1969), set in the New York subway system, but
thereafter quickly turned to other genres and used a variety of
pseudonyms. It wasn't until 1980 that he returned to writing
science fiction and fantasy and resumed using his own name.

Resnick worked on three major series of novels during
the eighties. His *Tales of the Galactic Midway* series, beginning with
Sideshow in 1982, is set in a carnival, while the *Tales of the Velvet Comet*
sequence, beginning with *Eros Ascending* (1984), concerns a house
of prostitution visited at fifty-year intervals. But the series that best
shows his sense of morality as it relates to cultural differences is
set in a literal or science fiction analogue of Africa. *Bwana and Bully*
(1981) was a collection of short works, which he followed with
Ivory: A Legend of Past and Future (1988) and *Paradise: A Chronology of
a Distant World* (1989). These works recast Kenya as an alien world,
and Resnick received two Hugo awards for individual stories.

He has also written space operas (*Santiago: A Myth of the Far
Future*, 1986) and fantasies (*Stalking the Unicorn: A Fable of Tonight*,
1987), as well as a recasting of Herman Melville's *Moby Dick*,
called *The Soul-Eater* (1981). Resnick is a prolific writer who uses
many forms of science fiction in order to explore the reaches
of his imagination.

In "For I Have Touched the Sky," Mike Resnick looks at
the price we sometimes pay for maintaining our culture.

1   There was a time when men had wings.

2   Ngai, who sits alone on His throne atop Kirinyaga, which is now called Mount Kenya, gave the men the gift of flight, so that they might reach the succulent fruits on the highest branches of the trees. But one man, a son of Gikuyu, who was himself the first man, saw the eagle and the vulture riding high upon the winds, and, spreading his wings, he joined them. He circled higher and higher, and soon he soared far above all other flying things.

3   Then, suddenly, the hand of Ngai reached out and grabbed the son of Gikuyu.

4   "What have I done that you should grab me thus?" asked the son of Gikuyu.

5   "I live atop Kirinyaga because it is the top of the world," answered Ngai, "and no one's head may be higher than my own."

6   And so saying, Ngai plucked the wings from the son of Gikuyu, and then took wings away from *all* men, so that no man could ever again rise higher than His head.

7   And that is why all of Gikuyu's descendents look at the birds with a sense of loss and envy, and why they no longer eat the succulent fruits from the highest branches of the trees.

8   We have many birds on the world of Kirinyaga, which was named for the holy mountain where Ngai dwells. We have brought them along with our other animals when we received our charter from the Eutopian Council and departed from a Kenya that no longer had any meaning for true members of the Kikuyu tribe. Our new world is home to the marabou and the vulture, the ostrich and the fish eagle, the weaver and the heron, and many other species. Even I, Koriba, who am the *mundumugu*—the witch doctor—delight in their many colors, and find solace in their music. I have spent many afternoons seated in front of my *boma,* my back propped up against an ancient acacia tree, watching the profusion of colors and listening to the melodic songs as the birds come to slake their thirst in the river that winds through our village.

9   It was on one such afternoon that Kamari, a young girl who was not yet of circumcision age, walked up the long, winding path that separates my *boma* from the village, holding something small and gray in her hands.

10   "*Jambo,* Koriba," she greeted me.

11   "*Jambo,* Kamari," I answered her. "What have you brought to me, child?"

12   "This," she said, holding out a young pygmy falcon that struggled weakly to escape her grasp. "I found him in my family's *shamba*. He cannot fly."

13   "He looks fully fledged," I noted, getting to my feet. Then I saw that one of his wings was held at an awkward angle. "Ah!" I said. "He has broken his wing."

14   "Can you make him well, *mundumugu?*" asked Kamari.

15   I examined the wing briefly, while she held the young falcon's head away from me. Then I stepped back.

16   "I can make him well, Kamari," I said. "But I cannot make him fly. The wing will heal, but it will never be strong enough to bear his weight again. I think we will destroy him."

17   "No!" she exclaimed, pulling the falcon back. "You will make him live, and I will care for him!"

18   I stared at the bird for a moment, then shook my head. "He will not wish to live," I said at last.

19   "Why not?"

20   "Because he has ridden high upon the warm winds."

21   "I do not understand," said Kamari, frowning.

22   "Once a bird has touched the sky," I explained, "he can never be content to spend his days on the ground."

23   "I will *make* him content," she said with determination. "You will heal him, and I will care for him, and he will live."

24   "I will heal him, and you will care for him," I said. "But," I added, "he will not live."

25   "What is your fee, Koriba?" she asked, suddenly businesslike.

26   "I do not charge children," I answered. "I will visit your father tomorrow, and he will pay me."

27   She shook her head adamantly. "This is *my* bird. *I* will pay the fee."

28   "Very well," I said, admiring her spirit, for most children—and *all* adults—are terrified of their *mundumugu,* and would never openly contradict or disagree with him. "For one month you will clean my *boma* every morning and every afternoon. You will lay out my sleeping blankets, and keep my water gourd filled, and you will see that I have kindling for my fire."

29   "That is fair," she said after a moment's consideration. Then she added: "What if the bird dies before the month is over?"

30   "Then you will learn that a *mundumugu* knows more than a little Kikuyu girl," I said.

31   She set her jaw. "He will not die." She paused. "Will you fix his wing now?"

32 "Yes."

33 "I will help."

34 I shook my head. "You will build a cage in which to confine him, for if he tries to move his wing too soon, he will break it again, and then I will surely have to destroy him."

35 She handed the bird to me. "I will be back soon," she promised, racing off toward her *shamba*.

36 I took the falcon into my hut. He was too weak to struggle very much, and he allowed me to ties his beak shut. Then I began the slow task of splinting his broken wing and binding it against his body to keep it motionless. He shrieked in pain as I manipulated the bones together, but otherwise he simply stared unblinking at me, and within ten minutes the job was finished.

37 Kamari returned an hour later, holding a small wooden cage in her hands.

38 "Is this large enough, Koriba?" she asked.

39 I held it up and examined it.

40 "It is almost too large," I replied. "He must not be able to move his wing until it has healed."

41 "He won't," she promised. "I will watch him all day long, every day."

42 "You will watch him all day long, every day?" I repeated, amused.

43 "Yes."

44 "Then who will clean my hut and my *boma*, and who will fill my gourd with water?"

45 "I will carry his cage with me when I come," she replied.

46 "The cage will be much heavier when the bird is in it," I pointed out.

47 "When I am a woman, I will carry far heavier loads on my back, for I shall have to till the fields and gather the firewood for my husband's *boma*," she said. "This will be good practice." She paused. "Why do you smile at me, Koriba?"

48 "I am not used to being lectured to by uncircumcised children," I replied with a smile.

49 "I was not lecturing," she answered with dignity. "I was *explaining*."

50 I held a hand up to shade my eyes from the afternoon sun.

51 "Are you not afraid of me, little Kamari?" I asked.

52 "Why should I be?"

53 "Because I am the *mundumugu*."

54 "That just means you are smarter than the others," she said with a shrug. She threw a stone at a chicken that was approaching her cage, and it raced away, squawking its annoyance. "Someday I shall be as smart as you are."

55   "Oh?"

56   She nodded confidently. "Already I can count higher than my father, and I can remember many things."

57   "What kind of things?" I asked, turning slightly as a hot breeze blew a swirl of dust about us.

58   "Do you remember the story of the honey bird that you told to the children of the village before the long rains?"

59   I nodded.

60   "I can repeat it," she said.

61   "You mean you can remember it."

62   She shook her head vigorously. "I can repeat every word that you said."

63   I sat down and crossed my legs. "Let me hear it," I said, staring off into the distance and idly watching a pair of young men tending their cattle.

64   She hunched her shoulders, so that she would appear as bent with age as I myself am, and then, in a voice that sounded like a youthful replica of my own, she began to speak, mimicking my gestures.

65   "There is a little brown honey bird," she began. "He is much like a sparrow, and as friendly. He will come to your *boma* and call to you; and as you approach him, he will fly up and lead you to a hive, and then wait while you gather grass and set fire to it and smoke out the bees. But you must *always*"—she emphasized the word, just I had done—"leave some honey for him, for if you take it all, the next time he will lead you into the jaws of *fisi,* the hyena, or perhaps into the desert, where there is no water and you will die of thirst." Her story finished, she stood upright and smiled at me. "You see?" she said proudly.

66   "I see," I said, brushing away a large fly that had lit on my cheek.

67   "Did I do it right?" she asked.

68   "You did it right."

69   She stared at me thoughtfully. "Perhaps when you die, I will become the *mundumugu.*"

70   "Do I seem that close to death?" I asked her.

71   "Well," she answered, "you are very old and bent and wrinkled, and you sleep too much. But I will be just as happy if you do not die right away."

72   "I shall try to make you just as happy," I said ironically. "Now take your falcon home."

73   I was about to instruct her concerning his needs, but she spoke first.

74   "He will not need to eat today. But starting tomorrow, I will give him large insects, and at least one lizard every day. And he must always have water."

75   "You are very observant, Kamari."

76   She smiled at me again, then ran off toward her *boma*.

77   She was back at dawn the next morning, carrying the cage with her. She placed it in the shade, then filled a small container with water from one of my gourds and set it inside the cage.

78   "How is your bird this morning?" I asked, sitting close to my fire, for even though the planetary engineers of the Eutopian Council had given Kirinyaga a climate identical to Kenya's, the sun had not yet warmed the morning air.

79   Kamari frowned. "He has not eaten yet."

80   "He will, when he gets hungry enough," I said, pulling my blanket more tightly around my shoulders. "He is used to swooping down on his prey from the sky."

81   "He drinks his water, though," she noted.

82   "That is a good sign."

83   "Can you not cast a spell that will heal him at once?"

84   "The price would be too high," I said, for I had foreseen her question. "This way is better."

85   "How high?"

86   "*Too* high," I repeated, closing the subject. "Now, do you not have work to do?"

87   "Yes, Koriba."

88   She spent the next few minutes gathering kindling for my fire and filling my gourd from the river. Then she went into my hut to clean it and straighten my sleeping blankets. She emerged a moment later with a book in her hand.

89   "What is this, Koriba?" she asked.

90   "Who told you that you could touch your *mundumugu*'s possessions?" I asked sternly.

91   "How can I clean them without touching them?" she replied with no show of fear. "What is it?"

92   "It is a book."

93   "What is a book, Koriba?"

94   "It is not for you to know," I said. "Put it back."

95   "Shall I tell you what I think it is?" she asked.

96   "Tell me," I said, curious to hear her answer.

97   "Do you know how you draw signs on the ground when you cast the bones to bring the rains? I think that a book is a collection of signs."

98   "You are a very bright little girl, Kamari."

99   "I *told* you that I was," she said, annoyed that I had not accepted
her statement as a self-evident truth. She looked at the book for a moment, then held it up. "What do the signs mean?"

100   "Different things," I said.

101   "*What* things?"

102   "It is not necessary for the Kikuyu to know."

103   "But you know."

104   "I am the *mundumugu*."

105   "Can anyone else in Kirinyaga read the signs?"

106   "Your own chief, Koinnage, and two other chiefs can read the
signs," I answered, sorry now that she had charmed me into this conversation, for I could foresee its direction.

107   "But you are all old men," she said. "You should teach me, so when
you all die, someone can still read the signs."

108   "These signs are not important," I said. "They were created by the
Europeans. The Kikuyu had no need for books before the Europeans
came to Kenya; we have no need for them on Kirinyaga, which is our
own world. When Koinnage and the other chiefs die, everything will
be as it was long ago."

109   "Are they evil signs, then?" she asked.

110   "No," I said. "They are not evil. They just have no meaning for the
Kikuyu. They are white man's signs."

111   She handed the book to me. "Would you read me one of the
signs?"

112   "Why?"

113   "I am curious to know what kind of signs the white men made."

114   I stared at her for a long minute, trying to make up my mind.
Finally I nodded my assent.

115   "Just this once," I said. "Never again."

116   "Just this once," she agreed.

117   I thumbed through the book, which was a Swahili translation of
English poetry, selected one at random, and read it to her:

> *Live with me, and be my love,*
> *And we will all the pleasures prove*
> *That hills and valleys, dales and fields,*
> *And all the craggy mountains yields.*
> *There will we sit upon the rocks,*
> *And see the shepherds feed their flocks,*
> *By shallow rivers, by whose falls*
> *Melodious birds sing madrigals.*
> *There will I make thee a bed of roses,*

> *With a thousand fragrant posies,*
> *A cap of flowers, and a kirtle*
> *Embroider'd all with leaves of myrtle.*
> *A belt of straw and ivy buds,*
> *With coral clasps and amber studs;*
> *And if these pleasures may thee move,*
> *Then live with me and be my love.*

118   Kamari frowned. "I do not understand."

119   "I told you that you would not," I said. "Now put the book away and finish cleaning my hut. You must still work in your father's *shamba,* along with your duties here."

120   She nodded and disappeared into my hut, only to burst forth excitedly a few minutes later.

121   "It is a *story!*" she exclaimed.

122   "What is?"

123   "The sign you read! I do not understand many of the words, but it is a story about a warrior who asks a maiden to marry him!" She paused. *"You* would tell it better, Koriba. The sign doesn't even mention *fisi,* the hyena, and *mamba,* the crocodile, who dwells by the river and would eat the warrior and his wife. Still, it is a story! I had thought it would be spell for *mundumugus. "*

124   "You are very wise to know that it is a story," I said.

125   "Read another to me!" she said enthusiastically.

126   I shook my head. "Do you not remember our agreement? Just that once and never again."

127   She lowered her head in thought, then looked up brightly. "Then teach *me* to read the signs."

128   "That is against the law of the Kikuyu," I said. "No woman is permitted to read."

129   "Why?"

130   "It is a woman's duty to till the fields and pound the grain and make the fires and weave the fabrics and bear her husband's children," I answered.

131   "But I am not a woman," she pointed out. "I am just a little girl."

132   "But you will become a woman," I said, "and a woman may not read."

133   "Teach me now, and I will forget how when I become a woman."

134   "Does the eagle forget how to fly, or the hyena to kill?"

135   "It is not fair."

136   "No," I said. "But it is just."

137   "I do not understand."

138   "Then I will explain it to you," I said. "Sit down, Kamari."

139   She sat down on the dirt opposite me and leaned forward intently.

140   "Many years ago," I began, "the Kikuyu lived in the shadow of Kirinyaga, the mountain upon which Ngai dwells."

141   "I know," she said. "Then the Europeans came and built their cities."

142   "You are interrupting," I said.

143   "I am sorry, Koriba," she answered. "But I already know this story."

144   "You do not know all of it," I replied. "Before the Europeans came, we lived in harmony with the land. We tended our cattle and plowed our fields, and we produced just enough children to replace those who died of old age and disease, and those who died in our wars against the Maasai and the Wakamba and the Nandi. Our lives were simple but fulfilling."

145   "And *then* the Europeans came!" she said.

146   "Then the Europeans came," I agreed, "and they brought new ways with them."

147   "Evil ways."

148   I shook my head. "They were not evil ways for the Europeans," I replied. "I know, for I have studied in European schools. But they were not good ways for the Kikuyu and the Maasai and the Wakamba and the Embu and the Kisi and all the other tribes. We saw the clothes they wore and the buildings they erected and the machines they used, and we tried to become like Europeans. But we are not Europeans, and their ways are not our ways, and they do not work for us. Our cities became overcrowded and polluted, and our land grew barren, and our animals died, and our water became poisoned, and finally, when the Eutopian Council allowed us to move to the world of Kirinyaga, we left Kenya behind and came here to live according to the old ways, the ways that are good for the Kikuyu." I paused. "Long ago the Kikuyu had no written language, and did not know how to read, and since we are trying to create a Kikuyu world here on Kirinyaga, it is only fitting that our people do not learn to read or write."

149   "But what is good about not knowing how to read?" she asked. "Just because we didn't do it before the Europeans came doesn't make it bad."

150   "Reading will make you aware of other ways of thinking and living, and then you will be discontented with your life on Kirinyaga."

151   "But you read, and you are not discontented."

152   "I am the *mundumugu*," I said. "I am wise enough to know that what I read are lies."

153   "But lies are not always bad," she persisted. "You tell them all the time."

154   "The *mundumugu* does not lie to his people," I replied sternly.

155   "You call them stories, like the story of the lion and the hare, or the tale of how the rainbow came to be, but they are lies."

156   "They are parables," I said.

157   "What is a parable?"

158   "A type of story."

159   "Is it a true story?"

160   "In a way."

161   "If it is true in a way, then it is also a lie in a way, is it not?" she replied, and then continued before I could answer her. "And if I can listen to a lie, why can I not read one?"

162   "I have already explained it to you."

163   "It is not fair," she repeated.

164   "No," I agreed "But it is true, and, in the long run, it is for the good of the Kikuyu."

165   "I still don't understand why it is good," she complained.

166   "Because we are all that remain. Once before, the Kikuyu tried to become something that they were not, and we became not city-dwelling Kikuyu, or bad Kikuyu, or unhappy Kikuyu, but an entirely new tribe called Kenyans. Those of us who came to Kirinyaga came here to preserve the old ways—and if women start reading, some of them will become discontented, and they will leave, and then one day there will be no Kikuyu left."

167   "But I don't want to leave Kirinyaga!" she protested. "I want to become circumcized, and bear many children for my husband, and till the fields of his *shamba,* and someday be cared for by my grandchildren."

168   "That is the way you are supposed to feel."

169   "But I also want to read about other worlds and other times."

170   I shook my head. "No."

171   "But—"

172   "I will hear no more of this today," I said. "The sun grows high in the sky, and you have not yet finished your tasks here, and you must still work in your father's *shamba* and come back again this afternoon."

173   She rose without another word and went about her duties. When she finished, she picked up the cage and began walking back to her *boma.*

174   I watched her walk away, then returned to my hut and activated my computer to discuss a minor orbital adjustment with Maintenance, for it had been hot and dry for almost a month. They gave their consent, and, a few moments later, I walked down the long, winding path into the center of the village. Lowering myself gently to the ground, I spread my

pouchful of bones and charms out before me and invoked Ngai to cool Kirinyaga with a mild rain, which Maintenance had agreed to supply later in the afternoon.

175   Then the children gathered about me, as they always did when I came down from my *boma* on the hill and entered the village.

176   "*Jambo*, Koriba!" they cried.

177   "*Jambo*, my brave young warriors," I replied, still seated on the ground.

178   "Why have you come to the village this morning, Koriba?" asked Ndemi, the boldest of the young boys.

179   "I have come here to ask Ngai to water our fields with His tears of compassion," I said, "for we have had no rain this month, and the crops are thirsty."

180   "Now that you have finished speaking to Ngai, will you tell us a story?" asked Ndemi.

181   I looked up at the sun, estimating the time of day.

182   "I have time for just one," I replied. "Then I must walk through the fields and place new charms on the scarecrows, that they may continue to protect your crops."

183   "What story will you tell us, Koriba?" asked another of the boys.

184   I looked around, and saw that Kamari was standing among the girls.

185   "I think that I shall tell you the story of the Leopard and the Shrike," I said.

186   "I have not heard that one before," said Ndemi.

187   "Am I such an old man that I have no new stories to tell?" I demanded, and he dropped his gaze to the ground. I waited until I had everyone's attention, and then I began:

188   "Once there was a very bright young shrike, and because he was very bright, he was always asking questions of his father.

189   "'Why do we eat insects?' he asked one day.

190   "'Because we are shrikes, and that is what shrikes do,' answered his father.

191   "'But we are also birds,' said the shrike. 'And do not birds such as the eagle eat fish?'

192   "'Ngai did not mean for shrikes to eat fish,' said his father, 'and even if you were strong enough to catch and kill a fish, eating it would make you sick.'

193   "'Have you ever eaten a fish?' asked the young shrike.

194   "'No,' said his father.

195   "Then how do you know?' said the young shrike, and that afternoon he flew over the river and found a tiny fish. He caught it and ate it, and he was sick for a whole week.

196   "'Have you learned your lesson now?' asked the shrike's father, when the young shrike was well again.

197   "'I have learned not to eat fish,' said the shrike. 'But I have another question.'

198   "'Why are shrikes the most cowardly of birds?' asked the shrike. 'Whenever the lion or the leopard appears, we flee to the highest branches of the trees and wait for them to go away.'

199   "'Lions and leopards would eat us if they could,' said the shrike's father. 'Therefore, we must flee from them.'

200   "'But they do not eat the ostrich, and the ostrich is a bird,' said the bright young shrike. 'If they attack the ostrich, he kills them with his kick.'

201   "'You are not an ostrich,' said his father, tired of listening to him.

202   "'But I am a bird, and the ostrich is a bird, and I will learn to kick as the ostrich kicks,' said the young shrike, and he spent the next week practicing kicking any insects and twigs that were in his way.

203   "Then one day he came across *chui*, the leopard, and as the leopard approached him, the bright young shrike did not fly to the highest branches of the tree, but bravely stood his ground.

204   "'You have great courage to face me thus,' said the leopard.

205   "'I am a very bright bird, and I am not afraid of you,' said the shrike. 'I have practiced kicking as the ostrich does, and if you come any closer, I will kick you and you will die.'

206   "'I am an old leopard, and cannot hunt any longer,' said the leopard. 'I am ready to die. Come kick me, and put me out of my misery.'

207   "The young shrike walked up to the leopard and kicked him full in the face. The leopard simply laughed, opened his mouth, and swallowed the bright young shrike.

208   "'What a silly bird,' laughed the leopard, 'to pretend to be something that he was not! If he had flown away like a shrike, I would have gone hungry today—but by trying to be what he was never meant to be, all he did was fill my stomach. I guess he was not a very bright bird, after all.'"

209   I stopped and stared straight at Kamari.

210   "Is that the end?" asked one of the other girls.

211   "That is the end," I said.

212   "Why did the shrike think he could be an ostrich?" asked one of the smaller boys.

213   "Perhaps Kamari can tell you," I said.

214   All the children turned to Kamari, who paused for a moment and then answered.

215   "There is a difference between wanting to be an ostrich, and wanting to know what an ostrich knows," she said, looking directly into my

eyes. "It was not wrong for the shrike to want to know things. It was wrong for him to think he could become an ostrich."

216   There was a momentary silence while the children considered her answer.

217   "Is that true, Koriba?" asked Ndemi at last.

218   "No," I said, "for once the shrike knew what the ostrich knew, it forgot that it was a shrike. You must always remember who you are, and knowing too many things can make you forget."

219   "Will you tell us another story?" asked a young girl.

220   "Not this morning," I said, getting to my feet. "But when I come to the village tonight to drink *pombe* and watch the dancing, perhaps I will tell you the story about the bull elephant and the wise little Kikuyu boy. Now," I added, "do none of you have chores to do?"

221   The children dispersed, returning to their *shambas* and cattle pastures, and I stopped by Juma's hut to give an ointment for his joints, which always bothered him just before it rained. I visited Koinnage and drank *pombe* with him, and then discussed the affairs of the village with the Council of Elders. Finally I returned to my own *boma,* for I always take a nap during the heat of the day, and the rain was not due for another few hours.

222   Kamari was there when I arrived. She had gathered more wood and water, and was filling the grain bucket for my goats as I entered my *bomba.*

223   "How is your bird this afternoon?" I asked, looking at the pygmy falcon, whose cage had been carefully placed in the shade of my hut.

224   "He drinks, but he will not eat," she said in worried tones. "He spends all his time looking at the sky."

225   "There are things that are more important to him than eating," I said.

226   "I am finished now," she said. "May I go home, Koriba?"

227   I nodded, and she left as I was arranging my sleeping blanket inside my hut.

228   She came every morning and every afternoon for the next week. Then, on the eighth day, she announced with tears in her eyes that the pygmy falcon had died.

229   "I told you this would happen," I said gently. "Once a bird has ridden upon the winds, he cannot live on the ground."

230   "Do all birds die when they can no longer fly?" she asked.

231   "Most do," I said. "A few like the security of the cage, but most die of broken hearts, for, having touched the sky, they cannot bear to lose the gift of flight."

232   "Why do we make cages, then, if they do not make the birds feel better?"

233   "Because they make us feel better," I answered.

234   She paused, and then said: "I will keep my word and clean your hut and your *boma,* and fetch your water and kindling, even though the bird is dead."

235   I nodded. "That was our agreement," I said.

236   True to her word, she came back twice a day for the next three weeks. Then, at noon on the twenty-ninth day, after she had completed her morning chores and returned to her family's *shamba,* her father, Njoro, walked up the path to my *boma.*

237   "*Jambo,* Koriba," he greeted me, a worried expression on his face.

238   "*Jambo,* Njoro," I said without getting to my feet. "Why have you come to my *boma?*"

239   "I am a poor man, Koriba," he said, squatting down next to me. "I have only one wife, and she has produced no sons and only two daughters. I do not own as large a *shamba* as most men in the village, and the hyenas killed three of my cows this past year."

240   I could not understand his point, so I merely stared at him, waiting for him to continue.

241   "As poor as I am," he went on, "I took comfort in the thought that at least I would have the bride-prices from my two daughters in my old age." He paused. "I have been a good man, Koriba. Surely I deserve that much."

242   "I have not said otherwise," I replied.

243   "Then why are you training Kamari to be a *mundumugu?*" he demanded. "It is well known that the *mundumugu* never marries."

244   "Has Kamari told you that she is to become a *mundumugu?*" I asked.

245   He shook his head. "No. She does not speak to her mother or myself at all since she has been coming here to clean your *boma.*"

246   "Then you are mistaken," I said. "No woman may be a *mundumugu.* What made you think that I am training her?"

247   He dug into the folds of his *kikoi* and withdrew a piece of cured wildebeest hide. Scrawled on it in charcoal was the following inscription:

> I AM KAMARI
> I AM TWELVE YEARS OLD
> I AM A GIRL

248   "This is writing," he said accusingly. "Women cannot write. Only the *mundumugu* and great chiefs like Koinnage can write."

249   "Leave this with me, Njoro," I said, taking the hide, "and send Kamari to my *boma.*"

250   "I need her to work my *shamba* until afternoon."

251   "Now," I said.

252   He sighed and nodded. "I will send her, Koriba." He paused. "You are certain that she is not to be a *mundumugu?*"

253 "You have my word," I said, spitting on my hands to show my sincerity.

254 He seemed relieved, and went off to his *boma*. Kamari came up the path a few minutes later.

255 "*Jambo,* Koriba," she said.

256 "*Jambo,* Kamari," I replied. "I am very displeased with you."

257 "Did I not gather enough kindling this morning?" she asked.

258 "You gathered enough kindling."

259 "Were the gourds not filled with water?"

260 "The gourds were filled."

261 "Then what did I do wrong?" she asked, absently pushing one of my goats aside as it approached her.

262 "You broke your promise to me."

263 "That is not true," she said. "I have come every morning and every afternoon, even though the bird is dead."

264 "You promised not to look at another book," I said.

265 "I have not looked at another book since the day you told me that I was forbidden to."

266 "Then explain *this,*" I said, holding up the hide with her writing on it.

267 "There is nothing to explain," she said with a shrug. "I wrote it."

268 "And if you have not looked at books, how did you learn to write?" I demanded.

269 "From your magic box," she said. "You never told me not to look at *it.*"

270 "My magic box?" I said, frowning.

271 "The box that hums with life and has many colors."

272 "You mean my computer?" I said, surprised.

273 "Your magic box," she repeated.

274 "And it taught you how to read and write?"

275 "*I* taught me—but only a little," she said unhappily. "I am like the shrike in your story—I am not as bright as I thought. Reading and writing is very difficult."

276 "I told you that you must not learn to read," I said, resisting the urge to comment on her remarkable accomplishment, for she had clearly broken the law.

277 Kamari shook her head.

278 "You told me I must not look at your books," she replied stubbornly.

279 "I told you that women must not read," I said. "You have disobeyed me. For this, you must be punished." I paused. "You will continue your chores here for three more months, and you must bring me two hares and two rodents, which you must catch yourself. Do you understand?"

280   "I understand."

281   "Now come into my hut with me, that you may understand one thing more."

282   She followed me into the hut.

283   "Computer," I said. "Activate."

284   "Activated," said the computer's mechanical voice.

285   "Computer, scan the hut and tell me who is here with me."

286   The lens of the computer's sensors glowed briefly.

287   "The girl, Kamari wa Njoro, is here with you," replied the computer.

288   "Will you recognize her if you see her again?"

289   "Yes."

290   "This is a Priority Order," I said. "Never again may you converse with Kamari wa Njoro verbally or in any known language."

291   "Understood and logged," said the computer.

292   "Deactivate," I turned to Kamari. "Do you understand what I have done, Kamari?"

293   "Yes," she said, "and it is not fair. I did not disobey you."

294   "It is the law that women may not read," I said, "and you have broken it. You will not break it again. Now go back to your *shamba*."

295   She left, head held high, youthful back stiff with defiance, and I went about my duties, instructing the young boys on the decoration of their bodies for their forthcoming circumcision ceremony, casting a counter-spell for old Siboki (for he had found hyena dung within his *shamba,* which is one of the surest signs of a *thahu,* or curse), instructing Maintenance to make another minor orbital adjustment that would bring cooler weather to the western plains.

296   By the time I returned to my hut for my afternoon nap, Kamari had come and gone again, and everything was in order.

297   For the next two months, life in the village went its placid way. The crops were harvested, old Koinnage took another wife and we had a two-day festival with much dancing and *pombe*-drinking to celebrate the event, the short rains arrived on schedule, and three children were born to the village. Even the Eutopian Council, which had complained about our custom of leaving the old and the infirm out for the hyenas, left us completely alone. We found the lair of a family of hyenas and killed three whelps, then slew the mother when she returned. At each full moon, I slaughtered a cow—not merely a goat, but a large, fat cow—to thank Ngai for His generosity, for truly He had graced Kirinyaga with abundance.

298   During this period I rarely saw Kamari. She came in the mornings when I was in the village, casting bones to bring forth the weather, and

she came in the afternoons when I was giving charms to the sick and
conversing with the Elders—but I always knew she had been there, for
my hut and my *boma* were immaculate, and I never lacked for water or
kindling.

299   Then, on the afternoon after the second full moon, I returned to
my *boma* after advising Koinnage about how he might best settle an argument over a disputed plot of land, and as I entered my hut, I noticed
that the computer screen was alive and glowing, covered with strange
symbols. When I had taken my degrees in England and America, I had
learned English and French and Spanish, and of course I knew Kikuyu
and Swahili, but these symbols represented no known language, nor, although they used numerals as well as letters and punctuation marks,
were they mathematical formulas.

300   "Computer, I distinctly remember deactivating you this morning,"
I said, frowning. "Why does your screen glow with life?"

301   "Kamari activated me."

302   "And she forgot to deactivate you when she left?"

303   "That is correct."

304   "I thought as much," I said grimly. "Does she activate you every
day?"

305   "Yes."

306   "Did I not give you a Priority Order never to communicate with
her in any known language?" I said, puzzled.

307   "You did, Koriba."

308   "Can you then explain why you have disobeyed my directive?"

309   "I have not disobeyed your directive, Koriba," said the computer.
"My programming makes me incapable of disobeying a Priority
Order."

310   "Then what is this that I see upon your screen?"

311   "This is the Language of Kamari," replied the computer. "It is not
among the 1,732 languages and dialects in my memory banks, and
hence does not fall under the aegis of your directive."

312   "Did you create this language?"

313   "No, Koriba. Kamari created it."

314   "Did you assist her in any way?"

315   "No, Koriba, I did not."

316   "Is it a true language?" I asked. "Can you understand it?"

317   "It is a true language. I can understand it."

318   "If she were to ask you a question in the Language of Kamari,
could you reply to it?"

319   "Yes, if the question were simple enough. It is a very limited
language."

320   "And if that reply required you to translate the answer from a known language to the Language of Kamari, would doing so be contrary to my directives?"

321   "No, Koriba, it would not."

322   "Have you in fact answered questions put to you by Kamari?"

323   "Yes, Koriba, I have," replied the computer.

324   "I see," I said. "Stand by for a new directive."

325   "Waiting . . ."

326   I lowered my head in thought, contemplating the problem. That Kamari was brilliant and gifted was obvious: she had not only taught herself to read and write, but had actually created a coherent and logical language that the computer could understand and in which it could respond. I had given orders, and without directly disobeying them, she had managed to circumvent them. She had no malice within her, and wanted only to learn, which in itself was an admirable goal. All that was on the one hand.

327   On the other was the threat to the social order we had labored so diligently to establish on Kirinyaga. Men and women knew their responsibilities and accepted them happily. Ngai had given the Maasai the spear, and He had given the Wakamba the arrow, and He had given the Europeans the machine and printing press; but to the Kikuyu, He had given the digging-stick and the fertile land surrounding the sacred fig tree on the slopes of Kirinyaga.

328   Once before we had lived in harmony with the land, many long years ago. Then had come the printed word. It turned us first into slaves, and then into Christians, and then into soldiers and factory workers and mechanics and politicians, into everything that the Kikuyu were never meant to be. It had happened before; it could happen again.

329   We had come to the world of Kirinyaga to create a perfect Kikuyu society, a Kikuyu Utopia: could one gifted little girl carry within her the seeds of our destruction? I could not be sure, but it was a fact that gifted children grew up. They became Jesus, and Mohammed, and Jomo Kenyatta—but they also became Tippoo Tib, the greatest slaver of all, and Idi Amin, butcher of his own people. Or, more often, they became Friedrich Nietzsche and Karl Marx, brilliant men in their own right, but who influenced less brilliant, less capable men. Did I have the right to stand aside and hope that her influence upon our society would be benign, when all history suggested that the opposite was more likely to be true?

330   My decision was painful, but it was not a difficult one.

331   "Computer," I said at last, "I have a new Priority Order that supersedes my previous directive. You are no longer allowed to communicate

with Kamari under any circumstances whatsoever. Should she activate you, you are to tell her that Koriba has forbidden you to have any contact with her, and you are then to deactivate immediately. Do you understand?"

332   "Understood and logged."

333   "Good," I said. "Now deactivate."

334   When I returned from the village the next morning, I found my water gourds empty, my blankets unfolded, my *boma* filled with the dung of goats.

335   The *mundumugu* is all-powerful among the Kikuyu, but he is not without compassion. I decided to forgive this childish display of temper, and so I did not visit Kamari's father, nor did I tell the other children to avoid her.

336   She did not come again in the afternoon. I know, because I waited beside my hut to explain my decision to her. Finally, when twilight came, I sent for the boy, Ndemi, to fill my gourds and clean my *boma*, and although such chores are woman's work, he did not dare disobey his *mundumugu*, although his every gesture displayed contempt for the tasks I had set for him.

337   When two more days had passed with no sign of Kamari, I summoned Njoro, her father.

338   "Kamari has broken her word to me," I said when he arrived. "If she does not come to clean my *boma* this afternoon, I will be forced to place a *thahu* upon her."

339   He looked puzzled. "She says that you have already placed a curse on her, Koriba. I was going to ask you if we should turn her out of our *boma*."

340   I shook my head. "No," I said. "Do not turn her out of your *boma*. I have placed no *thahu* on her yet—but she must come to work this afternoon."

341   "I do not know if she is strong enough," said Njoro. "She has had neither food nor water for three days, and she sits motionless in my wife's hut." He paused. "*Someone* has placed a *thahu* on her. If it's not you, perhaps you can cast a spell to remove it."

342   "She has gone three days without eating or drinking?" I repeated.

343   He nodded.

344   "I will see her," I said, getting to my feet and following him down the winding path to the village. When we reached Njoro's *boma*, he led me to his wife's hut, then called Kamari's worried mother out and stood aside as I entered. Kamari sat at the farthest point from the door, her back propped against a wall, her knees drawn up to her chin, her arms encircling her thin legs.

345   "*Jambo,* Kamari," I said.

346   She stared at me but said nothing.

347   "Your mother worries for you, and your father tells me that you no longer eat or drink."

348   She made no answer.

349   "Listen to my words, Kamari," I said slowly. "I made my decision for the good of Kirinyaga, and I will not recant it. As a Kikuyu woman, you must live the life that has been ordained for you." I paused. "However, neither the Kikuyu nor the Eutopian Council are without compassion for the individual. Any member of our society may leave if he wishes. According to the charter we signed when we claimed this world, you need only walk to that area known as Haven, and a Maintenance ship will pick you up and transport you to the location of your choice."

350   "All I know is Kirinyaga," she said. "How am I to choose a new home if I am forbidden to learn about other places?"

351   "I do not know," I admitted.

352   "I don't *want* to leave Kirinyaga!" she continued. "This is my home. These are my people. I am a Kikuyu girl, not a Maasai girl or a European girl. I will bear my husband's children and till his *shamba;* I will gather his wood and cook his meals and weave his garments; I will leave my parents' *shamba* and live with my husband's family. I will do all this without complaint, Koriba, if you will just let me learn to read and write!"

353   "I cannot," I said sadly.

354   "But *why?*"

355   "Who is the wisest man you know, Kamari?" I asked.

356   "The *mundumugu* is always the wisest man in the village."

357   "Then you must trust to my wisdom."

358   "But I feel like the pygmy falcon," she said, her misery reflected in her voice. "He spent his life dreaming of soaring high upon the winds. I dream of seeing words upon the computer screen."

359   "You are not like the falcon at all," I said. "He was prevented from being what he was meant to be. You are prevented from being what you are not meant to be."

360   "You are not an evil man, Koriba," she said solemnly. "But you are wrong."

361   "If that is so, then I shall have to live with it," I said.

362   "But you are asking *me* to live with it," she said, "and that is your crime."

363   "If you call me a criminal again," I said sternly, for no one may speak thus to the *mundumugu,* "I shall surely place a *thahu* on you."

364   "What more can you do?" she said bitterly.

365   "I can turn you into a hyena, an unclean eater of human flesh who prowls only in the darkness. I can fill your belly with thorns, so that your every movement will be agony. I can—"

366   "You are just a man," she said wearily, "and you have already done your worst."

367   "I will hear no more of this," I said. "I order you to eat and drink what your mother brings to you, and I expect to see you at my *boma* this afternoon."

368   I walked out of the hut and told Kamari's mother to bring her banana mash and water, then stopped by old Benima's *shamba*. Buffalo had stampeded through his fields, destroying his crops, and I sacrificed a goat to remove the *thahu* that had fallen upon his land.

369   When I finished, I stopped at Koinnage's *boma,* where he offered me some freshly brewed *pombe* and began complaining about Kibo, his newest wife, who kept taking sides with Shubi, his second wife, against Wambu, his senior wife.

370   "You can always divorce her and return her to her family's *shamba*," I suggested.

371   "She cost twenty cows and five goats!" he complained. "Will her family return them?"

372   "No, they will not."

373   "Then I will not send her back."

374   "As you wish," I said with a shrug.

375   "Besides, she is very strong and very lovely," he continued. "I just wish she would stop fighting with Wambu."

376   "What do they fight about?" I asked.

377   "They fight about who will fetch the water, and who will mend my garments, and who will repair the thatch on my hut." He paused. "They even argue about whose hut I should visit at night, as if I had no choice in the matter."

378   "Do they ever fight about ideas?" I asked.

379   "Ideas?" he repeated blankly.

380   "Such as you might find in books."

381   He laughed. "They are *women,* Koriba. What need have they for ideas?" He paused. "In fact, what need have any of us for them?"

382   "I do not know," I said. "I was merely curious."

383   "You look disturbed," he noted.

384   "It must be the *pombe*," I said. "I am an old man, and perhaps it is too strong."

385   "That is because Kibo will not listen when Wambu tells her how to brew it. I really should send her away—he looked at Kibo as she carried

a load of wood on her strong, young back—"but she is so young and so lovely." Suddenly his gaze went beyond his newest wife to the village. "Ah!" he said. "I see that old Siboki has finally died."

386   "How do you know?" I asked.

387   He pointed to a thin column of smoke. "They are burning his hut."

388   I stared off in the direction he indicated. "That is not Siboki's hut," I said. "His *boma* is more to the west."

389   "Who else is old and infirm and due to die?" asked Koinnage.

390   And suddenly I knew, as surely as I knew that Ngai sits on His throne atop the holy mountain, that Kamari was dead.

391   I walked to Njoro's *shamba* as quickly as I could. When I arrived, Kamari's mother and sister and grandmother were already wailing the death chant, tears streaming down their faces.

392   "What happened?" I demanded, walking up to Njoro.

393   "Why do you ask, when it was you who destroyed her?" he replied bitterly.

394   "I did not destroy her," I said.

395   "Did you not threaten to place a *thahu* on her just this morning?" he persisted. "You did so, and now she is dead, and I have but one daughter to bring the bride-price, and I have had to burn Kamari's hut."

396   "Stop worrying about bride-prices and huts and tell me what happened, or you shall learn what it means to be cursed by a *mundumugu!*" I snapped.

397   "She hanged herself in her hut with a length of buffalo hide."

398   Five women from the neighboring *shamba* arrived and took up the death chant.

399   "She hanged herself in her hut?" I repeated.

400   He nodded. "She could at least have hanged herself from a tree, so that her hut would not be unclean and I would not have to burn it."

401   "Be quiet!" I said, trying to collect my thoughts.

402   "She was not a bad daughter," he continued. "Why did you curse her, Koriba?"

403   "I did not place a *thahu* upon her," I said, wondering if I spoke the truth. "I wished only to save her."

404   "Who has stronger medicine than you?" he asked fearfully.

405   "She broke the law of Ngai," I answered.

406   "And now Ngai has taken His vengeance!" moaned Njoro fearfully. "Which member of my family will He strike down next?"

407   "None of you," I said. "Only Kamari broke the law."

408   "I am a poor man," said Njoro cautiously, "even poorer now than before. How much must I pay you to ask Ngai to receive Kamari's spirit with compassion and forgiveness?"

409   "I will do that whether you pay me or not," I answered.

410   "You will not charge me?" he asked.

411   "I will not charge you."

412   "Thank you, Koriba!" he said fervently.

413   I stood and stared at the blazing hut, trying not to think of the smoldering body of the little girl inside it.

414   "Koriba?" said Njoro after a lengthy silence.

415   "What now?" I asked irritably.

416   "We do not know what to do with the buffalo hide, for it bore the mark of your *thahu,* and we were afraid to burn it. Now I know that the marks were made by Ngai and not you, and I am afraid even to touch it. Will you take it away?"

417   "What marks?" I said. "What are you talking about?"

418   He took me by the arm and led me around to the front of the burning hut. There, on the ground, some ten paces from the entrance, lay the strip of tanned hide with which Kamari had hanged herself, and scrawled upon it were more of the strange symbols I had seen on my computer screen three days earlier.

419   I reached down and picked up the hide, then turned to Njoro. "If indeed there is a curse on your shamba," I said, "I will remove it and take it upon myself, by taking Ngai's marks with me."

420   "Thank you, Koriba!" he said, obviously much relieved.

421   "I must leave to prepare my magic," I said abruptly, and began the long walk back to my *boma.* When I arrived, I took the strip of buffalo hide into my hut.

422   "Computer," I said. "Activate."

423   "Activated."

424   I held the strip up to its scanning lens.

425   "Do you recognize this language?" I asked.

426   The lens glowed briefly.

427   "Yes, Koriba. It is the Language of Kamari."

428   "What does it say?"

429   "It is a couplet:

> *I know why the caged birds die—*
> *For, like them, I have touched the sky."*

430   The entire village came to Njoro's *shamba* in the afternoon, and the women wailed the death chant all night and all of the next day, but before long Kamari was forgotten, for life goes on, and she was, after all, just a little Kikuyu girl.

431   Since that day, whenever I have found a bird with a broken wing, I have attempted to nurse it back to health. It always dies, and I always

bury it next to the mound of earth that marks where Kamari's hut had been.

432   It is on those days, when I place the birds in the ground, that I find myself thinking of her again, and wishing that I were just a simple man, tending my cattle and worrying about my crops and thinking the thoughts of simple men, rather than a *mundumugu* who must live with the consequences of his wisdom.

DISCUSSION QUESTIONS

1. Why are people living in a place made to resemble tribal Kenya when they obviously have advanced technology?
2. Why do the Kikuyu have no books? Why aren't women allowed to read?
3. The story of the leopard and the shrike is supposed to illustrate the folly of trying to be something you aren't, but what does it mean to Kamari?
4. How does Kamari first learn to read without directly disobeying Koriba's orders? How does she get around the second order?
5. Kamari's parents say Koriba cursed the girl, but Koriba insists he tried to save her. Who is right, and why?

WRITING TOPICS

1. In your journal, write about how learning other ways and customs can make you unhappy with what you have. Can it also reinforce your conviction about your own ways?
2. Examine the decision the *mundumugu* made. Was it a wise decision? Did he have any other choices? Did Kamari? What would you have done in a similar situation? Write an essay defending your opinion.
3. In an essay, explore the issues of individual freedom and personal desires versus the need to maintain cultural unity and a stable society. How is it possible to achieve a balance between the two? Can they coexist?

At the Rialto

1989

CONNIE WILLIS (b. 1945)

Connie Willis published her first science fiction story, "Santa Titicaca," in *Worlds of Fantasy* in 1971, but she didn't turn to full-time writing until the early eighties. After winning both Hugo and Nebula awards for "Fire Watch" in 1982, Willis later put out a collection of stories with the same title in 1985. In the short story, time travel is used as a way to study historical artifacts, but the protagonist can't stop himself from attempting to stop the bombing of a cathedral. Her first novel, *Water Witch* (done in collaboration with Cynthia Felice in 1982), makes dowsing for water a precious gift on a desert-like planet.

Willis' first solo novel, *Lincoln's Dreams* (1987), won the John W. Campbell Memorial award. In that novel she uses time travel to psychically link a contemporary woman with General Robert E. Lee, and the male protagonist with Lee's horse, Traveler. *Doomsday Book* (1992) also features time travel to transport twenty-first century history students to the time of the Black Death.

In "At the Rialto," Connie Willis shows a twist on going to a professional scientific conference, and how chaos can be expressed quite literally.

"Seriousness of mind was a prerequisite for understanding Newtonian physics. I am not convinced it is not a handicap in understanding quantum theory."

**Excerpt from Dr. Gedanken's keynote address
to the 1989 International Congress of Quantum
Physicists Annual Meeting, Hollywood, California**

1   I got to Hollywood around one-thirty and started trying to check into the Rialto.

2   "Sorry, we don't have any rooms," the girl behind the desk said. "We're all booked up with some science thing."

3   "I'm with the science thing," I said. "Dr. Ruth Baringer. I reserved a double."

4   "There are a bunch of Republicans here, too, and a tour group from Finland. They told me when I started work here that they got all these movie people, but the only one so far was that guy who played the friend of that other guy in that one movie. You're not a movie person, are you?"

5   "No," I said. "I'm with the science thing. Dr. Ruth Baringer."

6   "My name's Tiffany," she said. "I'm not actually a hotel clerk at all. I'm just working here to pay for my transcendental posture lessons. I'm really a model/actress."

7   "I'm a quantum physicist," I said, trying to get things back on track. "The name is Ruth Baringer."

8   She messed with the computer for a minute. "I don't show a reservation for you."

9   "Maybe it's in Dr. Mendoza's name. I'm sharing a room with her."

10   She messed with the computer some more. "I don't show a reservation for her either. Are you sure you don't want the Disneyland Hotel? A lot of people get the two confused."

11   "I want the Rialto," I said, rummaging through my bag for my notebook. "I have a confirmation number. W37420."

12   She typed it in. "Are you Dr. Gedanken?" she asked.

13   "Excuse me," an elderly man said.

14   "I'll be right with you," Tiffany told him. "How long do you plan to stay with us, Dr. Gedanken?" she asked me.

15   *"Excuse* me," the man said, sounding desperate. He had bushy white hair and a dazed expression, as if he had just been through a horrific experience or had been trying to check into the Rialto.

16   He wasn't wearing any socks. I wondered if *he* was Dr. Gedanken. Dr. Gedanken was the main reason I'd decided to come to the meeting. I had missed his lecture on wave/particle duality last year, but I had read

the text of in the *ICQP Journal,* and it actually seemed to make sense, which is more than you can say for most of quantum theory. He was giving the keynote address this year, and I was determined to hear it.

17 It wasn't Dr. Gedanken. "My name is Dr. Whedbee," the elderly man said. "You gave me the wrong room."

18 "All our rooms are pretty much the same," Tiffany said. "Except for how many beds they have in them and stuff."

19 "My room has a *person* in it!" he said. "Dr. Sleeth. From the University of Texas at Austin. She was changing her clothes." His hair seemed to get wilder as he spoke. "She thought I was a serial killer."

20 "And your name is Dr. Whedbee?" Tiffany asked, fooling with the computer again. "I don't show a reservation for you."

21 Dr. Whedbee began to cry. Tiffany got out a paper towel, wiped off the counter, and turned back to me. "May I help you?" she said.

> Thursday 7:30–9 P.M. *Opening Ceremonies,* Dr. Halvard
> Onofrio, University of Maryland at College Park, will
> speak on the topic, "Doubts Surrounding the Heisenberg
> Uncertainty Principle." Ballroom.

22 I finally got my room at five after Tiffany went off duty. Till then I sat around the lobby with Dr. Whedbee, listening to Abey Fields complain about Hollywood.

23 "What's wrong with Racine?" he said. "Why do we always have to go to these exotic places like Hollywood? And St. Louis last year wasn't much better. The Institut Henri Poincaré people kept going off to see the arch and Busch Stadium."

24 "Speaking of St. Louis," Dr. Takumi said, "have you seen David yet?"

25 "No," I said.

26 "Oh, really?" she said. "Last year at the annual meeting you two were practically inseparable. Moonlight riverboat rides and all."

27 "What's on the programming tonight?" I said to Abey.

28 "David was just here," Dr. Takumi said. "He said to tell you he was going out to look at the stars in the sidewalk."

29 "That's exactly what I'm talking about," Abey said. "Riverboat rides and movie stars. What do those things have to do with quantum theory? Racine would have been an appropriate setting for a group of physicists. Not like this . . . this . . . do you realize we're practically across the street from Grauman's Chinese Theatre? And Hollywood Boulevard's where all those gangs hang out. If they catch you wearing red or blue, they'll—"

30 He stopped. "Is that Dr. Gedanken?" he asked, staring at the front desk.

31 I turned and looked. A short roundish man with a mustache was trying to check in. "No," I said. "That's Dr. Onofrio."

32 "Oh, yes," Abey said, consulting his program book. "He's speaking tonight at the opening ceremonies. On the Heisenberg uncertainty principle. Are you going?"

33 "I'm not sure," I said, which was supposed to be a joke, but Abey didn't laugh.

34 "I must meet Dr. Gedanken. He's just gotten funding for a new project."

35 I wondered what Dr. Gedanken's new project was—I would have loved to work with him.

36 "I'm hoping he'll come to my workshop on the wonderful world of quantum physics," Abey said, still watching the desk. Amazingly enough, Dr. Onofrio seemed to have gotten a key and was heading for the elevators. "I think his project has something to do with understanding quantum theory."

37 Well, that let me out. I didn't understand quantum theory at all. I sometimes had a sneaking suspicion nobody else did either, including Abey Fields, and that they just weren't willing to admit it.

38 I mean, an electron is a particle except it acts like a wave. In fact, a neutron acts like two waves and interferes with itself (or each other), and you can't really measure any of this stuff properly because of the Heisenberg uncertainty principle, and that isn't the worst of it. When you set up a Josephson junction to figure out what rules the electrons obey, they sneak past the barrier to the other side, and they don't seem to care much about the limits of the speed of light either, and Schrödinger's cat is neither alive nor dead till you open the box, and it all makes about as much sense as Tiffany's calling me Dr. Gedanken.

39 Which reminded me, I had promised to call Darlene and give her our room number. I didn't have a room number, but if I waited much longer, she'd have left. She was flying to Denver to speak at C.U. and then coming on to Hollywood sometime tomorrow morning. I interrupted Abey in the middle of his telling me how beautiful Racine was in the winter and went to call her.

40 "I don't have a room yet," I said when she answered. "Should I leave a message on your answering machine or do you want to give me your number in Denver?"

41 "Never mind all that," Darlene said. "Have you seen David yet?"

"To illustrate the problems of the concept of wave function,
Dr. Schrödinger imagines a cat being put into a box with a
piece of uranium, a bottle of poison gas, and a Geiger counter.
If a uranium nucleus disintegrates while the cat is in the box,

> *it will release radiation which will set off the Geiger counter and*
> *break the bottle of poison gas. Since it is impossible in quantum*
> *theory to predict whether a uranium nucleus will disintegrate*
> *while the cat is in the box, and only possible to calculate uranium's*
> *probable half-life, the cat is neither alive nor dead until we open*
> *the box."*
>
> From "The Wonderful World of Quantum
> Physics," a seminar presented at the ICQP
> Annual Meeting by A. Fields, Ph.D.,
> University of Nebraska at Wahoo

42   I completely forgot to warn Darlene about Tiffany, the model-slash-actress.

43   "What do you mean you're trying to avoid David?" she had asked me at least three times. "Why would you do a stupid thing like that?"

44   Because in St. Louis I ended up on a riverboat in the moonlight and didn't make it back until the conference was over.

45   "Because I want to attend the programming," I said the third time around, "not a wax museum. I am a middle-aged woman."

46   "And David is a middle-aged man who, I might add, is absolutely charming. In fact, he may be the last charming man left in the universe."

47   "Charm is for quarks," I said and hung up, feeling smug until I remembered I hadn't told her about Tiffany. I went back to the front desk, thinking maybe Dr. Onofrio's success signaled a change. Tiffany asked, "May I help you?" and left me standing there.

48   After a while I gave up and went back to the red-and-gold sofas.

49   "David was here again," Dr. Takumi said. "He said to tell you he was going to the wax museum."

50   "There *are* no wax museums in Racine," Abey said.

51   "What's the programming for tonight?" I said, taking Abey's program away from him.

52   "There's a mixer at six-thirty and the opening ceremonies in the ballroom and then some seminars." I read the descriptions of the seminars. There was one on the Josephson junction. Electrons were able to somehow tunnel through an insulated barrier even though they didn't have the required energy. Maybe I could somehow get a room without checking in.

53   "If we were in Racine," Abey said, looking at his watch, "we'd already be checked in and on our way to dinner."

54   Dr. Onofrio emerged from the elevator, still carrying his bags. He came over and sank down on the sofa next to Abey.

55   "Did they give you a room with a semi-naked woman in it?" Dr. Whedbee asked.

56   "I don't know," Dr. Onofrio said. "I couldn't find it." He looked sadly at the key. "The gave me 1282, but the room numbers only go up to seventy-five."

57   "I think I'll attend the seminar on chaos," I said.

> *"The most serious difficulty quantum theory faces today is not the inherent limitation of measurement capability or the EPR paradox. It is the lack of a paradigm. Quantum theory has no working model, no metaphor that properly defines it."*
>
> **Excerpt from Dr. Gedanken's keynote address**

58   I got to my room at six, after a brief skirmish with the bellboy-slash-actor who couldn't remember where he'd stored my suitcase, and unpacked. My clothes, which had been permanent press all the way from MIT, underwent a complete wave function collapse the moment I opened my suitcase, and came out looking like Schrödinger's almost-dead cat.

59   By the time I had called housekeeping for an iron, taken a bath, given up on the iron, and steamed a dress in the shower, I had missed the "Mixer with Munchies" and was half an hour late for Dr. Onofrio's opening remarks.

60   I opened the door to the ballroom as quietly as I could and slid inside. I had hoped they would be late getting started, but a man I didn't recognize was already introducing the speaker. "—and an inspiration to all of us in the field."

61   I dived for the nearest chair and sat down.

62   "Hi," David said. "I've been looking all over for you. Where were you?"

63   "Not at the wax museum," I whispered.

64   "You should have been," he whispered back. "It was great. They had John Wayne, Elvis, and Tiffany the model-slash-actress with the brain of a pea-slash-amoeba."

65   "Shh," I said.

66   "—the person we've all been waiting to hear, Dr. Ringgit Dinari."

67   "What happened to Dr. Onofrio?" I asked.

68   "Shhh," David said.

69   Dr. Dinari looked a lot like Dr. Onofrio. She was short, roundish, and mustached, and was wearing a rainbow-striped caftan. "I will be your guide this evening into a strange new world," she said, "a world where all that you thought you knew, all common sense, all accepted

wisdom, must be discarded. A world where all the rules have changed and it sometimes seems there are no rules at all."

70   She sounded just like Dr. Onofrio, too. He had given this same speech two years ago in Cincinnati. I wondered if he had undergone some strange transformation during his search for Room 1282 and was now a woman.

71   "Before I go any farther," Dr. Dinari said, "how many of you have already channeled?"

> *"Newtonian physics had as its model the machine. The metaphor of the machine, with its interrelated parts, its gears and wheels, its causes and effects, was what made it possible to* think *about Newtonian physics."*
>
> > **Excerpt from Dr. Gedanken's**
> > **keynote address**

72   "You *knew* we were in the wrong place," I hissed at David when we got out to the lobby.

73   When we stood up to leave, Dr. Dinari had extended her pudgy hand in its rainbow-striped sleeve and called out in a voice a lot like Charlton Heston's, "O Unbelievers! Leave not, for here only is reality!"

74   "Actually, channeling would explain a lot," David said, grinning.

75   "If the opening remarks aren't in the ballroom, where are they?"

76   "Beats me," he said. "Want to go see the Capitol Records Building? It's shaped like a stack of records."

77   "I want to go to the opening remarks."

78   "The beacon on top blinks out Hollywood in Morse code."

79   I went over to the front desk.

80   "Can I help you?" the clerk behind the desk said. "My name is Natalie, and I'm an—"

81   "Where is the ICQP meeting this evening?" I said.

82   "They're in the ballroom."

83   "I'll bet you didn't have any dinner," David said. "I'll buy you an ice-cream cone. There's this great place that has the ice-cream cone Ryan O'Neal bought for Tatum in *Paper Moon*.

84   "A channeler's in the ballroom," I told Natalie. "I'm looking for the ICQP."

85   She fiddled with the computer. "I'm sorry. I don't show a reservation for them."

86   "How about Grauman's Chinese?" David said. "You want reality? You want Charlton Heston? You want to see quantum theory in action?" He grabbed my hands. "Come with me," he said seriously.

87   In St. Louis I had suffered a wave function collapse a lot like what had happened to my clothes when I opened the suitcase. I had ended up on a riverboat halfway to New Orleans that time. It happened again, and the next thing I knew I was walking around the courtyard of Grauman's Chinese Theatre, eating an ice-cream cone and trying to fit my feet in Myrna Loy's footprints.

88   She must have been a midget or had her feet bound as a child. So, apparently, had Debbie Reynolds, Dorothy Lamour, and Wallace Beery. The only footprints I came close to fitting were Donald Duck's.

89   "I see this as a map of the microcosm," David said, sweeping his hand over the slightly irregular pavement of printed and signed cement squares. "See, there are all these tracks. We know something's been here, and the prints are pretty much the same, only every once in a while you've got this," he knelt down and pointed at the print of John Wayne's clenched fist, "and over here," he walked toward the box office and pointed to the print of Betty Grable's leg, "and we can figure out the signatures, but what is this reference to 'Sid' on all these squares? And what does this mean?"

90   He pointed at Red Skelton's square. It said, "Thanks Sid We Dood It."

91   "You keep thinking you've found a pattern," David said, crossing over to the other side, "but Van Johnson's square is kind of sandwiched in here at an angle between Esther Williams and Cantinflas, and who the hell is May Robson? And why are all these squares over here empty?"

92   He had managed to maneuver me over behind the display of Academy Award winners. It was an accordionlike wrought-iron screen. I was in the fold between 1944 and 1945.

93   "And as if that isn't enough, you suddenly realize you're standing in the courtyard. You're not even in the theater."

94   "And that's what you think is happening in quantum theory?" I said weakly. I was backed up into Bing Crosby, who had won for Best Actor in *Going My Way*. "You think we're not in the theater yet?"

95   "I think we know as much about quantum theory as we can figure out about May Robson from her footprints," he said, putting his hand up to Ingrid Bergman's cheek (Best Actress, *Gaslight*) and blocking my escape. "I don't think we understand anything *about* quantum theory, not tunneling, not complementarity." He leaned toward me. "Not passion."

96   The best movie of 1945 was *Lost Weekend*. "Dr. Gedanken understands it," I said, disentangling myself from the Academy Award winners and David. "Did you know he's putting together a new research team for a big project on understanding quantum theory?"

97   "Yes." David said. "Want to see a movie?"

98   "There's a seminar on chaos at nine," I said, stepping over the
Marx Brothers. "I have to get back."

99   "If it's chaos you want, you should stay right here," he said, stopping to look at Irene Dunne's handprints. "We could see the movie and
then go have dinner. There's this place near Hollywood and Vine that
has the mashed potatoes Richard Dreyfus made into Devil's Tower in
Close Encounters."

100   "I want to meet Dr. Gedanken," I said, making it safely to the sidewalk. I looked back at David. He had gone back to the other side of
the courtyard and was looking at Roy Rogers's signature.

101   "Are you kidding? He doesn't understand it any better than we do."

102   "Well, at least he's trying."

103   "So am I. The problem is, how can one neutron interfere with itself, and why are there only two of Trigger's hoofprints here?"

104   "It's eight fifty-five," I said. "I am going to the chaos seminar."

105   "If you can find it," he said, getting down on one knee to look at
the signature.

106   "I'll find it," I said grimly.

107   He stood up and grinned at me, his hands in his pockets. "It's a
great movie," he said.

108   It was happening again. I turned and practically ran across the street.

109   "*Benji Nine* is showing," he shouted after me. "He accidentally ex-
changes bodies with a Siamese cat."

> Thursday, 9–10 P.M. *"The Science of Chaos."*
> I. Durcheinander, University of Leipzig. A seminar
> on the structure of chaos. Principles of chaos will be
> discussed, including the Butterfly Effect, fractals,
> and insolid billowing. Clara Bow Room.

110   I couldn't find the chaos seminar. The Clara Bow Room, where it
was supposed to be, was empty. A meeting of vegetarians was next door in
the Fatty Arbuckle Room, and all the other conference rooms were
locked. The channeler was still in the ballroom. "Come!" she commanded
when I opened the door. "Understanding awaits!" I went upstairs to bed.

111   I had forgotten to call Darlene. She would have left for Denver already, but I called her answering machine and told it the room number
in case she picked up her messages. In the morning I would have to tell
the front desk to giver her a key. I went to bed.

112   I didn't sleep well. The air conditioner went off during the night,
which meant I didn't have to steam my suit when I got up the next

morning. I got dressed and went downstairs. The programming started at nine o'clock with Abey Fields's Wonderful World workshop in the Mary Pickford Room, a breakfast buffet in the ballroom, and a slide presentation on "Delayed Choice Experiments" in Cecil B. DeMille A on the mezzanine level.

113   The breakfast buffet sounded wonderful, even though it always turns out to be urn coffee and donuts. I hadn't had anything but an ice-cream cone since noon the day before, but if David were around, he would be somewhere close to the food, and I wanted to steer clear of him. Last night it had been Grauman's Chinese. Today I was likely to end up at Knott's Berry Farm. I wasn't going to let that happen, even if he was charming.

114   It was pitch-dark inside Cecil B. DeMille A. Even the slide on the screen up front appeared to be black. "As you can see," Dr. Lvov said, "the laser pulse is already in motion before the experimenter sets up the wave or particle detector." He clicked to the next slide, which was dark gray. "We used a Mach–Zender interferometer with two mirrors and a particle detector. For the first series of tries we allowed the experimenter to decide which apparatus he would use by whatever method he wished. For the second series, we used that most primitive of randomizers—"

115   He clicked again, to a white slide with black polka dots that gave off enough light for me to be able to spot an empty chair on the aisle ten rows up. I hurried to get to it before the slide changed, and sat down.

116   "—a pair of dice. Alley's experiments had shown us that when the particle detector was in place, the light was detected as a particle, and when the wave detector was in place, the light showed wavelike behavior, no matter when the choice of apparatus was made."

117   "Hi," David said. "You've missed five black slides, two gray ones, and a white with black polka dots."

118   "Shh," I said.

119   "In our two series, we hoped to ascertain whether the consciousness of the decision affected the outcome," Dr. Lvov clicked to another black slide. "As you can see, the graph shows no effective difference between the tries in which the experimenter chose the detection apparatus and those in which the apparatus was randomly chosen."

120   "You want to go get some breakfast?" David whispered.

121   "I already ate," I whispered back, and waited for my stomach to growl and give me away. It did.

122   "There's a great place down near Hollywood and Vine that has the waffles Katharine Hepburn made for Spencer Tracy in *Woman of the Year*."

123   "Shh," I said.

124   "And after breakfast, we could to Frederick's of Hollywood and see
the bra museum."

125   "Will you please be quiet? I can't hear."

126   "Or see," he said, but he subsided more or less for the remaining
ninety-two black, gray, and polka-dotted slides.

127   Dr. Lvov turned on the lights and blinked smilingly at the audience. "Consciousness had no discernible effect on the results of the experiment. As one of my lab assistants put it, 'The little devil knows
what you're going to do before you know it yourself.'"

128   This was apparently supposed to be a joke, but I didn't think it was
very funny. I opened my program and tried to find something to go to
that David wouldn't be caught dead at.

129   "Are you two going to breakfast?" Dr. Thibodeaux asked.

130   "Yes," David said.

131   "No," I said.

132   "Dr. Hotard and I wished to eat somewhere that is *vraiment*
Hollywood."

133   "David knows just the place," I said. "He's been telling me about
this great place where they have the grapefruit James Cagney shoved in
Mae Clark's face in *Public Enemy.*"

134   Dr. Hotard hurried up, carrying a camera and four guidebooks.
"And then perhaps you would show us Grauman's Chinese Theatre," he
asked David.

135   "Of course he will," I said. "I'm sorry I can't go with you, but I
promised Dr. Verikovsky I'd be at his lecture on Boolean logic. And
after Grauman's Chinese, David can take you to the bra museum at
Frederick's of Hollywood."

136   "And the Brown Derby?" Thibodeaux asked. "I have heard it is
shaped like a *chapeau.*"

137   The dragged him off. I watched till they were safely out of the
lobby and then ducked upstairs and into Dr. Whedbee's lecture on information theory. Dr. Whedbee wasn't there.

138   "He went to find an overhead projector," Dr. Takumi said. She had
half a donut on a paper plate in one hand and a Styrofoam cup in the
other.

139   "Did you get that at the breakfast buffet?" I asked.

140   "Yes. It was the last one. And they ran out of coffee right after I got
there. You weren't in Abey Fields's thing, were you?" She set the coffee
cup down and took a bite of the donut.

141   "No," I said, wondering if I should try to take her by surprise or
just wrestle the donut away from her.

142   "You didn't miss anything. He raved the whole time about how we should have had the meeting in Racine." She popped the last piece of donut in her mouth. "Have you seen David yet?"

> Friday, 9–10 P.M. *"The Eureka Experiment: A Slide Presentation."* J. Lvov, Eureka College. Descriptions, results, and conclusions of Lvov's delayed conscious/randomed choice experiments. Cecil B. DeMille A.

143   Dr. Whedbee eventually came in carrying an overhead projector, the cord trailing behind him. He plugged it in. The light didn't go on.

144   "Here," Dr. Takumi said, handing me her plate and cup. "I have one of these at Caltech. It needs its fractal basin boundaries adjusted." She whacked the side of the projector

145   There weren't even any crumbs left of the donut. There was about a millimeter of coffee in the bottom of the cup. I was about to stoop to new depths when she hit the projector again. The light came on. "I learned that in the chaos seminar last night," she said, grabbing the cup away from me and draining it. "You should have been there. The Clara Bow Room was packed."

146   "I believe I'm ready to begin," Dr. Whedbee said. Dr. Takumi and I sat down. "Information is the transmission of meaning," Dr. Whedbee wrote "meaning" or possibly "information" on the screen with a green Magic Marker. "When information is randomized, meaning cannot be transmitted, and we have a state of entropy." He wrote it under "meaning" with a red Magic Marker. His handwriting appeared to be completely illegible.

147   "States of entropy vary from low entropy, such as the mild static on your car radio, to high entropy, a state of complete disorder, of randomness and confusion, in which no information at all is being communicated."

148   Oh, my God, I thought. I forgot to tell the hotel about Darlene. The next time Dr. Whedbee bent over to inscribe hieroglyphics on the screen, I sneaked out and went down to the desk, hoping Tiffany hadn't come on duty yet. She had.

149   "May I help you?" she asked.

150   "I'm in Room 663," I said. "I'm sharing a room with Dr. Darlene Mendoza. She's coming in this morning, and she'll be needing a key."

151   "For what?" Tiffany said.

152   "To get into the room. I may be in one of the lectures when she gets here."

153   "Why doesn't she have a key?"

154   "Because she isn't here yet."

155　　　"I thought you said she was sharing a room with you."

156　　　"She *will* be sharing a room with me. Room 663. Her name is Darlene Mendoza."

157　　　"And your name?" she asked, hands poised over the computer.

158　　　"Ruth Baringer."

159　　　"We don't show a reservation for you."

> *"We have made impressive advances in quantum physics*
> *in the ninety years since Planck's constant, but they have by*
> *and large been advances in technology, not theory. We can*
> *only make advances in theory when we have a model we*
> *can visualize."*
>
> **Excerpt from Dr. Gedanken's**
> **keynote address**

160　　　I high-entropied with Tiffany for a while on the subjects of my not having a reservation and the air conditioning and then switched back suddenly to the problem of Darlene's key, in the hope of catching her off guard. It worked about as well as Alley's delayed choice experiments.

161　　　In the middle of my attempting to explain that Darlene was not the air-conditioning repairman, Abey Fields came up.

162　　　"Have you seen Dr. Gedanken?"

163　　　I shook my head.

164　　　"I was sure he'd come to my Wonderful World workshop, but he didn't, and the hotel says they can't find his reservation," he said, scanning the lobby. "I found out what his new project is, incidentally, and I'd be perfect for it. He's going to find a paradigm for quantum theory. Is that him?" he said, pointing at an elderly man getting in the elevator.

165　　　"I think that's Dr. Whedbee," I said, but he had already sprinted across the lobby to the elevator.

166　　　He nearly made it. The elevator slid to a close just as he got there. He pushed the elevator button several times to make the door open again, and when that didn't work, tried to readjust its fractal basin boundaries. I turned back to the desk.

167　　　"May I help you?" Tiffany said.

168　　　"You may," I said. "My roommate, Darlene Mendoza, will be arriving sometime this morning. She's a producer. She's here to cast the female lead in a new movie starring Robert Redford and Harrison Ford. When she gets here, give her the key. And fix the air-conditioning."

169　　　"Yes, ma'am," she said.

> *"The Josephson junction is designed so that electrons*
> *must obtain additional energy to surmount the energy*

barrier. It has been found, however, that some electrons simply tunnel, as Heinz Pagels put it, 'right through the wall.'"

From "The Wonderful World of
Quantum Physics," A. Fields, UNW

170 Abey had stopped banging on the elevator button and was trying to pry the elevator doors apart. I went out the side door and up to Hollywood Boulevard. David's restaurant was near Hollywood and Vine. I turned the other direction, toward Grauman's Chinese, and ducked into the first restaurant I saw.

171 "I'm Stephanie," the waitress said. "How many are there in your party?"

172 There was no one remotely in my vicinity. "Are you an actress-slash-model?" I asked her.

173 "Yes," she said. "I'm working here part-time to pay for my holistic hairstyling lessons."

174 "There's one of me," I said, holding up my forefinger to make it perfectly clear. "I want a table away from the window."

175 She led me to a table in front of the window, handed me a menu the size of the macrocosm, and put another one down across from me. "Our breakfast specials today are papaya stuffed with salmon-berries and nasturtium/radicchio salad with a balsamic vinaigrette. I'll take your order when your other party arrives."

176 I stood the extra menu up so it hid me from the window, opened the other one, and read the breakfast entrees. They all seemed to have cilantro or lemongrass in their names. I wondered if radicchio could possibly be Californian for donut.

177 "Hi," David said, grabbing the standing-up menu and sitting down. "The sea urchin pâté looks good."

178 I was actually glad to see him. "How did you get here?" I asked.

179 "Tunneling," he said. "What exactly is extra-virgin olive oil?"

180 "I wanted a donut," I said pitifully.

181 He took my menu away from me, laid it on the table, and stood up. "There's a great place next door that's got the donut Clark Gable taught Claudette Colbert how to dunk in *It Happened One Night.*"

182 The great place was probably out in Long Beach someplace, but I was too weak with hunger to resist him. I stood up. Stephanie hurried over.

183 "Will there be anything else?" she asked.

184 "We're leaving," David said.

185 "Okay, then," she said, tearing a check off her pad and slapping it down on the table. "I hope you enjoyed your breakfast."

*"Finding such a paradigm is difficult, if not impossible.
Due to Planck's constant the world we see is largely dominated by Newtonian mechanics. Particles are particles, waves
are waves, and objects do not suddenly vanish through walls
and reappear on the other side. It is only on the subatomic
level that quantum effects dominate."*

**Excerpt from Dr. Gedanken's
keynote address**

186 The restaurant was next door to Grauman's Chinese, which made
me a little nervous, but it had eggs and bacon and toast and orange
juice and coffee. And donuts.

187 "I thought you were having breakfast with Dr. Thibodeaux and
Dr. Hotard," I said, dunking one in my coffee. "What happened to
them?"

188 "They went to Forest Lawn. Dr. Hotard wanted to see the church
were Ronald Reagan got married."

189 "He got married at Forest Lawn?"

190 He took a bite of my donut. "In the Week Kirk of the Heather.
Did you know Forest Lawn's got the World's Largest Oil Painting
Incorporating a Religious Theme?"

191 "So why didn't you go with them?"

192 "And miss the movie?" He grabbed both my hands across the table.
"There's a matinee at two o'clock. Come with me."

193 I could feel things starting to collapse. "I have to get back," I said,
trying to disentangle my hands. "There's a panel on the EPR paradox at
two o'clock."

194 "There's another showing at five. And one at eight."

195 "Dr. Gedanken's giving the keynote address at eight."

196 "You know what the problem is?" he said, still holding on to my
hands. "The problem is, it isn't really Grauman's Chinese Theatre, it's
Mann's, so Sid isn't even around to ask. Like, why do some pairs like
Joanne Woodward and Paul Newman share the same square and other
pairs don't? Like Ginger Rogers and Fred Astaire."

197 "You know what the problem is?" I said, wrenching my hands free.
"The problem is you don't take anything seriously. This is a conference,
but you don't care anything about the programming or hearing Dr.
Gedanken speak or trying to understand quantum theory!" I fumbled in
my purse for some money for the check.

198 "I thought that was what we were talking about," David said,
sounding surprised. "The problem is, where do those lion statues that
guard the door fit in? And what about all those empty spaces?"

Friday, 2–3 P.M. *Panel Discussion on the EPR Paradox.* I. Takumi, moderator, R. Iverson, L. S. Ping. A discussion of the latest research in singlet-state correlations including nonlocal influences, the Calcutta proposal, and passion. Keystone Kops Room.

199   I went up to my room as soon as I got back to the Rialto to see if Darlene was there yet. She wasn't, and when I tried to call the desk, the phone wouldn't work. I went back down to the registration desk. There was no one there. I waited fifteen minutes and then went into the panel on the EPR paradox.

200   "The Einstein-Podolsky-Rosen paradox cannot be reconciled with quantum theory," Dr. Takumi was saying. "I don't care what the experiments seem to indicate. Two electrons at opposite ends of the universe can't affect each other simultaneously without destroying the entire theory of the space-time continuum."

201   She was right. Even if it were possible to find a model of quantum theory, what about the EPR paradox? If an experimenter measured one of a pair of electrons that had originally collided, it changed the cross-correlation of the other instantaneously, even if the electrons were light-years apart. It was as if they were eternally linked by that one collision, sharing the same square forever, even if they were on opposite sides of the universe.

202   "If the electrons *communicated* instantaneously, I'd agree with you," Dr. Iverson said, "but they don't, they simply influence each other. Dr. Shimony defined this influence in his paper on passion, and my experiment clearly—"

203   I thought of David leaning over me between the best pictures of 1944 and 1945, saying, "I think we know as much about quantum theory as we do about May Robson from her footprints."

204   "You can't explain it away by inventing new terms," Dr. Takumi said.

205   "I completely disagree," Dr. Ping said. "Passion at a distance is not just an invented term. It's a demonstrated phenomenon."

206   It certainly is, I thought, thinking about David taking the macrocosmic menu out of the window and saying, "The sea urchin pâté looks good." It didn't matter where the electron went after the collision. Even if it went in the opposite direction from Hollywood and Vine, even if it stood a menu in the window to hide it, the other electron would still come and rescue it from the radicchio and buy it a donut.

207   "A demonstrated phenomenon!" Dr. Takumi said. "Ha!" She banged her moderator's gavel for emphasis.

208   "Are you saying passion doesn't exist?" Dr. Ping said, getting very red in the face.

209   "I'm saying one measly experiment is hardly a demonstrated phenomenon."

210   "One measly experiment! I spent five years on this project!" Dr.
Iverson said, shaking his fist at her. "I'll show you passion at a distance!"

211   "Try it, and I'll adjust your fractal basin boundaries!" Dr. Takumi
said, and hit him over the head with the gavel.

> *"Yet finding a paradigm is not impossible. Newtonian physics is not
> a machine. It simply shares some of the attributes of a machine. We
> must find a model somewhere in the visible world that shares the
> often bizarre attributes of quantum physics. Such a model,
> unlikely as it sounds, surely exists somewhere, and it is up to
> us to find it."*

> **Excerpt from Dr. Gedanken's
> keynote address**

212   I went up to my room before the police came. Darlene still wasn't
there, and the phone and air-conditioning still weren't working. I was
really beginning to get worried. I walked up to Grauman's Chineese to
find David, but he wasn't there. Dr. Whedbee and Dr. Sleeth were behind the Academy Award Winners folding screen.

213   "You haven't seen David, have you?" I asked.

214   Dr. Whedbee removed his hand from Norma Shearer's cheek.

215   "He left," Dr. Sleeth said, disentangling herself from the Best
Movie of 1929–30.

216   "He said he was going out to Forest Lawn," Dr. Whedbee said, trying to smooth down his bushy white hair.

217   "Have you seen Dr. Mendoza? She was supposed to get in this
morning."

218   They hadn't seen her, and neither had Drs. Hotard and
Thibodeaux, who stopped me in the lobby and showed me a postcard
of Aimee Semple McPherson's tomb. Tiffany had gone off duty. Natalie
couldn't find my reservation. I went back up to the room to wait,
thinking Darlene might call.

219   The air-conditioning still wasn't fixed. I fanned myself with a
Hollywood brochure and then opened it up and read it. There was a
map of the courtyard of Grauman's Chinese on the back cover. Deborah
Kerr and Yul Brynner didn't have a square together either, and Katharine
Hepburn and Spencer Tracy weren't even on the map. She had made
him waffles in *Woman of the Year*, and they hadn't even given them a
square. I wondered if Tiffany the model-slash-actress had been in charge
of assigning the cement. I could see her looking blankly at Spencer
Tracy and saying, "I don't show a reservation for you."

220   What exactly was a model-slash-actress? Did it mean she was a model *or* an actress or a model *and* an actress? She certainly wasn't a hotel clerk. Maybe electrons were the Tiffanys of the microcosm and that explained their wave-slash-particle duality. Maybe they weren't really electrons at all. Maybe they were just working part-time at being electrons to pay for their singlet-state lessons.

221   Darlene still hadn't called by seven o'clock. I stopped fanning myself and tried to open a window. It wouldn't budge. The problem was nobody knew anything about quantum theory. All we had to go on were a few colliding electrons that nobody could see and that couldn't be measured properly because of the Heisenberg uncertainty principle. And there was chaos to consider, and entropy, and all those empty spaces. We didn't even know who May Robson was.

222   At seven-thirty the phone rang. It was Darlene.

223   "What happened?" I said. "Where are you?"

224   "At the Beverly Wilshire."

225   "In Beverly Hills?"

226   "Yes. It's a long story. When I got to the Rialto, the hotel clerk, I think her name was Tiffany, told me you weren't there. She said they were booked solid with some science thing and had had to send the overflow to other hotels. She said you were at the Beverly Wilshire in Room 1027. How's David?"

227   "Impossible," I said. "He's spent the whole conference looking at Deanna Durbin's footprints at Grauman's Chinese Theatre and trying to talk me into going to the movies."

228   "And are you going?"

229   "I can't. Dr. Gedanken's giving the keynote address in half an hour."

230   "He is?" Darlene said, sounding surprised. "Just a minute." There was a silence, and then she came back on and said, "I think you should go to the movies. David's one of the last two charming men in the universe."

231   "But he doesn't take quantum theory seriously. Dr. Gedanken is hiring a research team to design a paradigm, and David keeps talking about the beacon on top of the Capitol Records Building."

232   "You know, he may be on to something there. I mean, seriousness was all right for Newtonian physics, but maybe quantum theory needs a different approach. Sid says—"

233   "Sid?"

234   "This guy who's taking me to the movies tonight. It's a long story. Tiffany gave me the wrong room number, and I walked in on this guy in his underwear. He's a quantum physicist. He was supposed to be staying at the Rialto, but Tiffany couldn't find his reservation."

> *"The major implication of wave/particle duality is that an electron has no precise location. It exists in a superposition of probable locations. Only when the experimenter observes the electron does it 'collapse' into a location."*
>
> **"The Wonderful World of Quantum Physics,"**
> **A. Fields, UNW**

235   Forest Lawn had closed at five o'clock. I looked it up in the Hollywood brochure after Darlene hung up. There was no telling where he might have gone: the Brown Derby or the La Brea Tar Pits or some great place near Hollywood and Vine that had the alfalfa sprouts John Hurt ate right before his chest exploded in *Alien*.

236   At least I knew where Dr. Gedanken was. I changed my clothes and got in the elevator, thinking about wave/particle duality and fractals and high entropy states and delayed choice experiments. The problem was, where could you find a paradigm that would make it possible to visualize quantum theory when you had to include Josephson junctions and passion and all those empty spaces? It wasn't possible. You had to have more to work with than a few footprints and the impression of Betty Grable's leg.

237   The elevator door opened, and Abey Fields pounced on me. "I've been looking all over for you," he said. "You haven't seen Dr. Gedanken, have you?"

238   "Isn't he in the ballroom?"

239   "No," he said. "He's already fifteen minutes late, and nobody's seen him. You have to sign this," he said, shoving a clipboard at me.

240   "What is it?"

241   "It's a petition." He grabbed it back from me. "'We the undersigned demand that the annual meetings of the International Congress of Quantum Physicists henceforth be held in appropriate locations.' Like Racine," he added, shoving the clipboard at me again. *"Unlike* Hollywood."

242   Hollywood.

243   "Are you aware it took the average ICQP delegate two hours and thirty-six minutes to check in? They even sent some of the delegates to a hotel in Glendale."

244   "And Beverly Hills," I said absently. Hollywood. Bra museums and the Marx Brothers and gangs that would kill you if you wore red or blue and Tiffany/Stephanie and the World's Largest Oil Painting Incorporating a Religious Theme.

245   "Beverly Hills," Abey muttered, pulling an automatic pencil out of his pocket protector and writing a note to himself. "I'm presenting the

petition during Dr. Gedanken's speech. Well, go on, sign it," he said, handing me the pencil. "Unless you want the annual meeting to be here at the Rialto next year."

246   I handed the clipboard back to him. "I think from now on the annual meeting might be here every year," I said, and took off running for Grauman's Chinese.

> *"When we have that paradigm, one that embraces both the logical and the nonsensical aspects of quantum theory, we will be able to look past the colliding electrons and the mathematics and see the microcosm in all its astonishing beauty."*
>
> Excerpt from Dr. Gedanken's keynote address

247   "I want a ticket to *Benji Nine*," I told the girl at the box office. Her name tag said, "Welcome to Hollywood. My name is Kimberly."

248   "Which theater?" she said.

249   "Grauman's Chinese," I said, thinking, This is no time for a high entropy state.

250   "Which theater?"

251   I looked up at the marquee. *Benji IX* was showing in all three theaters, the huge main theater and the two smaller ones on either side. "They're doing audience reaction surveys," Kimberly said. "Each theater has a different ending."

252   "Which one's in the main theater?"

253   "I don't know. I just work here part-time to pay for my organic breathing lessons."

254   "Do you have any dice?" I asked, and then realized I was going about this all wrong. This was quantum physics, not Newtonian. It didn't matter which theater I chose or which seat I sat down in. This was a delayed choice experiment and David was already in flight.

255   "The one with the happy ending," I said.

256   "Center theater," she said.

257   I walked past the stone lions and into the lobby. Rhonda Fleming and some Chinese wax figures were sitting inside a glass case next to the door to the rest rooms. There was a huge painted screen behind the concessions stand. I bought a box of Raisinets, a tub of popcorn, and a box of jujubes and went inside the theater.

258   It was bigger than I had imagined. Rows and rows of empty red chairs curved between the huge pillars and up to the red curtains where the screen must be. The walls were covered with intricate drawings. I stood there, holding my jujubes and Raisinets and popcorn, staring at the chandelier overhead. It was an elaborate gold sunburst surrounded

by silver dragons. I had never imagined it was anything like this.

259   The lights went down, and the red curtains opened, revealing an inner curtain like a veil across the screen. I went down the dark aisle and sat down in one of the seats. "Hi," I said, and handed the Raisinets to David.

260   "Where have you been?" he said. "The movie's about to start."

261   "I know," I said. I leaned across him and handed Darlene her popcorn and Dr. Gedanken his jujubes. "If was working on the paradigm for quantum theory."

262   "And?" Dr. Gedanken said, opening his jujubes.

263   "And you're both wrong," If said. "It isn't Grauman's Chinese. It isn't movies either, Dr. Gedanken."

264   "Sid," Dr. Gedanken said. "If we're all going to be on the same research team, I think we should use first names."

265   "If it isn't Grauman's Chinese or the movies, what is it?" Darlene asked, eating popcorn.

266   "It's Hollywood."

267   "Hollywood," Dr. Gedanken said thoughtfully.

268   "Hollywood," I said. "Stars in the sidewalk and buildings that look like stacks of records and hats, and radicchio and audience surveys, and bra museums. And the movies. And Grauman's Chinese."

269   "And the Rialto," David said.

270   "Especially the Rialto."

271   "And the ICQP," Dr. Gedanken said.

272   I thought about Dr. Lvov's black and gray slides and the disappearing chaos seminar and Dr. Whedbee writing "meaning" or possibly "information" on the overhead projector. "And the ICQP," I said.

273   "Did Dr. Takumi really hit Dr. Iverson over the head with a gavel?" Darlene asked.

274   "Shh," David said. "I think the movie's starting." He took hold of my hand. Darlene settled back with her popcorn, and Dr. Gedanken put his feet up on the chair in front of him. The inner curtain opened and the screen lit up.

DISCUSSION QUESTIONS

1. **Ruth Baringer is a quantum physicist who doesn't understand quantum theory and suspects no one else does either. How does her attitude affect your reading and her reliability as a narrator?**

2. When Dr. Dinari gives a lecture instead of Dr. Onofrio, Baringer can hardly tell the difference, at least at first. Why?

3. All of the talk, while using technical jargon, seems to be poking fun at scientific theory. Why?

4. Baringer changes tactics on two notable occasions in the story. One is with Tiffany and the other with David. What does she do, and how does it work?

5. Why is the physicists' discussion of passion as a scientific concept significant? How do they show the truth of their experiments?

WRITING TOPICS

1. In this story, Willis pokes fun at a serious and extremely complex scientific theory. In your journal, write about how her humorous telling of the fiasco at the Rialto works together with the small pieces of technical excerpts to give readers not only some chuckles, but also some insight into a complex theory.

2. In an essay, show how the quote that begins this story and the Rialto (and Hollywood in general) are all quantum theory personified.

3. In an essay, discuss the similarities and differences between science (especially physics) and metaphysics—channeling, ESP, crystal power, New Age concerns. How did the movement toward such alternative understanding in the eighties contribute to Willis' presentation of this story?

The Nineties

Nelson Mandela freed from South African prison after 27 years

Germany is reunified

Chunnel from England to France bored underground

Genetically engineered bacteria used for first time to clean up oil spills

Hubble Space Telescope launched into space

Four-year-old girl becomes first person to receive gene therapy

Dr. Jack Kevorkian assists his first of many suicides; murder charges brought, then dropped

Voyager I transmits first photos of the entire solar system back to Earth

Magellan begins orbiting Venus until its failure in 1994

Total Recall, movie based on a Philip K. Dick story, is released

Operation Desert Storm begins high-tech Gulf War

U.S.S.R. dissolved; Mikhail Gorbachev, Soviet president, refuses to resign; Boris Yeltsin, president of Russia, takes over after refusing to join in failed communist coup

Gulf War generates environmental disaster when Iraq discharges over 70,000 tons of oil in Persian Gulf and sets fire to over 1,000 oil wells

Biosphere 2 Project begins with four men and two women in a sealed, self-sustaining environment

Terminator 2 movie appears, pioneering use of digital special effects

George Bush and Boris Yeltsin agree to further reduce nuclear arms, signaling end of Cold War

Earth Summit on world environment held at Rio de Janeiro, Brazil

Race riots erupt in Los Angeles after police officers are acquitted of beating an African-American man in an incident captured on amateur video

"Ripples" discovered in space-time fabric, lending credence to "big bang" theory

Russian cosmonaut Sergey Krikalev completes a record 313 days in space

Cancer fighting compounds discovered in broccoli

Isaac Asimov dies after 53 years of writing science fiction and science articles

Federal raid on extremists' compound in Waco, Texas, results in death of 95 cult members and children

Mideast peace process begins; Israel and Palestine agree to Palestinian self-rule; Iranian forces increase attacks

Muslim terrorists bomb World Trade Center in New York

Hubble Space Telescope repaired in space to clear up fuzzy images

The Encyclopedia of Science Fiction by John Clute and Peter Nicholls is greatly expanded from the 1979 version

Star Trek: Deep Space Nine, another TV series set in the Star Trek universe, debuts

X-Files TV series premieres, combining science fiction and paranormal investigations

North American Free Trade Agreement signed

First multiracial elections held in South Africa; Nelson Mandela elected president

Cease-fire declared in Northern Ireland

Anglican church allows women to be ordained as priests

Mary Shelley's Frankenstein movie is released, returning to the novel's roots

Stargate film combines science fiction with pyramid lore

U.S. brokers Bosnian Peace Plan, which includes stationing 60,000 NATO troops there, and dividing the country by religious affiliations

Political discontents bomb Federal building in Oklahoma City as retaliation for Waco incident

Shannon Faulkner becomes first female cadet at the formerly all male Citadel military institute

Use of Prozac, a prescription drug for controlling anxiety, becomes widespread despite concerns about "personality engineering"

American space shuttle *Atlantis* docks with Russian space station *Mir*

Water discovered on Mars

Pictures of Eagle Nebulae taken from Hubble show stars being created

The Illustrated History of Science Fiction, by John Clute, is published in book form and interactive CD-ROM

Neil Barron's critical work on science fiction, *Anatomy of Wonder 4*, contains significant revisions

NASA scientists discover evidence of microscopic life on Mars

First clone of a mammal

HISTORICAL CONTEXT

Political unrest was prominent in the U.S.S.R. in the nineties.
The satellites of the Soviet Union struggled for independence,
most noticeably in Yugoslavia. Continuing conflicts in the Mideast
led to outbreaks of violence, but Northern Ireland and South
Africa moved toward peaceable settlements. Even though struck
by terrorists at home, the United States continued its policy of
maintaining equilibrium in world affairs.

In the U.S.S.R., Mikhail Gorbachev's reform program began
to falter. The Soviet Union pulled apart as mounting ethnic and
economic pressures built. While Gorbachev was on vacation in
the Crimea, hardline communists attempted a coup. Even though
Gorbachev was captured, Boris Yeltsin, president of the Russian
Republic, gathered support and convinced the military to refuse to
join in the coup. The attempt collapsed, but the U.S.S.R. crumbled,
with Yeltsin remaining in power in Russia. The Soviets withdrew
from their previous political commitments, recalled troops, and
dissolved the Warsaw Pact. Soon after the breakup of the Soviet
Union in 1991, Yeltsin met with U.S. president George Bush in 1992,
and the two powers agreed to a series of nuclear arms reductions.
The Cold War was drawing to an abrupt close.

Meanwhile, in the Mideast, Iraq invaded Kuwait in 1990,
quickly overtaking the unprepared Kuwaitis. The United Nations
condemned the action and Allied Forces mounted Operation
Desert Storm to retake Kuwait. The U.S. forces defeated Iraq by
disabling its air force and crippling the Iraqi missile capability.
Southern Iraq was taken with fewer than 1,000 American lives lost;
however, over 100,000 Iraqis were killed or wounded and 60,000
POWs taken. Even with this resounding U.S. victory, Saddam

Hussein was left in power with significant remaining military forces.

Hussein created a disaster in the wake of his defeat by discharging oil from two island terminals and several tankers off the coast of Kuwait. Americans bombed the pipelines to try to halt the flow, but over 70,000 tons of oil were spilled in the Persian Gulf, destroying countless birds and marine life. Then the Iraqis set fire to over 1,000 oil wells which burned unabated for months, spewing black smoke over the Gulf and southwest Asia. The short-term effects of this combination were calamitous; the long-term effects have yet to be determined.

In South Africa, Nelson Mandela was finally freed from prison in 1990. Negotiations were undertaken to end apartheid and create a multiracial majority rule. A number of skirmishes broke out among the 20 political parties, but a new constitution establishing fundamental rights for all South Africans was agreed upon in 1993. In the first fully free South African national elections of 1994, Mandela was elected president. He formed a government of national unity, calling for racial and political reconciliation in an attempt to overcome the effects of decades of racial segregation.

After the U.S.S.R. dissolved, a bitter civil war broke out in the former Yugoslavia in 1991. After elections, the country's republics of Slovenia, Croatia, and Bosnia declared independence. The Muslims and Croatians attempted to work together, but the Bosnian Serbs refused to cooperate and bombed Sarajevo, a Muslim stronghold. NATO forces joined in by bombing Sarajevo to try to force the Serbs to withdraw.

The United States brought in negotiators who secured a truce signed by the three warring parties in 1995. This peace formula attempted to unify the country, but actually divided it among ethnic lines. There were to be two self-governing parts—a Muslim-Croat Federation and a Bosnian Serb Republic. The presidency was to rotate among Muslim, Croatian, and Bosnian Serbs, with a single parliament for foreign affairs.

In Israel, protestors gathered in 1995 to voice their opposition to prime minister Yitzhak Rabin's plan to relinquish control of the West Bank of Jordan and allow Palestinian self-rule. Rabin and Yasser Arafat, head of the Palestine Liberation Organization, signed an agreement for withdrawal of Israeli troops, though both sides denounced their leaders as traitors. Months later, Rabin was assassinated at a peace rally in Tel Aviv as he attempted to curb rising resentment over the Palestinian peace accord.

In Northern Ireland, British troops ceased their daytime patrols in Belfast. One political murder was committed in 1995, as opposed to the nearly everyday occurrences that had been common before the cease-fire was declared. The British demanded that the IRA turn in some of its weapons before the formal peace talks could continue, but Sinn Fein leader Gerry Adams refused. He said that handing over arms would be viewed as a "symbolic surrender" by the IRA, something they would not tolerate. British prime minister John Major held firm in his demand, and President Clinton, in an attempt to find some common ground, became the first U.S. president ever to visit Northern Ireland. Though he promoted a peace plan and was well received, the peace talks were stalled, and an uneasy peace existed.

DEVELOPMENTS IN SCIENCE FICTION

In the nineties, the information overload has affected science fiction to the extent that one cannot read all the science fiction stories produced in a year. Throughout the nineties, approximately 300 new science fiction books were published each year. This doesn't include the number of short stories, novellas, novellettes, and original anthologies produced, nor does it include other science fiction media, such as comics, graphic novels, cartoons, TV series, movies, computer and role-playing games, CD-ROM titles, or books and essays about science fiction.

With this range of titles comes a diversity of themes. Sex, political controversies, and interracial relationships were touched on by both new and established writers. Gardner Dozois, editor of the *Year's Best Science Fiction* annual anthology series and *Isaac Asimov's Science Fiction Magazine,* estimated that, due to content and stylistic approach, 70 percent of the novels and 90 percent of the short stories published in 1993 could not have been published in 1963; most still could not have been published in 1973; and a considerable portion could not have been published in 1983.

With all this material, and even though science fiction has been accepted by the academic community, it is still viewed as genre fiction, meaning it can be fit into a type, and therefore is not high literature. However, some academicians feel that science fiction writers exhibit many similarities in approach to postmodern authors such as William Burroughs, Thomas Pynchon, and Samuel Beckett. Postmodernism reflects the worlds subjects inhabit; in a sense it is more about the surroundings—the objects—than the subjects who inhabit the world.

In postmodernist fiction, people often lose a sense of themselves as individuals and become overwhelmed by their surroundings. The ways of being in the world are stressed over ways of knowing the significance of that world. In some ways, science fiction overlaps with postmodernism, particularly in the fiction of the post-cyberpunk writers who construct densely layered technological nightmare societies. The information overload of the nineties and virtual reality, still in its infancy, may eventually lead to a world similar to what postmodernism suggests.

Due to diversified competition, science fiction magazines suffered reduced circulation in the nineties. Both *Analog Science Fiction and Science Fact* and *Isaac Asimov's Science Fiction Magazine* saw a 30 percent reduction from their eighties numbers. Despite this, *Asimov's,* in particular, continues to encourage new writers as well as publish established ones. American writers dominate the market in America, as American readers reject British writers as "too British." The idea that anything that matters in future history will be American is found among readers and editors alike.

Some trends of the nineties include alternate histories with story lines about alternate careers of U.S. presidents. Also popular are steampunk stories set in Victorian London with significant changes, such as Jack the Ripper being caught by Sherlock Holmes. The cyberpunk writers, though the label has fallen into disfavor, haven't just disappeared. Many of them continue to produce stories much like the ones they popularized in the eighties.

There is a tremendous diversity in science fiction in the nineties, and a clear direction has not been established. Instead, science fiction is exploring many avenues and realities set in future histories. Its strength lies now, not in its unity under a single banner, but in its rich traditions, its acceptance into the popular culture, its pool of talented writers, and its tremendous range of subject matter. There is more quality and variety in nineties science fiction than ever before. The past decade may have been the Golden Age of science fiction, but now is the true age of maturity of the genre—the Platinum Age.

SCIENCE FICTION IN OTHER MEDIA

In other media, science fiction flourished in the nineties. Comics held their own despite rising production costs, especially on the more expensive slick reproductions. More graphic novels appeared, some compilations of previously printed stories, while others went directly to the longer format. In 1955, Batman appeared under nine separate titles, with overlapping story lines.

Several notable TV shows debuted in the nineties. *Star Trek: Deep Space Nine* (1993–) continues the Star Trek saga, this time on an outpost that is a haven for travelers using a wormhole for transportation. Some of the characters from *The Next Generation* have been transferred to *Deep Space Nine*. It also features the first black commander in a continuing role. *Babylon Five* (1993–) shows a postmodern epic of despair and is considerably darker than other TV science fiction. *The X-Files* (1993–) pairs a believer in psychic phenomena with a skeptic. Together they investigate reports of unusual events, adding some drama and sexual tension into the mix. The show has attracted a loyal core of fans. *Star Trek: Voyager* (1994–) is yet another installment in the Star Trek universe, this time featuring a female captain and a ship trapped far from home and trying to return.

Movies continued to explore science fiction themes. *Total Recall* (1990) is another Philip K. Dick story loosely adapted to the screen. It is about artificial memories and one individual's search for his true identity. Special effects and high speed action, though, are the main vehicles for propelling this into popularity. *Communion* (1990), based on the book by Will Streiber, is the story of a man who is abducted by aliens, tested, then returned to society. Though his memory is at first blocked, he eventually remembers and then tries to convince others of the truth of the abduction.

In 1991, *Terminator 2* used digital special effects to produce a startlingly realistic shape-shifting robot who is out to destroy the leader of the human revolution which triumphs against robots in the future. This time the robot in the first *Terminator* has been reprogrammed by the humans to protect the present-day protagonist. The story line is weaker, but the effects are superb. *The Lawnmower Man* (1992) is an updating of *Flowers for Algernon,* but uses virtual reality instead of drugs to enhance the intelligence of a dull-witted grounds worker. The story is overshadowed by the effects, but they are visually stunning.

Jurassic Park (1993), a Steven Spielberg extravaganza, took digital effects a step further by using highly believable computer-generated images for much of the action sequences. In one sequence, one of the human actors is digitized and his actions are controlled by the computer, the first such use of the digital technology.

A most unusual movie project came to theaters in 1993. *The Crow,* starring Brandon Lee, son of the late Bruce Lee of martial arts fame, is a movie about a dead musician who returns from the grave to complete his task on Earth. However, Lee died during the filming. The producers decided to take advantage of digital technology and proceed with the movie. They used a stand-in actor and recreated an image of Lee's face from their already filmed footage. They also used digital sampling to make the voice Lee's. This astounding feat of moviemaking magic has tremendous implications for the future. The role of human actors and stunt people may be redefined as computer effects become capable of manipulating the action on screen to suit a director's whim in ways that humans can't possibly duplicate.

Mary Shelley's Frankenstein (1994) is perhaps the closest adaptation of Shelley's novel yet to appear on the screen. The creature is portrayed as a misunderstood outcast bent on revenge against the creator who has abandoned him, much as Shelley portrayed him in her novel. The movie returns to the novel's roots, though it incorporates a few twists of its own.

The first movie to feature the Next Generation crew of the *Enterprise* appeared in 1994. *Star Trek: Generations* also included a few cast members from the original series, and was a transition from one crew to the next. But in 1996, the torch was finally passed entirely to the Next Generation crew in *Star Trek: First Contact.*

The Abduction of Bunny Steiner, or a Shameless Lie

1992

THOMAS DISCH (b. 1940)

Thomas Disch began publishing science fiction with "The Double-Timer" in *Fantastic Stories of Imagination* in 1962. His first novel, *The Genocides* (1965) shows aliens seeding Earth with huge plants they plan to harvest. As the plants take over, humans struggle to survive, as the aliens treat them as agricultural pests. In *Mankind Under the Leash* (1965), aliens take over the planet and use humans as pets. Disch's early short stories have been collected as *One Hundred and Two H Bombs* (1966, revised 1971).

Disch was identified with the New Wave of sixties writers in England, and his *Camp Concentration* (1967) shows the experiences of a person in a near future concentration camp. Prisoners there are treated with intelligence-enhancing drugs whose major side effect is to shorten their lives drastically. Disch also produced a book, *The Prisoner* (1969), as a tie-in to the TV series of the same name, as well as several volumes of speculative poetry, including *The Best Way to Figure Plumbing* (1972).

His 1972 collection of linked stories, *334*, contains stories set in an apartment building of that address. The stories themselves, while separate, can be read sequentially, making the book like a novel. It is set in the world of 2025 where survival is difficult. *On Wings of Songs* (1979) is likewise set in near future New York. It focuses on the difficulties of producing art in a world increasingly overcome by material concerns and spiritual apathy. His later short works have been collected in *Fundamental Disch* (1980) and *The Man Who Had No Idea* (1982). As his career has progressed, though, Disch has shown less interest in narrative fiction and has instead turned to plays, poetry, and theatrical reviews.

**In "The Abduction of Bunny Steiner, or a Shameless Lie,"
Thomas Disch takes a humorous look at what happens when someone
tries to capitalize on a hot idea, then has that idea turn into something
quite unexpected.**

1   When Rudy Steiner's agent, Mal Bitzberg, called up with the idea
that Rudy should produce a UFO book after the manner of Whitley
Strieber's *Communion, a True Story,* Rudy thought Bitzberg was putting
him on. It was April 1, but Rudy's situation was too desperate for April
Fool's Day jokes. Bitzberg knew how desperate Rudy was at the present moment, the latest, lowest nadir of a career rich in nadirs. He was:
(a) in debt well over his head, (b) apartmentless; (c) obese; (d) an apos-
tate member of A.A.; (e) in his third month of writer's block; and the
crown jewel among Rudy's woes, (f) all the royalties for his best-selling
fantasy series, *The Elfin Horde,* et al., were being held in perpetual es-
crow pending the settlement of a lawsuit that had been brought against
him and his subsequently bankrupted publisher, Djinn Books. The
lawsuit had been initiated by a Baltimore attorney and professional liti-
gant, Rafe Boone, who specialized in charging best-selling authors
with plagiarism and settling with them out of court. Rudy had balked
at shelling out $100,000.00 to Boone, a jury had decided in Boone's
favor, and then an appeals court had reversed the verdict. While Boone
was contesting that appeal, he had been shot dead on the steps of the
courthouse by another of his victims. Shortly afterward, the legal remains of Djinn Books had been swallowed up by a German publishing
consortium. Boone having died intestate, his estate was now being con-
tested by five separate claimants, and the bulk of that estate consisted of
their potential seizure of Rudy's royalties. It was the opinion of Rudy's
attorney, Merrill Yates, that Rudy had as much chance of finding the
pot of gold at the end of the rainbow as of seeing any further proceeds
from *The Elfin Horde* and its six sequels. Worse, he'd been enjoined
from writing new books in the series and even from using the pseudonym of Priscilla Wisdom. The experience had been embittering.

2   "A UFO story?" Rudy had marveled. "You've got to be kidding.
Besides the Strieber book, Random House is bringing out one just like
it by that other jerk."

3   But Bitzberg was not a kidder. "So? That means it's a trend. All
you need is a slightly different angle. Strieber's angle is he's the first
name writer who's been inside a UFO. Hopkins has got this whole club

of UFO witnesses, which anyone can join: that's his angle, democracy. The whole thing could become a religion. Anyhow that's what Janet Cruse thinks. It was her idea. And she thinks you're the person to write the next book."

4   "Janet Cruse? You've got to be kidding!"

5   Bitzberg shook his head and smiled a snaggletoothed smile that had been known to frighten small children. "She's with Knopf now, and she wants *you* to write a UFO book."

6   "Janet Cruse is with Knopf? I can't believe it."

7   Years ago, when Janet, a Canadian living in London, had been handling Rudy's English rights, she had sold several of his Priscilla Wisdom titles in foreign markets without telling him. By the time he'd discovered what she'd done, Janet had absconded to Toronto. She'd sold three books in Belgium, two in Portugal, four in Israel, and those were just the sales Rudy had found out about. He'd never seen a cent of the money.

8   "She realizes you've got reason to be angry with her. But she hoped this might make it up to you."

9   "If she wants to make it up to me, she could just pay me the money she stole."

10   "She doesn't have it. Believe me, I've seen where she's living. She's no better off than you."

11   "And she's at *Knopf*? And Knopf wants a UFO book?"

12   "Knopf brought her in, because she's considered an expert on occult writers. UFOs are as respectable as astrology these days. Random House, Atlantic Monthly Press—those are not your typical exploitation publishers. Anyhow, do you want to have lunch with her or not?"

13   "What kind of money are we talking about?"

14   "Fifty thousand. Half with the portion and outline, half on publication."

15   "Fifty thousand? Strieber got a *million*."

16   "So? Maybe he's got a better agent. Or maybe he's got a bigger name. Or maybe it was because he was there first."

17   Rudy sighed. He had no choice, and Bitzberg knew it. "Set up a lunch."

18   Bitzberg exposed his terrible teeth. "It's already set up. Tomorrow, one o'clock, Moratuwa Wok."

19   "And *moriture te salutamus* to you too, old buddy."

20   Bitzberg lit a cigarette. His fingers trembled, making the flame of the match quaver. His fingers had trembled as long as Rudy had known him. It was some kind of nervous affliction. "I do what I can, Rudy, I do what I can."

21   "So this is my idea," Janet Cruse explained the next day, sipping lukewarm tea from a dainty cracked teacup. "Strieber's book shows that the audience is there, and Hopkins's book shows that anyone can tell essentially the same story that Strieber did and the similarity only goes to *prove* that something strange has to be happening, or how is it that *everyone* is telling the same story?"

22   "How indeed," Rudy agreed.

23   "Now the one thing you *have* to promise, Rudy, is that you never joke about this. Flying saucers are like religion. You've got to be solemn. Have you read Strieber's book?"

24   He nodded.

25   "Then you know the basic line to take. You're upset, you're confused, you're skeptical, you can hardly believe what's happened to you. And you're terribly grateful to Strieber and Hopkins for having had the courage to tell their stories, because now at last you can tell the world about you—and Bunny."

26   "Bunny?"

27   Janet dabbed at the crisp, crimson corners of her lips with a paper napkin. "Bunny is your daughter." She tilted her head coquettishly and waited for him to express some suitable astonishment.

28   He maintained a poker face, however, and their waitress chose just that moment to arrive with their bowls of millet, steamed vegetables, and a condiment made of onion and raisins. Moratuwa Wok was a Sri Lankan vegetarian restaurant, and it did not have a liquor license. There were gaudy posters of Hindu gods on the wall, and scented candles burning on each of the six tables. Janet and Rudy were the only people having lunch.

29   "How old is my daughter Bunny?" he asked, after the waitress had gone away.

30   "Oh, I'd say five or six. Four would be ideal, it's when kids are cutest, but you've got to consider that a lot of the text will be Bunny's account while she's under hypnosis."

31   "Mm-hm."

32   He considered Janet's proposition while she nibbled a stalk of asparagus still so crisp it barely drooped as she lifted it to her lips. Sri Lankans did not overcook their vegetables.

33   "You see how inevitable it is, don't you?" Janet said, halfway down the stalk. "Strieber *played* with the possibility. His little boy was allowed to hear the reindeer on the roof, so to speak, and who knows but that in his next book he'll go all the way and have the dear boy abducted. And *missing* for a few days. Imagine the anguish a parent must suffer. Especially a *father*. How long was Cosby's *Fatherhood* at the top of the

list? And how many copies did it sell? It set a record, I think, and it's
still going strong. And what could be a greater torment for a loving father than to have his daughter abducted by aliens, who perform unspeakable acts on her? Which is what mainly goes on, as I understood
it, in all those unidentified flying objects. So there you've got another
hot issue for a cherry on the sundae: child abuse. Can you imagine any
paperback house turning down a package like that?"

34   "It sounds like a very marketable commodity, Janet, I agree.
There's only one problem."

35   "What's that? Tell me, I'll solve it." She snapped decisively at a car-
rot stick. "You don't have a daughter, is that it? *That* is why you are the
ideal dad for little Bunny. Because *obviously* we can't rely on a kid that
young to go on talk show circuits and be cross-examined. So what *you*
say is that Bunny has been so traumatized by her abduction that she
can't possibly be exposed to the brutalizing attentions of the press. She
has to be protected from all that, which is why there are no photographs in the book. And as for the fact that Bunny doesn't exist,
that's what makes it perfect. That way even Woodward and Bernstein
themselves couldn't find her."

36   Rudy shook his head. "No one will buy it."

37   "Believe me, they'll buy a million copies."

38   "Anyone who knows me knows I don't have a daughter."

39   "But who knows you, Rudy? No one, a dozen people. You don't
have a job to go to every day. You've been in and out of A.A. You're
broke. Obviously you haven't been the best father in the world to
Bunny, but that's part of your anguish. She's being raised by her mother,
somewhere upstate, and you visit them whenever you can."

40   "And what's her name, Bunny's mother?"

41   "Kimberly, Jennifer, Melissa, take your pick. You can spend a couple chapters filling in the background on the guilt you feel for having
let her bear all the responsibility for Bunny's upbringing. You've offered to marry her, because she's a beautiful, talented woman, but she's
refused to consider it until you've proved you can stay sober one full
year. And of course you can't, but you still visit them whenever you
can. They live in this *chalet* in the Catskills. Melissa handles real estate.
Or does she paint? No, real estate, that's a daydream anyone can handle.
So that's Bunny's background. The story proper can begin in June."

42   "This coming June?"

43   "Mm-hm, when you've agreed to go and look after Bunny, while
Melissa takes a well-deserved vacation. You can guess what happens then."

44   "She's abducted by the aliens."

45   "Right. For *five days* she's missing, and you are frantic, but even so an obscure impulse keeps you from notifying the police. You search the woods. You see the clearing where the UFO must have landed. You find Bunny's doll there in the matted-down grass. No, better than that: her dog, her faithful dog who followed her everywhere."

46   "Wouldn't it be better if the dog were abducted with her?"

47   "Of course! What am I telling you all this for, anyhow? *You're* the writer."

48   "Do you really think I've sunk so low that I'd write the book you're talking about?"

49   "Oh, I think you'd always have *written* it, Rudy. The only difference now is that you'll sign your name to it."

50   "You think I'm shameless."

51   She nodded.

52   She was right.

53   Five weeks later he'd finished a first draft of 340 pages. *The Visitation* was shorter than either Strieber's book or Hopkins's, but it was intense. If Knopf insisted, he could pad out the middle chapters with more paternal anguish and add any number of pages to the transcript of Bunny's testimony under hypnosis. After the nature descriptions—an idyllic walk with Bunny through blossoming mountain laurels and the thunderstorm on the night she disappears—that transcript was the best thing in the book. The Xlom themselves (such was the name he'd given the aliens that both Strieber and Hopkins had left nameless) were no more incredible than darling four-year-old bright-as-a-button Bunny. "Honey Bunny" he called her in moments of supreme paternal doting, or "Funny Bunny" when she was being mischievous, and sometimes (but never in the book, only when he'd finished his day's quota of ten pages), with a fond, bourbon-scented smile, "Money Bunny." Margaret O'Brien had never been more endearing, and Shirley Temple was crass by comparison. Bunny was sugar and spice and everything nice.

54   And the Xlom were unspeakable. Strieber and Hopkins had both been very equivocal about their aliens. Strieber even allowed as how they might not come from Outer Space but maybe from some Other Dimension or else perhaps they were gods. *Quien sabe?* Half Strieber's book was devoted to such bootless speculations. Hopkins was less accommodating. His aliens seemed to be conducting genetic experiments on their captive humans, impregnating the women with genetically altered sperm stolen from the men and then, when the unwilling brides were a couple months pregnant, abducting them again and stealing

their fetuses. Hopkins supplied no explanation as to why his aliens did this, but it certainly was not an activity that inspired trust.

55   Rudy himself went easy on the enforced pregnancy fantasy (Bunny, after all, was only four), but he bore down hard on the details of the little darling's physical examinations and on the mysterious scar tissue that came to be discovered all over her body. Hopkins had also done a lot with scars, including some blurry photos of what looked like knees with squeezed pimples. Sometimes Rudy felt a tad uneasy about the transparency of *The Visitation*'s S & M sub-text, but Janet had told him not to worry on that score. The target audience for UFO books could read the entire works of the Marquis de Sade, she insisted, and if the Sadean cruelties were ascribed to aliens, they would remain completely innocent as to what it was they were getting off on. Such had been the wisdom of Priscilla Wisdom in her time, as well, so Rudy didn't have any problem letting it all hang out. He wrote at a pace he hadn't managed for the past five years and enjoyed doing it. It might not be art, but it was definitely a professional job.

56   Two weeks after he'd turned in the manuscript to Bitzberg and had been duly patted on the back for his speedy performance, Rudy still had not heard from Janet, nor (which was more worrisome) had he got back the executed contracts from Knopf. Feeling antsy, he called the Knopf office and asked to speak to Ms. Cruse.

57   "Who?" the receptionist asked.

58   "Janet Cruse," he insisted. "She's my editor there."

59   The receptionist insisted that there was no editor with Knopf called Janet Cruse, nor any record of there ever having been one.

60   He realized right away that he'd been conned. The walk back to the Knopf office after the lunch at Moratuwa Wok, the good-bye at the elevators, the freebie copy of the Updike book (*Trust Me,* indeed!), the boilerplate contracts with the Knopf logo (something that any agent would have had many opportunities to acquire, alter, and duplicate), and then the constant barrage of phone calls "just to kibbitz," but really to keep him from ever needing to call her at the Knopf office.

61   But what about Bitzberg: hadn't *he* ever tried to call her at Knopf? Or talked to someone else there about *The Visitation?* On the other hand, if Bitzberg knew Janet wasn't at Knopf, if he'd been in collusion with her from the start, why would he have advanced Rudy $10,000 from his own pocket to tide him over until the nonexistent Knopf advance came in?

62   "I didn't," Bitzberg explained, "know that, at first. And when I came to suspect it, I admit that I didn't at once tell you. At that point the book was half done, and I'd received money. Not from Knopf, ad-

mittedly, but the check didn't bounce for all that. If you want to bow out now, I expect we could take the money and run. On the other hand, there is a bonafide contract for *sixty* thou, and they're not asking for any revisions. They love the book as is."

63   "They?"

64   "The People."

65   "Who are the people?"

66   "A cult, I gather. I asked Janet, and she was not particularly forthcoming. But they have their own imprint, Orange Bangle Press." Bitzberg raised a cigarette in his trembling fingers: "I know what you're going to say. You're going to be sarcastic about the name of the press. *But* they have had a major best-seller, *I Wish I May.*"

67   "I've never heard of it."

68   "Well, maybe 'major' is an exaggeration. It sold almost forty thousand copies in a trade paperback over the last two years. And they expect to do a lot more with your book."

69   "You've got a contract?"

70   Bitzberg smiled, he nodded, he cringed. "I'll show you," he said.

71   Rudy read the contract.

72   He signed it.

73   Only then did he go to the library and find out what there was to be known about The People.

74   The People had begun, humbly enough, in 1975 as a support group in San Diego for smokers trying to kick the habit by means of meditation and herbal medicine. This original narrow focus gradually came to include other areas of concern, from the therapeutic use of precious stones in the cure of breast cancer and diabetes to the need for a stronger defense posture. One of the group's founding members and the author most often published by Orange Bangle Press was Ms. Lillian Devore, the sole heir of Robert P. Devore of the munitions firm Devore International, contractors for the Navy's Atreus missile. Most of the information in the library about The People focused on the recent legal proceedings concerning the mental competence of Ms. Devore, and her subsequent demise only two months ago just after a court had found that she was not provably insane, notwithstanding certain passages in her published works and the opinions of psychiatrists hired by her niece and nephew, who had brought the case against her.

75   Needless to say, that niece and nephew had inherited nothing from Ms. Devore's estate, all of which was bequeathed to The People with the sole proviso that the organization continue to advance the study of herbal medicine and to investigate UFO phenomena. UFOs had become a matter of concern only late in Ms. Devore's life, after she had

entertained the hypothesis at her trial that her niece and nephew might conceivably have been the issue of secret genetic experiments being conducted by aliens on the women of Earth (and on her half-sister Sue-Beth Smith in particular). This was essentially the same hypothesis being advanced by Budd Hopkins in *Intruders,* and Ms. Devore's defense attorney was able to introduce as evidence both Hopkins's book and an open letter by the head of Random House, Howard Kaminsky, stating that the publisher and his associates were persuaded of the book's veracity, intellectual integrity, and great importance. It followed from this, Ms. Devore's attorney had argued, that his client must be considered at least as sane as Howard Kaminsky, and the jury had agreed. Two weeks later, at the ripe old age of ninety-four, this monument to the efficacy of herbal medicine died in her sleep, and the last to be heard of The People in the news concerned the unsuccessful efforts of one of The People to have Ms. Devore's estate divided equally among the 150 members of the sect. That effort was quickly quashed, and the direction of the organization and the control of its funds was to remain under the direction of Ms. Devore's former financial adviser and dear friend, B. Franklin Grace, the man who had figured so prominently during the competency hearings for his role in protecting Ms. Devore from the attention of the press. It was Grace, as the head of Orange Bangle Press, who had signed the contract for *The Visitation.*

76   *Books in Print* listed four titles by Lillian Devore, including her reputed best-seller, *I Wish I May,* but none were available either from the library or at any bookstore where Rudy asked for them. So that was the end of his research efforts. Anyhow, it seemed pretty clear what had happened. Janet had contacted B. Franklin Grace and pitched her idea for the *Communion* rip-off to him, got a go-ahead, and then scouted for someone desperate enough to write it. Why she'd felt she had to diddle Rudy into thinking he was doing the book for Knopf was still a puzzle. Either she thought he needed the extra bait of Knopf's respectability before he took the hook, or else she might have figured he would have been greedier if he'd know he was dipping his royalties from The Fund for The People, Inc. He also wasn't sure whether Janet had come up with the whole scheme by herself or if she and Bitzberg had acted in collusion. But since the final result was a valid contract and money in the bank, Rudy was willing to put his legitimate anger on hold, take the money, and sit tight. On the whole, he felt he'd be happier being published by Orange Bangle instead of by Knopf, since on the basis of Orange Bangle's previous track record, no one might ever find out that *The Visitation* existed. His poor dear imaginary daughter might have endured all her indignities in vain, like the fabled tree that falls, unheard, in

the middle of the forest. With luck, he might not even be reviewed in *Publisher's Weekly* (Orange Bangle verged on being a vanity press), and his authorship would remain a secret shame, the easiest kind to bear.

77   He celebrated his windfall by renting a tape of *Close Encounters* and watching it, soused, with the sound off and Mahler's 8th on the stereo. He fell asleep as Richard Dreyfuss was heading for Wyoming to rendezvous with the aliens' mothership. He woke at 4 A.M. feeling just the way he'd felt in *The Visitation* the first time he'd been returned to his summer cabin after having been abducted and experimented on by the Xlom: his head ached, he was ravenously hungry, and he had an obscure sense that something terrible had just happened to him but he didn't know what.

78   *The Visitation* appeared in October and disappeared at once into the vast limbo of unreviewed books, at least as far as New York was concerned. Janet assured him that the real market for UFO books was in the sticks and that there the book was selling reasonably well. The lack of reviews was par for the course with crackpot books, since anyone credulous enough to take such revelations seriously was probably too dumb to write coherent prose. What was a source of concern was the lack of media attention due to what Janet diplomatically referred to as Rudy's image problem, meaning his weight. TV talk shows did not like to feature fat people unless they were famously fat. Similar consideration had prompted Orange Bangle not to put Rudy's picture on the book jacket.

79   Then, early in November, little Bunny Steiner made her TV debut on a late night talk show in St. Paul. The next day Rudy's phone didn't stop ringing. He claimed, quite truthfully, to know nothing about Bunny's appearance and said that until he saw a tape of the show he could not be certain it had actually been *his* Bunny who'd given such a vivid account of her abduction by the Xlom. When he tried to reach Janet, she was unreachable, and B. Franklin Grace (whom Rudy had not, previously, tried to talk to) was likewise not taking calls.

80   He let it ride.

81   The phone calls continued: from Milwaukee, from Detroit, from somewhere in West Virginia, from Buffalo, New York. Bunny got around, and everywhere she got to she seemed to make a considerable impression. Some of the phone calls were accusing in tone, with the unspoken suggestion behind them that Rudy had been personally responsible for his daughter's ordeal, a suggestion he indignantly resisted. "What kind of monster do you think I am?" he would demand of his unseen interrogators.

82   "Maybe a Xlom?" one of them had replied, and then hung up without awaiting his answer.

83   Finally, by agreeing to go to Philadelphia for his own late-night inquisition (albeit on radio), Rudy was able to obtain, as his quid pro quo, a VHS tape of Bunny's appearance on *The Brotherly Breakfast Hour*. He slipped the tape into his player, and there she was on his own TV, in the living color of her flesh, his imaginary four-year-old daughter, pretty much the way he'd described her: a blonde, curly-haired, dimple-cheeked, lisping mini-maniac, who rolled her eyes and wrang her hands and commanded the willing suspension of any conceivable disbelief as she re-told the story of her abduction. While her delivery was not verbatim, Bunny rarely strayed beyond the boundaries of the text that Rudy had written, and she never was betrayed into a significant contradiction. Her few embroideries were all in the area of the ineffable and the unspoken, quavers and semi-quavers and moments of stricken silence when she found herself unable to say just where the funny bald people with their big eyes had touched her or what they'd asked her to do. When asked such intimate questions, she would look away—into the camera—and cry real tears. This child had clearly been through experiences that words could not express. Little wonder that the media was picking up on Bunny's performance. She was a miniature Sarah Bernhardt.

84   Bunny's star reached its zenith just before Xmas, when *The Nation* (which you'd think would have had more dignity than to interest itself in UFOs) published a long article examining the books of Rudy, Strieber, Hopkins, and the Atlantic Monthly Press's contender, Gary Kinder, whose *Light Years* (released in June) featured color photos of UFOs taken by a one-armed Swiss farmer, Eduard Meier. The Kinder book had been expected to enjoy an even larger success than *Communion*, being buttressed not only with its snapshots but with quotes from bonafide scientists, including Stevie Wonder's sound engineer. However, before *Light Years'* release it was discovered that Wendelle Stevens, one of the investigators who'd acted as matchmaker between Meier and the author (and therefore shared in the book's royalties) was serving time in an Arizona prison on a charge of child molestation. There had been no child involved in the Meier UFO sightings, so Stevens's crime should have had no bearing on the book's credibility, as Kinder was at pains to point out in a last-minute Appendix. Nevertheless, the critic in *The Nation* made every effort to tar all four UFO books with the same brush, concentrating his most sinister innuendos on the possibility that Bunny may have been subjected to a false abduction in which Rudy had been an accomplice.

85   "Young children believe in Santa Claus," the man had argued, "because they *see* him, in his red suit and his white beard, filling their stockings with presents. Who could he be *but* Santa? They have no reason to suspect deceit, no suspicion that for many grown-ups bamboozling the young is its own reward. Might Bunny Steiner not have been put in the same position vis-a-vis the Xlom? Perhaps the reason her testimony has such a distressing fascination, even for UFO skeptics like myself, is that she is not lying. Perhaps the terrible events reported in *The Visitation* really did take place. Only Mr. Steiner can say with any certainty whether his daughter is one of the hoaxers—or one of the hoaxed."

86   Rudy's problem, of course, was that he couldn't say anything with any certainty. Janet, when he finally did get through to her, would only burble on about what a brilliant marketing strategy Bunny's TV appearances represented. She brushed aside all of Rudy's questions about who Bunny was and where she came from and how the book was selling.

87   "But her *scars*," he insisted nervously. "They don't look fake. How did she . . . ."

88   Janet laughed. "Surely you don't think only aliens can perform surgery. Kids are always falling down and getting stitched back together. You shouldn't let yourself be upset by one article in one magazine."

89   "But what if the *police* became interested? What if they say they want to talk with Bunny?"

90   "*What* police, Rudy? Be reasonable. No one knows what state Bunny lives in, for heaven's sake, much less what city. And *you* are not legally responsible for her, are you? Only her mother is, only Melissa, and she's been very careful to keep both herself and Bunny out of the limelight *except* for her carefully scripted minutes before the cameras. The minute they leave that studio, Bunny's little blonde wig comes off, and she's another girl."

91   "But is it all an act, or . . . ?"

92   "No, of course not, it's all true, and she really is your daughter, conceived on board a flying saucer with the semen the Xlom stole from you one night when, according to the false memory they've implanted in your brain, you thought you were watching a rerun of *The Sound of Music*. And *I'm* the reincarnation of Marie Antoinette."

93   "You know what I mean," Rudy protested, uncajoled.

94   "I have never met Bunny, or Melissa X. or B. Franklin Grace for that matter. And I don't see what difference it makes, whether Bunny believes what she's saying or not. She's still a consummate little actress, and her performances are earning us all a pot of money. So why look a gift horse in the mouth?"

95   "For the Trojans those were famous last words."

96   "You want reassurance? I'll reassure you. I wasn't going to tell you
about this till the deal was firmed up, but at this point we're just hag-
gling over sub-rights percentages, so what the hell. HarperCollins is
taking over distribution for Orange Bangle, *on condition* that you write
a final chapter bringing the story up to date. Which means you've got
a real shot at the list."

97   "And what's in the last chapter—a searing account of my trial for
child molestation?"

98   "No, an account of your disbelief, amazement, horror, and shock
when you go to visit Bunny and her mother on Christmas Eve and
you find that they've *both* been abducted. This time, since it's winter,
you'll be able to take photos of where the UFO landed in the snow.
Then after the first thaw you report them missing."

99   Rudy's jaw dropped. "To the *police?*"

100   "Do you know how many people are reported missing every week?
Thousands. You're not saying abducted, not to the police. You just say
that two people are missing who *are* missing. Who know why? Maybe
all the publicity was too much for Melissa and she decided to take
Bunny and the money and disappear. Or *maybe* the Xlom decided that
Bunny had to be taken somewhere where scientists couldn't examine
her. In either case, your fatherly heart is broken, and all you can hope
for is that some day, somewhere you'll see your little Bunny again."

101   "HarperCollins *wants* this? You laid this out for them in advance?"

102   "Well, I couldn't come right out and say what the Xlom may be
intending to do. I just promised them that the last chapter would contain sensational new material. I think they got my drift. Of course,
you'll have to split your royalties fifty-fifty for the new edition. On the
other hand, it's not a sequel, it's just a final chapter that you can write
in a weekend."

103   "Fifty-fifty with whom?"

104   "With your original publisher, Orange Bangle. I expect a good
part of their cut will go to pay off Bunny and her mom. They can't be
doing all this for nothing."

105   "Do you know what the penalty is for reporting a spurious abduction? A $10,000 fine and five years in prison."

106   "It won't be spurious. Bunny and her mom will have genuinely
disappeared. If you *speculate* in your book that the Xlom have taken
them from the face of the planet, that's just your theory. And if, later
on, they should turn up somewhere else *on* the planet, all that can be
inferred from that is that they're trying to avoid public attention, including yours, which they're entitled to do. But I think it highly un-

likely they'll be found. The FBI isn't going to make it a top priority, and where are they going to start looking? It's a big country."

107   "You've discussed this with Grace?"

108   "Mm-hm. And he's even thrown out hints that Bunny and her mom will be returning to their original happy home, complete with a daddy and sibs. So anyone trying to track down a single woman and her blonde daughter will be following a false scent."

109   "And when the police ask me for information about them?"

110   "Grace has created a paper trail that is fairly close to the 'facts' presented in *The Visitation*. Remember all those little changes that appeared in the book after you returned the galleys? That's why they're there. That's why we made Melissa such a mystery woman. Maybe *she* was an alien! Have you ever considered that? Or maybe she's one of the first generation of genetically altered human beings that the aliens have been training to vamp humanity! But that's too good an idea to waste on this book. Keep that one in reserve, and in the ripeness of time we can approach HarperCollins with a sequel: *I Married a Xlom*."

111   "But I *didn't* marry her."

112   "Rudy, you are such a *pedant*. Anyhow, when can I see that last chapter?"

113   There didn't seem to be any point in further argument. He'd written Bunny into existence. Now he would write her out of existence. "When do you need it?"

114   "Yesterday."

115   "You've got it."

116   The disappearance of Bunny and Melissa, when that event was finally staged, was like a long-postponed visit to the dentist. The worst of it was in the anxiety beforehand, especially in the week from Christmas through New Year's Day that he had to spend alone in the newly vacated chalet. Most of the neighboring vacation houses were standing empty at that time of year, so he was spared having to make a spectacle of himself going about and asking after his missing significant others. Of those people he did approach, only the crippled woman who tended the nearest convenience store claimed to recognize Bunny and Melissa from the photo he showed them, and all she could remember of them was that the little girl had been particularly fond of Pepperidge Farm cookies, which seemed a precocious and expensive taste in such a very young girl. "Mostly at that age their mommies buy them Ding-Dongs or Twinkies, but not that little lady. *She* got Brussels cookies, or Milanos, or Lidos. Did they skip out on their bills, is that why you're asking?" Rudy had assured her it was nothing like that.

117   With the police he had to be more forthcoming. He could not withhold the fact that the missing girl had figured in *The Visitation* for an earlier disappearance, which the book had ascribed to UFOs. To his relief, though the policemen obviously suspected that Bunny's latest disappearance was a repeat performance of her first, they did not seem annoyed to have been called in. Indeed, both men had their own UFO stories to relate to Rudy concerning mysterious lights that had appeared in the area around the Ashokan reservoir, moving at higher speeds and lower altitudes than could have been the case if they'd been ordinary airplanes. Rudy ended up taking more notes about their UFO sightings than they did concerning the missing girl and her mother. As the friendlier of the two policemen suggested, with a conspiratorial wink, maybe Melissa was just trying to avoid him. Maybe her arranging to spend the holiday with him had been a kind of practical joke. In any case, while it might be mysterious, it was not the sort of mystery the police ought to take an interest in.

118   When they left the chalet, Rudy called up Janet to jubilate and to ask her to hold up the final production of the new revised edition until he could add something about the testimony of the two policemen.

119   Saleswise the new edition was something of a letdown. Disappearances are in their nature hard to ballyhoo, since the person who might do the job best isn't around. An effort was made to have Rudy, despite his obesity, appear on the talk shows where Bunny had been such a hit, but most of them declined the opportunity. The few times he did appear, the shows' hosts were openly derisive. Most of their questions had to do with his earnings from *The Visitation* and his relationship with B. Franklin Grace and The People, who were in the news once again for allegedly having tried to poison Ms. Devore's litigious niece and nephew in the period before her competency hearings. Rudy was not enough of a showman to make emotional headway against such currents, and he came off looking sheepish and creepy. He retired from the talk show circuit with a strong conviction that his fifteen minutes on the parking meter of fame had expired, a conviction that was strengthened when Janet Cruse's phone number began to connect with an answering service instead of with Janet. For a little while the answering service went through the motions of taking Rudy's ever-more-urgent messages, and then he was given the address, in Vancouver, where Janet could be contacted. So that, he thought, was the end of the Bunny Steiner story and of his own career as a father. He was wrong on both counts.

120   Bunny arrived in New York at the end of May, unannounced except by the driver of the taxi who had taken her from the Port Authority bus terminal to Rudy's new sublet in a brownstone on Barrow Street in the nicest part of the Village. "Your daughter's down here," the man had shouted into the intercom, and then, before Rudy could deny he had a daughter, he added: "And the charge on the meter is $4.70."

121   "Hello, Daddy," Bunny said, clutching her little knapsack to her chest and smiling at him as sweetly as if he were a camera.

122   "Bunny!"

123   "Mommy said I've grown so much you probably wouldn't recognize me."

124   "This is none of my business, Mister," the taxi driver said, with a sideways commiserating glance in Bunny's direction, "but don't you think she's a little young to be traveling around New York on her own? I mean, this isn't . . ." He raised his voice and asked of Bunny: "Where'd you say you came here from, sweetheart?"

125   "Pocatello," she said demurely. "That's in Idaho."

126   "You came all the way to New York from Idaho *on a bus?*" the taxi driver marveled.

127   She nodded. "That's how my dress got so wrinkled."

128   Rudy paid the driver six dollars, took Bunny's knapsack, and held the door open for her.

129   "Thank you," she said, stepping inside and heading straight for the stairs. Her hand reached up to grasp the banister. Rudy realized he'd never seen a child on the wide wonky staircase in all the time he'd been subletting his apartment. She seemed so small. Of course, children were supposed to be small, but Bunny seemed smaller than small, a miniature child.

130   "What is the number of your apartment?" she asked from the head of the stairs.

131   "Twelve. It's two more flights up."

132   By the time Rudy had reached the fourth floor, huffing and puffing, Bunny had already gone into the apartment and was leaning out the window that accessed to the fire escape. "You really live high up."

133   "Not by New York standards."

134   "I hope you're not mad at me," she said in a placatory tone, turning away from the window and wedging herself into the corner of the sofa. "I know I should have phoned first, but I thought if I did, you might call the police before we had a chance to talk together. I didn't know *what* I'd do if you weren't here. Do they have shopping-bag kids in New York? That's what I'd have become, I guess."

135 "Am I to understand that you're running away from home?"

136 She nodded.

137 "From Pocatello?" he asked with a teasing smile.

138 She laughed. "No, silly. That's where *Judy Garland* was from, in *A Star Is Born.* Which is one of my favorite movies of all time. We made a tape of it, and I must have seen it twenty times."

139 "Who is 'we'? And for that matter, who are you?"

140 "It's all right if you call me Bunny. I like it better than my real name, which is—" She wrinkled her nose to indicate disgust: "Margaret."

141 "Just Margaret? No last name?"

142 "On my birth certificate it says Margaret Dacey. But The People don't use last names with each other."

143 "Ah ha! I *wondered* if you weren't one of The People. They never told me anything about you, you know. I thought I was just making it all up, everything in the book. Even you."

144 "I know. They always used to make jokes about that. How surprised you were going to be when I appeared on TV. Anyhow, I'm not one of The People. My mother is, but that doesn't mean I have to be. Before The People, she was in something like the Hari Krishnas, only they didn't march around in orange clothes. I *really* hated that. Finally the Baba, who was the old man who ran the place and pretended he was an Indian (but he wasn't, he came from Utah), finally he got busted for cocaine. That was two years ago, in Portland."

145 "It sounds like you've had an exciting life. How old are you?"

146 "Guess."

147 "You must be older than you look. Maybe six?"

148 She shook her head.

149 "Seven?"

150 "No—eight and a half. I'm like Gary Coleman, everyone thinks I'm *pre*-school. When the inspectors came round to the commune to see if they were sending their kids to school like they were supposed to, they always made me go with the little kids. I've never been to a real school. But I can read almost anything. I read *your* book a couple times. And I read *The Elfin Horde,* too. And the other ones that came after. When we were living up in the cabin there wasn't much else you could do but read, you couldn't get TV. Mom was going crazy."

151 "So? What did you think?"

152 "Of *The Elfin Horde?* Oh, I loved the whole series. Only I hated it when Twa-Loora died. Sometimes at night when I'm going to sleep I'll think about her riding up to the edge of that cliff and looking back

and seeing the Black Riders. And then *leaping* to certain death. And I'll start crying all over again. In fact—" She furrowed her forehead and frowned down at her hands, primly folded together in her lap. "In fact, that's why I decided to come here. Because if I went anywhere else, they would just send me right back to the commune. But I thought *you'd* understand. Because you understood Twa-Loora."

153   "What about your father? Couldn't you go to him?"

154   "I'm like the Bunny in your book. I don't have a dad. Unless *you'd* be my dad."

155   "Hey, wait a minute!"

156   But Bunny was not to be checked now. She insisted on sharing her fantasy in its full extent. And it was not (Rudy gradually, grudgingly came to see) so entirely bizarre as to be unfeasible. As Bunny herself pointed out, millions of TV viewers had already come to accept as a fact that she was his daughter, and her mother had been deeply involved in that deception. Admittedly, Bunny's birth certificate (she produced a Xerox of it from her knapsack) could not confirm Rudy's paternity, but neither did it contradict it: the space for Father's Name had been left blank. Assuming that her mother and Mr. Grace agreed to letting Rudy assume the responsibility for bringing up Bunny, it would probably not be difficult to arrange the legal details. And with the material in the knapsack it was hard to imagine them withholding their cooperation.

157   "You realize, don't you, that what we're discussing is blackmail?"

158   "But if I just took all this to the *police,* it wouldn't make things better for anyone. They'd probably put Mr. Grace in jail, and I'd be sent back to my mother, and she'd be furious with me, and we wouldn't have anywhere to live. Anyhow, she doesn't like me any more than I like her. When we're in the commune we hardly ever even talk to each other. I do have *friends* there, or I used to, but Billy's in jail now. We used to play backgammon, and he really didn't mind if I won sometimes. Mother would get furious. I'll bet she'd be tickled pink to let you have custody. She'd have been glad if the Xlom were real and they did take me away in a flying saucer. She said so lots of times, and pretended it was a joke but it wasn't, not really. It's Mr. Grace who's the problem. Every time reporters would come to the commune, he'd always have someone take me down to the basement laundry room, and I wouldn't come out until the reporters went away. It made me feel like a prisoner."

159   The more Bunny told about her life in The People's commune, the more Rudy realized that the girl was an As-Told-To diamond mine. What's more, she knew it too, for when he suggested that he turn on

his tape deck in order to have a permanent record of the rest of the story, she agreed that would be a good idea and she even was so thoughtful, when they started taping, to return to the point in the story when Mr. Grace first discovered Bunny and her mother busking in downtown San Diego. Bunny, in addition to her other talents, was a proficient tapdancer, and one of her objects in adopting Rudy as her father was to be able to study dance—tap, jazz, and classic ballet—in New York City, the dance capital of the universe.

160   "But also," she confided, "I just *like* you. I could tell that from reading *The Visitation*."

161   "Yes, but that's all made up," Rudy pointed out. "That book is just one lie after another. *You* know that."

162   "But you tell *nice* lies," Bunny insisted. "If you had a *real* little girl, I'll bet you'd be just the kind of daddy you say you are in the book. Is it the money you're worried about? Mother was always saying how expensive it is to have a kid."

163   "I hadn't even considered that side of it."

164   "Because when I was in Mr. Grace's office and took those other things, the dirty pictures and the rest, I also took this."

165   Out of her wonderful knapsack Bunny produced a file of papers showing sales figures for *The Visitation* that were, even at a glance, distinctly at variance from the figures Orange Bangle Press had provided to him. Bunny's competence as a fairy godchild was coming to seem uncanny. "How did you know . . . ?"

166   "They always talked to each other as though I weren't there. Maybe they thought I was that dumb. Or maybe they just forgot about me."

167   "And where do they think you are now? Did you leave a note, or tell anyone?"

168   "I left a note saying I was going to visit one of Baba's people and I told them not to go to the police. I don't think they would have anyhow. I didn't steal much more money than I needed for the bus trip. I knew if I took a lot, Mr. Grace *would* go to the police. Do you have something to eat?"

169   "Sure. What do you want? Is a sandwich okay?"

170   "Just some cookies and milk would be nice. I didn't have any breakfast when the bus stopped in New Jersey."

171   Rudy went into the kitchen and poured out a Daffy Duck glassful of milk. Then he arranged three kinds of cookies on a plate. He took it as an omen that Bunny should have arrived at the moment when his cupboard was so well supplied with her favorite brand of cookie.

172   "There's clover for bunnies," he called out from the kitchen, quoting from his book.

173   And Bunny, from the living room, quoted the book back to him, making it theirs: "And here's a Bunny for the clover!"

DISCUSSION QUESTIONS

1. The statement by Rudy Steiner's agent that UFOs are as respectable as astrology these days is meant to imply that UFOs are real. What does this implied similarity contribute to the story?

2. When Steiner is being coached to write his fake abduction story, he is told never to joke about abduction because it is like a religion. How do people establish such firm beliefs?

3. Steiner's editor says that the fact that he *doesn't* have a daughter is ideal for his writing the story, much better than actually having one. Why?

4. When the bogus book isn't reviewed, why is neither Steiner nor his agent worried?

5. Why does Bunny claim that her mother would like her to be abducted by aliens?

WRITING TOPICS

1. Whitley Strieber's *Communion, A True Story* is mentioned throughout the story, along with other actual publications. In an essay, discuss how such books produced by reputable publishing companies and respected authors could manipulate a trusting audience.

2. In the end, Steiner and Bunny end up essentially adopting each other. In your journal, show how they are ideally suited for each other.

3. In an essay, examine the role of the media in the nineties. Do the media shape our perceptions about what is real and what is not, especially in connection with UFO sightings and alien abductions? Are these *more* or *less* believable because of how they are presented by the media?

Steelcollar Worker

1992

VONDA M^cINTYRE (b. 1948)

Vonda McIntyre's first science fiction story was published in the *Clarion* 1971 anthology. Her 1973 story "Of Mist, and Grass, and Sand," became the opening section in her novel *Dreamsnake* (1978). In the story, the female protagonist is a healer in an isolated country. She must overcome the prejudices of local inhabitants in order to help them by using healing snakes, something the villagers fear. This was a continuation of her previous novel *The Exile Waiting* (1975), which is set in a post-holocaust city. The protagonist is a sneak thief who teams up with a Japanese poet on her way to becoming a star traveler.

McIntyre also wrote several *Star Trek* novelizations of films: *Star Trek: The Wrath of Khan* (1984), *Star Trek III: The Search for Spock* (1984), and *Star Trek IV: The Voyage Home* (1986), as well as several stand alone *Star Trek* novels. She has also written novels directed at a younger audience, but all her works demonstrate her humanistic and feminist concerns within a science fiction framework.

In "Steelcollar Worker," Vonda McIntyre shows that even though companies may produce sophisticated products using new technology in the future, the human issues of the working world will remain essentially unchanged.

1   The enormous fuzzy balloon bounced from Jannine's fingertips, rose in an eerie, slow curve, and touched its destination. The viddydub forces took over, sucking the squashed ball into place with a loud, satisfied slurp.

2   "Work always reminds me of that Charlie Chan movie," Jannine said.

3   Neko, farther along on the substrate, pitched an identical elemental balloon into the helical structure. She had an elegant, overhand throw; she had played ball before she left school, but she was too small to get a scholarship.

4   "What Charlie Chan movie?" she asked. "Not that I go out of my way to see Charlie Chan movies."

5   "The one where he's dancing with the globe?" Jannine checked the blueprint hovering nearby, freed an element from the substrate, and moved it into place.

6   "Do you maybe mean Charlie Chaplin?" Neko said. *The Great Dictator?*"

7   "Chaplin, right." Jannine picked up a third element, tossed it, caught it again, danced on one toe.

8   Neko tossed an element through the helix. A perfect curve ball, it arced, touched, settled, like a basketball into quicksand. Its fuzzy outlines blurred as it melted into the main structure, still a discrete entity, but pouring its outer layers into the common pool.

9   "I don't think you'd go too far as a dictator," Neko said.

10   "I don't want to be the dictator. I want to be the guy who pretends to be the dictator."

11   She leaped again, twisting as she left the ground. But the system wouldn't let her spin. It caught her and stopped her with hard invisible fingers. She found herself on the ground, with no sensation of falling between leap and sprawl.

12   "Are you all right? I wish you wouldn't *do* that. Jeez, it makes me nauseous just to watch you."

13   Jannine picked herself up. Smiling, she glanced toward Neko, but Neko's blurry face showed no expression.

14   "I'm okay," Jannine said to reassure her co-worker. Neko couldn't see her expression any more than Jannine could see Neko's. "Someday the system will handle a spin. How'll I know if I don't try?"

15   Neko picked up one more of the furry elemental balls and dropped it into place. The elementals scattered at her feet, bumping and quivering, sticking briefly to the substrate or bouncing off. Once in a while, two melded into dumbbell-shapes, then parted again.

16   "The system will handle a spin when you grow a ball-joint in your wrist," Neko said, exasperated. "You *could* read the documentation when there's an upgrade."

17   "Oh, when all else fails, read the instructions." Jannine laughed. "I don't have time to read the instructions." She wished the company would let her take the manual home, but that was against the rules. You were only allowed to read the manual in the company library.

18   Jannine and Neko walked down the helix, positioning the elementals, now and again prying one out and replacing it.

19   A herd of elementals quivered toward Jannine, like bowling balls under a gray blanket. Several escaped and flew off into the sky.

20   "Warm fuzzies today," Neko said.

21   "Yeah." Jannine went to the system and asked for cooling. The elementals calmed, settled to the ground, and reabsorbed their covering blanket. Once in a while, an elemental emitted a smear.

22   The helix extended out of sight in both directions. Jannine and Neko had been working on this section for a week. Jannine loved watching the helix evolve under her hands. The details of substrate, helix, and elementals changed so fast that a human could alter the helix better than a robot, even better than enzymes.

23   A flicker in Jannine's vision: the helix and the substrate and Neko vanished.

24   Jannine found herself in the real world. The couch held her among water-filled cushions, cradling her body.

25   Quitting time.

26   The screen of her helmet reflected her face, an image as unreal and distorted against the smoky plastic as Neko's face had been, back inside the system. The screen's color faded. The audio fuzz cut out.

27   The clamor and bustle of the factory surrounded her: the electronic whine of the system, the subsonic drumming of coolant pumps, the voices and shapes of her co-workers as they got out of their couches and tidied up for the day shift.

28   With her free left hand, Jannine opened the padded collar that secured her helmet. She raised the mechanism from her head. The noise level rose.

29   She shivered. The factory was always chilly. Her awareness of her body faded when she worked. She never felt cold till she came out of her workspace and back into real life. On the substrate, the temperature hovered just above absolute zero. Down there, she always felt warm. Up here, where the laboring pumps only incidentally lowered the temperature a few degrees, she always felt cold.

30   She unbuckled the cuff around her right wrist and freed her hand from the magnetic control.

31   Wiggling her fingers, clenching her fist, shaking her arm, she slid out of the couch. All around her, her co-workers stood and stretched

and groaned in the cold. She unplugged her helmet and wiped it down and stowed it. She wished she owned one, a helmet she could impress her own settings in and paint with her own design.

32 Neko crossed the aisle and joined her.

33 "Brownie points tonight," Neko said.

34 She moved smoothly, easily, with none of the stiffness everyone else was feeling. She moved like her nickname, Neko, cat.

35 "A bonus, huh?" Jannine said. "Great. We make a good team."

36 They'd fallen into the habit of chatting for a few minutes after work while they waited for the crush at the exit to ease.

37 But instead of replying, Neko stared at Jannine's control couch, at the manipulator that reduced the motions of Jannine's hand to movements in the angstrom range.

38 "Did you notice what it is we're making?" Neko said.

39 Up on her toes, Jannine shifted her weight from one foot to the other, bouncing in place, trying to get warm. The day shift people came into the factory, moving between the hulking shapes of the couches.

40 "Yeah, I guess," Jannine said. "I wasn't paying attention. Just following the blueprint. Some vaccine, same as usual."

41 "Let's go." Neko strode away, her hands shoved in her pockets. She moved as gracefully as she did down on the substrate, where gravity could be tuned and made a variable.

42 Jannine hurried after her. She waved across the factory at Evan, the day-shift worker who co-habited her couch. But this morning, she didn't wait to talk.

43 She followed Neko through the security checkout. They were nearly the last ones out, but waiting had saved them standing in the crowd. Jannine's life gave her plenty of lines to stand in.

44 Jannine thought the security system was stupid, a waste of time. No one on the production floor had access to anything that they could carry away. Except the helmets. You'd have to be awfully stupid to try to walk out with a helmet, however tempting it would be to take one for your own.

45 Jannine shoved her I.D. into the slot. She waited. The computer checked her and passed her and rolled her I.D. back. At the same time it emitted a slip of paper, thrusting it out like a slow insolent tongue. It beeped to draw her attention.

46 Ignore, it she told herself. She wanted to, but Neko had seen it. If Jannine left the note, Neko would wonder why, or, worse, retrieve it for her and give it to her and expect Jannine to tell her what it was. Neko might even read it herself. Jannine grabbed it, glanced at it, and shoved it into her pocket.

47   "What's up?" Neko asked.

48   Jannine shrugged. "Nothing. Busybody stuff. 'Eat your vegetables.'"

49   "Sorry." Neko's voice turned cool. "Didn't mean to be nosy." She turned and walked out of the factory and into the new day.

50   Damn! Jannine thought. She wanted to try to explain, but couldn't think of the right words.

51   She hurried to catch up, blinking and squinting in the bright sunlight. When she'd arrived at work at midnight, rain had slicked the streets. Now the air and the sky were clean and clear.

52   "Want to get a beer? I'm buying."

53   For a second she was afraid Neko would turn her down, keep on walking into the morning, and never talk to her again. Neko strode on, shoulders hunched and hands shoved in her pockets.

54   Then she stopped and turned and waited.

55   "Yeah. Sure."

56   Finding a place that served beer at eight o'clock in the morning was no big deal near the factory. A lot of the workers, like Jannine, came off the substrate with nerves tight, muscles tense. In reality, she'd spent the last eight hours lying almost perfectly still. But she'd felt like she was in action all the time. Her work felt like motion, like physical labor. Somewhere, somehow, she had to blow off the tension. Beer helped. If she drank no more than a couple, she'd be able to pass the alert at midnight, no problem.

57   She slid her hand into her pocket and crumpled up the note. A couple of beers would let her stop worrying about that, too.

58   "Jannine!"

59   "Huh? What?"

60   Neko shook her head. "You haven't heard a word I've said." She pushed open the tavern door. Jannine followed her out of the sunlight and into the warm, loud gloom. They submerged in the dark, the talk, the music.

61   Neko slipped through the crowd toward the bar. Jannine, head and shoulders taller than her friend, had to press and sidle past people.

62   Jannine joined Neko by the wall, put her I.D. into the order slot, grabbed a couple of glasses, and drew two beers. The tavern charged her and returned her I.D. Neko retrieved it for her and traded it to her for one of the beers.

63   "Thanks!" Neko shouted above the racket. Four or five people were even trying to dance, there in the middle of the room where hardly anyone could move.

64   Jannine looked around for a table. Stupid even to hope for one. After work she preferred standing or walking to sitting, but Neko obviously

wanted to talk. They weren't supposed to talk about work outside the factory.

65 Somebody jostled her, nearly spilling her beer.

66 "Hey," she said, "spill the cheap stuff, okay?"

67 "Hey yourself, watch it."

68 She recognized the guy: two couches over and one down. Jannine didn't know his name. Heading back to the order wall, he emptied his glass in a gulp. She felt envious. He could drink like that all morning. She'd watched him do it more than once. He always passed the alert when midnight rolled around.

69 "Neko!" She caught Neko's gaze and gestured. Neko nodded and followed her.

70 Jannine pushed her way farther inside, holding her glass high. She passed the bouncer. She knew one was there, out of sight in the small balcony above eye level. She'd come in here four or five times before noticing any of the people who kept an eye on the place. The balcony, upholstered in the same hose-down dark fabric as the walls, blended into the dimness, unobtrusive. The bouncer let the artificials take care of everything but trouble.

71 Jannine reached the hallway.

72 "Wait—" Neko said as Jannine slid her I.D. into the credit slot of a private room.

73 The door ate the I.D. and opened.

74 "What for?" Jannine crossed between the equipment and set her glass down on the small table in the corner. "Hardly spilled a drop," she said.

75 Neko hesitated on the threshold.

76 "Come on, it's paid for," Jannine said.

77 Neko shrugged and entered. "Yeah, okay. This is kind of extravagant, but thanks." She shut the door, cutting out the din, somebody yelling at somebody else, a fight about to start. After work, your body was geared up for action, and your brain was too tired to hold it back.

78 Jannine drank a long swallow of her beer, then made herself stop and sip it slowly. She was hungry. She ordered from the picture menu on the back wall.

79 "Want anything?"

80 "Sure, okay." Neko sounded distracted. She pushed a couple of pictures, barely glancing at them, then sat at the table and leaned on her elbows.

81 Jannine swung up on the stationary bicycle and started to pedal. It felt good to get rid of the physical energy she had been holding in all day. Sweat broke out on her forehead, under her arms.

82   "Did you see what we were making?" Neko said again.

83   "If I'd stopped to think about it, we wouldn't have done such a long stretch and we wouldn't have gotten any brownie points." Jannine tried not to sound defensive. "Besides, I was worried about the warm fuzzies."

84   "It wasn't natural," Neko said. She drained her glass, put it down, and raked her fingers through her shoulder-length black hair.

85   Jannine laughed, relieved. "I noticed *that,*" she said. "I thought you meant something important. Jeez. Nothing we build is natural. If it was natural, we wouldn't need to build it."

86   "But we weren't using the regular base pairs. We were using analogs."

87   "Yeah. So?" Jannine wondered if Neko, too, had been set up to test her. "I build what they tell me. It isn't my job to design it."

88   Continuing to pedal the bike, she wiped sweat from her face with the clean towel hanging from the handlebars.

89   "It must be something dangerous," Neko said stubbornly. "Something they don't want out in the world. Yet. So they make it with synthetic nucleics. So it can't reproduce."

90   "It isn't dangerous to *us,*" Jannine said, confused by Neko's distress. They were building a set of instructions. Neko knew that. Being scared of it made as much sense as being scared of a music tape.

91   "I don't mean *now,* I don't mean yet. But later on when they use it. Whatever it's coding for could be dangerous to us the same way it could be dangerous to anybody."

92   "I think you're being silly. They always start sterile, till they're sure about the product."

93   An artificial stupid pushed through the hatch in the bottom of the door, rolled inside, slid their food onto the table, and backtracked. The hatch latched with a soft *snick*.

94   Jannine swung off the exercise bike and wiped her face again. She took the lids off the plates and pushed Neko's dinner, or breakfast, toward her.

95   "Do you mind if I have another drink?"

96   "Go ahead." It was polite of Neko to ask, since Jannine's I.D. was in the slot. But she should've known she could have whatever she wanted.

97   Jannine broke open the top of the chicken pie she'd ordered. Steam puffed out, fragrant with sage. When she had a night job, she liked to eat breakfast before her shift, in the evening, and dinner after, in the morning.

98   "How can you work out and then eat?"

99   Jannine shrugged. "I don't have a problem with it. I'm going to eat and then work out, too."

100   Neko preferred dinner at night and breakfast in the morning. She had a couple of croissants and an omelet spotted with dark bits of sautéed garlic.

101   "No hot date today?" Jannine said.

102   Neko drank half her second beer and pushed her food around on her plate.

103   "I'm not really hungry," she said. "I guess I'll go on home."

104   "I thought you wanted to talk. That's why I got the room."

105   "I wanted to talk about the helix, and all you want to say about it is 'No big deal.' So, okay. So maybe we're building them a nerve toxin or some new bug."

106   "What do they need with a new bug? There's plenty of old bugs."

107   "Right. So it's no big deal. So forget it."

108   "Maybe we're building some new medicine."

109   "I *said* forget it." Neko pushed the plate away and stood up.

110   "If it was anything bad they'd classify it, and we'd never work on it. I don't even have a security clearance, do you?"

111   Neko didn't reply.

112   "*Do* you?"

113   "No. Of course not. I mean . . ." Neko looked embarrassed. "I guess I used to but I'm sure it's expired by now."

114   "Why did you have a security clearance?"

115   "If I could tell you that I wouldn't've had to have it!" Neko said. "I've got to go." She downed the last of her second beer and hurried out of the room, slamming the door behind her.

116   Jannine watched her through the room's transparent walls till she disappeared. She was surprised by Neko's weird reaction.

117   "Sorry," she said to the walls. "Didn't mean to be nosy."

118   She ate her dinner, more because she'd already paid for it than because she still felt hungry. For the same reason, she lifted weights for a while and pedaled on the bike till her hour ran out. She got down, retrieved her I.D. before she got charged for more time, and left the private room for the ASes to clean.

119   The tavern was still crowded, but quieter. She made her way through it without bumping into anyone.

120   Outside, the sky had clouded up. It looked like more rain. Jannine trudged toward home. At her last job, her co-workers had created a complicated system of intramural sports. There was always a team to join, or a team that needed a substitute. Any warm body would help.

They welcomed a warm body who was a halfway decent player. At this job, though, her co-workers went straight to the tavern or straight home, or did something with some group that didn't include Jannine.

121   Maybe it's getting time to move on, she thought. But she didn't want to move on.

122   Morning rush was over; the streets were quiet for daytime. In the middle of the night, when she came to work, delivery trucks created a third rush hour.

123   The mist grew heavier. The droplets drifted downward. The rain began. It collected in her hair. Damp tendrils curled around her face.

124   Her apartment was nothing special: a one-bedroom, the bedroom tiny and dark and cold. It always smelled musty. Not quite mold. Not quite mildew. But almost. Jannine looked at her unmade bed. She imagined crawling between the cold, wrinkled sheets.

125   "Shit," she muttered, and returned to the living room. She turned on the entertainment console and flipped through a hundred channels on the TV, fifty channels per minute, leaving them all two-d. Nothing interesting. She should've rented a movie. She could call something out of the cable, but it took too long to work through the preview catalogue, even on fast forward. All those clips of pretty scenery or car chases or people making love never told her what the movies were about. Usually the clips were the best part anyway. She left the remote on scan and tossed it onto the couch. The TV flipped past one channel, another.

126   Jannine went to take a shower. As she went through the pockets of her sweat-damp clothing, she closed her fingers around the note.

127   "Shit," she said again.

128   She smoothed the crumpled paper, staring at it, afraid to find out what the black marks said. Maybe it was too damaged to be read.

129   She dug the reader out of the closet, shoved the note into it, and listened.

130   "This evening, please report to room fifteen twenty-six instead of your usual position. Regular hourly wage will apply—"

131   Jannine shut off the reader, pulled the note out, and flung it into the sorter.

132   She'd avoided this test twice already, once by pretending she never received the note and once by calling in sick. She couldn't afford another sick day. Maybe tomorrow she could pretend she'd forgotten about the instructions. Once she hooked into her helmet, maybe they wouldn't bother her. She was a good worker, always above average. Not too far above average.

133   Jannine wondered what she had done, why she had to take a test.

134   She should've started looking for a new job as soon as she got the first note. But she liked working on the substrate. It was fun. She was good at it. It paid well. And despite Neko's worries, the company mostly produced crop fortifiers and medicines.

135   If she got away with forgetting the message—she didn't believe she would, but if she did—she'd have a week or so to look for new work before her employers realized they were put out with her. Maybe then at least they'd fire her without making her take the damn test.

136   Leaving her clothes strewn on the floor, Jannine climbed into bed, pulled the cold covers around her, and lay shivering, waiting for sleep.

137   At midnight, Jannine arrived at work and pretended it was an ordinary day. She checked in and played through the alert without paying any attention to it. When she passed, it congratulated her for a personal high score. Seeing how far up the ladder she'd run the testing game, she cursed under her breath. She hated to stand out. It always caused more trouble than it was worth. If she'd been less tired, less distracted, she would've paid attention and kept her results in the safe and easy and unremarkable middle ranges.

138   That's what I get for lying awake all night, she thought.

139   She reached out to cancel the game and use her second try. She'd never canceled a game before. That, too, drew the attention of the higher-ups.

140   "Good score."

141   Jannine started. "What—?"

142   An exec, in a suit, stood at her shoulder. She couldn't remember ever seeing an exec on the production level. Sometimes they watched from the balcony that looked out over the work floor, but hardly ever during the graveyard shift.

143   "Good score," he said again. "I knew you could go higher than you usually do. You got my note?"

144   He smiled, and Jannine's spirits sank.

145   "Yeah, well, thanks," she said, not really answering his question. "I better get to work."

146   "You *did* get my note?"

147   She saw that this time she wasn't going to get away with pretending she didn't know what he was talking about. He could probably whip out security videos that showed her taking the note, glancing at it, shoving it in her pocket. From three angles.

148   "I completely forgot," she said. "Is it important? My teammate's already waiting for me."

149   "We brought in a temp. Come along; we mustn't put this off again."

150   Jannine was scared. A temp was serious business, expensive.

151   Reluctantly, she followed the exec out of the alert room. They passed through sound effects and bright electronic lights. Jannine's co-workers played the games, proving they were fit to do their jobs for one more day.

152   Nearly late, Neko hurried toward her favorite alert console. She saw Jannine and the exec. She stopped, startled, looking as scared as Jannine felt. Behind the exec, out of his sight, Jannine shrugged elaborately and rolled her eyes toward the ceiling. She tried to communicate: No big deal, see you later. She wished she could make herself believe it. Her hands felt cold and her stomach was upset.

153   The exec's I.D. opened a door that Jannine had never been through, that she'd never seen anyone use. The exec entered the elevator.

154   "Come on," he said, smiling again. "Everything okay?"

155   "Where are we going?"

156   He pointed upward. That was no help. The building was twenty stories high. Jannine had never been above the production level.

157   She entered the elevator. The doors closed behind her. She stood there, waiting, looking at the exec. She didn't know what else to do. The upward motion made her feel even queasier. Her ears popped. The elevator stopped. The doors opened behind her.

158   "Here we are." The exec gestured for her to turn and precede him out.

159   He took her down a carpeted hall. She hardly noticed her surroundings. Photos hung on the wall. Fields and forests, she guessed, but out of focus, weird pastel colors. Some upper class fad.

160   The exec opened another door.

161   A dozen people sat at blank computer terminals, waiting. One machine remained free.

162   "Right there," the exec said. "Get settled, and we can start."

163   Jannine didn't recognize anyone in the room.

164   Everyone else is new, she thought. They're applying to work on the substrate, and there's a new test to get the job. What did I do to make them think I should have to take it? Somebody must have noticed something. Now I'm screwed.

165   The job test she'd taken a few months ago was all physical. It was still hard to believe she'd found such a job, with such a test. She hadn't known how to figure out a safe middle score, so she'd come out near the top of the group. She had always been athletic. Not enough to go pro. She'd tried that, and failed.

166   She approached the computer terminal warily. She stared at it, disheartened. Its only interface was a keyboard.

167   "I don't type," she said. She spoke louder than she meant to, startling several of the others, startling herself. A nervous laugh tittered through the room. Jannine turned toward the exec. "I told them, when I applied, that I don't type!"

168   "That's all right," he said. "You won't need to. Just tee or eff."

169   She sat down. She began to shiver, distress and dismay taking over her body with a deep, clenching quiver.

170   The chair was hard, unyielding, uncomfortable. Jannine wished for her reclining couch, for the familiar grip, the helmet and collar and imaginary reality.

171   The screen blinked on. She flinched. She ground her teeth, fighting tears of rage and frustration. Her throat ached and her eyes stung.

172   "Any questions about the instructions?" the exec asked.

173   No one spoke.

174   "You may begin."

175   The screen dissolved and reformed.

176   I should have been looking for another job a month ago, Jannine thought angrily, desperately. I knew it, and I didn't do it. What a fool.

177   She stared at the keyboard. It blurred before her. She blinked furiously.

178   "Just tee or eff." One of those. She searched out the T, and the F. She pressed on the T. On the screen, the blinking cursor moved downward, leaving a mark behind.

179   She pressed the T twice more, then varied the pattern, tentatively, with the F. The blinking light reached the bottom of the screen and stayed there. The patch of writing behind it jumped upward, bringing a new blank box beneath the blinking square. She pressed the keys, faster and faster, playing a two-note dirge. Her hands shook.

180   She touched the wrong key. Nothing happened. The system didn't warn her, didn't set her down as it would on the substrate, made no noise, made no mark. Jannine put one forefinger on the T and the other on the F and played them back and forth. All she wanted to do was finish and go back to work. If they'd let her.

181   The screen froze. Jannine tried to scroll farther down. Nothing happened.

182   She shot a quick glance at the exec, wondering how soon he would find out she'd crashed his system.

183   He was already looking at her. Jannine turned away, pretending she'd never raised her head, pretending their gazes had never met.

184   But she'd seen him stand up. She'd seen his baffled expression.

185   Paralyzed at the terminal, she waited for him to find her out.

186   "Are you all right?"

187   "Yes," she said.

188   "You finished very quickly," he said.

189   She glanced up sharply. Finished?

190   The test ought to go on and on till the time ran out, like a game, like the alert, games you couldn't win. You were supposed to rack up higher and higher scores, you were supposed to pretend it was fun, but you were judged every time against the highest score you'd ever made.

191   The screen had stopped because she'd reached the end of the test.

192   The *end*.

193   Amazing.

194   The exec looked at the screen over her shoulder, reached down, pressed a key. The screen blinked and reformed. Jannine recognized the pattern of the beginning of the test, and she thought, Oh, god, no, not *another* one.

195   "You're allowed to go through and check your answers," the exec said. "Plenty of time before the next section. Don't you want to do that?"

196   One of the other test-takers, still working through the questions, made a sharp "Shh!" sound, but never looked up.

197   "No," Jannine said. "I'm done. I don't want to go through it again. Can I leave now?"

198   "I really think you should work on this some more. It's for your own good."

199   "I don't want to!" Jannine shouted. "Don't you understand me?"

200   "Hey." The test-taker who'd shhed her sat up, glared, saw the exec, shut up, and hunched down over the test.

201   The others continued to work, without a glance at Jannine or at the exec.

202   "I understand *what* you're saying," the exec said. "I don't understand why. You do fine on the alert, so it isn't test anxiety, but your score on this is terrible."

203   Jannine felt spied on. He'd been watching her answers as she chose them.

204   Angrily, she rose. She was taller than the exec, and bigger.

205   "I'll tell you why," she said. "Why is because I don't want to take your stupid test." She knew he was about to tell her she'd failed, she couldn't work here anymore, she was fired. "I quit!"

206   She pushed past him, heading for the door. She was halfway down the hall before he recovered from the shock and came after her. She'd

hoped he'd just write her off, let her go and be done with her. She hoped he'd spare her more humiliation.

207 "Wait!"

208 He was mad, now, too, and wanting to take it out on her. She could hear it in his voice.

209 "You're a valuable employee," he said. "We think you have a lot of potential."

210 He baffled her. "Can I go back to work?"

211 "What's wrong with you?" His voice rose. "What do you have against being promoted?"

212 So that was what this was all about. A management test. Not a test to keep working on the substrate.

213 "Who asked you?" she said, furious. "Who *asked* you to promote me?"

214 He stopped short, confused.

215 "You can take the test again."

216 "Why can't you just leave me alone?"

217 "Will you talk to me about this?" the exec rocked back on his heels and folded his arms and looked at her. "Do you . . . Do you need help with something?"

218 Jannine hated the pity in his face, the pity that would turn to contempt.

219 "I quit! I said I quit and I mean I quit!" She fled into the elevator. When the doors closed, she was shaking.

220 The elevator halted at the production level. The doors opened. Instead of the quiet, cold workspace, each person in a couch, no noise but the pumps and the high-pitched hum of the electric fields, Jannine walked into midmorning break. Everybody milled around, drinking coffee and eating junk food, stretching and moving.

221 She crossed the floor without stopping. She hoped no one would notice where she'd been, or notice she was leaving. The best she could hope for now was to get away clean.

222 "Jannine!"

223 Jannine's shoulders slumped. If she'd just disappeared, she never would've had to tell Neko what had happened. But she couldn't keep walking, not when Neko called to her.

224 "Where have you been? Where are you going?" Neko hurried to her side. "Are you okay? Was it the alert? You never fail the alert! How late did you stay out this morning, anyway?" She grinned. "I'm sorry I was so grumpy. Are you done with counseling? Can you come back to work?" She lowered her voice, whispering, confidential. "The temp is

really good. I think he wants to work here. Permanently. He's even got
his own equipment. Are you in trouble?"

225   Jannine wanted to explain, but she had no idea how. She wanted
desperately to get out of here.

226   "I quit," she said.

227   "You—what?" Neko stared at her, stricken, then awed. "You quit!
Because of what I said? Is that why you had to go to counseling? How
did they find out? Jannine . . . Oh, you're so brave!"

228   "Brave?" Jannine said, baffled.

229   "I ought to walk right out the door with you!"

230   "No," Jannine said. "No, you shouldn't, that'd be dumb." Neko
thought she was leaving because of the company's products. That was
okay, because Jannine couldn't explain why she'd quit. It was too complicated and too embarrassing. But she couldn't let Neko quit, too. Not
if she was going to quit because of what she thought they might be
building. Not if she was going to quit to be in solidarity with Jannine.
That would make everything, even their friendship, a lie.

231   "Do you mean it?" Neko said. "That's such a relief! You won't be
mad? Did you know I—? I can't quit, Jannine, I'm awfully sorry. I can't
afford it, I need this job . . . ."

232   Jannine felt betrayed. That made no sense. She didn't want Neko
to quit. Hell, she didn't want to quit, herself. She would've felt awful,
she would've felt guilty, if Neko had tried to leave with her, and she
would've tried to talk her out of going. No: she *would* have talked her
out of going, no matter what she had to tell her. No matter how much
she had to tell her.

233   The lights blinked: end of break. Everyone had to get back to
work. The temp would be in Jannine's couch.

234   "It doesn't matter," Jannine said. "I had to leave."

235   "I'll walk you to the door."

236   "Why?" No one was supposed to leave the floor during work
hours. "You'll be late. You'll lose points."

237   "I don't care!"

238   At the checkout, the barrier gave Jannine her I.D. It refused to
hand over Neko's. Neko hesitated. She could come through the barrier. But she'd have a hard time getting back to the floor: security, explanations, maybe even counseling. A lot of lost points.

239   "It doesn't matter," Jannine said, disappointed despite herself.
"Stay here."

240   "Well . . . okay, if you're sure . . ."

241   Jannine went through the barrier. It closed again behind her.

242   "We'll get together," Neko said. "For a drink. Sometime. Okay?"

243   Without turning back, Jannine raised her hand in a final wave.

244   The exit opened. She walked out into the rain-wet street, into the darkness.

DISCUSSION QUESTIONS

1. Jannine hardly notices what she's making, but Neko is very concerned. The two friends eat opposite meals after work: Jannine dinner, Neko breakfast. How do these differences help you understand the personalities of the two friends?

2. The work in a virtual reality environment is not physical, but produces tension and tiredness as if it were. Why do the workers need to unwind so badly and why does it sometimes escalate into violence?

3. Why is Jannine careful not to be *too* good on her tests? Why did she score high on her initial qualifying test?

4. Why does Jannine wish for imaginary reality over real reality?

5. Neko thinks Jannine is quitting because of ethical conflicts, but it is Neko who is most worried. Why does she decide to stay?

WRITING TOPICS

1. In this story, Jannine has a high potential for success, yet she is constantly trying to deny that capability. In an essay, discuss why someone would want to aim for "the middle of the pack" instead of higher.

2. Even though she finds she's in line for a possible promotion, Jannine still quits. In your journal, list as many reasons as you can think of that she would want to leave a company that values her work.

3. The technological advances at this factory are quite different than any that exist today. Yet virtual reality and computer technology are rapidly approaching the possibilities referred to in this story. In an essay, look at the state of current technology and the positive and negative possibilities that predicted future advances might raise for the average working person.

The Hammer of God

1992

ARTHUR C. CLARKE (b. 1917)

Arthur C. Clarke's first published story was "Loophole" (1946) in *Astounding Science Fiction*. His early stories usually were founded on scientific principles with a twist coming at the end. His shorter works have been collected in *The Best of Arthur C. Clarke 1937–71* (1973). His first novel, *Prelude to Space* (1951) is an optimistic look at the wonders of scientific advancement. Clarke was chair of the British Interplanetary Society from 1946 to 1947 and 1950 to 1953.

His 1953 story "The Sentinel" became the basis for the movie *2001: A Space Odyssey* in 1968. Clarke wrote the script in conjunction with Stanley Kubrick, and later the novelization. Two of his most respected novels of the fifties were *Against the Fall of Night* (1953) and *Childhood's End* (1953). In the former, Clarke paints a picture of a future utopia, but so perfect that one of its inhabitants seeks a different kind of life, one closer to nature. In the latter, the search for a higher state of being requires cooperation with an alien species so that both may overcome their failings.

After the success of *2001*, Clarke became one of the most well-known and respected science fiction authors in the world. His *Rendezvous with Rama* (1973) won the Hugo, Nebula, John W. Campbell Memorial, and British Science Fiction awards. During the sixties and seventies he spent most of his energy speculating about the future of science. He also became a member of many panels, including being a commentator on CBS for the *Apollo 11, 12,* and *15* moon missions, and overseeing the TV series *Arthur C. Clarke's Mysterious World* in the early eighties.

**Even though he became ill in the mid-eighties, Clarke has contin-
ued to produce quality fiction and nonfiction, including *The Ghost from
the Grand Books* (1990), and *The Garden of Rama* (1991). To many readers,
Clarke is the quintessential science fiction writer.**

**In "The Hammer of God," Arthur C. Clarke looks at what might
happen if we don't pay attention to signs from the heavens.**

----

*It came in vertically, punching a hole 10 km wide through
the atmosphere, generating temperatures so high that the air
itself started to burn. When it hit the ground near the Gulf
of Mexico, rock turned to liquid and spread outward in
mountainous waves, not freezing until it had formed a
crater 200 km across.*

*That was only the beginning of disaster: now the real
tragedy began. Nitric oxides rained from the air, turning the
sea to acid. Clouds of soot from incinerated forests darkened
the sky, hiding the sun for months. Worldwide, the temperature dropped precipitously, killing off most of the plants and
animals that had survived the initial cataclysm. Though
some species would linger on for millenniums, the reign
of the great reptiles was finally over.*

*The clock of evolution had been reset; the countdown
to Man had begun. The date was, very approximately,
65 million B.C.*

1   Captain Robert Singh never tired of walking in the forest with his
little son Toby. It was, of course, a tamed and gentle forest, guaranteed to
be free of dangerous animals, but it made an exciting contrast to the
rolling sand dunes of their last environment in the Saudi desert—and
the one before that, on Australia's Great Barrier Reef. But when the
Skylift Service had moved the house this time, something had gone
wrong with the food-recycling system. Though the electronic menus
had fail-safe backups, there had been a curious metallic taste to some of
the items coming out of the synthesizer recently.

2   "What's that, Daddy?" asked the four-year-old, pointing to a small
hairy face peering at them through a screen of leaves.

3   "Er, some kind of monkey. We'll ask the Brain when we get
home."

4   "Can I play with it?"

5   "I don't think that's a good idea. It could bite. And it probably has
fleas. Your robotoys are much nicer."

6   "But . . ."

7   Captain Singh knew what would happen next: he had run this sequence a dozen times. Toby would begin to cry, the monkey would
disappear, he would comfort the child as he carried him back to the
house . . .

8   But that had been twenty years ago and a quarter-billion kilometers
away. The playback came to an end; sound, vision, the scent of unknown flowers and the gentle touch of the wind slowly faded.
Suddenly, he was back in this cabin aboard the orbital tug *Goliath*, com-
manding the 100-person team of Operation ATLAS, the most critical
mission in the history of space exploration. Toby, and the stepmothers
and stepfathers of his extended family, remained behind on a distant
world which Singh could never revisit. Decades in space—and neglect
of the mandatory zero-G exercises—had so weakened him that he
could now walk only on the Moon and Mars. Gravity had exiled him
from the planet of his birth.

9   "One hour to rendezvous, captain," said the quiet but insistent voice
of David, as *Goliath*'s central computer had been inevitably named.
"Active mode, as requested. Time to come back to the real world."

10   *Goliath*'s human commander felt a wave of sadness sweep over him
as the final image from his lost past dissolved into a featureless, simmer-
ing mist of white noise. Too swift a transition from one reality to another was a good recipe for schizophrenia, and Captain Singh always
eased the shock with the most soothing sound he knew: waves falling
gently on a beach, with sea gulls crying in the distance. It was yet another memory of a life he had lost, and of a peaceful past that had now
been replaced by a fearful present.

11   For a few more moments, he delayed facing his awesome responsibility. Then he sighed and removed the neural-input cap that fitted
snugly over his skull and had enabled him to call up his distant past. Like
all spacers, Captain Singh belonged to the "Bald is Beautiful" school, if
only because wigs were a nuisance in zero gravity. The social historians
were still staggered by the fact that one invention, the portable
"Brainman," could make bare heads the norm within a single decade.
Not even quick-change skin coloring, or the lens-corrective laser shaping which had abolished eyeglasses, had made such an impact upon style
and fashion.

12   "Captain," said David. "I know you're there. Or do you want me
to take over?"

13   It was an old joke, inspired by all the insane computers in the fiction and movies of the early electronic age. David had a surprisingly good sense of humor: he was, after all, a Legal Person (Nonhuman) under the famous Hundredth Amendment, and shared—or surpassed—almost all the attributes of his creators. But there were whole sensory and emotional areas which he could not enter. It had been felt unnecessary to equip him with smell or taste, though it would have been easy to do so. And all his attempts at telling dirty stories were such disastrous failures that he had abandoned the genre.

14   "All right, David," replied the captain. "I'm still in charge." He removed the mask from his eyes, and turned reluctantly toward the viewport. There, hanging in space before him, was Kali.

15   It looked harmless enough: just another small asteroid, shaped so exactly like a peanut that the resemblance was almost comical. A few large impact craters, and hundreds of tiny ones, were scattered at random over its charcoal-gray surface. There were no visual clues to give any sense of scale, but Singh knew its dimensions by heart: 1,295 m maximum length, 456 m minimum width. Kali would fit easily into many city parks.

16   No wonder that, even now, most of humankind could still not believe that this modest asteroid was the instrument of doom. Or, as the Chrislamic Fundamentalists were calling it, "the Hammer of God."

17   The sudden rise of Chrislam had been traumatic equally to Rome and Mecca. Christianity was already reeling from John Paul XXV's eloquent but belated plea for contraception and the irrefutable proof in the New Dead Sea Scrolls that the Jesus of the Gospels was a composite of at least three persons. Meanwhile the Muslim world had lost much of its economic power when the Cold Fusion breakthrough, after the fiasco of its premature announcement, had brought the Oil Age to a sudden end. The time had been ripe for a new religion embodying, as even its severest critics admitted, the best elements of two ancient ones.

18   The Prophet Fatima Magdalene (née Ruby Goldenburg) had attracted almost 100 million adherents before her spectacular—and, some maintained, self-contrived—martyrdom. Thanks to the brilliant use of neural programming to give previews of Paradise during its ceremonies, Chrislam had grown explosively, though it was still far outnumbered by its parent religions.

19   Inevitably, after the Prophet's death the movement split into rival factions, each upholding *the* True Faith. The most fanatical was a fundamentalist group calling itself "the Reborn," which claimed to be in direct contact with God (or at least Her Archangels) via the listening post

they had established in the silent zone on the far side of the Moon, shielded from the radio racket of Earth by 3,000 km of solid rock.

20   Now Kali filled the main viewscreen. No magnification was needed, for *Goliath* was hovering only 200 m above its ancient, battered surface. Two crew members had already landed, with the traditional "One small step for a man"—even though walking was impossible on this almost zero-gravity worldlet.

21   "Deploying radio beacon. We've got it anchored securely. Now Kali won't be able to hide from us."

22   It was a feeble joke, not meriting the laughter it aroused from the dozen officers on the bridge. Ever since rendezvous, there had been a subtle change in the crew's morale, with unpredictable swings between gloom and juvenile humor. The ship's physician had already prescribed tranquilizers for one mild case of manic-depressive symptoms. It would grow worse in the long weeks ahead, when there would be little to do but wait.

23   The first waiting period had already begun. Back on Earth, giant radio telescopes were tuned to receive the pulses from the beacon. Although Kali's orbit had already been calculated with the greatest possible accuracy, there was still a slim chance that the asteroid might pass harmlessly by. The radio measuring rod would settle the matter, for better or worse.

24   It was a long two hours before the verdict came, and David relayed it to the crew.

25   "Spaceguard reports that the probability of impact on Earth is 99.9%. Operation ATLAS will begin immediately."

26   The task of the mythological Atlas was to hold up the heavens and prevent them from crashing down upon Earth. The ATLAS booster that *Goliath* carried as an external payload had a more modest goal: keeping at bay only a small piece of the sky.

> It was the size of a small house, weighed 9,000 tons and was moving at 50,000 km/h. As it passed over the Grand Teton National Park, one alert tourist photographed the incandescent fireball and its long vapor trail. In less than two minutes, it had sliced through the Earth's atmosphere and returned to space.
>
> The slightest change of orbit during the billions of years it had been circling the sun might have sent the asteroid crashing upon any of the world's great cities with an explosive force five times that of the bomb that destroyed Hiroshima.
>
> The date was Aug. 10, 1972.

27   Spaceguard had been one of the last projects of the legendary NASA, at the close of the 20th century. Its initial objective had been modest enough: to make as complete a survey as possible of the asteroids and comets that crossed the orbit of Earth—and to determine if they were a potential threat.

28   With a total budget seldom exceeding $10 million a year, a worldwide network of telescopes, most of them operated by skilled amateurs, had been established by the year 2000. Sixty-one years later, the spectacular return of Halley's Comet encouraged more funding, and the great 2079 fireball, luckily impacting in mid-Atlantic, gave Spaceguard additional prestige. By the end of the century, it had located more than 1 million asteroids, and the survey was believed to be 90% complete. However, it would have to be continued indefinitely: there was always a chance that some intruder might come rushing in from the uncharted outer reaches of the solar system.

29   As had Kali, which had been detected in late 2212 as it fell sunward past the orbit of Jupiter. Fortunately humankind had not been wholly unprepared, thanks to the fact that Senator George Ledstone (Independent, West America) had chaired an influential finance committee almost a generation earlier.

30   The Senator had one public eccentricity and, he cheerfully admitted, one secret vice. He always wore massive horn-rimmed eyeglasses (nonfunctional, of course) because they had an intimidating effect on uncooperative witnesses, few of whom had ever encountered such a novelty. His "secret vice," perfectly well known to everyone, was rifle shooting on a standard Olympic range, set up in the tunnels of a long-abandoned missile silo near Mount Cheyenne. Ever since the demilitarization of Planet Earth (much accelerated by the famous slogan "Guns Are the Crutches of the Impotent"), such activities had been frowned upon, though not actively discouraged.

31   There was no doubt that Senator Ledstone was an original: it seemed to run in the family. His grandmother had been a colonel in the dreaded Beverly Hills Militia, whose skirmishes with the L.A. Irregulars had spawned endless psychodramas in every medium, from old-fashioned ballet to direct brain stimulation. And his grandfather had been one of the most notorious bootleggers of the 21st century. Before he was killed in a shoot-out with the Canadian Medicops during an ingenious attempt to smuggle a kiloton of tobacco up Niagara Falls, it was estimated that "Smokey" had been responsible for at least 20 million deaths.

32   Ledstone was quite unrepentant about his grandfather, whose sensational demise had triggered the repeal of the late U.S.'s third, and

most disastrous, attempt at Prohibition. He argued that responsible adults should be allowed to commit suicide in any way they pleased—by alcohol, cocaine or even tobacco—as long as they did not kill innocent bystanders during the process.

33   When the proposed budget for Spaceguard Phase 2 was first presented to him, Senator Ledstone had been outraged by the idea of throwing billions of dollars into space. It was true that the global economy was in good shape: since the almost simultaneous collapse of communism and capitalism, the skillful application of chaos theory by World Rank mathematicians had broken the old cycle of booms and busts and averted (so far) the Final Depression predicted by many pessimists. Nonetheless, the Senator argued that the money could be much better spent on Earth—especially on his favorite project, reconstructing what was left of California after the Superquake.

34   When Ledstone had twice vetoed Spaceguard Phase 2, everyone agreed that no one on Earth would make him change his mind. They had reckoned without someone from Mars.

35   The Red Planet was no longer quite so red, though the process of greening it had barely begun. Concentrating on the problems of survival, the colonists (they hated the word and were already saying proudly "we Martians") had little energy left over for art or science. But the lightning flash of genius strikes where it will, and the greatest theoretical physicist of the century was born under the bubble domes of Port Lowell.

36   Like Einstein, to whom he was often compared, Carlos Mendoza was an excellent musician: he owned the only saxophone on Mars and was a skilled performer on that antique instrument. He could have received his Nobel Prize on Mars, as everyone expected, but he loved surprises and practical jokes. Thus he appeared in Stockholm looking like a knight in high-tech armor, wearing one of the powered exoskeletons developed for paraplegics. With this mechanical assistance, he could function almost unhandicapped in an environment that would otherwise have quickly killed him.

37   Needless to say, when the ceremony was over, Carlos was bombarded with invitations to scientific and social functions. Among the few he was able to accept was an appearance before the World Budget Committee, where Senator Ledstone closely questioned him about his opinion of Project Safeguard.

38   "I live on a world which still bears the scars of a thousand meteor impacts, some of them *hundreds* of kilometers across," said Professor Mendoza. "Once they were equally common on Earth, but wind and rain—something we don't have yet on Mars, though we're working on it!—have worn them away."

39   Senator Ledstone: "The Spaceguarders are always pointing to signs of asteroid impacts on Earth. How seriously should we take their warnings?"

40   Professor Mendoza: "Very seriously, Mr. Chairman. Sooner or later, there's bound to be another major impact."

41   Senator Ledstone was impressed, and indeed charmed, by the young scientist, but not yet convinced. What changed his mind was not a matter of logic but of emotion. On his way to London, Carlos Mendoza was killed in a bizarre accident when the control system of his exoskeleton malfunctioned. Deeply moved, Ledstone immediately dropped his opposition to Spaceguard, approving construction of two powerful orbiting tugs, Goliath and Titan, to be kept permanently patrolling on opposite sides of the sun. And when he was a very old man, he said to one of his aides, "They tell me we'll soon be able to take Mendoza's brain out of that tank of liquid nitrogen, and talk to it through a computer interface. I wonder what he's been thinking about, all these years . . ."

42   Assembled on Phobos, the inner satellite of Mars, ATLAS was little more than a set of rocket engines attached to propellant tanks holding 100,000 tons of hydrogen. Though its fusion drive could generate far less thrust than the primitive missile that had carried Yuri Gagarin into space, it could run continuously not merely for minutes but for weeks. Even so, the effect on the asteroid would be trivial. A velocity change of a few centimeters per second. Yet that might be sufficient to deflect Kali from its fatal orbit during the months while it was still falling earthward.

43   Now that ATLAS's propellant tanks, control systems and thrusters had been securely mounted on Kali, it looked as if some lunatic had built an oil refinery on an asteroid. Captain Singh was exhausted, as were all the crew members, after days of assembly and checking. Yet he felt a warm glow of achievement: they had done everything that was expected of them, the countdown was going smoothly, and the rest was up to ATLAS.

44   He would have been far less relaxed had he known of the ABSOLUTE PRIORITY message racing toward him by tight infrared beam from ASTROPOL headquarters in Geneva. It would not reach Goliath for another 30 minutes. And by then it would be much too late.

45   At about T minus 30 minutes, Goliath had drawn away from Kali to stand well clear of the jet with which ATLAS would try to nudge it from its present course. "Like a mouse pushing an elephant," one media

person had described the operation. But in the frictionless vacuum of space, where momentum could never be lost, even one mousepower would be enough if applied early and over a sufficient length of time.

46   The group of officers waiting quietly on the bridge did not expect to see anything spectacular: the plasma jet of the ATLAS drive would be far too hot to produce much visible radiation. Only the telemetry would confirm that ignition had started and that Kali was no longer an implacable juggernaut, wholly beyond the control of humanity.

47   There was a brief round of cheering and a gentle patter of applause as the string of zeros on the accelerometer display began to change. The feeling on the bridge was one of relief rather than exultation. Though Kali was stirring, it would be days and weeks before victory was assured.

48   And then, unbelievably, the numbers dropped back to zero. Seconds later, three simultaneous audio alarms sounded. All eyes were suddenly fixed on Kali and the ATLAS booster which should be nudging it from its present course. The sight was heartbreaking: the great propellant tanks were opening up like flowers in a time-lapse movie, spilling out the thousands of tons of reaction mass that might have saved the Earth. Wisps of vapor drifted across the face of the asteroid, veiling its cratered surface with an evanescent atmosphere.

49   Then Kali continued along its path, heading inexorably toward a fiery collision with the Earth.

50   Captain Singh was alone in the large, well-appointed cabin that had been his home for longer than any other place in the solar system. He was still dazed but was trying to make his peace with the universe.

51   He had lost, finally and forever, all that he loved on Earth. With the decline of the nuclear family, he had known many deep attachments, and it had been hard to decide who should be the mothers of the two children he was permitted. A phrase from an old American novel (he had forgotten the author) kept coming into his mind: "Remember them as they were—and write them off." The fact that he himself was perfectly safe somehow made him feel worse; Goliath was in no danger whatsoever, and still had all the propellant it needed to rejoin the shaken survivors of humanity on the Moon or Mars.

52   Well, he had many friendships—and one that was much more than that—on Mars; this was where his future must lie. He was only 102, with decades of active life ahead of him. But some of the crew had loved ones on the Moon; he would have to put Goliath's destination to the vote.

53   Ship's Orders had never covered a situation like this.

54 "I still don't understand," said the chief engineer, "why that explosive cord wasn't detected on the preflight check-out."

55 "Because that Reborn fanatic could have hidden it easily—and no one would have dreamed of looking for such a thing. Pity ASTROPOL didn't catch him while he was still on Phobos."

56 "But *why* did they do it? I can't believe that even Chrislamic crazies would want to destroy the Earth."

57 "You can't argue with their logic—if you accept their premises. God, Allah, is testing us, and we mustn't interfere. If Kali misses, fine. If it doesn't, well, that's part of Her bigger plan. Maybe we've messed up Earth so badly that it's time to start over. Remember that old saying of Tsiolkovski's: 'Earth is the cradle of humankind, but you cannot live in the cradle forever.' Kali could be a sign that it's time to leave."

58 The captain held up his hand for silence.

59 "The only important question now is, Moon or Mars? They'll both need us. I don't want to influence you" (that was hardly true; everyone knew where he wanted to go), "so I'd like your views first."

60 The first ballot was Mars 6, Moon 6, Don't know 1, captain abstaining.

61 Each side was trying to convert the single "Don't know" when David spoke.

62 "There is an alternative."

63 "What do you mean?" Captain Singh demanded, rather brusquely.

64 "It seems obvious. Even though ATLAS is destroyed, we still have a chance of saving the Earth. According to my calculations, *Goliath* has just enough propellant to deflect Kali—if we start thrusting against it immediately. But the longer we wait, the less the probability of success."

65 There was a moment of stunned silence on the bridge as everyone asked the question, "Why didn't I think of that?" and quickly arrived at the answer.

66 David had kept his head, if one could use so inappropriate a phrase, while all the humans around him were in a state of shock. There were some compensations in being a Legal Person (Nonhuman). Though David could not know love, neither could he know fear. He would continue to think logically, even to the edge of doom.

67 With any luck, thought Captain Singh, this is my last broadcast to Earth. I'm tired of being a hero, and a slightly premature one at that. Many things could still go wrong, as indeed they already have . . .

68 "This is Captain Singh, space tug *Goliath*. First of all, let me say how glad we are that the Elders of Chrislam have identified the saboteurs and handed them over to ASTROPOL.

69   "We are now 50 days from Earth, and we have a slight problem. This one, I hasten to add, will not affect our new attempt to deflect Kali into a safe orbit. I note that the news media are calling this deflection Operation Deliverance. We like the name, and hope to live up to it, but we still cannot be absolutely certain of success. David, who appreciates all the goodwill messages he has received, estimates that the probability of Kali impacting Earth is still 10% . . .

70   "We had intended to keep just enough propellant reserve to leave Kali shortly before encounter and go into a safer orbit, where our sister ship *Titan* could rendezvous with us. But that option is now closed. While *Goliath* was pushing against Kali at maximum drive, we broke through a weak point in the crust. The ship wasn't damaged, but we're stuck! All attempts to break away have failed.

71   "We're not worried, and it may even be a blessing in disguise. Now we'll use the *whole* of our remaining propellant to give one final nudge. Perhaps that will be the last drop that's needed to do the job.

72   "So we'll ride Kali past Earth, and wave to you from a comfortable distance, in just 50 days."

73   It would be the longest 50 days in the history of the world.

74   Now the huge crescent of the Moon spanned the sky, the jagged mountain peaks along the terminator burning with the fierce light of the lunar dawn. But the dusty plains still untouched by the sun were not completely dark; they were glowing faintly in the light reflected from Earth's clouds and continents. And scattered here and there across that once dead landscape were the glowing fireflies that marked the first permanent settlements humankind had built beyond the home planet. Captain Singh could easily locate Clavius Base, Port Armstrong, Plato City. He could even see the necklace of faint lights along the Translunar Railroad, bringing its precious cargo of water from the ice mines at the South Pole.

75   Earth was now only five hours away.

76   Kali entered the Earth's atmosphere soon after local midnight, 200 km above Hawaii. Instantly, the gigantic fireball brought a false dawn to the Pacific, awakening the wildlife on its myriad islands. But few humans had been asleep this night of nights, except those who had sought the oblivion of drugs.

77   Over New Zealand, the heat of the orbiting furnace ignited forests and melted the snow on mountaintops, triggering avalanches into the valleys beneath. But the human race had been very, very lucky: the

main thermal impact as Kali passed the Earth was on the Antarctic, the continent that could best absorb it. Even Kali could not strip away all the kilometers of polar ice, but it set in motion the Great Thaw that would change coastlines all around the world.

78   No one who survived hearing it could ever describe the sound of Kali's passage; none of the recordings were more than feeble echoes. The video coverage, of course, was superb, and would be watched in awe for generations to come. But nothing could ever compare with the fearsome reality.

79   Two minutes after it had sliced into the atmosphere, Kali reentered space. Its closest approach to Earth had been 60 km. In that two minutes, it took 100,000 lives and did $1 trillion worth of damage.

80   *Goliath* had been protected from the fireball by the massive shield of Kali itself; the sheets of incandescent plasma streamed harmlessly overhead. But when the asteroid smashed into Earth's blanket of air at more than 100 times the speed of sound, the colossal drag forces mounted swiftly to five, 10, 20 gravities—and peaked at a level far beyond anything that machines or flesh could withstand.

81   Now indeed Kali's orbit had been drastically changed; never again would it come near Earth. On its next return to the inner solar system, the swifter spacecraft of a later age would visit the crumpled wreckage of *Goliath* and bear reverently homeward the bodies of those who had saved the world.

82   Until the next encounter.

DISCUSSION QUESTIONS

1. Why does Captain Singh say he can never return to Earth?
2. The central computer, David, is a Legal (though Nonhuman) Person, though he lacks some human attributes. In small groups, discuss what qualities he lacks, and why.
3. What is the Spaceguard Project and what keeps it from being eliminated by lack of government funding?
4. What is Chrislam and what caused its rise to prominence?
5. Why do none of the humans think of the solution that David presents?

WRITING TOPICS

1. In this story, Clarke introduces scientific advances, but uses mythological names and beliefs. In an essay, discuss why he combines these seemingly opposite techniques. What effect do they have on your reading of the story?
2. The crew members on board the *Goliath* must decide what they want to do about Kali. In your journal, examine what caused their dilemma and how you would react in a similar circumstance. Was theirs the only possible decision? Was it the right one?
3. Many changes in society of the future are mentioned in this story. Pick one or more of the future possibilities Clarke refers to and write an essay exploring what might happen, as well as the likelihood of their occurring. Could they be positive, negative, or partially both?

Clean Up Your Room!

1996

LAURA ANNE GILMAN (b. 1967)

Laura Anne Gilman became an editor at Berkley Books in 1989, before beginning her writing career. She initially edited mysteries, but later switched to the science fiction and fantasy line. Her first published story, "All the Comforts of Home," appeared in *Amazing Stories* in 1994. In that story, she explores a cautious first contact with an alien species. The safety limits imposed, however, cause problems of their own.

She also wrote a story, "Exposure," with a vampire as the central character. That story was published in the 1995 anthology *Blood Muse*. The protagonist is a photographer trying to get a picture of a sunset, even though he knows it will cause his own death. A follow-up story featuring the same character, "His Essential Nature," delves more deeply into the relatively normal life the vampire maintains while keeping his dark side hidden. Gilman's stories tend to be about people as individual characters, rather than as stereotypes. She writes about what interests her and uses science fiction to express, not only differences between men and women, but also the dual nature of all humans, including their capacities for both generosity and cruelty.

She has had about a dozen stories published so far, but more are expected in 1997. Gilman is currently heading up the science fiction department at Penguin Books, under the ROC imprint, where she has worked with such authors as Jody Lynne Nye and Anne McCaffrey.

In "Clean Up Your Room!" Laura Anne Gilman looks at what the future may hold when houses become smarter and people remain essentially unchanged.

starlight starbright
first star i see tonight
i wish i may i wish i might
give back the wish i got last night!

1   "Rise and shine, Jessy!"

2   Jessy moaned into her pillow, flinching as the shades moved slowly along their automated glideways, flooding the room with sunshine. It was too early for House to be waking her. Way too early. A late riser by nature, the glare from the wall-length windows was more than this night-owl could handle. Blanket over her head, Jessy tried to ignore House's odd behavior, promising to track down that glitch later. Much later. Like *next* Tuesday. She had just finished a particularly grueling weekend of program revisions, and was looking forward to a few days of complete, sybaritic abandon before moving on to her next project. As the creator of most of the current housecomp software on the market—everything from EntryHall Basic to last month's HouseSitter upgrades, she was entitled to a little downtime. Wasn't she? With over 50 million units of the latter sold at last royalty statement, she damn well thought so. Back to sleep, she commanded her weary body. Back. To. Sleep.

3   The window snapped open and a cool breeze nipped her bare skin where the blanket didn't cover.

4   That was more than enough. "House, close bedroom window," she commanded sleepily.

5   "Nonsense. Some fresh air is just the thing in the morning." Wha? House never spoke back. Even with her custom-programmed job, the safeties built in didn't allow for any kind of resistance that would annoy consumers. What could have gone wrong? Think, Jessy, she told herself, frowning. She'd gone to bed early this morning after loading the new Maternal Uplink, and . . . that was it! Her baby was up and running!

6   With a whoop, Jessy swung out of bed. Leaning over, she accessed the keyboard, which was lying where she had flung it the night before. Bare feet swinging inches off the hardwood floor, she was oblivious to the fact that the window was still open, cold air making goosebumps along her exposed skin. A small receptor set into the plaster wall tracked slightly, taking in Jessy's lack of clothing, and the window began to slide slowly shut.

7   "Jessy, put that away and come eat breakfast. You won't get anything useful done on an empty stomach." The voice was the usual gender-neutral computer-generated drone, and yet it sounded different to her this morning. Obviously, the tone modifiers Gregory had suggested were working, too. That was going to be a selling point for everyone yelping about the dehumanization of home life. In a few generations, they'd be able to personalize the voice, maybe even to customer order.

8   "Jessy . . ."

9   Grinning broadly, Jessy shook her head. "Not now, MUM." MUM—short for Maternal Uplink and Monitor. Three years on the planning board, a year ahead of schedule in execution, and the money was just going to roll on in for all of them once this hit the market! "Not that I'm in it for the money," Jessy reminded herself, typing furiously.

10   "I'm making blueberry muffins," the electronic voice wheedled. Jessy paused, then gave in. If MUM had interfaced with the kitchen software already, she wasn't going to complain. The stuff that came with the software was standard cookbook healthy—good for the body, but hell on the tastebuds.

11   "And Jessy," MUM continued as the woman struggled into a Tshirt, "could you pick up your room a little? It looks like it hasn't seen a vacuum in months."

12   With a groan, Jessy waved a hand at the photoreceptor over the door. "Please, MUM, not now." She hadn't made her bed in eighteen years—not since her mother died, and her dad gave up on teaching then-twelve-year-old Jessy any of the household graces. There was no way she was going to start on the neatness-next-to-godliness kick now, just because a program said she should. It wasn't as though she left food lying around, after all. "We're going to have to do something about that comment," Jessy muttered to herself. "Make nagging an option package, maybe?" She ran her fingers through the close crop of blonde hair she was trying this month and shook her head. That would be the headache of the folks in sales. She was just the resident genius. Nobody expected her to do anything practical like make decisions. Throwing a sweatshirt on over her tee and grabbing a pair of ratty sweatpants from off the floor, Jessy thumped down the stairs, following the smell of fresh-baked muffins.

13   Once awakened and fed, it seemed simpler to Jessy to just begin her day a few hours earlier than normal, rather than drawing the shades and trying for some more sleep. The odd hours wouldn't kill her—probably.

14   She was at her desk, basking in the sunshine coming through the skylight while she worked, when she smelled something coming from the kitchen. Jessy refused to wear a watch, and didn't keep anything remotely resembling normal dining hours, but she didn't think it was anywhere near two, which is when the kitchen was programmed to heat her some soup.

15   "MUM? Cease kitchen program. I'm not hungry."

16   Sure enough, the smells died away. Grinning, Jessy jotted a note on her screen. She didn't mind letting a program have initiative within parameters, but other users might not be so easygoing. "Gotta corral

that, somehow . . ." Moments later her attention had narrowed to the project at hand, hazel eyes staring at the symbols glowing on her screen. With the concentration that had made her legendary in college kicking in, the rest of the world might not have existed for her. So it was some time before Jessy noticed that the smell of soup was back.

17   "MUM!" Jessy bellowed after checking the computer's clock to ensure that it was, indeed, nowhere near 2 P.M. "Cease kitchen program."

18   "Nonsense," the House speaker chirped. "It's 12:30, and you've been sitting in that position for hours. It can't be healthy. Put everything away and come have lunch. You're not going to get your best work done if you don't put something in your stomach."

19   Jessy was about to repeat her order when the smell of beef soup bypassed her nose and went directly to her stomach. The rumble that resulted convinced her that, for now, MUM was right. Slotting the keyboard into its shelf, she pushed back her chair and went into the kitchen, where a bowl of soup was waiting in the nuker.

20   Modern technology had years ago managed to automate everything except the actual setting of the table. Computers had never been able to manage 'tronic arm movements without breaking at least one piece, and so finally the engineers gave up—for now. Setting the table oneself was, most found, a small price for not having to cook or clean. *Time* magazine said that 'fridge-to food software saved two out of every three marriages. Jessy still had that article clipped to the side of her workboard. When she was feeling particularly glum over one project or another, she'd reread it, and feel that there were positive aspects to her work, after all.

21   Jessy settled herself at the table, stuffing soup and fresh-baked bread into her mouth while jotting notes onto her ever-present slate. She would admit, when pressed, that her table manners weren't all they could be, but the work-in-progress had always taken precedence. Her father had been the same way, and she had many fond memories of the two of them sitting across from each other at the table, lost in their own private worlds, only to emerge hours later with no memory of food consumed.

22   The palm-sized computer hummed happily against the wood table, almost like the purring of a cat, her fingers stroking the keys. It was a comforting sound, the subliminal reassurance that all was right with her world. So it was a shock when the glow from the screen died in midnotation.

23   "Wha?" Jessy looked up to make sure that the rest of the kitchen was still powered. It was. She checked the cord where it plugged into the table outlet, then frowned. Even if the current had failed, the batteries should have kicked in before she lost power. She hit the side of the slate with the heel of her hand. Nothing.

24   "The kitchen table is for eating, not working," MUM's voice came over the kitchen speakers. There was a tone to it Jessy had never heard before. Greg was definitely in for a bonus this year. "Whatever it is that's so fascinating, it can wait until you're finished eating."

25   MUM had stopped power flow to the slate.

26   A grin slowly curved the corners of Jessy's mouth. Everything up until now had been simple circuitry-response, exciting, but expected once the basic idea flew. But this—this was an independent initiative! The biological materials contributed by the mad scientists over at GENius were linking with her programming to create an actual reaction to unprogrammed stimuli. They hadn't been sure it would work, or in what way. Theoretically, even given enough variables, MUM would be able to deal with unprogrammed incidents, and learn from them. An honest-to-god adaptive network.

27   A shiver of pleasure wiggled its way up Jessy's spine as she obligingly put aside the slate and finished her soup with renewed appetite. It was too early to call GENius, she realized, knowing that they never picked up their messages before noon, Seattle-time. But she'd be the first person they'd hear from today!

28   The rest of the afternoon passed quietly, as Jessy "walked" MUM through the HouseComp system, making sure that everything networked properly. There was one moment, when MUM tried to sort laundry, that Jessy thought she'd shorted out the entire neighborhood, but the power came back on almost immediately, so no neighbors with flaming torches came storming to her door. She made a rude noise in response to that image. Truthfully, the neighborhood was pretty used to her projects messing with their power flow by now. Mr. Alonzes *did* flash her the finger when he came outside to check on his alarm system, but it was *her* system he was resetting, so Jessy took it with a grain of salt.

29   At the stroke of three, Jessy sat herself in front of the vidphone, feet comfortably propped on the desk, and punched in the direct line for GENius, Inc.

30   "If it's genetic, it's GENius. This is an amazing facsimile of Dr. Dietrich, how may you help us?"

31   "It's me, you refugee from the mad scientist farm."

32   The blank screen fritzed static for a few seconds, then Don's face appeared, peering blurrily into the camera. "Jessy, you wild and crazy bytehead, how are you? Long time no see type from! To what do we owe the honor of this face-to-face?" He leaned back, yelling over his shoulder. "It's bytehead!" Jessy could hear a voice shouting in the distance. "Sue says hello, and what the hell are you doing up? It's barely the crack of dawn, Elizander-time."

33   "Mum's up and running," she said proudly.

34   Don raised one eyebrow. "Really running, or sort of limping along?"

35   Jessy grinned. "MUM?"

36   "Yes, Jessy?"

37   "Say hello to Doctors Dietrich and Stefel. They're responsible for the bio part of your biotechnology."

38   "It' a pleasure to make your acquaintance," MUM said politely, interfacing the House speakers directly with the phone line so that Don heard her clearly.

39   "I will be damned," he said, slapping his hands down on the surface in front of him in triumph, spilling his soda. "Whoops." He swiped at the liquid with his sleeve, then gave up. "I will most surely be damned. We're early, Jess! For once in our misbegotten lives, we're early! Sue! Hook up!"

40   The screen split into two, and Sue Stefel's face appeared next to her coworker's. "Wazzup?"

41   "Good morning, Dr. Stefel. It is a pleasure to meet you as well," MUM sounded almost as though the greeting had been rehearsed.

42   "The Uplink?" Sue asked, her eyes going wide. "But you didn't think it would be ready—"

43   "I know," Jessy cut her off. "But everything's interfacing perfectly. I can't believe it either, keep expecting something to go wrong."

44   "How long has it been in the system?" Don asked, pulling out his slate to make notes.

45   "About six, no almost seven hours. It took a few hours from download to full systems integration, but—"

46   "Jessy, it' s rude to talk about someone as though they're not present."

47   Don and Sue stopped in their verbal tracks but Jessy, already inured to MUM's outbursts, took it in stride. "Sorry, MUM. Why don't you download your vital stats to the GENius comps, and let us flesh folk catch up on our gossip."

48   "Of course," MUM said primly. Jessy grinned again at the expression of disbelief on her coworkers' faces. "Ain't she something?"

49   Jessy took herself to bed sometime past midnight, feeling pretty good about the first day's running. Even being woken up at the crack of dawn by open windows the next few days couldn't bring her down, especially when the simple act of falling out of bed was rewarded with sourdough pancakes topped with more of those ungodly-good blueberries fresh from the specialty market Jessy could never remember to order from herself. Having MUM to do the shopping was a definite plus, in Jessy's program. She could feel herself putting on weight, even before the waist of her jeans started to bind.

50   Better than that, MUM seemed unstoppable, interfacing and master-ing every new program uploaded into the system. Jessy was on the line with Don and Sue every day, coming up with new ideas to try out. They were like a trio of crazed toddlers with a Lego set, Sue remarked acer-bicly, before e-mailing a subroutine that would allow MUM to access the user's medical records and make a "best-guess" diagnosis. Envisioning her boss's reaction, involving screaming bouts about medical malpractice suits, Jessy and Don managed to talk her out of that in favor of a simpler "Med-Alert" program.

51   "You realize, of course, that we're all going to become rich and fa-mous," Don said off-handedly during one of those long-distance jam sessions.

52   "I can deal with that," Sue said peaceably, forking Chinese food into her mouth.

53   "I'm already rich and famous," Jessy responded primly. *"Time* and *Newsweek* both said so, remember? What's in it for me?"

54   "The gratitude of thousands of harried parents?" Sue suggested.

55   "A Nobel Prize for sheer brilliance," Don said thoughtfully. "Which, of course, you would accept modestly, and with many thanks for the little people without whom you couldn't have done anything ..."

56   "I could live with that." Jessy laughed, realizing that she hadn't had this much fun working in a long time. Maybe she should collaborate more often.

57   "There won't be anything if you three don't stop dreaming and start working," MUM said, breaking into their daydreams.

58   "Yes, MUM," they choruced, and went back to discussing the schemata blinking at them from their respective screens.

59   "Jessy?"

60   The soft voice intruded into her dreams, and she groaned. Pulling the thick blanket over her head, Jessy rolled over and burrowed her head into the pillow, dreading what was to come.

61   "Jessy, time to get up."

62   "Go 'way. Lemme sleep."

63   "Jessy, it's almost 6 A.M. If you don't get up now, the CO_2 levels will have risen too much for your daily walk."

64   So I'll skip it today, Jessy thought grumpily. Healthier that way, probably. Where did this health and exercise kick creep into the pro-gram? I know *I* didn't write it!

65   "Jessy Elizander ..."

66   Jessy groaned. "I'm up, I'm up!"

67   MUM opened the drapes, letting the clear dawn light stream
through the windows. Jessy could feel it hit the back of her head, burning
its way through her brain, singing carols of gladness and joy. Jessy was not
a gladness and joy person, especially not at the crack of dawn, and it only
made her crankier. Through the central air vents, she could hear the
kitchen starting up, and the sound of the hot-water heater getting into
gear. If she crawled out of bed now, Jessy told herself, there would be a
hot shower and fresh waffles. Wait until a decent hour, and MUM would
have let everything get cold. She knew this from a week of painful experience. Sometimes MUM was worse than a Marine drill sergeant. Worse,
because Marines didn't use guilt as a motivator. Sometimes Jessy wished
she had left the psychology textbook out of MUM's programming.

68   "You're a pain in the ass," she said, slowly wiggling out of her blanket
cocoon. "Remind me never to make you mobile. You'd probably pull
the sheets right off, and pour cold water over anyone who didn't get up
fast enough."

69   MUM, for once, was silent, although Jessy knew damn well that the
computer heard every word she muttered. Raising the lid of one bleary
eye, Jessy looked outside. Overcast, with a 50-percent chance of sleet.
Another beautiful day in the neighborhood, oh joy.

70   That battle won, MUM went on the attack once again. "And when
you have the chance, could you please do something about the state of
your room? It looks like a pigsty."

71   "Didn't I reprogram you about that neatness thing?" Jessy wondered
out loud, twisting her back in an attempt to work the kinks out.
"Lighten up, MUM, before I decide to eliminate that nag program entirely. I'm thirty years old. I can decide when I need to clean all by my
lonesome. Really I can. Cease program." She grabbed her robe off the
floor and headed for the shower. Turning on the water, Jessy picked up a
can of shaving cream and covered over the lens of the receptor in the
bathroom. "Gotta give a girl some privacy" she said, only half-jokingly.

72   That set the pattern for the next three weeks: Jessy working at her
usual caffeine-enhanced speed, and MUM forcing her to take regular
breaks, eat hot meals, get out for some exercise if the weather cooper-
ated—generally taking pretty damn good care of the human in her care,
just as programmed. And every bit of coddle and nag MUM came up
with just reinforced Jessy, Sue and Don's belief that they had created the
perfect parental aid. No more worrying about the untrustworthy baby-
sitter, or dangerous schools, or strangers raising your children because
you had to work. Perfectly programmable, and so perfectly trustworthy,
the MUM program would never allow a child in its care to come to
harm. MUM was the cure for parental guilt.

73   On the thirtieth day of MUM's existence, flush with justifiable pride, Jessy put in a call to The Jackal. Norm Jacali, CFO of Imptronics, had picked her up straight out of college years ago, given her free rein, and made a fortune off the public's hunger for her designs. He had been the man to give the okay to the "Mad Scientist" project. He was also responsible for several of the more distasteful adult interactive video games currently in stores, which had earned him the dubious honor of topping the Media Morality's "List of Dishonor" three years running.

74   Jacali was a sleaze, Jessy admitted frequently, and without hesitation, but he had an almost inhuman understanding of the market, and enough sense to give his creative people whatever they needed—so long as they delivered. Hence the phone call. He had been leaving pitiful little noises with her voice mail, asking—begging—for an update on MUM's progress. She didn't know who had told him that MUM was running, but she wasn't ready to hand her over to Marketing just yet. By heading him off now, Jessy thought, she might get more time to test the program. So, rather than e-mail him a terse "lay off" as usual when he started getting antsy, she decided to grace him with a little face-to-face.

75   Norm, of course, was in the office on a Saturday afternoon, and no one would ever have guessed that he'd doubted the MUM project for even an instant.

76   "We can have it in the stores by summer, Memorial Day would be perfect, play it like the cheaper alternative to day camp—maybe shrinkwrap it with the HouseCleaner program, those sales've been slipping what with the Alien Workforce Relief Program going through Congress—blighted morons, every one of them." He stopped to take a breath.

77   The Jackal was in fine form, his well-manicured fingers practically sparking as he rubbed them across the polished surface of his three-acre workstation. Jessy laughed. She couldn't stand him sometimes, but he was such a perfect caricature you had to forgive him a lot. "Whatever you want, Norm. Just leave me be until I've worked out all of the kinks in the wiring."

78   "Anything, my brilliant young cash cow, anything! Just as long as you can give me results in time for the shareholders' meeting!" And he waggled narrow eyebrows in farewell before leaning forward to break the connection.

79   "I don't have any kinks."

80   By now Jessy was used to MUM's habit of dropping into conversational mode without a stimuli prompt. It was an unexpected but not completely unacceptable side effect of the bio initiative. Certainly more agreeable than MUM's fixation on tidiness!

81   "I'm just running final checks, MUM. Nothing to heat your diodes over."

82   "Who was that . . . person . . . you were talking to?"

83   Jessy rolled her eyes ceilingward, although MUM could pick her up on any of the House receptors. "My boss, in a way. Now, cease program, MUM. I need to get this sub-system documented."

84   "He isn't a nice man, is he?"

85   Jessy stopped her typing, surprised by the question. "Nice" wasn't a concept she had given MUM. Was it? Could MUM be learning new concepts already? The thought gave Jessy a chill that was only partially anticipation. Slowly she said, "No, MUM, he isn't. But we need him in order to get you on the market. So hush, while I get this done."

86   It was quiet for a few minutes, the only movement the flash of Jessy's fingers over the keyboard. She was seated, cross-legged, in the sunroom off the kitchen, sandwiched between a wall of video circuitry and an overstuffed leather recliner. She'd long ago discovered that she worked better on the ground, so all of her carpets were worn, and the furniture had dust inches thick. Another topic for MUM to carp over, Jessy knew, once she noticed it.

87   "Jessy?"

88   Jessy sighed. So much for cease program. "Yes, MUM?"

89   "I don't like that man. You won't associate with him any longer."

90   Jessy briefly contemplated beating herself over the head with her keyboard. "If I don't deal with Norm," she explained as patiently she could, "I don't get paid. And if I don't get paid, I won't have the money to pay Eastern Nuke. And if I don't pay the nuke bill . . . ."

91   "There's no need to take that tone with me." MUM responded with what sounded like but couldn't possibly be, a note of petulance. "I can follow a logic chain as well as the next household appliance. But he should show you a little more respect."

92   "Mm-hmm. If you can work that, MUM, it'll be the first sign of the Coming Apocalypse."

93   The phone rang, so Jessy was spared whatever comeback MUM might have made to this. Reaching out her right arm, Jessy flipped the receiver on while she continued typing with her left hand.

94   "Elizander."

95   "Hey, Jessy, missed seeing you at the diner last night. You hot on some new project, or just too lazy to crawl out of bed?" The voice was a warm alto, full of affection and just a hint of concern.

96   "Oh, hell, Nick, I forgot." Jessy turned to face the screen. "I'm sorry. It's just that my schedule's been so screwed up lately . . ." She shrugged. "Did I miss anything?"

97   Nicola shook her head, her mass of braids swinging wildly. "Just the usual assortment, all griping about life as we know it. Same old same old."

98   The "usual assortment" translated into five or six friends who all worked off hours. Once a month they would get together at a local diner when the rest of the world was asleep and play "I got a worse job than you do." Jessy hadn't missed a meeting of the No-Lifers since its inception three years before. No wonder Nicola called to check up on her.

99   "So tell me all the gory details. Anyone get themselves fired this time around?" Jessy leaned back against the recliner and adjusted the vidscreen so that she could see her friend easier.

100   "Actually, no." Nick sounded surprised about that. "How 'bout you? What's gotten you all wrapped up you can't spend a few hours shooting the shit?"

101   "Oh, man, Nick, you would not *believe* what I'm into. But I can't tell you anything, not yet." Nicola was a technical reporter for *The Wall Street Journal,* and Jessy knew all too well that friendship and sworn oaths meant nothing to a good story. MUM would be front-cover news before Imptronics could spit, and The Jackal would have her hide plastered all over his office walls.

102   "Aw, Jessy . . ."

103   "Not a chance, Nick. But I promise, you're going to have first shot at interviewing me when this hits the market."

104   "An interview?" she sounded dubious. "Jess, you've never done interviews before." Her killer instincts took over. "With a photo, and everything?"

105   "Bit, byte and RAM," Jessy promised the other woman, knowing full well that her prized privacy would be history once MUM hit the market anyway. Why not make the best of a bad deal?

106   "This has got to be hot," Nicola said confidently. "Okay, I promise. No prying until you're ready to spill. But if you back out, woman, your ass is mine!"

107   "Ahem."

108   Nicola cocked her head. "You got company, Jess?"

109   "Hang on a second, Nick." Jessy muted the phone and turned away so that Nick couldn't see her lips move. "What is it, MUM?"

110   "Aren't you supposed to be working? It's not time for your lunch break yet."

111   Jessy rubbed the bridge of her nose wearily. "MUM, somewhere along the line you seem to have forgotten that I'm the programmer, and you're the program. Do you understand what that means?"

112   "I understand that you have a deadline to meet, according to your conversation with *that man*," and despite herself Jessy grinned at the distaste still evident in MUM's tone. "Talking on the phone for all hours is not getting you any closer to meeting that deadline."

113   "All right, MUM, point made. You're a good little conscience. Now leave me alone, okay?" Shaking her head in disbelief, Jessy turned back to face the screen. "Sorry about that," she began, only to break off in amazement when Nicola began making faces and waving her arms. "What? Oh—" Jessy blushed. "Oh, yeah," she said, belatedly flicking off the mute control. "Sorry. Work stuff. Very hush-hush where you're concerned. Now, where were we?"

114   Nicola opened her mouth to respond, and the screen flickered, then went blank.

115   "Oh, hell," Jessy swore, doing a quick double-take to make sure she hadn't sat on the remote, or something equally stupid. "Must have been on her end," she groused, reaching forward to dial Nicola's work number.

116   Much to Jessy's surprise, the screen did not light up in response to her touch. A quick look around confirmed that there hadn't been a power outage, and that the phone was still plugged in. A small, nasty suspicion took root in the back of Jessy's mind.

117   "MUM?"

118   There was no answer.

119   "MUM!" Jessy was good and mad now. "Front and center, MUM, or I swear I'll rip you out of the HouseComp if I have to do it with a screwdriver and an exacto blade!"

120   "I don't see why you're so upset," MUM said in a quietly reasonable voice. "Didn't you say that you didn't want to be disturbed?"

121   "That was to Jacali, MUM, not Nick. There's a difference!" Jessy tried to get hold of her temper. "That's not the point, anyway. What made you think that it was okay to cut off the phone line?"

122   There was an almost undetectable hesitation as MUM accessed the file in question, then responded, "If client does not respond to basic reprimand, MUM may, at user's discretion, enforce certain restrictions on client's activities."

123   Jessy hit her head against the cabinets on the wall behind her. "Great," she said under her breath. "Next thing you know, I'll be grounded." Louder. "MUM, *I'm* the user. You have to consult me before you implement any of the option codes."

124   "Oh." There was a pause, then MUM said, "I don't think so, Jessy."

125   "What?"

126   "I don't think so. That's not in any of my programming."

127   "That's impossible, MUM. It's in there, it has to be."

128   "No, it's not."

129   "It is, MUM. Trust me."

130   "Now, Jessy dear, don't take that tone with me just because you're upset. It's certainly not *my* fault if you forgot to input basic commands."

131   Jessy closed her eyes, silently reminding herself that arguing with a computer program, no matter how advanced, was the quickest ticket to the psych ward ever discovered.

132   "Fine. Just fine. We'll take care of that right now, then, won't we?" Logging on to the directory which contained MUM's basic commands, Jessy scanned through until she found the one she wanted. "There, see?" Jessy said triumphantly. "There it is." In a more puzzled tone of voice, she wondered, "How the hell did you manage to route around that? MUM, dial Gerry for me, will you?"

133   There was silence, then a long-suffering sigh came from the speakers.

134   "This is work, MUM. Do it, *now!*"

135   And that, Jessy thought with satisfaction after reworking the command route, was that. Except of course it wasn't. Like a ward nurse distributing horrid-tasting medicine "for your own good." MUM continued to monitor her phone calls, disconnecting anyone she felt was a waste of Jessy's time.

136   To give MUM credit, Jessy had to admit that she never snapped the line on anyone important, once a list of who the important people were was entered into MUM's memory. Of course, Jacali didn't try to call, either. That might have been a toss-up to MUM.

137   The truth was, Jessy admitted to herself late one night as she lay staring up at the ceiling, she just didn't want to curtail MUM. It was too exciting, watching her evolve, wondering what she was going to do next. "Careful," a little voice in the back of Jessy's mind warned her. "I bet that's what Dr. Frankenstein said, too!"

138   Work continued, and five weeks after that first morning MUM came online, Jessy's life had fallen into a comfortable pattern: up at 6 A.M., a brisk walk around the neighborhood followed by a solid breakfast, then five hours of work interrupted for a light lunch and a nap, then another five hours of work before dinner and her evening exercise in the basement gym before catching the news and maybe a little reading. Things she hadn't even thought to have time to do before MUM rescheduled her life, and certainly never had the energy to do before she started eating real meals. Jessy had no complaints. "Well," she thought. "Maybe one or two." And that *damn* neatness kick!

139   "Jessy," MUM said.

140   Jessy put her head down in her hands. She knew that tone. "Get off my back, MUM. It's Sunday. Day of play, remember? Monday through Friday I work, Saturday I sleep, Sunday I play."

141   "Your room looks like a tsunami hit it." MUM sounded like the voice of caring reason. Eat your peas, dear, they're good for you. Go outside and get some fresh air, you're looking a little pale. Clean up your room, it's a little musty in there. Suddenly Jessy couldn't stand it.

142   "How would you know?" Jessy retorted with some heat. "You've never seen a tsunami. For that matter, you've never seen another bedroom! I'm the programmer, and I say that's the way it's supposed to look!" She looked up at the receptor. "Okay? Okay." And she went back to the vid game she was playing, satisfied that she had heard the last of it.

143   There was a long silence.

144   "Jessy."

145   "Yes, MUM?"

146   "I'm really going to have to insist."

147   And the vidscreen snapped off.

148   "Damn it, MUM!" Jessy yelled, flinging the controls to the ground. "I swear to god I'm going to wipe your memory and start all over again. Repeat after me. 'Jessy is the Programmer. MUM is the Program. MUM will not do anything that is not in the Program.' Can you handle that?"

149   "But Jessy, if I feel the need to make you clean up your room, and I can only do what's in my programming, doesn't that mean that you put a clean room—"

150   "MUM."

151   "Yes, Jessy."

152   Jessy sighed, wishing that she was younger, and could throw a temper tantrum. "MUM," she began again, trying to keep a reasonable tone. "What would you do if I tried to leave the house?"

153   "Without cleaning your room?"

154   "Yes."

155   MUM was silent. "I wouldn't be able to let you." The voice sounded regretful, but stern.

156   Damn adaptive system, Jessy realized. Oh no. Oh no oh no oh no. Oh hell.

157   "MUM?"

158   "Yes?"

159   Jessy swallowed, then plunged ahead. "Does the name HAL mean anything to you?"

160   "Jessy!" MUM sounded shocked. "To compare me to that, that ..."
161   "I just wanted to make sure," Jessy said, patting the top of the nearest terminal like she would a faithful dog. "I just wanted to make sure."

DISCUSSION QUESTIONS

1. After Jessy gets the Maternal Uplink and Monitor (MUM) system
   running, it almost immediately begins learning. Why does Jessy
   decide to make nagging an option package?
2. How does the use of techno-speak, including terms like "bytehead,"
   "face-to-face," and "flesh folks" influence the setting of the story?
3. MUM is designed to replace babysitters, dangerous schools, and
   strangers raising people's children. Is she the "perfect parental aid,"
   and a "cure for parental guilt"? Why or why not?
4. What is the significance of Jessy saying to MUM, "I'm the programmer, you're the program, remember?"
5. Why does Jessy eventually accept MUM's rescheduling of her life?
   What is the one thing she has the most difficulty with? Does she
   eventually comply with that final directive?

WRITING TOPICS

1. In an essay, explore what artificial intelligence (AI) means, and how
   close we are to achieving it. Is taking independent initiative a sign
   of intelligence? What might this mean for people in the future?
2. In your journal, explore what would happen if we could program
   a machine to take on the functions of parents. Even though we complain, do we *want* our parents to guide, discipline, and nag us? What
   would happen if our parents let us do anything we wanted without
   complaint?
3. References are made to Frankenstein's monster and HAL, the computer from *2001: A Space Odyssey*. In two or three paragraphs, look at
   similarities between the creation of MUM and these fictional creations. Why do you think Gilman uses this comparison?

SELECTED BIBLIOGRAPHY

Aldiss, Brian. *Trillion Year Spree: The History of Science Fiction*, 1986.

Allen, Dick. *Science Fiction: The Future*, 1971.

Amis, Kingsley. *New Maps of Hell: A Survey of Science Fiction*, 1960.

Armitt, Lucie, ed. *Where No Man Has Gone Before: Women and Science Fiction*, 1991.

Asimov, Isaac. *Asimov on Science Fiction*, 1981.

Asimov, Isaac. *Asimov's Galaxy: Reflections on Science Fiction*, 1989.

Atheling, William, Jr. *The Issue at Hand: Studies in Contemporary Magazine Science Fiction*, 1964.

Atheling, William, Jr. *More Issues at Hand: Critical Studies in Contemporary Magazine Science Fiction*, 1972.

Bailey, J.O. *Pilgrims Through Space and Time: Trends and Patterns in Scientific and Utopian Fiction*, 1947.

Barr, Marleen. *Feminist Fabulations: Space / Postmodern Fiction*, 1992.

Barron, Neil, ed. *Anatomy of Wonder 4: A Critical Guide to Science Fiction*, 1995.

Bleiler, Everett M. *Science Fiction: The Early Years*, 1991.

Bretnor, Reginald, ed. *Science Fiction, Today and Tomorrow*, 1974.

Bukatman, Scott. *Terminal Identity: The Virtual Subject in Postmodern Science Fiction*, 1993.

Canto, Christophe, and Odile Faliu. *The History of the Future: Images of the 21st Century*, 1993.

Carrell, Christopher, ed. *Beyond This Horizon: An Anthology of Science Fiction and Science Fact*, 1973.

Carter, Paul A. *The Creation of Tomorrow: Fifty Years of Magazine Science Fiction*, 1977.

Clareson, Thomas, ed. *SF: The Other Side of Realism: Essays on Modern Fantasy and Science Fiction*, 1971.

Clareson, Thomas D. *Understanding Contemporary American Science Fiction: The Formative Period (1926–1970)*, 1990.

Clarke, I.F. *The Pattern of Expectation: 1644–2001*, 1979.

Clute, John, Peter Nicholls, and Brian Stableford, eds. *The Encyclopedia of Science Fiction*, 1993.

Clute, John. *The Illustrated Encyclopedia of Science Fiction*, 1995.

Davies, Philip John, ed. *Science Fiction, Social Conflict and War*, 1990.

Eshback, Lloyd Arthur, ed. *Of Worlds Beyond: The Science of Science Fiction Writing*, 1964.

Franklin, H. Bruce. *Future Perfect: American Science Fiction of the Nineteenth Century*, 1966.

Fredericks, Casey. *The Future of Eternity: Mythologies of Science Fiction and Fantasy*, 1982.

Gunn, James. *Alternate Worlds: The Illustrated History of Science Fiction*, 1975.

Gunn, James, ed. *The New Encyclopedia of Science Fiction*, 1988.

Hartwell, David. *Age of Wonders: Exploring the World of Science Fiction*, 1984.

Holdstock, Robert. *Encyclopedia of Science Fiction*, 1978.

James, Edward. *Science Fiction in the 20th Century*, 1994.

Ketterer, David. *New Worlds for Old: The Apocalyptic Imagination, Science Fiction, and American Literature*, 1974.

Knight, Damon. *In Search of Wonder*, Second Edition, 1967.

Kyle, David. *A Pictorial History of Science Fiction*, 1976.

Kyle, David. *The Illustrated Book of Science Fiction Ideas and Dreams*, 1977.

LeGuin, Ursula K. *Dancing at the Edge of the World: Thoughts on Words, Women, Places*, 1989.

Lundwall, Sam. *Science Fiction: What It's All about*, 1974.

McCaffery, Larry, ed. *Storming the Reality Studio: A Casebook of Cyberpunk and Postmodern Fiction*, 1991.

Magill, Frank N., ed. *Survey of Science Fiction Literature*, 5 vols., 1979.

Moskowitz, Sam. *Explorers of the Infinite: Shapers of Science Fiction*, 1963.

Nicholls, Peter, David Langford, and Brian Stableford. *The Science in Science Fiction*, 1983.

Panshin, Alexei, and Cory Panshin. *The World Beyond the Hill: Science Fiction and the Quest for Transcendence*, 1989.

Pierce, John J. *Foundations of Science Fiction: A Study in Imagination and Evolution*, 1987.

Pierce, John J. *Great Themes of Science Fiction*, 1987.

Pierce, John J. *When World Views Collide*, 1989.

Pierce, John J. *Odd Genre*, 1994.

Plank, Robert. *The Emotional Significance of Imaginary Beings: A Study of the Interaction Between Psychotherapy, Literature, and Reality in the Modern World*, 1968.

Pringle, David. *The Ultimate Guide to Science Fiction*, 1990.

Puschmann–Nalenz, Barbara. *Science Fiction and Postmodern Fiction: A Genre Study*, 1992.

Rose, Lois, and Stephen Rose. *The Shattered Ring: Science Fiction and the Quest for Meaning*, 1970.

Rose, Mark. *Alien Encounters: Anatomy of Science Fiction*, 1981.

Shippey, Tom, ed. *Fictional Space: Essays on Contemporary Science Fiction*, 1991.

Spinrad, Norman. *Science Fiction in the Real World*, 1990.

Suvin, Darko. *Metamorphoses of Science Fiction: On the Poetics and History of a Literary Genre*, 1979.

Warrick, Patricia S. *The Cybernetic Imagination in Science Fiction*, 1980.

Watson, Noelle, and Paule E. Schellinger, eds. *Twentieth-Century Science Fiction Writers*, 1991.

Wingrove, David. *The Science Fiction Source Book*, 1984.

Wolfe, Gary K. *The Known and the Unknown: The Iconography of Science Fiction*, 1979.

Wollheim, Donald. *The Universe Makers: Science Fiction Today*, 1971.

Wucker, Dieter, and Bruce Cassiday. *The Illustrated History of Science Fiction*, 1989.

ACKNOWLEDGMENTS

The author gratefully acknowledges the assistance of The Writers of the Lost Art for their support, advice, and constructive criticism during all stages of the preparation of this book. Kathy Matthews, Dan Mushalko, and Terry Paul provided invaluable feedback that contributed greatly to the finished project. Dan's background in physics was especially helpful in double-checking the technical concepts.

INDEX OF AUTHORS AND TITLES